France under the Germans

France under the Germans

Collaboration and Compromise

Philippe Burrin

Translated from the French by
JANET LLOYD

THE NEW PRESS / NEW YORK

LIBRARY OF CONGRESS CATALOG CARD NUMBER 96-69742
ISBN 1-56584-323-1

First published as *La France à l'Heure Allemande: 1940-1944* by Editions du Seuil
Published in the United States by The New Press, New York
Distributed by W.W. Norton & Company, Inc., New York

Established in 1990 as a major alternative to the large commercial publishing houses, The New Press is a nonprofit American book publisher. The Press is operated editorially in the public interest, rather than for private gain; it is committed to publishing, in innovative ways, works of educational, cultural, and community value that, despite their intellectual merits, might not normally be commercially viable. The New Press's editorial offices are located at the City University of New York.

The New Press is deeply grateful to the French Ministry of Culture and Communication for its generous translation support.

Production management by Kim Waymer
Printed in the United States of America

9 8 7 6 5 4 3 2

Contents

Preface to the English edition

In the past two centuries, the Anglo-Saxon peoples have been spared the experience of occupation, whereas it has constituted a painful part of the recent history of almost all of the countries of continental Europe and continues to hold an important, or even central, place in their memories. This may explain the persistence, among the Anglo-Saxons, of a critical attitude compounded of moralism and their sense of possessing clear consciences where those European peoples are concerned, particularly the French whose behaviour during the Second World War is often the subject of ferocious condemnation. There are clearly also other reasons for this: irritation over French foreign policy of the Gaullist ilk or over the anti-Americanism that is certainly widespread in France. But there is a deeper reason that cannot be overlooked: the politics of the Vichy regime and its complicity in the Nazi crimes – first and foremost the Holocaust – are regarded, quite rightly, as so unworthy of the country that produced the Declaration of Human Rights as to besmirch its image, possibly irremediably.

Despite their distance from France, or perhaps thanks to it, British and American historians have made valuable contributions to the history of France's 'black years'. On the one hand, I should mention the analyses of Stanley Hoffmann (himself both a French and an American citizen), analyses which still, after thirty years, retain much of their incisive force, and the works of Robert Paxton, which remain an indispensable reference.[1] On the other, I should refer to the many studies of a more monographic nature, in particular those of Harry R. Kedward and John F. Sweets, that have cast new light on the life of French society during that period, often at a local or regional level.[2]

The present work acknowledges that twofold debt through the approach that it adopts, tackling now from the top, now from the bottom, the variety of ways in which French society adapted to the extraordinary situation constituted by its occupation by Nazi Germany. I have made use of the notion of accommodation so as to direct attention beyond the commonly accepted idea of collaboration that is seen in an essentially politico-ideological perspective. That perspective may be indispensable for giving an account of the action of the Vichy leaders and the attitude of those of their compatriots – the collaborationists – who adopted a position favouring *entente* with the conqueror; but it is unsuitabale for a satisfactory understanding of the far more numerous choices of adaptation made by French society as a whole.

The fact is that, right alongside behaviour that indicated a measure of commitment to collaboration, many French people lived through the occupation with the sole preoccupation of 'getting through it'. My aim has been to place such attitudes within their true context – that of a partially confused image of the occupier, an opaque future, disagreement as to the correct definition of the national interest, and the burdensome business of securing the necessities of life – and to explore their social and cultural origins. For any society, an occupation is a trial and, in a way, represents a moment of truth for it: all the tensions, frustrations and contradictions at work that undermine the social contract come to the surface, on top of which a way to live must be found, even in the presence of a foreign power intent upon persecution and extermination, and also bent upon enrolling support and neutralizing opposition. Despite their great diversity, there was not a single country in Nazi Europe that did not, to some degree, witness the emergence of accommodating behaviour. In the Conclusion to this work, I have tried to establish the parameters of that ubiquitous accommodation, partly imposed but partly voluntary. If Britain or even the United States had been subjugated and occupied, the proportion of enforced submission as compared to deliberate adaptation would perhaps have been different, but is it conceivable that such elements, including the second variety, would have been entirely absent?[3]

The reader may quarrel with the quasi-absence of the resistance in this study. But that absence is a natural corollary to the choice of a perspective designed to focus upon the analysis of the behaviour of adaptation, and it in no way signifies any undervaluation of the role of the resistance. Even if its military efficacy was limited, at least up until the middle of 1943, its moral and political impact was great right from the start. It seems to me that, far from diminishing it, this study of accommodation in effect further ennobles its role by contrast, by throwing into relief the lucidity and courage of the tiny minority of French people who did say 'no' to the occupier and did endeavour to translate that 'no' into actions.

This study's concentration on the experience of France may be regarded as another limitation. It would indeed have been good to produce more of a comparison with the experience of other peoples, in particular those in Western Europe. However, although a mountain of works exists on the subject, most are national monographs centred upon political and military history, so a comparison devoted to the greater or lesser degree of accommodation in a variety of societies would have very little data to go on. To the extent that the present work focuses upon a number of aspects seldom, if ever, studied – personal relations between the occupiers and the occupied, decisions to learn the occupiers' language, attendance at the lectures, exhibitions and concerts organized by them, etc. – and, more generally, endeavours to pinpoint the diverse reactions of one society, French society, it possibly provides some data that might one day prove useful in the composition of a systematic comparison.

Lastly, I should like to express my heartfelt thanks to my two publishers, André Schiffrin of The New Press (New York) and Christopher Wheeler of Arnold (London), for all their support and for their trust in me. I should also like to thank Janet Lloyd for her fine work of translation. I dedicate this book to my daughter Claire. If one day she comes to read it, she will understand how sorry I was not to have spent more time playing with her.

Philippe Burrin

Acknowledgements

THE completion of my research work owes a great deal to M. Jean Favier, the director general of the National Archives, and to Mme Chantal de Tourtier-Bonazzi, the director of its section of contemporary history, and also to all those in charge of the departmental archive centres that I was able to visit. I should also like to express my gratitude to the directors and staff of the archives of the Ministry of Foreign Affairs in Bonn, the Bundesarchiv in Coblenz, the Militärarchiv in Freiburg-in-Brisgau, the Institut für Zeitgeschichte in Munich, the archives of the Collège de France and the CDJC in Paris, and the librarians of the Institut d'Histoire du Temps Présent (Paris) and the IUHEI (Geneva).

My research has benefited greatly from the work of the departmental correspondents of the former Comité d'Histoire de la Deuxième Guerre Mondiale. I owe particular thanks to Jean-Pierre Besse, Claude Cherrier and Jacques Jarriot for having provided me with further information.

Finally, I wish to thank my friends and colleagues in Paris who have supported and encouraged me throughout this long endeavour: Jean-Pierre and Marie-France Azéma, Marie Chaix and Harry Matthews, Jacqueline Cauët, Nadine Fresco, Valérie Hannin, Stéphane Knémis, Denis Peschanski, Henry Rousso, Eric Vigne and Michel Winock.

Abbreviations

AF	Afrique Française
AFN	Afrique Française du Nord
AJA	Association des Journalistes Antijuifs
BNCI	Banque Nationale du Commerce et de l'Industrie
CFA	Comité France–Allemagne
CFTC	Confédération Française des Travailleurs Chrétiens
CGT	Confédération Général de Travail
CNRS	Centre National de la Recherche Scientifique
CO	Comité d'Organisation
CSP	Centre Syndicaliste de Propagande
DCA	Défense contre avions
EHD	Elsässischer Hilfsdienst
FST	Front Social du Travail
GC	Groupe Collaboration
GMR	Groupes Mobiles de Réserve
IEQJ	Institut d'Etudes des Questions Juives
IRA	Irish Republican Army
JAC	Jeunesse Agricole Chrétienne
JEN	Jeunesses de l'Europe Nouvelle
JOC	Jeunesse Ouvrière Chrétienne
LICA	Ligue Internationale contre l'Antisémitisme
LVF	Légion des Volontaires Français contre le Bolchévisme
MBF	Militärbefehlshaber in Frankreich
MSR	Mouvement Social Révolutionnaire
NRF	*Nouvelle Revue Française*
NSKK	Nationalsozialistisches Kraftfahr-Korps
OCRPI	Office Central de Répartition des Produits Industriels
OKH	Oberkommando des Heeres

OKW	Oberkommando der Wehrmacht
PCF	Parti Communiste Français
PDG	Président-Directeur Général
PFNC	Parti Français National-Collectiviste
PNB	Parti Nationaliste Breton
PNSF	Parti National-Socialiste Français
POPF	Parti Ouvrier et Paysan Français
PPF	Parti Populaire Français
PTT	Postes, Téléphone et Télégraphe
RNP	Rassemblement National Populaire
SA	Sturmabteilung
SD	Sicherheitsdienst
SFIO	Section Française de l'Internationale Ouvrière
SNCF	Société Nationale des Chemins de Fer
SOL	Service d'Ordre Légionnaire
STO	Service du Travail Obligatoire
TSF	Télégraph sans fil (radio)
UPR	Union Populaire Républicaine
USR	Union Socialiste Républicaine
VNV	Vlaamsch National Verband

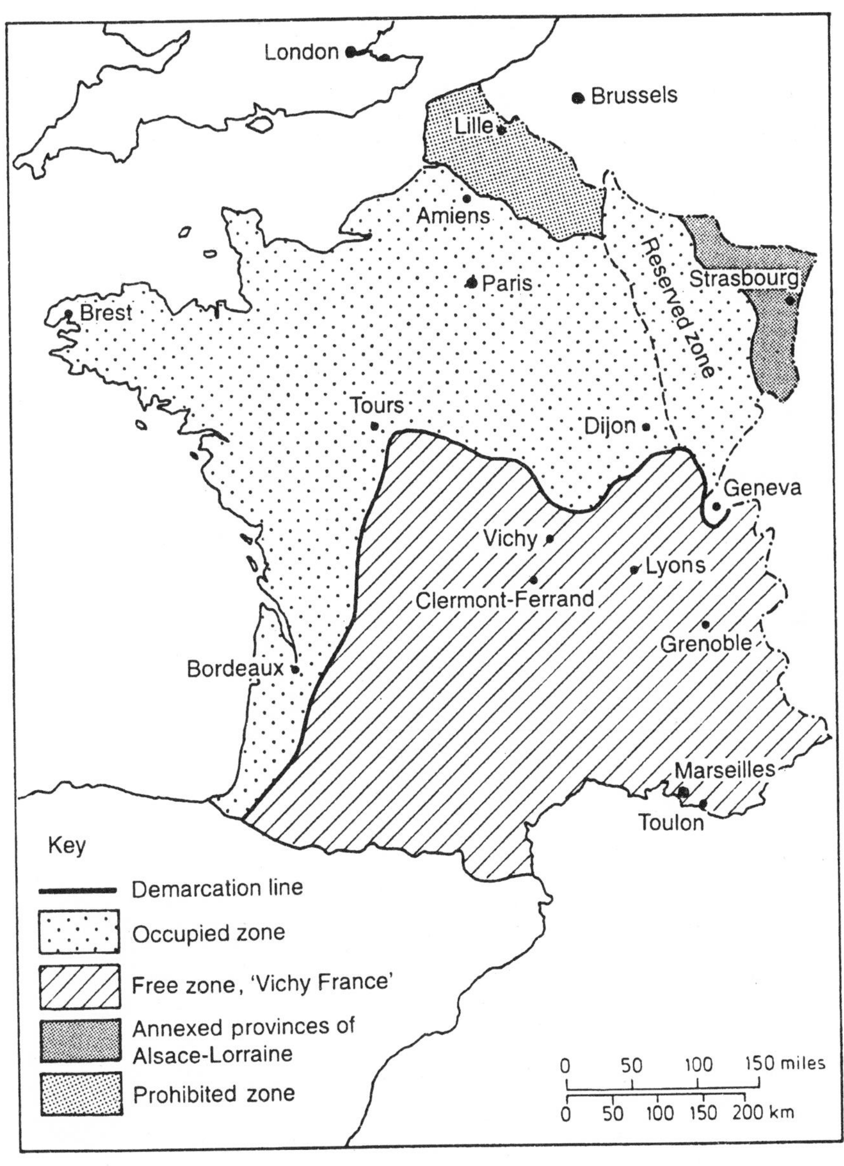
London
Brussels
Lille
Amiens
Paris
Brest
Reserved zone
Strasbourg
Tours
Dijon
Geneva
Vichy
Lyons
Clermont-Ferrand
Grenoble
Bordeaux
Marseilles
Toulon
Key
Demarcation line
Occupied zone
Free zone, 'Vichy France'
Annexed provinces of Alsace-Lorraine
Prohibited zone
0 50 100 150 miles
0 50 100 150 200 km

Occupied and Vichy France, 1940–2

Introduction

Foreign occupation constitutes a massive, brutal intrusion into the familiar frameworks of a society. It imposes authority and demands obedience founded upon neither tradition nor consent. It disrupts the networks and routines of collective life and confronts groups and individuals with choices which, in such circumstances, are very grave. In June 1940, a staggering defeat resulted in three-fifths of France passing under foreign domination, with the remaining two-fifths suffering the same fate in November 1942. The French found themselves living under the Nazi jackboot. Enemy troops were encamped on their soil, moved about their streets, went in and out of their houses. The enemy set the rules for daily life, even upset the temporal order: no sooner were they ensconced than the invaders imposed their own summer time. This presence, brought about by armed force and maintained by its threat, returned the French to one of those situations experienced by many peoples at one time or another, a situation to which France itself had been subjected, on a lesser scale, on several occasions in the past and one that other peoples too were living through at that moment in Nazi Europe.

The present work attempts to reconstruct the ways in which French people reacted to an extraordinary situation, and to rediscover how they behaved under the occupation and towards the occupiers. Total rejection of the occupiers was bound to be no more than marginal: a few departed to England, to join de Gaulle; others moved clandestinely to the free zone where a new government, itself a product of the defeat and occupation, imposed its law. But for the vast majority there seemed no alternative but to submit, bow before the triumphant force and adjust one's behaviour accordingly. Despite their secret defiance, even those determined to resist had to appear to compromise in the interests of their underground activities, as they waited for a superior force to bring liberation and to reset the clock. Accommodation was forced upon the French people, who had to choose the least of all evils and make concessions that might or might not prove compromising.

But accommodation was not always limited to its minimum forms, however elastic these might be. If it had been, the memory of this period would be less painful. The war left behind it death, ruins and physical suffering. The occupation, in contrast, inflicted wounds not so much physical as moral and political – wounds that have still not fully healed. In truth, such a situation puts society as a whole to the test, the more so when that society is riven by tensions and divisions, undecided as to what is right or just, or simply when the general interest is subordinated to the protection and promotion of personal or corporative interests. It is further aggravated when the occupying power intervenes to profit from this state of affairs, employing divisive tactics, seducing and soliciting at the same time as exploiting, repressing and persecuting; and that, precisely, was Nazi Germany's policy in France.

As a substantial minority saw it, there was no point in aiming for and sticking to a minimum degree of compromise. The kind of accommodation deliberately chosen by this minority was marked by indulgence for the powerful of the day, sympathy for certain aspects of their ideology and politics, a desire for agreement or *entente*, and offers to be of service to them or even to enter their service. Some simply judged it opportune to adapt in this way at a time when the enemy's victory appeared too extensive to be reversed; as they saw it, the French people had to resign themselves to living in the German hour. Others believed it indispensable to reach lasting agreement with yesterday's enemy; in their view, it was positively good for France to embrace the German hour.

The object of the present work is to produce a general review of those attitudes and patterns of behaviour, using both German and French sources, consulting personal diaries of the period that are far more revealing than later memoirs, and also drawing upon an abundance of other works, many of them of extremely high quality.[1] But make no mistake: there can be no question of dissolving the notion of collaboration within the general category of accommodation, for it represented its most obvious manifestation; it was, so to speak, accommodation raised to the level of politics. Rather, my intention is to cover all forms of adaptation, with a view to grading them and distinguishing their specific characteristics, seizing upon all kinds of different behaviour and complex motives so as to reconstitute the vast grey area that produces the dominant shade in any picture of those dark years.

We shall be focusing in turn upon three sections of French society, all of which manifested the basic elements of accommodation: that is to say a sense of constraint, material self-interest, personal compliance, and ideological convictions or connivance. The first section is the French government, which held a number of trump cards in power politics – a free zone, a fleet and the empire – and which, professing reasons of state that reflected a diplomatico-strategic line of thought and a desire to survive as a regime, used these trump cards as the basis for its policy of so-called collaboration. The second section is the civil society subjected to the occupation, in all the diversity of its groups and behaviour, right across the board from the Church to the universities, taking in business circles, enthusiasts for German culture and creators of French culture. Here, some may have considered it a virtue to make the best of a bad job, while others were only too ready to come to terms with the occupiers, anxious as they were to pull through, maintaining their personal positions or improving upon them, guaranteeing the present and safeguarding the future. The third section, within that civil society, is made up of the small but by no means negligible circle of politicians, journalists or ordinary French people who saw fit to commit themselves, playing politics in the presence of the occupier, expressing collaborationist opinions, professing agreement with the conqueror, militating in his favour, and even donning his uniform.

These three sections are all part of the same reality, although in their respective adjustments to the massive presence of the occupier there was room for considerable variations. Each evolved a predominating logic that developed its own rhythm and reached its climax in its own time. That is a fact that highlights not only the wide diversity and deep complexity of attitudes and behaviour but also another essential dimension of this period, namely its changes of perspective. Nothing illustrates this better than the evolution of the word 'collaboration' itself. Up until 1940 it meant work undertaken in common, participation in a common task. In no time at all it also took on the meaning of betrayal to the profit of the invader, or at the very least compromising with an occupying power: an astonishing enrichment of meaning through pejorative derision! The basis for the new meaning can be traced back to the speech made by Pétain on 30 October 1940, following his meeting with Hitler at Montoire, in which he declared: 'I am today setting out along the road of collaboration.' The word immediately passed into German (*Kollaboration*), and thence into every other European language.[2] From then on it carried a dark connotation that testified to rejection of a policy found controversial right from the start and eventually condemned without right of appeal. The shift in the meaning of this word that Pétain had used in a positive sense (for of course he did not mean to say 'I am today setting out along the road of disaster' or 'the road of betrayal') and that then became as black as ink and as heavy as lead makes one realize how important it is for us to understand how things looked at the time to people who did not know where they were going and many of whom could not really see the enemy clearly for what he was.

In the summer of 1940, the French had no way of foreseeing the four years through which they were about to live. The occupation did not begin with Oradour-sur-Glane. As always happens in adaptations to extraordinary conditions and in every period of rapid change, attitudes changed from one year to the next. The immediate past was unconsciously reconstructed so that, at the end of the road, it was quite natural to think that there had been clear and constricting choices to be made right from the start. Any history of this period should take into account just how opaque the future was, how quickly opinions can change, how much resolution can waver and how tempting accommodation must have seemed. The occupation put the whole of French society to the test. It gave rise to contrary reactions and to unclear, uncertain and ambivalent attitudes. Nobody was dispensed from making a choice.

1

The future of a defeat

DEFEAT struck France as lightning strikes a tree. The sight of so large an army overthrown in just a few weeks shook the French to their very depths. The world, hanging upon the event, was stupefied. Minds were haunted by the memory of Verdun. Another bloodletting was forseen and feared. Few French people, even pessimists, even defeatists, could have imagined so swift and complete a disaster. And how many Germans had dared to dream of it? Before the attack Hitler had displayed confidence and resolution, but his generals had followed him with apprehension: the Marne had not been forgotten, nor the long war that had followed. This time the fighting was short but proportionately more lethal: 92000 dead and over 200000 wounded on the French side, and half as many on the German side.

What contemporaries were to remember were the enemy's combined attacks with tanks and planes and the swift surrender of the French troops. But the outcome was not decided by uneven forces; the Germans' only superiority lay in their bombers. Nor was it caused by low morale on the part of the French troops: meeting the enemy face to face stifled uncertainty and self-questioning. Most of the routs began only once the lines were broken. The defeat was the result of weak organization on the part of the high command, errors committed in battle and above all the fearful discrepancies in the strategic ideas of the two sides. An enemy well practised in mobile warfare was confronted by French military leaders with a Maginot-line mentality.

The aftermath of the defeat was equally spectacular. France requested an armistice, gave itself a new government, and adopted a new line in foreign policy. Those choices were made by dismissing as many alternatives. The summer of 1940 was certainly a season of profound upsets. But while the defeat was inflicted from outside, the changes that followed resulted from deliberate French choices and the abandonment or rejection of other courses of action. The country's new leaders wanted to make a new start both internally and externally. They thereby committed France to a future that went beyond all calculations and predictions.

The German attack began on 10 May. One month later, on 13 June, the French government, in flight before the enemy's advance, faced a moment of truth. Should they halt the hostilities? The military situation appeared hopeless. The country was splitting at the seams on every side, a mass panic reminiscent of the Great Fear of 1789 having cast millions of refugees on to the roads. Paul Reynaud, the leader of the government, faced up to the situation as well as he could. He was energetic and intelligent (Hitler was not another Kaiser Wilhelm I, he declared, but a new Genghis Khan, and this war would assume world-wide dimensions), but when put to the test he was found wanting. His choice of men was unfortunate and he weakened at the critical moment.

On 18 May he had called upon Marshal Pétain to serve as vice-president of the Council. The next day he dismissed Gamelin, commander-in-chief of the French armed forces, and replaced him by Weygand. On 5 June he again reshuffled his government, pushing out his old rival Daladier and bringing in, alongside Charles de Gaulle upon whose firmness he could count, men from his own entourage: Paul Baudouin and Yves Bouthillier, who had opposite inclinations. On 12 June, Weygand argued in favour of an armistice. The next day, at the Council of Ministers, Pétain, who had come around to the same view, threw his authority behind him.

The government now found itself divided, not so much over continuing the struggle in metropolitan France, which nobody now believed possible, but over how to halt the fighting and what to do next. Reynaud wanted the army to capitulate and the government to move to North Africa. Weygand, in the name of the honour of the army, vehemently refused: where responsibility for the disaster lay was clear and the government should accept it fully. In rejecting even a unilateral cease-fire, Weygand was not simply defending an anachronistic concept of military honour: he was demanding an armistice, and doing so in the most peremptory fashion. His military point of view was mixed with decidedly political considerations. He had hinted at these on 12 June: 'This country must no longer be left rudderless; troops must be kept to preserve public order, for it could come under grave threat tomorrow.'[1] Three days later he again disclosed them when, in answer to Reynaud who pointed out that Holland had done exactly what he was being asked to do, he replied that Holland was a monarchy, not the kind of republic where governments follow one upon the other in rapid succession.[2] In short, a democracy has no right to ask for sacrifices from the nation, let alone from the army.

Although he was certainly defying the civil authorities, Weygand was a soldier. If Reynaud had dismissed him, he would have given way. But Pétain's arrival on the scene was more serious: when he made his position clear, the old marshal was in effect declaring himself as successor. Like Weygand, he was judging the situation from a political as much as a military point of view. It was both illusory and dangerous to continue fighting, he warned on that 13 June: to do so would spread panic in the army and that would destroy it once and for all. The notion resurfacing here was that of the army as the guarantor of order, the army that represented 'all that is best in the nation'.[3] Furthermore, he declared, if the government abandoned the soil of France it would be 'deserting'; it would thereby certainly forfeit the recognition of the French people who, deprived of their 'natural defenders', would be delivered up to the enemy. Finally, if it clung to the illusion of reconquest by the allied forces, it would rule out any 'rebirth' of the country (the idea of a change of institutions rears its head at this point). The only thing to do was to stay put and accept the suffering: 'A French rebirth would be the fruit of that suffering.' He, Pétain, was determined to stay, 'outside the government if necessary', so as to share the fate of his compatriots.[4]

The choice between fighting on and an armistice was certainly a difficult one. But at this juncture when the French government, with the enemy hard on its heels, was fleeing to Bordeaux, the options were not clearly set out, weighed up and taken in. Both the present and the future were perceived through a filter of hopes, preconceptions and unconfessed resentment, the troubling influence of which encouraged a policy of 'every man for himself'. It was in vain that the British government gave assurances of its will to fight, exhorting the French to continue the common struggle and promising that France would eventually be restored. Those reassurances, exhortations and promises were now powerless to halt the flow; in fact, they even encouraged the slide towards an armistice. Past grievances surged up: England had dragged France into the war without itself being ready and then had not made a fair contribution; and here it was demanding that France should fight to the last man, when it had pulled its own troops out of Dunkirk and withheld its air power! Deep down, nobody believed Britain capable of holding out for long; in fact, it was even suspected of harbouring darker designs. Already on 4 June, Pétain had told the American ambassador, Bullitt, that having allowed the French to sink in disaster, England, on the strength of its air and sea power, would proceed to sign a compromising pact over the back of its prostrate ally.[5] He could hardly have underestimated the resolution of the British more.

Following the Council of Ministers on 13 June, the ground gave way beneath Reynaud's feet. Opposing him, the military, eventually joined by Admiral Darlan, the leader of an intact fleet, closed ranks; and meanwhile a group of parliamentary representatives led by Laval were clamouring dissent. All around Reynaud the ranks were thinning; even some of those loyal to him were urging him to lay down arms. Reynaud was probably fearful of a split within the government, with some leaving the country, others remaining with Pétain. Nor could he obtain from foreign powers the support that he sought from them in a series of moves which, in truth, cast doubt upon the strength of his own resolution. He tried to persuade the British to release him from his promise not to conclude a separate armistice and to persuade the Americans to bring military assistance to their allies. He seemed to doubt both the need to continue the struggle alongside England and the latter's ability to stand fast without American support.

On 15 June, the Council of Ministers met again in Bordeaux, and antagonistic positions were again adopted. An ingenious solution suggested by Chautemps seemed to offer a way out of the impasse: why not find out the conditions for an armistice? If they proved unnacceptable, everyone would agree to move out. But the next day Pétain, exasperated by the continuing indecision, announced his resignation. Reynaud thereupon withdrew, without proceeding to a vote and even advising President Lebrun to call upon the Marshal who, for his part, was ready with a ministerial list. Foreign Affairs went to Baudouin, National Defence to Weygand, the Admiralty to Darlan. Laval, who had wanted Foreign Affairs, remained on the touch line.

No time was lost in requesting an armistice and at the same time enquiring as to the conditions for peace. 'Every man for himself' had become state policy. On 17 June, Pétain announced on the radio that he had approached the enemy and called for an end to hostilities. Even before receiving a reply, he considered the war to be at an end. To be sure, he was determined not to sign if Germany insisted upon the fleet being handed over or upon occupation of the whole of metropolitan France or any part of the French empire.[6] But he was still personally resolved to remain whatever happened. If the conditions proved unacceptable, the government would depart but he himself would stay to share the fate of his compatriots. On 17 June, he announced that he was offering France 'the gift of his own person to attenuate its misfortunes'. He thus cast himself in the role of protector of his country, even in the event of total occupation. Once Hitler had agreed to an acceptable armistice, he would take on the role of reformer of the nation without, however, abandoning that earlier one – a promise that he was indeed to honour after the occupation of the free zone in November 1942.

On 18 June, a new voice was heard over the airwaves: it was that of Charles de Gaulle, who had arrived in London to carry on the policies of Reynaud. There, he found himself in the company of state and government leaders who had also chosen exile and the struggle, placing their trust in resistance on the part of France and England. But de Gaulle himself was a rebel who, in the name of a superior duty, had broken his allegiance to what was still the government of the Republic.[7] In his appeal, he put his superiors in the dock for having evaded their military responsibilities by seizing political power. One lost battle did not put an end to a war that was encompassing the whole world and he, General de Gaulle, called for the struggle to be continued until final victory was won.

Those two appeals, made with one day's interval between them, marked out the terrain on which the French were to clash. Both speeches contained the word 'resistance'. For Pétain, France, thanks to the 'magnificent resistance' of its army, had fulfilled its obligations. Resistance, a military matter, was now a thing of the past; France had no accounts to settle with its British ally. For de Gaulle, resistance, while also of a military nature (for civil resistance had not yet entered his field of vision) carried a moral value: it was a 'flame' that 'must not and shall not be extinguished'. Pétain fixed his compatriots' attention upon the 'painful times' they were living through, upon the decision, announced 'today', to stop fighting. De Gaulle included both past and present in his vision of a future that was all that mattered but the outcome of which was no more than probable, the date of its accomplishment uncertain: the vision was of 'one day producing victory', 'one day crushing our enemies'. Pétain addressed himself to the groups whom he enumerated in a significant order: the army, former combatants, the people. The institutions of France were not mentioned; but the blueprint of a new France was surfacing. De Gaulle appealed to the military and the engineers and armament workers who were to be found in England: the first priority was war and victory. Pétain resorted to the language of emotion and affliction, introducing compassion and pity into the political register. De Gaulle ignored sentiment, denounced the inadequate mechanical forces responsible for the defeat and evoked the floods of fire and steel that would bring victory.

Two men, two messages, two missions. Both were figureheads, each believing that it was he who embodied France. Both were symbols of the divorce of the army from the Third Republic, which Pétain condemned for bringing forth defeat, de Gaulle for resigning itself to the armistice. De Gaulle was breaking with legality; but was not Pétain himself a potential rebel, having in advance refused to leave France? If Reynaud had predominated and reached North Africa, would he not have attempted to play politics with the occupying power, just as Leopold III, the king of the Belgians, did? The appeals of 17 and 18 June placed the French people at a parting of the ways, with a choice between immediate relief or war to the bitter end, a redeeming resignation or regeneration in an armed struggle, a France made over in a new image or a victory to be won.

The French request lay in Hitler's hands. If he had played Ghengis Khan the course of events would have been different. But he knew how to be Kaiser Wilhelm I when it suited him. In the same way, he had at first strung the German conservatives along, then dumped them. For the time being, he made no distinction between the fate of France and that of England; the French who were counting on a separate peace had entirely failed to understand his policies. His plan was simple and he rallied Mussolini to it, forcing him to give up his extravagant pretensions and claims to the left bank of the Rhône,

Corsica and Tunisia in return for having kicked an enemy that was already down. Hitler knew that total occupation was well within his power. But he also knew that it would force the French government out of metropolitan France. Despite the help that Franco was offering him, at a price, he was at this point not keen to risk himself in North Africa. And, above all, he was afraid that England, cheered by the support of another fleet along with the French empire, would dig its heels in, continue the struggle and thereby prevent him from liberating the troops in the West for the reckoning in the East. A moderate armistice would neutralize France and the last trump cards that she held. It would spare the victor a heavy administrative task. Once isolated, England might be persuaded to enter into negotiations and desist from playing any role on the continent.

The armistice was presented to the French at Rethondes, in the very railway carriage in which the Reich had been forced to accept defeat in 1918. Not for the world would Hitler have missed that moment. Having in person received the delegation of the vanquished and handed them the armistice agreement, he left them with Keitel, his chief of armed forces. The French read the document and transmitted its contents to Bordeaux. Its terms were reckoned to be tough but not dishonouring; they did not contravene the conditions laid out by Pétain. After the delegates had in vain requested a few modifications and sought equally vainly for clarification as to the future conditions for peace, they were instructed to sign.

According to the terms of the armistice agreement, three-fifths of the territory of metropolitan France were to be occupied. The dividing line ran obliquely from the Spanish frontier up as far as Tours, then sloped eastwards towards Geneva. By occupying the northern half of the country and the entire Atlantic seaboard, Germany appropriated the richest and most highly populated part of metropolitan France. In conformity with the Hague Conventions, to which its delegates took care not to refer explicitly, within this zone the Reich would exercise the rights of occupying power, while the French government, for its part, pledged the collaboration of its administration.

On a military level, the armistice agreement provided for the demobilization of the defeated French armed forces, apart from a few units detailed for the maintenance of order, and prohibited the manufacture of war equipment. Part of the weaponry was to be handed over to the conqueror, the rest stored under guard. The Germans had initially insisted that the airforce be handed over but now allowed – as their sole concession – that it should simply be disarmed. As for the fleet, it was to be disarmed in the ports where it was anchored in peace time, several of which were situated in the occupied zone. The Germans solemnly swore not to use it during the war and not to lay claim to it when the peace treaty was signed. That was as much as they were prepared to vouchsafe with regard to the future; the French would simply have to trust Hitler's promises. Apart from all this, the defeated nation agreed to pay the costs of occupation, without any precise sum being specified. After an ineffectual attempt to discuss the matter, it also agreed to hand over any German refugees asked for; and until such time as a peace agreement was signed, it also agreed to Germany's holding hostage the two million prisoners that it had captured.

The implementation of this agreement was overshadowed by the signing of an armistice with Italy, which the French refused to recognize as a victor but which the Germans did not wish to offend. The meeting took place in Rome, and the Italians forced themselves to show the moderation desired by Hitler. Their zone of occupation amounted to no more than fifteen or so communes straddling the frontier. They were to oversee the disarmament of the French army in North Africa, Syria and Somalia. As a colonial power themselves, they agreed that the demobilization here was to be no more than partial.

On 25 June, these armistices came into force. A few days later, the guns were again booming. This time the shells were British and they were pounding the French fleet moored at Mers el-Kébir near Oran in Algeria. Several ships were sunk, others seriously damaged and close on 1300 French sailors were killed. As soon as they had seen the French moving towards a separate peace, the English leaders had become concerned as to the fate of the fleet. They could not trust the German assurances and were not inclined to accept the word of the French leaders, headed by Darlan, who swore that they would not allow their ships to fall into the hands of the Germans. How could they be certain that these men, whose anglophobia was becoming increasingly marked, would not yield to threats or – even worse – would not make use of their fleet to buy clemency from their victors?

Rather than live with this sword of Damocles, Churchill preferred to destroy it. By this brutal operation, prompted by alarm verging on panic in the face of his own precarious strategic position, he made his intransigent determination to continue the struggle abundantly clear not only to Hitler, but also to the Americans and his own compatriots. One result of his gesture, which took the risk of provoking a confrontation with a former ally, was to confirm the choices made by the new French leaders. It shocked much of French public opinion, which presented it as a further justification for its desire to halt the struggle. It also made the task of the rebel French general in London virtually impossible.

The armistice was to become increasingly controversial. After the war, Vichy's supporters defended it with fragile and anachronistic historical excuses: they claimed that by saving North Africa from occupation by the Axis powers, it had safeguarded the chances of an allied landing and thereby laid the foundations of the German defeat. In the summer of 1940, however, nothing could have been further from the minds of men who were scornfully dismissing any idea of British resistance. The choice of an armistice needs no subtle explanations: only quite exceptional leaders would have resisted such an easy way out. Politically, it satisfied most of the population, desperate for a return to peace. Militarily, it made it possible to limit the destruction and to salvage whatever was salvageable: part of the metropolitan territory, the empire, the fleet and a tiny army. In contrast, the price for continuing the struggle would have been high: virtually the entire metropolitan army captured, the fleet exposed to air attacks, North Africa threatened, possibly conquered – and all for the sole satisfaction of making the Germans pay dearly for crossing the Mediterranean. Diplomatically, it provided a margin of manoeuvre, avoided increased dependence on England and held out the hope of favourably disposing the conqueror.

One reason why those considerations prevailed was clearly that others were found to add their weight to them. The grudges held against England were compounded by the expectation of imminent defeat. Germany seemed destined to uncheckable, irreversible success: even if England did hold out, it would never regain a footing on the continent. But would the conqueror allow a life to the conquered? By ceasing to fight and abandoning its British ally to its fate, France was facilitating a general German victory and ran the risk of itself being stifled in a Europe dominated by Hitler. But, however hard Pétain expected the peace to be, he clung to the belief – as he told Bullitt on 1 July – that France would be able to survive in a Nazi Europe: in a subordinate position, to be sure, but with honour, since it would be in Germany's interest to win its goodwill.[8]

Meanwhile, on the other side of the scales, what was de Gaulle offering? Loyalty to alliances, a proud vision of France, its standing and its mission, and the conviction that in a Nazi Europe it would certainly be fatally reduced. But, as de Gaulle well knew, pride and foresight, even lucid foresight, do not provide adequate bases for policies. Strategically, he was counting on a triple development: betting on Britain's will and ability to hold fast, on the conflict assuming world-wide proportions through the intervention of the United States and the collapse of the German–Soviet *entente*, and on the final superiority of the allied forces. In contrast to Pétain's, his vision was wide and far-sighted and he was able to rise above the conventions and limitations of his education, social milieu and profession. History proved him right. But at the time, many French people found Pétain more of a comfort.

The French leaders followed their decision to stop fighting with a new one. On 25 June, Pétain addressed his compatriots to inform them of the implementation of the armistices. In the very same breath, he announced the beginning of a new order and bade them help him to set up a 'new France'. 'The government remains free, France will be administered solely by Frenchmen.' The reform of the nation was a French affair; there was no need to wait for a peace treaty that would surely not be long in coming.

The switch in foreign policy did not inevitably have to be accompanied by a change of regime. However, for the new French leaders, the two decisions went hand in hand. It was patently clear that Pétain and Weygand were fearful of all-out war: they believed it would destroy not only the army but the entire structure of society, all of which would play into the hands of their enemies. An obsession with anticommunism and with order more generally was the powerful motivating force upon which the whole history of Vichy rests. Nor can there be the slightest doubt that, through the trails of smoke left by the disaster, they soon imagined they glimpsed a possibility for national reform, which in its turn required a degree of sovereignty. Although they may not have been preponderant, these considerations were certainly germane to the decision to favour an armistice.

Pierre Laval played a key role in the operations that resulted in the change of regime. On 23 June, Pétain had brought him into the government as vice-president of the Council. Laval, with his reputation for Auvergnat cunning, knew how shaky his own position was in a milieu where parliamentary representatives were not exactly considered God's gift to mankind. Seeing that Pétain had no clear idea as to how to proceed, he offered his own services to get Parliament itself to effect the change. While not much love was lost between the two men, the power of common interests that linked them was to prove both strong and pliant. Laval wanted to secure a favourable peace; Pétain wanted a new order for the country.

So far, everything had been decided by two or three dozen political or military leaders. However, the reform of the country's institutions involved over 600 members of Parliament, almost all the nation's representatives, some of whom had been elected in 1936, while the Senate was a mirror reflection of rural France. Having convoked both chambers to a National Assembly in Vichy, to which the government had by now moved, Laval set about finding a majority. The aim was to vote full powers to Pétain to promulgate a new constitution. Laval used every cunning tactic in his book to hook, retain and convince, making much of the need for the French to adapt their institutions to the regimes of their conquerors if they were to win moderate peace terms from them. He met with no serious opposition, and had no difficulty in sidelining any counter-proposals designed to safeguard the role of Parliament and republican principles. Any idea of France leaving the war yet remaining republican was pushed aside. And so it was that another leap in the dark was taken. On 9 July, the National Assembly almost unanimously adopted the principle of revising the constitution. On the following day, a strong majority invested Pétain with full powers.

In the wake of their ministers, most backbenchers now also took the easy way out. The shock of defeat, which had rekindled a more or less strong disaffection with the republican regime, the temptation to lay all responsibility for future decisions at Pétain's door, the desire of some members to demonstrate overwhelming solidarity so as to favour French chances when it came to peace negotiations – everything encouraged them to quit as a body in return for a few formal concessions from Laval: one allusion to the Republic, and ratification of the future constitution by the assemblies that it created. At this point nobody, not even in the small leftist minority that had voted against full powers for Pétain, voiced any criticism of the armistice or warned against the illusion of an early peace.

Hardly had the parliamentary representatives left Vichy than Pétain, in his promulgation of a series of constitutional acts, revealed what use he intended to make of the powers granted to him. The old marshal assumed the functions of head of state and full governmental powers and designated Laval as his successor. The only power he denied himself was that of declaring war, for which it would be necessary to obtain prior 'agreement from the Legislative Assemblies'. Laval had promised as much on 10 July, in response to fears aroused by the anglophobic attitude of the new leaders. Even when Pétain exceeded the terms of his mandate, no protests were heard, not even from the president of the Republic, who had been packed off home, or from the presidents of the two chambers, Herriot and Jeanneney.

The new authority stepped forward draped in the mantle of legitimacy. Amid the general disarray and the chaos engendered by the defeat, its great advantage was that it existed and promised to heed the cries rising from the shattered nation. It stepped into a remarkable political void: with the sole exception of the French communists, who had very little clout, the political parties had vanished from the scene. The way was open for national renewal, and the path that it would follow was soon made clear: the administration was to be purged, freemasonry banned, those responsible for the defeat punished, communists and Gaullists hunted down, certain French citizens deprived of their nationality, and a 'Jewish Statute' drawn up.

Right from the start Vichy provoked opposition in various quarters, but for the time being that opposition was dispersed and covert. It also aroused dissidence within its own ranks, amongst men who had so far supported it. The first 'men of Vichy' had identified themselves at Bordeaux. In Vichy itself, they emerged fully, campaigning with Laval at their head and uniting in support of a text produced by the deputy Gaston Bergery, which called for a new order within and, externally, for collaboration with the conqueror. The motion was supported by close on one hundred parliamentary representatives hailing from right across the political spectrum. As their own particular contribution to the establishment of the new regime and one that would assure them a place in it, a number of them, led by Bergery and Déat, tried to set up a single party. But Pétain turned the plan down, and the group disintegrated. Many of its supporters, led by Déat, went off to Paris. There, with the encouragement of the occupying power, a multi-coloured group of dissenters was soon formed: some considered the internal policies of Vichy too reactionary, others thought them too soft, and all found its policy of collaboration too timid. Had there been a French government in exile or a government that had signed the armistice yet remained republican, such a movement would have materialized anyway. But the existence of the new regime gave a specific impulse to its emergence and development. By using the defeat as an opportunity to change the country's institutions, instead of making the survival of the nation its priority, Vichy gave rise to dissent over the content of those changes. It was easy for the occupying power to exploit this.

France now entered upon an era of divided allegiances. In the summer of 1940, Vichy held pride of place. Its leaders embarked upon internal reforms before anything was fixed externally and with the postulates on which their policies rested yet to be verified. There can be no doubt that one reason why they accepted defeat so easily was that mentally they were ready both to switch direction in the country's external policies and also to change its internal structures. Militarily they were one war out of date; politically they were two wars behind, confusing Hitler with Bismarck in their hopes of a peace that would certainly be hard but from which France could arise once more, just as it had in the past.

The Third Republic had been born of a defeat and also died from one. In 1870, the Republican party, set in the saddle by Napoleon III's military failure, refused to bow down and instead continued the struggle as well as it could. In 1940, the basis of the new regime was a precipitate acceptance of defeat and future subordination. The grave-diggers of the Republic had belatedly learned a lesson from 1870–71. There would be no all-out war to engender more communes, no snipers to engender social disorder; but instead a return to peace, a return to order, a return to France.

2

An undecided present

Happy the government whose actions chime with the desires of those governed! The armistice was popular, and the change of regime was not unpopular. Pétain was seen as a saviour. In the parts of the country where the Germans installed themselves, minds were pacified remarkably quickly. The booted and helmeted enemy was surprised by its civil reception. The career of what was soon to be known as the Vichy government began at its peak, and the occupation began with a pleasant surprise. The French people were relieved to emerge from the tunnel of war. Dazed and groping, they thereupon entered another tunnel, even longer, much darker and more stifling.

Continue the struggle? That was medicine for strong constitutions only. Possibly only in the north, where the fighting had been fierce and the dislocation of the armies had not been witnessed, would people ready to take it have been found. Meanwhile, the millions cast on to the roads as refugees longed for an end to their wanderings and routed soldiers were hoping the cessation of hostilities would bring an end to their Odyssey or release from captivity. People in the south, swamped with both of these categories, feared a continuing struggle that would expose them to the same fate. Nothing seemed as important as stopping the fighting, reuniting families and returning to normal.

The defeat sanctioned by the armistice came as a shock, provoking general consternation, and there were many who wept or raged. But the sense of relief was equally evident. Perhaps it had been ripening for weeks. Saint-Exupéry, looking back in 1943 on his own war of May–June 1940, remembered a military France gripped by 'a kind of gut terror' and a civilian France determined not to resist and receiving the Germans with 'a terrible "ouf" of relief'.[1] This was perhaps an exaggerated view of the widespread desire not to prolong the agony. Edmond Duméril, a teacher of German in Nantes, who found himself attached to the prefecture as an interpreter, was a patriot who was deeply shaken by what had happened. Yet on 18 June, following Pétain's appeal to cease fighting, even he was writing in his diary: 'They say that some of the military would like to go on blowing up the Loire bridges; but to what end? We must hope that the armistice conditions will be accepted soon, to avoid further destruction.'[2]

In some people the armistice provoked an initial reaction of rejection, later to subside into bitter resignation. Guy de Pourtalès was following the national drama from his home in Switzerland. His son, who had been called up, had been killed; it would be several weeks before the news reached him. Pourtalès deplored the armistice, poured scorn on Pétain and was relying on de Gaulle, hoping that the fleet would rally to him quickly.[3] By the end of June, he reckoned that his hopes were in vain. Next, he was appalled by the British attack at Mers el-Kébir, which made the armistice decision seem acceptable to many and strengthened an already widespread anglophobia. When de Gaulle asked him to set himself at the head of 'Free France' in Switzerland, Pourtalès declined. Despite his distaste, the only thing to do was fall in with Pétain. 'France must not be divided with the Germans as occupiers. We must present them with a united national front. Once our African colonies had rallied to Pétain and the French fleet had been attacked by the English, the opposition had lost the day.'[4]

The French were much less concerned with the change of regime than with the end of the fighting. But some certainly welcomed it. For others, it tempered their bitterness: could it be that misfortunes do sometimes come singly? That was the initial reaction of conservatives who were not necessarily hardened reactionaries and many of whom later changed their minds. Paul Claudel, who had left for Algeria, thinking that the struggle would continue, returned home crushed by the armistice and its 'terrible, shameful conditions (the surrender of all refugees)', but then allowed the developments in Vichy to raise his spirits a little: 'My consolation lies in witnessing the end of this foul parliamentary regime that for years has been eating away at France like a generalized cancer. At least this is the end of the Popular Front, the CGT, the processions with raised clenched fists, the manifestos signed by communists and Catholics alike, the foul tyranny of the bars, freemasons, foreigners, and little schoolmasters. At least, let us hope so!'[5]

A pyramid could be erected from such quotations, some of which come even from the small circle of those first to resist, who are as harsh as any in their condemnation of the Third Republic. The regime disappeared amid massive discredit because it was linked with a past of social unrest and political divisions that seemed to have paved the way for the disaster. Should we conclude that the French people applauded the burial of the Republic? Had they been consulted, they might well, as in 1871, when the Germans held twenty-five departments, have voted for the peace party. They might have acclaimed Pétain, countenanced introducing more authority into the constitution and accepted a Roman-type dictatorship in the interval. But a total break with republican principles? A minority did desire the death of 'the whore', and a majority accepted the idea of a new order; but nobody warned them that it would erase the achievements of the Revolution. The face of the new government was still hazy, the swelling refrain of authoritarianism fell upon the ears of a bemused population. And that refrain was coming from the lips of respected people, starting with Pétain himself, whose presence made everything acceptable. Besides, Pétain did not hold up any mirror to a future with a government that would cling against all reason to the politics of collaboration and express its exasperation in militia-based repression. At this juncture, the French were grateful to him for having brought the fighting to an end, for lending the defeated country his prestige and for offering them words of compassion. Pétain was the one fixed star on a collapsed horizon, the man who could restore the four cardinal points for them: the defeat was irretrievable; it was necessary to accept the inevitable and build anew.

So none of what people such as Weygand so much feared came to pass. Though they turned against armed resistance, the French did not turn against social order. Their reaction was to cry treachery, to point the finger at those they considered guilty, and to beat their breasts in an impulse of contrition that suited the interpretation of the defeat suggested by Pétain.[6] Nor was their reaction unique in the Western Europe now overrun by the German armies. The Belgians and the Dutch experienced the same vacillation, bitterly criticizing their departing governments and resigning themselves to an accommodation with the victor:[7] Pétainism without Pétain, as you might say. In besieged England, de Gaulle was keenly conscious of his solitude. Of the 15000 French soldiers and sailors that the undertow from the French campaign had stranded there, only a few hundred joined the Free French forces: the vast majority chose repatriation to Vichy France. And even amongst the handful of French who did take the path of exile, to England or to the United States, Gaullism was to elicit at least as much doubt, opposition or even fierce hostility as encouragement and support.

While cheers were greeting an old marshal in a spa as he set about imposing his cure upon France, another part of the country was becoming acquainted with its occupiers. These were not greeted with bread and salt as they were to be a year later, in some regions of the Ukraine. But nor were they fired upon: the *franc-tireurs* of 1870–71 had produced no descendants.

On 19 June, at half past midday, in Nantes, Duméril heard a loud clamour and witnessed the arrival of the first green uniforms. 'What stern, morose faces beneath the low helmets that make them look so fierce! And there were French people thoughtless enough to line the streets to see them.' By late afternoon the cafés were closed, telephones had been cut off and the first posters were announcing a curfew and enforcing the temporary occupation currency. In the centre of town, Duméril noticed a knot of Germans. 'The soldiers were surrounded by civilians who were trying to interview them, without a trace of animosity, while the Germans took photographs of them.'[8] François Mauriac had the same experience in the south-west and wrote of 'spectators looking as excited as at the Tour de France', going on to exhort his compatriots to show a little dignity: 'Have eyes that see nothing.'[9]

The first days dragged by in anxiety. The occupiers picked out hostages – from amongst the local élites, according to the traditional formula – who were to be held responsible for the attitude of the population. They requisitioned as they pleased, leaving behind them premises filthy and vandalized, and in some cases victims violated. Exactions and looting were common enough, afflicting a rural population already sorely taxed by floods of refugees, which now rediscovered the ancient law of seizure that respected neither thresholds nor property rights. In Eure-et Loire, where Jean Moulin, who was himself beaten up, was prefect, the mayor of Prasville wrote on 9 July: 'Order is maintained, the looting is no longer by civilians. Convoys of Germans (soldiers) are living off the land – taking over houses to stay in, strewing straw in every room, to sleep on. They throw the furniture out, make free with the kitchen without so much as a by-your-leave, seize meat, wood, etc. They grab hay, straw and oats to feed their horses. They are the absolute masters.'[10] Then, as the furious waters of the invasion settled into regular channels, the anger and terror died down. The German authorities were the first to show concern to take their troops in hand, seeking now to present an attractive face – that of a victor bringing help to the refugees and re-establishing essential services.

In the larger towns and in Paris, which had been deserted by most of its inhabitants, the troops installing themselves caused less trouble, but the inhabitants found their crossroads bristling with placards in German, the swastika flag flying over public buildings, and soldiers crowding the shops and doing the rounds of the monuments. Paul Léautaud, who had decided to stay in his house at Fontenay-aux-Roses, with his cats, dogs and monkey, spotted his first soldier at the entrance to the Luxemburg Gardens. 'I felt nothing. I did not even pause to glance at him.' The next day one of his friends, a woman, paid him a visit. 'She was bowled over, affronted, sickened by the Germans' entry into Paris, shamed, dishonoured by it. Couldn't get over my serenity, my indifference.' For Léautaud, the defeat was in the order of things, the price of a whole backlog 'of mistakes and incompetence'; and it would result in hard conditions for France. But the future was not entirely dark. 'Now we have a long period of peace before us. Germany will be so strong!' So why not 'celebrate the peace' with a bottle of champagne and cakes?[11]

After the first moments, people were on the whole agreeably surprised. They felt reassured by the correct behaviour of the troops and the diligence of their officers, who were quite prepared to take action against lapses of discipline. At home in Pernand-Vergelesse, on 20 June, Jacques Copeau noted: 'The peasants are calm. Glad to have escaped the danger. Very impressed by the good behaviour of the invaders and their perfect efficiency.' The villagers were amazed not to be subjected to a wave of barbarians, as they were expecting. They noted the distressing contrast between the shattered French armies and the conquerors. One of his contacts told him, 'These people are happy. They are taking in the harvest.'[12]

Similar positive comments were to be heard on all sides, accompanied by unflattering criticisms of all things French. Even people of non-conformist inclinations succumbed to the general tendency. Galtier-Boissière found 'the faces of the German officers more intelligent than our own. These are no bemonocled dandies or sword-rattlers', and went on to declare: 'The Germans who have chosen the military profession are intelligent men, whereas, with us, they are all imbeciles.'[13] Similar reactions had been noted after the 1870 defeat, as can be seen from the following words addressed by a Frenchman to the German writer Theodore Fontane: 'Paris is outrageous. We are crazy. Look at the way we live: between the absinthe bottle and the billiard table or the billiard table and the absinthe bottle. That's the French nation for you! And what is the consequence? We have no great men; we have no ideas. Ideas: there is the cause of your superiority.'[14]

The earliest reports of the Germans, for their part, note that people are 'much impressed by the discipline' of the troops and that 'many French people express their appreciation regarding the relations of cameraderie that exist between our officers and the ordinary soldiers'.[15] For decades clichés had been circulating concerning the invaders' technical superiority and their sense of organization; and these now acquired a new lease of life. On the other hand, others suddenly fell into disuse. Where were the invaders of 1870, or even of 1914, with all their heavy trappings, who trailed such a strong whiff of leather and tobacco behind them? Now the comments focused upon the Germans' youth, their health, their passion for breaking into song, and their obsessive cleanliness that caused soldiers to gather around every fountain and seemed to rid them of the repulsive smell of the invasion.

Hatred, in general, was remarkable for its absence. In his precious account of the exodus, Léon Werth notes that the word 'Boches' has virtually disappeared and that women talk of not 'the Germans', but 'the soldiers', 'as if a kind of equivalence existed between all the armies of the world'.[16] He notices how quickly and easily people get used to their presence. On 1 July, Simone de Beauvoir, who had recently returned to Paris, went out to the suburbs for the day and then hitched lifts to get back to town. 'When the car drew up near a bridge, a German soldier threw us a bar of chocolate from his lorry. Others were chatting gaily with pretty girls. The chap driving the car said to me: "Plenty of little Germans are going to be made!" I have heard that said ten times or more, and never with any blame implied. "Well, it's nature", said my chap, "You don't have to speak the same language for that". I have seen no hatred anywhere, only panicky alarm among villagers, and when their fear subsided, their eyes were wide with gratitude.'[17]

In the free zone, where armistice control commissions were overseeing the disarming of the French troops, the Germans similarly noticed that they were not objects of hatred. They registered the existence of anglophobic and antisemitic feeling and detected in some circles a desire for an *entente* with Germany. They concluded that the general hope was for a return to normality and a rapid peace.[18]

Just as there were some who welcomed the new government, there were also some – admittedly, a minority – who approved of the German order. In Paris, Cardinal Baudrillart, despite his deep-seated germanophobia, feared the communards even more than the Prussians. On 23 June, he noted in his diary: 'Right now, we need the Germans here, to restore a measure of order.'[19] Some rejoiced openly that France had found a master, as did, for instance, a man heard by Yves Farge to say, in June 1940: 'Now the French will learn what order is!'[20] In late August, Guy de Pourtalès, whose distrust of the 'defeatists of Vichy' was increasing daily, encountered a couple of compatriots. 'Our discussion was somewhat heated. Hitler frightens them far less than Stalin does. Anything rather than bolshevism is the cry of these two comfortably-off bourgeois who tremble for their money, their houses and their peace of mind. And so much the worse for France: it will suffer (but then suffering is good and useful); it will be poor (but then poverty is an element of strength); it will be reborn only very slowly (well, let it take twenty, thirty, fifty years if it has to, what does it matter?), but above all, no bolshevism. If England is victorious, won't we see Blum, Mandel, freemasonry, the Popular Front, the Reds, all returning to France? . . . Rather Hitler, any day. Rather the German occupation. So, quick, quick, let's have done with the war, even if it ends in victory for Hitler.'[21] During the exodus, a similar view had been expressed in more forthright and brutal fashion to Léon Werth: 'It'll be a protectorate, like Morocco . . . We'll be no worse off, we'll work as we used to.'[22]

The prevailing mood was one of resignation and acceptance. It was accompanied by an appeal for discipline and austerity, the identification of those deemed guilty, and widespread self-flagellation. The shock of defeat had not worn off, people were still crushed by the impression of strength given by the German forces. But even if more and more people soon began to hope for victory for England, they remained in grave doubt as to the chances of their hopes being realized. Where were the steadfast spirits in the summer of 1940? There were not many who swam against the tide of this bitter or morose resignation often shot through with hopes of a possible future in a German Europe and delusions as to Hitler's intentions. In their letters and diaries many writers support the prevailing climate of opinion, without necessarily going so far as the resentful Drieu La Rochelle, to whom the defeat gave a certain amount of satisfaction,[23] or Jacques Chardonne who on 26 June wrote: 'I am no fonder of the Germans than before, nor of their regime, and I do not believe that it will get far in France. I do not like them, but I am resigned . . . Their occupation has been remarkably decent. I think they want France as a friend. And that seems to be the policy of the Pétain government. It is also mine, for I am not determined to make the worst of everything and I will not call down unnecessary evils upon our heads.'[24]

But what about a man such as François Mauriac, who stood up against Francoism in Spain, at the price of a painful conflict with the conservative catholicism that had nurtured him? On 25 August, Henri Guillemin heard him declare, à propos of de Gaulle: 'Purely symbolic, his intransigence. Very fine, but inoperable.'[25] Shocked by the defeat and revolted by Mers el-Kébir ('Mr Winston Churchill has united France against England – perhaps for many years'),[26] Mauriac was trying to see his way forward. On 25 June, he wrote: 'We are so storm-tossed that our feelings change from one day to the next. And no doubt it would be wise to keep quiet and wait for our destiny to become clearer.' The opinions that he did express certainly reflect his uncertainty. 'Nothing can be set up in France until we are free again. All that is being done, thanks to the presence of the foreigner, will be swept aside. I truly believe that. In our country, it is the destiny of right-wing ideas, even the most equitable, even the wisest of them, never to triumph except as a result of the misfortunes of our country. The commonplace of governments brought in on enemy luggage vans is, alas, a historical truth . . . Yet all we can do today is adopt a policy of collaboration, in so far as is possible. However, I doubt whether the essential condition, which would be to have a government that the Germans would respect, can be met by our present leaders, . . . Alas!'[27]

And what about Gide? Overwhelmed by the fall of France, he was so affected by the spectacle of the German victory that he could not repress his admiration for Hitler, even as he recognized how calamitous it was, nor fail to wonder whether it might not usher in better times, even though he knew that the Nazi regime denied the values to which he himself most clung.[28] His view of his compatriots was not flattering: 'If German domination were to secure us affluence, nine out of ten French people would accept it, three or four of them most cheerfully.' He then formulated his own line of conduct, one that he would not be alone in following: 'To seek agreement with the enemy is not cowardice, but wisdom, as is accepting the inevitable . . . What would be the point in battering ourselves against the bars of our cage? To suffer less from the cramped nature of the prison, the only thing to do is to keep to the space in the centre.'[29]

Like Mauriac, Jacques Copeau was turning over confused ideas in his head. The war had been inevitable and the French had salvaged their honour; victory would have rewarded an evil regime. But even if the defeat presented an opportunity to rebuild on new foundations, did it not place France at the mercy of its conqueror? Copeau, like Gide, was wondering what Germany's intentions were ('Germany will heed only its own interests in maintaining our divisions and encouraging our mistakes unless, perhaps, it needs a strong, healthy France, to further its world policies') and was veering from one possibility to its opposite to find the correct answer ('Is Hitler about to astound us by his magnanimity and seize the chance to reveal his greatness?').[30] He then proceeded to speculate upon a conciliatory peace to which France could respond by purging itself of 'old historical rancours' and by abandoning any idea of 'military and political hegemony'.[31]

Alain, the voice of democratic individualism and mistrust of the authorities, also fell victim to Hitler's fascination and set about reading *Mein Kampf*, which led him to write on 23 July 1940: 'For my part, I hope the Germans will win because the likes of de Gaulle must not be allowed to triumph in our country.'[32] Even Jean Paulhan, high priest of the *Nouvelle Revue Française* (*NRF*), who soon joined the resistance, was not entirely proof against the vacillation that so characterized the summer of 1940. He hoped for an English victory, while not altogether believing in it, and admired de Gaulle while finding some good in Pétain, whom he did not altogether trust: 'I really like de Gaulle and what he says. But Pétain's work, on the whole, could be useful. (And heaven help the English.)'[33] No wonder men such as Jean Guéhenno suffered in their isolation.[34]

While most French people put up with the situation morosely, in the occupied zone some were more welcoming to the invader. Every walk of social life saw the appearance of patterns of behaviour that went well beyond the minimal adaptation that circumstances demanded. Some believed open accommodation to be necessary, others positively favoured it, and yet others were satisfying a thirst for revenge.

Industrialists who had been working for the national defence were visited by German officers who brought them military orders. The first contact was usually stiff and menace-laden, ending with formal notice to deliver. Acquiescence was not hard to elicit. The industrialists were anxious about an economic reconversion that promised to be painful. All that held them back was fear of condemnation by the government. Schneider declared that, in the interests of his workers, he would not refuse to take orders; but he would prefer to make locomotives rather than war materials. If the Germans wished him to produce war materials, they would have to obtain authorization from the French state. It was not long before an order was accepted, for heavy presses used in the manufacture of aircraft bombs. As the German officer involved remarked, the director of Schneider's knew full well that presses of this kind were not used for making typewriters. However, he made no objection to this order which 'would pass unnoticed by most of the work force'.[35] Other industrialists were even more anxious to please. The director of Gnome and Rhône was not only prepared to turn out complete aircraft engines, but suggested going in person to seek authorization from the government.[36]

Alfred Pose was the director general of the Banque Nationale pour le Commerce et l'Industrie (BNCI), one of the largest banks in the country. Keen to reopen its counters as soon as possible, in which he was at one with the occupiers, he set off, armed with a free-pass, to rally branches throughout the occupied zone. He even obtained permission to travel to Alsace-Lorraine and on his return wrote as follows to his contact in the military administration: 'I was able to assess the exact position of the banking question in those provinces and, when the Dresdner Bank approached us, I issued instructions with a view to engage in discussions that will certainly have to be continued either in Paris or in Germany.'[37] Pose had decided to sell the bank's Alsace-Lorraine branches before the conclusion of the peace treaty, with its expected territorial losses, further reduced their value. Clearly determined to ingratiate himself with the conquerors, he suggested to the official in the military administration responsible for the banking sector that he should put at the latter's disposal his bank's department of financial and economic studies.[38] Meanwhile his assistant went the rounds of the occupation services to let them all know that the BNCI was prepared for 'the most intense collaboration with the German banks'.[39]

Not all businesses were as upfront as the BNCI. But almost all were anxious to avoid bankruptcy, even if this meant going after money regardless of where it was to be found. The purveyor of office equipment to the German embassy, who had lost his client in September 1939, obligingly made himself known once again: 'Our services are able to cater for all your needs in the way of typewriters, calculators and duplicating machines, as in the past.'[40] A translating agency, keen to help these poor foreigners communicate with the native population, informed the military command that it provided 'all translations from all languages, in particular French to German and vice versa, more speedily and economically than any other concern in Paris'.[41] Other firms were anxious not to incur any suspicion. On 13 August 1940, the management of the Félix Potin company sacked a manageress whom it had employed for forty-two years. The lady was Jewish; it was a great shame, but 'if we keep Israelites in our upper personnel, the Germans will seize our business'.[42] At this date, neither the occupying authorities nor Vichy had yet made any moves against the Jews

There seemed, on the face of it, no reason why the workers should be keen to please. Mindful of the high moments of the Popular Front, the Germans were prepared for hostility, even for passive resistance. But those who had fled returned to the occupied zone: for example, the Renault workers encountered by Maurice Martin du Gard, who declared, 'We're off to work for the Boches, but what the hell! We have to live.'[43] In the autumn of 1940, a German report stressed that the workers had manifested a 'striking' desire to return to work, even in factories working for Germany, so fearful were they of unemployment.[44]

The world of culture displayed a similar desire to return to normal and, in some cases, a similar eagerness to appear in a favourable light. On 9 July, Léautaud, working at the *Mercure de France*, was told by his director of 'a marvellous idea': 'an edition, at a price within everybody's means, of the biographical section of Hitler's *Mein Kampf*, to show the origins and development of the great man'.[45] Bernard Grasset, who found himself in the free zone, was moving heaven and earth in order to get back to Paris, not without seeking assurances that the occupying power would not exact reprisals for earlier works (he was bitterly regretting having published Hitler's personal enemy, Strasser) and that it would refrain from ordering him what to publish. Through intermediaries, he made it known that he held healthy opinions. He assured the German journalist Friedrich Sieburg that his 'attitude towards authority was very close to that which inspired the actions' of the government of the Reich and that he felt 'the same scorn for the regime that had led France to the abyss'. Meanwhile to Alphonse de Chateaubriant, who stood in good favour and whose new weekly, *La Gerbe*, he wished to publish, he declared, hand on heart, 'You know, my dear Chateaubriant, that I am a true Frenchman, with none of those unhealthy connections that the Germans so rightly condemn . . . However far back you go in both branches of my family, you will find neither a Jew nor a Jewess. It is perhaps useful to make this quite clear.'[46]

The same desire to please filtered down from publishers to booksellers. On 27 August, French police, accompanied by German police, seized anti-German books that appeared on a list – the first version of the 'Otto list'. Here is the German report on the exercise: 'The shopkeepers without hesitation handed over the books for which we asked. Furthermore, many of them offered us other works with anti-German contents that did not apear on the list.'[47] The compliance of some and the anxiety of others not to run any risks halved the work of the occupiers.

When Goebbels visited Paris on 1 July, Serge Lifar did the honours at the Opéra. Seemingly enchanted by the club-footed minister, the star dancer was keen to invite him to the new season's opening show. He therefore begged Ambassador Abetz to send him an invitation. 'Over the past years, I have devoted myself to a study of questions relating to dance and its history, and I hope soon to be able to present to Dr Goebbels my views on the prospects now opening up for dance in Germany.' Lifar fancied his chances as the Führer of European dance. At the German embassy, his letter provoked disquiet: might he be a Jew? After making enquiries, it proved possible to breathe again: Lifar was of Russian extraction. Goebbels was not able to return to Paris, but no matter: the dancer performed at the embassy on 3 September before an audience of high-ranking officers gathered to honour von Brauchitsch, the commander of land forces and the victor in the French campaign.[48]

In the world of politics, the parties were playing dead. Only the communists were at all active. But the descendants of the communards had left their grandparents well and truly behind them in the cemetery of Père Lachaise. The clandestine *Humanité* was so keen to re-emerge into public light that its issue of 19 June reproduced the German military communiqué of the day in exactly the same fashion as the newspapers that appeared with the blessing of the occupying power.[49] In other issues, it called for fraternization. Thus, on 4 July, it declared: 'It is particularly comforting, in these sad times, to see many Parisian workers chatting in a friendly way with German soldiers, either in the streets or in the corner bistro. Well done, comrades; keep it up, even if it does not meet with the approval of certain bourgeois who are every bit as stupid as they are harmful.'

But if the political parties had disappeared, there was no shortage of politicians trying to make the most of the new situation. And amongst those who were to be the leading lights of collaborationist Paris was to be found even a future member of the resistance, Loustaunau-Lascau. In his memoirs, he stated that he escaped to Vichy on 16 August 1940. However that may be, 17 August found him writing to the German embassy to request an interview: 'I am ready to form, with my friends, a new government within the framework of a doctrine which, as you know, was closely related to the ideas of the totalitarian States.' Claiming to have Pétain's support, he requested to be told of the victor's intentions: if it was a matter of concluding an honourable peace, he was prepared to collaborate; if not, he would melt into the background and silence.[50]

There were some, silenced since the run-up to the war, who now applauded the German victory. They included both Breton and Alsation separatist leaders. The former, who had been condemned to death in the 'phoney war' and had taken refuge in Germany, now returned in the wake of the occupying power; the latter owed their release from French prisons to it. Also included were antisemites who had gone so far as to ascribe more importance to the fight against the Jews than to the defence of the French nation. On 3 August 1940, one of them, who claimed to be a worker and a comrade-in-arms of Henry Coston, wrote as follows to Julius Streicher, one of the most extreme antisemites in the Nazi party: 'Sir, it is with good reason and for carefully deliberated motives that I venture to ask you to tell me how I can make contact with German groups fighting against Judaism.' Having listed his own services to the cause, he continued: 'Today I bless your people's victory because I know it is a civilizing one and, above all, that it will cure the French people of its most virulent malady: ignorance concerning the Jewish and masonic problem! As a war veteran myself, I am aware of the horrors of battle. My thoughts have been with all those noble victims who fell . . . Murder between Aryans, to the advantage of the Jews . . . If we had won this war, the Celtic Aryan race would have become totally European-negroid, that is to say indigenously Jewish.' The letter ends with a 'I am Hitlerian!'[51]

The French were curling up as if in a shell. The will to fight had gone, all was vacillation. On looking back, this summer was to be seen as a time when anything was possible, the best and also the worst. In September 1942, Bousquet, the chief of police in Vichy, paid a visit to Daladier, who was in prison, and told him of his own view of the defeat: 'Waves of ragged, retreating soldiers, disarmed and looting the villages. Then the arrival of the German army, orderly, disciplined, powerful and well-behaved; hence the French people's sympathy towards them. According to him, France could easily have been persuaded to collaborate with Germany at that point.'[52] Guéhenno, with a totally opposite attitude, remarked on 12 December 1941: 'One year ago, public opinion, weak and soft, was prepared to agree to anything. Vichy and Berlin together have by now contrived to make the entire country aware of its servitude.'[53]

By early autumn 1940, there was a palpable change in the atmosphere. The records from every quarter register a growing hostility towards the occupying power and a spreading hope of victory for the British. It was a massive, if not general tendency, but it did not resolve the confusion in people's minds and still left room for a widespread desire for accommodation.

On 19 October 1940, after speaking with Ramuz, Pourtalès in Switzerland wrote as follows: 'We have . . . more or less the same reactions: amazingly saddened by the sudden volte-face following the armistice, the end of traditional liberalism, the war against the Jews; Pétain staked everything on a German map, believing it would certainly prevail. And now people are asking, "But will it?" Ramuz told me sadly, "I no longer recognize the face of France".'[54]

3

A present past

WHY was there no massive, immediate rejection of the armistice, no hostility towards the government that signed it, no opposition to the policies that it introduced? Why such indecision *vis-à-vis* even the occupying power, to which some people adapted with such zeal? It is understandable that defeat came as a shock, the behaviour of the Germans as a surprise. But what about all the idolatry of the aged Marshal, the tendency to hope for a rapid return to normality and, in some cases, the arrangement or even *entente* sealed with the enemy, and the hesitations over the true nature of the Nazi regime? The French seem to have been weary of fighting, incapable of looking squarely at the enemy and thirsty for withdrawal and consolation.

They had the best of reasons for opposing Nazi Germany, and in opposition the best opportunity to restore unity. Such opposition would have provided a rallying point for the germanophobia of the national right, the liberalism of the centre, the antifascism of the left, and the antiracism and antipaganism of the Catholic world. In 1939 such a convergence had indeed appeared to be taking place. Then, the French had closed ranks – witness the popularity of Daladier, who was supported virtually on every side, even by the Church. An atmosphere of national unity swept the country, and measures such as the family code and the Marchandeau law repressing racism and antisemitism testified to a desire for a new start and a determination to prevent the national pact from being undermined. In September 1939, public opinion was behind the government and, although a certain lassitude crept in after a few months, the German attack stiffened people's resolve.[1]

The aftermath of the defeat revealed the fragility of that solidarity.

No doubt the event in itself was sufficiently traumatizing to force into being the idea that this was not simply one lost battle in a continuing war but rather a defeat that marked the end of one world and the beginning of another. But it would not have occasioned such an interpretation had not public opinion continued, beneath the concord of the phoney war, to foment all the doubts of the preceding decade – doubts that now caused people to hesitate as to what choice to make and that, in the eyes of many, made it acceptable to value reconstruction above liberation. A refusal to accept defeat and a determination to fight on would have been made possible by common values, a willingness for sacrifice in order to preserve them, and a sense of national fraternity. These, though, were conditional upon people harbouring no illusions regarding the enemy, placing their hopes and faith in their ally and maintaining solidarity with the other peoples of Europe who were also threatened by Nazi hegemony. What was needed was a tragic imagination capable of envisaging the future rather than an obsession with the past and self-pity, along with all the cheap hopes that such self-pity encouraged.

In August 1914, Charles Maurras, an expert on divisiveness, had written: 'The intensity of our external struggle will always depend to some extent upon the depth of the peace we have managed to promote among ourselves.'[2] How was it possible to stand together and face down the enemy when compatriots were divided, with differing opinions as to citizenship and uncertain as to the place and mission of their country in the world? In every respect the 1930s had undermined the cohesion of French society, recreating old cleavages and complicating them further with new confrontations. This was an unprecedented crisis and it struck extremely deeply because it simultaneously affected both the socio-political equilibrium of the country and also its international stance.

Ever since the nineteenth century, France had been notable for the relaxed pace of its modernization, which had favoured the maintenance of a relatively stable society underpinned by a large peasantry and prosperous middle classes. However, the aftermath of the Great War undermined this stability.[3] The growing rural exodus extended the suburbs and swelled a proletariat deeply conscious of a sense of exclusion. The devaluation of the franc, followed by the great depression, made the bourgeoisie insecure and poorer: the number of domestic servants dropped by over a quarter between 1911 and 1936. The formation of a national market and the circulation of ideas unsettled inherited modes of life and loosened the grip of traditional authorities. Through the works of Gabriel Le Bras and Canon Boulard, the Church suddenly discovered a pagan France, or at least a France undergoing a process of dechristianization, particularly amongst the working class and urban youth. On top of all this, the arrival of many foreigners, whose number almost doubled between 1921 and 1931, introduced an element of competition and anxiety with regard to the French national identity.

It is not hard to see that tendencies such as these must have unsettled those who clung to the past and reinvigorated the reactionary aspirations of the bulwarks of resistance to modernization represented by the aristocracy, the rural élites, the Catholic Church, and a section of employers. But equally perturbed were the 'new strata' upon which the Third Republic had been constructed: the self-employed and members of the liberal professions, who had placed their trust in a well-balanced France and moderate social mobility, were now looking back to the past as to a golden age and were beginning to claim protection and professional guarantees. The situation that they confronted led some of them to become politically active on the far right; for many who still adhered to orthodox republican choices it nurtured a sense of malaise and nostalgia upon which Pétain was able to capitalize after the defeat.

The fear of social change was strengthened by political developments. It is quite true that before 1914 the Third Republic was unstable at governmental levels and marked by strong ideological antagonisms, but at least it favoured the social status quo. But the aftermath of that war, which brought economic and financial matters to the fore, made many feel more dependent upon the state, whose aid seemed proportionately more precious and whose dominion more important. In 1924 and 1932, the radicals' accession to power, with the parliamentary support of the socialists, was enough to provoke serious revolt on the right. The victory of the Popular Front unleashed even stronger reactions, given that it raised the threat of a change in the system and was accompanied by unprecedented social unrest. With hindsight, it is easy to see that the institutions were not really seriously threatened by either side. Nevertheless, the experience had increased disaffection *vis-à-vis* the parliamentary republic and had prompted profound shifts of position: regression on the part of the Catholics towards the antiliberal and antimodern bases of their culture and on the part of the liberals towards their original élitism and distrust of universal suffrage, and even amongst genuine republicans a flagging support for democratic liberties.[4]

The political system remained intact, but the atmosphere that surrounded it was imbued with increasingly alien values.[5] Anti-communism, even within the ranks of the Popular Front, became a widespread, if not dominant passion:[6] communism that brought with it threats to institutions, social equilibrium, religion and the country's very security. Liberalism, the optimism of which was impaired by the great depression, was seriously losing ground, a fact that did not go unnoticed by some of its supporters. Individualism was increasingly out of its depth amid a wave of plans for social organization along technocratic, interventionist or corporatist lines, and visions of communal well-being drawn from conservative thinking or non-conformist grafts on to Christianity. And on top of this, there was all the sanitarian, natalist, populationist and eugenistic thinking which, encouraged by anxiety concerning the birth-rate decline, was conditioning people to think in terms of a social body and collective cures.[7] Alexis Carrel, in a work that won immediate fame (*L'Homme, cet inconnu*, 1935), encouraged this tendency. And Giraudoux ran very close to it when he pleaded for a sanitarian and carefully planned reconstruction of the country: a France made healthy by a 'racial policy', embellished by parks, festivals and exhibitions, and rallied around grandiose spectacles.[8] All these ideas set a high value on contributions from élites, scholars, and 'natural' experts and authorities, and promoted a widespread reaction against individualism in the name of collective imperatives and indivisible solidarities.

The political experience of the 1930s left in its wake a complex array of attitudes. On the right, it left a sediment of resentment, the gravity of which the historian Marc Bloch recognized in 1940, whilst serving in the army. Drawing attention to the 'chasm of prejudice that a section of the bourgeoisie is creating between itself and ordinary people', he added: 'I am afraid that none of us has fully appreciated the unbelievably powerful, tenacious and unanimous reaction that the Popular Front provoked among such people. We should remember this date – almost as important as the June Days [of 1848] – as one of the most critical moments in the history of France.'[9] No more than a few weeks later, Bloch was to be savouring the pertinence of his comparison, for just as people had rallied to the saviour of that moment, Louis Bonaparte, they were now rallying to Philippe Pétain.

On the left, the Popular Front had left behind it disappointment that was reflected in waning militancy, particularly in the trade unions, whose membership plummeted in 1938–39. The climate of disillusionment was encouraged by Daladier's government taking back many of the advantages won in 1936 and the new splits in workers' parties that hardened following the German–Soviet pact, disorienting many communists and dealing a massive blow to anti-fascism. It is important to take this into account just as much as the resentment felt on the right, for it was deeply to affect the reactions of the working classes up until about 1943, when a new wave of mobilization began. What with resentment on one side and demoralization on the other, on the eve of the war many people on both sides felt a profound aversion to party struggles that was reinforced by the spectacle of the Spanish tragedy, which nurtured a keen yearning for national unity. It was upon this foundation that the column of Pétain's glory was to rise.

The internal struggle had been compounded by the external crisis, placing the country in a most unenviable position. England, whose international situation was equally threatened, possessed greater internal stability. The other European powers were dictatorships, some of which, such as Italy and above all Germany, were enjoying growing power along with increasing popular support. France, divided internally, was facing an increasingly acute global challenge externally. Nazi Germany was speedily throwing off the shackles of Versailles, and meanwhile Italy's ambitions were asserting themselves in the Mediterranean, and Japan was expanding in the Far East. Never had the general situation seemed more threatening, never the risk of losing everything so probable. The League of Nations was clearly impotent in the face of Japan's aggression in Manchuria, followed by Italy's in Ethiopia. France's alliances were open to question: under threat from German and Italian expansionism, her small allies seemed more dangerous than useful. And the idea of establishing new links was profoundly divisive, for fascist Italy was anathema to the left, especially after its aggression against Ethiopia, the USSR equally so the right, once a victory for the Popular Front became a real possibility. England was still supportive, but could it be counted upon? Its balance of power policy, which had led it to sign a naval pact with Hitler in 1935, set many French teeth on edge.

During these years, international politics forced itself upon the attention of the French. Hitler's moves were front-page news and pictures of the wars in Ethiopia and China, let alone Spain, fostered the widespread anxiety that had first emerged right at the beginning of the decade when the idea of another war first began to haunt people's minds and create the 'pacifist depression' in which French nationalism was soon to become paralysed.[10] The Great War had left such deep wounds. The army of the dead cast a leaden shadow, and the cohorts of war-wounded drew attention to the scars left by a conflict whose memory the veterans' associations kept very much alive. Combativeness had by no means disappeared but a pacifist anxiety, a sense of 'What's the point?' that inclined people to resignation rather than sacrifice sounded a constant underlying note in public feeling. During the phoney war, the French accepted their trials but were anxious that they should cost as little as possible and rapidly come to an end.

Underlying everything was the exhaustion of a great power conscious of its decline, both demographic and economic, and fearful of a loss of status. It had taken a European coalition and two decades of war to bring down first revolutionary, then Napoleonic France. In 1870, Prussia had been strong enough to effect this on its own; in 1914, it had taken a world coalition and four years of desperate fighting to conquer Germany. It is true that, after 1870, France found some compensation in the expansion of its empire, which attained its zenith in 1919. But this did not blot out the memory of the way in which its powers had been diminished, let alone conceal the undeniable fact that victory had been won only thanks to the participation of its powerful allies or that the most the Treaty of Versailles could do was defer the conquered enemy's resurgence. The only choice left to France was between a policy of permanently keeping Germany down, for which – as soon became apparent – it lacked the means, or alternatively a policy of conciliation which, if maintained long term, risked turning it into a satellite. The two countries could only have been made to see that cooperation was in both their interests if the United States and Russia had brought their weight to bear upon European politics. As they did not, Germany, following the example of Japan in the Far East, made the most of the historical loophole provided by the abstention of the two potential superpowers and launched itself upon a conquest of European hegemony designed to enable it to play the role of a world power.

In the decade following the armistice, France's fortunes had risen, but for the next thirty years its power steadily declined, a fact that contributed to the fall of three political regimes. In the 1930s the French lived through the painful experience of being a conservative power that had more to lose than to gain from another war and on that account hovered between conciliation and firmness. The French cinema of the late 1930s testified to the effects of that uncertainty, reflecting in its representation of the external world 'a fundamental scepticism and a deep fear in the face of growing perils'.[11]

There were other indications too of this feeling of weakness, first and foremost the French sensitivity to foreign models. In the period between the wars a considerable number of French intellectuals eyed the new regimes of Europe with fascination when, that is, they were not making pilgrimages to Rome, Moscow or Berlin. France was decrepit, its message outdated or inappropriate, modernity lay elsewhere. One indication of this was the reception given to the political gestures that characterized the political scene at this time: the extended arm borrowed from Italy and Germany, and the raised clenched fist received from the German Communist party, which had invented it as a response to the Nazi salute. These were adoptions that testified to a lowering of national frontiers or at any rate to their permeability to common emotions, values and attitudes.

Another indication was a tightening in the definition of the national identity, a desire to recentre on a France understood in the most narrow, quasi-ethnic sense. Xenophobia and antisemitism, both long-standing tendencies, were on the rise, affecting virtually every sector.[12] What could be more telling than their eruption among writers such as Moraud, Giraudoux, Jouhandeau and Céline? One perceptive observer, Father Bonsirven, noted in 1936: 'A latent antisemitism reigns virtually everywhere, almost unconsciously, a mixture of mistrust, repulsion and prejudice.'[13] This antisemitism could all too easily serve to define identity since it fed on the familiar currents of the Christian tradition, xenophobia and opposition to the Republic, and was moreover fuelled by the international situation which helped to diffuse an image of the warmongering Jew – the Jew prepared to sacrifice France to defend his own race and interests, or Stalin.

The hesitancy and uncertainty, not to say paralysis, that were rooted in the double crisis affecting the country were also reflected in the somewhat unaggressive attitude that the French displayed towards the Nazi danger, despite the fact that traditional nationalism and recent memories of the long years of war had left a deep imprint upon the image of France's neighbour. People's minds were bogged down with the antinomies of law and brute force, and civilization and barbarity, along with a whole battery of clichés: the ponderousness of the Germans, their gregariousness, their obedience, their sentimentality, and also their energy and capacity for hard work and organization. And these were clichés that were all the more rigid given that so few French people had any direct experience of the neighbouring country. The same applied even in French scholarly circles: in advanced education, there were three times fewer German specialists than the number of French specialists in Germany.[14]

Germany's image was slightly improved by the attempts at reconciliation made, following Locarno, by the left, a minority of Catholics and a few industrialists.[15] But by 1930, and particularly once the Nazis had come to power, it suffered again, provoking a general mistrust tinged with trepidation. The power of Germany was feared, and the politics of the new regime were of a kind to increase that fear. Contrary to what is often claimed, the French public were provided with good information even if not many had read *Mein Kampf*. But although the press warned of danger, it was neither specific about it nor did it fully recognize where it lay. The very mass of negative clichés obscured the novelty of the phenomenon, and those who were forming public opinion further distorted it by forcing it to fit their own particular political images. For the democrats the Nazi government was that of a militaristic police-state, a kind of jackbooted Bonapartism – an image to which the liberals added that it practised economic interventionism of a kind that brought it close to socialism. Meanwhile the Marxist left ridiculed Hitler, mocking him for being a puppet of the great capitalists and taking care to distinguish between the German people and their regime – which is something that the nationalists, with their view of a Germany that never changed, certainly refused to do. Claudel, who had read *Mein Kampf* at the beginning of 1934, forthwith condemned 'the hideous spawn of Luther'. Like Maurras, who called Nazism 'the Islam of the North', he saw Hitler creating 'at the centre of Europe a kind of Islamism, a community that turns conquest into a kind of religious duty'.[16]

The French had been alerted to Nazi expansionism, but they failed to grasp how radical it was. Their incomprehension was occasioned partly by the blurring of perception effected by a bourgeois, democratic society faced with a regime that set a high value on heroism and fighting. Also at work was the blurring of perception due to historical experience, which made it difficult to conceive that war might entail rather more than shifting the odd frontier and exacting the payment of tribute. How could the French not have found it difficult to conceive that Nazism denied even the secular trend towards a world of nation-states? They had not realized that it aimed to incorporate within its empire not only all German minorities, but also other peoples held to be Germanic (the Flemish, the people of Luxemburg, the German Swiss, the Dutch, the Danes and the Scandinavians), regardless of their national identity; that, furthermore, it aimed to conquer an immense 'vital space' in Eastern Europe, at the cost of the Slav nations, whose élites were to be liquidated while the rest of their populations were either reduced to slave labour or expelled to make room for German colonizers; or finally that it was determined to eliminate, through exile or extermination, whole peoples to whom it refused the right to live in Nazi Europe, namely the gypsies, and above all the Jews. The confused image of the new German regime made it even more difficult to conceive of such upheavals, for its truly Nazi centre emerged only gradually from the conservative and reactionary matrix that surrounded it. Meantime, its leaders further increased the confusion by their many declarations of peaceful intent towards neighbouring countries, thereby buying themselves time to rearm so as eventually to use the language of force.

For most French people, while there seemed no reason to expect anything good from Nazi Germany, neither did there appear to be grounds for expecting the worst. The French crisis clearly encouraged people to bury their heads in the sand. The resurgence of German power accentuated the feeling of weakness experienced by many, while the 'pacifist record' repeatedly played by the Nazis fostered the hopes of men of peace such as Roger Martin du Gard who, following the remilitarization of the Rhineland, wrote 'I cling to my belief in a certain sincerity in Hitler's desire for peace. I sometimes sense an accent of authenticity in his words that moves me despite myself.'[17] The aspiration towards normality was fed by each successive government, each of which, in its concern for *détente*, gave its blessings to the many meetings organized between the two countries. In 1937–38, France was Germany's first partner in sporting events.[18] Even after war had broken out, hope persisted. Sartre, who had been called up, noted in 1940 that there were many in his regiment who were still hoping for an 'arrangement'.[19]

The general desire for peace and the sense of national weakness were compounded by confused vision engendered by the political crisis. Alongside groups intransigent in their rejection of the Nazis – the antifascist left, the Christian Democrats, all kinds of nationalists, and those persecuted by the regime – there were extensive areas of mixed opinion to be found. The Germanist Henry Lichtenberger, who himself advocated reconciliation between the two countries, in 1936 wrote as follows: 'People here float between a thousand contradictory feelings ranging from decided horror, through mistrust and anxiety, to curiosity mingled with sympathy or regret that in France we do not have a "strong man" of Hitler's ilk.'[20]

The tendency to detect 'merits' in Nazism, along with plenty of repugnant and deplorable aspects, was particularly – although not exclusively – prevalent on the right, above all in Catholic circles. Its positive points were considered to be its discipline, its community spirit, its taste for effort and self-sacrifice, the restoration of morality in public life, and its antiliberalism and antimarxism. *La Croix* condemned Nazism, in conformity with the views of the Pope, but its condemnation was relativized by the absolute anathema against communism and the approval that it expressed for certain aspects of the German regime: the repression of pornography, the restoration of the family, and its agricultural policies. During the phoney war an acute observer of the German scene, the Catholic Robert d'Harcourt, himself affected by the same combination of seduction and repulsion, wrote that 'many excellent French people' regarded the Nazi dictatorship as order, feeling a sympathy that he explained by 'a passionate desire for French cleanliness' and in which he detected an inferiority complex in the face of a 'strong' political regime that had achieved a certain restoration of morality on the other side of the Rhine.[21]

Hatred, it must be said, was not much in evidence, even absent. The rising tide of dangers had not rekindled detestation of the Boche. Novelists who set their works in Germany or wrote about it conveyed a 'positive and generous image'.[22] In the cinema, too, Germany was on the whole treated favourably. Films about earlier wars did not show the invader: the German threat was faceless, providing no focus for hatred. In general, up until the end of 1938, German characters and German culture were presented in an honourable and sympathetic light (as in Jean Renoir's *La Grande Illusion*, for instance). Instead of any attempt to provoke hostility against Germany, 'a soothing germanophilia coexisted alongside a minor current of anti-German feeling'.[23]

This confused attitude tinged by fear of war, the unease engendered by the French crisis and the curiosity that 'the German experience' provoked led to Nazi Germany arousing more interest than the Weimar Republic had. In the 1920s, fewer than 30000 French people crossed the Rhine each year; in 1931–2 close on 50000 did. After briefly falling in 1932, that figure doubled, reaching 105410 in 1936, then again fell slightly to 98833 in the following year.[24] The increased flow of visitors cannot be explained by economic relations, for these were certainly on the wane, despite the fact that friendly relations were established between a number of chambers of commerce.[25] Exchanges between schools and universities followed a similar curve. There were ten French teachers in Germany in 1930, thirty-nine in 1939; three lectors in 1932, nineteen in 1939. In 1931, the pen-friend system established connections between 4661 French and German schoolchildren; that number fell to 821 in 1934, then rose to 5933 in 1938.[26] Interchanges between schoolchildren and students of the two countries also increased considerably, through holiday courses and visits organized by various institutions and associations – war veterans' associations, the SNCF, Catholic schools and JOC (delegations of which visited (*Hitlerjugend* camps in 1938) and French boy scouts (who joined many camps up until the end of 1938).[27] During the school year of 1936–37, a total of 3000 young French people crossed the Rhine to Germany.[28] In further education, meetings between the two countries were resumed in 1936, after being frozen for three years. In 1937–38, fifty-six German academics took part in congresses or colloquia in France, and certain universities (Lyons and Lille) set up exchange programmes.[29]

These figures, though modest, are by no means insignificant. Nazi Germany aroused interest, particularly among bourgeois, who alone possessed the means to travel and were in a position to send their children on holiday courses. Most exchanges of this kind were still with the Anglo-Saxon countries; the mass of French people were as well disposed towards the English as they were ill disposed towards the Germans. But just as rejection of Nazi Germany was, in some quarters of the population, hesitant and ambivalent, similarly sympathy for England was tinged with an anglophobia the most outspoken manifestations of which, through their very excesses – for example, Henri Béraud's outburst at the outbreak of the war in Ethiopia – sometimes distracted attention from its dissemination. In the French colonial army and the navy, in particular, the *entente cordiale* and the war alliance had not eliminated antipathies of long standing, which had been revived by the disappointments of the post-war years. Irritation was felt at England's failure to understand France's thirst for security and the fact that, instead of being supportive, it played France and Germany off against each other in the name of a shortsighted balancing policy. For many French people, England was an ally by necessity rather than affection. In French novels of the period, England is the object of a general misrepresentation or of indifference loaded with prejudice; and at both extremes of the political spectrum the image of perfidious Albion remained as highly coloured as ever. Unadulterated egoism, secret services intriguing on every side, the tentacular domination of the City: all were clichés that rested on the same bases as the myths of the Jewish or masonic plot and that were purveyed in many successful works; while novels that were anglophile, of which there were not so many, adopted a somewhat defensive tone. The same went for the cinema and satirical cartoons in the newspapers, where the British were never presented to their advantage.[30]

The French entered the war with fragile cohesion, a so to speak existential *angst* and a confused view of both their ally and their adversary. On top of this, they then found themselves experiencing something completely different from what they had been fearing: after the shock of defeat, they entered upon an occupation of indefinite duration and for which they were most unprepared. During the 1930s it had not been hard to imagine what another war would be like. People's imaginations were fed by the recent past – immobile fronts and the mud of the trenches – or images of an apocalyptic future – chemical warfare in the skies annihilating the major cities of Europe.[31] Unsurprisingly, an occupation had hardly even been envisaged. The general image purveyed of the earlier conflict was that of battle under a rain of steel, and far less attention was paid to the trials of the northern regions that had been invaded (clearly, this situation would be reversed after 1944). In those areas, it is true, memories had not faded, kept alive as they were by recollections published both immediately after the armistice and also subsequently, in a new wave, during the 1930s,[32] and above all by monuments and commemoration ceremonies, which devoted much attention to the fate of civilians (taken as hostages, deported, executed, etc.) and celebrated their resistance, as in the case of Louise de Bettignies, a fine example of 'the heroic women of the invaded areas'.[33]

However, most French people had but a hazy notion of life under the occupation and only relatively few images to draw upon, provided by scattered sources of information such as family stories and school literary texts (Alphonse Daudet's *Contes du lundi*, Maupassant's short stories about the war of 1870–71, Barrès' *Colette Baudoche*, for example). It was such fragile channels as these that made known examples of patriotic courage and transmitted a code of basic conduct pertaining to the attitude that it was seemly to adopt in the presence of the invader.[34] All this was a very far cry from the rich collection of representations that the Second World War was itself to produce and leave as its heritage, the wide repertory of roles (the collaborator, the Resistance member, the wait-and-see people), the register of wartime activities (the black market, the work of saboteurs, and so on) and the images of the war's aftermath (the purging of some and the glorification of others).

Even where memories of the past were substantial and vivid, the light that they cast upon the future was inadequate. In 1935, Maxence Van der Meersch published his novel *Invasion 14*, a panorama of life in northern France under the German jackboot, which presented a wide assortment of characters and social circles: the resistant *patron*, the courageous priest, black marketeering peasants, unscrupulous profiteers. Nearly all the arguments produced following 1940 to justify either people's defiance or their adaptation were already formulated in this work: it shows both those who say 'They are stronger' and 'We'll have to put up with it' and those who rebel and seek ways of keeping hope alive and taking positive action. For some, the 'invasion' – the term 'occupation' was not used then – has the effect of revealing them to themselves, by impelling them to patriotic sacrifice. For others, it is an opportunity to settle old scores, for social revenge, and for 'getting rich quick'.

In some ways, this vigorously realistic novel, written from a Christian humanist point of view, might have been written after 1944. Its description of the resistance lacks virtually nothing: a priest sets up a radio post to pick up the French and English news, produces a clandestine newspaper called *Fidélité* and forms a 'network' divided into cells of three. It describes the initial enthusiasm manifested at the liberation, the destruction of all symbols of the enemy's presence, the rough handling meted out to prisoners and 'Boche's tarts' and, later, the great disappointment at the limited purges, the rush for jobs, and all the obscure heroes so quickly forgotten. ('Parasites have swarmed over the achievements of the sincere. Those who did nothing are kings.')[35] The book's conclusion is disillusioned; even with its declaration of faith in God and humanity, it was not of a kind to stiffen resolution in the face of new trials and tribulations.

In other ways, this novel records what is very much an experience of the past. The reader realizes that what had changed from one war to the next was a matter not so much of resistance, but accommodation. The author did describe instances of the latter, but all were determined by individual or social characteristics that had nothing to do with politics or ideology. National identities were unassailable and the only contacts with the enemy were due to familiarity arising from cohabitation, the weakness of the flesh or the lure of gain. There was nothing to cause the invader to be seen as a saviour, or even a possible partner. This was a crucial difference that gave that earlier occupation, amid the fighting that continued to rage, a character all of its own.

Around 1938, the approach of war prompted a resurgence of the theme of invasion, this time in works of propaganda with none of the richness of Van der Meersch's novel. Thus, the film *Deuxième Bureau contre Commandatur* evoked struggles between the French and the German secret services in an invaded village in northern France. The Germans are represented as brutal and rapacious, as depicted in the propaganda of the Great War: they imprison, torture, deport, execute. They are opposed by a French population united in their defiance and hatred, including the prostitute who, while selling her body, 'does the dirty' on her clients. National allegiances create an unbridgeable gap even between a French priest and a German one.[36]

In the autumn of 1939, just after the declaration of war, a novel by Raymond Queneau appeared. It was entitled *Un rude hiver* and it possessed a dimension that had been absent from *Invasion 14*. By pure coincidence Queneau had unwittingly become the author of a 'war novel'. As he noted in his diary, 'What one writes may acquire a prophetic sense.'[37] His antennae had indeed carried him further than he realized. The novel harks back to the earlier war, presenting a lieutenant convalescing in Le Havre, a hardened reactionary and a 'defeatist' who does not like the conflict that is dragging on and nurtures sympathies for Germany that are not unrelated to his disgust with the Republic, the Jews and the freemasons. One day he reveals his innermost feelings to a German spy: 'Well, Monsieur Frédéric, do you know what France needs to be rescued from decrepitude and chaos? You don't? Really? Well, I'll tell you. She needs a German protectorate, that's what she needs!'[38] Without the atmosphere that prevailed in these late 1930s could Queneau possibly have imagined one of his characters expressing such a frustrated and flabby hope for France's salvation, through defeat and the imposition of a German protectorate? And what an echo there was to be in the words of the woman who said to Werth in June 1940, 'It'll be a protectorate like Morocco . . . We'll be no worse off, we'll work as we used to . . . ' Whereas *Deuxième Bureau contre Commandatur* painted an enemy about whom there could be no doubt and against whom French people united because they knew their duty, Queneau's novel introduced the unsettling idea that the enemy might have friends and that not everyone defined the good of the country in the same fashion. In the tunnel into which they were stumbling, the French had only flickering lights by which to find their way.

4

The masters of the moment

THE autumn of 1939, when Queneau's novel appeared, also saw the publication of Hermann Rauschning's *Hitler m'a dit* ('Hitler told me'). The former leader of the Nazi party of Danzig, then in exile, reported that, seven years earlier, Hitler, looking forward to the future war between Germany and France, had explained that it was to be short and that in it he would thoroughly exploit the weapons of division and demoralization. He had made no secret of his opinion of his adversaries: 'I shall come to France as a liberator. We shall present ourselves to the French *petite bourgeoisie* as the champions of a fair social order and eternal peace. Those people do not want any more to do with war and greatness.' And he declared himself convinced that he would find allies on the spot: 'I shall long since have established contacts with men who will form a new government, a government that suits me. We shall find plenty of men of that kind. We shall not even need to buy them. They will come to us of their own accord, driven by ambition, blindness, partisan discord and pride.'[1]

Hitler imagined the French weary to the point of longing for a protectorate and so divided that some politicians would already be on his side. To anyone seeking to understand the politics of collaboration, his vision presents something of a caricature of the situation, yet up to a point it was premonitory: it was true that there would be Frenchmen who would make advances to the conqueror and would seek to come to an agreement with him. But neither a mad rush into submission such as Hitler was in advance scornfully gloating over nor a preconcerted national treason are needed to explain this. The real explanation is simple: the French political scene already included options, positions and preferences of a kind to make it probable that some would seek accommodation with Nazi Germany following a defeat. If the events of the 1930s caused French society to vacillate in its resolution and inhibited its ability to resist and to fight, they also led some politicians to cherish solutions which, in the event of defeat, they would be able to proffer as targets or remedies to their disoriented compatriots.

Some of these politicians had even gone so far as to bring the frontiers of France into question. This separatism stemmed from the regionalist movements that had emerged towards the end of the nineteenth century, at a time when at least one-third of the population did not speak the French language.[2] The centralizing policies of the Republic and the process of modernization had been met by a counter-movement dominated by the clerical right, which combined resistance to democracy and laicism and, later, also to socialism, with its struggle to preserve rural and Christian society.[3] After 1918, there was a new surge of regionalism, influenced by Wilsonian principles. Although the clerical hold remained strong, a new generation now emerged which, in the course of the 1930s, veered towards separatism. This radicalization was encouraged not only by the French crisis and the victory of the Popular Front, the heir to the detested Jacobins, but also by the rise to power of a number of fascist regimes. Glorified by their successes, they were seen as models that mobilized support around a nationalist ideology. And by virtue of the challenge that they presented to the international order, they were also regarded as potential allies whilst they, for their part, were certainly not averse to encouraging unrest of a kind to weaken France.

Nazism, in particular, was to become an object of fascinated attention. Of course, it did claim to speak for a Europe of ethnic groups, so as to support its objective of reuniting all Germans, and it was prone to represent France as an altogether artificial conglomerate: 8 million Occitans, 1600000 Germans, 1450000 Bretons, 400000 Corsicans, 200000 Flemings, 200000 Catalans and 150000 Basques, making a total of 12 million individuals of other than French ethnicity.[4] The French separatists were well placed to form an understanding of Nazism that came closer to its essentials than did the image of Hitler as a 'man of order', but their view also incorporated a measure of delusion. For the Nazis intended to reclaim 'Germanic' blood even in France. On that point, the works of German scholars were already clear enough.[5] How could the

Alsatians and the Flemings possibly realize their desire for a national life when the Nazis regarded them as peoples whose destiny was to be restored to the Reich?

Three regionalist movements were particularly affected by this radicalization. The movement for Corsican autonomy, with its irredentist tendencies, need not detain us, for it was very weak and the island was to be occupied, very briefly, by the Italians, from autumn 1942 to autumn 1943.[6] Flanders, a frontier zone, had a long-standing regionalist movement, but the conditions did not favour it. In the 1930s, only a very small minority of the 300000 odd Flemings (130000 of whom were Belgian) spoke nothing but Flemish.[7] Unlike the Basques and the Catalans, who were also situated astride frontiers, the Flemings were spread over three different countries: France, Belgium and Holland. It was a position that nurtured the 'Thiois' idea, the dream of a Greater Netherlands stretching from Frisia to the Somme. Here the clerical influence remained unadulterated (another unique feature), its continuing strength ensured by a priest, Jean-Marie Gantois, who in 1926 created the Flemish League of France, pledged to a cultural and linguistic reawakening.[8] In the following decade, the abbé slipped towards separatism and rallied to the idea of a 'Greater Netherlands' that laid claim even to territories (Artois and part of Picardy) that did not belong to the linguistic area of Flemish, on the pretext that their inhabitants were Flemish by blood before they were Romanized.[9] The adoption of such ethno-racist views testifies to the contamination of Nazism, which was likewise reflected in the hardening of the criticisms directed against Latin France, in the name of the superior qualities of Nordic blood, and in the racist and antisemitic passages of the work that the good Abbé Gantois published under a pseudonym in 1936 (*Le Règne de la race*, Sorlot).

In Alsace, in 1931, over 700000 people declared themselves to be solely German-speaking, nearly 800000 were bilingual and 200000 spoke only French.[10] Here, regionalism rested upon a more solid basis. The Alsatians who, under the influence of the Catholic Church, had fought within the German empire to preserve their identity, again raised the standard of autonomism during the 1920s, when republican France sought to separate the Church from the state. Despite restraining efforts on the part of the hierarchy, the Catholic community of Alsace was particularly affected by this, including a number of the leaders of the Union Populaire Républicaine (UPR), the main Alsatian party.

Autonomism had also won over a branch of the French Communist party, which was at that point supporting Alsace's right to self-determination. Caught up in this movement, certain local leaders, in particular the deputies Charles Hueber and Jean-Pierre Mourer, clashed with the party leadership and subsequently became dissidents. Soon marginalized and swept aside in the chaos of the 1930s, their group swung to the extreme right. Autonomism became separatism, and antiparliamentarianism was converted into solidarity with Nazi Germany.[11] The right wing did not escape a similar radicalization. The UPR declared its national allegiance, although its autonomist wing did not forswear its aspirations; but the autonomist party of Karl Roos veered towards Nazism, as did – even more decidedly – Hermann Bickler, who in 1936 founded a party along the lines of the Nazi model.[12] On the eve of the war, most autonomists still respected the national framework, but a minority dreamed of an independent Alsace allied to Nazi Germany, while a few (such as Friedrich Spieser) favoured being quite simply attached to the Reich.

In Brittany, where close on one million people spoke Breton in the period between the wars, regionalism had resulted as early as the late nineteenth century in the creation of many Breton associations organized by local élites, priests or royalists. After the war, their place was taken by younger people grouped around the newspaper *Briez Atao*, who had not been born into traditionalist circles and who (a sign of the times, this) were in favour of a confessional neutrality. The Autonomist party that they founded in 1927 demanded far-reaching autonomy, envisaged at this point within the framework of a federal recomposition of Europe. However, as early as 1931 a nationalist tendency was emerging, led by Olier Mordrel and François Debauvais, and this eventually led to the creation of the Breton National party. From this point onwards, although most of the regional movement concentrated on promoting Breton culture, inspired particularly by people such as Yann Fouéré, the nationalist faction speeded up its radicalization. The racial links between the Celts and the Germans were emphasized and the 'Nordic super-race' and the two groups' 'common blood' were exalted. Meanwhile Mordrel designed a programme according to which the future administration was to be limited to Bretons and all foreigners were to be expelled.[13] With such excellent inclinations, the Breton leaders were bound to interest the Nazi regime, which was already supporting the Alsatians. On the eve of the war, contacts even included deliveries of arms through the intermediary of the IRA. The Breton nationalists had taken over the motto 'The enemy of my enemy is my friend' from their Irish cousins, upon whom they modelled themselves.[14]

In the France of 1939, separatism was numerically no more than a minute force: a few thousand Bretons and Alsatians and a few hundred Flemings, surrounded by incomprehension and for the most part with no support from the clergy. It was nevertheless a disquieting force because of the extremism of its ideas and because, given the right circumstances, it might draw more support from the far wider field of regionalism. The French authorities were not insensitive to this danger. In September 1939, Gantois' movement was dissolved and the abbé was despatched to the army. In Alsace, fifteen leaders, including one priest, were arrested for dealings with the enemy; Karl Roos was condemned to death and shot at the beginning of 1940. The Breton leaders Mordrel and Debauvais, who left for Germany on the eve of the outbreak of war, were condemned to death in their absence.

Within the field of national politics, too, positions had been adopted that were to influence future developments. To be sure, the supporters of the regime established in the summer of 1940 by no means constituted a team united around a coherent programme and ready to seize their chance without more ado. Long-standing enemies of the Republic found themselves alongside members of the republican élite who had been converted to authoritarian principles, and admirers of fascism rubbed shoulders with traditional nationalists for whom the most urgent priority of all was to turn the French away from the foreign models that were dividing them. The development of these men's ideas had been neither synchronic nor rectilinear. Many of them, who had originally defended closer links with Germany, had condemned Hitler's imperialism during the phoney war. The shock of the defeat, the impression made by the German victory, the weakness of the British, and the fanning of ambitions had all played their part. At the time of his arrival in Vichy at the beginning of July, Déat was envisaging a limited political change: a regime with two or three parties.[15] A few days later, he was defending the idea of a single party, on the model of the totalitarian states.

Collaboration was not the ineluctable outcome of positions adopted earlier any more than it was seen, in that summer of 1940, in the guise that history was later to confer upon it. The men who were to win fame – if one can call it that – were setting out along a path as yet unknown to them, which led they knew not where. But they were pointing in a direction for which the past few years of longing for national reform and desiring reconciliation with Nazi Germany had already prepared them.

National reform was a theme that had long been purveyed by nationalism, whether of an integral or a populist nature. The crisis of the 1930s had imparted a new stridency to Maurras' criticisms, swollen the ranks of the right-wing leagues of Taittinger and La Rocque, multiplied the small groups attracted by fascism and Nazism, and encouraged the *putsch*-like tendencies of Deloncle and his Cagoule (the pre-war terrorist group). It had also purveyed dissent on the left, pushed radicals such as Bergery, Jouvenel, Fabre-Luce and Luchaire, socialists such as Déat and Marquet, and even the communist Doriot to chance their luck with movements whose common ambition initially was to unite the left against fascism but which soon found themselves swept towards positions of support for a national union. All these men were impelled by a desire, stimulated by the fascist regimes, for a reconstituted political community capable of restoring to the French common aims, values and sentiments.[16]

This longing for a national renewal was in most cases linked with a desire for reconciliation with Germany although what was envisaged here ranged from peaceful coexistence, through an *entente cordiale*, all the way to an alliance. The common denominator was the desire to avoid a war. After 1918, reconciliation had been the theme of the left, and so it remained for those who refused to swap pacifism for antifascism. From 1935 onwards, in a movement the reverse of that which was bringing former men of the left round to the idea of national renewal, it won over a section of the right, which thus shifted from nationalism to a kind of neo-pacifism. Here, as with public opinion, the desire for peace and the sense of France's weakness were both influential, as were a view of Nazism that concentrated mainly on its 'merits', and the interaction of external and internal politics, in particular with regard to the Communist party and the Soviet alliance. But, more than with public opinion, all this was felt acutely and in a – so to speak – concentrated way.

The association of reform and conciliation made for a composite picture. It included, on one side, men of the left who had more or less broken with the parliamentary regime and who wanted peace – even with Nazi Germany; on the other side, nationalists who, valuing a renewal of the country above all else, were anxious to maintain peace even if it meant healing the breach with Germany; and in the middle, people concerned first and foremost with social stability and peace in Europe. That reform and reconciliation should be associated was clearly not inevitable. Faced with real danger, a man such as Pierre Brossolette, who had been close to Luchaire up until 1934, or de Gaulle, who had been close to Déat in 1935–36, set firmness before reform. However, there was always a strong chance that men who, even after Munich, persisted in linking reconciliation and reform both publicly and privately would opt for collaboration after defeat.

Prominent among supporters of an *entente* with Germany were the members of the Comité France–Allemagne (CFA). Otto Abetz had been the prime mover in setting this up. While organizing meetings between young people of the two countries in the late 1920s, he had got to know Jouvenal and Luchaire. He had rallied to the Nazi regime, putting his knowledge of France at the service of the Reich's Youth Organization and Ribbentrop's office, an agency set up by the future Minister for Foreign Affairs to spread German influence abroad. In France, Abetz soon gained entry to all kinds of circles thanks to his discretion, his affability and a streak of non-conformism that was presumably at least in part calculated. In 1945, Merleau-Ponty wrote that Nazi Germany had delegated a number of 'ambiguous representatives' to France in the pre-war years. He was thinking of Karl-Heinz Bremer, a lecturer at the University of Paris who later played his part in cultural politics under the occupation, who in 1938 was prone to declare: 'I am an old radical.' 'By dint of speaking loud enough', Merleau-Ponty commented, 'one could get him to make concessions on all the principal articles of Nazism.'[17] It is a description that is equally applicable to Abetz although, it should be added, such behaviour can only have produced an effect on French people already predisposed to be impressed by it.

Abetz's first success came when he made contact with the two main organizations of war veterans and persuaded their leaders, Jean Goy and Henri Pichot, to make the journey to Berlin to meet Hitler. The latter said all the right things: he spoke of trials and tribulations experienced in common, solidarity between all war veterans, and Germany's desire for peace. In the autumn of 1935, the Comité France–Allemagne was set up. Its honorary members included Ambassador Noulens, representing the Quai d'Orsay (the name of Paul Morand, who had been very active in creating the Comité,[18] did not appear among its leading lights), academicians (Pierre Benoit, Luc

Bertrand, the Duke of Broglie), Senator de Chambrun, Professor Georges Brouardel (Académie de Médecine), the Germanist Henri Lichtenberger, the journalist Etienne Fougère, the *député* Montigny, the writer Jules Romains, and the composer Florent Schmitt (a member of the Institut de France). Foremost amongst the members of the administrative council were veteran war leaders (Goy, Pichou, Randoux); parliamentary representatives (Henry Haye, Charles Pomaret, Jean-Michel Renaitour, Scapini); journalists and writers (F. de Brinon, Vincent Delpuech, Emile Roche, Jouvenel, Drieu La Rochelle, Benoist-Méchin); and a number of other well-known figures (Gustave Bonvoisin, the ambassador Léon Noël, Ernest Fourneau, Monsignor Mayol de Lupé, Chappedelaine, J. de Castellane and Melchior de Polignac).[19]

The Comité France–Allemagne was a showcase of 'notables' unsullied by any scabrous personalities and with a reassuringly centre-right political image. Admittedly, it had the approval of the government, then presided over by Pierre Laval, and continued to be supported by his successors. Its aim was to bring together the élites of both countries, so its membership was limited, probably comprising no more than a thousand individuals.[20] However, it was extremely active. It organized trips to Germany for parliamentary representatives, municipal officials (Lille and Bordeaux), figures in the public eye, and writers.[21] It put on events in Bordeaux, Lille, Lyons, Marseilles and Nice (whose deputy mayor Jean Médecin was a member of the Comité).[22] It held congresses such as the one at Baden-Baden in June 1938, on the theme of 'the contribution of Germany and France to the cultural life of Europe'. As well as Brinon, Fourneau, Melchior de Polignac and Scapini, the speakers included the writer Pierre Benoit, the architect Auguste Peret, and performers Mary Marquet, Jacqueline Delubac and Sacha Guitry.[23]

The motives of the members of the Comité incorporated pacifism, germanophilia and philonazism in variable doses. The spectrum ranged from the commitment to peace and the European *entente* of a Jules Romains, whose position was close to radicalism but whose desire for reform had been kindled by certain aspects of Nazism, all the way to the philonazism of people such as Fernand de Brinon. Between these two poles could be found men such as Louis Bertrand, who was sufficiently alarmed by the situation in the spring of 1935 to go to Berlin to declare his beliefs: namely, that it was imperative for France, Germany and Italy to unite so as to block communism. The people he spoke to could not resist pointing out that it was from

Barrès that Bertrand had inherited his seat in the Académie Française.[24]

The theme of Franco-German reconciliation could accommodate quite a wide variety of political tendencies – which was precisely the point that the Comité was keen to make, presenting itself as a body of people of goodwill anxious to reveal the peace-loving and friendly face of Nazi Germany. The mouthpiece of the Comité, the *Cahiers franco-allemands,* aimed to disarm the mistrust of the French. Its tone was moderate, and its columns were open to people of varied opinions. Edouard Herriot and Georges Duhamel agreed to write for it. Its German contributors hammered home the Reich's desire for peace and its role as a bastion against communism. They embroidered upon the theme of the complementarity of the two countries and drew a contrast between a healthy, orderly, dynamic Germany with a great future before it, and a fragile, unstable, corrupt France that ought to content itself with a subordinate role. They harped upon a European *entente* founded upon respect for individual identities and a division of spheres of influence, suggesting that France should withdraw from European affairs to concentrate upon its empire.[25]

However, with such a wide diversity of motives, its members' commitment was sensitive to developments in the two countries' diplomatic relations. After the *Kristallnacht,* Pichot wrote a violent article denouncing Nazi antisemitism and the danger hanging over Europe.[26] Jules Romains, Bertrand de Jouvenel and others drew the same conclusion and resigned. But others were still not discouraged. In January 1939, the actress Cécile Sorel called at the German embassy to say that she desired *entente* between the two countries and would like to perform in Berlin before Hitler, as she had before Mussolini.[27] In that same month, the *Cadre noir* of Saumur, led by General de La Laurencie, a member of the Comité, took part, for the first time since the war, in a tournament in Berlin attended by Hitler and Göring.[28] And in high summer, Prince de Beauvau-Craon, the chairman of the Paris Polo Club, another supporter of Franco-German *entente,* travelled to Germany in an attempt to maintain sporting relations despite the mounting crisis.[29]

The CFA incorporated only a fraction of the supporters of Franco-German *entente.* Some were deliberately held at a distance from it; others chose to remain apart. The former included the leaders of small fascist groups and antisemitic chapels. André Chaumet, Henry Coston, Jean Renaud, Darquier de Pellepoix and Clémenti all went off to solicit recognition and funding from German agencies. Even

Bucard's Francist party, the most solid of such organizations despite its limited membership of no more than a few thousand, after having expressed its unconditional approval of Italian fascism, begged for financial help, complaining of the miserliness of the French bourgeoisie.[30] Within these marginal organizations, admiration for all forms of fascism was expressed without reserve: a fascist regime would set France on its feet once more and would ensure the formation of a close alliance with Italy and Germany, directed against England and, above all, the Soviets. Behind this project, which was based on the hope of hitching the fortunes of France to the nations bent on prey, can be detected the internationalization of nationalism that had developed following the appearance of communism. Bucard and his like did not shout 'Heil Hitler' as the communists yelled 'Long live Stalin.' Nevertheless, the solidarity with fascist regimes that their attitudes reflected indicated that the French extreme right had reached a turning point. The racist and antisemitic chapels were, logically enough, in the vanguard of this movement pushing for recomposition that put the struggle against a common foe before the salvation of a nation too degenerate to oppose it successfully. This was a bridge leading to satellization, if not treason, as is shown by the case of Paul Ferdonnet, 'the Stuttgart traitor', who emerged from just such a background.

Céline, for one, was part of this tendency, however much he denied any political commitment. His pre-war pamphlets (*Bagatelles pour un massacre, L'École des cadavres*) preached a very coherent racism. The reason why he sweepingly condemned the left, the bourgeoisie, the Church and the extreme right, not forgetting his whipping boy Marshal Pétain, was that they were all blind to the racial problem and the warmongering of the Jews. The solution that he offered was an alliance with Nazi Germany, in the name of their common racial roots conceived along the ethnoracist lines of the Alsatian, Breton and Flemish separatists. 'France is Latin only by chance, through a fluke, through defeat . . . it is Celtic, three-quarters Germanic.' Céline even went on to forestall any objections, forthrightly retorting: 'Are we afraid of absorption? We shall never be more absorbed than we are right now. Are we to remain slaves of the Jews, or shall we become Germanic once more?'[31]

The nationalist right kept its distance from this racist fringe. It wanted not an alliance but an *entente*, reconciliation or quite simply coexistence. This was the position of Maurras, a mortal enemy of the Republic but at the same time an impenitent germanophobe. In 1937, he sounded the alarm in his book *Devant l'Allemagne éternelle*, subtitled *Chronique d'une résistance*. France wants no more to do with war, declared Maurras, yet it will have to take up arms. Once defeated, it would undergo a fate reminiscent of ancient times, when a conqueror had the right to dispose of everything and everyone as he pleased. 'Hitlerian racism will subject us to the all-powerful reign of his Horde', he wrote, after warning, 'On 1 January 1934, a certain law on sterilization came into effect. If it affects a Native of the Reich, can we believe that a defeated Foreigner could easily escape it?'[32] But these sagacious observations were submerged beneath the idea that there is nothing new under the sun: Nazism was simply an avatar of the old eternal Germany. The fact that the articles collected in this work all dated from before 1914 testifies to the caricatural immobility of the author.

Maurras's call to 'resistance' might have carried more weight had he not, at the very same moment, been supporting a policy of conciliation that he justified by the dilapidated state to which democracy had reduced the country. Having spent his whole life tetchily drawing attention to France's steep decline, he seemed unable to contain his satisfaction, faced with a situation that so strikingly confirmed all his predictions. To him, national defence no longer seemed acceptable without some kind of general reform. His position would have been less ambiguous if he had not laid claim to the same enemies as Nazism. He was manifestly more inclined to rejoice over the blows that assailed them than to make common cause with them against the national enemy. It is hardly surprising that his young disciples of *Je suis partout* succumbed to the fascination of Nazism without his seeing fit to recall them to order.[33]

In the nationalism of the right-wing leagues, antigermanism remained strong, if tempered by the French crisis. La Rocque, while mistrusting Germany, manifested a certain ambivalence with regard to Nazism, in which he recognized some elements worthy of respect: order, unity and discipline. He kept an open mind on reconciliation but refused to make any sacrifices that might endanger France's position and, by and large, went along with the line that successive French governments adopted.[34] In these circles, Doriot was the only one who openly declared himself in favour of an *entente*. He had become a neo-nationalist out of hatred for communism, and could not bring himself to adopt any firm position that would require the support of the USSR and would, on that account, contradict the central theme of his politics. Unlike the other leaders of the extreme right, he did have a world vision, a legacy from his communist past, which took account of the rise of extra-European powers, Japan in particular, and convinced him, along with men such as Fabre-Luce and Jouvenel, that a regrouping of forces would be necessary if Europe was to retain its place on a competitive planet.[35] So it was that, in 1937, he defended the idea of action on the part of the European powers to block the expansion of Japan in China and to turn the latter into a European preserve.[36] It would be a means of diverting Nazi ambitions into directions less harmful to French interests and also a way to foster anticommunist solidarity in Europe, a solidarity that would eventually be turned against the Anglo-Saxons. Despite all this, however, in 1939 he felt obliged to recognize the need to block Germany and, during the phoney war, to take a traditionally nationalist line.

Conciliation also had its supporters in the centre and on the left. In the centre, they ranged from liberals such as Flandin, through Chateau, Bergery, Frot, Montigny and Monzie, to neo-socialists in the Déat mould. In their internal politics, these men all shared disquiet or repulsion in the face of the Popular Front, a deep anticommunism, and a measure of scepticism if not genuine disaffection with regard to the parliamentary regime. Déat and Bergery made no secret of their desire for reform along social and national lines, Déat being particularly keen on the organization of society and the creation of a collective surge of energy. Even Flandin was wavering in his attachment to liberalism and was inclining towards reform. As early as 1933, he admitted in a German magazine that liberalism was out of date and parliamentarianism had degenerated into a caricature of its former self.[37]

It would not be fair to say that these men idealized Nazi Germany. But they all dreaded war on account of France's weakness, fearful of another bloodletting and of playing into the hands of the communists. This made them cling to the hope of some kind of arrangement, even if it entailed abandoning certain positions. Some, led by Flandin, were thinking in terms of a redefinition of spheres of influence, a French retreat from Central and Eastern Europe and withdrawal to its empire. Others, such as Déat, favoured an economic reorganization of the contintent, designed to decrease tensions since, as they saw it, Nazi dynamism found its source in fundamental economic needs. Both groups clung to a belief that tensions could be relieved by acting in concert. The word collaboration was used with the meaning of working together, on an equal footing, as can be seen from Monzie's article entitled 'Collaborer avec l'Allemagne? Oui, c'est possible' [Collaborate with Germany? Yes, it is possible] (*Paris-Soir*, 26 May 1937).

On the left, for the pro-conciliation minority, national reform, in the traditional sense, held no appeal. This minority nevertheless did betray a considerable disaffection *vis-à-vis* the regime, which originated from an anticommunism heightened by competition with the French Communist party, a latent anglophobia, and intense pacifism. For years, the left had been deploring French nationalism and the conciliators were not prepared to change their line, even in the name of antifascism, particularly when this was preached by the French communists. Needless to say, even if their counterparts on the right were agonizing about France's standing, they for their part showed scant concern for power politics or European equilibrium.

Foremost in this minority were the so-called integral pacifists, a number of whom ahd been ardent 'revisionists', that is to say had favoured a revision of the Treaty of Versailles. They rejected the thesis that Germany was responsible for the outbreak of the First World War, denounced the role of French nationalism in the rise and victory of Nazism, and even looked with a measure of indulgence upon the latter's *faits accomplis*, regarding them as a natural reaction to the injustice that Germany had suffered. Félicien Challaye, for instance, a leading member of the League for Human Rights and a long-standing anticolonialist was, in 1933, already declaring that 'foreign occupation would be a lesser evil than war'. Prepared to believe in Hitler's pacifism right up until the last moment (since he visited Germany in 1938), he was inclined to ascribe quite a number of virtues to the Nazi regime as compared to 'plutocratic pseudo-democracy'.[38]

Other men of the left went along with national defence but, in the face of the current danger, preferred to abandon collective security and foreign alliances and fall back upon defence solely of the national territory. Such was the attitude of the anticommunist minority of the CGT, which fell in behind Belin and the *Syndicats* magazine. Belin, in October 1936, wrote: 'We are for European peace in so far as that is possible and, if it proves impossible, if some misfortune strikes, we shall be for French peace.'[39] It was also the attitude of the minority wing of the SFIO, grouped around Paul Faure, the secretary general of the party, whose idea of remedying German expansionism through an improved economic organization of Europe failed to conceal his fundamental isolationism. Some socialists even credited Nazism with 'merit' for having rallied the German people, restored its faith and confidence, and constructed an economic system beyond capitalism. Within the SFIO, the tiny 'Redressement' tendency (Zoretti, Lefranc, Albertini and Soulès) detected in the fascist regimes a 'pre-socialist structure' that compared favourably with the plight of 'plutocratic' France. Here too there existed a belief in remedying the situation through an 'economic collaboration' that would make it possible to rein in the 'dangerous dynamism' of neighbouring regimes and that presupposed reorganizing France partially along the lines of national self-sufficiency.[40]

Then there was the 'establishment', which supplied the regime born of the defeat with its principal leaders. They were men who had behaved with discretion before the war, either by choice or by necessity, a fact that was to serve them well, particularly Pétain, who had not been drawn to break his reserve even by several press campaigns on the theme of the country's need for a saviour. From time to time, however, he had seen fit to express some enlightening views. In a newspaper interview that he gave not long before the elections of 1936, he praised La Rocque's Croix-de-Feu and called for national unity, which can definitely not have been taken for encouragement to vote for the Popular Front. He compared France, which needed to rediscover a 'mystique', with Italy and Germany, both countries whose inhabitants believed in one. 'We, for our part, are full of doubts. The trouble is that ours is not a material crisis. We have quite simply lost faith in our destiny.'[41] Already he was sold on the idea of decadence and convinced of the need for radical reform. In 1938, he even declared that victories sent the French to sleep, while defeats shook them awake.[42] He turned the experiences of his own generation into doctrinal arguments, just as if some historical cycle necessarily linked 1870 and 1918. Mentally, he was already prepared to accept defeat on the grounds of the promise of regeneration that it held out, seeing another conflict as but one in a series of Franco-German clashes rather than an episode of world-wide war, just as he regarded Nazism as no more than the legacy of pangermanism, rather than an unprecedented form of racist imperialism.

In the 1936 interview, he had made known his opposition to the Franco-Soviet pact. An unpublished document discovered in the Italian archives and relating to a conversation with the Italian ambassador in Paris on 28 February 1936 – at the time of the war in Ethiopia and the sanctions against Italy – sheds a disquieting light on his diplomatic preferences. Pétain claimed to be in no doubt that Italy would emerge from the conflict better off than before, since in Mussolini it possessed a man who knew what he wanted, unlike the democratic governments, whose indecision was pitiful. Having added that he would quite understand if the Italians decided to leave the League of Nations, an organization in which he had never believed, he launched into a diatribe against England that impressed the Italian diplomat all the more in that it was delivered with calm and serenity: 'England has always been France's most implacable enemy.' It had fought alongside France only when this served its own interests, after which it had taken Germany's part. 'For all these reasons, I tell you that France has two hereditary enemies, the English and the Germans, but the former are older and more perfidious. That is why I should incline towards an alliance with the latter, which would guarantee absolute peace in Europe, especially if Italy joined in that alliance. Then it would be possible to solve all the problems that have so far remained insoluble, because a better distribution of the British colonies would make it possible to provide wealth and work for all.'[43] We should no doubt make allowances for the bitterness left by the previous year's clashes with England, and not mistake these words for a real programme. But when a man talks like that at the age of eighty, surely he is expressing thoughts that he has long been turning over in his mind. On the evidence of these declarations of his, Pétain seems to have been much closer to a Doriot than to a Maurras.

As for Laval, in the immediate run-up to the war, he was a man scarred by the fall of his government in 1936. This native of Auvergne had several times served as a minister, twice been president of the Council, was a successful businessman and also the Senator for Aubervilliers, and he placed the greatest confidence in his own abilities. Like another of the parliamentary republic's rejects, André Tardieu, he resentfully turned against the regime that had made his rise possible.[44] An Italian agent who saw him on several occasions in 1938 describes him as an embittered man, constantly harking back to his time in office, condemning the series of mistakes made after his departure and laying the blame on the French people who, he said, would now have to drain its cup to the dregs, adding that he wanted 'to be recalled to power' and that when he was he would resort to any means to remain there.[45] In the meantime, he was trying to set up a Pétain government. His attempt was not successful but on one point the episode was illuminating. In April 1938, when reporting to his Italian contact that he was making progress with his Pétain project, he confessed that things were nevertheless not going altogether smoothly: 'The Marshal has a will of his own and inflexible ideas, and great diplomacy is needed to make him see reason.'[46] The remark neatly sums up how future relations between the two men were to continue.

Laval believed that, with himself in charge, the external situation of France would have been much improved. However, his political record for 1935–6 provides no basis for such optimism. The wiley Auvergnat had tried to contain Nazi revisionism using both dissuasion – continuing negotiations with the USSR, moving closer to Italy, and tightening links with England – and conciliatory gestures towards Germany designed to make it move towards France: in short, he had tried to please everybody but ended up with inconsistent policies.[47] But he had certainly indicated that he was no stickler for intransigence and that he believed it possible to come to some arrangement by dint of policies in which parliamentary conditioning (through negotiation one can always reach agreement) combined with a *realpolitik* that was as scornful of principles as it was limited in its effects (by leaving Mussolini a 'free hand' in Ethiopia, he showed that he was perfectly prepared to reach agreement at the expense of others, without seeming to realize the full extent of the Italians' greed). Right up until the outbreak of war, he believed that the key to the situation lay in Rome, as if Mussolini could possibly not draw closer to Germany for reasons of both interest and ideology, given that German power was bound to upset the status quo and that he, Mussolini, would do better out of that than out of haggling with the democratic powers. During the phoney war, Laval was the life and soul of the group in the Senate fighting for a bloodless peace, as were Flandin, Déat, and Bergery in the Chamber of Deputies.

For Admiral Darlan too, the paths that he would follow in the future were already marked out in pre-war days. In a memorandum dated 22 January 1939, he declared himself in favour of avoiding a conflict with Germany and Italy, justifying his position with arguments that prefigured his line of reasoning after the defeat. 'For twenty years, the foreign policy that we have been pursuing has been illogical, landbound and exclusively European, whereas it should have been realistic, maritime and world-wide . . . Above all, we must preserve our empire. Everything else is of secondary importance. So, providing Germany does not support Italy in its claims, we should leave it free to act as it will in the East.'[48] As for Weygand, as early as October 1938, he had favoured withdrawing from the Polish alliance.[49] He was very close to Pétain in his internal politics and, along with Abel Bonnard, Bernard Fay and René Gillouin, was an organizer of the Committee for National Unity for the Reconstruction of France, a movement founded in March 1936 with principles that looked forward to the national revolution.[50]

All these men faced the phoney war with their earlier hopes dashed. Most decided to keep quiet as public opinion swung round, but their thoughts did not change and meantime a minority in Parliament was criticizing England, quietly pushing for a bloodless peace and hoping that Germany would turn against the USSR. The defeat set them free and encouraged them, in the name of necessity, to try out politics that had won their preference years earlier. In the summer of 1940, against a background of lassitude, delusion and misunderstandings, they launched themselves into remodelling their country and seeking an *entente* with Nazi Germany, thereby at a stroke repeating all the errors of judgement of the pre-war years.

PART I

Reasons of state

FOUR months after the defeat of France, Hitler and Pétain met in the small town of Montoire. Their handshake was flashed round the world and gave rise to a cloud of questions. One week later, Pétain addressed his compatriots, announcing that he was 'setting out on the path of collaboration'. The word was thus solemnly consecrated, but it was destined for an astonishing future. When Pétain gave it the stamp of his official approval, he meant it to refer to inter-state relations. In Nazi Europe, France was the only great power that Hitler crushed. It was an exploit that he was not to repeat either with England or with the Soviet Union. But France retained a government that controlled part of the metropolitan territory, a large fleet and a considerable empire. The collaboration of which Pétain spoke was indissociable from the margin of manoeuvre that those trump cards afforded, despite the massively uneven balance of forces.

Collaboration was a policy adopted by a weak power confronted by a strong one; but it was a policy for all that, that is to say a choice. In this case it was justified by reasons of state and was claimed to ensure not just a future for France, but the only future that would be good for it. The situation was quite different from that of, for instance, Denmark, another country that retained its government but which was totally occupied and left with no external trump cards. The Danish government made concessions to the occupier, some of which violated its neutrality: for example, in 1941, it authorized members of the Danish army to join a unit of the Waffen-SS; it also signed the anti-Komintern pact and outlawed the Danish Communist party. But it never laid claim to a policy of collaboration. It refused to commit its own future so long as the war continued, and it continued to act as a shield to the Danes.

The decision facing France was not simply a choice between Pétain and de Gaulle. To continue the struggle alongside England was not the sole historical alternative. France could have opted for an armistice government that remained republican, and sought to protect its trump cards – the free zone, the fleet, and the empire – deciding that the last word would not have been said so long as England continued to resist. Such a government would have been subjected to no less German pressure than Vichy was, and the teams of collaborationists in Paris would no doubt have been even more tightly packed and even more extreme. It would have been forced to take painful decisions, on economic matters for example, and on the provision to Germany of raw materials and manufactured articles from the free zone, instead of maintaining a total separation between the two zones. On the other hand, with its trump cards providing it with the means to damage German interests, it could have forced the conqueror to make an extremely careful calculation as to the advantages and inconveniences of total occupation. Ultimately, the rope would have snapped, at the latest when the Anglo-Saxons disembarked in North Africa. Meanwhile, such a government would have had to bend in the wind and make concessions that might later be judged to have been compromising, but at least it would have avoided mortgaging the future by seeking reform under an occupying power and in the midst of an ever-widening conflict. It would not have been shackled to the ball and chain of a new regime. And it could have resoldered the country together by re-entering the war when the chance presented itself.

The leaders of Vichy were neither proud nor perspicacious enough to choose, as de Gaulle did, to continue the struggle alongside England, but nor were they modest or cautious enough to adopt a policy of minimal involvement with Germany, from which they would have been able to extricate themselves in time. Their choice of collaboration implied an endeavour to restore French power through *entente* with a Nazi Germany that was still at war, an obstinate attempt to get the peace treaty revised before it had even been signed, and to regain, circumstances permitting, at least some of what had been lost in the defeat. It was, certainly, a policy adopted for reasons of state, based upon diplomatico-strategic arguments and inspired by a desire to restore national power. But, right from the start, it was also prompted and more and more constricted by concern for the regime itself. In the last analysis, faced with a choice between state power, which would have meant opting for the Anglo-Saxon camp, and political survival, which tied it to the occupying power, Vichy chose the latter, even if the price to be paid was vassaldom.

In August 1944, Pétain assured his compatriots: 'Even if I have not been able to be your sword, I have tried to be your shield.' But he might have addressed that remark more truthfully to Hitler. Over four years, particularly during the first two, he had vainly offered to be the shield of Nazi Europe against the Anglo-Saxon world, in return for an advantageous peace treaty.

5

France for itself alone

THE new regime installed itself in Vichy as if in a temporary camp until such time as the return to Paris forseen in the armistice agreement could take place. The tasks it faced were pressing and overwhelming. More or less everywhere administration was breaking down, with economic life so disorganized that pockets of famine were developing. The external situation brought no reassurance: France's neighbours were gathered for the kill, and the occupier held its victim by the throat. The directions taken went along lines laid down in the 1930s: reform and conciliation were the order of the day, this time with France as part of Nazi Europe.

The internal policies of the new regime took shape amid some confusion and in an improvised fashion. The manner of its constitution gave it a number of unusual features, the effects of which were to remain indelible. What came to power was not a political party, certainly not a party of the totalitarian type, with militants and organizations ready to serve it in society, but a makeshift team united on a number of options and making the most of an astonishing political vacuum to put together a hotchpotch of ideas and aims.[1]

Pétain was the main prop of this regime, both by reason of his extraordinary popularity and also because it was he who defined the principles of the new order. The 'national revolution' that he heralded was a rehash of late nineteenth-century nationalism, which asserted the pre-eminence of the collectivity over the individual and deduced from that the twin necessities of a purging and a restructuring of national life. The purging resulted in the banning from public office of any French citizen born of a foreign father, the dissolution of all secret societies, a statute discriminating against French Jews, and the internment of foreign Jews. The restructuring which was designed to produce longer-term effects, was marked by taking in hand and strengthening 'natural communities', that is to say families, professions and regions – all considered to be formative frameworks for a stable, well-ordered society.

It would be mistaken to assume that Pétain's popularity implied support for his doctrine, for it had less to do with his ideas than with his personality and what it represented.[2] He himself encouraged people generally to identify themselves with him, appealing to both their republican and their Christian sentiments. The former element went with the image of the hero of the Great War and also with that of educator and teacher, in this instance of national rehabilitation; the latter emphasized the father of the family, the good shepherd, the Christ-like figure 'making a gift of his own person'. This saviour, at once glorious, paternal and suffering, called forth a wave of devotion fuelled by the most archaic sources of personal power: here at last was a public figure who could be loved. What many remembered most from his speeches were the words of consolation: the motherland still upright in the midst of defeat, the value of work even with the economy in chaos, the importance of the family at a time of separations. It was a many-sided popularity that gave Pétain a long-lasting appeal that he did much to foster by presenting himself as the best possible option in the face of the occupier, a guardian of peace in the midst of raging war.

Surrounding the column of strength represented by Pétain were pillars of the regime drawn from the upper echelons of the administration. Public service was a factor of order and worship of the state was part of its tradition; the national revolution echoed the values and grudges of some of its leading lights. The military, to whom the defeat appeared to have given a new strength, thronged the corridors of power. Delivered from civil control, their ambition was to fashion the nation in their own image. Alongside them, in positions of authority, were top-ranking civil servants from the central administration, in particular its economic and technical sectors: sweet revenge for experts and technocrats weary of muddled interventions from parliamentary politics and who had been scandalized by the erratic economic policies of the Popular Front.[3] Vichy was really not so much a triumph for Maurras's type of ideas; rather, it testified to the authoritarian metamorphosis of some of the republican élites.

The regime constructed a platform for itself, on the basis of a combination of various political and social demands. Beyond the restricted but by no means negligible circle of confirmed antidemocrats, it exploited the authoritarian regression of large sectors of the population, beginning with the Catholics, whose support for the Republic had been much hedged about by reservations. It appealed to the restorative aspirations of many French people who dreaded a future of large towns, mobs of workers, and new-fangled *mores*. It placed its faith in the antiliberalism of social strata in which the great crisis had instilled a lasting disquiet: a large proportion of employers, many peasants, and a whole series of professional groups, such as doctors, architects and executives. It also strove to win over circles particularly affected by the defeat, such as the families of prisoners of war and those particularly sensitive to Pétain's personal prestige, such as former combatants.

It did not add up to a clear-cut, solid, well-balanced construction although it did encourage some to believe, for a while, that they could shore up the entire structure by dint of their own small efforts. Fragility was, so to speak, the regime's in-born defect. It was not just a matter of the lack of a coherent team and coherent ideas, which made for competition between different cliques and conflicting tensions; it also stemmed from the precariousness of the situation, which was at odds with the very nature of Pétain's project: instead of a retreat from the times and the world outside into quiet, healing reform, there would be the breathless speed and pressure of events as conflict rapidly intruded into the 'square meadow' [*le pré carré*] of France, where her people were supposed to be tapping new sources of energy. Furthermore, the division of the country into separate zones each of which soon developed a climate of its own rapidly reduced 'Vichy France' to nothing but the free zone. And even there, uncertainty as to the outcome of the war and the unpopularity of collaboration eroded Pétain's prestige: the national revolution turned into a contradiction of the nationalism that it professed. Finally, the increasingly oppressive occupation rendered social and political reform futile. The conscription of labour for Germany managed to kill any remaining interest in the Labour Charter, even in the eyes of its supporters.

Early on the leaders of the regime felt the need to create a political link with the population. In the summer of 1940, they created the Légion des Combatants Français, designed to bring together all former combatants; then, at the end of the year, they set up a consultative assembly composed of 'notables', known as the

National Council. The idea of a single party resurfaced from time to time, but did not win Pétain's approval. The aim of his social project was to reform people's minds and for this it depended upon the beneficent effect of natural communities. Militant activity could only reactivate the political virus, and a single party would alienate the Church, the 'notables' and the Légion.[4] The Milice, the paramilitary force created by Vichy late in the day, was conceived as a praetorian guard, although it escaped nobody's notice that Darnand's ambition was to turn it into a state party. None of these solutions achieved their objective: the population distanced itself, and resistance grew. What was remarkable was that the more support for it shrank, the more the dictatorship, instead of altering its line, hardened it.

A few people played roles of central importance in this regime, unrestrained by any popular controls, yet as fundamentally unstable as the defunct parliamentary republic and where the occupying power was soon taking a hand in the interplay of cliques. Philippe Pétain, aged eighty-four, was a soldier deeply marked by the Great War, which had hauled him out of obscurity and created his frame of reference. After Montoire, in a letter thanking Cardinal Baudrillart for declaring his support for the policy of collaboration, he wrote, à propos of the French people: 'I want them to trust me blindly, as three million of them did in the past, when I was their commander as they faced the enemy. Later, they will come to understand what my plan was.'[5] He was a man of order through and through: when the blind trust that he required slipped away, he brandished a big stick. Later, in August 1941, speaking of 'the true malaise' that afflicted the French people, he was to declare: 'In 1917 I put an end to mutinies; in 1940 I put an end to the rout. Today it is from yourselves that I wish to save you.'[6]

He clung fiercely to the power that had come to him so late. The veneration directed towards him convinced him that he was the embodiment of the whole nation and imbued him with a sense of infallibility. His handling of affairs, for which he had scant experience, reflected his personality. He was by nature prudent, distrustful, secretive, and touchy. To quote Du Moulin de La Barthète, one of his closest advisors up until 1942: 'With his taciturnity and his changes of mind, he spreads a light smokescreen before him.'[7] Because he was prone to listen to the opinions and advice of others, sometimes he seemed vacillating and erratic. But he clung tenaciously to his own ideas. It should be added that he was always careful to distance himself from men or measures whose unpopularity might rub off on himself. He was protective of his own prestige, even at the cost of coherence, and was adept at adapting his pronouncements to please his listeners.

His chief priority was the national revolution. He defined its principles, pressed for their application, and urged rigour in the face of obstacles, being only too inclined to 'detect opponents to his work on every side'.[8] He considered those opponents to be the freemasons and, above all, the communists. Where the Jews were concerned he was prudent in public, being anxious to avoid any appearance of religious persecution or alignment with the conqueror. But he could be trenchant in governmental deliberations, as when, in October 1940, he demanded that the Jews be totally excluded from national education and justice.[9] In response to protests, he implied that the Jewish Statute had been forced upon him by the Germans. That is certainly what he told the Chief Rabbi in March 1941, in the course of a conversation in which his antisemitic feelings surfaced clearly.[10] He never opposed any hardening of anti-Jewish legislation, limiting himself to intervening in a few individual cases.

The unexpected prolongation of the war forced him to devote much time to foreign affairs. Setting the importance of 'regeneration above that of resistance',[11] he sought above all for a way to stabilize the regime, oscillating between the hope that collaboration would pay dividends and the fear that it would rebound against his national revolution, in particular if it dragged France into the war alongside the Germans, thereby definitively alienating public opinion. He accordingly moved with great prudence to achieve the objective that he had fixed for himself, although here too, when communicating with neutral powers he liked to stress his weakness, given the margins of manoeuvre, declaring: 'I cannot navigate; I simply surf.'[12] At any rate, his political choices and his temperament combined to prevent him from changing course. He may not have gloried in the defeat, but he seemed to derive a morose satisfaction from it, constantly reminding his compatriots of their condition as a conquered nation and exhorting them to a resignation that he claimed to be redemptive. 'Each day I remind myself that we have been defeated', he declared in 1942, scandalizing some of his listeners.[13] His character, his view of the world, and his project of renovation all disposed him to endurance rather than confrontation or even risking confrontation. Although he sought compensation for his successive sell-outs, he would settle for very little. The France that he embodied was humble, scared, and accepting of its loss of status ('Demographically', he declared, 'France is no longer a great power; it is no more than first of the middling powers'[14]), a France that was counting on revival in the long term, meanwhile incurring the risk of being crushed if Hitler won the day.

Laval, aged fifty-seven, was the regime's second-in-command. It was he who paved the way for it and he, alone, who paid the price for it before a firing squad. Right from the start, he had a bad reputation: he was seen as a climber, a shady fixer, the man of deflation and discredited pro-Italian politics, and ultimately as Pétain's evil genius. The contrast between the two men's personalities emphasized this role of evil counsellor. Laval was a politicking man through and through, a man for clientèles, a manoeuvrer who believed that money, flattery and intrigue ruled the world and who made abundant use of all three. The new regime was not altogether to his taste, with too many military old fogeys and sour reactionaries, too much theoretical hostility towards parliamentary rule. But even if he scoffed at the rituals performed before the altar of the national revolution, he did feel at ease with a dictatorship. Embittered by his period in the wilderness, he now insisted that the art of government meant using a big stick and that in the life of every nation there comes a time for purges. As for the rest, he went along with the regime's choices, including its antisemitism. For him, antisemitism was not a gut reaction, but he had certainly absorbed the prevalent xenophobia and prejudices. At any rate, he sacrificed the Jews to the needs of his own politics with a lack of scruples and deep indifference, the consequences of which we shall be examining later.

He used all the tricks of his trade, but was also bold and prepared to back his intuitions. He had one bugbear – England – and one ambition – to negotiate peace with Germany. His self-confidence was remarkable. He was convinced of his own powers as a negotiator once he came face to face with a high-level German spokesman. In July 1940, when Laval, about to make his first trip to Paris, was told by Pétain that the Germans had a low opinion of him, he retorted unperturbed that they were afraid of being outwitted.[15] This Talleyrand of Aubervilliers was not one for piling up dossiers; he believed in ongoing discussion and in winning confidence by making gestures and promises. He was capable of warmth and charm, a skilful lawyer who believed any case could be pleaded and won, even before a conqueror whose worship of brute force stood in for a philosophy. Laval had policies that he would never abandon, methods that he would never discard, an ambition too thrusting not to be alarming.

Darlan, aged fifty-nine, was the military man who counted. The defeat had, for the first time ever, made the fleet France's principal weapon. The admiral now found himself pushed to the fore, in a position where he could revel in his taste of power. Unlike Pétain, he was neither a moralist nor a pessimist. But he too, without a qualm, wrote off the Republic that he had faithfully served. He was to make an important contribution to the technocratic side of the national revolution, chiefly through his support for the action of ministers such as Marion and Pucheu.

As a man, he was cold, gruff, suspicious, authoritarian, totally lacking in charisma, vain, and extremely vulgar, with an embarrassing taste for luxury. He had a clear mind and a trenchant pen, a sense of organization and decisiveness. But beyond that? According to Benoist-Méchin, who worked closely with him for a year, 'his mind was limited, he was short-sighted and not particularly cultivated. His intelligence, which was eminently practical, was that of a good staff officer, adequate for concocting a military plan, carrying out an order, fulfilling a duty. But beyond that, he had nothing much to offer.'[16] He had helped to build up the fleet before the war, but had done so very much in the spirit of the 'old navy' of armoured ships with cannon, taking little interest in more recent weapons such as radar and remaining blind to the crucial role that was to be played in the coming war by aircraft carriers and the DCA (anti-aircraft defence).[17] His powers of analysis were equally limited on the political level: his view of the Anglo-Saxons was stubbornly prejudiced; and his great impressionability where German successes were concerned led him to favour brutal and risky policies. What distinguished him from both Pétain and Laval was a greater sensitivity to prevailing circumstances and a pragmatism that stopped him from sailing against winds and tides. All the same, he was sufficiently caught up in his own game to need a whole series of adaptative moves before switching to the side of the Allies in the autumn of 1942.

Alongside Darlan was Weygand, the Minister for National Defence, seeking to retain the prerogatives of the defeated army. In his soul he was a reactionary, stubborn, intractable and excessive, with a knack for aggravating everybody. He clashed with Laval more and more frequently. 'All parliamentarians are scoundrels', he would jeer, to which Laval would retort, 'And all military men are cretins.'[18] In late August, he lost his temper in the presence of the American naval attaché: 'I can do nothing more since the Marshal is being pressed by a pig-merchant.'[19] In September, Pétain got rid of him by appointing him delegate general to French Africa, a strategic position that Weygand was able to exploit to get his voice heard, until he was dismissed in 1941. Explosive in his criticism, capable of putting a brake on the policy of collaboration, but just as sold on the national revolution as Pétain himself, he really had no serious alternatives to suggest. His successor at National Defence, General Charles Huntziger, continued to try to raise morale by distributing decorations. Darlan judged him to be 'a nut',[20] but he did none the less play a noteworthy role in collaboration, which was obliterated by his accidental death in November 1941. Since he disappeared and Darlan was assassinated, the responsibility of the military in Vichy's policies has never been fully recognized.

Around that kernel, a series of ministerial teams revolved. Some of their members, teachers or high-grade clerks, came from the administration, others were entrepreneurs or were based in professional associations. Some were picked more or less at random. They made up a curious portrait gallery ranging from the likes of Joseph Barthélémy, Minister of Justice, who was invariably prepared to sacrifice his legal scruples, to fascists such as Paul Marion, the colourful chief of propaganda, and included activists such as Pierre Pucheu, a *normalien* who had moved into industry and was proud of his success there – an 'impulsive, unstable, authoritarian' man who imagined 'that his slightest move generated new impulses in the country'.[21] In important matters these people carried little weight. They were treated as clerks by Pétain, as technicians by Darlan – as Du Moulin wrote of his government, they were 'well brought-up, almost dumb men'[22] – and as vassals by Laval. Pétain both reigned and governed until 1942, at which point he twice conceded prerogatives to Laval. Right up to the end, on important matters nothing could be done without his approval.

Vichy condemned the parliamentary democracy because it placed the destiny of the nation in the hands of mediocre men. However, the mediocrity of the Vichy leaders was no less pronounced and was furthermore not subject to the limitations that even Claudel found himself looking back upon with nostalgia in the spring of 1941.

'Those politicians at least had two qualities: humanity – otherwise they would not have been elected – and a wise fear of Parliament, public opinion and so on.'[23]

While the regime was attempting to shore itself up, in the outside world it was feeling its way through a darkened landscape in which the sole ray of light was the considerable diplomatic recognition that it received, from the USSR and above all from the United States, with whom its leaders were anxious to maintain the best of relations. This apart, there were nothing but worries. The British established a blockade and supported the Gaullists, who rallied French Polynesia, the Cameroons, and the whole of French Equatorial Africa except Gabon. The empire, already coveted by the Italians and the Spaniards, was now also threatened by Japan, which extracted permission to station troops in Tonkin in exchange for a fragile assurance that it would respect French sovereignty. Early in 1941, even Thailand seized the opportunity to take over several provinces in Laos.[24]

And there was a more immediate threat, for the occupying power was revealing how little it respected the armistice agreement. It hermetically sealed the demarcation line, forbidding all movement between the agricultural south and the industrial north. Within the occupied territories, it proceeded to carve up regions in a way that further destroyed the country's unity and boded ill for the future. Alsace and Lorraine were now effectively annexed, with the German customs posts shifted back to the 1914 frontiers. The departments of Nord and Pas-de-Calais, whose economic importance was considerable, were brought under the military command of Brussels.

Developments were equally alarming elsewhere, in the territory that fell under the military command in Paris. In the north-eastern region, refugees were forbidden to return and a German company active in the germanization of the Polish territories, known as *Ostland*, appropriated the land left vacant. Everywhere, the occupying power interfered with administration, imposing niggling regulations, insisting that every change of personnel and all laws promulgated in the *Journal officiel* be submitted for its approval. It assumed authority over the press, the radio, the cinema, and all news agencies, using them for its own propaganda and for attacking Vichy without compunction, even appearing to support the communists and sanction Breton separatism. It laid a heavy hand on the economy, seizing a huge war booty that reached well beyond the military sector, and entering upon a large-scale requisitioning programme. Mountains of raw materials, both semi-finished and finished products, tools, and even assembly lines were despatched to Germany. The ultimate blow came on 8 August when it demanded 20 million Reichsmarks per day in occupation costs, at an exchange rate inflated by at least one-third as compared to pre-war days. On top of its looting and requisitioning, it took to placing orders and, for settling the account, it imposed a clearing agreement: if economic life was to pick up, it would be necessary to give credit for exports to Germany.

In Vichy, following Mers el-Kébir, the early signs of this high-handedness were registered with consternation, but most anger there was concentrated against the English. Darlan, infuriated by the damage done to his fleet, pressed for reprisals, going so far as to suggest that France and Italy should mount a joint attack against Alexandria, a suggestion that Italy turned down.[25] Diplomatic relations were broken off and Gibraltar was bombed, and there the matter rested; but the incident had clearly emphasized the extent to which foreign policy had been revised. Encouragement to pursue that revision came when the conquerors, alarmed by the pugnaciousness of the British, halted the disarmament of the fleet. The lesson that Vichy learned from this was that any improvement in its situation *vis-à-vis* the occupier depended upon it persisting in its antagonism towards its former ally.

Meanwhile more of the risks were surfacing. On 15 July, Hitler demanded that a number of key strongholds in North Africa be ceded to him. First it had been the fleet, and now it was the empire that was threatened, this time by the Germans. The matter of the reply to be given brought to light considerable disagreement over the extent to which foreign policy should continue to be revised and what concessions should be made to conciliate the conqueror. Weygand, intransigent when it came to the preservation of the empire pleaded for a flat refusal; Laval argued that it was not possible to manoeuvre on both the English and the German fronts simultaneously and that the former should now be abandoned. 'As for the German front, he recognized the difficulties . . . France must not be allowed to be broken up. Everything else was illusory.' Darlan and Baudouin supported him. Darlan noted, 'General Weygand is still protesting that we must not be browbeaten. But positions have already been taken up. The Marshal is even talking of "declaring war on the English". It has been pointed out to him that he cannot.'[26] The majority approved Pétain's sending a letter to Hitler, proposing that his demand be discussed within a general framework, in the form of a 'free negotiation', so that the two countries could 'devote more thought to whatever can unite them than to that which has for so long set them in such bitter opposition'.

Hitler never replied and let the matter drop. Preoccupied by the struggle against England, he ignored the French leaders' efforts to enter into dialogue. Faced with the question of whether to go further than what was required by the armistice, they opted in favour of doing so because they were keen to acquire military means, to make the conqueror trust them, and to pave the way for the least disadvantageous peace treaty possible. Their reply to Hitler did not rule out military collaboration in the form of providing him with bases in the empire. But their perspective was above all economic, if only because they believed the end of the war to be imminent. From this time on the term 'collaboration' loomed large in both their words and their thoughts. On 26 July, in a confidential memorandum, Baudouin, the Minister for Foreign Affairs, declared his support for 'lasting collaboration with Germany' that would make it possible to create 'a new Europe', collaboration that would operate primarily on an economic level, conceding nothing on a political or moral level.[27] Bouthillier, the Minister for National Finance and Economy, was similarly inclined and told German diplomats that France wished to become integrated in the new European economy.[28]

In these early weeks, a race was on to find the best placed negotiator. It was won by Laval, who managed to bend the ear of Abetz. He intimated to him that he would like to meet Göring and, as if to lend weight to his request, went on to say that he wished to create a single party, to take action against the freemasons and to exclude Jews from the administration.[29] He hoped that France's adaptation, of which he believed the conqueror would approve, would guarantee its credentials and prove that it had broken with the past. At his first meeting with Abetz, he assured him of his desire to integrate France into the new order and to practise 'collaboration with no reservations'. He told Professor Grimm of his desire for a total defeat of the English, which would diminish the bill to be footed by France. Even if it had to concede a great deal in the peace treaty, some kind of recuperation should be possible at the expense of the British empire.[30]

Of all the new leaders, Laval was the most forthright on collaboration: France should distance itself from England, draw closer to Germany and even help her, in exchange for considerable returns, so as to persuade Germany that it was in her interests to deal generously with defeated France, and eventually to play Germany off against Italy, the object of general resentment; and if England crumbled, France could make up for its own losses at England's expense. But though Laval was the most forthright, the presuppositions upon which his behaviour rested were shared by them all. France's defeat was definitive and England's was bound to follow soon. In the face of the ineluctable hegemony of Germany, wisdom dictated damage limitation through a show of goodwill and voluntary adhesion to the new order, preferably before England's collapse or, worse, before it sued for a compromise peace. The era of a disastrously sentimental and ideological foreign policy was over; the time had come for realism, French egoism and reasons of state to triumph. Abroad, as at home, it was necessary to 'think French' and rely on oneself alone. Although Maurras's influence was essentially limited, it was his motto that Vichy adopted: 'France for itself alone.'[31] This brand of nationalism, which dissociated itself from the continuing war and other oppressed peoples, accepted amalgamation into a Europe reorganized by the conqueror. But just as collaboration necessarily implied a partnership, 'the new Europe' was only acceptable if it respected France's interests.

The men of Vichy shared four objectives, which they rated in orders that varied from one period to another: protection, sovereignty, status, and the regime.[32] Protection was an urgent, basic, immediate motive. It was necessary to halt the looting of the occupied zone, stand between the occupiers and the population, and obtain the release of the prisoners of war. This was a goal close to Pétain's heart, the one that he invoked to justify his desire to remain in France, even under total occupation. Had he limited himself to that one objective, things would clearly have turned out very differently. In the short term, this protective mission had the approval of both officials and the ordinary people and it provided the basis for the somewhat equivocal support given to a policy described by some as 'a policy of presence', by others as 'a policy aiming for the least of evils'. For a time it allowed even those determined to resist to entertain a hope of recovery.

Sovereignty was an objective seriously affected by the occupation of part of the territory and, even more, by the interventionism of the occupying power, something that was to increase rather than abate the longer the war lasted. The reaction of the French state was to strive to recuperate its administrative authority and limit the occupation to its military aspect. Its efforts, justifiable enough in international law, also and above all reflected a mentality that set a high value on the state, the regulated functioning of the administration and, through this, control over the population. But the French leaders, so insistent upon the need for a return to the values of order and authority, found themselves wrongfooted by the occupying powers that dealt high-handedly with the officials in the occupied zone, rendering it quite plain that it was they who made the law.

Recuperation of the standing of France was a longer-term objective for Vichy, but was certainly not absent from its preoccupations in the short term either. For its leaders, particularly the military amongst them, recovery meant first and foremost, as it had for the Germans after 1918, the restoration of its armed forces: this would constitute a basis for status, a guarantee of prestige, a foundation for power politics and also, in the immediate instance, an indispensable means of defence against attacks from the English and encroachments by the Gaullists. Restored rank for France also meant equality and reciprocity in its dealings with its conqueror, even if it was accepted that the defeat would have to be paid for.

Last but not least, the fourth objective was to secure a future for the regime. The French state born of the armistice needed to prove that its external policies were viable. Closer ties with the conqueror were important in the short term because of any ensuing relief that would enable it to win over public opinion. They were also important in the long term: a relatively lenient peace would give a conservative system a chance to work; incorporation in a Nazi Europe would also be helpful, given the similarity of its regimes and the defeat of all adverse principles. The regime's survival was a deep preoccupation that encouraged collaboration by making the occupying force appear as a factor of order, if only because it alone could provide the means of ensuring it. Huntziger was particularly sensitive to this, and on 30 August wrote to Weygand as follows: 'The internal situation of France, which the Marshal does not appear to suspect, demands that a force strong enough to maintain order be set up without delay.'[33] In the following February, he told a German correspondent that it would be necessary 'to deal with serious disturbances when the occupation came to an end'.[34] At the time of the *Relève* (Replacement Programme), when French workers were sent to Germany in exchange for the release of prisoners of war, Pétain told Pastor Boegner that 'one of the good effects of the workers' departure will be to weaken communism, which is "all the rage" in France'.[35] A year earlier, Bouthillier had already summed up this whole state of mind when, in response to Bertrand de Jouvenel, who told him that the regime's reforms ran the risk of being discredited by a foreign policy that the country did not want, he had retorted sharply: 'Do not delude yourself that internal policies can be divorced from external ones. It is the presence of the Germans that has given us a chance to carry out our internal programme of reform and is making it possible to do so.'[36] As can be imagined, when the moment of truth came, views such as these were to limit the implementation of that famous *raison d'état*.

On the other hand, it is also clear that internal policy was not the sole factor in determining the choice of collaboration. This followed just as much from a particular analysis of the situation, a particular calculation as to the future and a particular view of the conqueror: all were elements that were mixed with the preoccupation with survival but at the same time were relatively autonomous. And the analyses and calculations were all erroneous on crucial points: the possibility of the war assuming world-wide proportions was not taken seriously enough when estimating how long it would last; England's weakness was exaggerated, as were her evil designs on France if she proved victorious; the importance of the trump cards held by France was overestimated, as was her ability to hang on to them in the event of a prolonged conflict; and, finally, there was no understanding of either the Nazi regime or Hitler's long-term intentions. On this last point, Vichy clung to a distorted pre-war image of Nazism. It regarded Nazism simply as a prolongation of pangermanism, genuinely admired it for its military achievements, and was deeply impressed by the 'merits' of its regime, as it never tired of repeating in meetings with Nazi representatives.[37] So impressed was Vichy that it was even inclined to claim an ideological affinity, not so much with the racist core of Nazism, but with the whole baggage of ideologies that Nazism shared with conservative currents of thinking. In September 1940, Pétain gave the *Revue des deux mondes* (15 September 1940) an article in which he explained that liberalism, capitalism and collectivism were 'foreign products' that France, 'left to itself, quite naturally rejects'. He then went on to declare: 'And when it comes to examine the principles that ensured the victory of its adversaries, it will be surprised to recognize everywhere in them its own best qualities, its own most pure and authentic victory . . . The national socialist idea of the prime importance of work and its essential reality, as opposed to the fiction of monetary symbols, is something that we find it all the easier to accept, given that it is also part of our own classical heritage.'

Pétain thus chose to stress a secondary aspect of Nazism, meanwhile implicitly recognizing that its military victory had given it the status of an ideological reference. Above all, he professed recognition of a kinship that stemmed from a rejection of the same adversaries. This professed kinship between the new French regime and the Nazi regime, which admittedly did not efface a strong distinction between their principles on certain important points, was to produce a distorted image of the conqueror and was to operate as a ball and chain upon the exercise of Vichy's *raison d'état*.

A more accurate appreciation of the conqueror sometimes surfaced in the regime's channels of communication, but without much effect. In February 1941, Doyen, the president of the French armistice delegation in Weisbaden passed on a study that his team had produced on 'the Third Reich and its western frontiers'. Drawing its evidence from the German press and other German publications, it showed that the Reich's ambitions embraced the whole of northern France and it concluded with a disturbing prognosis of the conqueror's intentions. 'A France without army or fortresses and committed to a policy of collaboration might, at a pinch, offer sufficient guarantees. But this seems to be a chance unprecedented in history that is likely to impel the present leaders [of Germany] to adopt the safest solution, which would be to reduce our own country to its simplest expression, by annexing all or part of the former territories of the Holy Germanic Empire. With a selection of the right authors, both history and geography could be made to justify everything, and the transplantation of entire populations, by now common practice for the national socialists, could render anything possible.' The conclusions drawn were by no means optimistic as to the efficacy of Vichy's policies. 'The more or less complete realization of this programme is totally unaffected by *our* policies and simply depends upon the possibilities that the outcome of the war against England could open up for the Reich. It will depend upon the greater or lesser extent to which it will find itself free to do as it wishes in mainland Europe.'[38]

6

The machinery of occupation

With hindsight, it is easy to see how wrong Vichy was about the conqueror. Short of assuming the French leaders to have been totally lacking in judgement, it is perhaps more interesting to work out the reasons for their false perception. At the time, a number of elements, seen through certain lenses, might have encouraged a belief that there was still a way out and the future was not yet decided. Of course, things would have gone differently if England had given up the struggle in 1940. The Carthaginian peace that Hitler would then have inflicted upon France would have wiped out any preconceptions encouraged by the armistice and would have discredited those who, despite everything, would have been prepared to turn France into a satellite. It is interesting to speculate what, in those circumstances, would have become of the word 'collaboration' that was already beginning to circulate. However, peace was to be put off until later. Instead of immediate total humiliation, Vichy was to face German politics of a pliant, clever and tempting kind – tempting, that is, for whoever was ready to be tempted.

Following the armistice, turmoil reigned in Berlin in all the ministries, as they were invited to formulate their peace demands. The many memoranda put forward amounted to a new Treaty of Versailles: a colossal tribute should be paid, considerable annexations should take place, and economic and financial forfeits should be exacted.[1] In the topmost echelons of the Nazi hierarchy, ambitions went even further. France's defeat was seen as sweeping away three centuries of German impotence, consummating the defeat of the ideas of 1789, and opening up the way to a racial remodelling of the continent that would be completed by victory over the USSR.

In *Mein Kampf*, Hitler had made his ideas and feelings about Germany's neighbour perfectly clear. His hatred was solid, nurtured by a rudimentary view of history and poisoned with scorn for the French people's lack of racial awareness and their 'negrification'. At the same time, as amongst the German élites, all this was tempered by a certain respect for the past and culture of this neighbour. The war against France had not been primarily motivated by a thirst to annex territory: the vast expanses of the East would suffice. However, a chance to round things off was not to be missed, particularly when it could easily be justified by racism. In private, Hitler was prone to speak of annexing a vast, formerly German area stretching from Flanders across to Burgundy. Had he realized his dream, France would have been subjected to large-scale population movements. In July 1940, a German newspaper referred to a plan to expel six million inhabitants from northern France. On several occasions Hitler spoke of installing Germans from South Tyrol in Burgundy; and Himmler worked on this idea, which would have turned the Jura, the Doubs and the Haute-Saône into a territory of the Reich placed under the authority of the SS.[2] But, for the rest, Hitler never intended to annihilate France, as he did Poland, both as a state and as a nation. He was content to diminish it by lopping bits off, and dividing it against itself by exerting lasting influence upon its economy and culture: in short, by rendering it inoffensive and, to that end, eliminating the Jews there, as everywhere else in Europe.

Over the following years, this attitude remained unchanged. But as early as the autumn of 1940, the course of the war was requiring him to adopt certain tactical ploys. Having decided to crush the USSR in the following spring, so as to extend his strategic bases, bring England to heel and realize his ideological aims, Hitler deemed it inopportune to allow his conquered foes fully to perceive the fate in store for them. It was, on the contrary, vital to encourage them in their hostility towards their former ally in Africa and to obtain their assistance in eradicating that ally's presence from the Mediterranean. At every level, German negotiators accordingly now introduced variations on the themes of collaboration and the new European order. Hitler himself on several occasions requested help from France for particular projects, holding out the hope of thereby earning a better fate. Yet he never committed himself as to the future in any way, and kept reciprocity for favours rendered to the strictest minimum.

Of course, he was hampered by his alliance with Mussolini, who kept a jealous eye on a *rapprochement* that could only be to his own cost. But above all, he was deterred by his own distrust. He could not believe that France would renounce power politics, that she would not one day turn against him any weapons that he might allow. Besides, valuing strength above all as he did, he was haunted by the fear of appearing weak. On 31 January 1942 he accused France of seeking to profit from the difficult times he was going through. As Talleyrand had, France aimed to emerge from defeat undamaged, while Hitler was prepared to make a settlement only from a position of strength.[3] With such thinking, he was bound to dash Vichy's hopes. Instead of making deals, Hitler was to become increasingly intransigent, thereby committing to destruction not only his own country but also any foreign regimes clinging to its coat tails.

By keeping quiet as to his ultimate objectives and making a purely tactical show of openness, he was, for two years at least, to encourage a number of hopes not on the French side alone, but also on the German. He remained faithful to the ideas expressed in *Mein Kampf* by acting in this way: cunning and deception are just as essential to a great statesman as are strength and violence. Just as he had manipulated the German conservatives by allowing them to hope to share power and stabilize their positions, he dangled before the French conservatives the lure of a mutually profitable arrangement, meanwhile glorying in his perfidy and his power to impel others to their doom.

Hitler's subalterns went along with his game, nurturing an equal animosity towards France. Göring was interested solely in exploiting the economy of defeated France to the utmost. Goebbels welcomed the idea of a weak and disunited neighbour, applauding the idea of its future as a 'bigger Switzerland'.[4] Himmler, obsessed with racial purity, detested those mongrelized French. Later, alarmed at German military losses, he was to think of recuperating 'the German blood' that he sensed among them, in particular in French officers with Germanic names. He ended up proposing to create a French Waffen-SS. For men such as these, for whom the occupied countries were simply a field in which to play out their own rivalries, the existence of Vichy was a nuisance. They were obliged to take account of it, even though it deserved no more than crumbs from their table.

The position of Ribbentrop was rather different, for as the German conquests multiplied, his own ministry became less important. If only for that reason, he might even have welcomed the existence of a French state. In 1940–41, he found himself in agreement with military leaders worrying about British resistance and demanding it be eliminated before Germany launched its attack in the East. For such a strategy French help might prove valuable. Of course the military were arguing purely as strategists; the political concessions necessary to pay for such aid was no concern of theirs. Their point of view did not succeed in altering the course of events, but it did persuade Hitler to adopt a circumspect policy that, for him, held only a temporary value.

Meanwhile, the occupation machinery was being set in place. A German armistice commission based in Weisbaden was to supervise the implementation of the armistice agreement. Its Italian counterpart was located in Turin. Soon an economic commission was added. Its director was a pugnacious diplomat, Robert Hemmen, and it dealt with any questions that fell outside the framework of the agreement, in particular access to the resources of the free zone and the empire. In the spring of 1941 it was moved to Paris, testifying to the importance ascribed to economic relations between the two countries.

In the occupied zone, the principal source of authority was the 'Military Command in France' (the Militärbefehlshaber in Frankreich, the MBF), with headquarters in the Hotel Majestic. Its administration was divided into two general staffs. The first, with responsibility for military questions (repairing communication routes, guarding prisoners, army security, military justice) was directed by Hans Speidel, assisted by the writer Ernst Jünger. The second, with responsibility for administrative matters, was subdivided into two sections: a strictly administrative section, under Werner Best, and an economic section, under the direction of Elmar Michel. These covered every aspect of life in the occupied zone, across the board from surveillance of the administration to supervision of economic activity, and including measures for the spoiliation of the Jewish population. Attached to the MBF was the Wehrmacht armament service (the Wi. Rü.-Stab), which placed orders with French firms.

For administrative tasks, the MBF employed a civilian staff seconded from various ministries, major industries and professional organizations. In 1941 this consisted of 1500 officials,[5] assisted by military personnel, making up a total staff of about 22000. Order was maintained by security forces, the numbers of which varied considerably. The total dropped from 100000 men in December 1941 to 40000 in March 1942, then rose again to about 200000 by the end of 1943. But other German forces were also stationed in France: in 1942, operational troops numbered 400000 men, by early 1944 close on one million.[6]

This strong presence made it possible for the Military Command to carry out its mission: to provide for the security and supplies of the German forces, the maintenance of order, and the control and exploitation of the economy. It was a mission that was carried out by men who were professional soldiers and were responsible to the High Command of Land Forces (the OKH). It so happened that the MBF was headed by two cousins, in succession, both of them representative of their caste and its relations – at once tense and complicit – with the Nazi authorities. Otto von Stülpnagel was appointed in October 1940. Jünger describes him as combining the grace of a ballet dancer with the countenance of a 'melancholic and manic wooden Punch'.[7] He was a strict and punctilious man, feared by his subordinates. A stickler for his prerogatives, he tussled with determination with the other services. His test came with the executions of hostages ordered by Hitler, in response to the wave of attacks carried out against the occupying troops from August 1941 onwards. He disapproved of the sweeping nature of measures that deepened the gulf between the occupiers and the population and, having asked to be relieved of his responsibilities at the beginning of 1942, he withdrew, embittered that he, of all people, should have been criticized for 'weakness' or 'lukewarmness'.[8] His cousin, Karl Heinrich von Stülpnagel, had directed the German armistice commission in Wiesbaden for almost a year before taking command of an army on the eastern front. He was a cultured man who spoke good French, with the manners of a great lord, and was relieved when the SS took over his responsibility for maintaining order. He later played an important role in the plot against Hitler, imprisoning local SS officers in Paris on 20 July 1944. He was executed after making a suicide attempt.[9]

Both cousins were in their sixties and had served in the Great War. They stood for the traditional notions of order, regularity and efficiency. Jünger's diary reveals the lack of enthusiasm that met the rumours of the genocide of the Jews in circles such as theirs and the disgust felt for the bullies of the Nazi party. However, neither protested at or avoided tasks that violated international law. Antisemitic prejudice and above all anticommunism were part of their world of values, as was racism generally, which barred blacks from first-class compartments of the Metro and prohibited the return of Jews, blacks and Arabs to the occupied zone. The first Stülpnagel suggested replacing the shooting of hostages by deportation of the Jews and communists to the East. The second, while in Russia, had requested to direct the collective reprisals that were taken first and foremost against the Jewish population.[10]

Two other services placed under the control of the Majestic, but receiving their instructions from Berlin, implemented policies definitely stamped with the Nazi seal. Instructions for the Propaganda-Abteilung, responsible for orienting people's minds, came from Goebbels. Major Heinz Schmidtke, a personal friend of the minister, who directed 1276 employees[11] (in 1941) and four Staffeln set up in the provinces, was a positive caricature of a Prussian officer. He busied himself extending his authority even into remote corners of the cultural scene and establishing an influence that would survive the war. Goebbels' aim was to wipe out the cultural prestige of France in Europe and get the conquered French people to recognize the superiority of their victor.[12]

The second service was created by Himmler, who despatched to Paris a commando unit of twenty-five, led by Helmut Knochen, a man of thirty whose mission was to seek out, keep under surveillance and oppose 'ideological enemies of Nazism': Jews, Christians, communists and freemasons. For the time being Knochen carried little weight, since the MBF was the official policing authority. However, that did not prevent him from using methods with a definitely 'fire-and-brimstone' touch. In October 1941, for instance, he supplied explosives to French collaborationists, who proceeded to blow up seven synagogues, injuring several French people and two German soldiers. Stülpnagel was roused to fury and insisted, in vain, that Knochen should go. By himself resigning, he opened up the way for Himmler who, in the spring of 1942, appointed Karl Oberg, aged forty-five, to direct services of repression in France. Knochen thereupon became one of his two adjutants. The SS apparatus now swelled to about 5000 men.[13] It was a force that was by no means large enough for all the work there was to be done, a fact that made the help of the French police all the more appreciated.

Although the MBF was the key element in the occupation apparatus, the difficulties which it faced were considerable. Within its own framework it had to integrate not just military but also seconded civilian personnel, whose members tended to represent the views of the particular organizations from which they originated. Beyond that framework, not only did the airforce and the navy answer directly to Berlin, but the MBF's authority was undermined by the operational troops, which eluded its jurisdiction and behaved in a manner that frequently made for friction with the French population. These troops were younger and rougher, quick to requisition and to make massive purchases that upset economic life, and also to apply stringent sanctions in cases of sabotage or disobedience.[14] The MBF also had to keep an eye on the activities of the many services operating from Berlin, whether these constituted state organs or party offshoots, professional associations or private businesses, whose delegates sometimes made direct contact with their French opposite numbers (in 1944, 1200 German firms were active in France, about 500 operating in the construction field).[15] The MBF exercised uneven authority over the 80000 odd Germans brought into France by the occupation,[16] a figure that included the thousands of workers and technicians employed in naval yards and the railways. From the spring of 1942 onwards, the MBF's authority over the SS became no more than superficial, as did its control over the Sauckel recruitment organization, which soon numbered over a thousand employees brought in from the Reich.

Finally it had to get along with the German embassy, whose role went beyond relations with Vichy and also took in the political and much of the cultural life of the occupied zone. The team of diplomats headed by Abetz was young, dynamic and experienced. During the phoney war, it had devoted itself to demoralizing propaganda aimed at French soldiers.[17] Initially, Abetz's task was to advise the military commander of Paris on political and propaganda matters. At the beginning of August, Hitler appointed him ambassador to the military commander of France, with responsibility for all political matters, furthermore giving him the task of seizing Jewish works of art. After Montoire, he raised his delegation to the rank of embassy, but without accrediting him to Vichy since a state of war still existed. But Abetz was to link up with the French government and oversee its relations with other countries. The military authorities had to obtain his agreement on political questions. This gave rise to a certain amount of friction, since political and military problems tended to become muddled.[18]

One of the embassy's advantages was its compact size, although it was imposing enough by ordinary standards. In 1943, it consisted of 168 German employees and 54 foreigners, most of them French personnel. Including the services attached to it, in particular the German Institute, the total came to 568 employees, 367 of them Germans.[19] It enjoyed colossal means in the form of secret funds of one hundred million francs, allotted from the occupation expenses. Its organizational chart reveals the extent of its activities. Abetz's assistant, Rudolf Schleier, aged forty-one, was the oldest member of his team and also the most long-standing Nazi party member. He was responsible for management, war veterans and prisoners of war. He was a man who loved receptions, uniforms and decorations, and he had a good chance to indulge these tastes when he took over from Abetz for a year, after November 1942. The political section was directed by Ernst Achenbach, aged thirty-one, who had been posted to Paris before the war. He was intelligent, hard-working, and enjoyed the confidence of the ambassador, whose tactics he emulated and whose real substitute he was to be. According to Benoist-Méchin, his was 'a very keen mind, certainly much clearer than Abetz's'.[20] In mid-1943, he was recalled to Berlin because his wife was American and Hitler had decided that high-ranking officials with wives holding enemy nationality should be retired from positions of importance. It was a lucky decision for Achenbach's future career. He later became a liberal deputy, then a member of the European parliament, and would have been appointed European commissioner had not the French Nazi-hunters Serge and Beate Klarsfeld mounted a campaign against him.

Alongside a small economic section, an information section, directed by Rahn, sought to control matters to do with the press, the radio and propaganda, thereby competing with Propaganda-Abteilung, which Abetz wanted to restrict to military censorship. In the summer of 1942, he managed to relieve Propaganda-Abteilung of responsibility for literary and artistic affairs by attaching them to the cultural section of the embassy. The man in charge here was Karl Epting, aged thirty-five, who had been responsible for the German Universities Office in France before the war and after September 1940 had become the director of the German Institute created by Abetz. A recently signed-up member of the Nazi party, he became a zealous purger of the university. His task was to attract French intellectuals and diffuse German culture by organizing language courses, lectures and exhibitions. In these activities, the embassy benefited from the help of Friedrich Sieburg, a journalist on the *Frankfurter Zeitung* who was well known in France, and also that of Freidrich Grimm, professor of international law at the University of

Munster and legal advisor to the embassy, who used the many lectures that he gave under the aegis of the Groupe Collaboration to sound out public opinion.

Otto Abetz, aged thirty-eight, has left behind him the reputation of a francophile and the image of a lone dreamer clinging to the politics of collaboration. But it is one that neither the occupied French nor his own superiors were willing to swallow. Certainly he was a loner, at least after 1942, but as for the francophilia, it would depend on what one meant by the word. Abetz's political past was not associated with the extreme right, but he was never a social democrat, as has often been claimed. He was militant in the youth movements that were so typical of Germany in the period between the wars, and he believed in reconciliation with France, at the same time remaining convinced of the injustice of the Treaty of Versailles.[21] His efforts to promote closer ties with France in the early 1930s were not prompted solely by idealism: he sought financial aid for his purpose from the German Ministry of Foreign Affairs, a fact that suggests that he developed a taste for wielding influence very early on.[22]

When Hitler came to power, he had no trouble in adapting. By chance he came to the notice of Ribbentrop, who took him into his team in 1934. The following year, with Ribbentrop's encouragement, he became a member of the SS, in which he was to rise to the rank of brigadier general, which set him on the same footing as his superior in the diplomatic service, Secretary of State von Weiszäcker.[23] In 1937, he joined the Nazi party, seizing the chance of the reopening of its membership, which had been closed in May 1933 to avoid it being swamped with applications. Over these years, he had been adapting to the requisite mould, yet retained an easy manner that sometimes got him into trouble.[24] He was ambitious, a *bon viveur*, charming and affable; he loved France and loathed England, was rather unorthodox on racial questions and was given to describing himself as a 'diplomatic *franc-tireur*'. Ribbentrop liked him and made him his assistant, then early in 1940 transferred him to the diplomatic service.

His promotion to ambassador came as a reward for . . . what? He had established contact with Laval, for whom he soon felt sympathy, even affection. But in the summer of 1940 this 'Peterchen', as he called Laval, was of no great importance to Hitler, who could think only of crushing England. The explanation perhaps lies, rather, in his cast of mind, which was of a kind to appeal to the Nazi leader.

After the war, a member of his team compared him to a billiards amateur playing the ball off the cushion, a man of considerable slyness and not always a gentleman.[25] His taste for cunning and manipulation was evident as soon as he arrived in Paris, where he immediately suggested to the MBF that it should publish a communiqué declaring there to have been many attacks against British people residing in France and insisting that a stop be put to them. The attacks were a pure invention which, Abetz calmly explained, should serve to counter anglophile propaganda and, it was to be hoped, achieve 'the extremely desirable result of getting the French population to thrash a few British'.[26]

He entertained an ambitious view of his mission, which he submitted to Hitler in the middle of the summer. His plan was to use propaganda to prevent the French from uniting against Germany, playing upon a wide variety of political tendencies without hesitation and encouraging them in their 'hope or rather delusion of a possible *entente* with the Reich'. Also, German culture should be diffused through the creation of a German Institute and by means of articles in the press, translations of German works, and by organizing cultural events, meanwhile undermining French influence abroad. At the same time, the country could be weakened from within by encouraging the Breton movement and reawakening a sense of German identity in Flanders, Burgundy and Lorraine.

Politically, his ideal was permanent occupation of the country. This would be accepted by the French people provided the strongest opponents of Germany were exiled and the possessions of 'the warmongers' were sequestrated, that is to say all those – parliamentary representatives, freemasons, Jews, members of the clergy and journalists – who had called for arms to be taken up against the Reich. Abetz's thinking was completely Nazi, even if he did not go so far as to recommend the physical elimination of the French élites. Once all this was achieved, the Germans would only have to deal with the popular masses 'amongst whom the Führer already commanded considerable respect' and amongst whom it would be necessary to develop a European sense of identity. 'In exactly the same way that the idea of a peace was usurped by national socialist Germany and served to weaken French morale without damaging the combative spirit of Germany itself, similarly the European idea could be usurped by the Reich without prejudicing the claim to primacy in Europe, a primacy that national socialism has anchored in the German people.' In the event of Hitler not wishing to keep

France permanently, it would be necessary to introduce into the peace treaty a strict limitation on France's armed forces. It would then fall to Abetz to find the team prepared to sign that peace treaty.[27]

The new ambassador was true to himself with this combination of simplistic visions, primitive Machiavellianism, and trust in propaganda. Hitler did not go along with his long-term views but was sympathetic to his ideas on how to weaken France, as they coincided with his own. His directive to Abetz in that summer of 1940 was to reflect his attitude right to the end: France must be divided by all possible means and a great wedge must be driven between Vichy and the Anglo-Saxon countries.[28] To this he added an order to prepare for the expulsion of the Jews, an item omitted by Abetz, who had written to say that French opinion was already so hostile in this respect that there was no need to take any further action. The ambassador was no more than moderately antisemitic, but he was too anxious to please to attempt to apply a brake on anything Hitler suggested and, backed up by Achenbach, he was to play a notable part in the persecution, pressing Vichy to harden its line and supporting the SS in their work of execution as in that of repression in general: it is significant that he was excluded from the Paris part of the anti-Hitler plot. Initially, it did not occur to him that it would all lead to Auschwitz. But the path to Auschwitz was paved with a variety of intentions, not one of which, in truth, was good.

Abetz had attracted Hitler's attention. Thereafter, he was to meet with him personally so frequently – at least half a dozen times by 1942 – that this must be seen as reflecting the real favour that he enjoyed for a while. Perhaps, as one of his subordinates suggested, it was because he was adept at pandering to the dictator's tastes. When he was setting out for an audience, he would have a collection of saucy magazines prepared, and he used to encourage the publication of 'light' articles and drawings, saying that the Führer 'was very partial to that kind of thing'.[29] Or he would take along the plans of the new embassy that he wanted built on the Place de la Concorde, a project that the former professor of drawing knew would capture the attention of the failed painter. More seriously, Hitler valued him as a man who would not be a stickler for form, as were most of the diplomatic profession, which he detested as much as the legal profession and who, by creating political parties in Paris, had managed to bring into being an opposition to Vichy.[30]

Abetz tried to use his favour to get his leader to support the policies that he had devised. As he saw it, with the prolongation of the war Germany's interest lay in implicating conquered France in the war against England: not only would this provide welcome military support but it would also be a means of linking the interests of the two countries and would hasten the goal of reducing France to a 'satellite state' resigned to its 'permanently weakened position' in Europe.[31] To that end, it would be necessary to hold out the promise of a peace arrangement that would 'on the whole' safeguard the unity of the country but at the same time take precautions by establishing German bases on the Atlantic seaboard and forming a government committed to the German cause. In the whole occupation apparatus, Abetz was the only person with an overall view and who addressed the problem of long-term control over France. Rather than a diminished but irreconcilable neighbour he preferred a neighbour allowed to retain its own territory but which, in exchange, accepted becoming a protectorate of the Reich. This would involve the French to some extent sacrificing their nationalism upon the altar of the European idea – a theme upon which he was forever sounding forth.

He was obliged to recognize, with chagrin, that outside military circles his ideas were making little headway. He blamed the party leaders, who held him in disfavour, following the lead of Goebbels who accused him of being a 'speechifier' and a sickening francophile.[32] The root of the problem was clearly that Hitler, despite his seemingly receptive attitude, did not really believe in his ideas. Abetz himself reports in his memoirs that Hitler would stammer over the word *Kollaboration*, finding it hard to pronounce: a better clue to his state of mind would be hard to find.[33] The ambassador's reasoning rested upon the hypothesis that the French, or at least some of them, would go along with a voluntary vassalization. Hitler doubted that even collaborationists would resign themselves to the status of a protectorate. Eventually he grew irritated by the constant talk of concessions. On 27 February 1942, he told those close to him that he found Abetz too keen on collaboration, but he could not tell him openly of his own goals since the man had a French wife and there was no knowing whether he talked in his sleep![34] Abetz the manipulator had found his match in Hitler – a fact that is not particularly surprising. Was Hitler deliberately playing games with him? It was in all likelihood more a matter of slyness combined with a habit of not slamming the door shut, of putting off decisions, of behaving in such a way as to foster in his advisers the notion that they had the power to influence.

Once the SS arrived, the role of the embassy dwindled. To have a chance of success, if there ever was one, Abetz's policies required a less tense situation. Nevertheless, his team remained impossible to ignore, even after the *franc-tireur* ambassador was recalled to Berlin in November 1942. Although he eventually exasperated his superior, he had played a role of considerable importance in that he had fed Vichy's hopes of collaboration. Moreover, he had no compunction about implicating certain of the French in his own political game, – Laval and Déat first and foremost. He convinced them that France's fate depended upon a struggle between different tendencies within the Nazi regime and that it was important to form an alliance between the French and the German supporters of collaboration, so as to get things moving in the right direction.[35] A certain solidarity of interests, limited but real, was thus created on the basis of particular hopes and attitudes and a kind of complicit familiarity fostered, for instance, at the expense of Pétain, of whom, to the delight of the embassy staff, Laval always spoke mockingly.[36] From the French point of view, such solidarity inevitably appeared to hold out hope for some kind of a future, so long as Abetz had access to Hitler. However, it was undermined in advance by the double manipulation to which it was subjected: on the one side by Abetz, who had satellization, not partnership in mind; on the other by Hitler, who was encouraging his ambassador to aim for satellization but was in truth all along bent on crushing France.

Abetz's political game provides the strongest example of the interpenetration of interests that was an important element in relations between the occupiers and the occupied. To the extent that the services in Paris reflected and continued the struggles between tendencies in Berlin, transversal links were established between certain of the Germans and certain of the French, all of whom were seeking to further their own policies, positions and interests. Laval and Déat established links with the embassy, Darlan with the Kriegsmarine, businessmen with the economic section at the Majestic, certain collaborationists with the SS, and so on. This phenomenon may not have disrupted the chain of command, or confused allegiances, but it did encourage the idea that a margin of manoeuvre existed. When it came to important questions, the services in Paris did cohere as a block, but occasionally they cohered with Vichy against other German sources of influence. Thus, the MBF supported the French request for the reattachment of the northern departments, even if it did not succeed in overriding the military in Brussels, who had Hitler's support; and the MBF and the embassy, not without at least partial sucess, relayed French appeals for clemency when hostages were being shot in 1941. In early 1944, all the German services in France, including the SS, opposed further seizures of workers by Sauckel and supported Speer, who wanted to keep the French working in France. But Hitler came down mostly in favour of Sauckel.

The relative autonomy of the German services and the resulting tensions between their different points of view combined to lend credibility to the notion that collaboration was possible. Given that they came across Germans with varying interests and conflicting preferences, the French leaders fortified themselves with the hope that things were not yet fixed once and for all. They were not totally mistaken: even Hitler recognized the advantage in dealing circumspectly with France for the moment. But given that he was determined to crush his defeated enemy as soon as victory was his, and that he was to become ever more intransigent the worse things went for him, that hope was altogether deluded.

7

Montoire

Contrary to Vichy's prognoses, the war continued: England stood firm. When it had signed the armistice, Vichy had assumed that German victory was inevitable. Paradoxically enough, the resistance of the British increased its margin of manoeuvre, but also the risks involved. It was in this context that its politics took shape in the form that we now recognize: collaboration with the occupier in the midst of a continuing war.

In the autumn, the interests of Germany and France converged somewhat. Lacking superiority in the air, Hitler deferred invasion of England to some indeterminate future date. This setback, which he attempted to disguise, was made even harder to bear by the pugnaciousness of his enemy, which was making itself felt as far afield as the coasts of Africa, at the French empire's expense. In September, after rallying nearly all of French Equatorial Africa, an Anglo-Gaullist expedition attacked Dakar. The operation foundered upon the determined resistance of the forces of Vichy. For de Gaulle, this was a painful setback, but it sounded the alarm for Germany, which decided to eliminate the enemy before it could seize control of the southern Atlantic.

The 'new policy' was supported by the military, the leaders of the High Command of the armed forces, the OKW, in particular Jodl and Warlimont, and above all by Raeder, commander-in-chief of the navy. To all of them, the assistance of Vichy seemed indispensable. Vichy represented a minor, but by no means negligible factor of power. Its leaders might be tempted to re-enter the war, providing bothersome reinforcements for England. On the other hand, they might make Germany's task easier by providing bases on the Atlantic, closing the western Mediterranean, and exerting military pressure by defending their empire and reconquering their dissident colonies, not to mention the fact that their economic resources were assuming a greater importance the longer the conflict lasted.

Hitler's objective remained a settling of accounts with the USSR in the following spring. For him, the 'new policy' was of no more than secondary and temporary importance: it was a makeshift defensive ploy[1] that made it necessary to reconcile contradictory interests. In June, Hitler had scorned Franco's entry into the war, which the Spanish leader had been offering at a high price: namely in return for French Morocco and the region of Oran. Now though, his help would be necessary if the Mediterranean was to be sealed off, Gibraltar captured and Atlantic bases acquired. In return, however, French territories would have to be promised to Spain and this would dissuade Vichy from lending its support – support that would itself have to be paid for out of Italy's gains and by granting military reinforcements that might then be turned against the Axis powers, hence the idea of pulling off a double coup. By obtaining the right to station German troops in Spanish Morocco when Franco entered the war, Hitler would at a stroke be able to place French North Africa under surveillance, thereby diminishing the risk of a swing against Germany and also placing conquered France totally at his mercy.

Vichy, meanwhile, was facing up to the Anglo-Gaullist threat to the French empire. However, its forces were small and were controlled right down to the last shell. Covert advances accordingly now multiplied in both Paris and Wiesbaden. The French stressed their desire to defend themselves. They asked for the military means to do so and, in the same breath, also for a guarantee of respect for the integrity of the empire. The attack on Dakar, to which they riposted by bombing Gibraltar, put some beef into these advances, which now seemed to have some chance of success. The interests of the conqueror favoured the conquered, as is shown by the indefinite deferment of the disarming of the fleet and an authorization to rearm the airforce in North Africa. Vichy was immediately sensitive to this change,[2] as is shown by the fact that Pétain himself entered the arena. On 10 October, he made a speech in which he addressed an appeal to the conqueror. He spoke of France freeing itself from 'so-called traditional' hostilities: France wished to seek collaboration 'in all domains, with all its neighbours'.[3]

Two weeks later at Montoire, Hitler received first Laval on his own, then Laval and Pétain. In between those two meetings he travelled to the Spanish border, where he spoke with Franco, hoping to get him to agree to enter the war. At the meeting of 22 October, in response to Laval, who told him of his desire for loyal collaboration and his certainty of defeat for the British, Hitler spoke in general terms: France had lost the war and for this it would have to pay, but it might receive more generous treatment, in particular in Africa, if it made a contribution to the struggle against England.[4] Two days later, faced with Pétain, he repeated that to win the war he had no need of anyone else; but France might hasten that victory, in which case this would be remembered in its favour. Pétain expressed his desire to take back the Gaullist colonies and indicated that collaboration would be possible in this area. Laval pointed out that the French government could not declare war on England without approval from the National Assembly; nevertheless, there were other ways of achieving the same result, in particular by resisting attacks on the empire. He too stressed that it was necessary to proceed 'carefully and prudently'. Pétain wound up by declaring his admiration for Hitler and his immense successes.[5] Hitler had made no specific demands: he had asked for no declaration of war, no military assistance, no bases in the empire. The fact was that he had not obtained the commitment that he was hoping for from Franco, who had reverted to prudence. He had accordingly limited himself to sounding out Vichy's attitude; and he seemed relatively satisfied by what he discovered. The Vichy government had understood what he was interested in. Déat summed up what Laval had told him upon his return from Montoire as follows: 'No question of going to war against England; rather a matter of helping in the struggle against it, no doubt by making aircraft and by providing air and sea bases.'[6]

The photograph of Pétain shaking hands with Hitler prompted a wave of speculation. In truth, the meeting that had just taken place was a curious one: there had been no diplomatic preparation, none of the huge problems of the occupation had been discussed, and apart from a prudent communiqué, it had produced no results. Pétain accepted the principle of a collaboration, the modalities of which would be worked out as they went along; Hitler registered that France hoped that this would win it a more favourable outcome to the war. What the Nazi leader hoped was that this meeting, for which he arranged the maximum publicity, would bring home to the English the extent of their isolation. He also hoped that it would strengthen the isolationism of the United States, where the presidential campaign was in full swing; and that it would exert pressure on Spain and force it to a decision. Meanwhile, he had encouraged France to defend its empire and to commit itself against England. This would diminish the risk of a swing in the other direction and assure him of a strategic glacis that was cheap at the price. As for Pétain, he had eagerly seized the chance of a meeting for which he had been hoping, preferring a man-to-man conversation to a diplomatic exchange of views.

In a forceful speech delivered on 30 October he set the seal of official approval upon the politics of collaboration. Public disquiet made it difficult for him not to explain his position. Montoire, he declared, was a free meeting in the course of which 'a collaboration between our two countries has been envisaged'. Pétain stressed that the honour of France was safe, that his objective had been to maintain French unity, and at the same time to take up a position 'within the framework of the constructive activity of the new European order'. He expected collaboration to be repaid by better treatment for France, a better fate for prisoners, a reduction in the occupation costs, and a less rigid line of demarcation. His speech was formulated with great prudence: the government was 'entering upon the path of collaboration' and this must at once be 'sincere' and also 'exclude any thought of aggression', in other words exclude any declaration of war upon England. But the emphasis was clearly placed: 'this policy is my own', 'up until now I have spoken to you as a father. I am now speaking as your leader.' And the way forward was equally clearly indicated: whatever France's obligations towards the conqueror, it remained sovereign and its sovereignty 'obliges it to defend its soil, extinguish differences of opinion, and repress dissidence in its colonies'.[7] These three directives defined the field of collaboration as conceived by Pétain. It was necessary to unite the French in support of his policies, in order to inspire Germany with confidence. In the project of defence of the empire and reconquest of the Gaullist colonies, the interests of France and its conqueror converged, with the added advantage of restricting collaboration to a defensive framework. In protecting its own possessions or recovering them from a traitorous general, France was deploying no aggression against England; and if England were to react, the responsibility for whatever followed would be laid at its door.

Montoire gave the French leaders serious grounds for hope. Pétain demonstrated this by replacing Baudouin at Foreign Affairs by

Laval. Thanks to the military reinforcements that Germany would concede, Vichy would be able to defend its possessions and recapture its lost territories. The objective of the country's sovereignty tied in with the matter of its standing. The operation was all the more enticing in that it would be carried out solely by French forces and there would be no need to involve a German presence in the empire, since Germany had made no such demand. If the operation succeeded, France would be left better armed and rejoicing in the possession of all its African colonies. However, it did involve the risk of a clash with England in the event of it dashing to the aid of Gaullist troops that found themselves in difficulties. But that risk was counter-balanced by the hope of killing two birds with one stone, since the German interest in imperial affairs might be exploited to obtain a reduction in the occupation costs and promises with regard to the peace settlement, in particular a guarantee on the empire, which would save France from the greedy designs of Italy and Spain.

The hope of high-level negotiations was fostered by the announcement of a meeting with Ribbentrop, the date of which was then several times deferred. Meantime, Laval was making various gestures designed to demonstrate his goodwill, returning Belgian gold for instance, and ceding French interests in the Bor mines in Yugoslavia. In mid-November however, French hopes received an icy dousing: about 100000 people were expelled from Lorraine in a state of quasi-destitution. It was the most brutal violation of the armistice agreement yet, but the Vichy leaders regarded it above all as an embarrassment to current policies. Pétain did protest strongly, but that was chiefly because the Germans alleged that the operation had had his approval. In private, Laval did no more than request that it be suspended for a while: the expulsions could resume later, at a slower pace.[8] The government as a body adopted a similar attitude and, at the suggestion of Alibert and Baudouin, requested a deferral until the spring, proposing that batches of 10000 could then be expelled each month, so as to attract less attention, and that those expelled should be allowed to take their moveable chattels with them.[9] However, the operation went ahead with Hitler's personal sanction, thereby demonstrating that his French policies should not be mistaken for weakness and that he intended to implement them exactly as he pleased.

The empire was the immediate object of his preoccupations and here he considered negotiations to be useful, especially as adverse pressure persisted: Gaullist troops took possession of Gabon on 11 November. But there could be no question of allowing such negotiations to lead to any general discussion or even to any serious concessions. This was to be the model for all future negotiations. In late November Hitler sent Warlimont, one of the high-ranking officers of the OKW, to Paris, partly to find out how the French envisaged the reconquest of French Equatorial Africa, but also to discover their attitude to operations against the English colonies. In Vichy, the negotiations were welcomed. The military were expecting some restoration of their armed forces. Laval was also hoping they would make possible a more general discussion. It was a hope encouraged by the setbacks suffered by Mussolini, who had just attacked Greece. However, prudence was called for in such an important matter. So the course Laval adopted was to show goodwill but also to ask for more time, hoping thereby to obtain maximum military reinforcements and also to link these to a political settlement.

On 29 November, Laval and the French military leaders presented their plan to Abetz and Warlimont. It envisaged first increasing the defensive capacity of the empire and, next, the reconquest of the dissident territories, allowing one year to retake Chad. The French dismissed the hypothesis of a direct attack against any British territory, but Laval sought to soften the effect of this by indicating that it would be quite a different matter if England took any action hostile to France. The Germans were disappointed by the delays envisaged, and Abetz asked Vichy to produce a more aggressive version of its plan. On 10 December, another meeting took place. The French were now prepared to launch their offensive in Chad in the spring. But they still did not envisage attacking any English colonies except by way of retaliation in the event of London intervening to help the Gaullists. And Laval named a price: German support against any claims made by Italy, and a guarantee that the empire would be preserved intact. This time Abetz and Warlimont were favourably impressed and it seemed that their advice might fall upon the ears of a better disposed Hitler, for Spain had once again declined to enter the war. Three days later, however, Laval was sacked.

Public opinion interpreted 13 December as a rejection of Montoire. The Germans were not far from drawing a similar conclusion, but allowed themselves to be convinced of the contrary. In this complicated affair two things at least are clear: internal political considerations were predominant;[10] no changes in external policies were envisaged. Within the government, Laval was surrounded by distrust and hostility. Already in the autumn he had joked: 'I have 80 per cent of the country against me and 90 per cent of the ministers.'[11] He had bypassed Baudouin before taking his place. Judging his position to be insecure, he had had his eye on other portfolios, in particular that of Home Affairs, so Peyrouton had felt threatened.[12] Alibert and Bouthillier had another reason for disliking him: they regarded Laval as a blot on the national revolution.[13] But it was the fact that he ended up by alarming Pétain that was his undoing. The contrast in manner and personality between the two men was sharp, but hitherto this had not been enough to split them apart. But since Montoire, Laval had achieved nothing, not even the return to Paris that Pétain was so keen on. In the country at large he was very unpopular; and the Marshal was concerned for his own image. Worse still, the wiley Auvergnat seemed impatient to succeed him.[14] By the end of November it was an easy matter for plotters to persuade him that Laval was trying to separate him from his entourage and dispossess him of his authority: Déat's mounting attacks on the government were cited as evidence of this. In short, Bouthillier told Pétain, it is not a question of 'him or us', but 'him or you'.[15]

By acting as he did, Pétain converted a ministerial reshuffle into a veritable crisis. On 9 December he wrote to Hitler requesting him to agree to the replacement of Laval by Flandin. He assured him that he himself was 'more than ever a partisan of the policy of collaboration', and alleged that it was necessary to win the support of the population and that this would be facilitated by his own presence in Paris. However, he claimed, such a move had run into opposition, mostly as a result of Laval's 'intrigues', which 'together with other grave reasons, cause me no longer to trust him'.[16] In short, Pétain suggested, Laval was compromising the politics of collaboration; and he emphasized the difference between the policy and the man by claiming that it was he himself who was the policy's guarantee. The letter was not sent, probably so as not to spoil the meeting with Warlimont the next day.[17] But on the 13th the affair bounced back. Having said he would not go to Paris to receive the ashes of Napoleon's son, which Hitler was returning to France, Pétain allowed Laval to change his mind, no doubt because he could not resist the idea of going to the capital and being acclaimed there. It was a grave moment for the plotters: they joined forces to persuade Pétain that Laval was about to seize his chance to relieve him of his powers. At this, the Marshal took fright and dismissed his vice-president of the Council, who was immediately placed under arrest.

On 19 December, Pétain told Baudouin, 'I was wrong to move too late against Laval and when I did I acted in an explosive way. That is my temperament: I often delay for as long as possible but when the moment comes I act in a brutal fashion. My mistake lay in not giving Mr Pierre Laval clear warnings that would have spared him the surprise of Friday evening.'[18] In other words, Laval may have been under the impression that he had Pétain's approval right up to the last moment, so the whole affair was something of a psychodrama. It provides a good illustration of the intrigues of Vichy, Pétain's personality, and the influence of a court that knew how to play upon his most sensitive strings: his concern for his prestige, his fear of unpopularity, and his susceptibility to threats to his authority.

In any event, there was no question of breaking with or even modifying the policy of collaboration. We have already noted Pétain's assurances to Hitler on this score: he was not a cunning man and believed that words implied a commitment. The choice of Flandin, then in the good books of the Germans, was altogether in line with this. To the Americans both Baudouin and Flandin stressed disagreements over internal politics, although it would have been more in their own interests to suggest a move away from the politics of collaboration.[19] There can be no doubt that dissent existed – in the case of Bouthillier, over the matter of the Bor mines – over Laval's way of practising collaboration, as did anxiety as to how far he was prepared to go in it. But there is no evidence that such disagreements were any more than circumstantial, bearing mainly on modalities or competences.[20] And as for the anxiety, that concerned the possibility of things slipping out of control. At the heart of the crisis lay the question of the extent of Laval's power, not the policy of collaboration as such, certainly not collaboration as it had been practised up to this point.

Clearly, Laval was the link-man in relations with the Germans and, equally clearly, he intended to monopolize those relations to get them to serve his own political interests. But, contrary to the legend of him that was created after the war by former colleagues such as Baudouin, who were anxious to distance themselves from him by exaggerating their differences, his ideas were indistinguishable from those of the government as a whole. It is true that, quite apart from the fact that he was never keen to account for his dealings in detail, his negotiating style no doubt was more determined and more enticing. Laval readily expressed his hopes for a German victory and was never afraid to evoke the possibility of a war against England. But that was in order to show that he was ready to run great risks and was a way of justifying the size of the concessions he was seeking in return. And as soon as a discussion became serious, he would adopt a prudent and carefully calculated position. He resolutely ruled out the idea of a German presence in the empire;[21] and, as we have seen, he rejected the idea of a deliberate attack against the British empire.

Throughout the negotiations on Chad, he was flanked by military commanders and controlled by the government. There was no dissent at the preparatory meetings. The risk of a conflict with England was certainly worrying, but Laval, who dangled it as a lure before the Germans, did not consider it likely. He said as much on 7 December, at an armistice meeting attended by Pétain. His view was not challenged and those present thereupon decided to draw up a plan.[22] When he submitted this plan to Abetz and Warlimont three days later, he was accompanied by Darlan and Huntziger, who were in substance saying the same as he was, even if he came out with it more bluntly, as was his wont: 'France wants to recover its colonies and accepts the possibility of a war against England in Africa'; and 'Our fleet is armed so as to chase out de Gaulle and we hope that Germany will be victorious.'[23] He was solidly in agreement with the military leaders. They were not in the forefront of the plot that achieved his dismissal, and were subsequently the first to demand his return so that negotiations with Warlimont could resume. It should be added that these committed France to nothing in the immediate future, let alone to anything irreversible, and that the main hopes were focused upon a meeting with Ribbentrop. Finally, if the idea of recovering the Gaullist colonies thereafter no longer figured as an object of negotiation, even if it did from time to time resurface in declarations made by the Vichy leaders, the reason was that the Germans were no longer interested in the notion and were thereafter seeking aid of more immediate use to them in their war.

If Laval's sacking had nothing to do with the Chad affair, was it perhaps connected with secret overtures between the French and the English? The thesis of a double game has enjoyed an amazing run for its money. Like all myths, it is anchored in reality. Contacts between the two countries had been taking place since early autumn, on the initiative of the English who, after Dakar, favoured a relatively pliant line. The French would defend their empire; if England persisted in trying to get it to pass, by any possible means, into the hands of the Gaullists, Pétain would be forced into the German camp, and that would certainly not serve the interests of the British. London was keen to sound out Vichy's intentions, in the hope of finding a *modus vivendi*: it might be willing to relax the blockade in return for a promise to keep the fleet and the empire out of the hands of the Axis powers and not to seek to recover the Gaullist colonies.[24]

The most important intermediary, the Canadian diplomat Dupuy, saw Pétain for the first time on 24 November. The interview was on the whole discouraging. Pétain would not rule out ceding bases in the empire to the Germans, if sufficiently substantial concessions were forthcoming in return; he described this as 'passive collaboration'. As can be seen, even though the Reich had not made any such demand, he was already thinking about it and his attitude was more than merely conciliatory. On 6 December, Dupuy saw Pétain again, in the presence of Darlan, who made the following statement: Vichy would resist German pressure for an attack against the Gaullist colonies until February or possibly for even longer; there was no question 'now' of granting Germany the use of bases either in metropolitan France or in the colonies; the fleet would scuttle itself if Germany sought to seize it; it would not become engaged against the British fleet or the Gaullist colonies.[25]

It would take considerable imagination to detect evidence of any double game here. Vichy was too convinced of the power of the Germans and the weakness of the British – which London's approaches simply served to confirm – to be really impressed by the British. This is how Darlan summarized the episode in his diary: 'On 6 December, the Marshal sent for me to meet M. David [*sic*], a French Canadian. This gentleman told me he had been sent by Lord Halifax and said that the English had never doubted my word. I told him they had behaved like imbeciles. I confirmed that we were quite prepared to hit them hard if they attacked.'[26] The reason why Halifax was making much of the assurances Darlan and Pétain were claimed to have made was that they served to support the conciliatory line that he was then defending against Churchill. In reality, they merely referred to minimal positions that Vichy had adopted quite independently and that committed it to absolutely nothing in the future. If these initiatives in making contact held any interest for the French, it lay in finding out whether it would be possible to get the English to relax their blockade and to drop de Gaulle. On the latter point London's refusal, which was soon made clear, came as no surprise. As to the former matter, negotiations soon ground to a halt when London discovered that Flandin had told the Germans all about them and that they approved of them: increased supplies to France would give them the chance to seize even more. The English were forced to recognize that they were barking up the wrong tree in speculating on the existence of an anticollaborationist tendency in Vichy.

As for the United States, they certainly came into the calculations of the French. Their economic aid was welcome, as can be seen from the Murphy–Weygand agreement, concluded at the beginning of 1941, which facilitated supplies to French North Africa. Their influence might manage to moderate the pressure that England and Japan were exerting upon the empire, and their sympathy might carry weight when it came to a peace treaty. Roosevelt's conciliatory policy where Pétain was concerned, which upset a section of American public opinion and scandalized the British and the Gaullists, was dictated by a desire to neutralize the French fleet and empire, since any reinforcement of the Axis powers could only harm the interests of the United States. But as for pushing Vichy towards true neutrality, results were limited. Admiral Leahy, who was sent as ambassador, rapidly reached the conclusion that Pétain would not be renouncing collaboration, that he would never enter the war on the side of the Allies, and that he was likely to give in to Berlin on virtually everything.[27] In July 1942, a diplomat in his team warned Washington not to attach too much importance to the Marshal's protestations: 'Every time something goes wrong, every time there is an incident that might lead to his popularity being impaired or to him being seen as guilty in the eyes of History, Pétain pretends that he knew nothing, that Laval deceived him, abused him, mystified him, that everything was done behind his back . . . The old soldier is not without a certain cunning . . .'[28]

Within a few months Vichy was having to come to terms with an unexpected situation. A defeat for England looked less certain, but a defeat for Germany still remained totally improbable. The resistance of the British, far from prompting prudence, strengthened Vichy's original decision and confirmed its choice of collaboration. The war, which looked like continuing for an indefinite period, would surely incline the Germans to be conciliatory towards defeated France, whose margin of manoeuvre was increasing. 'Be strong', 'grow stronger' became the catch phrases. By clever use of the situation, France might be able to clamber a little way back up the slope and so find itself in a better position when it came to peace. All this presupposed inspiring the conqueror with confidence and demonstrating how help from his defeated neighbour could be in his interest: help voluntarily offered, but not for nothing; help that was substantial, but not unconditional.

In the notes and memoranda circulating in the ministries, government policy was defined as a policy of collaboration. The arguments for it, recorded for the benefit of negotiators, clearly set out its content and its contours. Collaboration was to be accorded primarily in the economic field, in such a way as to capitalize on the resources in which the Germans were interested, in particular those of the free zone and the empire. Next, on a political and diplomatic level, it would manifest itself by participation in 'the establishment of a new order in Europe'.[29] Stress was laid on the benefit to Germany of 'a close relationship with France which, if it is to be valuable, must appear to have France's free consent'.[30] One effect of this close relationship would be to diminish the passive resistance of other conquered peoples and to create uncertainty among neutrals, particularly the Americans, whose isolationism might thereby be strengthened. Relentless emphasis was then laid on France's role as a bridge between Europe and the United States. The argument in favour of collaboration also mentioned how important it was, in the interests even of Germany, that Vichy should obtain results, so as to carry with it the French people, 'the vast majority' of whom were hostile to the policies of Montoire, in which all they could see was collaboration 'between the farmer and his pig' or between 'a boot and a bottom'.[31]

Collaboration was to be unequivocal on the political and economic levels, but as limited as possible on the military level. Vichy's doctrine was defence of the empire against whoever attacked it, using solely French forces. Nobody wanted a war against England, for it would obviously not be in the interests of France, since it would be at the cost of the Antilles and Madagascar, would expose both metropolitan France and the empire to bombing raids without being able to retaliate, lead to a break with the Americans, irredeemably blacken the government in the eyes of public opinion, and make France wholly dependent on Germany.[32] But whereas belligerence would weaken France rather than strengthen it, exploitation of the

British and Gaullist threat, making the most of the balance of forces achieved by the two camps around the French empire, might make it possible to obtain various advantages: military reinforcements, a relaxation in the circumstances of occupation, and guarantees for the future. It was a delicate, difficult and dangerous policy, for the question was how to make the best use of limited trump cards which must not be lost and so ought not to be played.

Even on the military level it would be inaccurate to describe Vichy's politics as neutral. As Darlan clearly perceived, neutrality would require France to keep strictly to the armistice, and would rule out seeking military reinforcements from Germany, thereby – according to him – exposing the empire to covetousness on every side.[33] The most appropriate description might be non-belligerence, a formula that Mussolini had used to designate his own position during the phoney war, when he chose to remain outside the conflict while at the same time indicating his support for Germany by other means. Non-belligerence left France the option of pulling back towards neutrality, but equally that of pressing forward into belligerence. The latter option was present right from the start, when Laval mentioned acquiring compensation at the expense of the British empire, just as Mussolini had rushed to be in at the kill when France had been defeated. And it remained present thereafter, becoming even more of a likelihood in the wake of the Paris agreements, and at the beginning of 1942, when the government envisaged entering the war against the Anglo-Saxons. Belligerence was a choice that, in the end, Vichy never would take. All the same, for two years it remained a distinct and permanent possibility and, if it was never translated into action, the reason was essentially that Hitler was not prepared to move in that direction.

The form that the non-belligerence of the French state settled into was that of providing both indirect and direct aid. The indirect aid was a consequence of the situation: by defending the empire, Vichy prevented the English from scoring points, thereby facilitating Germany's task and ensuring that it possessed a strategic glacis that it was itself dispensed from garrisoning. It would have exerted still greater pressure on the British forces if it had set out to retake the Gaullist colonies. It is not hard to see why the occupying power responded quite generously to France's demands for reinforcements. Vichy's indirect aid to the Germans also took the form of military supplies produced first in the occupied zone, then, quite soon, also in the free zone, and other military material, which it agreed to hand over on several occasions in 1941.

Vichy's direct aid involved providing the Germans with bases in the empire. This question was first raised immediately after the armistice, when Hitler demanded bases in French North Africa. As we have seen, they were certainly not refused as a matter of principle. In the autumn this again obviously lay behind the negotiations concerning the empire. The German military regarded the use of French bases as an essential part of their 'new policy'. But at that point Hitler was waiting for Franco's reply. Had it been positive, with German troops stationed in Spanish Morocco, he would have been able to insist from a position of strength. It was Spain's refusal to enter the war, not the armistice of June 1940, that kept the Axis troops out of North Africa – something that was to facilitate the allied landings in the autumn of 1942.

In Vichy, the question was expected to resurface. Pétain mentioned it to Dupuy in November 1940, declaring himself ready to concede bases in return for adequate compensation. In May 1941, Pétain was telling Leahy nothing new when he explained that he would give no 'voluntary active military aid'. The implication was that at least he would willingly give passive aid, or even active aid if the Germans exerted serious pressure.[34] Without any doubt, his preference was for indirect aid, ideally in the form of a role for France that would pay dividends: a strong, rearmed, sovereign France maintaining a solid hold on its empire in defiance of the English, in exchange for a lenient peace. But even in advance he accepted the idea of providing direct aid, allowing Germany to make use of the empire either temporarily, for particular purposes, or indeed on a more enduring basis, provided considerable compensation was offered and the risks of English retribution were bearable. It was here that Pétain parted company with Weygand, who wanted to keep the Axis powers strictly out of the empire – despite the fact that since the summer he had himself gone beyond his formula of complying solely with 'the armistice, nothing but the armistice', given that that was the only way to strengthen the armistice army.

It is not hard to see that, so long as the government respected its doctrine of defence for the empire solely by French forces and so long as it did not openly support the German war, the hope of a readjustment, or even of entering the war on England's side, could be preserved in some hearts amongst the military, civil servants and even ordinary French people, who sought to reconcile their attachment to the national revolution with their hope for a German defeat, failing to see that – as Darlan pointed out – 'those two political attitudes were contradictory'.[35] There can be no doubt that, even in Vichy, among those who were supporting the government, there were some inclined to 'wait and see': people who wanted to know the identity of the victor before totally committing themselves or who, while hoping for an English victory, judged it opportune to deal tactfully with Germany until such time as the moment was ripe for a swing to the other side. Nor can there be any doubt that, for a while, this was indeed the interpretation put upon government policy – a fact that slowed down the erosion of Pétain's popularity.

But in truth 'wait and see' was never the policy of the Vichy leaders. Pétain, Laval and Darlan were too convinced that Germany was destined, if not to total victory, at least to lasting hegemony on the continent of Europe; and they were also convinced that the interest of France, as they conceived it, lay in conciliating the conqueror by offering aid that would be well repaid, thanks to the trump cards that remained in France's hand. The logic of this policy exerted such pressure that even Pétain, with his fear of positive action and his inclination to temporization, could do nothing but succumb to it, each time an opportunity to try to strike a deal seemed to present itself. It was the price that had to be paid for a policy that, in order to prolong the life of a regime, sought to revise the peace even before the conqueror had finished his war.

8

The Darlan era

THE sacking of Laval led to a crisis that dragged on for two months, thanks to Abetz's manoeuvres, Pétain's hesitations, and Hitler's lack of interest. The ambassador lost a valued ally and was alarmed for his own policies. While doing his utmost to get Laval reinstated, he also endeavoured to strengthen his own grip on French politics. On 16 December he went to Vichy and demanded that the government be reshuffled, with doubtful ministers eliminated. In the immediate instance he succeeded in getting La Laurencie, who had had Déat arrested in Paris, replaced by Brinon, whose pro-German sympathies were well known. He furthermore demanded that an executive be formed, composed of the most trustworthy ministers, Darlan, Laval, Huntziger and Flandin. This was designed to pave the way for Laval's reappointment and to further his own goal, which was that Pétain, whom he no longer trusted, should be limited to the function of head of state. At the head of the executive he hoped to see Darlan, of whom he had a good opinion and who, he hoped, would later become head of state, with Laval as head of the government.[1] With the admiral, he would be able to push on with his plan for a military alliance. As for Laval, who was furious with Pétain, it was easy to get him to go to Paris. The wiley Auvergnat placed himself under Germany's protection and thanked Hitler for getting him released.

For a moment, Hitler was alarmed. Might Pétain change camps? He resented the dismissal of a man whom he had met personally and who had identified himself with collaboration. He suspected that France was becoming more demanding as a result of the mishaps of Italy. To satisfy hmself, he received Darlan, who transmitted a letter in which Pétain repeated that he wished to continue to collaborate, but refused to recall Laval. Darlan, who was meeting Hitler for the first time, made the most of the opportunity to impress, not forgetting to throw a few bouquets in the direction of Abetz, who was seated at his side. Hitler, who was reassured, subjected him to a lecture and intimated that he would soon be making his position known.[2] His mind was already far away from France and the Mediterranean. On 13 December, he had signed the go-ahead for spring operations in the Balkans, designed to extend his grip over the region, following the discomfiture of the Italians; and on the 18th he had approved the plan of campaign against the USSR in the early summer. France was again of secondary importance; it was enough if it did not swing into the other camp, and to prevent that happening all that was necessary was to leave a ray of hope.

In Vichy, everyone was very worried at the vigorous reaction of the Germans, who closed the demarcation line and suspended all contacts. Ministers hurried about ringing doorbells and making reassuring noises. Darlan and Flandin asked for a meeting with Ribbentrop. Huntziger had it announced that his presence in the government guaranteed the continuity of collaboration and begged to continue his conversations with Warlimont.[3] Pétain himself was vacillating. He did not want to take Laval back under German pressure, but was at the same time afraid of ruining his policies. With the blockade persisting, he consented in principle that the Auvergnat should be taken back in a subordinate position. In exchange for a letter of apology, he even agreed to meet him. While waiting for Hitler to make his position clear, he hovered between fear of an impasse and hope of concessions. If the Germans wanted Laval, they should let it be known and offer a 'dowry' for him of 'advantages so remarkable that all of France will understand why I took him back'.[4]

At the end of January, Hitler at last spoke. He told Abetz that the politics of Montoire were forthwith suspended. Vichy was now to be put under pressure by having Laval kept in Paris and placed at the head of an opposition which might even go so far as to threaten to become a counter-government.[5] The ambassador then engaged in some of his own type of diplomacy. He was not going to give up the return of Laval without making Vichy pay for it at least by pushing out Flandin, about whom he had altogether reversed his opinion, ever since Flandin had opposed a ministerial reshuffle under German pressure. He thus entered upon a double manoeuvre attempting to manipulate both Vichy and Laval. On 30 January, he told Brinon that Hitler was on the point of breaking with collaboration; that, following Montoire, he had been resolved upon a generous peace but, through Vichy's fault, an extraordinary opportunity had been missed, and now it was a matter of not making things even worse. Without naming any names, he let it be understood that Laval's recall and Flandin's dismissal might avoid a definitive break.[6]

On that same day, he encouraged Laval to step up his demands, with the idea of increasing pressure on Vichy.[7] Laval asked for the post of head of government, Pétain being merely head of state, and the right to present him with a constitution for his approval. Laval believed that Hitler had decided to set him back in the saddle. He spoke to Déat of ministerial lists, envisaged a social policy that would bring him popularity, and spoke of constructing a motorway to link Paris and Berlin.[8] In Vichy the pressure was keenly felt, for the military had made their position clear. On 5 February, Darlan spoke in favour of Laval's return, winning over the entire government apart from Flandin.[9] At the embassy, the news evoked talk of a surrender: Vichy had proved weaker than had been expected; now it was important to prevent Laval coming to an agreement with his former colleagues.[10] Probably at the insistence of the embassy, Laval became even more inflexible in his demands.

With Ribbentrop on his heels, Abetz was finally able to resolve the affair. On 7 February, he let Darlan know what he should have told him a whole week before: Berlin was no longer insisting on Laval's return; in exchange, Flandin was to leave the government and Darlan was to become Pétain's successor. In return, the admiral acceded to a demand of Abetz's: he came to a secret agreement with Laval, promising to facilitate his return as head of government at a time that he and the ambassador should determine.[11] It was a consolation prize for Laval, who had been manipulated all the way along; and for Darlan it was a small price to pay for his promotion, which he seems to have been careful not to mention to Pétain. It was a promise that he would be able to defer honouring while proving to the Germans that they had no cause to regret the departure of the wily Auvergnat.

The crisis that began on 13 December had lasted almost two months. Having at first feared anti-German action, Hitler and Abetz changed their minds, seeing the efforts that Vichy made to mend relations. By accepting Laval's return, the French leaders showed that they were ready to carry on with the policies of Montoire at the cost of accepting Germany's interference in the composition of their ministerial teams. Only Hitler's decision prevented Laval's return, which would have dealt a serious blow to Pétain's popularity. But even without his return, the damage done was all too visible. The occupier had authorized the activity of political parties in Paris; the unity of the country looked further off than ever. In Laval, Abetz had discovered an ally who assured him of influence in all decisions relating to all governmental changes. During the crisis, Flandin, aiming for appeasement, had taken several important decisions, most notably to manufacture war materials in the free zone. In the same spirit, Peyrouton, the Minister for Internal Affairs, one of the plotters of 13 December, had handed over to the German police first the Thyssen couple, then the socialist leaders, Breitscheid and Hilferding. After the crisis, it was necessary to make new pledges. The Germans' theme song now was that by its actions, that is to say by unilateral concessions, France must prove the desire to collaborate that it so loudly proclaimed.

On 9 February, Darlan became vice-president of the Council. He concentrated in his own hands the navy, Foreign Affairs, Internal Affairs, the general secretariat of Information and that of the Council presidency. Apart from Huntziger, the new cabinet comprised partly 'notables', conservative Catholics or liberals (such as Bouthillier, Caziot, Barthélémy and Carcopino), partly young Turks, brought to Darlan by Benoist-Méchin, who was himself responsible for Franco-German relations. This group included Marion (Information), Pucheu (Industrial Production), Lehideux (Equipment) and Barnaud (general delegate for Franco-German economic matters). In the summer of 1940 these, along with Jacques Le Roy Ladurie, Victor Arrighi and Jacques Guérard, had grouped around Gabriel Le Roy Ladurie, the director of the Worms Bank, who was a former member of the PPF (as were several others in the group) and a man of considerable influence. The positions that they held were subordinate ones but were directly concerned with relations with the occupier.

In early April, they asked Abetz to transmit to Berlin a plan that they had composed, which had the approval of Darlan. This 'plan for a new order' envisaged an authoritarian France, integrated within a European whole through a customs union, and contributing to it the resources of an empire whose exploitation was to favour the flowering of 'a feeling of European solidarity'. Once it had stamped out Gaullist dissidence, a move that would bring into being 'the militia of the future sole Party', France would return to its maritime vocation. As the bridgehead on to the Atlantic, it would constitute 'Europe's shield', and for this it would need both a powerful fleet and a powerful colonial army. From being a symbol, Montoire was to become a reality: 'We wish to save France', they declared, 'and we beg the Führer to have faith in us.'[12]

Abetz passed on this text without comment, a fact that it seems reasonable to interpret as an indication of his reservations. The 'European' talk was a step in the right direction, but there was no question of either an alliance or subordination. He was afraid that, with the Worms team, he himself would lose ground and the economic section of the Majestic would profit. It was not surprising that he thereupon had the collaborationists of Paris, who distrusted Darlan, lash out at a 'synarchy' of businessmen taking over the state in order to pursue policies favourable to the big business 'trusts'.[13] The ambassador's goal remained the Laval–Darlan duo, but he was content meanwhile to settle for Darlan on his own. Darlan was a military man, neither pro-Church nor reactionary. His enthusiasm for collaboration, which he never tired of reiterating, seemed guaranteed by his anglophobia, and this, with luck, might lead to a state of war with England.

The admiral's ideas are expressed at length in the notes that he sent to Pétain. They had changed little since the preceding autumn. Collaboration must be above all political and economic. The empire must be defended solely by French forces, and France must be careful not to fire first on the English. Darlan admitted that, given the circumstances, defence of the empire amounted to military collaboration of a limited nature. He did not rule out extending it if, morally and materially, France was encouraged to do so by a reduction in occupation charges, a 'declaration on the integrity of the empire' and 'some kind of preliminary peace'.[14]

In his eyes, Germany's probable victory, France's weakness, and the logic of the initial choice ('if we continue the policy that led us to ask for an armistice, we are bound to collaborate')[15] were justification enough for collaboration. Darlan was convinced that a German victory would cost France less than an English one, and that Germany could be persuaded, in exchange for aid from France, both to limit its own territorial claims and to block Italian and Spanish ones. This view was encouraged by his belief that the occupying power was itself divided by divergent currents of opinion. According to Darlan, only some of the German leaders wished to crush France; others, including captains of industry and some of the military, desired *entente*; and others, namely the army, were still undecided.[16] Although he usually presented his own politics as the least of all evils, the admiral also nursed great hopes for the future of a France returning to its maritime and imperial vocation. In 1945, Abetz was to state that Darlan had told him, in private conversations, of 'his desire to see the French fleet become the most powerful one in the world and to ensure the defence by sea of the interests of the whole of Europe'.[17]

The Marshal appreciated him as a staff officer who kept him supplied with accurate memos, came for his directives and kept him informed of what he was doing. The two of them took major decisions together. On some points their views were clearly opposed, but this was of little consequence. In February 1941, at a meeting with Franco, Pétain declared that Germany would not be able to defeat England, for the resources of England were too great; the war would be a long one and would end in a compromise. In the opinion of Darlan, who was with him, the British fleet, then in the middle of the battle for the Atlantic, was nearly done for, and American aid would come too late; Germany had already almost won the war.[18] Pétain had a certain sympathy for the Americans, while Darlan made no secret of his scorn for them. In one respect, that scorn was shared by the Marshal. He was convinced of the military inability of the Anglo-Saxons – an old prejudice of a French infantryman. Neither believed the United States would enter the war.

Darlan thought that Germany would conquer, Pétain that it would not be conquered. Both reckoned France's interest lay in a speedy peace. The longer the conflict continued, the worse the country would be exploited, the greater the risk of social disorder and of the spread of communism, and the more the empire would be split up between the belligerents. For those reasons, especially following the German successes in the Balkans, they were inclined to pay a high price in order to conciliate the conqueror, offering military aid before such time as a victory or, even worse, a compromise peace with England, destroyed the value of their own trump cards. In one of the rare documents in which he set out his own concept of collaboration and clearly indicated where his own priority lay – 'to pluck out from French *mores* the causes that provoke defeats' – Pétain wrote that the country had to be strengthened for the end of the war, 'whoever the victor turns out to be'. But collaboration with Germany was necessary, whoever that was. An English victory, were it ever to come about, would take a long time, so it was essential, in the meantime, to prise a degree of liberty from the occupier. In the case of a German victory, the peace would have to be the best possible: so collaboration was even more justifiable, and was facilitated by the fact that the conqueror had to deal circumspectly with France because of the empire. Hence the conclusion: 'If Germany wins the war, we must have settled our fate with it before it no longer has any need of us.'[19] It was at this point that Vichy found itself upon the horns of a dilemma: to help Germany against England was to risk finding itself in Germany's power; not to do so was to risk being crushed by the conditions imposed for peace. So it was bound to help in the hope of advantages that would be impossible to revoke.

In the spring of 1941, Hitler was still keeping his back turned on France, despite the advice of diplomats and the military. It was out of the question to re-enter negotiations, he declared, since France was 'nurturing new hopes, as a consequence of Italy's weakness'.[20] Then came the German successes in the Balkans. The crushing of Yugoslavia and Greece, Rommel's recapture of Cyrenaica, and the seizure of Crete now disposed him to heed his counsellors. The navy still needed bases in the South Atlantic, to cut British lines of communication and to prevent seizure by the Anglo-Saxons. Keitel and Jodl still reckoned it necessary to strengthen the French empire; in the immediate future, they needed to get supplies to Rommel in North Africa. As for Ribbentrop, he wanted to help the government of Iraq against the English and, to do that, needed to pass through Syria.

On 26 April, Hitler announced to Abetz that he would receive Darlan in the first fortnight of May. The ambassador transmitted the message, not without playing it up. Hitler was wary. France would have to prove its desire to collaborate and it was already clear how it could do so: aid for Iraq, supplies for the Afrika Korps through Tunisia, and a base for German submarines on the west African coast.[21] In Vichy there was relief: the Germans were again doing the asking. To show his goodwill, Darlan agreed to sell Rommel lorries stockpiled in North Africa and to cooperate in the operation of assistance for Iraq. He asked for nothing in return for selling the lorries and, in exchange for the assistance to Iraq, contented himself with promises with no written undertakings, despite knowing the risks involved. He told Abetz that 'he was prepared to have public opinion label him as the man who lost Syria, so sure was he that he could obtain an improvement in Franco-German relations by supporting the German war effort in the Near East'.[22] Pétain wrote to Hitler telling him that he had welcomed the invitation addressed to Darlan 'with the greatest favour', going on to declare, 'In it I can see your desire to associate France in the construction of the European order now being envisaged. I would like to assure you that I share that desire.'[23]

On 11 May, Darlan was in Berchtesgaden. He praised the 'genius who created' the German army and 'the constructive, not destructive, spirit' of the conqueror of France. He displayed his credentials: the economic collaboration, the lorries ceded in Tunisia, the facilities made available in Syria. He asked for the weight of the occupation to be alleviated and for assurances on the empire. Hitler resumed his Montoire tune: Germany would win the war, it had no need of France; but France could help it to cut short the conflict, and England's defeat would be in its interests. In the immediate instance, what Hitler was interested in were Dakar, Syria and Tunisia. 'For something big, I will give something big. For something small, something small.'[24]

On his return to Vichy, Darlan obtained the government's approval. 'If we collaborate with Germany, without necessarily lining up alongside it to make deliberate war on England, that is to say if we work for Germany in our factories and allow it certain facilities, we can: save the French nation; reduce to a minimum our losses in metropolitan France and the colonies; play an honourable – or even important – role in the future Europe.' He stressed that it was in France's interest that 'the war be as short as possible'.[25] Vichy thus found itself back in the situation of the preceding autumn – helping Germany, and risking a clash with England – but now that situation was even graver: the 'facilities' meant using the empire for the German war. On 15 May, as after Montoire, Pétain, in a radio message, set the seal of his authority upon the Darlan–Hitler meeting, but this time without pronouncing the word 'collaboration', calling upon his compatriots to 'follow him, without a backward thought, along the paths of honour and the national interest'. He was expecting the success of the negotiations to allow France 'to rise above its defeat and preserve its rank in the world as a European and colonial power'.[26]

The negotiations that began on 21 May in Paris concluded with the signature of three protocols. The first, concerning Syria, fixed the concessions granted by Germany in exchange for the help already given by Vichy, that is to say its placing of aerodromes at the disposal of German and Italian planes, its handing over of stockpiled war material to Iraq, and the training of Iraqi soldiers in the use of French weapons (this last point had involved going well beyond the provision of mere 'facilities'). The second concerned aid to be given in North Africa: France was to supply materials to the Afrika Korps (lorries, food and artillery) and allow the use of the port of Bizerta and the Bizerta-Gabès railway line for the delivery of food supplies to Libya; in exchange, the Germans agreed to considerable reinforcements to the troops, the liberation of stockpiled military material and also of 7000 prisoners, including General Juin. The third, negotiated with the utmost difficulty, concerned the use of Dakar by the German fleet and airforce. Here, the risks were greater, for the Americans themselves might consider this as a threat to their security. No reciprocal military concessions at all were promised.

As in the previous autumn, the Germans wanted all this to remain on a purely military footing. Conscious of the considerable risks he was taking, Darlan insisted on a more general agreement. This was the subject of the additional protocol that he got Abetz to sign and in which he had the execution of the third agreement made dependent upon the granting of military reinforcements and political and economic concessions that would provide 'the means to justify, before the public opinion of the country, the possibility of an armed conflict with England and the United States'.[27]

These documents needed the approval of both governments. On both sides difficulties arose. Abetz, who had gone to Germany to seek support for the additional protocol, ran up against a categorical rejection from Ribbentrop. Even before hearing of this, Darlan, for his part, met with vehement opposition from Weygand when, on 3 June, he reported to the government on the state of negotiations. On 6 June, at a new Council of Ministers at which Weygand was present, he promised 'not to accede to any demands formulated by the Wehrmacht, before having received in exchange concessions so considerable that they transform Franco-German relations through and through'. The price that he communicated to Abetz was extremely high: sovereignty to be restored throughout French territory, with the exception of Alsace-Lorraine, which would have a special status; the costs of the occupation to be abolished; prisoners to be liberated; the empire to be guaranteed; and economic aid to be forthcoming from Germany.[28]

In truth, Weygand's opposition and Pétain's reluctance were

matching his own disappointment. He was well aware that the Paris protocols were unacceptable as long as the additional one was given no substance. He had also just learned, to his cost, not to put his trust in promises. The Germans, who at the time of the Iraq affair had agreed to reduce the occupation costs, were now insisting that payment should be made partly in gold and partly in foreign currency. They were also reducing the number of prisoners to be freed from 90000 to just over 30000. However, on 6 June, Darlan did not give up all hope in the Paris protocols: he fixed the price to be paid, and in doing so had the consent of Weygand who, possibly expecting a rejection, encouraged the stakes to be set very high. On 3 June, when the first Council of Ministers had met, the admiral had in fact set up a 'Negotiating Commission' composed of Benoist-Méchin, Barnaud, and Rear-Admiral Marzin, whom he entrusted with the mandate 'to pursue negotiations with the German civil and military authorities in order to finalize the Hitler–Darlan conversations of 10, 11 and 12 May'.[29] Then, on 9 June, he promoted Benoist-Méchin to the post of Secretary of State to the vice-presidency of the Council, which could certainly not be interpreted as an attempt to put the brakes on.

Negotiations on Bizerta and Dakar opened on 10 June, those on Dakar were soon postponed indefinitely by Hitler on account of the eastern campaign. Right from the start, the negotiations were blocked. To avoid immediate failure, discussions were held on the modalities of executing the Bizerta protocol, whilst awaiting agreement on its actual implementation. The French tried to use the lever of German needs in North Africa to force a preliminary discussion of the additional protocol, a discussion that seemed all the more imperative given that on 8 June the English, having stamped out the Iraqi rebellion, had attacked Syria. Benoist-Méchin was tirelessly stressing Darlan's willingness to go so far as co-belligerence, just as long as political and military concessions made it possible for him to justify this to the French people and the army.[30] The admiral himself requested several times to be received by either Hitler or Ribbentrop.

On 7 July, he again explained to Abetz that he desired to meet Ribbentrop and that he would give his agreement to transit through Tunisia as soon as his conditions were satisfied. His objective remained 'a change in the armistice status, without which France could not wage a real war against England'. Abetz's reply, on a familiar note, was that political negotiations would be facilitated by the implementation of the agreement on Bizerta. But Darlan was through with making gestures of goodwill, especially now that Syria was lost, with 1036 dead and 773 lost without trace from the Vichy forces.[31] Conscious of Abetz's impatience, Darlan informed him that he had summoned Weygand to examine the matter and would let him have an answer on 12 July[32]

On 11 July, Weygand was in Vichy, with a fair suspicion that he was to play the part of scapegoat. His notebook records: 'Darlan has taken an enormous step. He trusts the Germans less and is more conscious of his responsibilities *vis-à-vis* the Empire. Despite renewed German demands, there is no question now of giving them Bizerta or Dakar without first receiving the reinforcements and written guarantees that have been requested.'[33] On that same day, the Council of Ministers gave its approval to a note by Weygand. 'There is no question of breaking with Germany. So continuation of the negotiations already begun is indispensable for our military reinforcement. But no backing down on our political demands – and no giving in. We are in no hurry.'[34] As can be seen, Weygand was by no means opposed to negotiation. Like Darlan, he thought that the Axis powers needed the aid of France and that patience would be rewarded. The recent attack against the USSR and the expected German victory – underestimation of the USSR was so common – were regarded by all in a most favourable light. With his lines stretched and huge territories to satisfy his appetite, Hitler would be better disposed to paying for France's collaboration in the West.

On 12 July, the embassy was informed that the agreement on Bizerta would be put into effect only once political negotiations were completed. On the 14th, Vichy made it known in a verbal communication that it wished to obtain 'an essential modification to the Franco-German status'. Also communicated was 'a plan for a transitional pact', setting out an idea of Benoist-Méchin's that had Pétain's approval. Germany and Italy should grant France a transitional status, and give it a guarantee of territorial integrity for metropolitan France (with a special status for Alsace-Lorraine) and the colonies (except for former German colonies and with the reservation that some frontiers might be rectified, in particular in the Tunisian south). In short, the idea was to replace the armistice by 'a regime founded upon the sovereignty of the French state and France's loyal cooperation with Germany and Italy'.[35]

During the months that followed, Hitler, who was absorbed by the Russian campaign, had French affairs treated in a dilatory fashion. Abetz, looking ahead to after the expected victory in the East, was ruminating upon an idea to amalgamate the Vichy and Paris teams into a government that would join the Reich in liquidating the British presence in the Mediterranean. Meanwhile Darlan was tightening his authority over the government and the government's grip on the country. As the admiral explained to Pétain, he was convinced that if Hitler was hestitating to press on with collaboration, that was because he did not think that it was assured in France. What had to be done was persuade him 'that we are no longer the hereditary enemy', starting off by remedying 'the disorder in people's minds'.[36]

Even as he was purging the administration, making repression bite harder and dreaming of turning the Légion des Combattants into the basis of a single party, Darlan was seeking a way to rid himself of Weygand. The general thwarted his policies, infuriated him with his whims, and his dismissal would increase the trust of the Germans and perhaps make it possible to get negotiations going again. Pétain was reluctant. Weygand was to the Americans what Laval was to the Germans. But he was still anxious to get the policy of collaboration to pay dividends. On 17 November, he received Abetz, who had come to Vichy for Huntziger's funeral and told him he was ready to declare to the whole world that he recognized Hitler as Europe's guide, provided Germany would first tell him how it intended to settle its relations with France.[37] The next day, in response to renewed pressure from Darlan, he dismissed Weygand.

The Marshal, like the admiral, was keen to relaunch collaboration. Both testified to this in the three months that followed by taking decisions all too often eclipsed by the affair of the Paris protocols, although they are of at least equal importance to an understanding of their politics. To them, the moment for a relaunch seemed ripe because time was passing, they needed results, and they imagined that a favourable situation was taking shape. The difficulties that Germany had encountered on the eastern front strengthened France's position, as it faced the Anglo-Saxon world, and increased the importance of the assistance that it might provide in this context. It seemed to them that it was imperative to derive some profit from this situation before Hitler came to readdress the Mediterranean problem, once he had crushed Soviet resistance.

It was symptomatic that in November the government decided to prepare 'preliminary economic studies for peace negotiations'. It was thought that even if it were in vain to predict the outcome of the war, 'it is possible that before the total end of the conflict peace talks might be entered upon by certain countries, in particular France and Germany. It seems likely that, in the economic domain at least, agreements will be clinched before that time, agreements that will exert an important influence upon future political negotiations.' One passage in this study is most revealing as to the hopes being entertained: an advantageous arrangement was not ruled out even for Alsace-Lorraine. It was suggested that there were 'many' German figures of note who wished to find 'a way of settling this age-old matter of contention'. The solution would be to devise an economic solution for iron, coal and steel; this was 'one of the areas in which a Franco-German collaboration, within a European framework, would be most fruitful'.[38]

As in October 1940, Pétain let it be known that he would like to talk man-to-man with some high-ranking figure. On 1 December, a meeting with Göring took place. It was a fiasco. Darlan trotted out the additional protocol. Pétain demanded wide-ranging alleviation to the occupation regime. But Göring had come to discuss the situation in North Africa, where Rommel, after being thrashed by the British, was retreating towards Tunisia. Angered, he returned to the subject in Germany on 20 December with General Juin, through whom he asked the French government whether it was prepared to send Rommel food supplies immediately by way of Bizerta and to defend Tunisia alongside him, if the Africa Korps was obliged to take refuge there.[39]

On 22 December, Vichy replied that it was prepared to do so, requiring in exchange substantial reinforcements. 'In order to be in a position to respond to the inevitable British reactions', the French desired total liberty of manoeuvre in the western Mediterranean and in Africa.[40] Believing they had made a breakthrough, Darlan indicated that he was ready to go to Germany to continue discussions on a broader basis.[41] He probably reckoned it preferable to give way on the question of supplies through Tunisia rather than face a German ultimatum. No doubt he also thought it in France's interest to prevent a collapse of the Axis forces that would bring the British right to the French North African frontier. For that reason he agreed to help Italy, itself already sufficiently perturbed to make a gesture towards France, by selling it gasoline and guaranteeing a number of deliveries through Tunisia.[42] However, by consenting to Rommel entering Tunisia, and by considering fighting alongside him, Vichy was bound to invite the English to riposte wherever they could. The decision was all the more risky given that absolutely no guarantee was given that Tunisia would remain French.

For Ribbentrop, Vichy's demands were unacceptable. In his opinion the military freedom requested would restore to the French control of their coasts together with the possibility of rebuilding their land power in the empire. There could be no question of granting anything other than partial freedom to the fleet and even that would have to be in return for their stationing German troops in the French empire. On the other hand, it would be possible to make 'considerable' concessions at the political, economic and financial level.[43] This relative degree of generosity reflected the delicate situation in which Germany now found itself, placed between a North Africa that was eluding Rommel and an eastern front that was fast turning into a nightmare. One consequence of this was that France briefly recaptured Hitler's attention.[44] On 5 January 1942, Hitler held a lengthy discussion with Abetz, lending an attentive ear to what he had to say about the advantages of military collaboration and the idea of a preliminary peace agreement in the event of France declaring war on the Anglo-Saxon powers. Hitler's comments did not conceal the strength of his own mental resistance.[45]

However, Abetz hastened to strike while the iron was hot. He wanted to provide proof of Vichy's good intentions and persuade his leader to overcome his reservations. On 9 January, he got Benoist-Méchin to ask whether France was prepared to go to war alongside Germany in exchange for a peace treaty being drawn up. Three days later, he informed Berlin that the Council of Ministers had unanimously decided to declare war on England and the United States, following clarification of a number of political questions. In reality, there had been no deliberations on the part of the Council of Ministers, nor had any decision been taken in favour of unconditional belligerence. According to Benoist-Méchin's own testimony, the question was discussed in a small committee comprising Pétain, Darlan, Romier, Moysset, Pucheu and Bouthillier. Pétain, on the qui vive, backed away from the decision he was being asked to take. But the ministers present begged him for a positive response, which would make it possible to discover what Germany had to offer. Darlan argued that it would be folly to react negatively to the discussion and thereby 'renegue on all that we have done so far'.[46]

The Marshal allowed himself to be persuaded, demanding that it be made clear that France's entry into the war would take place in staggered stages, as reinforcement progressed.[47] As he had made clear last July, under no circumstances did he want general mobilization. At the very most, the armistice army might be used, reinforced by specialists and volunteers.[48] Darlan went off in a special train to Paris, to await Hitler's invitation, only to return in dismay a few days later.[49] Hitler had reverted to distrust and his obsession about not appearing weak. Rommel was re-establishing himself in Libya, and French aid was becoming less urgent. The German army was preparing the spring offensive, which was supposed to overcome the Soviet enemy. There would be time to return to the conversation later.

Although it all came to nothing, it is worth pausing to consider this episode. On the German side, this was the first time that Hitler was seen to hesitate and envisage the possibility of a settlement with France. But the attitude of the French is even more interesting. The Vichy leaders gave their reply on Tunisia in December and held their conversation on possible belligerence in January, when America had just entered the war (Berlin did not ask them to break off diplomatic relations although, as even Leahy believed, they would have been prepared to do so).[50] This suggests that their view was quite different from what we would now imagine it to have been.

The American fleet had received a heavy blow at Pearl Harbor and the Japanese were busy conquering South-East Asia, so the situation of the Anglo-Saxons was worse than ever. As for Germany, engaged in a war on two fronts from which it would probably not emerge defeated, it ought now to perceive the advantage of coming to an agreement with conquered France. The hypothesis of a compromise peace now became the great hope. In January 1942, Vichy was thinking not so much of declaring war on the Anglo-Saxons but rather of obtaining a favourable settlement from Germany by dint of getting the conqueror to realize the importance of France's role as a western shield, protected by which Hitler would be able to crush Soviet resistance once and for all. The hope of the French leaders was to kill two birds with one stone. With France politically satisfied and militarily strengthened, the Anglo-Saxons might be dissuaded from attacking French territories and persuaded to end the war with a compromise peace, and in this France would be well placed to play a mediating role.

Hitler's distrust spared France the agonies of implementing a painful decision. What concessions and promises would have sufficed to get France to follow Germany even in a defensive co-belligerence? Above all, France was spared the catastrophic consequences of entering the war, for this would assuredly not have altered the resolution of the Anglo-Saxons. The French leaders were carried away by scenarios whose realism was daily shrinking away to nothing. Not only were they mistaken about Hitler, they also underestimated the tenaciousness of the Anglo-Saxons and the missionary zeal of the Americans who, once they had entered the war, would stop at nothing short of the annihilation of their enemy.

After flaring up in January, the hope of a general settlement died away. The German silence once again became crushing, and was broken only by Hitler's vituperations over the Riom trial. Darlan was disadvantaged by his unpopularity. The army resented Weygand's dismissal; Pétain was tired of him. The Worms team wanted Laval recalled, as did the embassy, which hoped this would rekindle Berlin's interest in collaboration. In the spring, the crisis over the succession, which dragged on for several weeks, stirred up the factions of the Hôtel du Parc and underlined the role of the occupier, to whom everyone, including Pétain now turned for support or arbitration. Abetz was active in support of Laval, who wanted full powers. Leahy took Pétain to task and encouraged him to oppose this. Darlan tried to block his return, on the grounds of the opposition of the Americans, an argument that proved counter-productive with the Germans. There then followed lengthy negotiations over the powers of the Auvergnat, who eventually got what he wanted. Pétain was confined to his post as head of state, Laval became head of government, Darlan was put in charge of the armed forces and retained the title of successor to Pétain.

The Darlan era ended in weariness and disillusion. The admiral was embittered at losing control. The experience had shaken him and left him somewhat sceptical, as it had some of his collaborators. Pucheu, the go-getter, who in the summer of 1941 had been telling the Germans that Darlan, and Laval too, belonged to the past and that his role was to smooth the path to power for younger teams,[51] had become disenchanted. On 16 March, he told Déat the reasons for his pessimism, revealing a cast of mind conditioned by misplaced hopes and irreducible self-importance: 'The idea at the back of even Hitler's mind is one day to subject us to a *diktat*, and meanwhile to get all they can out of France, leaving it in a state of decline that prevents it from being dangerous. The only hope, according to P[ucheu], is that H[itler], whose subalterns are all mediocre men, will be persuaded by the facts to reconsider the situation of France and will one day realize that he cannot do without it and needs it; and that France will be willing, having been satisfied by a certain number of advantages.'[52]

9

Endless negotiations

WHERE had two years of collaboration got Vichy? Its efforts had been consistently unsuccessful: the armistice continued, there were no guarantees for the empire, no commitments as to France's future. But Franco-German relations were not simply a matter of high-level meetings and sudden surges of hope followed by long periods of frustration. At the lower levels, a dense and strained web of negotiations was covering every aspect of the country's life. Here, there were constant pressures, cascades of demands and bitter haggling: the French delegates were sorely conscious of the massively unequal balance of forces, confined as they were to a position which was further weakened by the dispersed framework of negotiations (Wiesbaden, the Hemmen delegation, the Majestic, the embassy, etc.). As for the Germans, whenever they wanted to change their line or had to, they passed the buck from one service to another. And the concessions that they dangled before the French were all too inclined either to disappear in the process or else to re-emerge much diminished. Meantime, the Germans promoted their own aims relentlessly; no sooner had the French negotiators agreed to something in principle than they insisted on its immediate application, then used this as a springboard for further demands. The French themselves were also quite capable of using the ploy of appealing to a superior authority, and they knew how to manipulate data and statistics, how to make counter-proposals and how to dawdle over executing whatever had been agreed.[1] But however appropriate such defensive tactics may be, they lose their value when needs are pressing, particularly when it is a matter of moving forward with a particular policy.

However, despite these handicaps, the picture – at least in the short term – was not entirely negative. Essentially, of course, France was structurally in the position of supplicant, but in certain matters and at certain moments it was the Germans who needed to ask for help. Then the French negotiators would discover a margin of manoeuvre that lent credit and support to their politics by producing a few results, until, that is, these were revealed in all their mediocrity and precariousness. Even in the most ordinary, day-to-day matters, state collaboration could not conceal the vain obstinacy with which Vichy clung to its objectives. By seeking to strengthen a half-occupied country in the middle of a seemingly endless conflict, in the face of an enemy bent on preparing for a Nazi Europe after the war, the leaders of the French state allowed themselves to be sucked into the spiral of satellization.

On the politico-administrative level, the gains were modest. The occupied territories remained divided into zones, with only very few modifications to the pattern allowed, such as the re-establishment of contacts with the northern departments attached to Brussels, and the de facto suppression of the north-east line in December 1941. Results were not impressive, as it was in the occupiers' interest to keep a very tight rein on everything. Vichy strove for recognition at least for its administrative sovereignty, doing so all the more insistently because of its cult of a particular set of values, foremost among them state authority.

The control that the Germans exercised over the administration was abusive. They issued orders on everything, intervened to get arrested people released or to seize prisoners whom they then treated as hostages, and either transferred or threatened officials who persisted in following the directives issued by their own superiors. The French state's response to this was to strive obstinately to protect its agents, re-establish its sovereignty, and get reality to coincide with its pretensions. In a circular dated 7 June 1941, Darlan declared categorically: 'The more the French government agrees to collaboration and practises it, the more Germany must be persuaded to restore the administration of the country to it.' Officials were told no longer to obey orders that were incompatible with the existing treaties – this meant the armistice agreement – without referring the matter to their superiors. In the autumn, the Germans more or less agreed to this: in principle, officials were responsible solely to their government. However, that certainly did not halt the abuses and infractions.[2]

In France, as elsewhere, it was in the occupiers' interests to get the native administration to work, to compensate for their own inadequate means, personnel and knowledge of the terrain. So they kept a close eye on it and maintained a tight control over it, having their say on all appointments or transfers of high-ranking officials and if necessary insisting upon dismissals: between 1940 and 1944 they got rid of sixteen prefects and fourteen sub-prefects and general secretaries.[3] It should not be imagined that, without Vichy, the situation would have been fundamentally different. The Dutch administration was not under orders from an antisemitic government; it nevertheless efficiently carried out the mission allotted it by the occupying power, namely to discriminate against, despoil, concentrate and deport the Jews of Holland. All the same, the existence of the French state did make a difference, and not solely because, in the name of collaboration, that state set the seal of its approval upon many of the measures taken by the occupying power. It also made the occupiers' task much easier. It purged the administration of people – Jews, freemasons and leftists – whom the Germans considered their enemies. Through its directives, its manipulation of promotions, and its threats of sanctions, it selected men loyal to its own politics, and brought civil servants into line and kept them there: thus Pucheu, the Minister of Internal Affairs, addressing the prefects on 19 February 1942, reminded them of 'the European aspect of their mission and the need for collaboration with Germany'.[4]

Vichy wished to keep its administration under tight control and protested as soon as there were incidents with or interference from the occupying power. As the Germans noticed, occasionally it even transferred high-ranking officials who had established 'too good relations' with the occupiers.[5] But the net result was to the advantage of the latter. In 1944, the MBF reckoned that the cooperation of the French services in the early months 'almost exceeded what was to be expected from the administration of an occupied country'.[6] At the end of 1942, it again noted with satisfaction that most high-ranking officials were prepared to continue collaborating, emphasizing that their attitude was all the more noteworthy given that this was opposed to the greater part of public opinion and that, in contrast, the attitude of lower and middle-ranking officials left room for doubt: underpaid and overworked as these were, they regretted the passing of the old regime and were hostile to collaboration.[7]

The difference Vichy made is particularly noticeable where repression is concerned. Here, the pressure exerted by the Germans coincided not only with its pursuit of sovereignty, but also its own ideological inclinations, which were close to theirs. As a result, the line between Vichy and the Germans became blurred. As a regime of order, the French state reckoned it knew all there was to know about repression; and it was keen to do the work itself. When the first communist assassination of a member of the occupying forces occurred, on 21 August 1941, the Germans set the retribution terms: either the French were to make amends by executing six people or else they would themselves shoot 150 hostages. In Vichy, it was decided to take the matter firmly in hand. First an antedated law with retroactive effect set up special sections to work alongside the courts; then the section thus created alongside the court of appeal in Paris condemned to death three communists who had been detained for minor offences, and these were summarily executed. When the magistrates refused to take any further steps, Pucheu created another special court, the State Tribunal, which completed the quota.

It was no doubt a matter of avoiding the shooting of hostages. Vichy preferred to murder communists itself rather than allow the occupying power to kill 'good Frenchmen' indiscriminately. The Germans were delighted by their decision: France had now trampled the liberal concept of the law under foot. The fact was that its leaders were keen to confirm the authority of the state and have it keep control of repression, even when it was a matter of punishing actions taken against the occupiers. They were also giving free rein to their fervent anticommunism, which itself was founded upon their basic values, in particular their obsession with order. In response to Barthélémy's reluctance, when faced with all-out repression, and his objection that the prisons were already full, Pétain replied: 'The firing squad will make you some room there.'[8] The Vichy leaders were also anxious to keep on course their politics of collaboration, which the assassinations were undermining by generating tension between them and the Germans (Darlan had just told Pétain that Hitler was hesitating to proceed further with France, on account of the 'disorder of people's minds'). But in the long run, as was predictable, Vichy was not even able to invoke its policies' successful results. Assassinations multiplied and, as French methods did not seem sufficiently expeditious, Hitler decided to have hostages shot by the dozen. Again, Pucheu was to be seen trying to replace people on the hostage lists by communists, as in the Chateaubriant affair.

On the score of antisemitism, the French state made no attempt to prove its superiority to the Germans.[9] As its leaders saw it, the struggle against 'the Jewish influence' was a matter for legislation rather than for the police. But the Nazis held a different view, which made the assistance of the French administration indispensable to them. Their objective was the elimination of the Jews, and even if the final solution – expulsion to some distant territory or extermination – remained indeterminate up until 1941, the process never varied: registration, despoiliation, segregation, concentration, deportation. In response to German pressure, Vichy extended its initial policy, in accordance with a logic which, once again, stemmed both from its desire to affirm its sovereignty and from an ideological connivance that was bearing increasingly poisonous fruits.

The basis for that connivance was Vichy's own initial and autonomous choice of antisemitic legislation. The statute of October 1940, which excluded Jewish citizens from public office and certain professions, was applied rigorously even in the free zone and North Africa, where the occupying power was absent and powerless. Without German pressure, Vichy would possibly have gone no further. But that pressure would have been much less effective had it not been for Vichy's policy of collaboration. The spiral began when, having ordered the registration and identification of all Jewish businesses in the occupied zone, the Germans imposed aryanization, that is to say the obligatory sale of all property held by Jews (by a decree of 18 October 1940). The French state feared an economic takeover and it was a fear that the looting of works of art by a team headed by Rosenberg seemed to justify. Vichy was, of course, more concerned to protect the national economy and patrimony than the rights of individuals. It accordingly agreed to oversee the appointment and work of administrators empowered to sell or liquidate the property of Jews. The MBF was only too pleased to accept this offer, as it saved it a great deal of work and also involved the French authorities in its anti-Jewish policy.

In early 1941, the occupiers put direct pressure on Vichy, demanding that it create an anti-Jewish office to coordinate and stimulate persecution in the occupied zone. Darlan eventually agreed and then, in a typical reflex, proceeded to create an organization designed to operate in both zones. He regarded this as a way of re-establishing control over the antisemitic policy as a whole, despite the risk involved in falling into line with the occupied zone. The general commissariat for Jewish questions was placed under Xavier

Vallat, who was a germanophobic nationalist but also a confirmed antisemite. The presence of the occupier did not seem to him a reason to defer the application of a French project, the purpose of which was to free the country of foreign Jews and to limit the 'influence' of national Jews through a series of professional exclusions.

Vallat laboured zealously to unify legislation. He seemed confident that he would manage to supplant German decrees by French laws. In the process, he extended to the free zone most of the measures affecting the occupied zone, introducing further professional limitations in a second 'Jewish Statute', in June 1941, and subsequently, in July, ordering the general registration and organization of all Jewish property. The French state, which had earlier declared that it intended to respect property, thus now excluded the Jews of the free zone from economic life. A few months later it went back on another of its undertakings, the maintenance of the distinction between French Jews and foreign Jews. At the Germans' request, it now made it obligatory for both groups to become members of the Union Générale des Israélites de France, an organization whose purpose was patently to prepare for segregation.

The French leaders were advancing down a path that led they knew not where. They did so under continuous German pressure, not without expressing reservations, sometimes attempting to apply the brakes, and occasionally protesting or expressing disapproval.[10] Nevertheless, they continued on down that path, without raising serious obstacles, mainly because they approved of its direction and of discrimination and the reduction of the 'Jewish influence', starting by the ejection of foreign Jews. Darlan and Vallat had heard of the plan at one point favoured by the Nazis to deport the Jews of Europe to some distant territory.[11] They approved of this idea, their only reservations being on the score of 'old French Jews'. On 10 March 1941, Darlan told Pastor Boegner that it was necessary to distinguish between 'three categories of Jews: foreigners, of whom I should like to see France rid; those recently naturalized – let them be ejected, I am all for that; and finally, Jews of long-standing French nationality, who have been assimilated and have served the country well. We do not want them to be badly treated.'[12] Besides, they wanted their collaboration policy to succeed. Given that they were already envisaging a Nazi Europe, why should they have raised difficulties over what they regarded as not only a minor matter, but one on which disagreement was merely a matter of degree, not one of principle? Their frame of mind was not of a kind to make them say 'no' when the demand for deportation eventually came.

The Vichy leaders had from the start paid great attention to the economy. Their obsession with social stability dictated that they should get industry going again immediately: unemployment affected over a million people. They were also concerned for the country's unity, which had suffered from the dislocation of commercial movements. They were fearful of German economic penetration and aspired to 'be strong', so as to face the post-war period in favourable conditions. But their negotiating position was undermined by the sealing of the demarcation line, by the English blockade that cut off overseas connections, and also by the suspension of trade with much of the continent. The Germans, the greatest threat to the economy, were also, through the orders that they placed, the only serious commercial outlet, but they were imposing three measures of extortion: an exchange rate inflated by over one-third as compared to 1939; occupation costs so high that they threatened to make prices escalate; and a clearing mechanism that forced vanquished France to pay for the commercial balance, that is to say the major proportion of all German orders. Yet Vichy still held a few cards. The occupying force was interested in a number of resources located in the free zone and the empire, in particular raw materials and colonial products; and for certain operations and certain kinds of production it needed the aid or agreement of the French authorities: the manufacture of military material, the ceding of shares, and the recruitment of labour.

The government's primary concern was to ensure the means of keeping control of the economy, by itself determining the apportioning of raw materials. Businesses were grouped by branches into organization committees (COs) and an apparatus was instituted to effect the distribution of raw materials (OCRPI). This authoritarian organization was set up not only to cope with immediate constraints, but also to respond to the new regime's desire to reform the national economy and to the need to prepare for becoming part of a German Europe. It too was designed to cover the entire country, at the cost of submitting to supervision by the occupying power.[13]

In an attempt to profit from Germany's interest, Vichy drafted laws that prohibited entering into certain operations with foreign nationals or made such operations subject to special authorization. At the same time, it tried to keep control of all trade. If the occupying power was to remain in a position in which it was obliged to make requests, it had to be prevented from entering into direct contact with individual French firms and, to that end, it was necessary to centralize orders and block the delivery of products from the free zone to the occupied one.[14] Given the circumstances, these efforts inevitably produced no more than meagre fruits. In the occupied zone the Germans refused to allow any centralization of orders and continued to approach firms directly; in the free zone, many industrialists and traders succumbed to the temptation to deliver to the conqueror products that were denied any other outlet by the English blockade.[15] Moreover, up until the point of total war in 1942–43, when a certain rationalization of the exploitation of occupied countries took place, the Germans' interest in the French economy was selective and sporadic, another fact that gave them the upper hand in negotiations.[16]

The French state had to be consulted where the non-occupied territories were concerned and also included in a number of negotiations that concerned the country as a whole. It thus took part in concluding major contracts for the delivery of raw materials and finished leather and textile products (the Kerl and Grunberg plans). Vichy's position was solid enough for it to force the acceptance of rules of fair exchange for German orders. The first of these was that the occupying power should supply the raw materials needed for the manufacture of ordered goods, apart from coal, which the Germans refused to provide although, in the case of certain orders placed in the free zone, it was forthcoming. Here, the French were in a better position, as the occupying power was definitely the one doing the asking.[17]

Vichy was extremely vigilant about preserving national capital. In October 1940, it ruled that all proposals to cede interests to foreigners must obtain authorization. It was not the case that this was automatically refused, but simply a matter of retaining control so as to be in a position to obtain fair remuneration and to strengthen Vichy's hand when it came to general negotiations.[18] When asked to give such authorization, the French authorities would insist on equivalent shares in German businesses (usually in vain) or on assurances as to its share of markets after the war (here, it was sometimes successful). In the main, what France received in exchange were deliveries of raw materials, orders placed with French industry, and patents and technological expertise.[19] In the settlement of accounts, Vichy asked that payment be made other than by deduction from the costs of occupation or through the clearing mechanism. In some cases, payment took the form of French loans previously held by foreigners.

German capital entered the economy via a number of routes: through the creation of companies with mixed capital (Francolor, France-Rayonne, Gazogènes, France-Actualités, etc.); through shares taken up in French companies, particularly in the media (such as Havas, the Hibbelen trust, which controlled close on fifty periodicals, and the publishing houses of Denoël and Sorlot); through the purchase of French interests abroad, in Germany, and above all in Eastern and South-Eastern Europe, regions that had now passed into the Reich's sphere of influence; and, finally, through shares bought in aryanized companies, in particular the Galeries Lafayette.[20] Vichy was to flatter itself that it had avoided the creation of German majority shareholders, following the unfortunate experience of the Francolor company, that is, in which it had ended by accepting a German majority holding in return for an assurance that this would not be regarded as a precedent. However, if the penetration of German capital remained very limited, in the main the credit for this did not belong to the French state. It was far more due to the relative lack of interest of the Reich's authorities, who were intent on immediate exploitation, and also to the prudence of German businessmen, who were uncertain of France's position in the new order and likewise of the eventual outcome of the war.

The occupying power was also interested in obtaining a work force and pressed Vichy to encourage the recruitment of voluntary workers for Germany. In March 1941, the government agreed to abrogate a law passed six months earlier, which had prohibited the French from working in the production of war material in foreign territories. (It had been partly aimed at the Gaullists.) But, with remarkable constancy, it did persist in refusing to give its official support to the recruitment of workers for Germany. From the autumn of 1941, however, that constancy began to crumble. The prolongation of the war in the East, which increased German needs, conjured up the spectre of requisitioning; an increase in the number of voluntary workers departing to Germany seemed preferable. Vichy now had the idea of converting French prisoners into civilian workers who would remain in Germany, or alternatively of a swap, in which prisoners were liberated in return for a consignment of workers. This was an idea that had already been suggested by Scapini in the autumn of 1940 and it was to be put forward again by Laval in the following year.[21] At the beginning of 1942, the government agreed to approve recruitment in exchange for the creation of an official organization to monitor French workers in Germany. The Minister of Labour, Belin, stressed that this was 'an action in which [the government] was deeply implicated'.[22] In early April 1942, Darlan even authorized the opening of German recruitment offices in the free zone. In this matter, in which the occupying power applied insistent pressure that later became far stronger than it had ever been regarding capital, Vichy did manifest considerable reluctance. That can be explained partly by its sensitivity to public opinion and partly by the fact that it was more concerned to keep the economy ticking over than to bring unemployment figures down by despatching workers beyond the Rhine.

Overall, results were sometimes good but more often bad, even in 1941, the brightest year for economic collaboration. This was the moment when the technocrats of Vichy were developing a number of grandiose projects, in particular the idea of European channels of communication.[23] Lehideux, who was responsible for industrial equipment, presented Benoist-Méchin with the most grandiose of such projects: it envisaged three great motorways – Bordeaux–Berlin, Cherbourg–Basle and Marseilles–Hamburg – complemented by waterways linking the Rhine, the Atlantic and the Mediterranean; and in France itself, sixteen highways converging from all directions upon Paris, where they would fetch up at sixteen monumental gates to be known as 'the gates of the Marshal'.[24]

All too conscious of the strong, unrelenting pressure applied by the occupying power, technocrats were greatly relieved when the German negotiators proved conciliatory, as they occasionally did, manifesting a desire for reciprocity or evoking the prospect of a balanced partnership. With respect to textiles, for instance, the German negotiator suggested that the forseeable shortfall in European production after the war would open up a profitable field for the industries of both nations.[25] Such moments were rare, but the most was made of anything that could be called reassuring. Towards the end of 1941, the heads of the Ministry of Industrial Production produced a series of notes to be incorporated in a file with the unexpected title: 'The aid given to the French economy by Germany.' To show that collaboration was not a one-way exercise, the technocrats made as much as possible of the German contribution: supplies of raw materials, technological assistance in the production of substitutes, and a few deliveries of finished products[26] – pretty meagre results, which reflected the massive inequality that obtained in deals struck between the two countries.

The machine was working again, it is true, and unemployment disappeared in the autumn of 1941. But though the economy was ticking over, it did so for the benefit of Germany, which in 1942 absorbed about one-third of the national revenue for 1938, then in the following year half of it.[27] At the end of 1941, France handed over food supplies (10 per cent of its wheat production, 15 per cent of its meat, 80 per cent of its champagne, 25 per cent of its colonial oils, 40 per cent of its cocoa); raw materials (55 per cent of its aluminium, 40 per cent of its bauxite, 90 per cent of its cement); and manufactured products (70 per cent of its products from engineering industries in the occupied zone, 90 per cent of products from its naval industries, 80 per cent from its aeronautical industry, and 70 per cent from its electrical industry).[28]

The French economy was turning over for Germany and was itself becoming steadily poorer. The replacement of raw materials was not respected: there were increasing delays and in many cases nothing at all was ever delivered. German orders were met by exhausting French stocks: the French population would get less coal and more restrictions.[29] At the end of 1941, the Germans recorded, quite correctly, that France's economic contribution came from the use of its productive apparatus, the exhaustion of its reserves and from keeping its own consumption down to the minimum.[30] From the spring of 1942 onwards, exploitation increased, and the margin of manoeuvre left to the French negotiators shrank even more.

At the interface between the economic and the military spheres, the manufacture of war materials was related to Vichy's policies of non-belligerence, as was the matter of 'facilities' in the empire. As early as August 1940, the government agreed to industries in the occupied zone executing military orders for Germany. The only category excluded was 'completed offensive material destined for the struggle against England'; and the limit set was a distant one. On 19 August, however, in a note to Weygand, Huntziger indicated that, provided concessions were forthcoming in exchange, even the manufacture of aggressive materials might be authorized.[31] The productive apparatus of the free zone was also being tapped. The Germans were very interested in the aeronautical industry. Vichy welcomed the idea of reactivating this vast branch, which before the war had employed 250000 people but which the armistice agreement had closed down. Military as well as economic advantages were involved here: if the Germans wanted planes, let them allow the French to build some for themselves. Hence the idea of a common programme with the product shared. The implications of such a decision were obvious: as Bouthillier said, 'The decision to work for the Germans in the free zone is the gravest action since the armistice.'[32]

Understandably, negotiations were particularly tough. At first Vichy tried for political concessions, but Flandin then withdrew from that position, being anxious to be recognized as keen to continue collaboration and also because of the priority that Vichy gave to the reconstitution of the French military forces. Negotiations then resumed within a more restricted framework, and in the second half of 1941 produced agreements that apportioned to the French one aircraft for every two that went to the Germans (essentially transport planes, as the Germans preferred to construct their own combat machines). The French also received authorization to construct a few civil aircraft and to pursue a programme of research.[33] A similar agreement was concluded for naval construction. Vichy obtained the liberation of about 30 per cent of the ships' hulls located in the occupied zone, to complete a few warships and build merchant ships, in return for constructing a number of items in both zones, including warships, for Germany.[34]

Achievements fell far short of objectives. In the aeronautical domain only about half of the quotas were met, and only 10 per cent of the naval programme had been completed by the time the disappearance of the armistice army, in November 1942, put an end to any shares at all for France.[35] The explanation for this lay in the dearth of both energy and qualified labour, problems of adapting to the construction of German models, and the fact that the occupying power privileged construction in the Reich. Notwithstanding, by the end of the war, the French aeronautical industry had produced 1540 aircraft and 4138 engines, to which should be added 5716 engines repaired (combining orders for the common programme and orders placed directly with French firms). This was a considerable proportion of the military transport planes at Germany's disposal.[36]

Vichy had also concocted a third common programme, which was not accepted. This involved the manufacture of war material in the free zone in order to resupply and modernize French forces. It was a programme heavily weighted in favour of France with regard to both share quotas (eight for one) and related conditions. It had been prepared amid the atmosphere of the Paris protocols and it both reflected Vichy's rising aspirations and testified to the importance that it ascribed to military improvements, even at the risk of becoming ever more deeply compromised. It was thus that Huntziger wrote as follows on the subject of this programme: 'For moral and psychological reasons, the French Government believes it essential that the German orders remain secret and be subsequently confused with the French orders.'[37]

It was in the re-equipment of the French armed forces, in the strict sense, that Vichy's policies produced their best results. Germany's interest in the defence of the empire was too great for it to skimp as much as usual. Assessing the situation in September 1941, the French delegate to the sub-committee for land forces in Wiesbaden spoke of 'indisputably advantageous results' à propos of the number of men and arms obtained for the defence of the empire: it is worth noting that in 1942, the airforce, which the armistice had destined for total disarmament, had 900 aircraft at its disposal, and the fleet could muster 56000 men, almost as many as before the defeat, instead of the 3000 decreed by the armistice.[38] However, the French delegate went on, this could be explained by the 'self-interested generosity' of Germany, which took good care that the advantages conceded did not exceed the framework of its own interests. And the head of the armament sub-committee commented: 'Germany's plan will be to compromise us by repaying us as cheaply as possibly.'[39]

Quite apart from the fact that the reinforcements granted were calculated down to the last detail and that the Germans retained the means to control how much they were used, chiefly through fuel allowances, these results suffered from another major weakness. This was that materials wear out and, in the modern age, military power presupposes free use of an extensive industrial base, abundant means of repair and upkeep, and continuous technological innovation, all of which, in the case of France, were severely limited by German controls and French penury. And the situation was compounded by yet another weakness: a shortfall in manpower in the armistice army. In the spring of 1942, the military realized, to their consternation, that it was impossible for them to retain the services of young men of the classes of '38 and '39, and that their demobilization would result, due to the lack of volunteers, in a deficit of between 55000 and 60000 men out of the authorized total of 100000! In the opinion of General Bridoux, the Secretary of State for War and a fervent collaborationist, 'the existence of a deficit of this magnitude would create an inadmissibly dangerous situation at a time when foreign activity to undermine the internal order and the security of the empire, already extremely strong, is likely to become twice as intense'.[40]

All in all, Vichy did wrest some advantages from all this endless negotiating, but they were limited, provisional, revocable, and always paid for in such a way as to implicate it ever more deeply in the politics of the occupying power. One exception to this might possibly be claimed: of the 1 500000 prisoners of war transferred to Germany, 600000 returned between 1941 and 1944. Vichy can take the credit for 220000 of them, the remainder being escapees or – in the case of the majority – the wounded and sick whose repatriation was covered by the Geneva Convention. However, it should be remembered that of that 600000, 90000 were men liberated under the conditions of the *Relève*, that is to say in exchange for France despatching three times as many workers to Germany. Moreover, that figure of 600000 also included many men – farmers, civil servants and technicians – whose liberation for professional activity in France also served German interests. So, really, only the liberation of the veterans of the 1914–18 war can be counted as an unconditional success.[41]

In general, the nature of German interests caused collaboration to produce far fewer results on the economic level than on the military level. The French people were hoping for improvements in their daily life, but the manufacture of armaments diverted resources away from civil needs and exposed the population and workers to bombing raids.[42] They dreaded a war against England; yet Vichy's determination to re-equip the military increased that risk, since it was against the Anglo-Saxons that the armaments that were conceded were likely to be used – as indeed transpired. In the end, much of this military equipment acquired at such cost was lost in the struggle against the Allies, first in Syria, then in North Africa, even before the fleet was so piteously scuttled in November 1942.

Shortly before the landings in North Africa, a number of high-ranking officials – military ones, it should be said – openly recognized the vanity of the government's policies. In September 1942, a note from the naval staff office observed that the growing demands of Germany 'are little by little reducing France to a situation almost as tragic as if, in June 1940, it had refused to sign the armistice and had accepted total occupation'. It continued as follows: 'The ruins caused by (even a total) occupation would not be much graver than they will be as it is, for Germany will in any case grind us down utterly in order to win its war.'[43]

10

The return of Laval

By recalling Laval in the spring of 1942, Pétain testified to his desire to press on with the policy of collaboration. Or, at least, he recognized that he could think of no alternative. In the East, a German offensive was imminent. In Vichy, it looked bound to succeed, at least in the conquest of resources without which the USSR would be forced to its knees and with which Germany would be strengthened. What could the Anglo-Saxons, who were everywhere on the defensive, do about that? Laval had obtained the extraordinary powers that he had demanded after 13 December. As head of government, he now appointed his ministers and assumed direction of governmental policy. As a security measure, he himself took on Internal Affairs, Foreign Affairs and Information. Darlan retained the title of Pétain's successor and was head of armed forces. He was humiliated by his semi-disgrace and could see his powers being whittled away. The new government comprised a number of the Marshal's faithful followers, part of the former Worms team, now increasingly disunited, and a bunch of Lavalists, some of whom were drawn from the personnel of the Third Republic: in short, a mixed group, including one jumpy academician, Abel Bonnard. There were fewer respectable 'notables', more committed collaborationists.

Pétain retained the power to promulgate a new constitution and the power to dismiss the head of government. He did not take kindly to the delegation of some of his former powers. His resentment on this score had strongly influenced his reluctance to recall a man whom he did not like but whose politics were now closer than ever to his own. On 19 April, when announcing the formation of the new government to the French people, he stressed that it would be operating under his authority. As if to wipe out the past, he recalled the role that Laval had played in the creation of the new order: 'Today, at a time as crucial as June 1940, I am once more joined by him, as we continue the task of national reform and European organization for which we together laid the foundations.'[1] The Marshal, who in January had been rattling his chains and speaking of 'semi-liberty', was now readjusting his képi.

Laval returned well aware of the difficulties awaiting him and still convinced that his policies were the right ones. At home, he stuck a number of irons in the fire, seeking to improve the standing of the government in the eyes of public opinion and to strengthen his own authority. To soften the reactionary image of the regime, which he regarded as one of the causes of its unpopularity, he sought support from formerly elected representatives, tried to persuade parliamentarians such as Marquet to accept portfolios, and resuscitated the general councils, under a different name. He busied himself winning over trade unionists and conciliating the world of labour. He reined back on the struggle against freemasonry, at the same time appointing a rabid antisemite, Darquier de Pellepoix, to replace Vallat. He slowed down the Légion des Combattants, whose zeal was irritating the administration and displeasing the general public. In public, he bandied about words such as 'socialism' and 'republic'.

But public opinion could no longer be bought off by words, as Laval was well aware; and he opted for 'a republic with muscle', ready to put the boot in to the press and the radio, a police force to stamp out opposition, and – why not? – a single party to enfold the population and serve as a praetorian guard. He had no more sympathy for activism than he had ever had. Militancy and propaganda left him cold, or suspicious. But after the experience of 13 December he could see the advantage of partisan support, if only to block the men of Paris, above all Doriot, who in the summer of 1942 made a bid for power. While encouraging 'big Jacques's' rivals, by offering them money, and while Benoist-Méchin, on his instructions, brought the Légion des Volontaires Français contre le Bolchévisme (Legion of French Volunteers against Bolshevism) under the direct control of the French state, in the free zone he played the card of the Service d'Ordre Légionnaire (the Legionary Service of Order), the activist kernel of the Légion des Combattants, whose leader, Darnand, he appointed delegate to the head of government.

Externally, Laval knew that it was no longer a moment for politics that took on the risk of a conflict with England by attempting to reconquer the Gaullist colonies or, even worse, by granting 'facilities' in the empire to the Germans. With the USSR, Japan, and the United States all in the war, it was doubtful whether Germany would win a total victory, but it would still be the greatest power in Europe, once it had conquered the USSR. That victory was probable, and also devoutly to be hoped for: it would leave the Reich winded, in possession of territories that would satisfy its appetite and enable it to turn the whole continent into a fortress. The Anglo-Saxons, given a hard time by Japan, would pull back from a long war, particularly if France received an honourable place in the new Europe. France would then be well placed to act as intermediary and – possibly – to mastermind a compromise peace.

Laval threaded his hypotheses on to his string of hopes: a German victory in the East in the near future, the Anglo-Saxons discomforted and weary of war, a Hitler who would listen to reason. His scenario did not embrace a far more probable hypothesis which suited neither his hopes nor his interests: namely, that the war would drag on in the East, the vice would close tighter in the West; while occupied France was squeezed like a lemon by the occupier, first the empire, then metropolitan France would be attacked by the Anglo-Saxons; France would become a battlefield; and Vichy would lose its last trump cards. One year earlier it had been a question of using what remained of French power in time to acquire the gratitude of a Germany poised for victory, at the same time obtaining the means to strengthen itself and, if possible, forestall any undesirable consequences of that victory. From the spring of 1942 onwards it became a matter of helping a Germany whose victory looked doubtful, but whose defeat was still improbable, meanwhile avoiding any compromising military situation, particularly in the empire, that would stand in the way of France playing a role as mediator. Hence Laval's emphatic references to the struggle against communism and his increased prudence where the Anglo-Saxons were concerned. Laval was now professing pacifism and declaring his refusal to plunge France into the war: it was a position that placed him in agreement with Pétain.

He explained to Admiral Leahy, on 27 April, that the war had become an ideological struggle between democracies and totalitarianisms, that France did not have to take sides, and that he himself was concerned only for the safety of his country. An *entente* with Germany seemed to him a realizable possibility; it would establish peace in Europe; and in any event, a German victory or, if possible, a negotiated peace would be preferable to an English and Soviet victory. He wished to maintain good relations with the United States; he would give Germany no military aid, but would defend the empire against an Anglo-Saxon attack.[2] The Americans were disinclined to believe him. Roosevelt recalled Leahy for consultations and despatched a representative to Gaullist France. He became more peremptory with respect to French possessions in the Caribbean, insisting upon the immobilization of the warships at anchor there and the imposition of extensive controls. He also expressed his approval of the English landings in Madagascar on the grounds that this would forestall Japanese occupation of the island. All these were severe blows for Vichy.

Laval endeavoured to reassure the Americans. Meanwhile, he was offering pledges to the Germans, at the very moment when Berlin was hardening its exploitation of the occupied countries. Göring wanted more deliveries of food: never mind if the French cried famine! Speer, the Führer's architect, now Minister of Armaments, was insisting upon increased military production. The Gauleiter Sauckel wanted French labour for the total war effort. The Wehrmacht, in need of cannon fodder, was forcibly drafting the young men of Alsace and Lorraine; Vichy protested in Wiesbaden, but said nothing in public. As for the SS, it wanted assistance in maintaining order and implementing the 'final solution to the Jewish question'. Abetz had to work hard to keep his end up: his plan for a satellite France called for finesse, tact and a few concessions; instead, the vice was being tightened.

Laval desperately needed some improvements. Even where his policies abroad were concerned, he had to throw some sop to public opinion if he was not to appear completely isolated. Moreover, quite apart from the concessions he was striving to obtain, the litany of which had varied little over two years – the liberation of prisoners, reattachment of the northern departments, a reduction in the occupation costs – he was anxious to get major negotiations going. However, the second-rank officials who came to plague him with demands slipped away as soon as he mentioned general policies. Naturally enough, he reverted to his usual methods, offering pledges in order to establish mutual trust. By now he was saying 'yes' to virtually everything, sometimes even before he was asked. On 12 May, he wrote to Ribbentrop: 'In our misfortune, I would like to tell you, spontaneously and simply, that France is prepared, so far as it can and without delay, to make its contribution to your efforts. I hope, consequently, that as many French workers as possible will take the place in your factories of those who are departing for the eastern front.'[3] Laval knew that Sauckel was about to demand workers from him. By offering France's cooperation, he hoped to open up the way to a summit meeting and subsequently be remunerated for it.

From April to October, Laval strove to obtain an interview with the German leaders. Obsessed with his aim and constantly presented with new demands, he took a number of crucial decisions, encouraged by the Reich's successes. Rommel had entered Egypt, the Wehrmacht was advancing towards the Caucasus. Surely German pressure would soon abate, he thought. On 26 June, he told the Council of Ministers: 'We are entering upon a difficult period: the period of "paying up". It will no doubt last for as long as the German eastern offensive continues. To defend the interests of France, the head of government and ministers will have to increase their efforts.'[4] They had to accept what they could not refuse, applying delaying tactics where possible, until such time as victory in the East led to a relaxation in demands, particularly for labour. Nobody in Vichy seemed prepared to recognize the risks involved in taking such a bet and adopting such methods. Admittedly, there was nothing new about Laval's policy: the protection of France, if not of the French people, the recuperation of sovereignty, the pursuit of rank, and survival for the regime had always been what made Vichy tick.

Laval paid less attention to military matters than Pétain and Darlan did. But, like them, he was opposed to a German presence in the empire, for it would complete the break with the United States; also, he was determined to defend French West Africa and North Africa, which were so unfortunately situated on the approaches to Europe. Then, in the spring and summer of 1942, Vichy was agog with rumours of an imminent 'invasion'. Its alarm was understandable, for this would present it with a dangerous choice: either not to resist, in which case Germany would occupy the whole of metropolitan France; or, on the contrary, to resist, appealing for German aid, and thereby finding itself at war with the Anglo-Saxons. Benoist-Méchin, who favoured the second solution, suggested planning for an appeal for German armed forces, but only at the very last moment. But Laval would not hear of this, fearing that the Anglo-Saxons would get wind of it.[5] As for the first solution, nobody supported it, at least not in public; it would amount to renouncing all Vichy's policies so far. All that remained was a bastard solution: to resist without aid, as energetically as possible, asking the Germans for arms but not for their armed forces – or at least to defer asking for the latter for as long as possible.

One after another, all the French leaders warned the Americans that they would defend the empire.[6] To render the warning more forceful, they requested more means of defence from Germany. Pétain appeared particularly exercised. At the end of May, he suggested to a German diplomat that they should hold staff-office discussions on the defence of the empire.[6] The Germans rejected the idea and proposed reinforcements for French West Africa in exchange for France ceding them neutral vessels immobilized in Mediterranean ports. Laval turned this down, as it would lead to French vessels in Anglo-Saxon ports being seized. Then the Anglo-Canadian attempt at a landing at Dieppe, on 19 August, made him think again. In exchange for France handing over the neutral vessels, French West Africa would receive reinforcements shortly before the allied landings.

The Dieppe operation confirmed Vichy's fears, but it was relieved and heartened by its failure. Pétain thanked von Rundstedt for the fine resistance of his troops and spoke to a German diplomat of 'this happy day that has pleased all the French'. In emotional mood, he then launched into a tirade against the English whom he held 'in horror' and who had done 'so much harm' to France. Laval's congratulations were phrased more forthrightly: 'Your success is also ours.'[7] This event resuscitated an idea that Pétain had voiced in the preceding weeks, namely that the armistice army should take part in the defence of the Atlantic coast of metropolitan France. The effect of creating this 'niche' would be to allow it a foothold in the occupied zone, at the cost of being associated with the occupying power against the Anglo-Saxons. Two days after Dieppe, the Marshal made this offer to Hitler in a letter whose authenticity was later to be challenged. Benoist-Méchin's memoirs clarify the matter. It was he, Benoist-Méchin, who had proposed the idea to Laval who, being reluctant, suggested referring the matter to the Marshal, expecting him to turn it down. But Pétain was won over by it, and Laval then rallied to its support, remarking that Hitler would not reply anyway (as, in effect, he never did), but it would still amount to a point in his favour once the day for settling accounts arrived.[8]

On the economic level, the German demands were insatiable. In Laval they had found a man who would never refuse, even over military products. He was asked to hand over half the munition stocks in the free zone; he agreed. He was asked to manufacture explosives in the free zone; he agreed. He was asked for 30000 railway carriages and 1000 engines, and also that large stocks of leather be handed over. Again, he agreed. Admittedly, after agreeing in principle, he embarked upon some hard bargaining. Laval was showing goodwill and hoping for the long awaited interview.

As for manpower, here he did have to haggle: French workers were quite a different matter from shares in the Bor mines. In May, Sauckel put in a claim for 350000 men, 150000 of them skilled workers. Laval had already agreed in advance to this when he had proposed to Ribbentrop that France should make its contribution to the struggle against communism by sending French workers to Germany. Once he had conceded the principle, he entered into fierce negotiations over the pay-off. He knew what trump cards he held: forced labour was a contravention of international law, and the MBF was reluctant to shoulder responsibility for this; the embassy was fearful of the reactions of public opinion and also of its own plan failing; everyone knew that without the consent of the French administration the operation would be impracticable. However, Sauckel possessed a serious means of exerting pressure: the threat of requisitioning in the occupied zone. It was a threat that Laval was anxious to avoid, so that French sovereignty could continue to be respected and also because if Sauckel proceeded it would show that his own politics had failed.

His efforts over the next few months were concentrated on limiting German demands, avoiding the French state having to resort to constraint, and obtaining as much as possible in exchange, if possible concessions that would impress public opinion. So it was that he came up with the *Relève*. France would provide the men requested on a voluntary basis in exchange for the liberation of one prisoner for every worker who went off to Germany. After negotiations, to avoid a trial of strength, he agreed to the much less advantageous rate of one prisoner for every three skilled workers. On 22 June, in a flamboyant speech, he announced the *Relève*. One passage of that speech was to be remembered by those who heard it: 'I desire victory for Germany because, without it, bolshevism would become established everywhere. France cannot remain indifferent in the face of the immensity of the sacrifices made by Germany in order to build a Europe in which we must take our place.' Even as he tried to play upon the anticommunism theme, Laval, by declaring that desire openly, offered Hitler a pledge that betrayed what poor cards he now held and also his own political obstinacy.

When voluntary recruitment failed, pressure resumed. At the end of August Sauckel, who was impatient, published a decree imposing forced labour upon all men and women in occupied Western Europe. Laval threatened to resign if this was applied in France, then made concessions. On 4 September, he pushed through a law mobilizing all men between the ages of eighteen and fifty and all unmarried women between twenty-one and thirty-five, to carry out such work as the government deemed 'useful in the superior interest of the nation'. There was no mention of despatching people to Germany. Rather than a German decree in the occupied zone, let there be a French law applicable in both zones! But at least Laval had tried to put off a use of force that could only alienate him further in public opinion. The interpretation that he put upon this law was that it simply implied being selected for the *Relève;* since it was not really requisitioning, he decided not to apply the sanctions provided for in the law. As Barnaud declared to the German negotiators, it would have been a different matter if the Germans had agreed to a one-on-one exchange. Had they done so, 'the Government would have reckoned that it had the right, from a moral point of view, to force departures upon the working class, even by forcible requisitioning'.[9]

Conscious of the unpopularity of all this, Laval wanted to show that he had acted purely in response to German insistence, and that it was in the interests of workers to obey a French law rather than be subjected to German force. It was an ultimatum that he was waiting for and that he got from Stülpnagel. On 20 October, in another speech, he referred to the necessary 'politics of *entente*' with Germany, carefully avoiding the discredited word 'collaboration'. He assured his listeners that an agreement 'remained possible, with honour and respect for the vital interests of our country'. Again he flourished the danger of a Soviet victory. Both his tone and his words were very defensive – something quite new for him. He stressed how important it was for France not to become a victim in Germany's victory and that it must, tomorrow, be able to take its place in an organized and reconciled continent. Above all, he exhorted workers to respond to the *Relève,* brandishing the threat of sanctions and extolling the choice of voluntary departure, with all the material advantages and the favourable consequences for prisoners that this involved, rather than 'forced labour from which only Germany would benefit'.[10] From December on, the police and the gendarmerie delivered requisitioning notices and sought out dodgers.

Ultimately, Laval did not gain much from his prevarications. Sauckel agreed that 100000 out of the 350000 asked for could work in France, on the building sites of the Todt organization. And it took six months to raise the contingent claimed, – a delay that owed far less to the dilatory tactics of the Vichy negotiators than to the lack of cooperation of workers and employers. Laval was counting on a victory in the East, but the German armies had still not crushed the Soviets. And meanwhile he had set the seal of official approval upon the delivery of a labour force and had become enmeshed in a system that would lead to obligatory labour for Germany.

The French people were less interested in the question of autonomy for the police force than in the recruitment of labour for Germany. Nevertheless, the record here sheds interesting light upon Vichy's obsession with sovereignty, a doggedness that was set not only to last but even to strengthen. It is also illuminating as regards the figure of the chief of police, René Bousquet, a young man (thirty-three in 1942) but one with years of administrative experience behind him, in the course of which he had entered the Laval network. In September 1940, he had been appointed prefect in the Marne; then, eleven months later, regional prefect for the Champagne. Competent, dashing and forceful, this spoilt darling of the Third Republic, who had many radical and masonic friends and had never shown any particular inclination towards authoritarian doctrines, provides a striking illustration of the way in which a fair proportion of the French state's civil servants rallied to Vichy. It is true that his career had accelerated at a rather improbable rate under the previous regime. In this respect, he resembled his SS counterparts, in particular Knochen, who had also enjoyed promotion at lightning speed. Without being an ideologue, Bousquet was a man sincerely won over to the national revolution, or at least to Laval's version of 'a strong-arm republic'.[11]

Prefect Bousquet was a well-informed and well-connected man, as was evident from his conversation with the Italian consul in Rheims in October 1941. The consul writes of Bousquet's 'frequent and quite intimate relations' with Laval and mentions that he was also well received by Darlan. He describes him as 'a person of rare intelligence, with political ideas well adjusted to the principle of agreement with the Axis'. Bousquet expressed approval of the fascist regime and paid it a compliment in passing: 'It is from you [the Italians] that we are learning that, without a single party, you cannot have an authoritarian regime.' He defended an egalitarian concept of collaboration 'which does not offend our sense of independence'. He was in favour of an agreement with Italy, 'within the Axis framework, of course', which would substitute a state of peace for a state of war, as should also happen with Germany. All that was needed was agreement on a few principles thanks to which it would be possible in due time to resolve all dependent problems, including territorial questions. It would be a kind of secret pact, which would be preceded by a formal agreement, to soften up public opinion.[12]

One year later, having become chief of police, Bousquet paid a visit to the imprisoned Daladier and explained the difficulties facing the policy of collaboration, which he himself fully supported. 'The government is trapped between the Germans, who are at once demanding and condescending, and French public opinion, which deludes itself and chases after fantasies.' Bousquet believed 'that the Germans are very strong'. He imagined them organizing the conquered Russian territories in preparation for the winter, invading Iraq and the Near East, and ejecting the English from the Mediterranean. 'Then Germany will organize Europe in accordance with the plan devised by the brains trust that works closely with Hitler, and will say to the Americans "Do you want peace? No? Then come and fight".'[13] His attitude in these conversations with the Italian consul and Daladier is typical of the man: self-confident to the point of arrogance; irritatedly condescending towards the French people, who understood nothing about anything; anxious for independence and reciprocity in what he held to be a realistic policy of collaboration; and convinced of the strength of Germany, albeit without any sentimental inclination towards the occupiers; in short, unemotionally accepting of an authoritarian regime.

Laval had found an experienced man he could trust, with first-hand knowledge of the difficulties of administration in the occupied zone, particularly regarding police matters, in which the Germans were interfering more and more. Both men wanted to restore the government's authority, and at the same time strengthen the police, in order to keep a grip on the country. Here, the recuperation of sovereignty went hand in hand with survival for the regime. The whole matter acquired increased importance with the arrival of Oberg, who started off by laying claim to control of the French police. But demoralized and inclined to passivity as it had been ever since the first hostage executions, what good would the police force be if obliged to take orders from a German? The basis for an agreement was in this way identified. Bousquet asked that the independence of the French police be respected, once it was 'reorganized on new bases and firmly led', and in return he promised active commitment 'against terrorism, anarchism, and communism, the common enemies of our two countries'.[14]

What he wanted to discontinue was any French participation, either direct or indirect, in matters to do with hostages or in any other mixed operations that were damaging to the regime, because these confused the two police forces in the eyes of public opinion. The German police must limit itself to repressing actions taken against the occupying forces. The French police would act to repress only resistance of a purely political nature. The two forces would cooperate in all cases that affected both the security of the French state and that of the occupier. He also wanted increased means: the creation of police schools, more arms, the reserve mobile units (GMR) extended to the occupied zone, trained for street fighting and equipped with armoured vehicles. He explained to Oberg that the GMR would be useful for restoring order and for covering the rear of German troops in the event of allied landings. The population of Paris would have to get used to 'a police that intervenes ruthlessly in cases of disruption' and were in for 'a shock at the sight of it'.[15]

Oberg did not reply until 23 July, when he by and large granted Bousquet's requests. On 8 August, the Oberg–Bousquet agreement was announced at a meeting of SS officials and regional prefects. With this agreement, which certainly did not make headlines in the newspapers, Vichy crossed a line. In return for the Germans refraining from interfering in their usual fashion, the French police would have to prove themselves to be unfailingly reliable and efficient. The agreement produced one side effect: from September 1942 on, the shooting of hostages was discontinued. The SS had itself come to the conclusion that it increased resistance, whereas sending people to concentration camps acted as a deterrent. In recognizing that France had enemies 'in common' with the occupying power, Bousquet and Laval formalized an ideological collusion that up until then had remained tacit. Far from this specification of tasks preventing people from confusing the two forces, it made it even clearer to the minds of those inclined to resist that the struggle against the occupier could not be dissociated from the struggle against Vichy.

The Jews did not figure among the 'common enemies' identified by Bousquet. Nevertheless, their fate became entangled with the question of the police. By March 1942, convoys had, with no intervention from Vichy, transported to the East 6000 Jewish men, at least 1000 of whom were French. In June, the railways' availability led Himmler to speed up the 'final solution' in Western Europe. The cooperation of Vichy and its police became essential. This was the point at which Bousquet began negotiations with Oberg. Laval was endeavouring to relaunch collaboration. When the SS asked them to organize round-ups, the leaders of Vichy, intent on making their policies succeed, followed a predictable line.

From the very start the Nazi police suspected that Bousquet would not be likely to refuse them anything in this matter. In May, learning from Heydrich that the non-French Jews interned at Drancy would soon be deported, he asked whether the foreign Jews interned in the free zone might not be taken at the same time.[16] He seems to have been acting purely on his own initiative, with the idea of getting rid of a burden over which his predecessors had shown so little concern that they had allowed over 3000 people to die. His question reflected a state of mind that was certainly not uncommon. In February, the German consul in Vichy reckoned, after many conversations, that 'the French government would be happy to get rid of the Jews somehow, without attracting too much attention'.[17]

When the SS demanded the arrest of 22000 Jews in the Paris region, 40 per cent of whom were French, Bousquet announced that Pétain and Laval did not want the police involved, adding an assurance that 'the French side had nothing against the arrests in themselves'. It was just that their execution by the French police would be 'embarrassing' in Paris. When the SS were insistent, Bousquet fell back upon a replacement formula: the police would deliver the total demanded by arresting foreign Jews in both zones. He stressed 'that, for the French government, such action was altogether unprecedented and it was very conscious of the difficulties that would ensue'.[18]

The next day, in Vichy, Pétain and Laval ratified the arrangement. Laval told the Council of Ministers: 'We must distinguish between French Jews and the rubbish sent here by the Germans themselves. The German government's intention seems to be to create a Jewish state to the East of Europe. I would not feel dishonoured if I one day sent to that Jewish state the countless foreign Jews who are in France.'[19] The Germans had originally planned to deport only adults. At Laval's request, they agreed that children should be taken with their parents. It is not hard to guess the head of government's line of reasoning here: splitting up families would have upset public opinion, and besides the children would have been a burden on the state: if the Germans wanted them, they were welcome to them all.

In Paris the police under the direction of the SS organized a huge round-up on 16 and 17 July that resulted in the arrests of 12884 people. In the free zone, Bousquet was busy, handing over first the foreign Jews interned in the regime's death camps, then other foreign Jews caught in the round-ups. To complete the promised quota, he rescinded exemption rules that he himself had fixed and increased controls. Thanks to French cooperation, between July and September the Germans were able to send 33057 people to Auschwitz.[20] Never again were they to obtain such massive cooperation or such a high score.

No knife was being held to Vichy's throat. Without the cooperation of the police, the SS were paralysed. They would have thought twice before provoking a crisis over a matter that in no way advanced the war effort and would divide the occupation services. However, the French leaders were perfectly willing to get rid of the foreign Jews. After the war, Knochen declared: 'In the various discussions that I held with the French authorities, it always seemed to me that the settlement of the Jewish question was in fact recognized and accepted by them, particularly where foreign Jews were concerned.'[21] Even at the time, Laval and Bousquet had no compunction about admitting this. In a diplomatic circular on the deportations, Laval stated that what were involved were measures of 'national prophylaxy'.[22] Meanwhile, Bousquet told Pastor Boegner, who had come to protest, that 'whatever the outcome of the war, the Jewish problem will have to be resolved', adding that all he was concerned about were the French Jews, who would be subject to 'strict obligations' and 'limited rights'; and, he added, 'The present unpopularity of the government will in the future be one of its greatest titles to glory.'[23]

The Vichy leaders were concerned for the French Jews for reasons of public opinion, prestige and sovereignty. But they were not so anxious for them that they felt obliged at the outset to state their refusal on principle, let alone ask for assurances in exchange for their action against foreign Jews. On the contrary, Laval and Bousquet rapidly accepted the principle of denaturalization for some French Jews.[24] To make out any serious defence for Vichy, you would have to believe that this regime that claimed to distinguish between 'good' and 'bad' Frenchmen, to the point of relieving over 150000 people of their nationality, possessed some respect for citizenship – which they did not. Their leaders were not clear as to where to draw the line where the Jews were concerned. But they took it for granted that the existing line was not satisfactory. If the Reich had continued to sweep from victory to victory, it would have become clear exactly where Pétain and Laval would have called a halt when defining which Jews counted as 'good' French citizens: probably just a handful of people saved by roots that went back over several generations.

It is not clear how much they knew of the fate of the Jews. The gas chambers of Auschwitz were just beginning to function and there were rumours of massacres of Soviet Jews, but could they have been expected to imagine a project to exterminate all the Jews of Europe? Perhaps not, but it certainly was easy to imagine the appalling nature of the future reserved for a population deported like cattle in the middle of a war. Public opinion was instinctive: the sight of manhunts, mothers bludgeoned by rifle butts to separate them from their children, the terrified herds of people and the enforced deportations, all made a deep impression, leading some bishops in the free zone to protest publicly and the bishops as a body to make formal representations to Pétain. In early September, Laval took all this into account and applied the brakes. He let Oberg and Abetz know that, in view of his agreement to hand over foreign Jews and all French Jews naturalized later than 1933, they should make no fresh demands of him.[25]

Then, as later, Laval would have liked the handover of Jews to be repaid by concessions. According to Knochen, whereas Pétain limited himself to intervening in just a few particular cases, without ever protesting on principle, Laval placed the matter on a 'business footing' and tried to use it as a bargaining counter, being prepared to give way on the Jews so long as he could thereby win concessions that would advance his own policies. In joking vein, he would often say, 'Why do you not get the Jews to work? I will give you any number of Jews, but leave me the French workers.' But for the Nazis the point was not primarily to make the Jews work for them: it was to exterminate them. The Vichy leaders made their task easier because *raison d'état* was stiffened by ideological complicity. Exactly the same applied to the agreement on the police, which the Germans made tacitly dependent on the French handing over the Jews and which was thereupon immediately signed.

Vichy's complicity with the occupying power had already been manifested in its imperial, military and economic policies. It was now extended to the domain of internal politics, partly because Laval, reining back on the imperial and military levels, was forced to make use of whatever was left, and partly because the growing weakness of the regime nudged it into tightening links with Germany. By recognizing that it possessed among its own compatriots 'enemies in common' with the occupier, and by delivering up some of the Jews resident in its own territory, the French state demonstrated its ideological solidarity with Nazi Germany. By so doing, it also demonstrated how limited was the protection that it claimed to offer. The circle of those whom it was willing to sacrifice was widening: first the people of Alsace and Lorraine, then the communists, whoever resisted, foreign Jews, some French Jews, etc.

11

Puppet Vichy

On 8 November, Anglo-Saxon troops landed in Morocco and Algeria. In Vichy, the news came as a shock. Since Dieppe, it had been thought that another such expedition would not take place before the following spring. The state of mind in which the French leaders faced this trial is betrayed by Pétain's words, three weeks earlier, to Prince Rohan, the director of *Europaïsche Revue.* As usual, he produced a catalogue of wagers and hopes. Pétain was expecting a German victory in the East, but rather than a total victory a stabilization of the front that would make it possible to establish a solid line of defence. He hoped that this time England would be discouraged, and that a compromise peace would be concluded under the aegis of the United States. If not, France would become a battlefield; and that he wished to avoid at any price.

His hope was that Hitler would put the winter pause to good use, 'return to politics', and begin at least the provisional construction of Europe. He stressed that, in a Europe that had switched militarily into a defensive mode, France hoped to find a place that would spare it from becoming a war zone. 'In exchange for the restoration of its sovereignty', he declared, France was ready to assume a role of great importance to Europe – that of a 'barrage' against the West. Pétain, who spoke disparagingly of the offensive capabilities of the Anglo-Saxons, reminding his listeners that he knew what it was like to be in command of them and was confident of repelling them. If France could perform the role of a 'western barrage', nobody would be able to land. 'For his own part', he would gladly go to war against the English, with whom he had scores to settle, but not against the Americans.[1]

Pétain reckoned the outcome of the war to be uncertain and was still hoping for a settlement with Germany that would restore

France's sovereignty and at the same time smooth the way for the much heralded compromise peace. With France voluntarily becoming part of the new Europe – a Europe on the defensive, so as to become compromised with the Axis as little as possible – and taking on the role of a defensive shield, the Anglo-Saxons would be deterred from prolonging the conflict, and France would be the natural intermediary in a compromise peace. But of course, for this to happen, the adversaries involved would have to conceive their own interests in the same fashion. Clearly, Pétain was quite incapable of perceiving the inexpiable nature of this war and also of seeing that it was only fortuitous circumstances, stemming from British weakness and Hitler's lack of interest for the French empire, that had made it possible for Vichy to prolong the deluded hope that the 'square meadow' of France could be taken out of the conflict.

The landings in North Africa brought Vichy face to face with the question that its leaders had been turning over in their minds for several months: what could be done in order not to lose everything? On 6 November, when the Anglo-Saxon convoys were detected but before their destination was known (they were thought to be making for Dakar), Laval spoke in terms that indicated his embarrassment to someone who told the Germans what he had said. Of course, he wanted to avoid a war with the United States, but he also wanted to defend Dakar, and this he could not do without assistance. In an emergency, he would accept German troops, so as to avoid the free zone being occupied. How much simpler it would all be, he sighed, if there were only the English to fight.[2] Laval would have some skilful acrobatics to perform if he was to avoid war with the United States and still preserve the empire and the free zone, at the same time taking care to contrive an arrangement with Germany – something that he and Pétain still believed possible. Vichy was clearly at sea, refusing to admit defeat, yet ready to bend if it could thereby salvage anything at all.

The landings received the threatened reception. Pétain gave the order to fire at the assailants. French resistance crowned with success would be the ideal outcome. But even if hopeless, resistance was imperative in order to dissuade Germany from interfering in the empire and occupying the free zone. The Germans and the Italians were indeed worried and were urging Vichy to stand fast, meanwhile preparing a counter-attack for which they needed bases in the empire. On that same 8 November, Hitler asked whether France had resolved to fight with him, breaking off relations with the Anglo-Saxons and declaring war on them: if so, he would be prepared to 'overcome all obstacles' alongside France. In Vichy, the government limited itself to pointing out that, through their own action, the United States had themselves broken off diplomatic relations. It gave permission for Axis planes to use North African airspace, but did not give authorization for them to land.

Laval assured the German consul that he was perfectly prepared to declare war, but still had to convince Pétain. He would like to meet Hitler to settle this matter and clarify the future. It was patently clear that he was unwilling to commit himself on the vague say-so of the Nazi leader. On the other hand, firm assurances and a guarantee of the integrity of both the empire and metropolitan France would help to strengthen the morale of French troops and, if the worst came to the worst, would make it easier to accept German aid and salvage something in the event of North Africa being lost. Laval was clinging to the hope that the emergency afforded him a means of pressure, and that the resistance of Vichy's troops and its possession of the fleet would be enough to produce results. Hitler agreed to receive him on the following day, 9 November. His intention was simply to encourage French resistance and obtain facilities so as to launch the Axis response. Already, in the evening of the 8th, he had insisted that air bases at Constantine and in Tunisia be made available. Laval gave in: it was preferable to allow Germans into the empire than lose the free zone. Having set out with the intention of using the French troops' resistance as a bargaining counter, he now found himself faced with a grave set-back. Hitler had no intention of opening political negotiations. The turn of events in North Africa in itself was enough to deter him from doing so.

The landings caught Darlan in Algiers, at the bedside of his sick son. Faced with the superiority of the enemy's forces, the admiral authorized a local suspension of armed action, while hostilities continued elsewhere in conformity with Pétain's orders. Darlan's reaction was typical of a Vichy leader: he feared an armistice might lead to occupation of the free zone and was clinging to the hope that some good might come out of the situation. On the 9th he wrote to Pétain as follows: 'We must avoid requesting aid from Germany, unless it replaces the armistice situation by a different, more advantageous formula.'[3] These were also the sentiments of the Marshal and, of course, of Laval, then on his way to Munich. However, the following day Darlan gave way to pressure from the Americans and ordered a general cease-fire. He was promptly disowned by Pétain, who reiterated his order to resist. The admiral bowed his head and declared himself the prisoner of the Americans.

At this very moment, Laval was meeting Hitler and Ciano. The confusion surrounding the situation in North Africa was clearing. The fighting was dying down, negotiations were taking place, and French resistance was almost at an end. Hitler had by now decided to occupy the free zone; first, however, he wished to prise from his visitor an agreement that would allow him to set up a bridgehead in Tunisia. The meeting was brief and icy. Laval repeated his desire for a German victory, stressing his 'fanatical determination' to assist in the struggle against communism; he reiterated his wish to collaborate, speaking of a necessary series of stages in the commitment of France's limited military means. Above all, he begged for 'gestures', suggested more frequent meetings with German leaders and that Germany should give some guarantee, at least on the empire. Hitler, who was irritated, interrupted him and demanded authorization to use Tunisia. Step by step, Laval retreated, asking at the very least for a guarantee against possible Italian claims (the expression on Ciano's face can be imagined). In the end he gave in, but not without covering himself. All Germany had to do, he said, was deliver an ultimatum. Vichy would accept it, merely registering a formal protest, which could be sorted out between the two governments.[4]

Hitler immediately launched his preparations for a German intervention in North Africa, then ordered the occupation of the free zone for the following morning. At dawn, Abetz went to wake Laval with the news. According to what he told Benoist-Méchin two days later, Laval was upset but then put a good face on it, saying, 'Those Jews on the Côte d'Azur are in for a nasty surprise!'[5] Certainly some people would be worse off than he. Still, he was returning empty-handed, having let the Axis troops into Tunis and now he had lost the free zone too.

Pétain was informed by letter, by Hitler who on this occasion managed to find a few words to soften the blow. The occupation was simply a precaution, he said; it did not end the armistice or in any way affect Vichy's sovereignty, and it would be lifted as soon as circumstances permitted. Pétain had no intention of opening fire on the Germans, as he had upon the Anglo-Saxons, nor did he intend to leave metropolitan France, despite the advice of his entourage, nor was he even going to cancel his order to resist in North Africa. The armistice army, with arms sloped, stood idly by, watching the arrival of the Germans. Pétain did read out a letter of protest to von Rundstedt, but hastened to add that he was only doing so as a sop to public opinion. Hitler's letter was not that of an enemy, he declared. A German diplomat present at this interview thought it noteworthy that the two marshals exchanged a cordial handshake at the beginning and the end of the meeting.[6] Pétain seized the chance to request that the Toulon base, where the fleet was moored, should remain in French hands – a last vestige of the free zone, as it were. Hitler and Mussolini consented to this in exchange for a promise from the chiefs of the base to the effect that they would take no action against the Germans and would defend themselves against any Gaullist or Anglo-Saxon attack.

Meanwhile, North Africa had slipped through Vichy's fingers. Learning that the Germans had crossed the demarcation line, Darlan decided to regain his freedom. After an abortive attempt to neutralize North Africa, he rallied to the Americans, who needed French help to repel the Axis advance in Tunisia and, in return for this, allowed the admiral to remain in charge of the empire. Pétain stripped him of all responsibilities and repeated his order to resist 'the Anglo-Saxon aggression', at the same time urging no opposition to the Axis troops in Tunisia.[7] There was no more talk of defending the Empire against 'all comers'.

Laval returned from Munich to a confused and tense situation. Pétain was being pushed to and fro by contrary influences. The collaborationist extremists, in Paris and in Vichy, were vociferous. They had got wind of Hitler's proposal of 8 November, which Abetz represented to them as an offer of alliance, and they violently condemned Laval for not having agreed to it with alacrity. All their factions were now united in calling for war against the Allies, a government reshuffle in their favour, and the despatch of a unit of volunteers to reconquer North Africa. Abetz, for his part, was manoeuvring for an unequivocal stand, believing that it would have a mollifying effect upon the Führer. On 15 November, the question of a declaration of war against the Anglo-Saxons was the subject of an exchange of views between Laval and his ministers. A minority, with Barthélémy as its spokesman, warned against the possible double consequence of generalized dissidence and civil war.[8] The majority, as in January, were in favour of aiming for a conversation with Hitler that would make it possible to clarify the alleged offer of an alliance. 'France would accept the Führer's proposal on two conditions: 1) that its sovereignty would be formally recognized; 2) that the Axis governments would maintain France's power both in Europe and in the empire. France should now in general no longer be treated as a defeated country but as an ally. To soften up public opinion, a precondition would be to obtain serious amelioration in the status of prisoners.[9]

Laval immediately communicated this news to the Germans, speaking of a 'reversal of alliances'.[10] The fact is that he was anxious to re-enter a summit discussion, respond to the pressure of the extremists, and obtain new powers from Pétain.[11] As it turned out, there was no declaration of war, and Laval acquired authority such as he had never had before and that was no longer counterbalanced by the presence of Darlan. Pétain delegated all powers to him and made him his successor if he himself became incapacitated, but imposed certain conditions. Laval had to promise not to commit France to a war, guarantee the safety of the people of Alsace-Lorraine and political detainees, and respect the country's spiritual traditions. Pétain appeared quite oblivious of the fact that he himself had signally failed in the implementation of this very programme. On 19 November, he announced the change to the French people: 'I remain your guide. You have only one duty: to obey. You have only one government: the one that I have empowered to govern. You have only one country: the one that I embody, France.'[12]

Meanwhile, the Axis powers were landing in Tunisia. Laval was keen to make it clear that he wished to defend what remained of the empire. He wanted to be present if or when the Allies were kicked out of North Africa. The Germans were to hold out in Tunisia for six months and this encouraged many hopes in Vichy. Laval was, as always, trying to obtain a territorial guarantee. So, to ensure a trouble-free landing for the Germans, he despatched Admiral Platon, an ardent collaborationist, to Tunisia. He supported the creation of an African Legion without, however, wishing to implicate the state officially: entering the war against the Anglo-Saxons was out of the question. On 22 November, he told Hitler that he was placing the Mediterranean merchant fleet at his disposal. He also informed him that he wished to make a contribution to the struggle against bolshevism and the reconquest of North Africa, and would like to discuss this with him and also, in particular, talk about a declaration regarding the maintenance of France's position and all its 'colonial potential'.[13]

Hitler did eventually receive him, but only to spring some nasty new surprises on him. He was still keeping a wary eye on the fleet at Toulon and, not long after consenting to leave it under French jurisdiction, he gave orders to prepare to seize it, not because he wanted the fleet for himself – he intended to make a present of it to the Italians, a fact that speaks for itself – but in order to eliminate the last element of uncertainty. He took this opportunity also to disarm the armistice army, which was vegetating in its barracks. On the morning of 27 November, his troops carried out their double mission. As ordered, the army submitted and the fleet scuttled itself. Vichy's doggedly pursued policy to restore its military might, dearly paid for and never used except against the Anglo-Saxons, reached its logical conclusion in self-destruction. The policy of 'France for itself alone' had been indissociable from the politics of collaboration.

The day before this operation, Ribbentrop had written to Laval to tell him it was impending. In this way, he added humourlessly, France would be in a position to acquire more trustworthy troops who might enjoy a 'cameraderie in arms' with Germany. He also told Laval that Hitler would soon be receiving him. That was enough to get him to swallow anything. Hitler, for his part, wrote to Pétain. It was a less tactful letter than the previous one, but did end with an assurance of his desire for collaboration and an offer of aid for the reconquest of the empire.[14]

By 27 November 1942, Vichy no longer had a free zone, nor an army, nor a fleet, nor an empire, apart from Tunisia, now in the hands of the Axis powers, and Indochina, held by Japan. Italy now occupied a substantial portion of metropolitan France: almost all the left bank of the Rhone, and Corsica, both regions that it had long been coveting. This was a sore irritation, made worse by the protection it afforded the Jews, in sharp contrast to the severity of the French state. On the German side, out of consideration for Vichy, the former free zone, now known as the southern zone, was declared to be not an occupied zone but a zone of operations. The organization chart of the German services became much more complicated. The MBF and the embassy had no powers in the southern zone; only the SS covered both zones. Militarily, full powers were exercised by the commander-in-chief of the western front (OB West), von Rundstedt. He installed in Lyons a commander of the France-Sud military region, with staff offices liaising with the prefectures, and a representative in Vichy, General von Neubronn. The armistice commissions were maintained despite there now being no French army. As for Hemmen, he became the French state's mentor in economic and financial matters; amid all this bustle, the occupation costs rose from 300 to 500 million Reichmarks a day. In principle, the Germans only had military rights in the zone of operations, where Vichy retained its administrative powers. But they soon extended their hold to cover every sector of public life.

The French state no longer held any of the trump cards upon which its politics of collaboration had been founded. It had become a fiction maintained by the wish of Hitler, who reckoned it 'clever' to keep on a Pétain government, as a kind of ghost, as he put it, to be pumped up from time to time by Laval, when it became completely deflated.[15] From the Germans' point of view, the disadvantages of the French state disappearing altogether were obvious. They would themselves have to administrate the country, and they lacked the personnel to do so. Furthermore, France would reunite against them, whereas Vichy kept the country divided and provided a target for some of the criticisms that would otherwise have come their way.[16]

For Pétain and Laval, a fiction was better than nothing at all, once they had turned their backs on all the other choices opened up by the events of November: namely, to leave metropolitan France and re-enter the war; to resign and be placed under house arrest; or to become a purely 'Red Cross' government that restricted its efforts to limiting the hardships of the occupation. Instead, they continued on the same track as before: rank, however insubstantial, was still worth striving for; sovereignty, which had virtually disappeared, seemed more desirable than ever; and as for the preservation of the regime, this was now their primary concern. In the summer of 1940, Pétain had declared that he would never abandon his compatriots, even under total occupation. Now he was as good as his word; but was he still a protector? Though he claimed to embody the nation, he refused to recognize the error of his policies and to give up his reforms so long as the course of the war still left him a few last hopes. Efforts to recuperate French sovereignty and to preserve the regime continued unflaggingly, but meanwhile the Milice and the STO rendered any claims of a protective rule completely hollow.

Laval had requested another interview with Hitler, justifying this on the grounds of the full powers he had just received and his desire that they should reach agreement as to how these should be deployed. His main preoccupation was to stabilize the enfeebled regime by obtaining concessions to soften up public opinion and freedom of action in internal politics, and by recuperating at least a few of the attributes of state sovereignty. As he was to explain to Ribbentrop, if he was seen to be simply a stooge of the Reich, his policies of collaboration would be ineffective.[17] On the score of alleviations, he was hoping that total occupation would at least wipe out the demarcation line and make it possible to re-establish the administrative unity of the country. He pressed for the prisoners to become civilian workers, the occupation costs to be kept at the earlier level, and for quotas of workers to be reduced in exchange for France producing double the quantity of munitions.

In internal politics, he wanted to impose censorship throughout the country and, above all, to eliminate competition from the parties in Paris and, in particular, defuse the challenge of Doriot, who was still launching bitter attacks against him. He would do so by gathering all factions into a single party, served by a militia and placed under his own direction. This was an idea very close to his heart and Abetz, who supported it, even suggested to his superiors that the policy of division pursued in the past should now be abandoned. It was a suggestion that got him recalled to Berlin for a year.[18] Laval also wanted an army. Pétain, too, was particularly anxious to acquire one, explaining to von Rundstedt that it was necessary both for the affirmation of French sovereignty and also for the success of Franco-German collaboration, to which he declared himself still committed.[19] Laval wanted there to be seen to be a French presence in North Africa, and asked for authorization for teams of volunteers, including a few officers and members of the SOL, to carry out operations of subversion and sabotage in the territories under Anglo-Saxon control.[20] Finally, he wanted to develop the African Phalange into the instrument of French participation in the reconquest of the empire, while still avoiding any official commitment. In short, he was suggesting a new deal: the German occupation to be restricted to the military domain in exchange for more help from the French administration, particularly in the maintenance of order, more assistance in the economic domain, and a symbolic French military presence in the struggle against the USSR and the Anglo-Saxons.

The meeting with Hitler took place on 19 December; it was the second in five weeks. Times of misfortune certainly seemed propitious for meetings with the Reich's leader, who wanted to 'reinflate' the French so as to get them through this bad patch. First Laval saw Ribbentrop, to whom he showed his list of desiderata, stressing the need for freedom of action in internal politics. He declared that he wanted to bring the French system into line with that of Germany and Italy. When received by Hitler, in the presence of Ciano, Göring, Ribbentrop and Abetz, he repeated his pleas, declaring his 'great admiration' for the leaders of the Axis. Hitler expressed distrust of France but personal confidence in Laval. However, an assassination attempt or a 13 December can happen so quickly! Prudence was called for, and Laval would be judged according to his actions.[21]

Laval seemed quite pleased with the interview. According to Barthélémy, he greatly valued Hitler's 'personal confidence'. 'This was a new departure. France had already been given one chance. Now it was being given another.'[22] Disappointment followed about ten days later. Not one of his demands was accepted, not even that the demarcation line be suppressed, although a little later it was somewhat relaxed. The Germans were ready to examine proposals concerning a new army and the African Phalange. But they refused to dissolve the Paris factions and forbade the creation of a single party. Hitler was not prepared to renounce his policy of division.[23]

Laval reacted bitterly to this decision, even called it a 'political defeat'. He was yearning to dissolve Doriot's party, yet was being set on the very same footing! He let it be known that if he could not suppress the Paris factions, he preferred to give up the idea of a single party.[24] However, he did not renounce his plan for an internal security force. A few days later, the Milice was created, by detaching the SOL from the Légion des Combattants. Laval now had an instrument to wield against the extremists in Paris. He calmed down Darnand, who was threatening to elude his control. In his resolve to defend the regime, he was united with Pétain. On 5 January 1943, the Marshal said of the SOL: 'Today, together with the police, they are the only organized force capable of maintaining order. If they did not exist, reason would dictate they be created, to bar the way to the hidden and evil forces that seek to destroy us.'[25]

In early 1943, Laval submitted his military proposals to von Rundstedt, writing as follows: 'The situation of the country indicates that we should plan for not just police measures to maintain order throughout the territory but veritable war operations designed to restore order wherever disturbances occur, particularly at the rear of German–Italian troop operations along the Mediterranean and Atlantic coasts.' Laval wanted to increase the numbers of the mobile guard from 6000 to 25000 men, then turn this into the core of a new army. He also requested reinforcements to guard communications and for anti-aircraft defence; and, finally, that an African Phalange

18000 strong be set up under the leadership of Darnand, to represent France's 'initial' participation in the reconquest of North Africa. In all, these armed forces would comprise about 50000 men.[26] The Germans responded by conceding a few reinforcements, where it was in their own interests to do so, such as for anti-aircraft defence against the Anglo-Saxons and for the mobile guard to put down resistance. As to the African Phalange, on Hitler's instructions, they prevaricated. Laval did not persist: recruitment had mustered barely 1500 volunteers.[27] However, they did grant Laval's request to recreate an army, by authorizing the formation of one regiment, the 1st regiment of France, as Pétain dubbed it. It was six months before this unit received a single weapon, as Laval had turned down the German armaments offered to him.[28]

The Germans' concessions came in dribs and drabs, but their demands continued to rain down thick and fast. Economic negotiations had eased a little since total occupation. But Laval had his hands full with Sauckel. Hardly had the first programme been met than he reappeared in Paris. Laval, who had declared that he could supply no more than 100000 men in the whole of 1943, now agreed to send 250000 by 15 March, but not without pressing for an improved rate of exchange for the *Relève*. He was obliged to content himself with a promise to convert 250000 prisoners into civilian workers once the contingent demanded was delivered. But it soon became apparent that the numbers promised could not be raised, and German pressure increased. On 16 February, the government promulgated the law on the STO (Service du Travail Obligatoire), mobilizing complete age-groups to be sent to Germany.

During the first half of 1943, Laval continued to plead for at least some commitment from Germany, failing a definite arrangement. On 9 March, he wrote to Hitler to remind him of all the efforts that France had agreed to make. He acknowledged that France had to pay for its defeat, and in this connection mentioned by name Alsace-Lorraine and Tunisia; he was also prepared to accept a customs union and a lasting German military presence on the Atlantic coast. But he did want the Axis to make a public declaration promising to make room for his country in the new Europe, in a position that would do justice to its continental and imperial past.[29] Once more, but for the last time, Hitler paid him some attention. In April, in Vichy, there were rumours of an imminent new 13 December. As these multiplied, Hitler alerted Pétain by letter. For good measure, he then received the head of government on 29 April. Laval pleaded for a United States of Europe, cooperation being preferable to constraint, and emphasized the need for a promise with respect to the future. Hitler snapped that he was not about to make France any presents or allow it to sit back placidly awaiting the end of the war. A stream of reproaches then followed. Laval left, downcast and disillusioned.[30]

The clouds were gathering all about him. Public opinion had definitively turned its back on him, the administration was faltering, resistance growing. The men of Paris continued their agitation; Darnand made advances to them and sought the support of the SS. Pétain's entourage, a seething nest of plotters, were drawing up plans for the compromise peace, that fleeting flash in the night, and all of these included the sacking of the head of government. In the summer, there was a swing in the fortunes of war. On the eastern front, the Soviets began their advance. In the West, in July, the Allies invaded Sicily and Mussolini was overthrown. In September, Italy capitulated; Corsica was liberated soon afterwards. A great wind of hope swept through Europe, and the departures for forced labour dried up.

Laval was sensitive to these changes. In August, when Sauckel came to demand 500000 men, he refused them, which suited Speer, who favoured leaving the French to work in their own country. Laval also reined in on the persecution of the Jews. Having signed the draft of a law that denaturalized French Jews from 1932 on, then agreed to alter that date to 1927, then also to widen the circle to include the spouses and descendants of those naturalized, even if these were originally of French nationality, on the day that Mussolini was toppled, he stopped the law from being promulgated. He continued to let the Germans use his police to arrest foreign Jews. But now he asked that, in exchange, French Jews be spared. Hence his irritation with the Italians, who were protecting 15 000 foreign Jews in their zone, and his complaints to the Germans, urging them to get them moved. He was all for straining relations between Germany and Italy; but above all, he wanted to use those foreign Jews to satisfy German demands.

The military turning point of 1943 instilled prudence. It did not lead Vichy to switch camps, or even to change course. Pétain and Laval did not swing over into the allied camp, as the Italian Badoglio did. Nor did they set about playing a double game, as most of Germany's Balkan allies did. Nor did they follow the example of the king of Denmark who, in August, suspended his functions. All the same, they were thinking of the future and of the transition to the liberation, which now seemed simply a matter of time. De Gaulle, recognized by the internal resistance, made a daunting challenge for legitimacy, sanctioned, in November in Algiers, by a meeting of the provisional consultative Assembly. Laval and Pétain were both separately meditating upon ways of updating their tactics that might enable them to face up to this challenge and trump the Gaullists. Having seen the Americans make deals first with Darlan, then with Badoglio, they felt there might still be hope for them. Paradoxically, the rush towards a republic resulted in a militia state.

Laval was the first to make a move. In November, he told the Germans that he wished to reshuffle the government, bring in some parliamentary representatives, and shift the regime in the direction of a republic. Pétain, meanwhile, who was, as a result of Hitler's veto, prevented from sacking Laval, decided to manoeuvre on his own particular ground, that of the constitution and the succession. Pressed by faithful followers of his, such as Auphan and Bouthillier, he grudgingly consented to alter the constitution plan that he had been tinkering about with for years, by paring away its authoritarian aspects and making room for universal suffrage. As for the succession, he decided in November to announce in a speech broadcast on the radio that this would be decided by the National Assembly, should he die before the new constitution came into force. When the Germans heard of this, they banned the broadcast. Pétain's reaction was to suspend his activities as head of state.

Ribbentrop sent Abetz back to his post to sort the matter out. In future, all changes to the law would have to be submitted for German approval. Laval was to reshuffle his cabinet in such a way as to guarantee collaboration. Men who could be trusted must be brought into the administration. The Germans considered the possibility of Pétain resigning with detachment and told him so, while reckoning it preferable to keep him in office. The head of state, who seemed annoyed above all at Berlin having made him wait for a response to his gesture, gradually gave way. On 5 December he announced that he was resuming office. At the end of the month he capitulated on the principle of a ministerial reshuffle, leaving its form to the discretion of Laval. Abetz had to tussle with Laval, who was no keener than Pétain on introducing extremists into the government. He ended up by accepting Henriot as Minister of Information and making Darnand responsible for the maintenance of order in place of Bousquet, who had prudently been beating a retreat ever since the autumn. The matter of Déat took rather longer, as Laval at first tried to confine him to a post of secondary importance. In March, Déat entered the government as Minister of Labour, in which capacity he was also responsible for the STO.[31]

With the envisaged return of the National Assembly, the regime came full circle, its failure patently clear. Even its leaders now doubted whether it could survive: the last of their objectives thus evaporated. But they failed to heed their doubts, and that disparity between their tattered convictions and the blanket protection that they extended to their hardening politics made their responsibility all the graver. Clinging to the notion of a miraculous compromise peace – having hoped that Germany's victory would not be absolute, they were now hoping that its defeat would not be total – they were above all determined to hang on to power. The maintenance of order was to them both a value and a principle of government. In the circumstances of the moment, it provided a guarantee of short-term survival. It remained the only basis for hope of a peaceful transition in the event of a successful invasion, since it provided them with a trump card for negotiation when faced with the returning *émigrés*. That was the last hope remaining to comfort Pétain, who still retained a semblance of popularity and an aura of respect.

At the beginning of 1944, Vichy finally entered upon the last home stretch. Its leaders were more or less without great expectations, but also without courage. They would have preferred a peaceful transition; they supported a policy for civil war. They wanted to distance themselves from the worst aspects of the occupier; they now allowed their name to confer legitimacy upon the most collaborationist team in the regime's history, lending their support to the Milice, urging it on and setting it an example. Spurred on by the extremists and a prisoner of his own politics, Laval donned the harness once again, as if he could see no alternative to rushing forwards, like Déat and Darnand. He accepted further demands from Sauckel and extended the requisitioning for labour to new categories. He hardened sanctions, going so far as the death penalty for officials who 'sabotaged' government policy. He turned over to the Germans prefectorial lists of Jews, French ones among them, and set his police to carry out arrests that no longer made any distinctions of nationality – in Bordeaux and Poitiers, for example – with the result that several thousand compatriots were delivered up to the Germans.[32]

Since 1942, collaboration had been whittled down to the sphere of internal politics. The trump negotiating card had once been a military force too dangerous to use, which had then ceased to exist. Now Vichy's trump cards were of a purely internal nature: men, Jews, and, increasingly, the maintenance of order, which protected the regime and even lent it a little weight when it came to dealing with the Germans. After tirelessly offering to act as the shield of Nazi Europe against the Anglo-Saxons, Vichy had become a shield for the Germans on French soil, and above all a shield for its leaders.

PART II

Accommodations

The occupation did not just bring into conflict the official negotiators of the two states, each with its own calculations, interests and trump cards. It also brought the invaders and the invaded society face to face. Here, the negotiating table was replaced by multiple points of contact, involving chance meetings as well as professional relations that had been initiated by one side or the other. There were many of these points of contact because French society was highly differentiated and its members – whether as groups or as individuals – were accustomed to defending their own interests, and also because the occupying power itself was pursuing a differentiated policy that combined incitement and solicitation as well as exploitation, repression and persecution. Even without the Vichy regime, French society would have had to confront this situation. The existence and politics of the French state simply stimulated a process of adaptation impelled by autonomous and, so to speak, spontaneous reflexes.

Between 1940 and 1942, amid more or less general dispiritedness, quite a number of compromises were reached. Through their attitude or their behaviour, many French people went half-way or even all the way to meet the occupying power and its policies. They did so without necessarily looking beyond to a political *entente,* and many, deep inside, must have been torn by mixed feelings or contradictory opinions. Four motives prompted such a movement: a sense of constraint, material self-interest, personal compliance and ideological connivance. Self-interest was the strongest of these; it was quite often tinged with ideological sympathy and combined with some compliance towards the conqueror. The constraint was seldom physical, usually more a matter of intimida-tion that fostered a diffuse fear in those under occupation, inclining them to avoid complications by behaving in an anticipatory fashion. The Jewish population, however, represents a different case. Here, the occupier did apply direct unequivocal constraint, and this gives the problem of accommodating behaviour a particularly dramatic aspect and creates a quite different situation. The Jewish 'notables' who agreed to direct the Union générale des Israélites de France and to take care of fellow Jews who were the victims of discrimination, despoiliation and proletarianization and were threatened with deportation, were faced with extremely painful choices and did not always make the right decisions. But it was hard to move all in one go beyond certain mental horizons and to take in the full extent of the danger. In any event, whatever they did they were not moved by subservience and certainly not by any ideological connivance.

Some accommodations resulted from the choices made by individuals, but in the case of associations and institutions they were a collective matter. Faced with the occupier, French people tended to behave as they did in social life, that is to say prompted by their habits, their mental attitudes and the force or lack of force of their national reflexes – which for some had been eroded by hard social conditions – and by the result of their weighing that national reflex against the need to protect their own personal interests. Furthermore, not all were hard pressed to the same extent by the politics of the occupier: defiance involved different things in different quarters, whether it was a matter of protecting oneself or protecting an institution, of responding to pressure or taking positive action to advance particular interests. However, the problem was always the same: namely, how far to go. In the next few chapters, we shall be examining the logic of this accommodation on the part of society, by cutting a series of sections through it. Not that they will exhaust the rich diversity of situations and choices, but they may enable us to understand how a host of coinciding interests, many of them limited and no more than occasional, produced the grey moral texture of those years, furthering the policies of the occupier and making life for certain of the occupied considerably easier.

12

Public opinion

BERNANOS, who had spent the war in Brazil, wrote after his return to France: 'If one could . . . plot a graph of the chances of an allied victory precisely, month by month, between 1940 and 1945, one would notice that, through a curious application of the old principle of elementary physics, that of communicating vessels, it coincided perfectly with the curve of the increasing numbers supporting a hypothetical Victory Party, first for a German victory, then for an allied victory.'[1] But this pamphleteer, who had penned a moral portrait of Vichy with such inspired violence, was mistaken about the attitude of most of his compatriots if he really thought them so anxious to be on the right side and so prompt to switch camps in consequence. His representation is close to another that is even more widely known, that of the metamorphosis of forty million Pétainists into forty million Gaullists. Neither does justice to French public opinion on collaboration. One should not only take account of its broad tendencies and how they evolved, but also understand their cohesion and internal force, as well as remembering the waverings and mobility of people's minds. As Claude Mauriac correctly observed, 'What French person would be capable of recognizing everything he or she thought and said (let alone did) under the occupation?'[2]

Dictatorships are always curious to discover the state of mind of the people that they gag. Vichy and the occupier were constantly monitoring the pulse of the French people. The German authorities had at their disposal the network of Kommandaturen and Propaganda-Staffeln, the antennae of the SD and the Abwehr, and the Wehrmacht armament service (the Wi., Rü.-Stab). They could also keep an eye on the free zone through the control commissions that went on their rounds to ensure that the armistice terms were being respected. Only the embassy was short of eyes and ears. In order not to be left out, it created an investigation service, employing Frenchmen who had manifested an interest in its propaganda material. In the summer of 1942, it had at its disposal 948 correspondents, 348 of whom were 'tried and tested collaborationists', who filled in forty-three questionnaires for it.[3] As for the French government, it possessed an administration that kept it minutely informed. In the free zone, where it had freedom of movement, it went so far as to poke its nose into private correspondence. Military men dispensed with their honour and listened in to telephone conversations, intercepted telegrams, and each week ploughed their way through several hundred thousand letters. This provided them with material on which to base syntheses that reflected in equal measure their desire to give an accurate account and their fear of causing displeasure.[4]

A cross-section of these sources shows, beyond any doubt, that the vacillation provoked in 1940 by the shock of defeat and the correct bearing of the Germans did not outlast the autumn, with its combination of British resistance, the aggravations of the occupation, and the prospect of a trying winter. From that moment on most of the population wanted victory for England and manifested towards collaboration sentiments that ranged from scepticism to hostility. From mid-1941 on, the German attack on the USSR, followed by the hostage executions, increased both the diffusion and the strength of that tendency. In 1942 the *Relève* and the allied landings in North Africa discredited collaboration definitively. Even the English bombing raids, which took their toll of more and more victims, did not reverse public opinion.

That is not really surprising. The conditions that played against Vichy were overwhelmingly unfavourable. Germany's image, which was riddled with negative clichés and prejudices, even if the early days of the occupation undermined these a little, faced a bulwark of negative tradition. At its foot, the policies of repression and persecution of the occupying power soon created a moat of hatred. It is true that the assassinations perpetrated by the communists were met, in the summer of 1941, by quasi-general disapproval; but the savagery of the ensuing repression soon changed attitudes. On top of all this was economic exploitation on a scale that exceeded all expectations. It was designed to impoverish the entire population and did indeed gradually come to affect even those who had at first managed to elude it.

The occupiers squeezed the country like a lemon and could only resort to propaganda to attempt to persuade the French that it was all for their own good. They did so with the greatest energy, turning out brochures, tracts and posters by the million, flooding the press and cinemas with images fabricated with care and sometimes with considerable talent. The embassy itself, for whom propaganda was certainly not the prime mission, distributed over 17 million different brochures, 10 million tracts, and 400000 copies of twenty-three different posters in the space of two years,[5] as well as launching itself into the production of films and plays and constructing a publications empire that eventually came to monopolize almost half the periodicals of Paris.[6]

Results did not measure up to all these efforts and such lavish expenditure. The occupiers were obliged to recognize the supremacy of the English and Gaullist propaganda. All they could do was try to limit its influence and dissuade the French from acting on their sympathies. So long as the German armies were sweeping all before them, Goebbels' propaganda machine was able to convey an image of power and destruction impressive enough to paralyse attempts at active resistance.[7]

As for the Vichy regime, it too had set up a considerable apparatus, under the direction of Marion. It was partly inspired by the propaganda of the conqueror and it suffered the same discredit.[8] The BBC broadcasts and the diffusion of rumours hostile to the occupier brought French people together and separated them from the occupiers and likewise from their government.

It was not long before the majority of French people rejected collaboration, but with significant variations from one zone to another. Let us leave aside Alsace and Lorraine, whose inhabitants were subjected to the reality of annexation and germanization. There, a powerful sense of abandonment prevailed, and the absence of public protests from Vichy was interpreted as acquiescence before a *fait accompli*. In the prohibited zone, the rejection of collaboration was both massive and immediate. Memories of the earlier occupation were revived by the measures – without equivalent elsewhere – that were taken there in the very first months: large numbers of hostages were taken; men were seized in the streets for deportation to the Reich and, in one locality, even women were rounded up, for gynaecological examinations. The reaction of public opinion to the last of these measures was so strong that the Germans discontinued such antiquated practices inherited from the previous occupation.[9] Here too, annexation seemed to loom, sharpening the sense of being ill defended by Vichy, whose political inclinations had nothing to recommend them to this bastion of socialism and trade unionism. Furthermore, the image of the English was traditionally favourable here, so that by and large everything combined to incline the population to condemn the armistice. Pétainism was to be found among the bourgeoisie, but in most cases it was accompanied by rejection of its foreign policies.

In the occupied zone, the rejection of collaboration was less immediate, but spread quite rapidly. In a report produced in September 1940, the military of the Wehrmacht's armaments service (the Wi. Rü.-Stab.) expressed a succinct but general and at the same time quite subtle judgement: 'The population is on the whole calm, occasionally welcoming, but most of the time reserved and to some extent positively hostile.'[10] As for the government, it was for the most part ignored, criticized or scorned. It was a long way away, appeared to be impotent, and was all for collaboration. At the end of 1940, the postal censorship summarized the situation as follows: 'For the people of the occupied zone, the very mention of the word collaboration evokes an image of the people of Alsace and Lorraine ejected from their homes and another, no less horrible, of impending famine.'[11] Pétain was spared, however, and continued to enjoy a degree of respect that was certainly denied to Laval. However, by the spring of 1941, the postal censorship was admitting that public opinion in the occupied zone was 'hardly at all favourable' to Vichy, and even that the 'aura' of the Marshal did not penetrate very far.[12]

In the free zone, opinion was divided over collaboration: rejection was neither general nor immediate. The inhabitants were more exposed to Vichy's propaganda, more affected by the popularity of Pétain who, they believed, would protect them against an undesirable extension of the occupation. His national revolution, which met with 'almost total indifference',[13] had little to do with his popularity; the regime stood high in public opinion because it spared them the presence of the Germans, was trying to improve relations between the two zones and also to get the prisoners repatriated.

Despite anglophilia, which increased, far more of the population than in the occupied zone followed the Marshal and continued to do so for longer,[14] albeit somewhat reluctantly. Thanks to Pétain's speech, Montoire left people feeling a mixture of hope and anxiety, rather than a general revulsion. The support for Vichy was nevertheless fragile and was accompanied by widespread scepticism. 'This collaboration with Germany, which many reckon to be impossible anyway ("the Boches are still the Boches, after all"), does not exclude general hope for an English victory, as only this can deliver France from the grip of the conqueror.'[15] At the end of the year, trust in Pétain increased, even in the occupied zone, with the sacking of Laval, which many interpreted as a check to collaboration and a sign of the profundity of the Marshal's thinking.

In the spring of 1941, the Paris negotiations, followed by the Syrian affair, to some extent dissipated illusions, at the same time sharpening opposed attitudes. A survey drew attention to 'the extremely grave repercussions that followed from collaboration, which created an increasingly deep division between supporters of this policy and opponents of it'.[16] Just as after Montoire, Pétain's speech, covering Darlan's meeting with Hitler in May 1941, was reassuring and encouraged a 'reasoned resignation' fed by the hope of concessions on the demarcation line and the prisoners'.[17] A turning point was reached with the German attack against the USSR, which was greeted with satisfaction by virtually everybody, some rejoicing at the destruction of communism, others at the weakening effect that this war might have upon the Germans, yet others for both those reasons at once. Although the effect of the first of these reactions was to give collaboration increased credibility, its appeal was still far weaker than the hope of Germany being defeated or exhausted, and both of the latter hypotheses were encouraged by the resistance put up by the Soviets. In August, surveys for the first time showed 'a noticeable fall in support for the policy of collaboration'.[18]

The German control commissions that operated in the free zone produced a similar picture of this development. In the previous autumn their members had noticed that anglophilia was growing, while support for the government was diminishing because of its external policies. At that time, they had encountered no hatred in their travels and seldom any insults.[19] In the summer of 1941, however, jeers came thick and fast, with young people yelling 'boches' or 'shits' at them.[20] They registered that there were many people who were expecting difficulties for the Germans in the East, and who were cheered by this. Vichy was coming in for more and more criticism; the government's standing in public opinion was 'low', and the Marshal himself was no longer spared.[21]

In Vichy, the change of atmosphere was noticed and prompted

Pétain to deliver his speech about 'the evil wind'. He thereby gave a leg up to the minority current of opinion that supported the national revolution, which thereafter hardened in its denunciation of those who opposed it. The situation continued to deteriorate none the less. 'The need for a policy of collaboration with Germany seems to be accepted by no more than quite a limited number of French people',[22] the second to last survey of the year reported. Pétain's position continued to weaken despite the fact that his prestige remained considerable and his stock rose from time to time, as after his speech of January 1942, in which he spoke of his 'semi-captivity'. In the spring of 1942, the control commissions observed that 'Down with Pétain' graffiti were no longer a rarity and that in many places his appearance on the cinema screen was no longer greeted with applause.[23]

Laval's return set off a new wave of doubts and speculation, in an atmosphere of reserve and distrust. But even at this date, part of public opinion remained unconvinced of the futility of all Vichy's efforts. However, it could not swallow Laval's speech. His wish for a German victory was greeted with 'intense emotion' and 'general stupefaction'.[24] In the autumn of 1942, the Vichy services recognized the failure of their official policies: 'In general, it is possible to detect in the attitude of those questioned the growing feeling that, all things considered, it would be better to adopt an attitude towards Germany that openly corresponds "to the wishes of the vast majority" of French people, even at the price of the risks involved, given that now the Reich "is in command in the free zone just as it is in the occupied zone". That solution would have the advantage of restoring the national unity that is compromised by the demarcation line.'[25] One month before the landings and Pétain's confirmation of his policies, many people had already come to the conclusion that there was no longer any justification for Vichy. Pétain's aura was, however, not totally dissipated. As a public figure, he continued to be respected to the bitter end by part of the population, which felt compassion for him and regarded him as a symbol of their suffering country. Meanwhile, a by no means negligible fraction, despite thinning ranks, continued to regard him as the country's leader and the emblem of a political struggle.

The majority tendency to reject collaboration left room for a current that favoured it, the importance of which, up until 1942, should not be discounted. Between September 1941 and May 1942, the postal censorship of the free zone read on average 300000 letters each week. The subject most frequently evoked – food supplies – concerned only 5 per cent of the letters: French people above all wrote about their families and their health. Depending on the weeks, between 2000 and 3500 letters (0.5 per cent to 1 per cent of the total) contained allusions to Pétain, the vast majority of them favourable. References to collaboration appeared in only 700 to 1000 letters (0.2 per cent to 0.3 per cent). Between 20 and 30 per cent of these were positively appreciative in 1941 and 25 per cent still were in April–May 1942.[26]

Although these figures cannot be claimed to rest on a representative sample, they do provide a rough indication that coincides with German estimates, which set rejection at 80 per cent. It does not seem too unreasonable to suggest that up until 1942 the current favouring collaboration concerned, on average, between one-quarter and one-fifth of the French people in the free zone, and between one-fifth and one-sixth of the country as a whole. This would, after all, amount to several million people, many more than the membership of the small collaborationist parties.

But to what, exactly, was that approval given? It would be naive to imagine that it was totally committed, coherent and continuous. Three major views of collaboration are detectable from the reports based on the Vichy censorship. The first was that of 'providential' collaboration. The defeat had revealed the enfeebled state of France; it provided a chance for reform accompanied by an *entente* with the conqueror. For some, the latter needed to be limited to political and diplomatic alignment; others went so far as to argue for a military alliance and co-belligerence against the Soviets or even against the Anglo-Saxons. Some reckoned that collaboration implied following the Nazi model, others simply that it was compatible with an authoritarian regime, as invented by France.

The second view of collaboration was of a 'realistic' variety: like it or not, German domination in Europe was there to stay. France had to adjust its politics if it wished to safeguard the future, beginning by defending its possessions against the Gaullists and the British. This position was frequently associated with the hope of a bloodless peace that would restore a dignified role to conquered France and procure it a favourable peace treaty with Germany, which seemed unlikely to be defeated. This was the major inspiration of Vichy's politics, but it existed alongside a current more influenced by the 'providential' view of collaboration (Benoist-Méchin, Marion, Bonnard, etc.). According to postal censorship, the second view (of realistic collaboration) was shared by some of the population. Thus, on 18 November 1941, a report ran as follows: 'People continue to be delighted that both the Germans and the Russians are suffering heavy losses. They are hoping that eventually France will act as an intermediary for a compromise peace.'[27]

The third view was of collaboration as an expedient: a policy accepted with suspicion and resignation, in the short term, in the hope of obtaining tangible alleviations to France's lot. Most French people did not believe, as Darlan did, that an English victory would be more costly for France than a German one. But they were not all confident of an English victory, and many feared what a lengthy war would cost them. Germany was not a trusted partner, but if a policy of accommodation could secure a few advantages, why not make the most of it? Just so long as the future was not compromised and, above all, France did not swing over into a war against the Anglo-Saxons.

It is patently clear that, out of these three views, support was strongest for the third, and weakest for the first, and that most French people tempted by Pétain's politics belonged to the third category. This fraction of the population followed the government, veering between hope, scepticism and resignation but prepared, in the last analysis, to allow themselves to be convinced. A synthesis of the reports of the prefects in the free zone, for November 1941, on the subject of collaboration, after noting that its supporters were still few in number, continued: 'On the whole, public opinion finds this policy repugnant; it will submit to it if forced to, considering it as a strictly provisional solution designed to play for time, to alleviate the weight of the occupation, and to obtain a number of immediate advantages (in particular the return of prisoners), but it will continue to hope for an Anglo-American victory.'[28] Vichy was aware that this was more or less the only remaining popular basis for its policies, and was all the more anxious to make them pay off.

The partisans of collaboration – if the word partisans can be used in conjunction with an attitude that was in many cases so soft, uncertain and lacking in confidence – seem to have been drawn mostly from the bourgeoisie and the middle classes, to judge from the scattered notations in the censorship reports. But they were also to be found amongst prisoners of war and their families, whom Vichy treated with considerable care. The postal censorship reports stress the Pétainism of these circles and their support for collaboration. In the autumn of 1941, one even stated that in the occupied zone support 'came solely from the families of prisoners of war'.[29] It still existed in November 1942, 'manifesting itself through their loyalty to the Marshal, the trust that most of them place in the head of government, and a quite general anglophobia'.[30] As for the prisoners still in the camps, their opinions were mixed: they were strongly attached to Pétain, but deeply divided over collaboration.[31] Repatriated prisoners, however, seem to have had a less equivocal attitude. According to the postal survey, 'a very large number of them support a policy of collaboration'.[32] The Germans' view of the situation was similar: they reckoned the liberated prisoners to be their best propaganda agents for collaboration.[33]

Vichy's politics had the support of no more than a minority, and even that was fragile, shaky and dwindling. One might have expected it to be altogether crushed by the majority opinion. However, rejection of collaboration was not necessarily either absolute or intransigent; and it certainly did not amount to a choice in favour of resistance. On the first of those two points, it seems legitimate to wonder whether, if the Germans had made more visible concessions, Vichy would not have been able to extend its basis and win over quite a few sceptics. That was certainly the hope of its leaders, possibly encouraged by the censorship reports, according to which if collaboration produced tangible results, it would rally the whole population.[34]

On the second point, it is worth pointing out that communicating vessels – to return to Bernanos' image – are hardly relevant where public opinion is concerned.[35] Rejection of collaboration and a distancing from Vichy did not increase the level of resistance – or only to a limited degree. Rather, they resulted in a degree of passivity that all observers found remarkable and which uncertainty about the future, the hardships of daily life, and the policies of both the French and the German authorities all did much to foster.

The most important thing to take into consideration is the uncertainty as to the outcome of the war. In the first year, that uncertainty was totally impenetrable and its effect was to make the French people literally huddle together for comfort. Most were praying for an English victory but can hardly have believed it likely, certainly not in the near future. Although that hope grew stronger as time passed, it was frequently dashed by the progress of the war. The excitement of the summer of 1941 and at the end of the year collapsed heavily at the beginning of 1942, then gave way to morose depression, as the German offensive in the East revived the disappointment felt at the inaction or reverses of the Allies. Even strong lucid minds, as well informed as was possible, went through crises of doubt up until the landings in North Africa.[36] A poignant example of the role of anticipation is supplied by the sudden collapse of the number of conscripted people departing for Germany, in the summer of 1943, as soon as Sicily had been taken by the Allies and Mussolini had fallen. In the first third of 1943 they numbered 179371; in the last three months, 12953.[37] Earlier most of those requisitioned obeyed orders; but later disobedience took over, as the turn of military events indicated that liberation was not far off. The ranks of the Maquis were swollen by young men who were then to face a testing winter. This 'average' reaction of public opinion provides the background against which to set the impressive courage of the tiny minority who had opted for resistance even in the first two years. To do so presupposed a quite unusual level of faith that does great credit to those men and women.

The trials of daily life were furthermore very real and, even as the military situation began, pitifully slowly, to evolve in the right direction, there were still no alleviations – in fact quite the reverse. When they spoke of the 'hard times' they were living through, French people restored full meaning to that over-used expression. What with frozen salaries and rising prices, real wages dropped by 37 per cent between 1938 and 1943 – and that is simply an average.[38] The weak and the disadvantaged were afflicted by penury that provoked growth problems amongst children, a higher death rate amongst the elderly, and a steep rise in accidents and sickness amongst workers, many of whom suffered from partial unemployment up until 1942.[39] On top of all this, virtually everywhere people had to endure painful separations, with families dispersed in different zones, prisoners of war held captive far away, and increasing numbers of displaced persons and refugees as a result of allied bombing raids on the Atlantic coast.

The existence of the Vichy regime compounded all these difficulties, for many considered it the legal, if not legitimate, government. For some people, the national revolution introduced confusion, hesitation on the score of the enemy, and doubt over priorities. Such approval as greeted Vichy's internal policies even led some of those who resisted right from the start, such as Frenay and General Cochet, to adopt acrobatic positions over Montoire.[40]

Pétain's popularity, even when it had eroded, militated against a rejection of collaboration and, even more, slowed down its translation into actions. A sense of lassitude in the face of the war that dragged on and on, and a longing for a speedy arrangement also encouraged vacillation among even those who definitely disapproved of collaboration.

Finally, the Germans, in their own fashion, also promoted passivity, in the first place through their victories, which encouraged the notion that accommodation was inevitable; then through their measures of repression, which became increasingly intransigent from the summer of 1941 onwards, and thereby underlined the perils of active opposition. In 1940 German military tribunals had condemned eight people to death; between January and September 1941 the figure was fifty-one; between September 1941 and March 1942, it jumped to 236, added to which, in that last period, hostage executions claimed 353 victims.[41] There was plenty to cow the French and they can hardly have derived much solace from comparing their lot to that of Central and Eastern Europe, if indeed they were even aware of it: in Serbia, in that same period between September 1941 and March 1942, 27905 people were executed, over 20000 of them by way of reprisals.[42] In France, reactions would certainly have been stronger if the Germans had continued to execute hostages selected from amongst the 'notables', as they had in the past. By executing Jews and communists instead, their aim – partly successful, it must be said – was to foster a certain complicit resignation. Amid all the repressive and exploitative aspects of its policies, it did leave some pockets of freedom, under surveillance of course, for example in the domain of culture and amusements, and these encouraged illusions of normality. It is interesting to speculate what would have happened if, as in Poland, schools, universities, cinemas, theatres and publishing houses had been closed down.

These conditions kept many French people cocooned right to the end. Rejection of occupation and collaboration existed alongside a desire simply to get through it all; for many people the phoney war lasted right through to 1944. Andrzej Bobkowski, a Polish *émigré*, who left an invaluable diary chronicling the occupation, noted in December 1940 that a factory cashier, hearing him talk of escape to England, retorted: 'One has to earn one's own little living, and that's all there is to it.'[43] It was an attitude that infuriated those who were resisting, sometimes to the point of despair. Guéhenno speaks of 'prostration' in February 1942, then, one year later, on the subject of obedience to the STO, declares: 'This entire country is by now nothing but a frightened protoplasm.' Finally, listening to the conversations of the pupils in his *lycée* in the spring of 1944, he comments: 'Still the same fear, the same rot. People are terrified. They are wary of everything, the Germans, the English, the Russians; all they can think about is "getting through" without coming to any harm; it is as if, to the great mass of this country, nothing matters except survival, at any price.'[44]

During the first two years at least, the attitude of the majority was as far removed from a firm, aggressive state of mind as was the attitude of the minority. So much was clear from the prudence and discretion shown by virtually everybody. In March 1941, Paulhan wrote: 'Have I told you that in the little bistro where I drink a coffee every morning in the company of five or six working men and women from the *quartier*, never the same ones, in all their thousands of complaints over three months I have never heard a single mention of the Germans. It's a matter of prudence, dignity, fear, perhaps a mixture of all three.'[45] General Doyen noted that a British victory was desired by the majority, but it was difficult to get any clear picture as people were so prudent. 'Those who favour Germany are not very proud of the fact anyway, and those who favour England are afraid of having their hopes dashed or fear to voice their opinion because of the possible consequences.'[46] In May 1942, Marc Bloch wrote to Lucien Febvre: 'One of the things that strikes me most today is how impossible it is for any of us to know what his closest neighbour is thinking and doing . . . One sometimes makes astonishing discoveries. I certainly have.'[47] Sometimes the motive for this prudence was a fear of being denounced, but often it was also a fear of being wrong or being labelled in public, so great was people's uncertainty and so persistent their confusion as to what was good or right, wise or opportune.

In the early days, collaboration was still simply an opinion that divided people. It disgusted many, but it was tolerated and one could agree to differ over it. In May 1941, Drieu sent his latest work (*Écrits de jeunesse*) to Guéhenno, dedicating it as follows: 'As a token of our perfect disagreement', which its recipient felt was 'rather nice of him'.[48] In February 1941, François Mauriac had written to Ramon Fernandez: 'Our political disagreements are as nothing to French people who drink from the same springs.'[49] One of the most notable effects of this atmosphere, more detectable in some circles than in others, was the tendency to hang back behind bolder spirits, keeping one's own counsel, so as not to stick one's neck out in the event of Germany losing the war, and at the same time keep a foot in the door in case it was victorious.

By mid-1941, differences of attitude were much sharper and references to the Dreyfus affair were frequent. The prefect of Finistère remarked in the autumn of 1941: 'We are back in the bad old days of the Dreyfus affair, with deep divisions even in families. People are classified as partisans either of collaboration or of General de Gaulle.'[50] And in December 1942 Claude Mauriac wrote: '"It's a new Dreyfus affair", my father told his brother Pierre, who was passing through Paris. They are themselves divided by such a chasm that they dare not talk to each other without extreme prudence.'[51]

As time passed, the reference to the Dreyfus affair lost its pertinence. Gradually, as the course of the war dissipated uncertainty and put a stop to the quarrels that this had occasioned, collaboration came to be regarded less and less as an opinion, and more and more as an act of treachery. By the summer of 1941, instead of looking back to the Dreyfus affair, people were already thinking in terms of punishment and purges. In July that year, Angelo Tasca, a socialist who had rallied to Vichy, noted with considerable alarm what he had heard from a Parisian contact: 'As soon as the Germans go, there will be deaths, many: thousands. Everyone is looking forward to the day when certain people will be torn to pieces.'[52] Such thinking was almost palpable at the end of the following month, when people learned of the assassination attempt against Laval and Déat. As Guéhenno noted, the people of Paris had 'great difficulty in concealing their joy', 'the joy of a horrifying hatred'. Paulhan had the same impression in a little bistro in the nineteenth *arrondissement*, where regulars, workers and unemployed men, were seized by a 'strange joy', deep and silent: 'I shall never forget that little old bookbinder who was literally *trembling* with joy, his normally wise countenance suddenly wild. That is how the Commune must have started, or at least been prepared for.'[53] The idea of retribution was everywhere. On 10 September 1941, Fernand-Laurent spoke to Jeanneney, the president of the Senate, of the need for a 'ministry of reprisals'.[54]

The summer of 1941 certainly marked a turning point, or rather the beginning of a turning point, one that developed gradually, not without reversals, and only reached its climax at the end of 1942. The atmosphere of those first two years, even then divided and polarized, with its undertow of silent hatred brewing and strengthening, but still crossed by many uncertainties, constituted the background to accommodations of many kinds.

13

The French and the Germans

IN THE part of the country that they held, the Germans stamped their mark upon the French landscape. They made their presence widely felt by being both seen and heard. Even when invisible, they invaded people's minds, even their dreams. The presence of the intruders, whether palpable or imagined, made it necessary for people to undergo a kind of apprenticeship in attitudes and modes of behaviour. The problem was forcefully and immediately posed whenever contacts were made, particularly when the occupier took the form of, not a compact military unit, but one individual clad in the enemy uniform. Not everyone could avoid such contacts. Some tolerated them, others accepted or even sought them. They were bound to occur in the context of the requisitioning of billets or of professional, social, sexual or romantic relations. In some cases the contact would be anonymous and indirect, as in the case of denunciations.

When it came to individual behaviour, faced with the Germans, the French were very much on their own. Memories of previous experiences where they existed, or, if they did not, some kind of instinct, sometimes prescribed a line of conduct. But when the occupier presented an attractive face, was he still to be treated in accordance with those ancestral reflexes? The politics of the new regime seemed to indicate that some kind of revision was in order, as did the vacillations of public opinion. The battle of representations that developed quite independently of any official intervention was symptomatic.

During the exodus, Léon Werth considered this question very carefully. He had been born in the Vosges, and remembered many stories from his childhood, such as the one heard many times over about an aunt for whom, in 1870, a German officer had arranged a meeting with her prisoner-husband. She had faced a dilemma of conscience: how should she thank him? With a discreet inclination of the head or by shaking his hand? In the event, she shook his hand, but thirty years later was still agonizing about it.[1] Werth watched as the first contacts took place, deploring those of his compatriots who did not feel 'that with each contact made with the German conqueror some measure, however small, of our dignity is at stake'.[2] That was the key word: dignity. The right thing to do was submit, without grovelling, not overstep a constrained obedience such as is due to any illegitimate authority: 'Whether to accept anything at all that the enemy cannot force upon you needs to be thought about very carefully.' But what if the enemy was insisting upon nothing and seemed friendly? Werth himself experienced one uncomfortable dilemma of this kind with a non-commissioned officer who tried to repay him for his companionship with packets of tobacco; and another when the soldiers billeted on his farm offered them a concert of gramophone records. Werth tried to reconcile his position as a conquered Frenchman with a minimum of civility: 'We constitute two separate groups without hostility, but also without overlap.'[3]

The question of the correct attitude to adopt was a key symbolic issue with regard to both the resistance and the collaboration that were burgeoning. In a text published in one of the first issues of Drieu La Rochelle's *NRF*, Chardonne sanctioned an attitude that involved good-heartedness in unfortunate circumstances, when he approvingly described a scene that he swore to be true, in which a vine-grower in the Charente said to a German officer: 'I would prefer to have invited you . . . But I can't change the way that things are. Enjoy my cognac, I offer you it with no hard feelings.'[4] Here, the enemy was promoted to the status of a guest, tomorrow possibly that of a friend. Chardonne knew that this was not the behaviour generally expected. Under furious attack, he riposted by turning the argument of dignity upside down: 'That gesture of the peasant went beyond the tradition of dignity; it broke through the fatal chain of disasters.'[5]

From the point of view of resistance, what you needed to do was designate the enemy clearly and recreate a standard image of him that would render any correct behaviour on his part irrelevant, check any misplaced civility on yours and deter you from making out an individual beneath the uniform. The behaviour prescribed boiled down to erecting a wall between the French and the Germans.[6] As early as July 1940, Jean Texcier, a militant socialist, produced 'a little manual on dignity' entitled *Conseils à l'occupé*. He recommended acting 'correctly' but without initiating any moves in the direction of the occupiers; pretending not to understand their language; discouraging their attempts to enter into conversation in French; refusing to watch the enemy parading; and turning a deaf ear to propaganda, even when it used the French press and radio. It was a code of conduct designed to influence thoughts as well as actions: a dignified attitude should not be accompanied by 'facile resignation'. It reflected the atmosphere of the first summer of occupation: no hatred, no calls to armed resistance, a peaceful tone and a sense of humour which, however, in no way undermined firmness. Civility was acceptable: of course one responded when asked a question in French or requested for a light.[7] The advice given was aimed at people whose contacts with the occupier were purely accidental and personal.

In *Le Silence de la mer*, Vercors turned from the street to the intimacy of the home, and set the standards higher. The novel is about a man and his niece who have a German officer billeted on them. Werner von Ebrennac is a composer; he loves France and would like to believe in a future *entente*. Despite their troubled feelings of sympathy, the French retreat into silence. The message of the story is twofold. It stresses, first, the dignity of rejection, embodied in particular by the girl, who refuses relations of any kind with this man who is the very embodiment of the good Germany, the Germany of thinkers and musicians; secondly, the impossibility of collaboration: even if the occupier, as a person, possesses every good quality, he is a cog in a machine designed to destroy France. Vercors depicts an enemy misled by the power that he serves and driven to the point of despair when he realizes this.

The image of the Germans against which Vercors was battling was probably not very widespread even during the first two years. Nevertheless, like Texcier's manual, his novel was emblematic of a situation in which the occupier's image was blurred and the reaction of the occupied confused. It was tempting to allow oneself to be taken in by appearances, to treat the enemy, if not as a guest, at least as a fellow man meriting civility and consideration. Deep down beneath this, lay a powerful longing to return to normal and an individualistic cast of mind disposed to distinguish the man himself from the country he came from and the regime he served. As Merleau-Ponty wrote, after the war, 'We had to relearn all the puerile ways of behaving from which our education had weaned us, judge people from their clothes, respond rudely to their well-mannered orders, live for four years alongside them but not for a minute with them, and remember that, under their gaze, we were not men, but "Frenchmen".'[8]

The battle of representations was also, indeed mainly, fought out in the insubstantial sphere of stories and rumours, which it is not easy for a historian to trawl. In the summer of 1940, rumours were rife about a failed attempt to invade England and German corpses washed up by the tide or consumed in slicks of burning oil: natural elements were providing a rampart for the English that guaranteed their invincibility. Myths circulated about the occupiers too, making people uncertain what to think of them. One of these came to the ears of a puzzled Léautaud: 'They say (?) that on the day the Germans arrived, in the Place de L'Hôtel-de-Ville, a Parisienne (in other words, a lady) went up to an officer and offered him a rose. The officer cast it to the ground and stamped on it, saying: "Madame, you are a bad Frenchwoman".'[9] Here, the occupier was portrayed as teaching the French a salutory lesson, for they were forgetting themselves.

The psychoanalyst Marie Bonaparte registered the confusion of the summer. 'Amongst many of the defeated, aggressive hatred gave way to a meek and fascinated admiration for their conquerors.'[10] That winter she collected stories that testified to the mental struggle in which people engaged to contradict the Germans' famous 'correct' behaviour. 'A German officer was billeted in a lady's home. He was charming, very pleasant . . . Upon leaving, he bade the lady farewell and thanked her, then added with a charming smile: "Yes, I'm sorry to go, as I should have been happy to see you all dead!" '[11] Already there were other stories that also looked forward to the departure of the Germans: the worst was yet to come; it was important not to be deluded. 'A nurse took care of a German officer. He was grateful and wanted to give her a present; she refused it. So instead, he presented her with a piece of advice: if the German troops left Paris, she should hide all her loved ones, as the Germans had received orders to massacre all the French. Like it or not, they would be obliged to obey.'[12]

Such stories expressed a reaction against a partially positive image of the occupier that continued to circulate and that was revived by the lightning campaign in the Balkans in the spring of 1941.[13] Two years on, even the talk of the discipline and bearing of the German troops of the early days, now a series of clichés, was still not quite worn out or entirely proscribed, although it had a struggle to surface amid the general sea of criticisms. In the summer of 1942, Léautaud recorded a conversation with the head of production at the *NRF*. 'Like myself, he praised the physical cleanliness, clean clothing and polite manners of even the ordinary soldiers. In contrast, he cited the example of a French soldier on leave whom he had come across with his cap askew, his hair dishevelled, a cigarette drooping from his lips, his shoes unpolished, walking along with no dignity at all.'[14] As for German organization, it continued to elicit praise in various quarters. In August 1942, Bobkowski wrote of a fellow factory worker who stuck up for the French on this score: 'The Germans try to stuff our heads with their greatness and genius, their sense of organization and their culture. But they have never been capable of organizing an honest, decent snack.'[15]

But those were the last flickers of appreciation. Following the hostage executions and the start of the deportations of the Jews, there was no longer any need to counter temptations to seek closer relations. The dignity of distance and silence, by now taken for granted, was overridden by appeals for active resistance. Distinctions between Germans and Nazis, ordinary people and leaders, the good and the bad Germany were all effaced. Hatred was increasing, as Guéhenno remarked in October 1942: 'I have seen hatred growing like a tree over the past two years. Now the time has come for it to bear fruit – and what fruit!'[16] It was a hatred that made people – even intellectuals inclined to pacifism – throttle back any positive remarks and concentrate on a murderous image that encompassed all Germans. On 1 December 1943, Charles Braibant described Claudel as 'suddenly as blithe as a lark', rubbing his hands in glee over recent bombing raids on Berlin. 'Whoever had heard us laughing at the thought of three thousand Germans, including women and children, dying in the space of a few minutes, whoever had heard us – he, the greatest Christian poet of his time, me, the apostle of international friendship – would have said, "Nazi Germany really must be a pack of wild beasts, if its crimes have wrought such changes in two hearts such as these!" '[17]

In *Boule de Suif*, Maupassant described in passing a village under German occupation in 1870, where soldiers carried out daily tasks alongside the women who had been left there on their own: 'Amongst poor folk, of course you have to help one another . . .

It's the high and mighty who are waging war.' One republican was moved to anger at the sight of this *entente cordiale* established between conquerors and conquered.[18] But such scenes were unlikely in 1940. Military training was more rigorous, and the Nazi regime's plan was for totalitarian control. Even if correct behaviour was still the order of the day, the same could not be said of fraternization which, anyway, was made exceedingly difficult by the language barrier. German soldiers had their own living quarters, places of leisure and of worship, even their own shops, and this considerably curtailed opportunities for contacts, particularly for the operational troops.[19] As for members of the military administration, outside the framework of work they were forbidden to frequent certain categories of French people, such as members of the government and journalists, and had to obtain authorization for other relations that were considered 'undesirable'.[20]

On the side of the occupied French, the majority was disinclined to seek contact of any kind. A general code of conduct, spontaneous and unformulated, prescribed not merely distance, but a positive strike of the senses, thanks to which the invaded managed to protect their integrity. Even one's eyes denied the Germans any rights. Guéhenno wrote: 'When you enter the Metro, we squeeze together to make room for you. You are an untouchable. I bow my head so that you cannot see where my eyes are directed and to deny you the joy of the flash of an exchanged look. There you are in the midst of us, like an object, surrounded by silence and ice.'[21] In September 1941, in the Place du Panthéon, Léautaud witnessed a scene of initiation into this code of behaviour. Some soldiers had arrived to visit the monument. 'A small group of little girls aged between five and ten passed me, led by a girl of about twelve. "Don't look at them", she ordered, "Don't look at them." They all crossed over to the pavement in front of the Library and continued on their way, their heads averted.'[22]

The rule of not looking was even stricter on loitering in order to see. In October 1942, passing in front of a requisitioned hotel, Léautaud heard a German orchestra playing. 'There was a whole crowd of us there, on the pavement, facing the wide open door to the courtyard, watching and listening. People were stepping into the road to pass by in both directions. I heard people saying to us, "Well, you loiterers seem to have time to waste, you fools." It gave me some idea of how Parisians in general are feeling.'[23] Clearly, the code of behaviour was not yet respected by everybody, but social pressure to observe it was increasing.

The occupiers of this 'blind town' soon sensed the icy atmosphere. In his letters, the writer Felix Hartlaub, posted to Paris from December 1940 to September 1941, described that all-encompassing, freezing silence evoked by Guéhenno. He and his colleagues never strayed beyond the centre of town, where every third person was on watch. The climate was 'arctic', he wrote on 1 June 1941, and each one of them knew they could never return alone when peace came.[24] Ernst Jünger discovered that, on the rare occasions when eyes were not turned away, a direct gaze from them could be hard to bear. Wearing his uniform, he one day entered a stationer's, where he was served by a girl who fixed him with a look of 'prodigious hatred'. That was the first time it happened. It was August 1942, and Jünger was upset, as if suddenly realizing his position.[25] One year later, he was used to the experience: 'Whenever I pass by in uniform, I catch looks filled with the deepest aversion coupled with a murderous longing.'[26]

The 'blind town' was nevertheless secretly observing the intruders. It noticed how the dashing, well-fed 'grey-green' soldier of the early days, whose bearing so crushed the frightened, hungry French,[27] gradually came increasingly to resemble them both in expression and in clothing, as if he was mutating, turning into one of the defeated whom he was soon to become. Yet amid that compact, disagreeable, 'greenish mass', it did occasionally happen that a look turned a German into an individual man. Over a period of days, Guéhenno observed the affection between one old soldier and his horse, and this reawakened memories of 'the good Germany'.[28] And here and there, in private diaries, the odd remark reflects a fleeting shock provoked by an instance of unexpected behaviour: 'Just now, in the Metro, an armed German soldier who was sitting down got up to offer his seat to Léon A—, having noticed the star pinned to his chest.'[29]

All the same, distance and rejection did not always rule out civility of a kind or even, occasionally, a kind of basic solidarity. The most common contact between French people and Germans would occur when the latter had lost their way. Sartre described the mixed feelings French people might have when rejection was at odds with a 'deeply implanted humanistic desire to be of service'. 'On such occasions, you decided according to the feel of the moment and either said "I don't know" or "Take the second turning to the right''. In either case, you moved off feeling discontented with yourself.'[30]

Léautaud, an indefatigable walker, mentions only three such chance encounters in his diary. He set one soldier on his way, talked to another in a library, and came across a third in January 1944: 'On the trip home there was a German soldier on the deck of the bus, a wretched fellow by the look of him and his equipment, nothing like the strong, handsome lads we have become accustomed to seeing. He spoke not a word of French, could only present the conductor with a scrap of paper on which was written ''Porte d'Orléans, Bus 94b''. All the other travellers on the bus deck tried to help him out, explain to him where he was going and where he should get off. Each time someone new boarded the bus, the conductor asked, ''You don't know German by any chance, do you? There's this fellow, here . . . ''.'[31]

That civility was addressed to a representative of the enemy who was on his own and lost, the sight of whom evoked a general quasi-instinctive pity. Such encounters sometimes did produce an impulse of solidarity, as in the following scene which struck Sartre: 'On the Boulevard Saint-Germain, one day, a military vehicle overturned, crushing a German colonel. I saw ten Frenchmen rush to free him. They hated the occupier, I am sure of it . . . But after all, was this an occupier, this man lying crushed under his car? And what were they supposed to do? The concept of the enemy is only ever completely firm and clear if that enemy is separated from us by a barrier of fire.'[32] In their own fashion, the scenes reported by Léautaud and Sartre convey the extent to which some French people could be disarmed and how deeply they yearned to keep the sphere of their own lives separate from that of the war.

Distance and silence did not constitute an inevitable pattern of behaviour. It all depended on whether or not the particular circumstances introduced a measure of elasticity as to the problem of civility, or whether Chardonne's recipe seemed appropriate. In either case, those involved usually manifested a discretion that testified to their awareness of the code of conduct and their concern not to attract the opprobrium of public opinion, which saw to it that the code was increasingly respected. Amid the ocean of deliberate indifference and hostile distancing, many isolated instances of contact clearly did occur up until 1942, but thereafter they were submerged by the rising tide of hatred. Ideological connivance played its part, but was not necessarily the deciding factor. Ingratiation and self-interest often carried the most weight, but even they left room for mental restrictions and private convictions that ran counter to the accommodating spirit.

The requisitioning of billets mostly affected bourgeois and rural circles. What was forced upon them was accepted with grumbles, or worse, by those who resented this intrusion of the general disaster amongst their own household gods. (Flaubert had experienced a similar humiliation in 1870: 'If you knew what it is like to have Prussian helmets all over your bed!'[33]) The imposition was even worse when the unbidden guests were uncouth or vindictive, as were some soldiers who, the better to keep themselves warm, would turn off or plug up the radiators of all the rooms inhabited by their French hosts.[34]

In general, both sides coped by making mutual adjustments, being anxious to cohabit with as little tension as possible. However embarrassing the situation, it did not necessarily create a void. Social pressures were kept outside by a home's walls, and there were many impulses apart from self-interest and favourable prejudices that made for some kind of exchange: curiosity about other individuals, a thirst for news, a desire to discover grounds for hope or confirmation for one's impulse to reject, when the latter was shaky, or, finally, simply an ingrained politeness that could not be suspended. The Mauriac family was obliged to take in an officer. He came to introduce himself. 'We all made an effort and summoned up the courage to pronounce whatever words we knew. Not least embarrassed was this big, bluff chap standing at attention, who clicked his heels and bowed on the slightest pretext. He wore an iron cross, the decoration presented for the French campaign. We told him Luce's husband was a prisoner. He did not dare to leave and we did not dare to indicate that he should. The minutes ticked by. It was unbearable. At last he went off to dine.' When he had finished his meal, the Mauriac family took their places in the dining room, telling the officer, who was leaving, that they would meet again in the drawing room. What an appalling evening! François Mauriac spoke of returning to Paris, and his son understood his feelings: 'Anything would be preferable to this promiscuity. How could one possibly not try by any means to escape from such a false situation?'[35]

Between February and June 1941, Ernst Jünger was travelling through the occupied zone with his regiment. Wherever they went, cohabitation worked well. Jünger was an engaging man, the very image of the officer in *Le Silence de la mer*. He, however, was not met by a sea of silence. For example, once he was billeted on a woman whose husband was a prisoner of war, and he must have made a good impression on her as she got him an invitation to one of her aunts and, a year later, sent him a chicken as a present. He also stayed with a peasant whose conversation enchanted him and who would ask him questions about himself ('Do you have a lady too?').[36] His experience was not an isolated one. In Brittany, the Thirty-fifth armoured unit noted in its report for April 1942 that the attitude of the population was correct but varied depending on whether one was in public or in private. 'Even in pro-German circles, people generally avoid being seen with Germans, whereas officers and men billeted on people get along well with them.'[37] This puts one in mind of Maupassant who, in *Boule de Suif*, describes the early days of the occupation of Rouen, in 1870, when the absence of the massacres that had been feared had relieved the atmosphere. 'In many families, Prussian officers would eat with the family. Some of them would be well brought up and, out of politeness, would commiserate with France, professing repugnance at having to take part in this war. People would appreciate such sentiments. Besides, one day they might need the man's protection . . . They told themselves that, after all, on the basis of the ultimate argument of French urbanity, it was still permissible to be polite in one's own home, so long as one showed foreign soldiers no familiarity in public.'[38]

As well as enforced cohabitation, there were various forms of free association that were, however, regulated by physical or social geography. The occupiers' presence was not everywhere of equal density. It was strong in major centres but thin in certain rural districts, where uniformed men seldom went. Furthermore, meetings between the two sides followed the pattern of social customs in general. It is hardly surprising that the world of workers was the least forthcoming. That was not solely because German troops were not as a rule stationed in the industrial suburbs, although they certainly kept an eye on them. It was also an effect of social customs and a tradition of rejection and suspicion *vis-à-vis* the authorities that could easily be switched to apply to the invaders. At the other end of the social scale, among the bourgeoisie, international experiences, similar education and manners, familiarity with diplomacy and intervention, and with invitations and hospitality all made for easier contacts, relations and liaisons.

Cafés provided a framework for sociability where the occupiers quite frequently became familiar figures, particularly in rural areas, as the historian Louis Chevalier noticed in his own village in the Vendée. Whereas peasants tended to continue to drink from their own barrels, sailors stuck to their usual habits and would frequent the hotel on the quayside. 'In the early days, they had pretended not to see the Germans, to behave as if they were not there . . . And then, as a result of getting used to one another as they swapped papers and drank in their separate groups, they would eventually chink glasses together and, after a bit of drinking, begin to address one another as "tu" and use one another's first names.'[39] The hotel proprietress, her daughter and the serving girls, who were not at all intimidating, acted as 'links' between them.

In Brittany and Normandy, on an investigatory trip at the end of 1940, the director of the extremely collaborationist agency Inter-France, discovered that a 'veritable chasm' separated the directors of newspapers favouring collaboration from public opinion, which was 99 per cent anglophile. Yet, he noted, with considerable irritation, that very same population maintained with the occupiers relations that were 'marked by the greatest cordiality'. Shopkeepers would welcome them effusively. 'In the towns – even the large ones – and even more in the villages, the German soldiers have their routines in various establishments (cafés and restaurants). They are known there, respected, and sometimes addressed by name, and it is not unusual to find the staff of the establishment treating them with not merely consideration but even a veritable sympathy – born of daily familiarity – that is manifested in a friendliness that a purely commercial interest could not justify.'[40]

In the larger cities, it was sometimes in cafés that contacts were made. Claude Mauriac notes in his diary, in March 1942, that a non-commissioned officer had spoken to him in a café, and he had not refused to talk with him. 'We were joined by a mutual sympathy, we were the same age, both young Europeans. Yet there was so much incomprehension, so much blood between us, so much hatred, that despite everything we both felt embarrassed and distrustful.' The German spoke of the desirability of collaboration. 'After the war', replied Mauriac. 'And even as he tried to chat with me as a friend, he was embarrassed by his uniform and was trying to distract my attention from it in any way he could.'[41]

Contacts in the way of business and conviviality amongst socialites concerned a much smaller circle of people, on both sides who were conscious of coming from the same background. Business relations, for which restaurants would provide a setting, absorbed the occupiers into practices familiar to the world of business affairs generally. German officers were useful to know, and a meal in a restaurant could facilitate arrangements in a way that a discussion in an office could not, at the same time avoiding the embarrassment of issuing a compromising invitation to one's own home. Countless meetings of this kind took place; even a man such as Charles Rist took part in some. Though hostile to Vichy and even more so to the politics of collaboration, Rist was at the same time a liberal from the upper bourgeoisie who continued to defend the interests for which he was responsible in his customary fashion, even making a few advances towards the occupier himself if necessary, yet never with any sense of placing his integrity and convictions at risk. As a member of several boards of directors, he worked hard to defend a bank upon which the occupiers had foisted a commissioner by the name of Falkenhausen. When he was received along with this man by the military officer responsible for the banking sector, in October 1940, Rist spoke in German, hoping thereby to find an understanding ear.[42] He established cordial relations with Falkenhausen and lunched several times with him – but never after 1942.[43] The commissioner was a cultured and sympathetic man, who helped him insofar as he was able.

To invite Germans into one's own home was more of a commitment: it meant treating the occupier as a guest. But Ernst Jünger's diary testifies to the relative frequency of such occasions. In October 1941, he lunched *ex officio* in the home of Brinon, who spoke mockingly of the 'Yids'. The guests included Sacha Guitry and Arletty: 'The mere word "cuckold" was enough to make her laugh; so in this company she was amused all the time.'[44] During the months that followed he was a guest of Sacha Guitry, Paul Morand (several times), Cocteau, Fabre-Luce and Florence Gould. The wife of the American railway magnate held a salon, where Jünger was received along with, most notably, Jouhandeau, Cocteau, Marie Laurencin and Giraudoux, and where the young Mauriac allowed himself to be taken one day in 1943, to lunch with Gerhard Heller ('After all, the champagne, and this "internationale" of sympathy and youth made it all too easy. I should not have been there'[45]). Jünger was no doubt an exceptional case. He was a writer with reservations about Nazism who had been translated into French. He belonged to the circle surrounding Stülpnagel, which was keen to get rid of Hitler before catastrophe struck. Picasso, whom he met in July 1942, judged him well when he said, 'Between the two of us, as we are, sitting here, we would negotiate a peace this very afternoon. This evening people could celebrate with illuminations.'[46] That no doubt partly explains how it was that he continued to receive invitations from French people to the last. But, at the beginning, could the officer really have been obscured by the writer?

The socialite circle was certainly not confined to this small community of men of letters. When questioned after the liberation, occupiers freely supplied the names of people who had entertained them in their homes as if the war were already over. They were motivated in a variety of ways: by a desire to ingratiate themselves and get to know those currently in power; by cosmopolitan inclinations or habits of caste, as in the case of certain aristocrats, who were members of a society that recognized its own across frontiers and that was well represented in the Majestic. Others did so through sympathy or admiration for the conqueror and what he represented. Yet others, such as business entrepreneurs, were after special facilities, as was, for example, Baron Jean Empain, the chairman of the Metro, who would invite Germans home now for one purpose, now for another: 'Some were for the Metro, some for food supplies, some for petrol.'[47]

Diplomats from the embassy also mixed in high society. After the war, Epting recalled in particular being the guest of Carbuccia, Count de Bourbon-Busset, Count Etienne de Beaumont, Baroness de Seillière, the marquis de Polignac, René de Chambrun (Laval's son-in-law), Chappedelaine, and Lambert de Guise.[48] Schwendeman, the press attaché, was a favourite of the Bunau-Varilla family, with whom he often spent the weekend. In his diary of social engagements, most of which relates to 1942–44, the names of sixty-four of his French hosts appear, ten of them aristocratic ones, including seven marquises and countesses.[49] Nor was the SS a victim of snobbism. Knochen remembered the hospitality of Mme Gould and also of the Dubonnet family, who invited him to their chateau just outside Paris. 'The houses of the Mumm and Polignac families held the two principal Parisian salons, where we were received and where the cream of society mingled.'[50]

We may rely on Fabre-Luce's testimony on the socialite scene and believe him when he remarks, à propos of these receptions: 'When

French and Germans meet in this way on an equal footing, they start off coldly but end up on cordial terms.'[51] He is also illuminating, in the style of La Bruyère, on the mixed reactions of Parisian high society. Hobnobbing with the occupiers would sometimes prompt carefully calculated social sanctions: 'Araminte has been to a German concert; she will no longer be invited to our musical evenings. Damis has been seen in Maxim's; we shall seat him at the end of the table. Clorinde has invited Germans to her home; in future we shall cut her.'[52]

On 9 July 1940, Copeau, on his way to Dijon, fancied he detected 'women beginning to get closer to the Germans', who were more attractive than 'the puny reformed French' and 'the skinny old men' still in town. He went on to remark how painful it was to see 'French virility submerged by this endless greenish wave'.[53] Under any occupation, sexual encounters are a sensitive matter. They affect deep strata of the collective subconscious and, because of what they come to symbolize, they evoke strong emotions: fear of losing one's partner; resentment of a threat to national virility that emphasizes the humiliation of defeat; suspicion of the weaker sex, which is felt to be taking its revenge with the aid of the all too aptly termed 'occupying power'. For the invaded, the only way to oppose the invader was by sealing off their senses, thereby defending and affirming their integrity. So it is not hard to see how deeply relations of this kind undermined that integrity and how forcefully they created a sense of defilement and contamination. At the liberation all these feelings were passionately unleashed in the shaving of women's heads, as if it was meant to purify the national body.

The main problem for the occupation authorities was controlling prostitution. The Nazi regime exacerbated a German obsession with venereal diseases that had already been evident in 1914–18 and that now caused them to reserve particular brothels for the exclusive use of the Wehrmacht. By the spring of 1941, twenty-nine of these establishments in the Paris region had been designated for the troops, and three for German officers:[54] no Jews or blacks; condoms obligatory; detailed rules of hygiene for the ladies, backed up by strict medical checks and surveillance whenever they left the confines of the house; and no licences given without permission from the Kommandatur. Each time a German soldier left a brothel he received a card bearing the name of the brothel, the date and the girl's first name. They were forbidden to infringe the obligatory distance from the natives by, for instance, giving them their photographs. Between 5000 and 6000 streetwalkers were also issued with bilingual cards that designated them for the exclusive use of the Germans. However, these measures failed to prevent an explosion of unauthorized prostitution. According to the German authorities, this involved between 80000 and 100000 women in Paris alone, as a consequence of poverty, separations and the pecuniary attraction of occupiers who possessed an overvalued currency. It was a major source of infection.[55]

The French accepted this venal trade philosophically. At the most, influenced by Maupassant,[56] they liked to tell themselves that these 'submissive girls', as the policemen called them, made their grey-green clients pay dearly for what amounted to the violation of their honour as French women, even if this was all in the day's work for them, by leaving them with an infection, as a souvenir. Other relationships were not looked upon with such indulgence. In his *Conseils*, the mild Texcier calls for violence solely in this connection. Whereas prostitutes were simply plying their trade by selling themselves to the occupiers, it was inadmissable that 'honest women' should dilly-dally with them. Such behaviour deserved the kind of punishment that the enemy himself meted out for it: 'Beyond the Rhine, the pretty lady would be publicly whipped.' The Germans had a head start in these matters. During the occupation of the Rhineland in the 1920s, women had had their heads shaved for sleeping with French soldiers.[57] From 1940 on, some sections of the Nazi party inflicted the same fate, in the public square, upon German women who had entered into sexual relations with foreign workers.[58]

In France, there was no authority responsible for discouraging relations between soldiers and natives. Many kinds of liaisons developed, ranging from fleeting chance encounters to full-blown love affairs. Michèle Bood's diary discloses the author, an anglophile schoolgirl, trying to flirt with young German soldiers.[59] Jünger's diary shows that it was not hard for kindred souls to come together. On 1 May 1941, there was a fling with a salesgirl: 'Paris offers you these kinds of meetings, almost without you having to seek them.'[60] Next, he got to know a dressmaker, who invited him home for her birthday: then there was a relationship with a woman doctor; eventually he succeeded a Luftwaffe major as the lover of Florence Gould.

Other well-known women also took German officers as their lovers. Arletty, for example, and Coco Chanel, whose behaviour can be put down to a number of explanations: a cosmpolitan past with an unhappy love life, political inclinations developed in the wake of the shock of 1936, and self-interested resentment that prompted her to exploit aryanization in order to recover control of a perfume company lost to Jewish competitors before the war.[61] But most of these women came from modest backgrounds, many of them actually being in the Germans' employ.[62] As maids, laundresses, waitresses, nurses or office workers, they were surrounded by soldiers and officers, and some of them allowed themselves to be tempted or seduced. Women working in direct contact with the public were also particularly exposed. Many of the 1000 odd female PTT employees, most of them young auxiliaries, who were investigated in the course of the professional purges during the liberation, had been accused of going out with German soldiers.[63] In *Hiroshima, mon amour,* Marguerite Duras gives a realistic description of a liaison that begins in a shop towards the end of the occupation. A seventeen-year-old girl is working in the family chemist shop. Her mother is away from home, and her embittered father is hitting the bottle. The town all around is empty of men. She is weary of the war, and the wastage of her youth 'sticks in her gullet'. One day a German soldier comes in for treatment. 'I bandaged his hand as I had been taught to, full of hatred.' He returns; she bandages him again. 'I never raised my eyes to him, just as I had been taught.' He lays siege to her; eventually she succumbs ('I became his woman in the twilight, in happiness, and in shame'). Thinking that nobody has noticed, they become careless. At the liberation, he is murdered; her head is shaved.[64]

It would be pointless to seek a single explanation for these love affairs, whether fleeting or of longer duration. The isolation of the wives of prisoners and others separated from their husbands; a desire to obtain favours or other advantages in a difficult material situation; a quest for protection or possibly a taste for adventure; the satisfaction of a grudge or a desire for revenge: there were many different causes, many different circumstances, but they all underline the precarious situation in which many French women found themselves, as is testified by the threefold increase in arrests of women in the Seine department between 1938 and 1944.[65] In some cases there may even have been political considerations involved. Take the case of a young girl in the Gard, born in 1924 and, living with her peasant parents, who welcomed the German soldiers with open arms when they invaded the free zone. Her flighty behaviour was compounded by the insulting nature of her remarks: 'The Germans are great, the French are dirty bastards. They'll show you!' In August 1943, she decided, probably as a result of her social ostracism, to go to work in Germany (a decision taken by quite a few women in her position). The day before she was due to leave, a cousin and four of his mates shaved her head.[66]

It is very hard to determine how widespread this phenomenon was. Between 10000 and 20000 women were probably punished for such liaisons in the course of judicial and professional purges, for the most part in rural departments.[67] In the countryside, everyone knows everything, and virtually nothing was forgotten at the liberation. In the towns, many liaisons, particularly fly-by-night ones and encounters in the early days of the occupation, left no trace and were forgotten. A minimum of several tens of thousands of French women engaged in sexual relations with the occupiers.

A similar uncertainty surrounds the fruits of those loves, despite an enquiry that the SS had the Propaganda-Abteilung organize in 1942.[68] The propaganda service was able to produce only estimates, the bases for which are unknown. For the region of Rouen, a figure of 3000 to 4000 children is suggested; a crèche is claimed to have been set up to help the mothers, a few of them the wives of prisoners, the majority girls engaged to German soldiers, who were planning to settle in the Reich after the war. The estimate for France as a whole is 50000 to 70000 children.[69]

When caught up in the purges, in self-defence some women drew attention to the anti-Nazi opinions of their lovers, or asserted that they were not German, but Austrian; they had not associated with any occupation regime or system, only with a man whose circumstances brought him close to those occupied. Others claimed that one's feelings were free, as was one's choice as to how to use one's own body. Yet others had clearly simply been looking for a source of help in hard times and had probably met up with a man who was likewise simply bent on getting through a bad patch, in a version of the *entente cordiale* between poor people that had so scandalized the republican in Maupassant's story. But in a love affair with a member of the occupying force a woman is always suspected of seeking to surround herself with the latter's power. The relationship implies protection, advantages and evasion of the common lot. Such behaviour was no doubt deeply related to these women's weaker sense of national duty and their relative lack of interest in public affairs – factors that were themselves a consequence of their enjoying fewer civil rights.

The last form of contact with the occupiers, which was indirect and anonymous, was denunciation, and it was considered the most reprehensible, as it involved making use of the occupier to settle old scores with one's compatriots. Denunciation is no doubt a phenomenon that is typical of troubled times; the liberation itself was by no means free of it. But by then the denunciations would be addressed to the authorities of a legitimate state, and the victim would benefit from the guarantees that this implied. Under the occupation, in contrast, a denunciation inevitably produced formidable results. Even when unfounded, it led to arrest, interrogation (an experience bound to be unpleasant, at best) and the risk of being used as a hostage or of being deported. If the circumstances of the person denounced happened to be irregular, the consequences were always dire.

The scale of this phenomenon is impossible to gauge, but it certainly existed. Some French people limited themselves (if that is the right word) to denouncing others to their own administration: the French police or French antisemitic organizations.[70] Others went straight to the occupier, behaviour that many prefects bitterly deplored. In the autumn of 1941, one prefect spoke of a positive flood of denunciatory letters and added that, in the opinion of the occupation authorities, 'virtually all the matters that have resulted in French people being condemned by German tribunals were brought to their notice through denunciations made by other French people'.[71] Even more common than denunciation itself were threats of it, brandished among neighbours or in the work place, to frighten or intimidate. Some of these threats were carried out. A strike broke out in the factories of Gentilly on 9 February 1942; the management threatened to denounce the strikers 'to the French and German police'. The following day, a number of workers were arrested; nine were deported to Germany.[72]

Many of these informers were motivated by self-interest: the lure of a reward, a desire to settle an inheritance quarrel or to acquire a property for oneself. But the major motivation was revenge: as in crimes of passion, those involved tended to be members of the same family or close relatives, warring spouses, unsuccessful rivals or detested neighbours. At the time of the purges, the *Berry républicain* carried a number of edifying examples. A forty-three-year-old labourer was denounced by a girl whom he had been pestering with his unwelcome attentions, and extricated himself from trouble by himself denouncing his own nephew, who had a secret cache of weapons (7 February 1945). A nineteen-year-old typist denounced her boyfriend, who had come home on leave from Germany and never returned, and who had then left her (21 December 1944). A couple of workers who had been turned out by their landlord denounced him for anti-German talk (24 December 1944). A café proprietress with a German lover denounced her husband (8 February 1945). A young man reprimanded by his father for the company he was keeping denounced his father for having hidden his rifle; the father was deported, and the son went off to Germany as a volunteer worker (22 February 1945).

Overall, women constituted a small minority of those purged, but they were over-represented in cases of denunciation. In Finistère, in fifty-four out of seventy-seven cases judged by a court of justice, the accused were women. In the Eure department, the accused were women in two-thirds of the 225 cases recorded. They were also in the majority in the sixty-three denunciation cases with a political motive, for example those in which allied parachutists or members of the resistance had been denounced.[73] Betrayal is the weapon of the weak and denunciation is doubly so: not only were the majority of those who resorted to it women, but many were women who belonged to disadvantaged social categories. People from the liberal professions, whether men or women, were very under-represented in such affairs.[74] Denunciation was the weapon of weak people who could not resist the temptation to make this source of newfound power play into their own hands.

14

The Church and the associations

Associations, as well as individuals, had to determine what attitude to adopt. All organizations possess a will to survive, want their presence and action to continue and hope to grow stronger and expand. Were they to give up those aims on account of the occupation? In the case of associations, the safeguarding of position and interests and, even more, the satisfaction of ambitions were hard to reconcile with a strike of the senses, as prescribed for individuals. The code of dignity was not rejected, but it was made more pliant, bent into a policy for survival: in other words, for accommodation. It is worth stressing the extent to which an institutional framework predisposes those involved to adapt, checks any determination to keep apart, and limits the taking of risks, even where there is no ideological connivance in play.

For some associations, even those without great ambitions, it was impossible to ignore the occupiers, given that they were pursuing an active policy of solicitation and intervention. A major case in point was the German embassy which, as well as having to 'keep in step' with the Majestic, had its own means of influence and manipulation, which it employed in the interests of its mission: namely to divide the French, to put pressure on Vichy and to instil a voluntary servitude. One instrument was essential for this policy: the MBF's decree of 28 August 1940 that prohibited associations from engaging in any activities without authorization. The occupying authorities certainly possessed the power to damage but, through Abetz, they also manifested a desire to attract and win over, making the most of converging interests. Associations that allowed themselves to be tempted found themselves in a triangular relationship, with the French state as the third party.

Paradoxically, the very earliest negotiations brought the occupiers into contact with one of their worst 'ideological enemies'. In the immediate aftermath of the defeat, the French Communist party was weakened by the imprisonment of many of its militants, disorganized by the exodus and the defeat, and deserted by most of its members. But it still had some of its cadres, its link with Moscow, where Thorez had taken refuge, a doctrine and an identity – enough for it to launch into negotiations that aimed to obtain authorization for the reappearance of *L'Humanité*, which meanwhile continued to be published clandestinely. The first advances, made on 18 June to the Propaganda-Abteilung, came to nothing: the French police arrested the emissaries of *L'Humanité*. The affair was revived by the intervention of Abetz, who was dying to fish in popular waters. With that very aim in view, he had just created *La France au travail*, a publication that attacked Vichy, capitalism, the Jews and the warmongers. On 22 June, he wrote to the MBF expressing his regret that censorship had failed to suppress news of those arrests. The occupying power should not appear to be giving its approval to anticommunist repression by the French police; or, if it did, other arrests of 'asocial' employers ought to be announced at the same time.[1]

On 25 June, the prefecture of police was ordered to release those arrested as well as several of their comrades. Negotiations now shifted to the embassy where, between 26 June and 13 July, three meetings took place. Two members of the central committee of the Communist party took part in these, Maurice Tréaud and the deputy, Jean Catelas, both controlled from a distance by Duclos. They explained that, in the newspaper they wanted to receive authorization to publish, they planned to support reconstruction and denounce the warmongers and British imperialism – in other words to pursue a policy of 'European pacification'.[2] When Abetz indicated that republishing *L'Humanité* was out of the question, they suggested reviving *Ce soir*.

Abetz's game is made clear in a memorandum he addressed to the MBF on 7 July, in an attempt to get his policies accepted. Rather than struggle against the 'communist danger' by arresting a few agitators, why not be more subtle: make contact with the leaders, try to win them over, and use them to organize the workers into getting the economy moving again; and, to this end, permit them to publish a newspaper? The communists he had met were prepared to discontinue the clandestine publication of *L'Humanité*, to submit the authorized organ to censorship before printing and to fall into line with *La France au travail* on political questions of importance. Of course, they were hoping to smuggle through their own doctrines under cover of pursuing an apolitical, antiplutocratic and anti-English line. But an attentive eye would be able to sift the merchandise in such a way that, thanks to this newspaper that they themselves wanted, the working class could be influenced to the advantage of German interests.[3]

Abetz's idea was greeted with hostility by the military in both Berlin and Paris. Nor did Hitler, whom he strove to win over in early August, look upon it favourably. He agreed not to take repressive action in the immediate future, since the communists were certainly helping to divide the French, but he asked the authorities to be ready to do so when the right moment came.[4] When Abetz returned, after a month's absence, he told his Communist party contacts the bad news. In an effort to keep his policies going, he suggested giving *La France au travail* a new look by taking on a few communist journalists. At this point the communists broke off relations. Thanks to Abetz's intervention, this whole affair had escalated instead of meeting a speedy end at the hands of the military. Abetz had shown poor judgement, probably because he had overestimated the real enough convergence between his own policies and those of the communists, as exemplified by the line pursued by the underground *L'Humanité*: criticism of Vichy, denunciation of the war, and attacks against England, de Gaulle, and 'other agents of English finance' that 'would like to see the French make war for the benefit of the City'.

As is clear from the Soviet archives,[5] on the communist side the initial go-ahead and also the subsequent order to withdraw came from Moscow. In the interval there had been a clash of views, complicated by delays in transmitting them. The reappearance of the newspaper had been part of a strategy for returning to operating in broad daylight and setting about the reconstruction of the communist apparatus, through the liberation of militants who were still imprisoned and a return to activity in trade unions, associations and municipal councils. For this strategy to work, the support of the occupation authorities was indispensable, and, thanks to the German–Soviet pact, that was no longer beyond the bounds of possibility. That, at least, was the calculation of the communists, who thereupon set about trying their luck. Here are two examples of the steps that they took: the railway workers asked Abetz for an 'audience with the German authorities', to get permission for their dissolved trade union to resume its activities and to obtain the restitution of their premises.[6] With a similar purpose, the Parisian leaders of the Friends of the Soviet Union addressed an appeal to 'Monsieur le Gouverneur militaire', taking care to assure him of their 'deepest consideration'.[7] The policy of a return to operating in broad daylight, without, however, dismantling the party's illegal apparatus, left Duclos a certain latitude of interpretation which he was, understandably, keen to exploit. The situation looked relatively promising following the harsh repression that the Republic had inflicted and that Vichy was keen to prolong. The party would be able to exploit the political void produced by the defeat and present itself as the defender of a population gravely affected by the disorganization of the economy. And it would be able to do this openly, thanks to the protection of an occupying power that was seeking ways of weakening the French government. In Moscow, in contrast, the discussions with Abetz had been greeted with disquiet, particularly by Thorez, who was fearful of being compromised. A return to broad daylight by all means, but not at the cost of sacrificing the party's identity and with the risk of being regarded as allies of the occupier. From his position at the centre of this affair, Duclos saw things rather differently, but was nevertheless wary. Once discussions had started it seemed difficult not to await Abetz's response, which was then delayed until 22 August. By then Moscow had ordered all contacts to be broken off.

The communist moves of the summer of 1940 were part and parcel of the party's policy to make the most of any means possible, whether legal or illegal, and its instinct to battle for power whatever the circumstances. France's defeat and the German–Soviet pact opened up the perspective, considered desirable in both Paris and Moscow, of reanimating the party, restoring a certain weight, if not dominance, to it, and – who could tell? – possibly the chance to negotiate a peace. In 1918, after all, to ensure the survival of his regime, Lenin had ceded important territories to Germany. These were undeniably politics of accommodation, but the communists remained on the qui vive and their form of accommodation, unlike other forms, was at least free of any ideological connivance. Furthermore, they held an unusual trump card, an underground apparatus that rendered any argument of institutional defence irrelevant. Once this episode was over, the French Communist party pursued its path on its own, becoming a target for general repression, since from October 1940 onwards the Germans gave the French police a free hand. The German attack on the USSR, the following June, caused the French Communist party to swing into the general armed struggle against the occupying power.

The Germans seemed to provide an umbrella under which to shelter from Vichy; and the communists were not alone in seeking cover beneath it. The associations of war veterans did likewise, once Pétain had absorbed them all into the Légion Française des Combattants. His decision was not to the liking of some of its leaders, who now found their positions under threat and were, besides, disillusioned with the politics of the new regime. Abetz, for his part, was against the idea of any organization that encompassed both zones and that might provide support for Vichy. So he got the MBF to ban the implantation of the Legion in the occupied zone and to authorize the operations of four separate organizations there.[8]

This whole affair displeased Pétain, who could see what the Germans were playing for (a 'status quo that favours them') and continued to fulminate against the veterans' leaders involved ('At a governmental level, I cannot tolerate private moves that undermine my authority').[9] The veterans had preferred the protection of the occupying power to the fusion desired by their own government. From that time on, Vichy blocked the funds of the former associations, so they were left with no alternative but to accept German money if they were to continue their activities and resume publishing their news sheets.[10] Abetz soon came to see that these allies were of little use to him: the membership was impressive (1.5 million in the occupied zone), but he judged it to have little internal cohesion.[11] That was his way of deploring the 'marshalism' of these circles and their hostility to any political action directed against Pétain. When it became known that one of the veterans' leaders, Rivollet, had joined Déat's RNP, protests broke out within his association, and he was forced to assure everyone that his action had been purely personal.[12] The only advantage to Abetz turned out to be a negative one, namely that a form of unification under the aegis of Vichy had been prevented.

Similar moves were made by the trade unions, with similar results. Abetz, always on the look-out for counter-weights to the new regime, inevitably took an interest in workers' associations, given that Vichy had dissolved their confederations and was moving towards the establishment of its own kind of organization (although, as it happened, this did not come about until the autumn of 1941, when its labour charter was promulgated). Once again, the embassy exerted pressure on the reticent military: Abetz declared that it was essential to authorize the trade unions before the institution – which he believed to be imminent – of a single organization designed to take their place; authorization for the trade unions would promote an image of Nazi Germany as the protector of the workers. Through the trade unions, he explained, it would be possible to offer the workers compensations to make up for the economic restrictions that they were suffering: winter benefits, children's playschools, organized leisure activities, all of which he proposed to finance by confiscating the possessions of Jews and warmongers.[13]

The military authorities feared repercussions in Vichy that would damage the policy of collaboration and, above all, thought trade unions might turn into a political force that would be impossible to control.[14] In December 1940, after many discussions, they eventually gave way, but banned trade unions of civil servants, in order to avoid antagonizing Vichy, which had prohibited them. The authorized trade unions would have to promise to limit themselves to defending the social and professional interests of their members. Seventeen CFTC federations and twenty-five federations of the CGT, as well as three independent trade unions, requested and received authorization to function.[15]

As with the war veterans, it was not hard for Abetz to prevent the creation of a single organization controlled by Vichy. But that is about all he achieved. As he saw it, the authorized trade unions, which it would be necessary to regroup, then fuse, under the direction of reliable men, were to encompass a disoriented working class and steer it towards collaboration, at the same time encouraging the recruitment of voluntary workers for Germany.[16] However, the various trade unionist families (the CGT, the Christians, the professional trade unions, and so on) proved unwilling to give up their particular identities and opposed the move to amalgamate them. This even failed in the case of the ex-CGT federations, which were split between those who approved of the presence of Belin in the government and those who opposed it.[17] The collaborationist tendency was very much in the minority here, and the decision of its leaders to create a centre of trade-unionist propaganda, soon to be attached to the RNP, underlined this parting of the ways. Besides, in the last analysis, the trade unions were handicapped by their weakness: according to the Germans, in the spring of 1941 there were only 400000 members in the occupied zone.[18] Workers were turning away from organizations that the ban on strikes and the wage freeze had stripped of power.

In contrast to the leaders of the associations of war veterans, the trade unionists' decision to request authorization from the Germans was not made in defiance of Vichy, which had not yet decided what to do about them. Through the mediation of his chief adviser, Froideval, Belin played an active role in angling for authorizations. In doing so he was motivated by his desire to retain influence over his colleagues and not to allow the workers of the occupied zone to drift into communism. He may also have hoped to implant pawns who favoured his own concept of professional organization, which was under challenge from the regime's corporatist wing. As for the leaders of the trade unions themselves, their motivations were very diverse. They all favoured making their presence felt, in order to save posts and positions, and they all welcomed the margin of manoeuvre *vis-à-vis* Vichy that the occupiers' tolerance offered them. None of them wanted to leave the field free for the communists, against whom they had struggled fiercely in the past. This was particularly true of the trade unions of the ex-CGT, whose leaders had made the most of the repression of communism during the phoney war, as a means to recover positions lost in the wake of 1936, and to settle old scores.

But beyond that, there was a parting of the ways between the collaborationist minority and a resistant minority which put itself on the map, in November 1940, with its 'Manifesto of French trade unionism', a profession of faith in the values of democracy and free trade unionism. The manifesto was distributed in the form of a circular, to which the occupying power turned a blind eye so as to undermine Vichy. Between these two extremes was an indeterminate mass of opinion probably not much in favour of a German victory but sufficiently anxious to secure a place in the new professional order to provide a measure of support for Laval. On May Day 1942, the leaders of eighteen ex-CGT federations addressed a public appeal to him, speaking of reconciliation between different peoples, condemning the assassinations of German soldiers, and looking forward to 'a new, pacified Europe' in which 'the honour and vital interests of France' would be respected.[19]

Abetz's policies presented a serious temptation. In February 1941,

André Delmas, the secretary general of the national trade union of school teachers, dissolved by Vichy, requested authorization for his organization in the occupied zone.[20] At first the idea was looked upon favourably by the occupiers, who were keen to oppose the clericalism of Vichy and were hoping to win the sympathy of teachers; then it was dropped, for fear of creating tension with the French government. Delmas, who was discreet in public but in private manifested a certain sympathy for Germany and collaboration,[21] continued to interest the embassy which, in the autumn of 1941, pressed Vichy to find him a place in the trade union of teachers that it was then thinking of creating. Delmas regarded the Germans as both protectors and partners who might help to orientate French politics, up until the turning point of 1942 when he quietly tiptoed away from the public stage.

Unlike the communists, the war veterans and the trade unions, the Catholic Church never sought refuge under the occupiers' umbrella; but it defended its interests in a fashion that made it, too, accommodating. As a social and spiritual, if not political, power, it was disposed to be hostile to Nazism, but it was at the same time linked with the new regime considerably more strongly than was required by its tradition of obedience to the established power. It is true that the politics of this regime surpassed all expectations: a programme for schools that brought God back into the classrooms and offered funding for private (i.e. Church) schools; measures to boost the family, restore standards of behaviour and encourage a return to the land, thereby fulfilling long-standing Church aspirations; and an authoritarian ideology that wrote off the mistakes of the pre-war period (as the bishop of Dax declared in February 1941, 'for us, the truly accursed year was not the year of our external defeat, but the year of our internal defeat, 1936').[22] In the new France, the Church rediscovered the principles by which it was defined: authority and hierarchy, shepherds guiding their flock. In rallying to Vichy, it did as other churches in Italy and Germany had done, by accepting a dictatorship so long as it promised to safeguard their rights and liberties. This acceptance was more than a little deluded, based on a recognition of common enemies, the reality of partial convergences and a tenacious hope of re-establishing a Christian society.

In defeated France, the Church felt it had the wind in its sails, in the early days at least. The political and social forces hostile to it had disappeared, removing much sorely felt competition. Catholics were present in the government and were playing an important role in new institutions, in particular in social and charitable organizations. At the grass-roots level a resurgence of piety was filling the churches. Parents were flocking to free education, which increased its share in primary schooling from 17.7 per cent to 22.6 per cent between 1939 and 1944, and in secondary schooling from 40 per cent to 53 per cent (the figures are those for 1932 and 1942).[23] Finally, Catholic youth movements were in full expansion, comprising in 1941 2.3 million out of a total of 2.5 million young people in youth organizations.[24] All this success was crossed by moments of disquiet, particularly under Darlan, when brakes were applied to aid for schooling and the question of a single youth association was raised. In the summer of 1941, the bishops spoke of the respect due to a legitimate power, adding 'but no feudalization'. In September, they forbade priests to hold positions as leaders in the Légion Française des Combattants.[25] The Church was not blind to the state of public opinion and was anxious to be seen to distance itself.[26] But its attachment to Pétain, the man of destiny, remained solid enough to withstand any test.

On collaboration, the Church remained extremely discreet, and at no point gave the government its approval publicly, as a body. One or two rare prelates offered their support after Montoire: the bishops of Arras and Verdun, and above all old Cardinal Baudrillart, who in the following year gave his blessing to the struggle against communism. In his opinion, collaboration 'took account of the existing realities'. It offered a serious chance for the future of the country. If it failed, it would be hard to avoid 'falling into evils even worse than those that have fallen upon us up to now'.[27] Not one of these prelates had a favourable, let alone a laudatory word for the occupier. All were concerned that their support should be reasonable and conditional: collaboration was the lesser evil and had to bring a lasting peace. All felt a deep concern about internal politics, which were strongly criticized by the professors of the Catholic faculties of Lille, who denounced the fallacious alternative: 'either defeat accepted in the hope of an internal renewal; or final victory, with the risk of a continuation of earlier political errors'.[28]

The silence of the upper echelons of the clergy was prompted by doctrinal reasons as well as by patriotism. Collaboration involved a regime whose ideology had been condemned by the Pope and against which French bishops had preached during the phoney war. They were also influenced by a desire not to affront public opinion and not to interfere in a domain that was the government's preserve. However, it is not really possible to speak of any positive hostility to such politics. Gaullists such as Monsignor Chevrot in Paris were few and far between. The most common position adopted was at the very least to leave the matter in Pétain's hands, as advised by *La Croix*, after Montoire.[29] In fact, it would have been awkward to express approval for the regime's internal policies and disapproval for its external ones. So the tendency was for the clergy to accept the latter in the name of realism or simply as an expedient – an attitude that was encouraged by a certain ideological convergence with the politics of the occupying power. When the men of the Dijon SD investigated thirteen episcopal offices in the north-east in the autumn of 1940, they discovered that a number of bishops approved of their action against freemasons, Jews and communists. The widest approval went to the measures against the Church's old enemies, the freemasons. The bishop of Verdun declared: 'On this subject I am in agreement with you and thank you from the bottom of my heart.' The bishop of Nancy, who said he supported 'supervised collaboration' – that is, supervised by the conqueror – expressed his 'particular gratitude to the German authorities for eliminating freemasonry'. The vicar general of Saint-Dié called Laval a good Frenchman, drew attention to the communist danger and declared that the policies of Montoire were the best possible solution for the country: 'At this moment what France needs is a just but firm hand.'[30]

Given the existence of such a trend in clerical thinking, it is hardly surprising that a minority approved of collaboration. Clerics who had dealings with the occupation services were no doubt a rarity, but there were a few: Canon Tricot of the Catholic Institute of Paris; Abbé Renaud, the parish priest of Saint-Monceau, who was collaborationist to the point of becoming hostile to Pétain and even to the Pope, whom he considered too soft in his protest against the Anglo-Saxon bombing raids, declaring that it would be no bad thing if a few bombs fell on the Vatican, to wake him up.[31] No more than a handful of priests became involved with collaborationist parties, supported autonomist organizations (Gantois and Perrot), or wrote articles for the Paris press (the Revd Gorce). But a higher proportion were favourable to the defence of Christian civilization against bolshevism, or went along with the hardening of the regime, out of loyalty to Pétain, even if they did not do so publicly.

It was, no doubt, only a minority that went so far, but their position was certainly not far distant from the average line taken by the clergy. Even if they did not give collaboration their approval, many of them supported it indirectly when they denounced Gaullism and resistance, encouraged the *Relève*, attended the inauguration of a German Institute, celebrated mass on the occasion of the anniversary of the LVF, or officiated at the funerals of collaborationists, in particular men of the Milice. Trust and obedience: without glorying in it, but in close order, the cadres of Catholicism followed Pétain.

Things would no doubt have been different had the occupying power manifested the full force of its hostility towards the Church from the start. On this point Abetz was every bit as committed as the SS. In October 1942, he reckoned that after the war the Church would be Nazism's most powerful enemy. There would be no more Jews left in Europe, he wrote, communism would have been destroyed, and freemasonry wiped out, along with all Anglo-Saxon influence. But the Church would still be there, so it was important to start fighting it there and then, by strengthening anticlericalism. It was, he explained, a view that he took good care not to advertise; indeed, he deliberately propagated the idea that Nazi Germany would like to reach agreement with the Church.[32] By way of a lure, the activities of Catholic organizations were tolerated in the occupied zone.

It was a tactic that proved quite effective where at least some of the upper clerical hierarchy were concerned. The highest regulatory body of the Church of France was the Assembly of Cardinals and Archbishops. Its role was one of coordination more than direction, and the division of the country had further hampered its effectiveness. The personalities of individual prelates were therefore of considerable importance, particularly those of cardinals Gerlier in Lyons, Liénart in Lille, and Baudrillart and Suhard in Paris. It was Suhard who was responsible for ensuring liaison with the occupation authorities.

On the eve of the outbreak of war, Suhard was a man convinced of the threat to Christianity that Nazism represented, but who condemned communism even more strongly and was, moreover, severely critical of the republican regime (on 20 October 1939, he wrote in his notebooks: 'Visited General Giraud: very elevated conversation about France and the need to recreate a mentality of order and dedication').[33] Haunted as he was by the irreligiosity of the masses, he welcomed a regime that was giving the Church favourable conditions for its missionary work of rechristianization.

Nevertheless, he was wary of becoming too involved with it, and in February 1941 declined appointment to the National Council. He explained that 'an attitude of loyal independence' would serve the government better, as it would allow the clergy to diffuse a spirit of obedience without appearing to be under orders to do so. Furthermore, such an attitude 'has already proved most helpful in France's relations with the occupation authorities. The Germans have manifested a deep respect for the conduct of Cardinal Suhard and the French clergy as a whole . . . One day such favourable dispositions might prove extremely useful in the course of general negotiations.' But the end of this document conveys the multiple identity of this prince of the Church: 'If the Marshal issues an order, however, the cardinal of France, mindful that he is a Frenchman, will obey.'[34]

Note the second argument in this document: a measure of distance from Vichy would facilitate relations with the occupiers. Suhard definitely had a positive view of both his own role and the attitude of the Germans. He went out of his way personally to present himself in a light that was agreeable to them. On 12 December 1940, he assured Abetz that the clergy were perfectly willing to use their influence in favour of collaboration, adding that there were points of convergence with Nazism that rendered compromise possible.[35] It was an idea that he reiterated in the autumn of 1943: the conflict between the German Church and the Nazi regime bore upon only the delimitation of the spiritual and the temporal orders, whereas communism represented 'a radical negation of all spiritual forces'.[36] Clearly, for the French Church, anticommunism constituted the principal point of convergence with Nazism. According to German sources, in July 1941 Suhard and Baudrillart suggested to their colleagues – without success – that they should follow the example of the German Church, and declare their public approval of the war against the USSR.[37] On 27 August 1942, Suhard pronounced the absolution at a solemn mass in Notre Dame in memory of members of the LVF who had died in the East.[38]

Given that he believed in the possibility of agreement, not only between the two countries, but even between the Church and Nazism, the cardinal was unlikely to be hostile to collaboration. In November 1941, his right-hand man, Monsignor Beaussart, acting as his spokesman, declared his conviction that 'collaboration is the only reasonable course for France and for the Church'. Beaussart also represented Suhard at the reception given by the embassy in honour of Göring, on 2 December 1941.[39] Offering his best wishes for 1942 to

Abetz, he declared his hope 'that the course of events makes it possible for our two countries to draw ever closer, with the greater understanding that will be the condition for total reconciliation'.[40] The word 'collaboration' was avoided in favour of an appeal for understanding on the part of the conqueror: provided this was forthcoming, reconciliation with Nazi Germany was deemed possible.

Not all the clergy were at one with Suhard. The Germans were not slow to register the hostility of the lower clergy, a hostility that is confirmed by other sources too, such as this letter addressed to Brinon at the end of 1941 by a vicar of Saint-Nicolas du Chardonnet, who declared himself 'horrified by the thinking of many members of the clergy in the capital. Poor fellows, they are hoping for the triumph of England and salvation for us by that means!'[41] In January 1941, Abetz detected two tendencies among the higher echelons of the clergy: one followed Suhard, favouring collaboration and hoping to extend the Church's pastoral activities, yet steering clear of the political domain; the other, which followed Gerlier, was anti-German and wanted to make the Church the pillar of the French state.[42] Abetz's interpretation of the divergence in the attitudes of these two prelates was that it masked a double game: in the occupied zone, they spoke of collaboration, while in the free zone they were critical of Germany. The ambassador was once again betraying his anticlericalism. Suhard and Gerlier genuinely did hold different views on the place of the Church in the new regime and also on the attitude to be observed towards the occupier, and the second of those divergences indicated partially different views of Nazism. However, when it came to action, Pétainism kept them both in line.

In public, Suhard acted with great discretion. He did not attempt to get the activities of Catholic movements authorized in the occupied zone, 'for fear of compromising himself *vis-à-vis* public opinion', according to Vichy.[43] What mattered most to him was simply that they carried on with their activities. Accordingly, he told them to keep out of trouble and whenever any problems arose with the German authorities, he intervened immediately. When premises of the JAC in Rennes were closed and two of its managers were imprisoned in May 1941, he first reminded Abetz of all his efforts to keep Catholic youth out of any activities 'that might give the occupying authorities cause for concern', then, in a tone of veiled menace, asked that 'this measure hostile to the Church of France' be rescinded.[44]

The resolution that he manifested in the defence of the interests of the Church contrasted sharply with his flaccid reactions to the persecution of the Jews. It was a flaccidity shared by the majority of French prelates, who accepted the Statute and refused to protest publicly against the great round-up of July 1942, so as not to expose the Catholic organizations to reprisals. (Even in the free zone, where no such risk existed, only a minority of bishops criticized the handing over of foreign Jews, in August.) In his official capacity, Suhard was obliged to write to Pétain about the matter; but in the nuncio's own opinion it was 'quite a platonic kind of protest'.[45] In private, if we are to believe what Laval and Bousquet told the Germans, he showed understanding regarding the deportation of foreign Jews.[46] Here again, there was a marked difference between his behaviour and Gerlier's. Laval, who saw them both in October 1942, reckoned that Suhard went along with his policies, whereas with Gerlier he had to plead hard for both his anti-Jewish policies and the Relève.[47]

The attitude of the high-ranking clergy provoked criticism from some Catholics. On 26 May 1942, Claudel sent Cardinal Gerlier a letter that must have produced quite an effect: 'I have read with great interest the account of the splendid official and religious funeral ceremonies for His Eminence Cardinal Baudrillard. A wreath offered by the occupation authorities was apparently to be seen on the deceased's coffin. Such homage was clearly the due of such a fervent collaborator. On the same day, I heard the report of the execution of twenty-seven hostages in Nantes. Having been loaded on to lorries by collaborators, these Frenchmen began to sing the *Marseillaise*. From the other side of the barbed wire, their comrades joined in. They were shot in groups of nine in a sandy hollow. One of them, Gaston Mouquet [*sic*], a lad of seventeen, had fainted. He was shot anyway . . . When the cardinal reaches the other side, the twenty-seven dead hostages, at the head of an army that is growing daily, will slope arms and act as his guard of honour. For that emulator of Cauchon, the French Church could not lay hands on enough incense. For those sacrificed Frenchmen, there was not a prayer, not a single gesture of charity or indignation. A day will come . . . Please accept my . . . Yours etc.'[48]

Among Catholics in favour of resistance, indignation was uncontainable. A 'Mémoire to the Bishops of France' produced in the summer of 1942 stressed the hostility felt by the majority of French people towards Vichy, which would 'instantly' be swept away in the event of a military reversal. Even Pétain's prestige was crumbling. By going 'well beyond traditional loyalism', the Church was exposing itself to grave risks. As for collaboration, every aspect of it was to be condemned: it constituted 'sinister trickery on the political level, grave error on the psychological level, betrayal of France on the spiritual level, apostasy on the religious level'. A victory for Nazism would 'signal religious persecution, state tyranny, and a pagan totalitarianism of which we have so far had no more than a foretaste'. It was imperative for the Church to stop praising Pétain, to protest against infractions of human rights and the anti-Jewish measures, and to warn against collaboration with Nazism. Even if such behaviour entailed risks, they would be preferable to being compromised.[49]

Even after November 1942, the message was not heeded. The higher echelons of the clergy remained loyal to the Marshal. In June 1943, Suhard wrote to him as follows: 'More than ever France needs you. With spirits in such disarray, it needs a voice to tell it which direction to follow.'[50] Nevertheless, with total occupation, the hardening of German repression and the weakening of the regime, the Church felt a stronger need to affirm its traditional protective role. In June 1943, it told Laval forthrightly of its opposition to the denaturalization of French Jews.[51] In early 1944, it got Suhard, who had often intervened in individual cases, to ask the embassy for an improvement in the lot of French people interned in Germany.[52]

For the rest, it continued first and foremost to look out for its own interests, conceived in the narrowest possible way. In early 1943, it faced a difficult decision in connection with the STO, a decision that even split the hierarchy and that extended Catholic resistance. The statement approved in May 1943 by the Assembly of Cardinals and Bishops declared that obedience was not a duty of conscience. Notwithstanding, on the whole it recommended submission. Timid though it was, that declaration for the first time dissociated the Church from the government. Even so, Suhard let it be known 'that this letter in no way constituted a declaration of war upon either the government or the occupying authorities', and that it was simply 'a lesser evil' that would prevent an outbreak of 'individual declarations' 'which would have led to much worse difficulties'.[53]

The cardinal feared reprisals on the part of the occupiers, and his fears were justified. Upon his intervention, the Germans agreed to liberate those arrested but warned that further arrests would follow if the clergy did not keep quiet about the STO and put a stop to the anti-German activities of its youth organizations.[54] The Church was also ready to exert pressure, as can be seen from its negotiations over the sending of almoners to Germany. Suhard did not hesitate to warn the embassy that unless agreement was reached the Church might accentuate its hostility to the STO, whereas concessions on the part of the Germans would make it possible to overcome the opposition of part of the clergy.[55] The Germans did indeed refuse to be conciliatory, but Suhard's threats remained a dead letter. All the same, this affair did show that the Church was capable of taking action when its own interests were at stake. The bishops decided as a body that twenty priests should secretly depart for Germany. It was a gesture that the churches in both Belgium and Holland were not willing to make[56] and it seems reasonable to regard it as an attempt to compensate for the absence of a condemnation of the STO on the part of the Church of France.

Suhard's prudent line was not unconnected with his own personal view of the conflict. In 1943, he made scornful remarks about the Americans in the presence of a German diplomat.[57] A few days before the allied landings, he wrote in his notebooks: 'As the conflict continues, it gives each of the belligerents allies that they fear and that make them fight against adversaries whom, deep down, they would like to have as allies.' Later he went on to say 'The United States may well become the most intolerable imperialist power the world has ever known.'[58] According to Abetz, he several times suggested 'that, because of the bolshevik danger that is becoming increasingly threatening, Germany ought to aim for an *entente* with England'.[59]

Even if other opinions and attitudes existed at the top of the Church hierarchy, they produced no practical effects. Admittedly, the Church of France gave no official support to the policies of collaboration. It even abstained from repeating the Pope's condemnation of communism. Its dignitaries certainly showed prudence in their relations with the occupier. Nevertheless, throughout those black years it remained silent on the score of Nazism, which the Pope had condemned, and also on the score of the crimes of the occupying power – the executions of hostages, the deportations of those who resisted, the persecution of the Jews – breaking that silence only (and to a minimal degree) on the subject of the STO. While public opinion was evolving from hostile passivity towards active rejection, the Church remained unmoved, playing into the occupiers' hands through both its silence and its recommendations of obedience. Its efforts to discipline the faithful did prove effective, at least in the first two years: from the time of the armistice up until September 1942, out of the 329 teachers arrested by the German authorities, only two came from free (Church) education, and only four out of the 339 pupils.[60]

Its covert defence of its own interests – 'the Church for itself alone', you might say, to return to Maurras's formula – partly explains its prudence. Was all that had been achieved with such pain to be allowed to be destroyed? Yet the Church of Belgium, despite its prudence and its tenacious defence of its own position, was more discriminating as to the limits of what could be accepted: it recognized the occupier as a 'de facto power', to which obedience was due 'within the limits of international conventions'. Consequently it did protest against the STO and draw attention to the incompatibility between Nazism and Christianity, and it also excommunicated Degrelle, the collaborationist leader.[61] In France, the existence of the new regime muddled all the cards. The Church regarded this as its historic chance to recover a central place in French society. Its attitude towards the occupying power was consequently dictated by its attachment to a regime that was itself dependent upon its association with the conquerer. A distorted image of that conquerer and his intentions, cleverly self-promoted, and a tacit but real ideological connivance, particularly on the score of communism, further determined the behaviour of the French clergy.

After 1942, the upper Church hierarchy knew that a defeat for Germany was probable and that there could hardly be a future for the regime. But it still remained attached to Pétain and continued as prudent as ever *vis-à-vis* the occupiers. The hope of a compromise peace, a pacific transition when liberation came, and order maintained up until that point partly explains its loyalty to Pétain. Above all, however, the prelates were bound by their own particular values and mental attitude. It was not only the Germans and Vichy that resistance challenged; it also threatened the foundations of authority itself, with the result that the Church was dissuaded from distancing itself from the French and German authorities. A parallelism of interests existed, which now had far less to do with political aspirations and was connected far more with the desperate protection of the values upon which the ecclesiastic institution was founded.

No clearer testimony to this could be found than the insistence with which, in the autumn of 1943, Suhard pleaded with the occupiers to allow Catholic organizations to continue to operate. He stressed that by this means he would be able to keep on steering Catholic youth towards pacific ends and deter them from engaging in resistance and terrorism, both of which he condemned absolutely. The occupiers got the message: 'In his view, maintaining these youth organizations is far less risky to us (the Germans) than dissolving them and leaving Catholic youth to its own devices.'[62] Suhard was afraid that young Catholics would become politically committed and slip towards resistance, of which he disapproved and which he failed to understand. Here is another example of that mentality at work: in October 1943, the Assembly of Cardinals and Archbishops condemned Catholic resistance for its deplorable 'attitudes of personal judgement and independence' and reminded the faithful of the exclusive authority of the hierarchy.[63] A determination not to allow the bases of obedience to be undermined and a fear of disorder and of playing into the hands of other forces all helped to block a decision to send almoners into the Maquis – until June 1944, that is, when the Pope intervened. For the growing minority of resisting Catholics, whose commitment to resistance was in fact safeguarding the future of catholicism, it was this kind of behaviour that was to prompt them, after the war, to question the authority of the hierarchy and to address themselves to the matter of the autonomy of a Christian conscience.

15

Business leaders

It is not at all easy to weigh up the attitude of the Church as against that of the employers, as these were two such very different worlds. At the liberation, the latter were treated much more harshly than the former, with political, social and national grudges all combining to condemn them as pillars of Vichy, exploiters of the working class, profiters from the occupation, if not positive allies of the occupying power. Employers as a group were pilloried; several of the most prominent were sent to prison. Subsequent nationalizations seemed just punishment for their collective unworthiness. The resentment against them stemmed from the trials undergone by a severely poverty-stricken working class, the group the hardest hit by German labour requisitioning and whose sense of social injustice had been sharpened by all the privations recently endured.

As a group, the employers, like the Church and the army, constituted a repository of authoritarian values, the restoration of which had seemed within reach. Acutely conscious of their prerogatives, and imbued with an extremely paternalistic sense of responsibility and a mentality more patrimonial than entrepreneurial, French employers had been shocked by the social movement of 1936 that had followed hard upon the great depression. Their agreement with the new regime was prompted at three levels: it was a foregone conclusion once the latter had affirmed the need for strong authority and signalled its intention to restore the social élites to the forefront of public life; it was easily established on the basis of a revaluation of business in which the work ethos would match that of the motherland and the family; and it was encouraged by the idea of a new organization of social relations, controversial in its design but in which the workers' representation would be limited, trade union autonomy would be checked, and strikes would be banned.

However, the employers' world lacked the fine simplicity of the Church and, even more, its powerful identity. Cleavages were as numerous as interests were diverse. There was a great distance separating those whose only thought was to keep their heads above water and those engaged in major business deals, whose calculations were based on a long-term view; and between these two poles were many intervening gradations. The only common denominator was a desire for business to prosper, for utilitarian aims, and pragmatic reasoning. Although a large majority of employers approved of the regime, not all did, nor were all of them in agreement on every point.[1] A certain anticapitalist rhetoric used on occasion even by Pétain – measures such as the dissolution of the Comité des forges, symbolic as this may have been; the law on limited companies; and the Labour Charter of Work, all set some teeth on edge. Above all, the policy of collaboration engendered doubts and prompted criticisms more or less rapidly depending on the zone. Like the Church, the employers as a group held back from siding openly against the occupiers right to the end. On the other hand, they did distance themselves from Vichy as soon as the hardening politics of the occupiers began to harm their interests. Anxiety about the aftermath of the liberation did not outweigh the desire to be delivered from occupation and all its constraints.

The executives of the organization committees (*comités d'organisation*: COs) constituted the most prominent section of the employers as a group during this period.[2] It was they who manifested the increasing power of employers and demonstrated the importance of their place in the new regime. They also found themselves playing a crucial mediatory role in relations with the occupation authorities, and hence in collaboration. When they set about this task right after the disaster of the defeat, they did not yet realize quite how difficult it would be.

The committees came into being in August 1940 in an economy severely disrupted by the defeat, disorganized by the frontiers drawn between one zone and another, cut off from most of its external contacts, and weakened by the tribute exacted by the occupying power. Committed to its vision of a strong and limited state, the new regime chose to harness the private economy to the regeneration of the country. The immediate task assigned to the committees was to cope with penury and, to this end, group together firms in the same branch of business, report on what means of production were available, and organize the distribution of raw materials. In the mid-term their role was to organize the economy by providing cadres and discipline (both key concepts for the regime) and also by rationalizing and modernizing it. This is where the influence of the technocrats made itself felt, as did the spirit of voluntarism that was later to infuse the industrial policies of the post-war period. In 1940, the guiding idea was to prepare businesses for competition in a German Europe by promoting *ententes* between French firms, making methods more efficient, and encouraging applied research.

The committees were placed in the hands of leading employers, most of them the heads of major firms, many of whom had held responsible positions in the pre-war trade associations. They gave younger, less well-known men a chance to come to the fore – managers in their forties such as François Lehideux on the CO for automobiles and bicycles, Jacques Guérard from insurance, Pierre Pucheu from the mechanical engineering industries. These were men who had already been supporters of an organized economy before the war and who now won their spurs and were subsequently given posts in the government. A circle comprising a few hundred business leaders was thus entrusted with a role of considerable importance. The Cos benefited from a delegation of public power that enabled them to impose dues upon those under their control and to propose sanctions. The control exercised by the state seemed limited in comparison to theirs, even though the state did appoint the members of these committees and monitored their activities through the mediation of a government commissioner who held a right of veto. Many contemporaries, particularly the heads of small or medium-sized firms saw all this as revenge and triumph for the 'trusts'.

On the face of it, this was a situation in which the major employers carved out a preserve of their own, obtaining the means to model the economy to suit their own rationalizing interests and to satisfy their own appetites for expansion. But it is worth pointing out that the leaders of these committees had to adjust to a situation that was neither of their own choosing nor necessarily to their liking. Before the war, vocational organization had been no more than a minor issue that attracted smaller and medium-sized firms in difficulties more than larger-scale employers who could cope well enough with competition and were concerned not to open up chances for state intervention. One advantage of the creation of the COs was that it blocked administrative interventionism. Furthermore, the disorganization of the economy and the presence of the Germans for an indeterminate period made consolidation seem an attractive solution, whether in order to exert pressure to obtain raw materials, to protect oneself against takeover attempts, or to orientate the reform of the national economy. Finally, it was believed that the committees would help to get activity going again and to reduce unemployment – important priorities for the employers as much as for the government, in the interests of social stability.

Big business thus strengthened its influence just at the point when the counter-balances of parliament, political parties, and trade unions had all disappeared. With political responsibilities, a hand in the allocation of raw materials, and access to high-ranking civil servants, its leaders certainly seemed in a good position to defend their own interests. But did they really have the power to promote these interests? In reality, with regard to both ideas and methods, their power was anything but united and their autonomy was certainly very limited. Cohesion within the various committees was uneven, as was the driving force of their leaders, whose ambitions varied widely. A minority took their task of rehabilitation and rationalization extremely seriously. Others were more concerned to protect and enhance their own vested interests, sometimes making use of aryanization to this end.[3] In 1943, the technocrats were to look back on their hopes with a somewhat disillusioned eye.[4] As it turned out, the day-to-day task of coping with the general shortages absorbed most of the committees' energies, and they were met with inertia, if not illwill by most firms, which tended to be dissatisfied with their allocation of raw materials, uncertain about which committee they were attached to (there were 141 of them at the end of 1941, 231 by 1944), and exasperated by the paperwork that swamped them and by the ever-expanding administrative apparatus, the costs of which they were expected to bear.[5]

Above all, the autonomy of the committee executives soon came under pressure from two quarters. On the one side, the occupiers, as the war dragged on, came to play a formidable role, controlling the distribution of raw materials, placing more and more orders and even, towards the end, deciding what should be produced, invariably to suit their own best interests. On the other, the French state assumed ever greater powers of control and direction, particularly through the distribution of raw materials, organized by the Office

Central de Répartition des Produits Industriels (Central Office for the Distribution of Industrial Products: OCRPI). The COs, which were thus reduced to a role of sub-distribution, found themselves tightly integrated into Vichy's politics of collaboration and, on that account, subjected to close surveillance. However overworked they may have been, the government commissioners managed to keep a close eye on all relations with the occupation authorities, issuing a stream of directives and checking on the progress of all negotiations.[6]

Relations between Vichy and the occupying power hinged upon the organization committees right from the moment of their creation, and both sides sought to use them to their own advantage. Had there been no French government, the Germans would have imposed an organization of this kind, just as they did in Belgium, Holland and the northern departments of France that were attached to Brussels. The creation of the COs provided them with exactly what they wanted: an instrument for collecting statistical information that seemed to be in very short supply but was indispensable if exploitation was to be efficient; a conveyor belt for the sub-distribution of raw materials, which saved them having to employ several hundred officials;[7] and a means of standardizing the economic structures of the two countries prior to incorporating France into Nazi Europe.

As Vichy saw it, if the task of the COs was partly to cope with shortages and establish the bases of the new national economy, it was also to interpose themselves between the occupying power and French firms. This was a role that became increasingly important as German orders increased in volume. Vichy imagined that by making the committees responsible for centralizing and meeting those orders, it would be possible to demonstrate how amply France was providing Germany with economic aid and to get this offset by substantial concessions. However, the occupiers were interested only in the advantages to themselves to be derived from the COs, and preferred to negotiate directly with French firms, upon which they had the means to exert daunting pressure. After several months of discussions punctuated by rows, Vichy was eventually forced to accept the *de facto* situation. German orders continued to be placed directly with the firms, and the COs were confined to giving advice and recording statistics.[8]

They nevertheless did play a noteworthy role in Franco-German relations. From the sources that exist, it is not possible to get a total and detailed idea of the points of view of their executives and their influence upon the politics of Vichy. However, the general impression given is that they simply went with the flow, sometimes dragging their feet, rather than actively pushing forward. They appear to have been keen to maintain permanent contact with the Vichy ministers, anxious to obtain governmental directives to cover themselves, and in general to have manifested an attitude that was deferent and prudent rather than confident and initiatory. The advice that they proferred was assessed piecemeal by negotiators who, in matters of importance, always subordinated it to government policy.

This docile integration of the COs can be explained in the first place by the legalism, protection and legitimation that state patronage extended to the relations between French employers and an occupying power that invariably exploited its own position of superior strength. It is also and above all explained by a strong convergence of interests. The committee executives were clearly keen to keep the economy working, defend their own branch of it, if not their own firm, and do their utmost to strengthen its chances of survival, whatever happened. To that end, most were prepared to make at least temporary concessions. Ideological support for Vichy was not a decisive factor although, in the early days at least, it was seldom altogether absent and did play its part in securing support for the government's line of action. Of course, Vichy took care not to appoint anyone of doubtful loyalty, and the Germans maintained vigilant surveillance, insisting on vetting appointments as if they were for civil servants, and sometimes ruling out executives who were deemed lukewarm or untrustworthy. Over the years, up to 1944, this resulted in a by no means negligible rotation of CO executives (in a sample of twenty-three committees, one-third at least were replaced),[9] although it is not possible to determine how many stood down or were simply removed.

A minority took a positive lead. These were certainly not marginal figures but nor can they be claimed to be particularly representative. Various reasons may be cited for their commitment: firm support for the policies of the new regime of a kind that, for example, led the secretary general of the CO of the hotel industry to convey to the MBF, after Montoire, his 'most ardent desire to make the spirit of collaboration that has just emerged effective and long-lasting';[10] or a specific sectorial interest (the occupiers did not solicit cooperation to the same extent from all the branches, and the interests of some branches inclined them to favour accommodation more than others). Some already had experience of cooperation with German businesses within a framework of international *ententes* or cartels. Others, ever since the pre-war days, had felt a need for closer ties to help them face up to common competitors – the Americans, for example, in the car industry. Finally, in some cases a desire for *entente* manifested by the corresponding German sector led, through the affirmation of a shared branch egoism, to the creation of transversal solidarities.

The theme of European economic organization, which was widely diffused by German propaganda and its French outlets, in particular by a newspaper such as *La Vie industrielle,* also encouraged such attitudes and, in 1941 at least, found a number of sympathizers. One was the chairman of the trade association of untreated leathers and skins, who dreamed of a 'United States of Europe' and, for the benefit of his own branch, sketched out a picture of an organization committee on a continental scale, a European and African centre for untreated leathers and skins.[11] Most of the CO executives did not allow themselves to be carried away by such visions. They were acutely aware of the situation and the uneven balance of forces and this led them to react to rather than initiate action, adjusting to a German policy that itself underwent considerable changes, evolving from the looting of the early days to exploitation, initially on a sectorial scale but subsequently of the French economy generally.

The 'sharing of experience' constituted one of the first contexts in which the committees came into contact with the occupation apparatus. In the interests of standardization and efficiency, the Germans wished to give the French the benefit of their own experience in coping with an economy blighted by shortages. To this end, the MBF officials appealed to the COs' opposite numbers, the 'economic groups' whose delegates were attached to the 'Centre in France for German economic organizations'. By early 1941, conferences were being organized to bring the French distributors and CO executives (for machinery, steel, iron, precision engineering and optical equipment, cars, etc.) into contact with the 'corresponding' German groups.[12] This was definitely in the interests of the French and, with much encouragement from the technocrats of Vichy, they declared themselves ready to follow the advice that was showered upon them. Bichelonne looked favourably upon the idea of holding meetings, in Paris and Berlin alternately, that would open up vast perspectives: substitutes for raw materials, the harmonization of standards, the organization of technical research, and even sharing together in 'the future European economic market'.[13]

These meetings became routine, involving a whole series of COs ranging from trade, through timber, to gas and electricity, and eventually widening to incorporate the chambers of commerce. In September 1941, the latter formed mixed commissions that met in Germany and France alternately. The purpose, here too, was to familiarize the French with the economic organization of the Reich and to work towards a standardization of ideas and methods. But short-term preoccupations were certainly also involved, such as the matter of professional training, which the occupiers wished to see developed in France.[14] The French chambers of commerce played along, often with a good grace. When the president of the Rennes Chamber of Commerce wrote to a German colleague to thank him for the welcome extended to its delegation, he expressed his wish to see 'these contacts continue, with the most desirable aim of extending economic relations between our two countries'.[15]

What the 'sharing of experience' really meant was a docile French pupil paying attention to the teaching of a learned German professor. Nevertheless, its importance was considerable, even if the French were not exactly fulsome with their thanks after the war. The Germans were well ahead in the struggle against the wastage of raw materials and the search for substitute products. They were more than willing to pass on their experience given that this aid served their needs in the short term, and their interests in the longer term; and for the French there were immediate advantages, hence the number of the meetings and the many journeys to Germany with a technological or economic purpose (from February 1941 on, French engineers and technicians were allowed to travel to the Reich to learn about methods of production).[16] In November 1941 alone, Germany was visited by delegations from the chamber of commerce, the chemical industry, the railways and the cable, aluminium, and aeronautical industries.[17] The period of occupation gave French industrialists and high-ranking civil servants an unprecedented opportunity to catch a glimpse, however limited, of the organization and production methods of their neighbour, the most industrialized country in Europe. The eventual gain to them is literally inestimable; it may well have been appreciable and appreciated at the time.

The placing of German orders created a second area in which the COs were involved. In the autumn of 1940, Göring declared that part of Germany's civil production must be transferred to the occupied countries, since Germany needed to concentrate on military production. This prospect provoked serious misgivings: German industrialists were reluctant to entrust orders to foreign firms that they did not know; they wanted to protect their own manufacturing methods; and they were afraid of giving competitors a head start in the post-war period, when they themselves would be faced with a painful reconversion.[18]

Although orders were placed directly with individual firms, the COs could be useful by creating a favourable climate for their acceptance; and that is exactly what the occupiers expected of them. Their executives accordingly sent round circulars of encouragement. Similarly, some pressed firms in their own particular branch to accept more orders: for example, the executive of the committee for medical equipment, whose efforts resulted in a considerable increase in material delivered to the Germans.[19] Some pleaded their cause in the newspapers, envisaging long-term collaboration or personally vouching for the German industrialists' desire for *entente*. For example, Pierre Pucheu, while executive of the CO of mechanical engineering industries, declared: 'The Germans have made quite clear their desire for economic *entente* between our two countries.' He stressed that these orders would provide employment for the workers, and set in train 'a policy of reconstruction established in full agreement with German industrialists, which will make it possible to replace the economic struggles of the past by ordered collaboration'.[20]

Committees were all the keener to promote the programme of German orders when their branch particularly needed them and the partners they had to deal with were conciliatory. The optical equipment and precision engineering industries had been sorely affected by the seizure of many of their machines. The Germans promised to return them in exchange for the accepting of military orders. It was an offer that was gratefully received: the CO declared its willingness to find out how much work could be taken on and to see that contracts were fulfilled with the utmost despatch. Its executive, Yvon, had formed a good opinion of the Germans and their intentions. In an interview, he emphasized the vital interest of orders for his branch, adding that German industry could perfectly well have kept them for itself. 'The altogether contrary path that is being followed, that of working in common, seems to be dictated more by a reasoned wish to prepare for the future peace than by an urgent desire to satisfy imperative needs.'[21] On instructions from the government, he tried to obtain the necessary raw materials from his opposite number, who refused them but promised to intervene on his behalf with the MBF. While this German branch had no intention of eating into its own allocations of raw materials, it did put pressure on the MBF to get it to favour this particular CO in the distribution of raw materials, thereby disadvantaging other sectors of the French economy. Clearly, collaboration could sometimes pay off and lead to partial solidarities. Small wonder that, upon his return from negotiations in Berlin, Yvon expressed his desire for 'very close collaboration'.[22]

The organization committees came into contact with 'economic groups' in another context too, that of agreements made between corresponding branches. The prolongation of the war had made it necessary to transfer orders to France. Agreements between corresponding branches of industry were part and parcel of the plans for German industry in the summer of 1940 when, in the expectation of an early peace, it was asked to draw up a list of its needs. Nearly all sectors asked that the obstacles to their exports to France be reduced or removed. Many, to reinforce their advantage, demanded that the creation or enlargement of French factories be banned, and even that some of them be closed. Others sought definitively to guarantee their own pre-eminence by acquiring holdings in France, particularly in the companies from which they had been ousted in 1918, and through agreements on the regulation of markets.[23]

The fulfilment of all these requests was deferred indefinitely, as was the peace treaty which was supposed to give them form. Nevertheless, a few agreements between corresponding branches were concluded, as well as some between cartels, for example on man-made textiles (France-Rayonne).[24] These branch agreements dated from the first months of the occupation and were, in practice, contracts for the delivery of raw materials or semi-finished products, accompanied by agreements on the regulation of markets: in order to obtain the former, the French were obliged to swallow the latter. In the paper and pottery industries, the French branch had to commit itself to sharing markets and to certain sales conditions, in exchange for immediate supplies of raw materials or an order. Here again, the Germans promised to intervene to obtain coal and raw materials for them.[25] The inequality of the forces involved in these agreements was patently obvious, and it would be a mistake to regard them as evidence of a desire for long-term collaboration.

Significantly enough, no agreements of this kind came to anything thereafter. In the field of electrical construction, for example, Siemens tried to set up a European cartel under its own direction, but discussions were dragged out, the days of German successes passed, and nothing was done.[26]

The case of insurance provides a good example of the pressures of the early days of the occupation. The CO of this branch was directed by Jacques Guérard, the PDG of an insurance company, a member of the Worms team, and a staunch supporter of positive and long-term collaboration. ('Collaboration', he declared, 'is not, or should no longer be, a way of getting through a few of the hardest years of our national existence at the least cost, a way of sparing us certain trials or tempering them, a procedure that, between ourselves, we make excuses for.')[27] As early as the autumn of 1940, his opposite number insisted upon the right for its members to operate in France, with the aim of taking over the part of the market held by British companies (101 companies and close on one-tenth of the total premiums paid for in 1938). Pressure was applied: the MBF appointed commissioners to the British companies who proceeded to treat them as enemy property, as a result of which sums due to French victims of war damage who were insured by them were frozen and in danger of being confiscated.[28]

In September 1940, the government had Gabriel Cheneaux de Leyritz, the director of insurance at the Ministry of Finance, who was also the government commissioner to the CO for insurance, announce that it accepted the principle of authorizing the establishment of German companies, provided France would benefit from reciprocity in Germany.[29] Negotiations began between the two COs and, in March 1941, a protocol was signed. The French accepted the establishment of twenty or so German companies, repeating their request for reciprocity; in other words, reciprocity was no longer regarded as a precondition. The Germans agreed to the appointment of provisional French administrators to the British companies, setting them under the supervision of the German commissioners. The form of the takeover of the British portfolios was not specified: it would either involve reinsurance by the German companies, with the reinsurer subsequently taking over the contracts, or else an enforced transfer to the German companies, after a delay for those insured to opt out.[30]

In the course of the months that followed, seventeen German companies were approved by Vichy. The French COs, anxious to bring the conditions of activity of these new competitors into line, managed to get them to recognize a common tariff, in return for a 10 per cent reduction for them for an agreed period, by way of a kind of implantation allowance. Nor did French goodwill stop there: the French insurance companies agreed to the creation of a company for the reinsurance of high risks, to be located in Munich (the *Pariser Zeitung* of 7 June 1941 ran the headline, 'French insurance frees itself from British domination'). Vichy also agreed to allow three German companies to acquire minority holdings in three French companies.[31]

The negotiations had gone well. Agreement was reached between the insurers all the more easily given that the interests of the French were not directly affected, since what the Germans would take over were spoils from the British. But Vichy was not satisfied with this state of affairs, for reasons that are interesting in that they testify clearly to Vichy's political objectives. There was insufficient protection: the German commissioners were continuing to block the payments due to the insured French people on the grounds that these funds were enemy property. France's sovereignty was not being respected: Vichy wanted German recognition of its right to regulate the insurance sector in France, whatever the nationality of the companies concerned. Germany, however, feared that its gains might be brought into question after the war and wanted a legal document to protect them; so they continued to block the British assets. Finally, France's standing was not being respected: the German government was evasive when faced with the demand for reciprocity that the French had put forward from the start and that had already been accepted by the German CO for insurance companies.[32]

In December 1941, Guérard and Cheneaux de Leyritz returned to the subject in Berlin. Guérard declared that 'collaboration between the two countries over insurance, of which he was a committed supporter, was every day running up against the same obstacle: the absence of reciprocity. This was the objection that was ceaselessly made to him in his daily work in France.' He requested authorization for the establishment of two or three companies. 'These companies would probably not do much business in Germany, but they were ready to make a few pecuniary sacrifices in the interest of the Franco-German cause.'[33] Although negotiations did make a little progress on the legal document, they never progressed any further on the question of reciprocity, even though Cheneaux de Leyritz, now chairman of the CO, returned to Berlin in 1942.[34]

The case of the automobile industry was an exception, for here the initiative came, not from the Germans, but from the executive of the French CO, Lehideux.[35] The position of this branch had been characterized by an almost immediate return to work and relatively few instances of dismantling: the Germans needed it for their motorized war. French car makers were thus able to compensate for the cessation of public orders, although they paid for this in other ways. Commissioners, later known as 'industrial commissioners', forced upon them manufacturing programmes that diverted them away from the production of cars for leisure – a serious handicap for the future. On 1 March 1941, an agreement signed in Berlin created a 'Transitional Committee for Collaboration in the European Automobile Industry' that embraced Germany, Italy and France. The long-term objective was to rationalize the production and distribution of cars and to fix relations with producers in the rest of the world (with American competition in mind). Five commissions were set up, which continued to meet regularly until September 1942.[36] The agendas of the meetings indicate quite clearly that their immediate purpose was to coordinate production to serve the Axis war effort. Lehideux wanted to lay down the foundations for a viable collaboration between industrial groups, on an equal footing, in an organized and rational fashion. The conquerors, for their part, made no concessions at all on their rights and moved towards the constitution of a cartel, the terms of which they would fix when the moment suited them. For the time being, they made the most of the goodwill of the French.

In the committee for cars as in the committee for insurance, the driving force of the executives, who were also militant collaborationists, played an important role. But, as can be seen in the case of insurance, the militants were tightly linked to high-ranking state officials. None of these negotiations led to any serious agreement. What they showed, as usual, was that on the German side the will to keep defeated France in its place was altogether intransigent and that government bodies, in particular the Ministry of the Economy, regularly intervened to introduce political corrections to the negotiations pursued in a pragmatic way between employers' organizations.

At this level, relations appear often to have been cordial, being founded on converging interests, although this did not prevent the Germans from making the most of the means of exerting pressure that the situation provided in abundance. After the aggressive spirit in which the initial contacts were made, there were many indications of goodwill.[37] In this connection, it is worth noting the following comments made by Norguet, the director of engineering industries for the Ministry for Industrial Production, at the end of 1941: 'In some of the Germans seeking *ententes* or stakes in French firms, it seems . . . possible to discern not always a desire for hegemony or domination, but on the contrary a desire to insure themselves against all eventualities. The fact is that some of them are uncertain of a German victory and of a continuing Nazi regime, or are acting as bourgeois seeking association with foreign bourgeois so as to influence the social state of their own country.'[38]

The last context in which the COs played a part was the *Relève*. By the beginning of the summer of 1942, the vision of a new European order had lost much of its sheen. The enforced exploitation of the economy, the closure of several thousand factories in order to concentrate the labour force (an operation to which the COs reacted with massive inertia, preferring to leave the responsibility to the state), and the beginning of German plundering of the labour force – all these things were darkening the outlook of the employers. So it was with palpable unease that the committee executives found themselves being asked by Laval to contribute to the success of the *Relève*.[39] By becoming agents of the government in this affair, they would be entering a minefield where their own interests were in peril.

To get this idea of voluntary labour for Germany to succeed, Laval asked the committee executives to encourage firms to promote the *Relève*, that is to say send teams of workers led by foremen and engineers to factories agreed upon by the French and German COs. The French COs were also to try to arrange for these men to join up with teams of prisoners of war who would be converted into civilian workers.[40] Laval was hoping to encourage recruitment by offering workers the chance to leave as a group, work and live in supervised conditions and be reunited with prisoner comrades. He dangled before the employers the hope of subsequently recuperating their workers, who would remain together and keep their hands in, working with their own particular skills.

In July, discussions started between the French and the German COs affected by the *Relève*. The German COs needed a labour force; the French COs, at the request of their government, tried to obtain 'special advantages designed to make the recruitment of volunteers easier'.[41] Accordingly, they presented their demands: that missions be sent to check on working and living conditions, and that French prisoners be transferred to the factories to which their comrades from France would be sent. On the first point, the Germans agreed in principle. On the second, their answers varied, as is shown by the negotiations of the two COs in particular (although it is not possible to tell whether their cases are representative).

The German executives of the CO for optical equipment and precision engineering refused outright.[42] Those of the CO for leather products were more amenable. Relations were strained at the economic level but cordial at the personal level. The French had visited Berlin in the spring. In September the Germans came to Paris where they received a princely welcome: visits to places of interest outside Paris, meals in the best restaurants, an evening at the Opera. In meetings with their French counterparts, they accepted the list of prisoners prepared by the French and promised to approach the Wehrmacht in an effort to get them sent to the factories that were to receive the volunteer workers of the *Relève.*[43] There seems to be no explanation for such a difference in attitudes, except perhaps a greater need for labour and a more open state of mind on the part of the German CO for leather. It proceeded to do its best, although without results. In the autumn of 1943 its director wrote to say, with palpable regret, that times were hard for him too: the authorities were withdrawing labour from his sector and diverting it to munitions.[44]

Beyond these negotiations, and once it became a matter of recruiting volunteers, the COs became extremely reluctant. Most limited their activities to passing on the appeals of the government. But a few did themselves make efforts, Georges-Jean Painvin, for instance, the leader of the chemical industries and also the PDG of Ugine and the Crédit Commercial de France, who personally urged his colleagues to find volunteers. To no avail, however: by October, fewer than a hundred workers had left for Germany, accompanied by an engineer from Ugine, although the branch had been asked to supply 7000 workers.[45]

When the STO was set up, the COs were relieved of their task of exhortation. But a number of them continued to intervene in this field, this time to preserve their own labour force and to improve the lot of any of their workers who had already gone to Germany. The COs for banks and insurance companies stand out here in that they did pursue a policy of protection, and did manage to diminish and delay requisition, mostly by drawing attention to their active relations with German firms and the help they were giving them.[46] When they ceased to benefit from preferential treatment, in the spring of 1944, they got their German counterparts to make sure that those requisitioned were sent to work in banks or insurance companies. As Cheneaux de Leyritz wrote on 30 May 1944: 'Not only am I anxious to protect the sector of industry for which I am responsible, but I also wish to maintain courteous relations with German insurance.'[47] No doubt these employers were indeed anxious to improve the lot of their employees, to spare them distasteful or dangerous work, and to give them the opportunity of useful training. But, as anyone can see, in reality, in pursuing such a policy, they smoothed the way for their departure and thereby facilitated the task of the occupying power.

Some of the COs remained hitched to the Vichy wagon to the bitter end, as is testified by a surprising episode that took place in the summer of 1943. Ever since late 1941, the Germans had been dangling the lure of a partnership with France in the exploitation of the 'territories of the East'. In reality, what they were after was immediate aid to reactivate certain sectors of industry. After being approached several times, in March 1943 Laval agreed to send out a number of firms, but in return requested to be allowed a share in the economy of the Ukraine.[48] At this very moment Germany's eastern front was beginning to crack. Yet in Vichy, imperturbably, an Eastern European Company was being set up. 'A French economic delegation in the Ukraine', under the direction of a paint manufacturer from Aubervilliers, Laval's former electoral fiefdom, dispatched two fact-finding missions with delegates from a number of the COs among their members. Their conclusions were not encouraging. 'Contrary to the hopes engendered by certain German statements, it is not proposed that France should create any major industrial or agricultural concerns in the Ukraine. Heavy industry and agriculture . . . seem to constitute "private preserves" for the exclusive use of German nationals. Our country is only called upon to provide temporary assistance in a few secondary branches.'

Bichelonne, who was supervising this affair, complained to the Majestic: France was being offered only contracts that were 'precarious and liable to be reversed or cancelled at the end of the war'(!), despite the fact that the French government had 'taken extremely liberal decisions to the effect that such profits realized by the industries established in the Ukraine as came to France would not be subject to fiscal taxation'. A few days earlier, Bichelonne had invited nine committees to subscribe to the capital of the East European Company. Five never replied. One declared that, in view of the military situation, there was no cause 'to hurry to set up the company' and requested time to think about the matter. But three committees (building and public works, the hotel industry, and the chemical industries) sent along their subscriptions. This creation of a latter-day 'East India Company' was an episode that came to nothing; but it shows that Vichy was not abandoned by everyone in the world of business.[49]

16

Captains of industry

At the liberation, there was one image that seemed to sum up the attitude of industrialists under the occupation: that of the Round Table lunches, regular meetings of French and German business men held at the Ritz. 'Treachery lunches', some people called them, and 'just see who is invited!', they said. The cream of industry celebrated with the occupiers, drinking to the profits of their consortiums in vintage wines: a sad image from Epinal, to which one might add, in a corner, a few down-and-outs contemplating these unworthy feasts with clenched fists.

Like their colleagues in other occupied countries, French employers faced the full drama of peoples subjected to occupation in an age of industrial warfare, when any assistance given to the occupying power could hasten its victory and enable it to assume lasting domination. Nowhere in Nazi Europe did rejection or abstention ever seem the inevitable choice, even where German policies were far more brutal than in France. The most common attitude adopted involved finding a means for those occupied to survive without providing too much assistance for the occupiers. It was a difficult exercise in which the scales tilted heavily to one side, putting employers in an uncomfortable position the moment they derived profit from the situation.

By the end of 1941, 7000 French firms were taking on German orders of either a civilian or a military nature. By 1944 that figure had doubled.[1] It included probably most of the firms with fifty or more employees (in 1936, 279 firms had over 1000 employees, 2473 had between 200 and 1000, 9188 had between 50 and 200), as well as some firms with between twenty-five and fifty employees. In other words, most industrialists of any importance were accepting orders from the occupying power, thereby supporting its war effort either directly or indirectly. But what was their state of mind as they did so?

Records kept by the German services in contact with them, in particular the Wehrmacht armament service (the WI. Rü.-Stab.) provide at least some information. Initial contacts were often abrasive. Alongside a few indications of goodwill, there was a reluctance that sometimes bordered on passive resistance. Industrialists manifested repugnance at accepting orders for munitions, or at least they did if the government had not given them the go-ahead. In fifty firms, the matter was resolved by the appointment of German commissioners, as in the cases of the major car manufacturers and the Schneider firm.[2]

By the autumn of 1940, the attitude of industrialists was reckoned to be 'relatively positive', or at least improved since July and August – an evolution that ran counter to public opinion in general, as the Germans noticed.[3] In early 1941, their reports noted the existence of 'a circle, admittedly small but expanding', of major industrialists disposed to integrate themselves into a continental economy under German control. Some were motivated by political convictions: any links thus forged might influence the conditions for peace and hence the future of France; some by economic calculations: French industry had not suffered great war damage, and German orders could facilitate rapid reconversion to civilian production, which would give it an advantage in the post-war European market. (That was a hope that was balanced by an equivalent fear of entrepreneurs on the other side of the Rhine.) It is worth noting that the Germans themselves did not exaggerate the importance of this circle of industrialists. They commented that their best allies in the exploitation of the French economy were the 'weariness and indifference' of a population that no longer bothered to argue over politics so long as it was provided with food and employment.[4]

By the spring of 1941 there was a noticeable tendency for relations between industrialists and the Germans to become more common. In region A (covering the north-west of the country), the Wi. Rü.-Stab. noted an increase in those visiting its offices. Following the initial reticence, a kind of routine became established. Entrepreneurs would call in to settle some difficulty, to ask for assistance or instructions, or to angle for an order. The fact was that much of the region's economic life was by then dependent upon German contracts.[5]

The change in atmosphere was noticeable at the German technical and industrial salon held in the Petit Palais from February to October 1941. The flow of orders that needed to be placed made it difficult to continue to approach firms individually, hence the idea of exhibiting the objects that the Germans most needed to be put into production and to let industrialists make their own choice. The operation was not assured of success, even allowing for the effect of the publicity put out by the CO and the blessing of Vichy (Brinon and Stülpnagel between them opened the exhibition). However, the German organizers were delighted with the results. Initially, the aim of the salon was to get major firms to volunteer to produce items needed by the Wehrmacht. This proved a 'very great success': 80 per cent of the 12000 objects exhibited found industrialists ready to produce them. Then it was the turn of the civil sector, aimed at small and medium-sized firms: 75 per cent of these objects found willing producers. Altogether, 10000 firms engaged in the production of machinery and in the electrical industry, mostly from the Paris region and the north-east, attended the exhibition and filed 26000 manufacturing proposals. At first the visitors manifested a very noticeable reserve, but this soon gave way to a more interested and positive attitude.[6]

Here, it was the industrialists themselves who were out seeking orders. Since the days immediately following the defeat, the situation had been reversed. However, by the summer of 1941, German records registered a change of atmosphere, which became even more noticeable by the turn of the year. Authorities in region A noted that even industrialists hitherto favourable to collaboration now seemed 'more reserved'.[7] It is quite true that speculation on the advantages of economic collaboration for France in general and for individual firms in particular had by now become unfashionable. Civil orders had been replaced by military ones. By the time the *Relève* was launched the Germans were in no doubt as to the negative state of mind of the employers' world, whose attitude was hardened by the course of the war, the stiffening of public opinion, and the discontent of the workers.

As to orders, different branches of industry were in unequal demand and were in need of them to varying degrees. Collieries, for example, were producing for a market in which demand far exceeded supplies. Their managers were making the most of this situation and were mining low-producing seams, to sell low-grade coal, keeping back the better material in order to be able to take on competition after the war.[8] Coal was essential for meeting German orders, but it was not sold to the Germans. In contrast, metallurgical production fell considerably; firms in this sector could survive only with German contracts. Not all employers were facing equal difficulties.

German orders presented undeniable advantages in business logic, for industrialists were concerned to survive or expand, to preserve their personal standard of living and their social position and furthermore – in the early days, at least – with the prospect of winter looming, they claimed to wish to protect their workers. German orders made it possible for them to get going again and soon to be working at full capacity. A number of factors increased the attraction of these orders: selling prices calculated in overvalued marks; in some cases, the acquisition of technological expertise or even manufacturing secrets from German clients anxious for the product to measure up to their demands; and, from the summer of 1941 on, guaranteed deliveries of coal and raw materials, and special food supplies for factory canteens. All this was particularly helpful for the larger firms, which could exploit subcontracting by providing work without allocations of raw materials: it was left to the subcontractors to find these by their own means. As shortages increased, and thousands of firms were forced to close as a result of the programme of concentration and the requisitioning of the labour force, German orders became quite literally vital.

The atmosphere in itself added encouragement, as could be felt in 1941. After the upheavals of war and the defeat, economic life was picking up again and seemed to be returning to normal. In some sectors, the pre-war level of production was even matched (for aluminium, coal, gas and electrical equipment). German power was at its peak, peace seemed just round the corner and the Vichy regime was offering legitimation and encouragement. Small wonder the occupiers detected a most favourable attitude towards collaboration amongst the employers working for them. However, it should be remembered that it was detectable only in a minority. Interest in German orders did not necessarily signify support, falling into line, or even a lasting resignation.

Even purely at the level of business logic, plenty of disadvantages were also involved. The effect of these orders was to break links with clients in the French marketplace that it might prove difficult to restore. To firms engaged in producing war materials they brought the risk of being bombed. Often they were not even truly profitable, particularly when they followed one after another in rapid succession, with a series of different specifications that made it necessary to make constant alterations in manufacturing methods.[9] Above all, the precariousness of the situation could never be forgotten: what would a future German Europe be like? Many businessmen were affected by these and similar concerns: industrialists orientated towards overseas markets and those for whom a German victory spelt greater competition; employers in the prohibited zone, who took the worsening of their lot for granted; and likewise those already damaged by the conqueror, for instance in the steel industry, which had been seized, looted and exhausted. Small wonder that a man such as de Wendel did not look favourably upon either the occupying power or even Vichy, whatever his conservative inclinations.[10] The same went for men like Schneider, whom the German victories deprived of all his branches in Europe.

French industrialists expressed their reticence in many ways. They asked for sizeable advances, into which the Germans read a desire to tie up as little of their own money as possible in deals of this type.[11] They tried to minimize any signs of voluntary cooperation: the Peugeot family, who were strong supporters of Pétain up until 1942, accepted neither supplies of extra rations nor German propaganda in their factories.[12] Faced with efforts to introduce German capital, they demonstrated 'the greatest reserve', reducing the number of successfully concluded deals to almost nothing.[13] They refused to cooperate in any way in the recruitment of labour, even in 1940 and 1941, when underemployment was widespread. In this connection, at the end of 1941, the armament service drew attention to 'the nationalist state of mind of the majority' of industrialists, who were careful not to extend their contribution to the German war economy beyond whatever was absolutely necessary to the survival of France.[14]

As soon as the requisitioning of labour began, they took active steps to defend their workers, partly out of entrepreneurial self-interest, but also out of patriotism and a concern for social peace. In the vast sector working for Germany, a tacit and awkward *entente* obtained between employers and workers. The 15000 odd firms of 1944 employed 1500000 workers, to which figure should be added 660000 who were subcontracted[15] – in total 20 per cent of the active male population (of 1936). Most of these workers benefited from exemption from the STO, a fact that prompted continuous requests for employment from young men who preferred to work for Germany in France rather than beyond the Rhine. This unity sanctioned by expediency, of which nobody was particularly proud, did not prevent working-class claims from building up clandestinely, preparing the way for a future wave of social militancy in the wake of the liberation.

Most industrialists took on German orders as a stop-gap, in accordance with business logic. But in a situation characterized by shrinking activity, many constraints and great uncertainty, which did not, to be sure, exclude the desire to make a profit and a wish to manage the future with an eye to the possibility of a German victory, some stood out by reason of their manifest greed or zeal, or because they agreed to the establishment of durable links with German partners. In the first of those two cases, seeking out the occupier as a client could clearly be criticized as unacceptable behaviour. In principle, there was a clear distinction between acceptance and solicitation. In practice, however, when it came to orders the line between the two was easily blurred. Eagerness was manifest when industrialists resorted to advertising in, for example, the *Pariser Zeitung*. It would be tedious to list the dozens of firms – quite apart from nightclubs and restaurants, which rented advertising space there on a continuous basis – that daily strove to bring themselves to the Germans' attention, the majority of them mechanical engineering firms, steelworks and public construction companies. And who but a German clientèle could Elizabeth Arden have been addressing when she stressed that her products were 'three times less expensive than abroad'?[16]

The situation was even clearer when orders were welcomed greedily, leading to a firm's productive apparatus being extended and its French clientèle being dumped; or when industrialists determined to keep their factories running whatever the cost actually offered to manufacture military material. Louis Renault, who could not have cared less about his workers being requisitioned, could not bear to see his machine tools seized. To prevent this, in early 1943 he declared himself prepared to manufacture armoured supply carriers or even tanks. 'Only one thing counts, me and my factory', he said, in connection with the *Relève*, 'Let others do as I do if they so wish!'[17]

In the second case, a French industrialist would become associated with a German partner, that is to say he might set up a company with mixed capital, or form a consortium to build a factory, or come to an agreement over the exploitation of a patent,[18] or establish some other kind of durable link. In 1941, a number of large department stores – Printemps, La Samaritaine, Les Nouvelles Galeries – negotiated with German counterparts (Karstadt, Erwege and Hertie) and, in some cases, concluded agreements over their mutual use of central purchasing agencies. It was not a matter of covering immediate needs: the contract between La Samaritaine and Hertie specified that it would become valid only when the peace treaty was signed. What these people had in mind was definitely long-term collaboration and, of course, a speedy German victory.[19]

A number of large firms established long-term liaisons of this kind. The initiative, it should be said, always came from the German side, often from IG Farben, the mammoth chemicals company. Unlike the thousands of other industrialists accepting German orders, here the parties already knew each other, in some cases from years back, mostly from having taken part in international *ententes* or cartels. It was German pressure that made the French government take part in these negotiations; and the entrepreneurs welcomed this, as most of them found themselves in positions of weakness. With not only markets, but also branches, holdings and licence agreements abroad, they had suffered from the collapse of their exports and external revenues. Furthermore, at least some of their factories were situated in the occupied zone or in other countries now occupied by Germany. The triangular situation of the firms, Vichy, and the Germans nevertheless worked out quite differently for different companies, depending on the attitudes of the industrialists involved.

The case of Michelin will serve as an example of a firm that chose to repulse the advances of the Germans, even if this meant diverging from government policy. In the summer of 1941, the unreliability of deliveries of rubber from Indochina prompted negotiations at state level. Germany suggested supplying synthetic rubber (buna) in exchange for a financial holding in the French sector. Concerned for the future of an economy more or less cut off from overseas, the French government was interested. The Michelin company, on the other hand, was not, if only because the Germans demanded that it hand over its assets in countries now under their control. The firm refused to abandon its Belgian branch or even to allow the Germans a minority holding in it. The Germans then shifted their efforts to Czechoslovakia and Holland; Michelin repulsed them, but without rejecting their proposals absolutely. It asked for guarantees of its continuing presence in those markets 'after the war', particularly in the Dutch market.[20]

Michelin accepted the risk of not receiving any supplies of buna and of being treated unfavourably in the distribution of rubber. In August 1941, one of its executives declared, in connection with its Belgian branch, 'I have made my choice: it is to sacrifice the present to save the future.' It was a position that related to political choices and only made sense in the context of a belief in, if not an improbable German defeat (as can be seen from the reference to 'after the war'), at least a less than total victory. Economically, given its supply sources, Michelin was inevitably hoping for an English victory. Besides, it was being offered a poor deal: a little buna in exchange for giving up its branches abroad. Anxious for the negotiations to succeed, Vichy did not put pressure on Michelin to give in, but it certainly gave it no encouragement to hold out.[21] As a result of Michelin's attitude, the whole affair in its initial form was later abandoned.

Other industrialists proved more pliant. The negotiations over Francolor, which began soon after the defeat, were marked by vindictiveness on the part of IG Farben. After 1918, German industry had lost control of the French market in dyestuffs, but never resigned itself to this situation, even when it was formally regulated and a cartel was set up in 1927. Now, with the tables turned, IG Farben was determined to regain its dominant position by amalgamating all the major French dyestuffs factories into a single company in which it would itself hold most of the capital. This company would be prevented from exporting and would furthermore be obliged to depend on IG Farben for supplies of all other products.

Learning of these demands at a meeting called by Hemmen in Wiesbaden, the industrialists concerned appealed to the government. They wished to avoid losing control; but the government's major concern was not to allow the creation of a precedent. In the end, it agreed to a German holding of 51 per cent in exchange for certain concessions: an assurance that this would not establish a precedent, and the appointment of a French chairman and French and German administrators in equal numbers. The Francolor company was set up in November 1941 and was placed under the direction of a man sympathetic to German aspirations.

The French industrialists had virtually no trump cards. IG Farben's superior industrial strength was overwhelming and it was not dependent on them in any way. Thanks to its access to the Majestic, it had the means to harm them or even to close down their factories. Besides, it was favoured by the atmosphere of the immediate aftermath of the defeat, when the Germans were not yet bothering to don kid gloves when dealing with the French. The industrialists affected, in particular Duchemin, the PDG of Kuhlmann, the major firm in this sector, were by no means pleased at losing control over their factories. However, when, upon hearing of the decision, they objected to the 'diktat' and protested to Vichy, their attitude was not unambiguous. Pucheu sharply reminded Duchemin that it was he who had empowered the government to decide in this affair. 'That decision may not have had your free consent, but nor was it imposed against your will. Not only did you at no point ask for negotiations to be broken off, but in the course of several of your approaches to my collaborators you manifested acute anxiety at any prospect of their failure.'[22]

Duchemin disclaimed any responsibility in the outcome, devolving it all upon the government. He may have done so with an eye to the future, in case the tide turned against the Germans. For the time being, thanks to the state's intervention, the hungry designs of IG Farben had been contained. Renewed activity for the factories was assured and by 1942 production had already risen to its pre-war level, making it possible to dispense a high dividend to shareholders. Finally, generous financial conditions had been obtained: IG Farben paid for its holding with a part of its own shares, ceded at a very favourable price. Then in 1942, the French industrialists made use of a right to buy shares that they had been granted at the same time and thereby collectively became IG Farben's fifth largest shareholder. This not only meant that damages were limited but furthermore ensured that, in the event of a German victory, they would benefit by being integrated into the giant German chemical industry.[23]

Rhône-Poulenc, with most of its factories in the free zone, was in a better position to resist the greedy approaches of Bayer, one of IG Farben's subsidiaries. The German firm wanted damages for the counterfeiting of its products in the past and the use of its protected brands. It also aimed to gain a measure of control over the French company, demanding first that a common distribution company be set up, in which IG Farben would be the majority shareholder and, later, that it should hold a minority share of the capital of the French firm itself. Rhône-Poulenc agreed to pay charges on a whole series of products and then, as a lesser evil, also accepted the idea of a distribution company (Theraplix, with 49 per cent German capital), which was given only partial control over its own products. All in all, in exchange for paying those charges and setting up a mixed company, it managed to protect its capital, limit Bayer's control over the sale of its products, and safeguard its right to export.

Rhône-Poulenc was, to be sure, defending its business interests, but this could not be called a last-ditch defence. The reason why it entered into these negotiations even though its position was not directly threatened, was that it judged it opportune to be conciliatory with a partner that could serve its interests in the event of a German victory. It suggested extending scientific and technical cooperation to other domains besides pharmaceutical products, such as plastic materials, resins and synthetic rubber, all of which appeared to have a great future and to which the German company could make extremely valuable contributions. It even suggested extending the system of charges by having both companies share mutually in the proceeds of the exploitation of the two groups.[24] The vigour of its outlay in investments and research, together with the fact that it took out double the previous number of patents are indications of its determination to succeed in a climate of increased competitiveness in an economic field less protected than in the past.

The company of Alais, Froges and Camargue, better known as Pechiney, was also drawn into negotiations at an early date. Except for the fact that one of its factories was situated in the occupied zone and a number of its assets had been confiscated in Norway, it was in an exceptionally favourable position. As one of the leading European producers of aluminium, it was a strong technical and commercial force. It held 80 per cent of the shares in the Aluminium Français cartel, the rest being in the hands of Ugine. Most of its installations and raw materials were in the free zone. And it was Germany that was doing the soliciting here, as its deficit in bauxite and aluminium, both essential for aeronautical production, was increasing – a fact that led it to negotiate with Vichy for delivery contracts. Pechiney, which took part in these negotiations, raised objections but was finally overruled by the state.

Those objections stemmed essentially from its business interests. The Pechiney executives, in particular its director general Raoul de Vitry, were not at all keen to deliver an increasing proportion of its products to Germany, when they could be perfectly well absorbed by the French market. Pechiney were afraid both of losing their French clientèle and of being blamed for handing over products useful to the national economy.[25] Nor did they like being forced to commit themselves, in a second contract, for one whole year up until 1 February 1942, without any clause providing for annulment in the event of a peace treaty being signed. Pechiney was fearful of finding its hands tied in industrial negotiations that might take place very shortly. Finally, it also feared that some of its deliveries to Germany might be used to supplant it amongst its own clients. One of the company's executives, in April 1942, went so far as to request from the German side an assurance that the aluminium would be kept for 'strictly military needs' and would not find its way to 'our own faithful clients'. Planes for the Reich were preferable to the loss of an export market.[26]

In 1941, Pechiney took part in another series of negotiations in which, guided by the same business logic, it adopted quite a different line. Whereas in the matter of contracts for aluminium it was trying to restrain the government with regard to both quantities and delivery dates, it now sought to persuade it to consent to a commitment that was greater than the government was ready to contemplate. In June 1941, Aluminium Français informed the government that a German consortium wished to build an aluminium factory in southern France and was disposed to accept Pechiney as an associate in this project, provided it could itself take a substantial holding in the business. If not, the factory might be built in Yugoslavia. The Aluminium Français group placed the decision in the hands of the government, leaving it in no doubt of its own preference: the government should accept. The arguments put forward by Pechiney were as follows: (1) the factory would take some time to construct and would not be completed before the end of 1942: 'It therefore seems that this project can have no influence upon the war'; (2) a refusal would lead to the factory being built elsewhere, weakening the position of French industry when it came to regulating markets when peace arrived. The Aluminium Français group suggested that, in exchange for supplying the building materials for the factory, the Germans should acquire obligations that would be converted into shares 'only if and when an agreement was concluded on the distribution of world aluminium markets'.[27] Through shares in principle agreed to but in practice deferred, and with conditions attached to them, the group sought a means of persuading the Germans, once peace arrived, to negotiate a regulation of markets that would respect its interests.

The Vichy leaders shared the industrialists' view of the advantages of this operation. However, fearing a repetition of the Francolor affair, they were anxious to limit German holdings to a minimum. On 4 September the Pechiney executives presented Barnaud with the outline of an agreement drafted in consultation with the German industrialists. The factory would have a French managing director, the capital would be 60 per cent French and 40 per cent German, with a possible extra 10 per cent for the Germans once a satisfactory arrangement on the division of external markets had been found. All the factory's products would be reserved for Germany for the duration of the war. Government delegates objected to the size of the German shares, judging them to be excessive. The industrialists explained that the German government wanted some rights, on account of the military importance of the factory's products. They added – and here a crack appeared in the facade – 'It is necessary to get the Germans to participate as much as possible in this business, the future of which after the war does not seem too assured, yet at the same time retain French control of the new company.'[28]

The firm's executives were trying to win, whatever the scenario. Having the factory built in France would increase their weight in peace negotiations, but this fact would probably be offset by over-production: hence the danger of sinking too much capital in the project. A large German holding would spread that risk and improve the French position when it came to regulating markets. Pechiney was, as it were, preparing its own little industrial peace treaty, trying to achieve a balance between its concern to keep control of capital and at the same time optimize its financial and commercial interests. The government's representatives, for their part, were 'stupefied' to discover that it would be possible to set up the business with French capital. They immediately considered state involvement, to the great alarm of the firm's executives, who regarded this as the thin end of the wedge for nationalization, and sent them off to revise the wording of the agreement with the German industrialists who, for their part, made no difficulties about giving up the idea of acquiring immediate shares.

According to the new bases of the agreement, approved by Vichy, the factory would be built by the French group and financed with state assistance, with the Germans providing the building materials. Its products would go exclusively to Germany for the next ten years (this settled the question of outlets). When peace arrived, both sides would seek to come to a satisfactory arrangement on markets, and if they proved successful, the German group would be able to claim a holding of up to 50 per cent. Two points of disagreement remained: the French industrialists wanted to scale down the forthcoming contracts for supplies of aluminium and obtain guarantees for their interests in the factory in Norway. As can be seen, they were aiming for the very utmost that could be squeezed from the negotiations. Then discussions broke down: the German government had intervened to insist upon an immediate 50 per cent share holding. Once again, the political dimension and the matter of national prestige had thwarted the pragmatic inclinations of the industrialists. Several months of discussions failed to resolve the impasse, for the Pechiney executives were no more disposed than Vichy was to admit a German element into their managing board. No more progress was made.

The part played by business considerations on the one hand and politics on the other varied from one set of negotiations to another. But it is hard to find examples in which political considerations led to decisions that ran counter to business logic, whereas business logic did sometimes lead to decisions which, on the face of it, might easily have been ascribed to political considerations. That can be seen in the case of Pechiney, whose managers were not Vichyst militants, unlike the Ugine executives. Raoul de Vitry later became one of the relatively few major employers who joined the resistance. What preoccupied him in 1941 was the future of his business, evaluated on the basis of the probability of an imminent German victory. The relative strength of his position, which was quite exceptional, may have led him to envisage competition in a German Europe quite optimistically. In the spring of 1941, Hemmen even declared that, given that the French aluminium industry was operating with lower running costs, it would be natural for it to increase production after the war, while the German industry cut back.[29] It was a declaration that was contradicted by the German government, which was bent on gaining control wherever possible. Perhaps it was as a result of all this that Vitry realized that resistance was imperative.

The militant Pétainism of Ugine's managing director, Georges-Jean Painvin, and of the executives of Rhône-Poulenc partly explains their greater inclination to commit themselves as to the future. In the summer of 1941, as the Michelin affair mentioned above dragged on, both these companies were negotiating with IG Farben over building a buna factory in the free zone. Artificial rubber was only of interest within the framework of a German Europe that would last. The investment envisaged for this project was far greater than for the aluminium factory; and it would take much longer to build, with the artificial rubber factory not planned to start production until the spring of 1945.[30] The industrialists were not blind to the uncertainty of outlets, but the state authorities, first and foremost Bichelonne, deemed the project of sufficient interest to warrant their undertaking to finance it. The matter was still under discussion in 1943.[31]

It was hardly surprising that the inclination towards accommodation manifested by these major industrialists at the economic level was also evident at the level of their relations with the occupying power. The most obvious example of business conviviality is presented by the Round Table lunches, although these represented no more than the tip of the iceberg. They were organized by the prince de Beauvau-Craon (a director of several companies and the chairman of both the Cercle Interallié and the Polo Club of Paris) assisted by François Dupré (the chairman of Grands Hotels Associés, director of the Plaza and the George V hotels, and an executive of Ford's), René de Chambrun (an advocate at the court of appeal and the son-in-law of Laval) and, on the German side, Carl Schaefer, the commissioner at the Banque de France.

Every three weeks from February 1942 onwards these lunches brought together at the Ritz fifty or so Germans and Frenchmen, the guests varying from one occasion to another. Leaders of the economic sector of the military administration and representatives of major German firms were seated between French businessmen or ministers (Laval, Brinon, Bichelonne, Bousquet, etc.), politicians (Déat) or writers and journalists (such as Fabre-Luce, Morand, Rebatet). As well as distributors (Henri Fayol) and the executives of organization committees (Raoul Ploquin), these businessmen included bankers (Ardant of the Société Générale; Pose of the Banque Nationale pour le Commerce et l'Industrie; André Laurent-Atthalin from Paribas); industrialists from the chemical industry (François Albert-Buisson of Rhône-Poulenc; Baron Pierre Hely d'Oissel of Saint-Gobain; Georges-Jean Painvin of Ugine; Roland Gadala of Pont-à-Mousson), from the car industry (Maurice Dollfus of Ford), from the electrical equipment industry (Pierre de Cossé Brissac of Matériel Électrique; Emile Girardeau of the Compagnie Générale du Téléphone sans Fil), producers of wines and spirits (André Dubonnet of Éts. Dubonnet; the marquis Charles Melchior de Polignac of Pommery champagne), department store proprietors (Cognacq, of La Samaritaine), and leading lights from the world of fashion (Lucien Lelong).[32]

These were employers from the sectors most involved in exchanges with Germany, men who carried weight within their own branch of industry and who had demonstrated their goodwill or, at the least, were not recalcitrant. It would perhaps be fair to say that they represented the Lavalist faction in the business world, not solely on account of the assiduous presence of Laval's son-in-law but also by reason of their view of the war, summed up well enough by Louis Renault's prognosis of it in February 1942: success for Germany's imminent offensive in Russia and a probable compromise peace between the Germans and the English, for fear of American hegemony.[33] It would no doubt be wrong to set them all on the same level or to ascribe firm convictions to them. Their presence was largely determined by the Germans' interest in whatever they produced, and their attitude was supported if not endorsed by the politics of Vichy. All the same, it was indicative of a certain state of mind. The lunches, started in February 1942, were discontinued in the autumn of that year, when the landings spread a chill. By January 1943, even René de Chambrun seems to have been demoralized to the point of confessing to Achenbach: 'It's tough, collaboration is'[34] (a comment, in French, recorded in a German report).

Some of the major employers were in no need of organized lunches to help them find their way to the occupation services. Marcel Boussac, the foremost textiles producer and also the foremost racehorse owner, is a case in point that is all the more interesting in that he was not an employer from the extreme right. He was close to Flandin and Bonnet, with centre-left contacts, an industrialist who did not come out badly from the Popular Front. Inflation and wage rises helped his business. As a 'social employer', he managed to avoid many difficulties. But Boussac was also the kind of employer who frequented political circles in order to see which way the wind was blowing and to protect his own interests, a businessman who never dissociated political influence from prosperous business, whatever the regime.

After the defeat, he put up 150000 francs to help Luchaire launch *Les Nouveaux Temps*[35] and busied himself getting horseracing going again. His horses were to be better fed than many French people, thanks to the German baron whom he employed to manage his stables. He was appointed to the National Council, probably at Flandin's instigation, then dropped from it in November 1941, and was a member of the CO for textiles. He came back into favour after the return of Laval, to whom he had easy access. In Paris he was in contact with all the German services, even the SS, which intervened to advance his interests in an aryanization affair.[36] After the war, Knochen stated that Boussac used to provide them with 'very important' information about the economic situation. Politically, he approved of Laval's policies, but criticized him for his 'lack of energy and above all for his weak hold over the economic administration of the country'. He 'was a partisan of absolute collaboration with Germany, in order to increase France's production from which our two countries could have profited simultaneously'.[37] Boussac lived out the occupation relatively unscathed. The purges of the liberation barely touched him, leaving him poised to become the richest man in France.

In normal times, employers do not tend to be attracted to political action, and their attitude did not change under the occupation. Very few were involved in the collaboration parties and those who were seldom figured in their front ranks. They were rather more visible in the Cercle Européen, founded in September 1941 by Edouard Chaux, then subtitled the 'Comité de Collaboration Économique Européenne' (the Committee for European Economic Collaboration). This was an organization that was unique on the Paris scene in that, for once, it set French and Germans on an equal footing, and likewise nationals from other countries linked with the Axis powers. The honorary committee included Laval, Brinon, Schleier, Achenbach, Dr Michel, and the consuls of Italy, Spain, Hungary and Portugal, as well as Déat, Doriot and their like. No more than a handful of businessmen were present: Gabriel Cognacq, the managing director of La Samaritaine, André Dubonnet, the manager of Éts. Dubonnet, René Lalou, the chairman of Mumm and the Éts. Dubonnet. The membership of the organization probably never exceeded 1500, 200 of whom were company directors. There were not many famous names among these: one director of Éts. Kuhlmann, and a few fashion designers such as Jacques Fath and Nina Ricci.[38]

Employers concentrated on keeping their businesses running. But when they did join a political party it was not always primarily to advance their entrepreneurial interests. Eugène Schueller, a combative employer in the 1930s, played an important role in Deloncle's MSR after the defeat. His commitment was that of a reformer of the economy who believed the time had come for the idea of proportional wages to prevail. In his case politics was not a means of improving his business affairs. The companies of which he was a director, in particular L'Oréal, whose sales quadrupled between 1940 and 1944, prospered thanks to French demand.

Schueller accepted German orders for the first time at the end of 1942, in small quantities, in order to minimize the requisitioning of his work force. At that point he had retired from politics.[39]

The employers were men who accepted the evidence of facts, although it took some of them longer to do so than others – even Renault himself. After being bombed for the third time, in September 1943, one of his executives realized that some internal spring had given way. 'Louis Renault, who is now convinced that victory has changed camps, seems to want to profit from this last bombing raid to cover his responsibilities both past and present. He would like to defer starting up again until forced to by measures taken by the German authorities, so as to be able to use these in self-defence when the time comes.'[40]

17

Money manipulators

THE banking profession is a discreet one. But the personal discretion of bankers may sometimes be found wanting and does not always lead to the right decisions. Paul Baudouin had moved from the Banque d'Indochine into the government. Then the Worms Bank team had raised the flag of 'synarchy' over Vichy. That was quite enough to pump wind into the sails of suspicion, which had already been billowing even before the war. On the left, as in anticapitalist circles on the right, many were convinced of the iniquities of the 'two hundred families': the shareholders of the Banque de France, who were believed to have ensnared the French economy in their nets. Banking was a concentrated profession, a fact that was certainly not in its favour. In the 1930s, out of some 2000 establishments, six (the Société Générale, the Crédit Lyonnais, the Comptoir National d'Escompte de Paris, the Crédit Commercial de France, the Banque Nationale pour le Commerce et l'Industrie and the Crédit Commercial et Industriel) monopolized 60 per cent of all deposits.[1] Other establishments – business banks (the Banque de Paris et des Pays-Bas, the Banque de l'Union Parisienne, and the high finance houses, Neuflize, Mirabaud, Vernes and Rothschild), which specialized in property administration and state and industrial investment – had for years been shrouded in a veil of secrecy.

Orleanism mixed with reaction predominated in these circles of powerful men, where inherited positions were beginning to pass away. The Republic was tolerated on condition that it was liberal (before the war, most bankers had remained unimpressed by the idea of a corporative organization).[2] Here, as elsewhere, authority was gaining ground. The bankruptcies caused by the economic crisis of the depression damaged the credibility of private banking which, furthermore, was also suffering from the competition of public and semi-public establishments providing credit, which were draining off an increasing proportion of deposits. Over and above all this loomed the threat of state control, an intolerable prospect so long as the Popular Front held the reins of power. One sign of the times was that the major banks – high finance in particular but also the Banque Nationale pour le Commerce et l'Industrie and the Banque d'Indochine – were prominent among the subscribers to Doriot's PPF between 1936 and 1938,[3] although this probably did not prevent them from simultaneously funding the moderate right, always their preference in fair-weather times. The banking profession was in the firing line, and at the liberation it was accused of having oiled the wheels of enemy exploitation. At that point, while the nationalization of the major savings banks went full steam ahead, some prominent bankers – such as Henri Ardant and Gabriel Le Roy Ladurie – were languishing in prison, meditating upon the ups and downs of the financial profession.

Upon arrival, the Germans immediately set up a Surveillance Office for banks. It was omnipotent, empowered to find out everything, suspend transactions, close banks down, and transfer sums as it pleased. It appointed commissioners to the Jewish and English banks. It set up enquiries into everything: structures and records, security portfolios, deposits of foreign currencies and precious metals. For the sake of convenience, it made use of the principal professional association, the Union Syndicale des Banquiers de Paris et de la Province. This served as a secretariat, sending out circulars and questionnaires and making it possible to economize greatly on personnel.[4] Once the French organization committee for banking was in place, two German officials, instead of the eight employed to start with, sufficed to supervise the entire sector together with its 80000 employees.[5] Instances of friction were exceptional, but there were a few – one in early 1941, when twelve executives of the Crédit Lyonnais were arrested and charged with attempting to withhold clients' accounts from the survey of foreign currency.[6]

After a few months of uncertainty, the Germans adopted a moderate policy. In doing so, they were probably partly influenced by the goodwill manifested by the French. Above all, however, they had become aware of the advantages to be gained from soft pedalling. The views of those in the military administration responsible for the banking sector, themselves bankers, prevailed. While insisting that Vichy should in principle authorize them to set up branches of German banks and obtain shares in French banking houses, in practice they gave up the idea of doing so. They had insufficient experience of French financial practices, and any attempt to divert French savings into German banks seemed doomed to failure. Besides, what would be gained by constraint? It was wiser to act with moderation and prepare for the future by establishing good relations with the French authorities and permanent contact with the leaders of the profession.[7] Unlike their colleagues in Belgium and Holland, apart from two exceptions, they contented themselves with sending representatives. No more than six banks, with twenty or so employees from the Reich, were represented in Paris during the occupation.[8]

French banking thus found itself in a most favourable position. It was unaffected by seizures of equipment and raw materials and by the introduction of 'industrial commissioners', nor was it under pressure to admit capital from the conqueror or to renegotiate its share of the market. Unlike the field of insurance, no greedy competitors intent on seizing Jewish or English spoils were implanted. Finally, there were no large losses abroad to be feared as few subsidiaries existed outside France. The sole vulnerable spot was the foreign shares portfolio. Although the occupying power certanly retained the means to inflict damage and impose constraints, the conditions for a return to 'business as usual' were more favourable than in any other sector of activity.

While the Germans were deciding on their policy, the French bankers were organizing their profession. The regulation that had repelled them before the war was now accepted without demur. The presence of the occupying power, its policies for establishing its own control, the risks of takeover on the one hand and the very illiberal orientation of the new French regime on the other were all elements that encouraged them to adapt of their own accord rather than be forced to do so by others. Besides, they had a further motive: the prospect of a new European order, which encouraged them to move closer to the structure of the German banking sector. As early as September 1940, the key man in this process of professional organization justified this by evoking the 'possible integration of our national economy within a wider framework'.[9] The managing director of the Société Générale and vice-chairman of the Union of Bankers, Henri Ardant, was an authoritarian and paternalistic boss whose opinions allied him to reactionary social catholicism of an antiparliamentary, if not antirepublican, orientation. As early as 1936 he had declared himself to be a partisan of a corporative organization.[10]

Setting up the CO for banking took nearly a year of negotiations with, not the occupying power, but the French state. Ardant, who was appointed chairman of the provisional committee, favoured a corporatist and oligarchic plan. His intention was to place the CO in the hands of the largest banks and see that it served their interests: it would limit competition between major banks, discourage public and semi-public credit, define the profession rigorously, and insist upon a minimum level of capital high enough to deny many establishments official recognition and also any right of appeal against rejection. The plan was so severe that it provoked considerable criticism from bankers more attached to free enterprise. It ran into stubborn opposition from representatives of both the state and the Banque de France, neither of which was at all inclined to allow the largest Paris houses a free hand.[11] The law of 13 June 1941, which set up the organization committee for banking, ratified a compromise reached in the course of a battle between plans and counter-plans: the CO's powers would be limited to private banks, the state would act as the authority exercising surveillance and receiving appeals, and the minimum capital required would be fixed at a very low level. The law nevertheless made it possible to build up a solid organization and to homogenize the profession considerably, albeit probably not as much as was desired by Ardant, whose rhetoric clearly betrayed the xenophobic and antisemitic inspiration of his policy of concentration.[12]

Before agreeing to this, the occupying power insisted on introducing into the law not only the principle of German shares in French banks, subject to authorization from the French state, but also a stipulation that the latter should undertake officially to accept any establishments that the MBF wished to see operating in the occupied zone. Two companies with German capital benefited from this: Aerobank, the only subsidiary of a German bank (the Bank der Deutschen Luftahrt AG) implanted in France during the occupation, with the mission of financing the Reich's aeronautical orders;[13] and a finance company (the Société de Crédits et d'Investissements), endowed with capital of 400 million francs for buying up firms and acquiring shares.[14]

Once the new law was promulgated and the organization committee for banking was set up, the occupying power abolished the

Surveillance Office. It was now served by a dependable French apparatus with considerable powers, directed by a man held in high esteem by all the Paris occupation services[15] and who made no secret of his desire to establish close links with German banking. In the spring of 1941. Ardant paid a visit to Berlin in his official capacity. A number of doors were slammed in his face, but this did not stop him, on his return, from declaring himself to be 'more than ever convinced that the French economy must seek collaboration with the German economy'.[16] In September, he was one of fifteen figures connected with the economy and business – most of them government delegates such as Bouthillier, Pucheu, Benoist-Méchin, Barnaud, Lehideux and Bichelonne, but also Painvin (chairman of the CO for the chemical industries), Carmichaël (chairman of the CO for textiles), Marcel Ferrus (chairman of the National Federation of Public Works), and Marcel Paul-Cavallier, of Pont-à-Mousson – invited by the embassy to a reception in honour of Landfried, the German Secretary of State for the Economy. Ardant distinguished himself by formulating hopes for the future that won instant approval from Pucheu and Bichelonne. Once victorious, he declared, Germany should have enough ambition 'to eliminate customs barriers within a vast European economic space and as soon as possible create a single European currency'. Landfried later told the embassy staff of his astonishment. He had not had any idea 'how deeply the idea of a European economy had become anchored in people's minds here'.[17]

Ardant continued to be attracted to Berlin and for more than a year the commercial attaché to the embassy strove to get him invited there. In March 1942 he wrote as follows: Ardant was 'not only the most influential French banker at this time', but also 'one of the Frenchmen closest to our own ideas'. Returning to the attack in October 1942, he argued that an invitation from the organization of German bankers would strengthen Ardant in the position that he was defending and would endorse his authority in the face of the criticisms of some of his colleagues.[18] In Berlin, however, while the idea appealed to German bankers, it was brushed aside by the Ministry of the Economy, which was very distrustful when it came to closer ties between the business circles of the two countries. The situation seemed to have reached an impasse when, at the beginning of 1943, the embassy learned that Ardant had gone to Germany with the support of the SS. The SS eventually consented to explain that the trip was designed to facilitate the sale of a French holding in Romania. The reason why the SS had helped the banker was in order to express its gratitude for the information that he supplied. After the war, Knochen confirmed this: 'Ardant gave us all the information we wanted from the point of view of both banking and finance.'[19]

In this way, the banking profession was organized under the leadership of the major banks and directed by a man very much trusted by the occupying power. Banking was a branch of industry largely protected against the greedy designs of the Germans. Over and above this, its economic lot was definitely enviable. The major banks recorded a steep increase in their deposits, greater than the increase in the official wholesale prices up until the beginning of 1944. This increase was occasioned by the dizzying growth of the money supply engendered by the occupation costs and the anaemic situation of the economy. Because business had slowed down so much, the banks could make less and less use of these large deposits by funding commercial transactions or granting credits. They therefore turned more and more to discounting government securities, thereby swelling their portfolios of state bonds. They furthermore made sizeable profits thanks to greater activity in the stock market. From the time of its reopening at the beginning of 1941 up until the beginning of 1943, the stock exchange went up and up. In the capital market, companies made the most of their easy financial circumstances and the fall in interest rates to refinance their debts, take out loans, and make capital increases.

Consequently, in the first two years at least, major banks showed excellent profits: declared profits rose mightily, reserves soared, and capital greatly increased.[20] They then ran out of steam, stagnated or slipped back. In 1944 decreases were more or less general. But even taking into account the depreciation of the currency, the major banks at least maintained their positions during this period. Theirs was a considerably better position than that of the industrial sector, affected by wear and tear on machinery and a dearth of investment; nevertheless, as everyone was aware, the situation was precarious.[21]

How much did 'German business' contribute to this prosperity? In August 1942, Charles Rist, upon emerging from a meeting of the board of directors of Paribas, noted bitterly: 'Business is either non-existent or connected exclusively with the war.'[22] Amid the economic stagnation, operations 'connected with the war' naturally loomed large, although those conducting the purges, who did not fail to look closely into the matter, albeit with a somewhat indulgent eye, had to admit that they affected the gross profits for the period only to a limited extent (between 5 and 15 per cent). The annual statistics are more revealing, however. They show that most of the profits were garnered during the first two years and that they then constituted a considerable proportion of profits (in the case of the Worms Bank, 24 per cent of the net profits for 1941):[23] later developments reflect not so much fewer opportunities to make profits as a concern, dictated by prudence, to limit commitment in this area.

In truth, profits are not necessarily the most interesting aspect here. Relatively unprofitable or even loss-making operations are just as revealing when it comes to defining a prevalent state of mind. According to the defence put up by the banks after the liberation, there were three main reasons for their involvement in German business. The first was to provide a service for long-standing clients who had agreed to take German orders and who, had they not done so, would have taken their business to competing banks. This is an argument that broke down in all cases in which the banks made efforts to attract new clients amongst firms working for Germany. The second was the attitude of the French government which, it was claimed, pressed bankers to take up a united position or even gave them orders to do so (for which evidence is hard to find, although it is true that the government did exert some pressure, most notably in the cases of mixed companies and aryanization cases – pressure to which the banks complied with a docility that went well beyond mere obedience).[24] The third was the clout of the occupying power, which made systematic refusal impossible for fear of the appointment of a commissioner who would have used his powers to finance even more German orders. This truly was a risk not to be underestimated, although the adoption of a common attitude would have limited it and forced the occupying power to depend more upon the services of the Aerobank.

A desire to safeguard the business, encouragement from Vichy, and German pressure: all these weighed more or less heavily depending on the particular point of view regarding the future that the banks adopted. German pressure was more imagined than real; and sanctions were the more feared because goodwill on the part of the occupying power seemed essential in a German Europe. As for Vichy, its encouragement was received all the more eagerly because its policies were by no means displeasing and because it appeared to have a long future before it.

Until the end of 1942 no banks at all rejected money connected with German business, not even the Comptoir National d'Escompte de Paris, one of the few banks congratulated on its reserve when the purges came: when, in October 1942, representatives of the Commerzbank in Paris requested more favourable conditions for its documentary credit, the Comptoir immediately offered reduced commission rates, declaring, 'We earnestly hope that the improvement we are making to our conditions will persuade you to reserve any new business for us. It will be assured of our unfailing meticulous attention.'[25]

There were at least two kinds of operation that sucked the major banks into the occupation machine. In the first place, they facilitated the liquidation of French holdings in central and Balkan Europe. The Germans insisted on their cooperation here, and Vichy gave them the go-ahead, its sole concern being to obtain real advantages in exchange, rather than payment through the clearing mechanism. The banks generally put their counters at the service of the Germans, and some of them set about encouraging their clients to sell such holdings. They had written off those investments anyway, some of which had already become 'lame ducks'; and the Germans were certainly not fussy about how much they paid. In December 1941, Jahan, the managing director of Paribas boasted to his board of directors of 'the excellent conditions' for the sale of some of his bank's shares 'in central Europe where, in view of the circumstances, it cannot at present continue to operate'.[26]

Second, the banks advanced credit to firms working for Germany. In particular they offered security, which was extremely useful to the occupying power, for it guaranteed the down payments which the banks undertook to repay should the contract not be honoured. The Germans thereby won time, since this meant that in many cases they could get work going immediately without needing to enquire into the solvency of the firms taking their orders. As for the banks, they received a commission commensurate with the risk that they were taking. It was a risk that was known to be of both a political and an economic nature, which explains why, according to German reports, a great deal of encouragement and not a little pressure was needed to persuade them to commit themselves seriously in this field.[27]

In other fields, the operations of banks indicate compliance or even eagerness on their part. There is no need to dwell upon the liquidation of subsidiaries in Alsace and Lorraine that the Banque Nationale pour le Commerce et l'Industrie and the Crédit Commercial de France (and they alone, apparently) sought to bring about as early as the summer of 1940, by setting up negotiations with German banks. Nor need we dwell upon the privileged role played by some establishments in financial transfers between the two countries. The Crédit Lyonnais, for instance, in the summer of 1940 received, in obscure conditions, a monopoly on the transfer of savings of voluntary workers in Germany. Shortly afterwards, the Ministry of Finance granted it, along with the Société Générale, the Banque Nationale pour le Commerce et l'Industrie and the Aerobank, a dispensation from the regulatory procedure for exports, which represented a very real favour.[28]

Other operations quite simply mortgaged the future. In this respect it is only fair to say that the Comptoir National d'Escompte was the only major bank that remained in the clear (since it refused to do so). One of the most noteworthy of these operations was the creation of a company designed to finance Franco-German business in the field of dyestuffs, artificial rubber and aluminium. The request came from IG Farben, which had already tried to set up such a scheme before the war. In the spring of 1941, Paribas, the Société Générale and the Banque de l'Union Parisienne all gave their agreement, while the Crédit Lyonnais turned to the state for advice. Barnaud's reaction was significant and very close to the distrustful attitude manifested by the German Ministry of the Economy with regard to Franco-German links in business affairs. He declared that the French government would be liable to embarrassment in future negotiations if technical problems had already been discussed directly between the industrialists and the German authorities and if financial problems had been resolved in advance by German groups and French bankers working together.[29] In the spring of 1942, an association (not a company) was finally set up by the four banks, its purpose being 'to finance IG Farben-Industrie's business in France'. Its headquarters were established on the premises of the Banque de l'Union Parisienne. The association was to operate for five years: the future of the Reich was still looking robust. It was to supply several hundred million francs in credit to companies linked with the giant German chemicals company, enabling it to extend its business in the French market.

A number of bankers went even further and took part in the establishment of Franco-German companies. Thus, in June 1941, the Banque Nationale pour le Commerce et l'Industrie, the Banque de l'Union Parisienne, the Crédit Commercial et Industriel, and the

Société Générale together acquired a majority share in the capital of the 'Industrie Cinématographique' company, alongside a minority German holding. And in March 1942, Paribas, the Banque de l'Union Parisienne and the Banque des Pays du Nord acquired half-shares in the capital of the new 'Radio Monte-Carlo' company.[30] In the field of gas generators, Paribas played a leading role, outstripping its rival, the Banque de l'Union Parisienne, which was entering into similar operations but committing itself more cautiously. The Germans considered it 'never very *deutschland-freundlich* (favourable to Germany)', on account of its close links with Schneider.[31]

Paribas had turned state loans to its advantage during the 'belle époque', and had made links with German banks that had caused it to be accused of antipatriotism in the Great War, before switching to lucrative colonial business and industrial investments of unequal profitability in the countries belonging to the *petite entente*.[32] Since the beginning of the occupation, it had been pursuing activities of every kind in the German business field, starting by guaranteeing most of the German insurance companies authorized to operate in France, while the Société Générale picked up the rest. In 1941, in partnership with a German firm, Paribas created the Société des Gazogènes Imbert (the Imbert Company of Gas Generators) and the Société de Carburants Français pour Gazogènes (the Company of French Fuels for Gas Generators). Its choice of investment was based upon the prognosis of a continental economy perpetually cut off from Anglo-Saxon petroleum supplies. Thanks to the lengthy duration of the war, the first company was profitable; the second, however, incurred losses of at least 100 million francs.[33]

It is hardly surprising that Paribas took such a prominent lead. With its substantial interests in Central and Eastern Europe, it was greatly affected by the cessation of French holdings abroad. And, bearing in mind its long record of consultation and cooperation with the French state – for whose external policies, it flattered itself, it provided valuable support when it was in its interest to do so – it would have been surprising to find it suddenly risking incurring its displeasure. But the fact is that, as in the case of Ardant, political preferences played their part in the promotion of its professional opportunism. The managing director of Paribas, Laurent-Atthalin held blatantly collaborationist opinions, and was sufficiently cheered by Laval's return to power to tell Charles Rist, on 12 September 1942, 'that he wished to collaborate thoroughly with the Germans'.[34]

Both German and French sources testify to a marked commitment to Germany on the part of a minority of bankers. In his diary, Rist, who sat on the boards of directors of several banks (Paribas, the Banque de Syrie, the Banque Ottomane, and the Suez Bank), provides some edifying glimpses of the state of mind of some of his colleagues, detecting hatred of the Republic, malicious delight at the humiliation of France, and an obsession with communism that caused some of them to insist, 'Bolshevism is far more to be feared than Hitlerism, and it is making progress throughout the country.'[35] In the summer of 1942, Rist felt that the majority of bankers 'were expecting and hoping for an allied victory'; 'those who are not, are the ones who consider themselves better informed or more intelligent'.[36]

After the war, the head of the Surveillance Office for banks, Carl Schaefer, recalled his 'friendly' relations with Pose and Jéquier, the managers of the Banque Nationale pour le Commerce et l'Industrie and the Crédit Commercial de France respectively, who invited him to dine with them in fashionable restaurants and also in their homes. He also mentioned meals taken with Ardant, who was no socialite, and lunches in the Paribas dining room.[37] When, in October 1941, the embassy organized a meeting with economic experts from the Reich, it invited three bankers (Pose, of the Banque Nationale pour le Commerce et l'Industrie; Henry Jahan, of Paribas; and Jéquier, of the Crédit Commercial de France), who were introduced as the representatives of 'the major Paris banks the most favourable to Germany', most of their colleagues being more reserved on the score of collaboration.[38]

The attitudes and convictions and, in some cases, the political aspirations of these men backed up their obvious concern for professional success and prompted them to manifest a clear desire for collaboration which, however, never led them to adopt positions from which they could not retreat if necessary. Pose was a professor of law turned banker who, according to one of his colleagues, possessed 'a superior intelligence combined with limitless pride and ambition'.[39] As soon as the Germans arrived, he hastened to make it plain that he would do absolutely anything to safeguard the interests of the bank that he had rescued with great panache before the war. He engaged the services of a former member of the Comité France–Allemagne to liaise with the occupation authorities and, by dint of going out of his way to be helpful and a shower of small gifts, he set about establishing cordial relations with the Majestic-based official responsible for the banking sector.[40] At the business level, he manifested an equally practical approach. A study of records at the beginning of 1943 was to come to the conclusion that, of all the French banks, the Banque Nationale pour le Commerce et l'Industrie 'was probably the one that contributed the most to Franco-German relations'.[41]

Yet Pose seems to have begun at an early date to doubt the fortunes of the German military power, for by early 1941 he was already predicting that the Anglo-Saxons would emerge victorious from a long war. At his bank, he protected Jewish employees affected by the Statute of June 1941, giving them work that they could continue to do off the bank's premises and making sure their salaries were paid.[42] So it was not too surprising that, in November 1942, finding himself by chance in North Africa, he joined forces with Darlan, becoming his (extremely untrustworthy!) Minister of the Economy. As a recent convert to monarchism, he then dragged the Comte de Paris into a plot that led to the assassination of the admiral.[43] He was made to pay professionally for his political ambition. In Paris, the Germans' reaction to his defection was to appoint a commissioner to head the bank whose development he had wished to ensure at any price.[44]

Set alongside the Banque Nationale pour le Commerce et l'Industrie, the Worms Bank was dwarfed. However, its reputation as a political bank enhanced its stature. It had been created to facilitate the business affairs of the Worms group which was active in naval construction, maritime services, and the coal trade and also owned shares in over a hundred companies (including the Ets. Jappy Frères, of which Pucheu was the general manager). The Worms house was run by three associates, among them Hippolyte Worms and Jacques Barnaud. It immediately attracted the attention of the German authorities by reason of its links with England (during the phoney war, Worms had led the Franco-English Committee for maritime transport) and because the third partner belonged to 'the Jewish race'. Despite this man's resignation, the German commissioner for the bank was retained on account of an extremely free interpretation of German regulations.[45] The reason for this was the Germans' desire to keep under surveillance and under pressure an establishment that wielded such influence in Vichy that the collaborationists of Paris mounted a noisy campaign against the 'synarchy'.

Gabriel Le Roy Ladurie was the salaried manager of the Worms Bank.[46] He was a clever, socially well-received man who relished his role as an *éminence grise* and was responsible for the bank's political reputation. As a Catholic and a royalist, he supported first La Rocque, then Doriot, then rallied to Reynaud whom he subsequently abandoned for the armistice party. After the defeat he gathered round him a circle whose mentor he became and whose members entered into contact with the German services that counted the most, namely the economic section of the Majestic and the embassy, where virtually the entire team was invited to dine on 20 January 1941: Le Roy Ladurie, Arrighi, Barnaud, Benoist-Méchin, Drieu, Lehideux, Marion and Pucheu.[47] A few weeks later Darlan took most of them on board his government.

The two German commissioners successively appointed to the Worms Bank produced basically unconflicting descriptions of Le Roy Ladurie. The first, Ziegesar from the Commerzbank, believed him to be a remarkable professional, 'the life and soul of the house' after Worms, and described him as a man convinced of the need for close economic collaboration between France and Germany. The second, Falkenhausen, from the Deutsche Bank, recorded a more complicated assessment of the man in the autumn of 1941. Le Roy Ladurie was not unconditionally either for or against Germany. He exploited the opportunities that the politics of collaboration presented to his country and his business, seeking to synthesize his patriotism as a Frenchman, his 'burning political ambition', and the material interests of the firm for which he was responsible, although for him those interests took second place. As for the question of whether or not he would definitively opt for collaboration, this would depend on how relations between the two countries developed and on how the military situation evolved. The scenario that had his preference, for political as well as economic reasons, was that of a compromise peace between Germany and England, which would leave France playing the role of an intermediary and still in possession of its empire. This was, of course, the main Vichy line, and it was also supported by most of the rest of the Worms team. It is interesting to note the importance that this concept attached to economic considerations, as Falkenhausen had noticed: the Worms Bank had too many interests on the Anglo-Saxon side to wish for a total German victory.[48]

Le Roy Ladurie knew from experience what the risks of such a victory would be. At the beginning of his period as commissioner, Ziegesar had brandished the threat of aryanization, in order to promote the idea of a German share holding.[49] This was an element in the situation that Le Roy Ladurie certainly had to take into account, but in truth it probably simply encouraged him in a direction that he had already taken for general political reasons and that he conscientiously stuck to in his professional activity. In the spring of 1941 he was a driving force behind the plan for a company designed to further Franco-German economic relations, in which can be glimpsed the prospect of a Europe of bankers and industrialists. Those involved on the French side were the Worms Bank, Jappy Frères, Davum (the sales company for the steel producing group, Marine et Homécourt), Pont-à-Mousson, and the Comptoir Fluvial du Nord et de l'Est; the German side included most notably the Commerzbank, and Mannesmann and Roechling. The plan was for each side to set up a company in which each would allow the other 40 per cent of the shares. The French company was created in August 1941, but the project foundered when the German Ministry of the Economy refused to authorize the constitution of the German company. The time for partnership had not yet arrived.[50]

Le Roy Ladurie never neglected his job as a banker, particularly his links with the Commerzbank, which dated from before the war and which he hoped to convert into a privileged relationship. Hence his concern to establish good personal relations, for example by presenting works from his own library as gifts to one of the managers of the German bank,[51] and above all his attempts to be of assistance professionally, accompanied by a stream of gestures of goodwill. Twice he agreed to lower commission rates ('We hope that, as in the past, you will be kind enough to reserve for us a large part of your business in France . . .').[52] He acted as adviser to clients from the Commerzbank who were keen to acquire shares in France.[53] He asked the Commerzbank to be his associate in the financing of German orders and to place up to 200 million francs worth of orders amongst his contacts, in exchange for which the Commerzbank could share in commissions.[54]

Le Roy Ladurie was even so considerate as to smooth the way for his sister company to enter the French market. The Commerzbank's office in Paris was installed on the premises of a finance company (the Société Privée d'Études et de Banque) which the Worms Bank owned and Le Roy Ladurie offered to sell. The German bank was interested: a legitimate French company would be more useful to it than a subsidiary handicapped by its origin. During August and September 1941, Le Roy Ladurie busied himself in efforts to obtain authorization from Vichy. He even tackled Bouthillier, who feared he would be creating a precedent by allowing a German bank to become implanted under the cover of a French finance company but finally agreed on the twofold condition that this company would not be sold on to another German bank and that it would abstain from acquiring shares in French banks. The Commerzbank accepted the conditions and obtained the support of the MBF. However, it ran up against a categorical refusal from the German Ministry of the Economy.[55]

In 1942, the barometer for military victory swung over to the other side, and the banker's ardour cooled, as did that of the rest of the Worms group which, following the landings in North Africa, was no longer represented in the government. Falkenhausen noted that, while his relations with Le Roy Ladurie were still pleasant, the latter's desire for collaboration had become doubtful: his fear of communism inclined him towards Germany, but his fear of losing the French empire was propelling him in the opposite direction.[56]

Drieu La Rochelle criticized Le Roy Ladurie for looking at 'the country's affairs just as he looked at the affairs of his bank'.[57] He was a political banker, certainly, but still a banker first and foremost who, as such, trimmed his sails when the wind changed. After November 1942, the Germans noticed a growing reserve on the part of the minority of bankers who had committed themselves to collaboration, including Ardant. In the summer of 1943, there was mounting criticism of the Société Générale, which thereafter became ever cooler with regard to German business.[58] As chairman of the CO for banks, Ardant devoted all his efforts to protecting the banking labour force, not without success (his employees were grateful to him and spoke up for him in the purges).[59] In April 1944, when this privileged situation was reconsidered, he spoke of resigning, prudently explaining to the Germans that this would be by way of a protest against the sabotaging of the French administration. Those in charge of the banking sector at the MBF were sufficiently exasperated to consider arresting him and replacing him by Laurent-Atthalin but eventually, with cooler heads, decided instead to prolong his mandate as chairman of the organization committee.[60] Behind the scenes, the resistance was now being courted.

In the corridors of power, the resistance was now being courted. In 1943, François Bloch-Lainé, treasurer for the movement in metropolitan France, constantly found himself being rebuffed when he approached banks for funds, even though, as he pointed out, he always chose those that were the least compromised. But by the beginning of 1944, money was pouring in, as were offers of premises and administrative facilities. It was not long before the finance committee of the resistance was meeting in offices made available by Paribas.[61] At the time of the purges, Le Roy Ladurie drew attention to his contribution of 4 million francs – this was his best defence, along with the search of his home by the German police in March 1944 and his incarceration in Fresnes prison for twelve days.[62] At the beginning of 1944, Ardent also threw himself into funding the resistance, simultaneously donating 50000 francs to the PPF, out of habit no doubt.[63] It was a reversal that smacked of a massive purchase of indulgences.

18

Rogues and menials

Behind the big bosses before whom ministerial doors opened and whom the Germans treated with a certain consideration were mixed ranks of respected wholesalers, arrant rogues, and drudges seeking a leg-up or better pay. The wholesale dealers who controlled goods with prices inflated by the shortages can be quickly dealt with. No need for elaborate entrepreneurial strategies or particular talents here: it was simply a matter of being in the right place at the right time – where the money flowed. Take the chairman of the interprofessional group responsible for fruit and vegetables: an exporter of dairy produce to Germany before the war, he now found himself appointed by Vichy to distribute German orders among the various unions in this branch of the market. It was a position that brought him remuneration amounting to 4 million francs; as a bonus, the occupiers granted him, personally, a monopoly over the export of fruit and vegetables to Alsace-Lorraine. So profitable was this branch of business that it attracted many newcomers. One wholesaler who had previously dealt in imports now quickly switched to exports; his business profits, about 10 million francs per year before the war, soared to a total of 738 million for the period of the occupation.[1]

The Germans were also interested in the drinks business. The chairman of the distribution committee for wines and spirits was, suitably, a Bordeaux man. He was another who by no means suffered under the occupation: his business profits increased sixfold. He was on 'my dear friend' terms with the German official responsible for the purchase of wines, and was in the habit of presenting him with the kind of little presents that keep such friendships going. In May 1942, for instance, it was a case of

Lafite, 'a nice little wine worthy of both he who gives it and he who receives it'.[2] This German was a contact worth having in many a situation. On 18 October 1943, the said chairman from Bordeaux asked him to intervene on behalf of a compatriot in difficulties: 'My dear friend, I have a young protégé in Stuttgart . . . who is a civilian worker. He is a genuine volunteer who wanted to go to work in Germany. He is very happy there but complains of being unable to find any wine, even though willing to pay for it. Do you know of an establishment in Stuttgart that would be willing to sell him a few bottles of French wine?'[3]

Alongside such respected figures, other individuals emerged from the gutter to make millions on the German black market. Once settled in France, the Germans had immediately opened purchasing offices. Each service wanted its own: the army, the navy, the airforce, the SS and military counter-espionage. Money, provided by the occupation charges, flowed freely, channeling into German hands products and supplies that had been hoarded and depleting the resources badly needed by French firms trying to meet the orders placed with them by the Reich. Göring was well aware of this monstrous wastage and in 1943 reluctantly intervened personally to put a stop to it.[4] The most important of these purchasing agencies was the Otto office, created by the Abwehr to provide it with a cover and financial ease. By the spring of 1941, it was employing 400 people. No paperwork, no administrative formalities, and no questions asked: its recipe for success was simple. Soon the docks of Saint-Ouen, three hectares of covered warehouses, were overflowing. Close on 200 strapping, highly paid lads checked the merchandise and loaded it up for Germany. After the war, the business turnover of this office alone was estimated at scores of billions of francs. Such opportunities attracted a flock of wheelers and dealers and middlemen of many nationalities, most of them with a police record. They included a few big fish such as Joanovici, born in Bessarabia, who had arrived in Paris in 1921 and had been one of the biggest scrap merchants in the Paris region before the war. Under the occupation he was to make an estimated 4 billion. Another was Michel Szkolnikoff,[5] a Russian Jew who had arrived in Paris in 1933 and had proceeded to seek his fortune in various kinds of business, some of which landed him in prison. The occupation provided him with a career well suited to his talents that at the same time assured him of undreamed-of protection against the French police and the racial laws. Szkolnikoff amassed billions and lived in grand style, with a place reserved for him at all the fashionable restaurants, and at home he had one of the best tables in Paris, where members of the SS and the military, seduced by the corrupt atmosphere, would come to carouse. His suppliers were of many kinds: even respected industrialists and wholesalers felt no qualms about reserving part of their produce for him. He made incredible profits, converting them into gold, jewellery or apartment blocks in Paris or on the Côte d'Azur. He invested a minimum of two billion francs in real estate alone, having amassed that sum in the space of three short years.

Between the respected wholesalers and the racketeers of every kind was a thick layer of mediocrity, a cohort of small firms ready to work for the king of Prussia himself if this would help them survive or give them a chance to make a profit. The German purchasing offices dealt with many assiduous suppliers, always keen to be of service: producers of preserves and purveyors of regional specialities, for instance, and one Paris manufacturer of springs who, with a taste for grovelling no doubt, signed a letter dated 4 January 1944 as 'your devoted servant, at your command'.[6]

In certain sectors, German demand attracted dealers like moths to a candle: dealers in antiques, for example, who were faced with barely resistible temptations. German buyers rolled up in their dozens, some of them figures of great importance like Göring. According to a report produced after the war by the American secret services, Paris was the busiest art market in Nazi Europe. Nearly all the Paris dealers made sales to the Germans, dozens of them supplying artefacts for the Reichsmarschall collection, frequently in contravention of rules designed to safeguard the national patrimony. Some even acted as middlemen between owners and German clients. And alongside the established antique dealers, many new middlemen hastened to infiltrate this market in which articles passed from one hand to another, often with extra zeros tacked on to their prices at each move, before finally taking the road for Germany.[7]

There was similar feverish activity in public works, where the German manna encouraged many a neophyte to set up a firm specially to receive it, and led established figures to use middlemen or to offer cut prices and sweeteners in order to secure contracts.[8] The clothing trade was also keen to be of service: one small-scale manufacturer of brassières, a trade association leader for this branch of industry, approached the Commerzbank for orders and received so many that, to meet them all, he formed a 'Paris consortium of brassière manufacturers', supervised by the corresponding German trade union.[9]

The German archives are crammed with hundreds of solicitations addressed to the 'Centre of German economic organizations in France', formerly the German Chamber of Commerce in Paris.[10] They probably came from quite small businesses, begging to represent German firms. In an economy in which the search for clients had been replaced by a search for objects to sell, this was a way of getting around shortages. But what went on was less innocent than it seemed, for the selection of representatives was vetted a good deal more rigorously than orders for manufactured goods were. The racial criteria of the Nazi regime were strictly observed: Jews could not represent German companies.

Faced with having to produce a 'certificate of Aryanity', candidates reacted in a variety of ways. One expostulated indignantly that he had been representing German firms for forty years and his word of honour ought to suffice: his candidacy was rejected. Some let it be known that, if that was the case, they preferred to withdraw. Those with fears would invent an unexpected deterioration in their health or a sudden change in their circumstances. Others simply broke off the correspondence. But the majority produced a certificate, albeit sometimes under protest, as did the officer who at first brandished his word of honour but knuckled under in the end.[11] Only a minority withdrew, but the fact that they did so is significant. Some people clearly did realize that the commercial link they were seeking to establish locked into the mechanisms of the political regime.

There were other ways of hitching up to the German wagon. One was by opening up one's company's capital to a German holding. Not very many people did this, far fewer than offered to represent German firms. Some of those who did were prompted by a desire to settle old scores. A shareholder of two cigarette-paper companies wrote as follows: 'We offer you loyal and sincere collaboration and would be grateful for the chance to extricate ourselves from all those English, Jews and freemasons.'[12] Usually it was a matter of keeping one's social footing, as in the case of one family in Le Havre, which swapped a majority German shareholding in its maritime insurance company for the right to keep the former proprietor in his post as manager.[13]

Many of these offers failed to find a taker. A Paris company producing serums and vitamins was prepared to allow a minority share to any German company that would supply it with the raw materials that it urgently needed. Its manager wrote to the Paris representative of the Commerzbank, whom he thanked for having told his clients of 'the desires of our board of directors with regard to collaboration', as follows: 'You know that our essential aim is to consolidate the future of our House through fruitful exchanges with Greater Germany'. However, although a few German companies did show some interest, none wanted to commit themselves, as the quality of the products was judged to be inadequate.[14]

Conversely, some French people could offer only their own entrepreneurial vocation, in the hope that the occupiers would provide them with a business. The profession of front man won sudden popularity during these years. Right to the very end, there were candidates for the job, seemingly unaffected by the changing circumstances. In 1943, the MBF registered ten cases of German capital invested in French firms that had received authorization from the French government and thirty-four others – for a total of close on 120 million francs – in which the identity of the shareholders was camouflaged.[15] The MBF not only tolerated but even encouraged a practice that, as early as 1941, caused teeth to grind in the Ministry of the Economy in Berlin: was the Reich of so little account that it was obliged to resort to intermediaries? The MBF's reply was that this would make it possible to get around Vichy's legislation and, in particular, to lay hands on Jewish property, without seeming to break Göring's promise to leave most of it to France.[16]

Jewish property was, of course, the reward that could be expected by these aspiring entrepreneurs. At least 10000 Frenchmen worked during the occupation as temporary managers of some 40000 despoiled Jewish businesses. In May 1944, when aryanization was near completion, there were still 5522 of these working alongside 110 German commissioners.[17] These jobs attracted a wide range of applicants, many of them incompetent, a fact that led to a rapid turnover. Some were antisemites of course, such as one man 'convinced of the importance of the Jewish danger and of its European character', who told the MBF of the 'moral satisfaction' that he felt as he converted his opinions into actions.[18] Some were crooks or swindlers, many of them with considerable experience. Some were traders down on their luck, seizing an opportunity to get back on their feet in the sales world.

Officially, a Vichy office was responsible for hiring these people, but applicants in their dozens approached the occupation authorities directly. The proprietor of an advertising agency, who had fallen on hard times, a war veteran with decorations and of 'pure Latin race', excused himself for not writing in German, expressing his confidence of soon being in a position to remedy this: 'If I were in continual contact with Germans, I should soon acquire an almost total knowledge of the language, or at least enough to read and understand it.' One lady, formerly the manageress of an engravings gallery, French, Catholic, abandoned by her husband and with her elderly father to look after, showed a similar willingness to cooperate: 'I am learning German and am beginning to be able to cope with it.'[19]

Moving on from such front men and temporary managers, we come to others with nothing but their physical strength to hire to the occupiers, either in France or in Germany. The armed forces had no difficulty in finding all the labour they needed. In the spring of 1941, the MBF administration employed close on 45000 French people; by the second half of 1942 the figure was not far off 70000, the vast majority working as domestic servants (cleaners, laundresses, waitresses, auxiliary nurses) or as cooks, secretaries, interpreters, mechanics or drivers.[20] Then there were also those working for other services: at the end of 1941, there were 160000 workers on German construction sites and some 100000 in concerns connected with the Wehrmacht. By 1944 500000 were employed by Wehrmacht services or in the Todt Organization.[21]

The latter figure includes an incalculable number of people taken on either forcibly or automatically because of the nature of their work, particularly during the last years of the occupation. But in 1940–42, most of these engagements were voluntary. As is attested by the swelling number of complaints from employers faced with what they considered to be unfair competition, tens of thousands of workers chose to quit steady jobs and enter the service of the occupying power. It is true that the conditions on offer tended to override hesitant scruples: a higher hourly wage, more hours of work per week, all sorts of incentives, privileged food supplies. In November

1941, manual labourers working for the Todt Organization were earning three times as much as those working for French firms.[22]

Others simply went off to work in Germany. In March 1941, close on 30000 volunteers were recruited in France. Their number increased to 121653 in January 1942, then reached 184652 by 31 May 1942, when the *Relève* came into operation. Up until November 1940, French nationals made up no more than a minority of these recruits. Most were foreigners – Poles, Russians, Italians, Slovaks, etc. – who were more footloose, less affected by the fate of France, and harder hit by unemployment as a result of the measures of nationalistic discrimination adopted by Vichy. Thereafter, the proportion of French nationals rose steadily, to over 80 per cent by the summer of 1941.[23] By June 1942, the total of volunteer workers of French nationality had risen to 132700.[24]

With the *Relève*, the volunteer system acquired the official blessing of the government, for each volunteer hastened the return of a prisoner. From October 1942 on, the selection procedure added the threat of sanctions to the pressure that was applied by the state and by some employers. In February 1943, the STO imposed rigorous obligatory selection upon entire age-groups. Yet the voluntary system still continued and the small eastward trickle of volunteer workers produced by this even increased in the last year, when French people who had placed themselves at risk by their collaborationist behaviour sought refuge in the Reich. In the first half of 1944 these even outnumbered STO workers (22247 as against 18347).[25] In July 1944, 3500 volunteers embarked upon the last-chance train journey.[26]

In all, at least 200000 French people went of their own free will to work in Germany (including the 32530 *Relève* volunteers who left between June and Octover 1942, before the introduction of the requisitioning of labour).[27] It should furthermore be pointed out that the figure given for voluntary workers up until June 1942 relates only to those who actually left for Germany. Between the moment of volunteering and that of departure at least 25 per cent more dropped out: 2 to 5 per cent were rejected following the obligatory medical examination, and a further 20 to 30 per cent simply melted away.[28] However, in relation to the overall population France still came at the bottom of the tables for Western European countries: by September 1941, for example, there were 48567 French volunteers compared to 28895 Danes, 92995 Dutch and 121501 Belgians.[29]

Volunteers were recruited essentially in the occupied zone, mostly in the Paris region (five-eighths of the total up until October 1941).[30] Several thousand came from the free zone: in the spring of 1941, Vichy authorized German commissions to recruit amongst the foreign internees. Professionally speaking, these were mostly unskilled manual workers: half were metal workers, over a quarter building labourers, the rest miners and agricultural labourers. However, the convoy of 25 March 1941, for example, also included two maîtres d'hotel, one typographer, seven cooks, three hairdressers, and two engineers.[31]

This employment was open to women, and by the spring of 1941 the proportion of female volunteers was beginning to rise steeply. In July 1942, of the 77000 French nationals working in the Reich, 23000 were women.[32] In September 1944, 42654 French women were on Geman territory.[33] Some had probably seized the chance offered for voluntary women workers to join their prisoner-of-war husbands.[34] Most were unskilled factory workers, the rest cleaners or shop employees. They had few qualifications and a lamentable standard of health. It is true that the medical examination for women was particularly rigorous: the German obsession with venereal contagion was given free rein, thereby slowing down recruitment. Only half these volunteers passed the medical examination without a hitch: between 10 and 15 per cent were definitely rejected, many on account of tuberculosis or, above all, venereal diseases (as against a general average of 2 to 5 per cent); one-third were placed on hold for further examinations or while they took a course of treatment.[35]

It may seem strange that French men and women should voluntarily emigrate to Germany just after the defeat and with their own country under occupation, and it is not easy to determine precisely what motivated them to do so. One obvious factor was persistent unemployment, at least in the early days (the official figure for those out of work in July 1941 was 230000). However, in the mid-term the curve of voluntary recruitment rose, while that of unemployment fell. The main motivation must have been the attraction of a higher wage and the favourable conditions attached that German propaganda delighted in emphasizing (a six-month contract, two weeks of paid leave for those whose contracts were renewed, the possibility to transfer up to 1500 francs per month to France). But there were other motives too: an urge to make a break, or a desire to escape from a delicate or difficult situation.

On the basis of scraps of information provided by the archives, many of those involved seem to have been people who had never got a good start in life, individuals poorly assimilated into a collective framework, whether at the family, the professional or the social level. In the Var, for instance, volunteers came not from the world of large factories or typical working-class trades, but from a young, 'floating' proletariat without training and without work.[36] The strong recruitment in Paris was also probably related to isolated or marginalized sectors of the population, where people seized upon a German contract, clinging to the idea of special rewards and possibly, either consciously or subconsciously, expressing their resentment against a country that had dealt with them harshly.

The case of Maurice Sachs, who left for Germany in the autumn of 1942, though somewhat flamboyant, is essentially quite typical. Sachs was a collaborator with Gallimard, a friend of Cocteau, Gide, Maritain and Max Jacob, who before the war had made a minor name for himself in the Paris world of letters. After the defeat, he became increasingly unstable, living from hand to mouth and burning the candle at both ends, eventually fetching up in a brothel for homosexuals before taking the road to Hamburg, concealing his Jewish origins.[37] Here are the courses taken by two other lives, this time of women, but similarly dominated by instability. The first is that of a young Parisian woman who left for Germany in 1941 where she was arrested and condemned to death for complicity in a robbery (German courts gave no quarter during the war). Brinon, who intervened on her behalf, pleaded extenuating circumstances: her concierge mother had worked her fingers to the bone to get her daughter through her *baccalauréat*; the girl had been seduced, then abandoned; her child had died in the exodus; she had an appalling medical history.[38] The second is the story of a young orphan who took a job as a cleaner at the Kommandatur and went out with German soldiers. She then moved to another town and became an assistant cook in a German camp and cleaner for an officer who dismissed her for theft. Next she became a maid at a Gestapo headquarters, from which she was sacked for giving cigarettes to prisoners. At the end of 1943, no doubt feeling that she had exhausted the possibilities in France, she went off to work in Germany.[39]

Up until 1942, strictly political motives seem to have figured relatively little. One of the cases in which they did play a part provides us with a somewhat misspelled letter addressed on 18 April 1941 to the Feldkommandatur of the Marne department, which reveals a whole social scene: 'Sir, I am riting you this letter, beging you to tell me if I could go to work in Germany in a munissions factory, as an unskilled worker or a labourer clearing a building site . . . I am eighteen and a half years old and I am sure I could be of use to you cos I have already worked 4 months as a factory hand in Tulle (Corrèze). So if its possible tell me at once and let me go to work for the Defence of Germany.' Having appended an address of farm labourers in the Marne, the young man added a postscript: 'PS. This is where I am, waiting for good news from you that will make me happy as I would find some friends I am an orphan and would like to get a trade for myself later.'[40] Once arrived in Germany, some of the volunteers joined the Amicale des Travailleurs Français, a creation of the German embassy. Around mid-1942, it regularly sent propaganda to 21652 families of volunteers, probably those who had joined the Amicale.[41] That would mean that one volunteer in seven had been making a political gesture, a gesture that was no doubt supported by material motives, perhaps a need for legal assistance or for means of supporting a family left behind in France.

But for them all the political dimension must have figured at least on the horizon: it would hardly have been possible not to see the implications of such a decision. And if the individual concerned was blind to these, parents, friends or neighbours would have taken it upon themselves to point them out. In October 1940, the landlord of a block of flats, learning that one of his tenants had signed up for Germany, had a row with him, declaring 'You and your dirty Boches, I shit on the lot of you', sentiments that the volunteer's wife promptly conveyed to the occupying authorities in a letter of denunciation.[42] As early as 1941, German reports were noting the ostracism that struck the volunteer workers either before their departure or upon their return,[43] especially when they made no secret of their decision and sang the praises of Germany.

For almost all the volunteer workers, this stay in the Reich was their first experience of another country and many of them seem to have been agreeably surprised by it, at least during the first year, as can be seen from the following letter sent by one worker to his parents at the end of 1940: 'When I arrived here I found it odd to be so well received, and I think that life here is far better than the life we led even before the war at home. For there is one thing that matters more than anything, everyone is equal, even for food, which is very good, and there are canteens for the workers the like of which I have never seen in France. It's only when you leave your own country that you can see that at home they have always stuffed our heads with nonsense. I assure you that I do not regret having come to work here.'[44] The German authorities were in no doubt of the positive opinions of most French volunteers and claimed in late 1941 that 90 per cent of them were well satisfied.[45] They were all the better pleased when they noticed the effect that the expression of such sentiments on the part of the volunteers had upon those close to them and on relations generally.[46]

Nevertheless, there were also complaints, and by the summer of 1941, hundreds of contracts were being broken.[47] The factory was not the one that had been promised, unforeseen deductions were made from wages, and working conditions and food and lodging fell short of expectations. There was homesickness to contend with and all kinds of difficulties of adaptation. The German population, although inclined to rate the French higher than other peoples, certainly the Italians, was not lacking in prejudices. Police surveillance did the rest. The authorities' reports present an almost caricatural image of the expatriates: wanton women, rowdy men, all full of ingratitude towards their hosts.[48]

Sometimes the volunteers encountered their compatriots. These were 'rather strained' meetings. The prisoners of war manifested 'deep distrust and a surly rancour' towards these French people who had chosen to offer the strength of their arms to help the very enemy that was holding them prisoners.[49] Yet some went down the same road when, in 1943, they agreed to be 'converted' into civilian workers.[50] The Germans were expecting higher production levels once they could openly employ this labour force in the manufacture of munitions, from which prisoners of war were banned under the Geneva convention. For those involved, the decision to become civilian workers brought with it a number of advantages: lighter surveillance, a wage and, above all, home leave. But there was a downside too: it meant falling out of step, swapping enforced confinement for the ambiguous position of a quasi-voluntary worker. Some 200000 prisoners agreed to be converted into workers, in conditions that were not always regular. No doubt the flow would have been even greater if the most important promise, that of a period of leave in France, had been honoured. But after two trial runs, the Germans changed their minds: at the end of April 1943, 43 out of the 1000 granted leave failed to return; in August 2000 out of 5000 did likewise.[51]

Finally, there was one form of work in Germany that combined voluntary labour on the part of the workers with German business on the part of their French employers. As early as the autumn of 1940, the Germans were encouraging the formation of teams of volunteers all recruited from the same firm. The firm forfeited a proportion of their then surplus work force and kept it in reserve for future use. The scheme was not a great success. By August 1941 no more than a dozen or so firms were playing along: altogether rather fewer than 3000 workers were involved. Most went to work for IG Farben, a great consumer of labour which, on that account, became a major cog in the concentration camp system.[52]

With the introduction of the *Relève*, this idea resurfaced, officially through Laval, but also in a quasi-private form. In the autumn of 1942, an association known as 'Panoma' was set up by six Paris roofing and piping firms. The Hamburg Chamber of Crafts gave them a one-year contract to repair damaged apartment blocks there. The work required a team of sixty workers to be sent, in return for which these firms would be exempted from labour requisitioning. They allowed themselves to be separated from some of their workers but, in contrast to firms affected by the *Relève*, they continued to employ them: Hamburg paid the wages of the workers to the association, plus a small sum to cover extra general costs.

Similarly, the 'Paros' association comprised fourteen Paris firms specializing in roofing, plumbing and heating. These were contracted for work to be carried out in Upper Silesia for two German firms, one of which was IG Farben. The members of the association contributed some capital and undertook to supply a number of workers. The statutes provided for profits to be shared between the associates, but after the introduction of the STO this arrangement seemed awkward. In April 1943, it was decided that profits would be shared out among the staff working in Germany.

The employers pointed out to their workers the advantages of higher salaries, sticking together as a team, frequent periods of leave, and the chance to meet up with prisoners of war now converted into civilian workers. Some of those conditions were imperfectly honoured or were altered with the introduction of the STO, which led to home leaves being discontinued. The workers who made the trip to Germany had, notwithstanding, taken their decision freely. On one point, the promises of the Germans were kept: the expatriates were out of the way of bombing raids. Those who were sent to Upper Silesia let it be known that they were pleased with their posting.[53] To that extent Auschwitz, which was bombed only once, in July 1944, was, after all, one of the safest places in the Reich.

19

Sprechen Sie deutsch?

In the year of our Lord 1759, the troops of the king of France occupied Frankfurt. The commander-in-chief acquired quarters in the home of one of the town's leading citizens. The latter, feeling inconvenienced and in sympathy with the Prussians, put up with this with a bad grace. His young son, on the other hand, enjoyed this interruption of routine, became fond of the French officer and assiduously frequented the theatre that followed the troops. His father reproved him. He disapproved of his son's passion for the theatre, believing that it boded ill for his future career. He was not bothered that the theatre in question was French. On the contrary, he became reconciled to the stage once he perceived the great progress that the young Goethe was making with his French.[1]

French was then considered the language of civilization that every well-born German ought to speak. The occupiers were soldiers; their theatre was designed neither to propagate the French language and the French culture nor to prepare for any political subjugation which, besides, could be imposed regardless of any knowledge of the French language. Not until the period of the French Revolution, several decades later, did culture become a deliberate means of political influence and domination. And several further decades passed before the knowledge of the French language through compulsory inculcation, conscription and the press generally, became a necessary mark of membership of the French nation. The France of the Third Republic used its language and culture as a tool of its external politics generally, as of its politics of occupation. In the Rhineland after 1918, as well as striving to deflect economic currents and steer them in its own direction, it tried to win over minds by creating a French-language magazine, introducing French performers from the world of the arts, setting up language courses and organizing exhibitions.[2]

When Germany occupied France in 1870–73 and then again in 1914–18, it did not adopt a similar course of action. Beyond the Rhine, a national identity had been forged by cohering around an ethnically centred German culture and language. It was only on the eve of 1914 that the imperial government embarked upon a cultural policy aimed at other countries and that looked beyond the German minorities. Its example was followed by first the Weimar Republic, then – more energetically – by the Nazi regime which thus, paradoxically, followed the lead of the French Revolution. Its values may have been in absolute contradiction but – like Italian fascism – it resembled its model in its taste for propaganda and its desire to mobilize the masses.

Once in the position of conqueror in 1940, it returned to the policies learned from France, only to reverse them against its model. It did so on an unprecedented scale, extending its efforts in every direction, with long-term designs. Would it have been so keen to purge and rewrite the history text books of conquered France if it had not been planning lasting domination and establishing a protectorate that would take the very culture of France under its umbrella? The Nazi regime addressed the French people in a number of forms, targeting various audiences and never losing sight of its objectives.

Day in day out, the occupying power dispensed its inflated propaganda on cinema screens and in the press. But it also employed means that allowed it to make its politics seem beguiling: rather than hammering home the message and trumpeting aloud its own praises, it beckoned and insinuated. Up until 1942, the French were provided with a succession of exhibitions conveying two messages: their future lay in their willing insertion into a German Europe; they shared the same enemies as the conqueror. The organization of these exhibitions was placed in French hands. From the sidelines, the Germans – usually the German embassy – provided the finance, steered and maintained control.

The first exhibition, managed by Jacques de Lesdain and Jean Marquès-Rivière, was designed to whip up prejudice against the freemasons. A delighted Abetz reported that in the first three days – this was mid-October 1940, four months after disaster struck – 120000 visitors queued at the doors of the Petit Palais, the lines sometimes stretching for 200 metres.[3] Everybody rushed to stare at objects, items of furniture, and documents seized from the Lodges. The centrepiece of the exhibition was a reconstruction of the temple of the 33rd degree of the Grand Orient of France. Hoardings and commentaries protested against the power of freemasonry and its hold over political life, revealing its English and Jewish connections and emphasizing its role in the decadence and defeat of France.

In the course of five weeks, this exhibition attracted 900000 visitors. It then toured the provinces where it was seen by a further 113930 people.[4] The embassy staff were delighted. They announced that they had made all these people see that the freemasons and the Jews were responsible for the misfortunes of their country and that its recovery could only be achieved by eliminating them and cleaving to the ideas of Nazi Germany.[5]

The theme of the exhibition exerted a strong pull, with its promise of revelations and all the publicity given to the list of masonic journalists and parliamentary representatives that was on sale in the form of a mini telephone directory. This exhibition, set out as simply as a fairground, was free, unlike those that followed it. Moreover, a number of measures taken by Vichy had just made the public particularly sensitive to its theme.[6] No doubt most of those who came to see it were simply curious, greedy for sensation and steeped in the widespread prejudices. Many were in modest circumstances and, the Germans noted, there were quite a few clerics (although in Bordeaux the bishop roundly refused to visit the exhibition).[7] A large minority consisted of people seriously hooked, willing to pay to attend the lectures laid on by Marquès-Rivière or for the catalogue that he had put together (of which 31472 copies were sold).

The second exhibition was shown in the Grand Palais between June and October 1941. It was called 'La France européenne' (European France), a title that saw off the concept of a French Europe. Conquered France had to recognize that it now held a subordinate place in a continent that Germany had won the right to lead. The exhibition was opened by Brinon, Stülpnagel, Laval and a representative of the archbishopric. It displayed the riches of the country, laying particular emphasis on its agriculture, which more or less allotted France its role in the new Europe that was presented in such an alluring fashion. The exhibition attracted 635000 visitors; 15000 of them took the trouble to listen to a political lecture on the same subject.[8]

Some of the same material was recycled in 'La vie nouvelle' (The New Life) (May–August 1942). Its themes were the family, work, town planning and the good life. The model farm was here replaced by a factory's garden of recreation, holding out the promise of a radiant future in the new Europe whose attractions and solidarity were lauded, the latter being illustrated by the work of volunteers in Germany and the struggles of the Legion of French Volunteers against bolshevism. Together, these two exhibitions, organized by the indefatigable Jacques de Lesdain, attracted as many people as the antimasonic exhibition in Paris, although the numbers attending the second were considerably lower than those for the first, being visited by 295925 people.[9] The spectacle of harmonious integration into Nazi Europe by now lay under the very noses of the French people.

Shortly before 'La France européenne' closed, the Palais Berlitz opened its doors to another exhibition, 'Le Juif et la France' (The Jew and France) (September 1941–January 1942).[10] It was organized by Captain Paul Sézille, the director of the Institute for the Study of Jewish Questions, an organization under the aegis of the embassy and the SD. The purpose of the exhibition, which used material from the Nazi exhibition, 'The eternal Jew', was to demonstrate the permanence of the Jewish presence and how the Jewish race had invaded national life. It did so by dint of many texts, drawings, photos and models designed to teach how to 'flush out Jews' and to encourage repulsion. The single message announced in capital letters on the front of the catalogue was 'Jews never could be, never can be, never will be assimilated to other peoples.'

Sézille boasted of a million visitors; the embassy recorded 250623.[11] Classes of schoolchildren were taken to it; members of the occupation services went; but most visitors were French people who went along of their own accord. The exhibition moved to Bordeaux in March–May 1942 (61213 visitors) and then to Nancy in July–August (33482).[12] In all, 345318 people saw it, far fewer than the numbers for the earlier exhibitions. The Germans did not attempt to prolong its life beyond the summer of 1942. The reactions provoked by the deportations threatened to make it a resounding failure.

Finally, 'Bolshevism against Europe' opened in March 1942 in the Salle Wagram. It was the idea of Propaganda-Abteilung, which did not want the embassy to occupy all the high ground. It made use of the services of a French group, Paul Chack's Comité d'Action Antibolchévique, but was eager to underline the patronage of the Reich and its allies in the struggle against communism (Italy, Hungary, Romania, Finland, Spain and Portugal). France, which did not figure on this list, insisted upon taking part; Brinon represented Pétain at the inauguration. Before it closed, as if to swell the numbers of visitors, the exhibition was visited by a number of only more or less willing groups: SNCF employees whom Propaganda-Abteilung wished to enlighten as to the communist danger,[13] and two or three thousand Parisian secondary school children brought along by 152 teachers who had thought it politic to respond to the suggestion of their minister, Abel Bonnard.[14] After Paris, where it was seen by 370000 people, the exhibition moved to Lille (160000) for July–August, then on to Bordeaux (140000) from October to December 1942.[15] It then toured the former free zone, where it continued to attract visitors. In Toulouse, between 6 May and 8 June 1944, a further 29855 people (10 per cent of whom were Germans) visited it.[16]

By the summer of 1942, the season of major exhibitions was over. The public never did get the chance to see one devoted to Albert Speer that Abetz was thinking of offering it. Those responsible for organizing propaganda sensed a change in the atmosphere and were afraid of a flop. Hitler, to whom all requests for authorization were referred, now became irritated by these exhibitions that had earlier flattered his taste for the spectacular. When, in the summer of 1942, Abetz sounded him out on the idea of a new exhibition entitled 'The Greatness of Germany', he lost his temper. While you are at it, he said, why not present the French with a collection of all the best German weapons? It was totally misguided to want to show them the achievements of Nazism and give them a chance to copy them. Germany's aim was to bring down France for good by keeping it divided against itself. Of course, you had to be cunning, you had to adjust the politics of the occupation to the circumstances, but the final objective had to remain unshakeable.[17]

In total, these large exhibitions attracted three million visitors by the end of 1942.[18] They had made the most of the public's addiction to art galleries, museums, theatres and spectacles of all kinds. Nevertheless, they had not managed to disguise the instigation and support received from the occupying power. Shortly after the opening of the antimasonic exhibition, Jacques de Lesdain received a letter from a woman who signed herself Marie-Françoise Defrance. It attacked him violently for acting as the agent of the occupier who 'respects neither God, nor honour, nor promises given' and it ended as follows: 'Monsieur, I do not know how much your writings earn for you, assuredly more than thirty pieces of silver: I am not calling you a Judas, the word is too weak; what I am saying is "You are a Pierre Laval".'[19]

It would be an exaggeration to read into this stream of visitors evidence of agreement for Nazi or Vichy propaganda, let alone a plebiscite in favour of collaboration. The exhibitions drew crowds because they were aimed at an equivocal curiosity and, above all, because they pandered to antipathies, prejudices and ideologies already present in a diffused, or sometimes concentrated form in French society. In its own way, their success indicates that a substantial portion of the population was sufficiently confused over what was at stake in the situation and their own choices, to be won over by the temptation of a connivance, however brief and limited, with certain aspects of the ideology of the occupying power. The uneven impact of these exhibitions reflects the varying degrees of that connivance. The subject of freemasonry was more popular than that of antisemitism or even anticommunism which, nevertheless, continued to the last to evoke interest. At the very least all this suggests that people had dropped their guard. From the occupying power's point of view, of course, this was an advantage, for it deflected attention on to those who were also its own enemies, thereby deferring outright rejection of its dominion.

Meanwhile, the so-called 'educated' public was also being targeted in other ways. It was presented with a prodigious collection of the most sophisticated products of German culture: a curious idea, it might be thought, at a time when the two countries were still in a state of war and the clash of arms was to be heard on all sides. However, those in charge of German propaganda were anxious to establish the superiority of their own culture in order to justify their claim to political dominance, to rally the French to them by promoting an illusion of collaboration, or, at the very least, to render them inoffensive by encouraging them to believe in a return to normal.

In this endeavour, Propaganda-Abteilung was again competing with the embassy or, to be more precise, with the German Institute created by Abetz in the autumn of 1940 and located in the Hôtel de Sagan, the former seat of the Polish embassy. Its director, Karl Epting, was a zealous organizer who was knowledgeable about Parisian society. The unbridled rivalry between the two services did not prevent them from adopting similar tactics and focusing on classical culture, making the most of reputations and tastes long since established. It was an attractive policy that sometimes led to misconceived intellectual gestures. Thus, in March 1942, Charles Vildrac, a future member of the underground Comité National des Écrivains (National Committee of Writers), attended a soirée for the German poet Rilke organized by the Institute and the Groupe Collaboration, in order to testify to his personal friendship with Rilke.[20]

Some cultural genres lent themselves to promotional ploys better than others did. The theatre was not particularly productive: the four German companies that came to perform plays in their original language failed to attract crowds. Propaganda-Abteilung then, with hardly any more success, concentrated its efforts on producing plays translated from the German.[21] Music was not affected by the language barrier, and German music enjoyed a great reputation. Several resistance novels, first and foremost *Le Silence de la mer*, seeking to keep French people on their guard, represented that music as the most powerful mode of *rapprochement* and warned them not to succumb to it. It was a seductive art that, by establishing communication, served as a political weapon.

On this point, the warnings of the resistance fell upon deaf ears. German concerts played to packed houses. In September 1941, the Berlin Philharmonic Orchestra was even obliged to lay on a third, extra, concert to satisfy the crowds.[22] It is true that the musical public had seldom been so indulged. The very cream of German musical life came to Paris: Eugen Jochum, Herbert von Karajan, Hans von Benda, Wolfgang Abendroth, Clemens Krauss, Hans Knappertbusch, the soloists Wilhelm Kempff, the young Elizabeth Schwarzkopf and Lore Fischer, as well as larger groups such as chamber orchestras.[23] The demand does not appear to have diminished with time. Between May 1942 and July 1943, the German Institute organized seventy-one concerts (thirty-one in Paris, forty in the provinces) – more than one a week.[24] The public had clearly decided not to deny itself this pleasure. Fabre-Luce wrote of one of these concerts: 'One is beyond wars, beyond nations.'[25] Wagnerian brass was certainly one means of smothering the cries of the tortured and the rattling fire of the firing squads.

Other programmes, exclusive to the German Institute, intermingled culture and politics. It may have seemed a long shot to expect to find a public for lectures placed under the aegis of the occupying power and delivered by German orators, even if they did express themselves in French, but the bet paid off. Between October

1940 and July 1941 alone, the German Institute organized forty-six lectures, twelve of them in the provinces.[26] The pace hardly slowed over the following two years, with a wide spectrum of subjects ranging from literature, through architecture, law, economics, history and philosophy, to medicine. Some of these lectures were devoted to classical aspects of the national culture: Hans-Georg Gadamer, for example, spoke on 'The people and history in Herder'. Many lectures presented a picture of 'the new Germany' or tackled subjects of current interest: for example, those of the economists Ferdinand Fried and Anton Zischka and the jurist Carl Schmitt.[27] Yet others were concerned with matters closely connected with Nazism, racism for example, on which major experts such as Eugen Fischer and Otmar von Verschner pronounced. Quite apart from their German patronage, most of them included a strong element of propaganda.

Epting made the most of the opportunity they offered to make new contacts and to promote relations. In September 1941, a lecture delivered to a 900-strong audience by Dr Leonardo Conti, the Reich's foremost medical authority, was followed by a reception attended by at least a hundred representatives of the French medical world.[28] In April 1942, Friedrich von Falkenhausen spoke on 'The Huguenots in Prussia'. Epting noted with satisfaction that this lecture had made it possible to attract for the first time – and, it may be added, definitely the last – a number of people from Protestant circles, generally hostile to both Vichy and the occupying power.[29] Charles Rist was present, accompanied by his German commissioner, who was related to the lecturer.[30]

Up until the summer of 1942, that is to say in one year and a half, the lectures attracted 25000 people in the capital alone;[31] the total for the whole of the occupation must have approached 50000. It truly was an astonishing success, bearing in mind the level of these talks, and one that far outdid the results obtained by the same organizer, Epting, before the war. Then, his efforts had been more or less wasted, attracting no more than a few thousand people in a whole year to the concerts and lectures that he put on.[32] It was as if military success had, at a stroke, crowned Nazi Germany with the laurels of high culture.

Words travel too, in invasions – *Ausweis, Ersatz, Kommandatur* – but these were unpleasant words, and Germany was keen for others to become known. And interest should not be one-way only: the occupiers wanted to acquire or improve their knowledge of the natives' language. In the spring of 1941, upon a request from the Majestic, the Paris education authorities made lecture halls available and appealed for volunteers: sixteen *lycée* teachers responded.[33] However, it was up to the conquered to make the first efforts. It may have been because Abetz and his people were already impressed by French culture, or because they came from southern Germany that they ascribed such importance to this matter. Whatever the reason, they worked with as much fervour to spread knowledge of the German language as their colleagues in Alsace-Lorraine did to suppress French.

At the embassy's request, Vichy made a few gestures: a second post of Inspector General of German was created, as existed for English; English and German were made the only languages whose study at school was compulsory.[34] But it was not state intervention that was the most effective in this domain: the decisions of parents were more important, for their choices reflected the image that society had formed of a language and the people who spoke it. In 1914, the pre-eminence that German had enjoyed in secondary education ever since the victory of the Prussian schoolteachers in 1870 disappeared overnight. The outbreak of war branded the enemy's language with infamy and raised that of France's ally, England, so high that it was never to lose ground again. On the eve of the Second World War, there were twice as many secondary schoolchildren learning English as there were learning German (about 60 per cent as against 30 per cent, and 10 per cent learning Italian or Spanish).

In 1939, the same phenomenon as in 1914 took place, although on a minor scale: German's share dropped from 29.2 per cent to 26.4 per cent.[35] Once again the enemy's language was rejected, as if acquiring it might contaminate French minds or impair the integrity of one's patriotism. But instead of that tendency growing, this time it was reversed: French attitudes did not remain as they were in the first autumn of the war. German crept back up to 27.8 per cent at the beginning of the school year in 1940, rose to 29.8 per cent in 1941, and eventually, in 1943, reached 31.4 per cent, its highest level since the First World War. In Paris its progress was even more marked: it rose from 30.9 per cent in 1939 to 38 per cent in 1941 (the latest date known).[36] Then the tendency (at the national level) was reversed: 27.9 per cent in 1943, 24.8 per cent in 1944, which brought it back down to the level of the 1920s; then a further plunge to around 20 per cent by the beginning of the next decade.

The changes may seem unimpressive, but in reality they were considerable. The figures relate to the whole of secondary education. But the pupils made their choices when they first entered it and were thereafter not allowed to change. The five-point increase between 1939 and 1942 thus means that German was the language chosen by the majority of new pupils and even that, in the leaps of 1941 and 1942, it reversed the two-thirds proportion that previously favoured its rival, English.[37] At that rate, within a few years it would have recovered first place. On the eve of the war one family in three was encouraging its child to choose German. After the defeat, two families in three were doing so. The change of attitude was not so much reasoned as a reflection of what was in the wind at that time; and that is what makes it interesting. It suggests that we should qualify the hypothesis that anglophilia was dominant in the bourgeoisie (secondary education at that time concerned only about 5 per cent of the eleven to seventeen-year-old group). Was it a matter of the impression left by the German victory, an impulse to emulate the Prussians, as after 1870, the better to stand up to them, or a nostalgia on the part of parents more of whom had themselves learned German rather than English? No doubt all these things, in variable quantities, came into it. At any rate, it is hard not to conclude that the inclination to adapt must have been quite widespread, even if reluctant. (Albert Fabre-Luce, a reliable observer, remarked in 1941: 'French bourgeois vituperate against collaboration, but they are learning German: so they must believe it has a long future.'[38])

Here is an even more remarkable fact: before the war, only 20 per cent of the girls had learned German, as against about 35 per cent of the boys. In 1940 and 1941 five times more girls than boys switched options. At the beginning of the school year in 1941 probably about one family in two, as against one in five before the war, put their daughter down for the German language course. That decision is all the more striking in that it is connected with the very sensitive domain of the choice of a spouse. By steering their daughters towards the language of the conquerors, some of the French bourgeoisie seems to have been acknowledging the latters' superiority, and the possibility of their becoming acceptable sons-in-law, as if despite themselves they seemed to be envisaging a future in which *entente* would be admitted into their very homes.

The interest in German spread beyond schoolchildren. It would be instructive to register all the courses that were organized by all kinds of institutions, ranging from chambers of commerce to the SNCF, in an effort to make it easier to work together.[39] There was no shortage of demand, as is shown by the boom in textbooks and French–German dictionaries and lexicons. And it embraced many different circles. On 15 December 1940, Bobkowski wrote: 'Many of my female companions in the factory are also learning German. The day before yesterday, one of them boasted that she was taking lessons: "*Ich lerne deutsch.*" "With officers or soldiers?" I asked her indifferently. She giggled stupidly and went off. And all because the mark stands at 20 francs.'[40]

The difficulty was finding a means of learning. The language schools had been taken by storm. In 1939, the Berlitz school had 939 students of German and 2470 students of English; in the autumn of 1941, the former numbered 7920, the latter 625.[41] Some French people wrote to the military administration, proposing an exchange of language lessons with the officers.[42] Others put personal advertisements in the newspapers, seeking a private teacher to give classes in their homes. The more fussy would specify 'Aryan and, if possible, of German origin'.[43]

The times were favourable for new methods, and Mimephone appeared on the scene, a humble harbinger of audiovisual methods, getting groups of students to drone in unison the phrases being pronounced on the screen. Its inventor bustled about in a demented fashion, doing the rounds of institutions, winning over the directors of navy schools and the staff officers of the Chantiers de la Jeunesse and the Légion Tricolore, and besieging the occupation services responsible for prisoners of war and the *Relève*. Everywhere he boasted of how his method could help create closer Franco–German relations, not forgetting the Ministry of Education, making sure it was aware of his successes: 3000 students in 1941–42, including forty or so teachers of English in Paris secondary schools and colleges who were keen to recycle themselves. (The Ministry judged the method to be mechanical and superficial.) By 1943, the language of the future had changed: the director of the 'Mimephone' was by then proposing 'the sounds of English through pictures'.[44]

Other French people with a sudden thirst for German decided to go straight to the top. By the autumn of 1940, Epting, who had attracted mere hundreds of students in the 1930s, found thousands enrolling for classes at the German Institute in Paris. He immediately set about creating Institutes in all the major cities of the occupied zone. Most were opened with great pomp before an audience of German and French authorities including, in Orleans and Poitiers for example, the prefect, the mayor, the bishop and a senior member of the university.[45] Following the occupation of the free zone, the network was extended to Marseilles, Toulouse and Lyons. By 1944 there were fifteen German institutes and fifty-six subsidiaries dotted around their neighbourhoods, serving Dax (thirty students enrolled for 1943), Saintes (thirty-eight), Arcachon (fifty-seven), Capbreton (twenty-three), Cholet (fifty) and Roquefort (eighteen).[46]

Some of the instructors were French, teachers of German from secondary schools or colleges, putting in extra hours of work. In Dijon these made up almost half of the fifty-one teachers. Some took their work extremely seriously. In Wassy (Haute-Marne), a village of 3500 inhabitants, a college professor increased his number of students from thirty-two in July 1942 to sixty-eight in May 1943, at which point he and his charges received a visit from the German in charge of the Dijon Institute, upon whom he depended. The visitor, much moved, reported that he had been greeted by the whole class, standing, who had proceeded to sing German renderings of *J'avais un camarade* and *Mon beau sapin*.[47]

Left to themselves, the Germans could never have coped with the huge demand. In the autumn of 1940, about 5000 students were enrolled. Many had had to be turned away for lack of room. One year later there were 12000 enrolled students. Once again Epting lamented having had to turn people away. He wrote to Abetz telling him that, with more teachers and more classrooms, a full 20000 students could have been accommodated.[48] In the autumn of 1942, there were nearly 15000 enrolled (at which date there were no more than 2500 in Belgium and 6000 in allied Italy).[49] Then the decline set in: 11000 in early 1943, 9500 in June 1943, just under 9000 in 1944. The extension of the network to the rest of the country had helped to check the decrease in numbers, which was more marked in Paris (6169 enrolled in December 1941, 3551 in June 1943),[50] whose share of the total fell from 50 to 35 per cent.

In their reports, the directors of the various institutes blamed the way the war was going and noted that their pupils had become the butts of teasing or social ostracism. But they also stressed the relative resistance to the trend. There was no sudden falling-off, just a slow, continuous drop in numbers, as in a good business going gently downhill, not without interludes of recovery. When the

German Institute of Marseilles opened in December 1943, 750 students flocked to enrol in the space of three weeks; and 330 in Toulouse in one week in April 1944.[51] In June 1944, the Paris Institute had almost 1000 students enrolling for its summer courses, due to start on 7 August.[52]

At least 30000 people must have taken courses of varying duration in some German Institute,[53] nearly all of them as individuals. Group courses – for junior nurses, the employees of large Paris department stores or those of German cinema firms (Agfa, ACA, Tobis), and for a few Parisian sections of the RNP or the Groupe Collaboration – involved no more than a few hundred people. The numbers of men and of women were virtually even, the women with a slight majority, which increased as time passed. Although a substantial fraction were schoolchildren,[54] most were adults and they came from a relatively wide social range.[55] Office workers accounted for nearly 40 per cent, half of them clerks (including civil servants), the other half secretaries and typists. A good third was composed of people with no profession (18.8 per cent), mostly women, otherwise schoolchildren or students (18.1 per cent). The world of proprietors and skilled workers accounted for almost 20 per cent (4.1 per cent traders or entrepreneurs; 5.6 per cent craftsmen or skilled workers, 9.5 per cent from the liberal or artistic professions), and then there were teachers and 'others' (2.7 per cent of each).

German courses attracted an urban and tertiary clientèle. Peasants were a rarity, as were workers (although 150 of the latter did follow a course in Paris in October 1942), and the clergy were almost totally absent. From the point of view of the social structure of the country, the clientèle of the German Institutes was heavily represented by the middle and upper classes, civil servants, particularly teachers, and above all members of the liberal professions, which were over-represented.[56] Together with the heads of businesses, secondary school pupils and students, the above account for half the total. On the other hand, it is worth underlining as remarkable the very presence of those employees, most of them women, and that small minority of manual workers, craftsmen or ordinary workers for whom this was their first attempt at learning a foreign language and from whom it must have demanded a serious effort, hard to sustain. These were the categories most affected by departures as the year wore on.

It is easy to attribute a utilitarian motive to many of these people, starting with the schoolchildren and students who needed to revise or were trying to catch up, having not chosen to study German at school in the first place. The same goes for employees, secretaries, shopkeepers, even civil servants: most were probably people who came into contact with the Germans in their work and who set themselves to learn their language of their own accord or at the suggestion of their employers or under pressure from them.[57] For other categories utilitarian motivation seems less obvious. What can have been the combination of reasons that brought to the Institute of Dijon, amongst the 1055 students registered at the end of 1941, 162 people without professions, eight retired people, five officers, nine doctors, four pharmacists, three judges, two barristers, three notaries, three architects, eight draughtsmen, ten engineers and three artists; and, in October 1942, in Paris, sixty-six secondary school teachers and eighty-five primary school teachers?[58]

Of course some, but probably a minority, must have been supporters of collaborationist groups. But most students did not come for political propaganda, plenty of which was already supplied by the press and the parties. It was essentially works of literature that were borrowed by the one thousand or so people who used the library of the Paris Institute in 1942–43. Fewer than ten books on the 'Jewish question' were taken out during that school year.[59] However, favourable prejudice and sympathetic curiosity were clearly involved at least in some measure, and the German Institute did all it could to strengthen these by dint of out-of-school activities, parties and receptions that were remarkably well attended: between May 1942 and July 1943, in all 7600 people took part in these.[60] Above all, the Institutes organized many cultural occasions, four or six each month, designed to communicate German culture and, little by little, purvey a vision of the Nazi world. For instance, in April 1941, the Paris Institute organized a showing of *Le juif, Süss*, which was attended by 3600 of its pupils.[61]

After November 1942, the clientèle of the institutes became less diversified, and their propaganda became more insistent. Some categories beat a proportionately greater retreat: the liberal professions, the independents, manual workers (craftsmen and particularly factory workers), and civil servants. Others were less sensitive to the atmosphere: shop employees, students, professionless people and women in general. The members of these categories seem to have regarded the German Institute as offering a service or cultural recreation rather than as a means of drawing closer to their conquerors, whereas other categories were more sensitive to this aspect. This may explain how it was that the decrease in the registration of pupils was so gradual at a time when membership of the collaboration parties was plummeting.

How many French people set themselves to learn German? Probably at least 100000 across the entire field, from secondary schools to German Institutes and including language schools, special courses and private tuition. One may well wonder what results it all produced: snatches of conversational German, disparate words and phrases, an embarrassing memory of ill-considered efforts? Besides, the decision to learn a language is a long-term commitment, the fruits of which are not to be harvested immediately. Would people have ventured to learn the language of their occupiers if they had known that their domination would end in a rout? Who knows to what extent acceptance of the new order and hopes of a privileged position in it lay behind all these efforts to acquire the language of Goethe and Hitler?

20

Intellectuals and self-preservation

Now, after considering the consumers of German culture, let us turn to the creators of French culture: the men of the arts, letters and sciences. They too had to face up to the choices and dilemmas presented by the occupation. Here too adaptation to the new conditions, in all its diversity of motivation, ranging from a sense of constraint to ideological conviction and taking in material interest and personal compliance, took many forms and went to varying lengths. We shall now attempt to analyse these, distinguishing different gradations of commitment. The following chapters will be devoted to the motives that led publishers and authors to make concessions so as to publish or be published; and we shall then examine the cases of artists, writers and academics who made advances to the occupying power.

In order to clarify what follows, let us begin by considering the choices made by people who felt no attraction to collaboration in any form, yet who decided to compromise and, to some extent, to adjust to the framework dictated by the occupiers. Many people blamed intellectuals for not adhering to the 'silence of the sea' despite the fact that their situation, less circumscribed by material considerations than that of the entrepreneurs, ought to have made it easier for them to do so. But, to a large extent, their behaviour can be analysed in a similar fashion as that for associations or firms. The fact is that they were not isolated up there in their ivory towers. They were in charge of much needed resources: a laboratory without which research could not continue, or a publication that circulated ideas and results. As soon as the occupying power began to take an interest in those instruments, they were obliged to come to a decision as to what line to take and what was acceptable, what unacceptable.

The history of the major intellectual establishments under the occupation has been kept very much under wraps, starting with that of the most prestigious of them. The Collège de France offers the most illustrious representatives of their own discipline the privilege of devoting themselves to their research, liberated from most university duties. In 1940, the director of the Collège was Edmond Faral, a specialist in medieval Latin literature. Immediately after the armistice, Faral hastened to establish contact with all professors. A prompt reopening of the Collège might prevent it being requisitioned and as a safety measure he decided to bring forward the beginning of the academic year. He made it clear to his colleagues that this was his own personal decision and that they were under no obligation whatsoever, in particular to return to Paris. 'It goes without saying that some of us, for particular reasons, might run risks (each must decide for himself) that nobody would dream of forcing upon them.'[1]

The task he had set himself was to preserve the institution. But this was soon engulfed in turbulence. Vichy's antisemitic legislation affected several of his members; and others were imprisoned by the Germans because of their anti-Nazi records (Langevin, Tonnelat and Wallon). Faral was clever, prudent and probably Pétainist, although he avoided making this obvious in his official correspondence. He applied Vichy's racist exclusions, without making full use of the legal clauses of exemption. Four professors were affected by those exclusions, and only in the cases of two did he press for an exemption.

But was he doing no more than applying the regulations? A text that he presented in January 1941 to the government delegation in the occupied territories, in which he attempted to repair the Collège's image following the arrests, contained the following passage: 'The Jewish question: no Jew has taught at the Collège de France since the beginning of the academic year. That decision was taken even before the law of 3 October 1940.' In the rough draft of this letter, the beginning of that last sentence, subsequently crossed out, ran as follows: 'The administration had taken that decision . . .'[2] Faral makes no mention of any German intervention. Whether or not, in his heart of hearts, he approved of the Jewish Statute and even if he had overemphasized his own personal role in this letter, all that makes no essential difference. His behaviour certainly shows how the implementation of the politics of discrimination was made much easier by a succession of particular decisions, some of them quite anticipatory. He manifested an equal concern to prevent any demonstrations against the occupying authorities. After Langevin's arrest a flysheet urging students from the Sorbonne to gather to demonstrate at the Collège de France was brought to his attention. He forthwith decided to close the gates and asked the police to set up a force to maintain order in front of the Collège. 'It is essential that no demonstration, even a silent one, should take place at the Collège de France', he wrote to the commissioner for the fifth *arrondissement*.[3]

It is only fair to add that almost all university authorities behaved in a similar fashion. Whether it was a matter of racial exclusion or of relations with the occupying power, prudence – if not compliance – inclined them to accept the situation without protest, or even to anticipate its demands. The assistant director of the École Libre des Sciences Politiques, Roger Seydoux, sought out Epting, 'to talk about the future of the institution'. Upon Epting's request, he eliminated all its Jewish or anti-German teachers.[4] Without even waiting for an official injunction from the occupying authorities or a directive from Vichy, he sacrificed some of his colleagues to ensure the survival of the institution for which he was responsible. At this point, he suggested to Benoist-Méchin that he should take over one of the courses.[5] The School was soon employing quite a few teachers from the new aristocracy, such as Borotra, Bichelonne, and the prefects Jean Legay and Jean-Pierre Ingrand. By the autumn of 1943, the wind was blowing the other way and Seydoux asked Joseph Barthélémy, a teacher of long standing who was about to return to his professional chair after resigning from his post as Minister of Justice, not to resume his teaching.[6]

Epting was received courteously, if not cordially, by the academic authorities. Even though he was far from being a top-ranking figure in the occupation apparatus, he was considered a man worth accommodating. Included in a list of those taking part in the breakfasts that he organized at the German Institute in January and February 1941 are the names of Joseph Denis, the director of the Office National des Universités et Écoles Françaises; Jean Baillou, the secretary general of the École Normale; Roger Seydoux; and André Siegfried, a professor at the Collège de France and the École de Sciences Politiques.[7]

Faral's policies do not appear to have caused any upsets in the Collège de France. No professors protested against the racial exclusions either as a body or individually, despite the fact that, with only a few exceptions such as René Leriche and Bernard Fay who was appointed director of the Bibliothèque Nationale and threw himself into the struggle against the freemasons, they did not approve of Vichy. A similar agreement seems to have obtained between the administrator and the professors regarding the problem of posts left vacant by the Jewish Statute and the German arrests. Should they be left vacant, as a silent protest? Or should they be filled again, even at the risk of seeming to approve of what was happening? The trouble was that leaving them empty might cause the government to reduce the Collège's budget or even to condemn the statutes of this establishment which was generally believed to be a hotbed of opponents of its policies.[8] Pétain produced a solution to the question of the vacant posts: replacements should be deferred, for fear of undesirables being elected: the choice could be avoided. However, Faral successfully countered this in favour of maintaining 'French strength'.[9]

The professors at least proved intransigent on the quality of their new colleagues. There was no question of co-opting candidates of uncertain merit, or even valid candidates whose election might be tainted by the backing of the authorities. After the liberation, Faral cited in his defence the barrage of objections that the Collège raised against several 'official' candidates, mentioning the names of Hourticq, Julia and Montandon.[10] The professors of the Collège de France behaved as most French university professors did, whereas in Belgium and Holland the purges unleashed public reactions of anger; but in those countries the purges had been imposed directly by the occupying power, whereas in France it had emanated from the government. Respect for legality, fear of sanctions, uncertainty as to the reactions of one's neighbours, and the opacity of the future all combined to clip the wings of protest. Academics fell back upon the justification of the defence of their institutions.

Hold fast, keep things going: this was the principle that, for each in his own way, ruled the behaviour of two professors of the Collège de France. One was Frédéric Joliot-Curie, the other Lucien Febvre. Both had been anti-Munich. It is worth studying these two in order to assess the variety and quality of the decisions that intellectuals had to confront in that period. Was there any one choice that the force of evidence rendered inevitable? Was it possible for the best choice to be anything other than whatever was the least unsatisfactory? These questions are particularly pertinent to the early days of the occupation, that period of retrenchment when the defeat weighed heavily on people's spirits and the German victories blocked the horizon. The interest of these two cases lies in their ability to convey an atmosphere that was soon to change, one in which a longing to return to normal was mingled with a desire to get through a trial of uncertain outcome as best one could.

In 1935, Frédéric Joliot-Curie received the Nobel Prize for chemistry together with his wife Irène, the daughter of Marie Curie. At the age of thirty-five, he was seen as one of the masters of French science, as was confirmed two years later by his election to the Collège de France. This dazzlingly successful scientist was also a politically committed man, like his teacher Langevin. He was active in the Socialist party, on the Committee of Vigilance of antifascist intellectuals, and in the League for Human Rights. Although close to the communists and anti-Munich, he dissociated himself from the French Communist party at the time of the German–Soviet pact. Under the occupation, he emerged as early as 1941 as one of the leading figures of university resistance, in association with the French Communist party. After the liberation, his commitment bestowed incomparable lustre upon the party. In 1950 it cost him his job as high commissioner for atomic energy.[11]

In the second half of the 1930s Joliot was already involved with atomic energy, pursuing research, in partnership with his wife, that placed France alongside Germany and the United States in the front rank in this field. At the beginning of 1939, researchers in these three countries arrived, virtually simultaneously, at the discovery of nuclear fission. Its possible consequences were immediately recognized: either a controlled chain reaction, producing electricity on a large scale; or an uncontrolled reaction, producing an explosive weapon of unprecedented power. When war was declared, nobody knew whether it would be possible to produce such nuclear weapons, and if so, how long it would take, or what their role in the conflict might be. The scientists of each country committed themselves deeply so as not to allow the enemy to get ahead. Seconded to National Defence, Joliot moved towards the construction of a nuclear reactor for which he collected stocks of uranium and heavy water, rather than a bomb, the production of which he judged to be too difficult. At the same time he embarked upon the construction of a cyclotron in his laboratory at the Collège de France.

At the time of the defeat, work on the reactor was still feeling its way and the cyclotron was not yet completed. The uranium and heavy water were despatched out of France, ahead of the German advance. Despite invitations to follow them, Joliot decided to stay. Since then, much speculation has been devoted to the weight of influence that he might have afforded his country had he taken part in the Allies' nuclear adventure.[12] In the summer of 1940, it was hard to see so far ahead, and Joliot seems to have been swayed by perfectly normal and immediate motives: reluctance to leave his dispersed family and his wife, whose health was not good; a sense of responsibility towards his team of research workers; fear of homesickness in England, which he did not know and whose language he did not speak; and in the background an impression that the German victory was so overwhelming that departure might lead to a lengthy exile.

On 14 July 1940 he wrote to his mother, telling her that the Germans were behaving 'correctly' and that he had gone to Vichy to seek directives. He wrote of the need for patience, his happiness at having located his family, and his hope of returning to Paris in the winter.[13] His letter conveys no hint of either approval or rejection of the new regime, which he regarded simply as the legal authority. If such was his first reaction, there was nothing exceptional about it, even for a left-winger, for at this point Vichy had not fully revealed its true face. The importance of reuniting his family and the need for patience were his two main themes. He felt it necessary to prepare for endurance – hanging on, holding fast for an indefinite period.

His return to Paris came about sooner than he expected. On 15 July, the laboratory of nuclear chemistry at the Collège de France was taken over by the occupying authorities. When told of this by Faral, who urged him to return, Joliot obtained orders from Vichy to go to Paris. For two weeks, in the company of the administrator, he was then engaged in lengthy negotiations.[14] Their opposite numbers consisted of a team led by General Eric Schumann, Keitel's scientific adviser, which included one familiar face, that of Wolfgang Gentner, a young physicist who had worked with Joliot from 1933 to 1935.

Victory gave the Reich a cheap opportunity to get on with its nuclear research. The Germans were disappointed to learn of the disappearance of the stocks of heavy water, but they had plenty of uranium, having recently seized all Belgium's supplies. Upon examining the nuclear reactor, they found that Joliot was hardly ahead of them.[15] But there was also the cyclotron being built in the basement of the Collège: nothing of the kind existed in Germany. At first the conquerors considered taking it to bits and removing it, but this idea ran into difficulties of a practical nature,[16] quite apart from the fact that it would deprive them of the expertise already gained by the French scientists.

The Germans told Faral and Joliot that they had the right to seize the material of a laboratory that had worked for national defence. But they added that they would not do so provided Joliot gave them a written undertaking to take in a team of German scientists, whose task would be to work 'with him' on a number of projects ('tests with the cyclotron, the general physics of the nucleus, and ways of setting the apparatus in motion'). According to Faral, Schumann 'stressed the fact that he spoke as a scientist, not as a military man; that the studies in which the Germans were interested were purely scientific and could be of no practical use in the war; and that, besides, the questions to be studied would be defined in advance and would in no way be of a kind to harm the national interests of France'. Should his proposal be rejected, the laboratory would be closed to the French and handed over to the German scientists, who would work there on their own 'until better days came along'.[17]

Faral and Joliot could have refused point blank or abstained from taking up any clear position, or at least placed the decision immediately in the government's hands. But instead they took the course of negotiating new wording for the undertaking demanded of Joliot before proceeding to ask for the authorities' stamp of approval. They had already made their decision: to preserve the use of the laboratory. However, the German *diktat* was unacceptable without assurances as to the non-military character of the research that would be pursued there, the freedom of the work of the French scientists, and the preservation of their material. According to the revised text that the French suggested to Schumann, the German scientists would work not 'with' Joliot, but 'alongside' him, and only 'on subjects the study of which is not contrary to the national interests of France' (the text then continued as above). The two professors furthermore demanded the introduction of a secrecy clause 'to avoid the risk of misunderstandings that might arise from misrepresentations'. They were understandably afraid of being exploited by German propaganda, but their attempts to make the operation to which they were consenting secret also betrayed their unease.

Once the other side had agreed to these alterations, the professors turned to Vichy, seeking approval from the government. However, Mireaux, the Minister of National Education responded negatively: 'This field of thought is a reserved domain. No. If the Germans insist, it will be said that we gave way under pressure.' Faral and Joliot then got hold of the government's delegate in the occupied zone, Léon Noel, who agreed to mediate in Vichy, while they prepared a more complete report for the minister, 'suggesting that he re-examine the question'. In the professors' view, the revised German directive should be accepted for a whole series of reasons: the character of the 'unilateral decision' that it retained and that testified to the constraint imposed; the fact that the questions to be studied 'in no way touch upon things to do with the war' (they were thus personally vouching for the assurances made by the Germans); the fact that Joliot would be in a position to make sure that the agreement was respected; the secrecy clause that 'prevents the conditions of work being used for any kind of political propaganda'; and, finally, the fact that the laboratory would be placed beyond requisitioning. Their conclusion ran as follows: 'Clearly, we cannot accept with a light heart. But a refusal on the part of the French would in all probability lead to more intransigent demands and more rigorous measures, the effect of which would be to exclude us from working and to dispossess us of our material.'

This report was submitted to Vichy on 18 August and two days later received a positive response on condition that in the obligation of secrecy an exception should be made for 'the head of the French state or any person designated by him'.[18] The government's decision at the prompting of the two professors was later to be severely challenged by Jules Basdevant, the legal adviser to the Quai d'Orsay, in whose opinion there were no legal grounds to justify Germany requisitioning scientific laboratories. Basdevant criticized Faral and Joliot for having suggested different wording for Schumann's directive: 'Although, formally, this was supposed to be a unilateral decision, the fact that they suggested the wording implies a degree of acceptance of the contents and hence acceptance of the right of the occupying power to rule on the functioning of the laboratory and to have German collaborators admitted there.' Given that despite the armistice a state of war still existed, these scientists could be accused of acting in intelligence with the enemy. Basdevant criticized the government's position no less forthrightly. To claim the right to information for the head of state was 'to ask for satisfaction on a particular, secondary point while abandoning far greater rights and even the priciple of those rights'.[19]

In order to continue to work in his own laboratory, Joliot had chosen – and pressed Vichy to choose – the path of acceptance. He found himself in the company of five German scientists, placed under the direction of Gentner, with the mission of completing the construction of the cyclotron and making it work. It was a remarkable situation, and Joliot took great care to organize it in such a way as to minimize the risks inherent in it. The workroom and a number of technicians, but not research assistants, were made available to the Germans. Each of them received their own workbenches and they were not permitted access to the rest of the laboratory except with permission from Joliot who, for his part, retained the right to move about as he pleased and could thus keep an eye on everything that was going on.[20]

However clearly defined, the situation remained a delicate one, and rumours of 'collaboration' were soon rife.[21] Langevin's arrest at the end of October 1940 did not help matters. Colleagues and students alike criticized Joliot for continuing to work when his master was languishing in prison. The physicist now told the Germans that in view of these criticisms he was stopping work. By doing so, he paralysed the activities of the German team, prompting the service responsible for it (the *Heereswaffenamt*) to urge the MBF to settle the Langevin matter. It pointed out that Joliot's cooperation had 'so far been satisfactory'. He was, no doubt, not much better than Langevin, whose anti-German sentiments he shared; but he was 'indispensable for the work in his laboratory, work whose ultimate goal was, of course, unknown to him'.[22] In early December, Langevin was transferred to house arrest in Troyes, and work was resumed in the laboratory. It is worth noting that Joliot's justification for his stopping work was the criticism of his colleagues, and it should be added that he never made Langevin's liberation a condition for his own resumption of work, but limited himself to asking that his lot be alleviated.[23] He behaved prudently, taking care not to expose himself to sanctions but at the same time availing himself of the unexpected lever placed in his hands – and he did so courageously, for not all the consequences were predictable. Clearly he continued to believe that the best policy was to hold on and endure, even if it meant having to put up with a most unpleasant situation.

An episode that took place at the beginning of 1941 may shed some light on Joliot's state of mind at that time. On 15 February

1941, Parisians discovered on the front page of Luchaire's newspaper, *Les Nouveaux Temps*, an interview entitled 'M. Joliot-Curie tells us that what needs reforming first is our attitude . . . We French scientists, passionately devoted to our country, must have the moral courage to learn some lessons from our defeat. What must we recognize? The decrease in the quality of the men who have become our leaders, a decrease that – alas – is more or less matched in every sector of creative activity.' The main thrust of the interview was an attack against the École Polytechnique, accused of having handicapped research and ruined the munitions industry by concentrating on producing 'stars' while despising practical applications. It was time to sweep away that 'hegemony' and to use 'different and useful talents wherever they are to be found'. Joliot cited himself as an example: he had studied modestly at the École de Physique et Chimie, then worked in a factory, which had 'disintoxicated him from abstractions' and 'cured him of a number of intellectual vices'.

The journalist may have exaggerated Joliot's views or coloured them with his own vocabulary, but he probably did not substantially misrepresent him. Besides, the hypothesis of a misrepresentation does not explain why he should have agreed in the first place to give an interview to a newspaper that made no secret of where its sympathies lay, when he could quite simply have declined. A few days earlier, the news programme for the occupied zone, under German control, had asked to be allowed to do a story about his laboratory and the German scientists working there, to illustrate 'a concrete case of technological collaboration'. Understandably, Joliot had no wish for such publicity and he categorically refused, getting the approval of the German service upon which his laboratory depended. The secrecy clause was proving useful.[24]

The interview in *Les Nouveaux Temps* really does seem to have been a *faux pas*. Despite the presence of the occupier, Joliot could not resist the temptation to set out his views and settle some old scores with an institution that he condemned for its intellectual behaviour and the use of its power and social status. But at the same time, he was expressing ideas that could be interpreted as agreement with Vichy: the call to learn a number of lessons from the defeat, the denunciation of intellectualism, the need for change. But in fact there was no agreement: the word Vichy was not pronounced, no sympathy for the new regime was expressed and there was no allusion to the occupying power. The interest of these declarations lies in the fact that they reveal a particular frame of mind. They show a Joliot sensitive to the tendency – so typical of 1940 – to seek out where responsibility lay and a longing to turn over a new leaf. Joliot's idea of renewal was clearly a far cry from that of Vichy. But what is symptomatic is that he was at this point concentrating upon renewal: the struggle against the occupying power was not yet seen as the absolute priority. In this respect, one may wonder whether, despite his condemnation of the Germano–Soviet pact, Joliot's point of view after the defeat was not close to that of the French Communist party, which regarded the war being fought out as a struggle between two imperialisms with little to choose between them.

However that may be, one cannot imagine him saying such things after the spring of 1941, once he had become engaged in active resistance. And, with that new attitude, it is hard to imagine him agreeing to cooperate with German scientists. But no doubt cooperation did have its convenient aspects as well as its drawbacks. It certainly did for Faral, who used it as an argument in 1941 when he was trying to persuade Vichy to let him fill the positions left vacant. ('The occupation authorities are well aware of the value of the scientific work being done at the Collège de France. As you know, as a result of a decision by the High Command, German officers and scholars have, since last August, been working individually in our nuclear chemistry laboratory, to learn from the knowledge of our own scientists').[25] Of course, Joliot's position was different, but the fact is that relations between him and his German colleagues were good, thanks to the presence of Gentner, who improved the living conditions of the French team and intervened to get Joliot released when he was arrested by the German police in June 1941 on suspicion of having links with the resistance. Had he been unmasked, even Gentner's protection would have been of no help at all to him.

The situation may have offered Joliot cover for his resistance, but it was nevertheless dubious. When he had assured the government that the questions that interested the Germans 'had nothing to do with war matters', Joliot had represented the situation in such a way as to help him to plead his cause. The work in connection with the cyclotron could hardly not have had military implications, even if these were not immediate. The construction of the apparatus was completed by the German scientists, who had essential parts sent from the Reich but who were also, in Gentner's opinion, assisted 'most efficiently' in their task by the French team and technicians.[26] Now, by setting up this particle accelerator and then getting it to work, at a time when they were only just beginning to construct a similar apparatus in their own country, the Germans gained time and, above all, valuable experience, particularly in two areas of military application: on the one hand, in the field of radiation, for they used the Paris cyclotron in their research into the use of radioactivity in war weaponry; on the other, in the field of the acceleration of particles for the cyclotron was theoretically able to produce tiny quantities of plutonium and these could be used as a nuclear explosive.[27]

Beyond these immediate uses, their interest in the cyclotron had to do with their own nuclear programme. It would have been impossible for Joliot not to understand this or for him to have underestimated the scope of this field of research, in which civil and military aspects were indissociably linked.[28] (It is striking to see how the atomic weapon was already beginning to be talked about under the occupation, both in scientific circles and also as a purely imaginary concept. In March 1942, Bobkowski overheard some concierges talking about the raids on Billancourt and claiming that the English had used 'atomic bombs' there.)[29] If there was any genuine miscalculation on Joliot's part, it was on the score of the role of nuclear fission in the current conflict. Joliot was convinced that several more years' research were necessary. It was an opinion that tended to be shared by the German scientists involved in the field, who were, it is true, influenced by their belief that the end of the war was not far off. That is why, at the beginning of 1942, the Reich's atomic programme was made to take second place to the development of rockets, whereas the Americans, on the basis of their contrary estimate that the war would be of long duration, did launch themselves promptly into the nuclear adventure.[30] It is clear, with hindsight, that if the Germans had taken that path, the work carried out in Joliot's laboratory would have been seen as contributing a small link in a process leading to the Nazi creation of a nuclear bomb.

Hold fast, hang on: for Lucien Febvre it was a matter not of a research apparatus but of a periodical that could only reappear if the conditions stipulated by the occupying power were accepted. The vast majority of university people did accept those conditions. Their absorption in their studies was a comfort to them; the language of scholarship created a carapace that isolated them from what was going on in the outside world and the insignificant circulation figures of their publications deterred the occupiers from paying much attention to them, although they were careful to keep a general eye on all that went on. So there was nothing particularly exceptional about the periodical that Lucien Febvre was keen to relaunch, apart from the fact that one of its two owner-managers was Jewish and, unless he was eliminated, a relaunch was out of the question. In contrast to Joliot's situation, there was no constraint to force a decision. Abstention from any decision would have entailed no consequences.

When Marc Bloch and Lucien Febvre founded *Les Annales d'histoire économique et sociale* in 1929, their ambition was to break the domination of political history, move the focus from individual events to the longer term and broaden the scope of history to include economics, sociology and psychology. Their new periodical soon earned itself a respected place through its innovatory approach, the quality of its articles and the acerbic pen that Febvre wielded against the old grey-beards of the profession. Its success affected the careers of both men, who had been professors in Strasbourg since 1919. Febvre was elected to the Collège de France in 1933, Bloch to the Sorbonne in 1936. Relations between the two men were close without being intimate, and sometimes tense, as in 1938, when Febvre accused his colleague of seeking to reduce him to the role of a brilliant second.[31]

Immediately following the defeat both men were in the free zone. Bloch was hard hit by the Jewish Statute and his patriotic feelings were deeply hurt. He applied for exemption and was one of the few who were granted it. Seconded first to the University of Strasbourg evacuated to Clermont-Ferrand, then to the University of Montpellier, he considered emigrating to the United States, but eventually rejected the idea for family reasons. As for Febvre, he was in Saint-Amour, close to Léon Werth. In the autumn, his wife visited Paris and Febvre relayed her impressions to Bloch: 'No newspapers, or rather a press "in French" that sinks to new depths of foulness', 'silent men and women, cast down, crushed', but fortunately, 'as always, the ordinary people behaving well' (the admirer of Michelet is detectable here). Febvre announced that he was returning to Paris, since the Collège de France was resuming its courses. 'What else is there to do? And besides, maybe the administrators are right: we must strengthen this front . . . But it is a bitter business.'[32]

Now he began worrying about the future of the periodical, turning over hypotheses in his mind. The first was to 'let things lie'. But there were risks and, after all, it would be a loss of influence and position – and just when the review could well turn a profit. The second was to request permission and be prepared to publish under the imposed conditions. But benevolent subjection was not their house style, quite apart from the fact that 'the claims of scholarly tolerance are nothing but words'. The third was to move the periodical to the free zone, or perhaps even to America, with Bloch. 'Perhaps. It's up to him. Except that the publication would lose its original character'; it would cease to be French and would be hard to obtain in France.[33] The idea of it reappearing in the occupied zone took hold of Febvre's mind and he proceeded to make enquiries and preparations. Bloch was extremely reluctant and suggested that it should come out in the free zone. In the spring of 1941, Febvre, who had made up his mind, wrote to his colleague urging him to accept his idea. There then followed a bitter and emotional exchange of views in which arguments for and arguments against clashed and became poisoned by unexpressed personal grudges.

In his letter to Bloch, Febvre was in full spate: 'The *Annales* wish to continue to appear' he wrote, personifying the periodical, 'But what are the conditions? They are difficult and hard – partly because of the attitude of the occupiers and partly because of a fatal mistake.' The 'fatal mistake', which now prompted a torrent of recriminations, was the contract that made Bloch co-manager and co-proprietor. 'That document has been causing me terrible problems for the past two months. It stands in the way of everything.' 'Without that absurd document, it [the periodical] would belong to Lucien Febvre, and that would be that. But the document is there. The business belongs to Marc Bloch *and* to L.F. . . . There is that document, a document absurd in itself, absurd in its entire gist. I allowed – *mea culpa*, and through my constant desire not to say no, to be conciliatory, frankly to accept what I did not like so as to avoid the bother of a disagreement – I allowed you to entrust its editorship to a man accustomed to all the cunning of a Conseil d'État.'[34]

Such tactlessness takes one's breath away. Febvre had nothing to say about the iniquities of the measures imposed by the occupying power and by Vichy; to do so would have weakened his own position. On the contrary, he went so far as to represent the will of the occupier and that famous 'document' as equal obstacles to the aspirations of the *Annales*. Reading his words, one has the feeling that only some last vestige of decency held him back from blaming

Bloch for being there at all – a Jew standing in the way of a project, the validity of which was beyond doubt. Even so, he made his position clear: he wanted the periodical to be published again and he wanted it to be in Paris. For this to happen, Bloch would have to stand down as partner.

One can imagine the distress of Febvre's colleague upon reading these pages. He would have to disappear from the periodical that he had created, deliberately efface the stamp of his own professional identity, having so recently had his patriotic feelings hurt. He replied that he had, with reluctance, considered publishing the periodical in the free zone; but he certainly did not wish it to reappear in the occupied zone or to do so without his name. How could Febvre even contemplate doing this? The censorship could become extremely dire. 'It will be necessary to purge the editorial committee, and probably also the contributors. But why should the Germans stop there?' True, censorship also existed in the free zone, 'but I can't help it, I shall always see a difference between a French censor, whatever his true allegiances, and a *feldgrau*. My dignity is less affronted by the former than by the latter.' And without his name? It was not in his character to give way. 'If our work had meaning, it lay in its independence, its refusal to be pressured by what Péguy. . . used to call "things temporal" . . . The suppression of my name would constitute an abdication. On this, believe me, nobody would be deceived.' If Febvre did not want a period of sleep, very well! It was up to him to create a new periodical, with another cover and, if need be, using the wartime funds of the *Annales*.[35]

Febvre reacted by expressing 'a bitter sense of moral dissidence'. 'The desire to hold fast – as much as possible, as well as possible: that was what gave me the strength to write you my last letter.' He would resign himself, he wrote, 'sick at heart'. However, he immediately returned to pleading his own cause. Create a new periodical? He would have to give undertakings to the occupier, make do without funding from the CNRS, abandon the subscribers who had paid their dues for 1941. Publish in the free zone? The *Annales* would then not be distributed in the occupied zone, it would not be able to 'reach the most suffering parts of France, those that really need it, those that are crying out for its help', whereas from Paris they could reach anywhere, even abroad.

Febvre sensed that he was making heavy weather of his attempts to undermine Bloch's position, founded as it was upon a reaction based on principle. So he reproached him for 'giving in to one of those "Myths of Purity" that had wreaked such countless ravages upon history', then proceeded to twist the argument of patriotism to his own advantage, speaking of the sacrifices that patriotism has a right to expect, and hammering home the accusation of desertion: first their desertion of their subscribers and readers. 'It is not on some unforseeable day . . . when, in a quite different climate, it might be possible to recreate the *Annales*, similar but not identical to what it was in the past – it is not then that those who love their periodical will be needing it.' Next their desertion of France itself: the reason why he was so saddened by the 'death sentence' pronounced by Bloch was 'because the *Annales* is a French periodical. And its death is another for my country.' 'For my country': the slip was typical and came as no surprise.[36]

Let us not dwell on the grandiloquence of some of Febvre's arguments, particularly the consolation that the periodical would bring to the 'most suffering parts' of the country – after all, Vichy held no monopoly over pathos – nor on the unspoken reference to Bloch's Jewishness, to which Febvre implicitly ascribed his colleague's refusal to see reason. Bloch was certainly not blind to that slur, for he riposted as follows: 'Do not think that I am obsessed, in everything, by the "Statute".' Even if he were not a Jew, he declared, he would have acted in the same way and refused to resign.[37] Febvre's *implication*, which bears the stamp of the period, conveys some idea of the crack in the facade of which plenty of Jews must have become aware, seeing the perception that even people who knew and respected them had of their choices.

But there was more to this dispute, and there is no reason to believe that it was not painful for Febvre as well. For him, what predominated was a fear that it would be much more difficult, or even impossible, to resume publication at some later date, and a concern not to forfeit its achievements – in the form of subscribers, reputation and influence – to the advantage of other historical periodicals. His sense of competition, his attachment to an enterprise that was going well, and an elevated idea of its mission were all powerful motives that may serve to explain his refusal to publish in the free zone, with the prospect of limited circulation. Finally, Febvre must have been anxious to preserve a cultural presence, faced with a future that seemed dauntingly uncertain.

In the eyes of Bloch, the politics of concession 'just to save something'[38] was wrong both morally and politically. But as he too was concerned for the periodical, rather than simply refuse on principle, he preferred to argue on the grounds of perils in the future: his elimination would be seen as compromising with the occupying power which would gradually tighten its grip and eat away at editorial freedom, etc. In the background one can perhaps detect a fear of being excluded from the common task: another unspoken aspect to this altercation. Linking everything together was a view of the situation that was not all that different from Febvre's except that it was accompanied by another sentiment: 'I do not know what the future holds, but I do not despair.'[39]

Although he repeated his reasons for opposing Febvre, in the end Bloch decided to give him a free hand.[40] A desire not to provoke a break and to deal tactfully with his colleague, whose arguments were forcing him on to the defensive, are probably reasons enough for his decision. In 1942, he was to find that, taking everything into consideration, it was a tolerable choice. The periodical went its own way, not without changing its format in 1942 and being renamed *Mélanges d'histoire sociale.* The occupying power, with other fish to fry, kept a no more than distant eye on it. In returning to familiar work (he contributed to the periodical under a pseudonym), Bloch seems to have found a flicker of comfort in his bleak trials. But before long the resistance was absorbing all his energies. In 1943 he went underground. In 1944 he was arrested, tortured, then shot.

By consenting to his own elimination, Bloch made it possible for the periodical to reappear. At the liberation, his martyrdom gave it a moral guarantee. The past was now seen in a new, distorted perspective by people who were professional historians, and who admittedly are not always the best equipped when it comes to immediate history. Febvre wanted to go back to the title of *Les Annales* and also to obtain some paper. In both cases, he had to justify the publishing of the periodical under the occupation. The Minister of Information happened to be Jacques Soustelle, a member of the editorial committee. 'I am certain', Febvre wrote to him, 'that all I need do is present this twofold wish to Jacques Soustelle for the Minister of Information to bestow both authorization and paper upon the *Annales* which, alone of all the French historical periodicals, for four years publicly maintained the spirit of "before", with the collaboration, right to the end, of Marc Bloch himself.'[41]

Let us pass over the altogether gratuitous dig at the other periodicals. The competitive spirit that had prompted Febvre to resume publication was certainly not dead. He now represented that publication under the occupation as an act of defiance, claiming that the periodical had been 'one of the most vibrant centres of intellectual resistance to the oppression'. And this was a claim that he supported by referring to Bloch's martyrdom, the resistance credentials of several members of the editorial board, and even the change of title in 1942, which he explained by a desire to elude 'Vichy's proscriptions regarding periodicals'.[42] On this point, the truth – simpler and less glorious – was that the occupying power had indeed imposed paper restrictions and Febvre's periodical, along with many others, had been a victim of this. But far from it being persecuted by Vichy, a commission for scholarly periodicals set up by the Ministry of National Education under Bonnard had, in May 1942, included it in a list of publications for which authorization to appear was 'urgently requested'.[43] It was when the response to this request turned out to be negative that Febvre had decided to switch to the title of *Mélanges*, which was not affected by the paper restrictions.

All signs of the hesitations and uncertainties of the time were erased, the past was presented in the best possible light, where necessary with the addition of a few extra touches,[44] and motives were transformed. In 1941, Febvre had forseen a lasting period of subjugation and had considered it advisable to adjust to it. He had wanted to keep his periodical going, just as Joliot had wanted to save his laboratory. It was a preoccupation that was shared by many owners of businesses, one that involved an effort to preserve normality and a pre-war atmosphere in order to render the present less harsh and to light the way to the future, and that contained no hint of sympathy for the conqueror. Nevertheless, his decision to republish rather than to stand by certain values and principles, and the resulting friendly aryanization were not without significance. To the extent that the decision took shape when the outlook was one of a probable, though certainly undesirable, German domination, it boiled down to acceptance of the prospect of a future in which there would be no more Jews.

21

Inter arma silent Musae

On 24 September 1944, Cocteau declared in his diary: 'Under the German occupation, France had the right and the duty to show its insolence, to eat, to shine, to defy the oppressor, and to say "You are taking everything away, but I still have it all".'[1] The arts and letters did indeed shine, bringing an oppressed people moments of distraction and delight. New names shot to stardom, new works entered the register of French culture. *Inter arma silent Musae*: amid the clash of arms the Muses are silent. But when their voices were raised, within the confines of the aviary constructed by the occupier, was it really to defy the oppressor?

After the liberation, Cocteau's thesis was much repeated. Every film made, every book published, every play performed had been a challenge flung by French culture in the face of the destroyers of all culture. As part of its foreign policy, the occupying power did indeed aim eventually to extinguish French influence in Europe. But in the meantime, it intended to profit from it in certain fields: thus, thanks to a system of linked quotas, the exportation of French films would, it was hoped, favour the penetration of the German cinema, until such time as it would have become strong enough to dominate the European market.[2] But in France itself German policy was not to make the local culture fall into line, as it was in 'Germanic countries', nor was it to stamp it out ruthlessly, as in Poland. On the contrary, the policy was to allow French culture to flourish in all its vigour and diversity, once it was purged of Jews and all those who opposed Germany, free from the rules that applied in the Reich. Léautaud recorded a remark made by Epting's assistant, Bremer, in response to criticism for having authorized a particular newspaper to appear. What Bremer said was: 'In our country, it would not be possible . . . There is no liberalism there. So we are treating ourselves to the pleasure here.'[3] Seldom has such a martial occupier been seen to cosset civilian morale with such solicitude.

Despite certain tensions between the various services (Propaganda-Abteilung, the 'School and Culture' section of the MBF, the embassy, and the German Institute, not to mention the SS, which became increasingly prone to interfere), the policy of liberalism under surveillance proceeded to pursue a number of goals. In the first place, its aim was to make it easier to maintain order, by keeping the French population amused; in 1942, Hitler issued a reminder that it was important to encourage the French to distract themselves and forget about the occupation.[4] Second, it was to encourage collaboration by promoting a belief that France had a cultural future in Nazi Europe; the shop window of Paris must sparkle in the eyes of the neutral peoples of Europe and America so as to encourage them to remain uncommitted onlookers. Finally, it was designed to stir up a ferment of decadence which, according to the Nazis, was fortunately already active, by exploiting all the cracks in French unity. Thus, in the occupied zone, some films authorized by the German authorities would elicit protests from religious leagues and would be banned by the prefecture for outraging French mores, a decision the occupiers would promptly cancel.[5] Discord was also deliberately fomented between the two zones: the Parisian shop window was designed to allure creative minds in the free zone and to underline the contrast between the blinkered censorship of Vichy and the tolerance of the occupiers.[6]

Publishers and writers were not slow to draw attention to this contrast.[7] The Germans were careful to stimulate the disgust felt for Vichy by most intellectuals, in order to encourage them to return to their peace-time work, just as if peace existed. It was tempting to do so, in the name of a lesser evil which here played into the hands of German control: for in terms of culture it was not the free zone that was free. The temptation was all the greater given that, stuck at home as they were, the French public formed a literally captive audience and one avid for culture as never before. On the side of the culture on offer, the lack of paper and energy shortages certainly imposed constraints, as in other fields, but the chain of cultural production was far less dependent upon resources futher up the pipeline. Culture was a French product, for French people, without a Germany levy, even benefiting from STO exemptions in the case of show business.[8] Artistic creators could now feel at ease on a stage where competition had been slashed by exiles, exclusions and repression or much thinned by the severance of relations with overseas countries, the banning of Anglo-Saxon films and also, soon afterwards, of all translations from the English language.

Unlike virtually every other domain of social life, the cultural scene was propitiated by the occupier within a space that was, to be sure, purged and kept under surveillance, but was also to a large extent left open. The paradox in this situation was that the films that were freest in tone and most aggressive towards the Vichy trilogy of values (labour, motherland, family) were produced by a German company.[9] Generally speaking, artistic creators were not subjected to pressure, let alone to demands on the part of the occupying power. They had only themselves to say 'no' to; and that was not easy when the censorship was liberal, demand strong and competition weak. Such an abnormally favourable situation could give the surrounding world an air of quasi-normality.

The publishing world can hardly be proud of its behaviour under the occupation. The best that can be said is that it above all followed a business logic. This was characterized by a desire to maintain acquired positions, by concern over competition, and by discomfort over transferring business to the free zone owing to Vichy's censorship and because the fixed assets and most of its public were situated in the occupied zone. As a consequence it found itself faced with an occupying power that, by dint of using both stick and carrot, made it dance to the German tune. So much was made clear from the start by the Otto list, drawn up on the basis of information provided by the publishers themselves as to the titles of works that might give offence. The occupying power saluted them in its introduction to this printed list, in which it ascribed to them 'a concern to establish the conditions necessary for a more accurate and objective appreciation of the problems of Europe'. However embarrassed they may have been, those involved, led by their union leader Réne Philippon, accepted the situation without demur so as not to damage essential negotiations relating to the censorship of published works. According to the terms of the agreement concluded in October 1940, they could continue to publish on their own responsibility, thereby avoiding preliminary censorship and the delays this would entail. They paid for this by promising to respect the Otto list and never to publish any work that might 'damage German prestige and interests' or any author whose works were banned in Germany.[10]

The staff of Propaganda-Abteilung were most appreciative of this compliance that dispensed them from having to impose their will by issuing decrees. This produced a problem for the publishers: if it looked as though they themselves had handed over the books on the Otto list, they might not receive compensation from the French state later on. They therefore requested, successfully, that once the books had been handed over, the Germans should *a posteriori* provide them with a certificate stating that the works had been seized.[11] As can be imagined, such a compliant attitude was a great help to the official responsible for the *Schriftum* (literature) group of Propaganda-Abteilung, Gerhard Heller. This zealous man, working at first on his own, later – from the spring of 1941 onwards – with two assistants, kept an eye on the publishers and his records up to date. When aryanization produced an opening, he suggested acquiring German shares in the Ferenczi and Nathan publishing house. He even took it upon himself to prevent the publication of Jewish authors before the MBF had issued any decrees to that effect (at first only German or *émigré* Jewish authors were banned). At the beginning of 1941, he explained to the publishers that, although there was no formal ban, it would not be timely to publish Jewish authors.[12] He does not appear to have had to raise his voice to make himself heard.

A similar situation obtained with regard to translations from the German language. In November 1940, Epting created a Franco-German commission composed of authors (Benoist-Méchin, Chateaubriant and Drieu), representatives of the publishers (Grasset, Payot and Plon – these were three houses that were looked upon favourably in 1941), translators and critics (Albert-Marie Schmidt and Maurice Boucher),[13] with the task of drawing up a list of German works that it would be desirable to translate. According to their mentors, the publishers displayed heartwarming goodwill.[14] About 300 translations from German appeared under the occupation, most of which were decided upon after the defeat.[15]

That figure represents a clear increase compared to the two years before the war, but was much lower than the zenith reached in the early 1930s, particularly in publishing houses traditionally active in translation. Several publishers produced on average more than they ever had before, as if they had only just discovered the interest and virtues of translation. That was the case for Mercure de France, Denoël, PUF and Masson, quite apart from Hachette, which the occupying power requisitioned.[16] The number of contracts signed, but not of translations published, provides an even more instructive picture, conveying both the general extent of this movement of adaptation and its timely evolution. No publishers reckoned they should refrain from acquiring at least a few translation rights. Most of the contracts were signed in 1941 or 1942: some were never honoured or not honoured until after the war. Let us leave aside the 'aryanized' publishing houses such as Balzac (formerly Calmann-Lévy), which bought up translation rights by the armful. Some houses signed contracts for more translations than they ever published: those were the keenest in the early days. Albin Michel, which only published one translation, had bought the rights for fourteen works; Fayard had signed eight contracts but was to publish only four translations; Payot had signed for twenty-eight and published fifteen; Grasset had signed for nine and published six, and so on. In other houses, the number of contracts was lower than that of published translations; these were firms with a literary vocation, which demonstrated their goodwill by publishing mostly classics. Gallimard bought the rights on fourteen books (nine in 1941, three in 1942, two in 1943) and published twenty translations. Aubier, which published thirty-four translations of classics, had bought only five works.[17]

Prudence went hand in hand with adaptation. Unlike in the 1930s, the works translated were noticeable for the absence of authors opposed to Nazism or persecuted by it. But most were classics; only a substantial minority were works authorized in Nazi Germany, and only a tiny minority were by Nazi authors in the strictest sense. Before the war, Sorlot had contracted to publish a French translation of Rosenberg's *The Myth of the Twentieth Century.* After the defeat, when the translation was ready, Mercure de France decided to compete for the honour of publishing this racist theorist. To the staff of the Institute, this seemed an excellent idea, given the superior standing of Mercure de France.[18] Denoël which, like Sorlot, agreed to accept German capital in the business, unsurprisingly published a selection of Hitler's speeches. But Flammarion was keen to share that privilege and let the German Institute know of this.[19] It was offered a work by Professor Grimm, with a Preface by Brinon (*The Political Testament of Richelieu,* 1941). Grasset wished to make Goebbels known and pestered the Institute people to grant it the contract, suggesting in passing that he might create a monthly collaborationist magazine, *L'Europe littéraire.*[20] Once he had obtained the contract and the translation was completed, Grasset tidied the idea away. Time had passed; it was by then December 1942.

In the interval Grasset had published some works by background figures: two works by Friedrich Sieburg and *Napoleon* by Philippe Bouhler, one of the leaders of the Nazi party. Plon and Flammarion treated the French public to modern economic and social works with a distinctly Nazi flavour (such as those by Anton Zischta, August Winnig and Ernst Friedrich Wagemann). The venerable Librarie Générale de Droit et de Jurisprudence held out for Carl Schmitt, 'the crown jurist' of the Nazi regime, one of whose works it had published before the war and two more of whose titles it now bought (his *Leviathan* and his *Begriff des Politischen*: the latter appeared in 1942 under the title *Considérations politiques*, translated and prefaced by William Gueydan de Roussel, an activist in the 'anti-judeo-masonic struggle'). Masson brought out the *Manuel d'eugénique et d'hérédité humaine* by Otto von Verschuer, one of the Nazi regime's most highly regarded geneticists (it was after working as his assistant that the infamous Dr Mengele went on to pursue his all-too-well-known career) and entrusted its translation to the racist ethnologist and theoretician George Montandon.

All the publishing houses naturally published works by French authors that favoured collaboration. An edifying glimpse of these is provided by *Le Miroir des livres nouveaux*, a collective catalogue circulated in the autumn of 1941, with the support of Propaganda-Abteilung. Among the publishers who patronized it were Albin Michel, Gallimard, Grasset, Payot, Plon and Stock, alongside several aryanized houses that were certified as respectable by being found in such good company. One-fifth of the authors promoted in this catalogue were German, first and foremost Hitler. Some were politically committed works (such as those by Drieu and Chateaubriant), others were literary works, by well-considered literary authors, of course.[21]

Finally, some publishers willingly met with German colleagues or visited Germany, Henri Flammarion for one.[22] By early 1941, the German Institute was encouraging the establishment of relations between medical authors in the two countries. Masson took part in a meeting held in Stuttgart in the summer of 1941, which set up a mixed committee to prepare for an exchange of contributions. Contacts were also established between scientific publishers, with PUF in the forefront on the French side.[23] But whether prompted by conviction or by self-interest, these meetings do not appear to have led to anything.

All in all, this was a profession that demonstrated a more or less general compliance, upheld by a substantial measure of ideological connivance. Many of the Paris publishing houses published speeches by Pétain, Laval and other members of the government. Some had sympathies with Nazism: Grasset, Sorlot, Denoël, Jacques Bernard of Mercure de France, and Chardonne, the manager of Stock. For a few, the occupation provided a shortcut up the ladder. Maurice Girodias was only twenty-one years old when he created the Éditions du Chêne, which soon became one of the best-known art publishing houses. In October 1941, he published *Le Meuble*, the first volume in a 'Collection de la tradition française', of which he sent a copy to Abetz, at the same time requesting an audience to discuss Franco–German cultural relations.[24]

Honour where honour is due: how could Gallimard remain absent from any general discussion on publishing during this period? His is a case all the more interesting in that it introduces a measure of complexity into any theory that would seek to explain the behaviour of publishers solely by reference to their political or ideological sympathies – Pétainism in most cases, Nazism in a few. How their respective, individual motives weighed against one another was certainly more complex and varied considerably from one publisher to another, even if this did not result in patterns of behaviour that differed noticeably from the average.

At the time of the defeat, Gallimard was in southern France, feeling extremely worried. As the publisher of Freud, Kafka and Thomas Mann, he was not expecting the conqueror to look too kindly upon him: he was indeed to be the publisher most affected by the Otto list. But he received appeals from his authors, who were anxious to be published and whom he feared would desert him for his competitors (Grasset in particular) who, one by one, were reopening for business. In October 1940, Gide heard from him. 'He is thinking of bringing out the *NRF* again and foresees having to make necessary changes for fear the Germans install themselves on the premises and take over everything. He seems to believe it easier to come to terms with them than with the Vichy government.'[25] The 'necessary changes' meant replacing Paulhan by Drieu on the journal and setting up a board of directors that included Gide, Giono, Montherlant and Saint-Exupéry ('What are needed are people likely to reassure the occupying power', Montherlant noted).[26] Following a brief period of confusion when the publishing house was closed by Propaganda-Abteilung,[27] Drieu took over the direction of the review, with the additional right to oversee the production of the whole house for a period of five years.

Gallimard had to make a number of concessions in order to reopen. Had he not done so, he would surely have felt that he was the only one to sacrifice himself, to judge by the acquiescence of so many authors and the bewilderment that in the early days led Alain, Éluard, Gide and Valéry all to appear in the pages of the new *NRF*. The episode of the closure was not allowed to be forgotten; the sense of being under threat was maintained throughout the occupation by the attacks that came from part of the collaborationist press. Gallimard continued to act in a conciliatory fashion. He published some political works, starting with Drieu's, but discouraged Rebatet, who offered him his scathing work, *Les Décombres*. He translated German works, mostly classics (Goethe and Hoffmann) and let this be known in the *Pariser Zeitung*: an announcement in German of French translations of German works![28] It was clearly a matter of sending out the right signals rather than winning extra readers. He did not neglect contemporary authors, buying the rights to fourteen works,[29] four of them by Jünger (three of which appeared under the occupation, although the fourth, the most political, *Le Travailleur*, was eventually published by Bourgois in 1989) and also Heidegger's *L'Être et le Temps* (not to be published until 1964). These were two authors who were, at the least, ambiguous towards Nazism and who were big names. But there was no Freud or Kafka to give his selection the mark of openmindedness, as there had been in the past.

Gallimard also tried to seize any opportunities offered, for instance where aryanization was involved. The trade association of publishers wanted to find a corporative solution for the publishing houses of Nathan and Calmann-Lévy, both to forestall any German penetration and to preserve the balance of the profession by preventing one of its members from becoming too big. When the corporative solution failed, a group of nine publishing houses (Gallimard, Plon, Flammarion, Grasset, Fayard, Albin Michel, etc.) made an offer, also without success. A number of publishers then tried to effect individual takeovers, first Fayard, who offered 2.2 million, making it clear that he intended to make Paul Morand the director of the house (it was important to inspire confidence), then Gallimard, who offered 2.5 million and a literary committee that would include both Drieu and Morand. In the end, Calmann-Lévy was sold to front men acting for the German embassy.[30]

However, Gallimard's policies were not able to magic all dangers away. In June 1941, the appearance of a novel by Violet Trefusis provoked the anger of the censors. In the spring of 1942, it was Drieu who made trouble, disillusioned with his position and wanting to abandon the directorship of the *NRF*. Gallimard, beside himself with worry, managed to persuade him to stay.[31] There was another crisis in July 1942 when a rumour, destined to be printed in *Je suis partout*, denounced the diffusion of the works of Jean-Richard Bloch, a Jewish writer and, what was more, one who had taken refuge in Moscow. When ordered to explain himself, the publisher protested that he had had absolutely nothing to do with it. 'In September 1940 we gave orders forbidding the delivery of any works by J. R. Bloch . . . It was a decision that we ourselves took despite the fact that no titles by J. R. Bloch appeared on the Otto list.'[32] Gallimard stressed that, although he had not withdrawn Bloch's works from sale, he had forbidden any further deliveries, even though under no obligation to do so. Here again, it is easy to see that the task of the occupying power would have been far more laborious without the assistance of Frenchmen concerned not to take any risks, who themselves extended the measures imposed by the Germans.

In August 1942, Gallimard was lunching with a diplomat from the embassy. He was vexed by the abandonment of the agreement of the autumn of 1940, which had left the decision of whether or not to publish to the publishers themselves, and also by the fact that that power of decision had now been transferred to a supervisory committee appointed by Vichy. The Germans had agreed to this because they saw an advantage in leaving the decision to refuse publication to the French, while they retained the ultimate right of authorization – and not only the right but also the means, through their allocation of paper. Gallimard was vexed because this change had been marked by authorization being refused for the re-publication of works by Fargue and Valéry, and he was afraid that well-known authors would decide to publish in Switzerland. 'He was sure that it was not the intention of the German authorities to force French publishing to emigrate', he explained; surely it would be judicious to revert to the earlier procedure?

Gallimard's chances of prevailing were slender, even taking into account his plea that it would be in the interests of both parties. Yet he was not dismissed as a man of no account. The German diplomat, mindful of the dissatisfaction felt with Philippon on account of his recent unwillingness to stick his neck out (in April 1941, opening the Rive Gauche bookshop, he had claimed it to be a model of collaboration between the two countries),[33] suggested replacing him by Gallimard – not that he harboured any illusions as to his 'weaknesses', but he thought that he would cooperate 'more openly and loyally with the German services than Philippon did'.[34] However, that was just a personal opinion and other officials would have opposed it vigorously, certainly after the end of 1942, when the publication of Saint-Exupéry and Aragon sparked off another flood of criticisms in the collaborationist press. In March 1943, the SD named Gallimard (along with Fayard, Cerf, Spes and others) in the category of publishing houses that might be closed down or whose activities might be considerably curtailed, with the STO in view;[35] nothing ever came of the suggestion, however.

Gallimard is an interesting case because he displayed no hint of the philonazism of a man such as Grasset or of the Pétainism of other publishers. In truth, it would have been surprising if he had, given that he had tried hard to avoid military service in the Great War.[36] He steered his course in no doubt whatsoever that the most preferable outcome of the war would be an Anglo-Saxon victory. But, quite simply, he was not a bold man and for the time being what mattered to him was to hang on to his publishing house and his authors. His behaviour, partly conditioned by his vulnerability, provides a fair illustration of one way of getting through those difficult times: protecting his every flank, jettisoning ballast and taking precautions, while at the same time not neglecting any chance opportunities that came his way, steering his course between the Charybdis of open compromise and the Scylla of costly intransigence.

Where would Gallimard and his colleagues have been without their authors? As it happened, there was not that much to choose from between the two groups. On the shelves of the bookshops, readers could find new books with the most glittering of names: Aragon, Audiberti, Bataille, Blanchot, Camus, Claudel, Éluard, Guillevic, Guilloux, Mauriac, Michaux, Paulhan, Ponge, Queneau, Romain Rolland, Sartre, Triolet, Troyat, Valéry and Vialar, not forgetting the earliest novels of Marguerite Duras (*Les Impudents*, Plon, 1943), Simone de Beauvoir (*L'Invitée*, Gallimard, 1943) and René Barjavel (*Ravage*, Denoël, 1943). Yet the position of authors was less exposed; they had no businesses to run; if difficulties arose, the censors blamed their publisher; most could survive without publishing.

On the other hand the temptation to do so was considerable, even irresistible, for the reasons noted above.

Was it right to publish? Here, the code of conduct did not seem to apply, since it was a matter of the French addressing the French, Guéhenno, however, was critical of the determination of writers to be published, a determination that they defended with every kind of plausible argument. 'They say, "French literature must continue". They think that they are that literature, they are French thought, and that these would die without them.' He, for his part, refused to forget that 'the whole of France, the whole of Europe is in prison'. So, 'now is the time to write for nothing, simply for pleasure'.[37] For the vast majority of authors, including academics, this was too demanding an attitude, for they were of the opinion that the publication of a book could not be regarded as recognition of the occupying power, let alone of its politics.

What did rapidly become a subject of debate and quite wide disagreement was publication in the periodicals. Here, the name of the press's director, the political line taken by the journal and the association of particular writers with it could all give pause for thought. As soon as it became know that Gide was intending to contribute to the new *NRF*, he received a number of extremely critical letters, which led him to withdraw. 'You do not realize what support you are thereby providing for enemy propaganda, your collaboration will be represented by them as proof of their liberalism', one of his correspondents wrote to him.[38] Many authors thought otherwise, and not only during the first two years. In the summer of 1940, Léautaud had nothing but sarcasm for colleagues who published in the controlled press, particularly 'reactionary writers, conservatives, officials, academicians, who celebrate the motherland, patriotism, honour, and other grandiose sentiments, such as Abel Hermant, Pierre Benoit, Abel Bonnard', while he, more of an outsider, a 'rebel', said 'not on your life'.[39] Only a few months later, he himself appeared in Drieu's *NRF* and also in *Comoedia*, a cultural weekly with a liberal image, encouraged by the occupier and designed to attract the literary *gent à plume*. The plumage displayed there was indeed abundant, and showy with it: Marcel Arland, in charge of the literary section, plus Paulhan, Jean Grenier, Valéry, Fargue, Cocteau, Audiberti and Giraudoux, some of whom were simply bent on distancing themselves from Drieu. In 1943, Paulhan was to write, 'I have not forgotten the time when collaboration with *C[omoedia]* on the part of Valéry, Claudel, and

Vildrac was a clear enough way of indicating their refusal to collaborate with the *NRF*.'[40]

The case of Paulhan provides an example of the diversity of the positions that might be adopted as well as of a cogent understanding of the ongoing basic problem. Writing to Louis Guilloux in 1941, he declared that in his view a writer could not be held responsible for the opinions of those writing on the page opposite. Keep silent so as not to play into the hands of the Germans? But what if one's contribution would do them a disservice rather than a service? Besides, if what they wanted were high quality publications, was not that a good reason to write, but badly?[41] There are plenty of twists and turns in these arguments, and Paulhan knew that they were not valid where some periodicals were concerned and that the close company of certain writers was truly not to be tolerated. It is hard to imagine him providing even literary articles for some political journals, as Marcel Aymé did for *Je suis partout*, and Colette and Morand did for *Combats*, the paper produced by the Milice. The attitude that he expressed, adopted by a man whose support for the resistance cannot be doubted and who stuck to his point of view at the time of the purges, shows that a margin of interpretation did exist, one that is, moreover, not easy to dismiss.

The question of the code of conduct became increasingly acute, leading at least those who favoured resistance to distance themselves altogether from the periodical press as from 1942. However, it did not deter the vast majority of authors from continuing to publish. On this point we should try to understand both the attitudes of the time and also the way that perspectives may have shifted since then. Authors were encouraged to publish by the appearance of normality that prevailed. The occupying power did not exercise a general censorship. Publishers took care of this and would only submit a manuscript to Propaganda-Abteilung if they had any fears or doubts. As for authors, even if they did not come into direct contact with enemy surveillance, they knew enough of its existence to impose a kind of self-censorship as they worked. All the same, their desire for normality was too strong to resist: liberty under surveillance was better than total silence. For all their claims to be illuminating the path ahead, intellectuals too needed to find their way. The easiest course was to return to work, busy oneself and try, by writing, to retain some control in a situation of impotence and in the face of an uncertain future. They were all the more prone to do this given that, ever since the late 1930s, the intellectual atmosphere had been one of withdrawal, disengagement and lack of involvement.

Even writers who were to become the spokesmen or representatives of commitment after the liberation were affected by this atmosphere during the first part of the occupation. A case in point was Sartre. He had avoided politics in the pre-war period, was impelled into the resistance by his experiences as a prisoner, then detached himself from it. He turned his back on the authorized press, which would have welcomed him with open arms, but published a book and had his plays performed. In 1943 he rejoined the resistance and this time stayed with it. His concern for his work and desire for success counter-balanced the call to action. But for Sartre a literary work was itself a commitment and certainly his message – even if not always clearly perceived – constituted a radical criticism of all authoritarian powers.[42]

For others, the path to commitment zigzagged amid confusion and temptation from one extreme to another. Since the end of the Spanish Civil War, Roger Vaillant, the former surrealist, had laid down his arms. In August 1940, in Vichy, he ran into Déat, who had been his philosophy teacher, and told him that 'his dream was of closer Franco–German intellectual contacts'.[43] The following year he was on the brink of joining the RNP. In 1942 he identified with Stendhal's attitude at the time of the Restoration, when 'the party that snuffed things out' triumphed: 'Nothing being done here can touch me', Stendhal had written, 'I am a passenger on this ship. All that matters is to have some tranquillity and some good shows to see.'[44] Not long after this Vaillant overcame his drug addiction and joined the resistance.

In some cases, accommodation went beyond simply publishing – when, for example, the price for publication was some concession, however symbolic, to the occupier. It was a price that both Mauriac and Duhamel paid. Since the defeat, François Mauriac had been consoling himself by writing. When invited by Drieu to contribute to the new *NRF*, he enthusiastically accepted, adding: 'I am not altogether in agreement with any of your articles. But your point of view does seem to me defensible. You alone – or almost alone – are in a position to play, with dignity and without recanting, a role useful to everybody.'[45] This provides an example of the attitude of, if not encouragement, at least comprehension for the collaborationists that prevailed in the early days. On 9 December 1940, furthermore, Mauriac told Guillemin that he was 'convinced that, for France, there was no policy except collaboration'.[46] However, at the sight of the first issue of the *NRF*, he took a grip on himself and withdrew his contribution.

When he had completed a novel (*Pharisienne*), he was pressed by his publisher, Grasset, to allay the suspicions of the occupiers by writing an article for *La Gerbe* or by paying a visit to Epting. He agreed to call at the German Institute, a decision that he described to his wife as 'just a gesture, one already made by Giraudoux, and that commits me to nothing, although it clearly does have some significance'. He was received by Epting and Bremer. 'They gave me a little lecture on the Europe of tomorrow. I understood that they would not be making any trouble for me.'[47] Out of prudence or gratitude he sent them a copy of his novel with a dedication – a gesture that became known and that returned to torment him after the liberation. But Bremer had not yet finished with him. First, he limited the edition of Mauriac's novel to 5000 copies, to the great indignation of Grasset, who tried hard to get this decision reconsidered. Next, he allowed a press campaign to develop, but prevented it from definitively antagonizing Mauriac and making him a martyr in public opinion. Two birds with one stone, he congratulated himself: the press campaign shows Germany's friends that they are supported, while the authorization for Mauriac's book to appear testifies to the tolerance of the occupiers. Then he banned the publication of any reviews of the novel, in an attempt to force Mauriac to take up a public position.[48]

Mauriac saw through these manoeuvres. Writing to his wife on 7 June 1941, he commented, 'Clearly they want to make me declare myself. They feel that I am sulking. I shall be obliged to declare my position: absolute loyalty with regard to the conqueror, an agree[ment] to collabor[ate], but reservation on the score of ideas and doctrine.'[49] In the event, he produced no public declaration, but probably made conciliatory noises in private. At any rate, the Germans lifted the limitation of the edition, to Grasset's great satisfaction: 25 000 copies were distributed within a few weeks. Mauriac's pliancy cannot be separated from his hesitation, which is typical of the period. Torn between resignation and resistance, and confused by the blows dealt to communism, he was tempted, as were other Catholics, to believe 'that Nazism, once victorious, might evolve; that is the impression left by all the conversations I have had with various members of the occupying force'.[50] Soon, though, he courageously made his decision – the only member of the Académie Française to join the active resistance. One of his works recalls the point when he reached his parting of the ways. His *Cahier noir,* published clandestinely by Éditions de Minuit in 1943 and one of the major works of the intellectual resistance, had started off as an *Examen de conscience* that Grasset had been expecting to publish; but the work then changed in both content and direction.[51]

Georges Duhamel was another French literary lion, no less regarded with suspicion by the occupiers who, in December 1940, seized his volume of memories of the exodus, *Lieu d'asile,* then already in print. In June 1941, Bremer reported that Duhamel had paid a visit to the German Institute with assurances that he had no intention of writing a single line against Germany. According to Bremer, Duhamel 'looked with interest upon the Germans' attempts to organize Europe in a new way and was convinced that, provided Germany did not falter as the Versailles victors had, the French would follow gladly'. These were prudent, conditional words, which did not rule out a subsequent evolution on Duhamel's part. The underlying purpose of his visit was to secure an authorization to publish, probably for volume IX of the *Chronique des Pasquier* and for an essay, *Confessions sans pénitence,* both of which appeared in the autumn of 1941. Bremer wound up his report by expressing his distrust.[52] What would he not have given to read Léautaud's entry in his diary a few days later, describing a meeting with Duhamel: 'I told him Valéry's anecdote about that German officer who wanted to suspend the payment of a military allowance to one particular woman, explaining "She gave all my men the clap". Duhamel did not find this at all funny. "She should have been decorated and persuaded to give all the Germans the clap", he said.'[53] Duhamel published nothing else under the occupation, and the authorities even banned the reprinting of his earlier works. As in Mauriac's case, his gesture would have been unthinkable later on.

Publication was sometimes achieved at the cost of cuts, as in the cases of Camus and Saint-Exupéry. Certainly, in their case what is interesting is not so much the cuts that they agreed to in order to be published, but rather their determination to be published in Paris. Camus, who was living in Algeria from January 1941 to August 1942, preferred the occupied capital to his publisher in Algiers. One novel, *L'Étranger,* and one essay, *Le Mythe de Sisyphe,* published by Gallimard in 1942, established his reputation and launched him on a dazzling career. For that to happen, a chapter devoted to Kafka in the latter volume had to be cut; but his desire to be published won the day. Camus was still feeling the disenchantment of the late 1930s, after his time in the Communist party. History soon caught up with him, however, and like Sartre he came to see that it was the resistance that reflected his own ideas.[54]

The case of Saint-Exupéry was more unusual, as he was living in America, where his book *Pilote de guerre* appeared in both French and English. But he was determined that it should be published in occupied France. That choice was not unrelated to his political ideas: he believed in a Pétain acting under constraint and who was 'saving "the substance" of the country by agreeing to cooperate'.[55] It is not only that choice on the part of the author that merits our attention, but also the Germans' authorization for him to be published. Saint-Exupéry was not unknown to the occupiers. Before the war he had twice visited Germany, the second time in 1939 when he was welcomed by Abetz, who organized a visit to the leadership schools for him and Henry Bordeaux, who produced an alarmed report (*Étapes allemandes*, 1939) on the visit.[56] Saint-Exupéry, who was severely critical of Nazism, was nevertheless confused and curious enough to take a closer look at it, and on a quasi-official visit, what is more. Two of his works, *Pilote de nuit* and *Terre des Hommes*, were translated in Nazi Germany and were warmly received there.[57]

In 1941, the *Pariser Zeitung* reported several snippets of news of him, the origins of which remain obscure but which testify to the interest that he aroused. In August, it announced his forthcoming return, 'one of the best and most sympathetic writers of France'; in October, it reported that his return had been deferred.[58] It is not surprising that his book was not automatically rejected or that it was authorized, after one anti-Hitler remark had been cut. The limitation of the edition to 2100 copies, on the other hand, indicates that German approval of him was already qualified. The book was immediately attacked by the press of the extreme right, then banned in February 1942. Neither the authorization nor the ban did the book an injustice, for there were two aspects to it – on the one hand, its profound humanism, its faith in the future, with the defeat presented as a possible chance for renewal and a promise of eventual victory; on the other, the decadence of the country, the inevitability of the defeat, its appeal for sacrifice and its prediction that recovery would be long and slow. All these themes had a Pétainist ring to them, the effect of which was to encourage acceptance.

Finally, publication could also be achieved at the cost of alterations that went beyond mere cuts, as happened in the case of Aragon's *Les Voyageurs de l'impériale*, a *fin de siècle* novel, mostly written before the defeat, in which Franco–German relations and the Dreyfus affair played a part of some importance and – now – of considerable delicacy. The manuscript, submitted by Gallimard to the German censorship in the spring of 1941, was rejected on account of the political past of the author, who was living in the free zone. The rejection was not definitive, however, and an expurgated version was ready by the autumn of 1941. The book did not appear until December 1942, following trouble with the Vichy censors even after its German permission had been granted. A further humiliation was that it appeared just at the moment when the critics were falling upon Saint-Exupéry. Gallimard, who had not announced it as forthcoming or given it any publicity, withdrew it from sale after just a few weeks. Aragon eventually produced a 'definitive edition' in 1947.[59]

The cuts made to the 1942 edition were considerable: more than twenty pages, two allusions to Heinrich Heine, whole passages on German espionage and, above all, on the Dreyfus affair.[60] Quite apart from Aragon's political record, which was quite enough to unleash unfavourable criticism, the reception of the book could have been embarrassing. This social novel constitutes an attack against the individualism of one man, a bourgeois and a parasite, who lived and was brought down amid his sterile concern for his ego, before being propelled into the great slaughter of 1914. This denunciation of a world without grandeur was something that a fascist might appreciate and commend, the more so given that antisemitism was an important theme, reflecting the atmosphere of the 1930s and all the more stark following the excision of any remarks implying criticism or conveying any distancing or irony on the part of the author.

The extent to which Aragon himself took part in the rewriting remains uncertain. After the war he declared that he had only agreed to minor alterations and blamed what had been done on some 'diabolically' clever German censor. ('No Frenchman would have had the ingenuity needed for those alterations').[61] It is now known that they were made by Paulhan and Gallimard on two successive sets of proofs. It does not seem likely that they would have acted totally on their own initiative, without consulting the author.[62] Whatever the truth of the matter, the real decision was taken following the German rejection in the spring of 1941. Aragon was told of this and his correspondence with Gallimard shows that he was impatient to see his book appear and was irritated by the delays.[63] By agreeing to expurgations, he had made his own decision, one for which there were no doubt many reasons: an author's vanity, financial needs, and possibly also the fact that, at this point, communists did not yet consider themselves at war with Germany. After that, he may have allowed things to take their course. When he received a printed copy and learned of the book's withdrawal, his reaction was not at all one of shock: his *Voyageurs* 'had suffered in the battle', he wrote to Paulhan, 'there were printing errors galore, to put it mildly. I hope this has not upset Gaston [Gallimard] too badly.'[64] Aragon seemed relieved that his book, which had so 'suffered in the battle', had been withdrawn. Without mincing words, a fair description of the struggle to be published would be: 'the author and the publisher both ran the gauntlet with lowered heads'.

The case of Aragon, torn between concern for his work and an impulse to commit himself in some way, provides yet another example of the general evolution of French society: from withdrawal towards a yearning for deliverance and, for some – Mauriac, Saint-Exupéry and Aragon himself – a movement towards fighting for deliverance. In the case of Aragon's novel, this produced an edition slashed by the censor's scissors which the author later sewed back together to produce the book's definitive edition. Between one and the other, the line dividing what was acceptable from what was not had shifted.

22

The signing-up of the Muses

When Göring came to meet Pétain in December 1941, Abetz gave a reception in his honour for which he himself drew up the guest list. Official figures and the upper crust of the political collaborationists made up the big battalions, leaving room, however, for the world of culture. Abetz thought of men of letters, journalists and writers: Brasillach, Blond, Luchaire, Crouzet and Bunau-Varilla, but also Pierre Benoit, Abel Bonnard, Jacques Chardonne, Alphonse de Chateaubriant, Drieu La Rochelle, Henry de Montherlant and Paul Morand. Nor did he forget people from the theatre: the actor and impresario Sacha Guitry, the actresses Arletty, Alice Cocéa, Danielle Darrieux, Annie Ducaux, Edwige Feuillère, Jacqueline Delubac and Yvonne Printemps, the singer Germaine Lubin, the dancer Serge Lifar, and the violinists Marius Casadesus and Jacques Thibaud.[1]

For these people, it was not just a matter of an accommodation for a particular purpose or of the price to be paid in order to appear on a controlled stage that was sometimes demanded of those not thought to be sympathetic towards the occupiers. For these were people who sought the company of the Germans, did them favours and attended functions organized under their auspices. To be sure, they constituted only a tiny minority, but many were famous figures, and they came from virtually every sphere. They claimed that it was purely in the service of French culture that they mingled with the occupiers, in the interests of closer Franco-German relations. Personal compliance and ideological connivance were definitely involved, but without necessarily generating any unshakeable convictions. These people were not militants, for the most part not even members of the collaborationist parties. But their attitude was such that, up until

1942, the German services had no difficulty in attracting them as guests or participants for the functions that they organized.

A small cohort of writers and essayists circulated around the embassy and the German Institute. Whether because of a natural prudence or discretion or a professional habit, or because they were only half won over or anxious to see 'which way the wind was blowing', all of them avoided the commitment of a Drieu or a Chardonne. First, let us consider the borderline case of Bertrand de Jouvenel. In the summer of 1940, he got in touch with Bergery and Déat and urged them to come to Paris, thereby furthering the designs of Abetz, with whom he had renewed contact and continued to meet, discreetly, over the next two years.[2] He was later to justify these relations with the claim that Vichy had entrusted him with an intelligence-gathering mission.

His book *Après la défaite*, published in 1941, contrasted the bankruptcy of France and the success of Germany since the Great War. Understandably enough, it was one of the few works translated into German at the time. Like Taine, Jouvenel offered a *Réforme morale et intellectuelle*, this one based on the new social sciences. Biopolitics, he wrote, would restore to France a population that would be healthy, strong and numerous – the word 'race' was not used. 'Geopolitics', a German science, would determine the country's role in conformity with its position and configuration. 'Psychopolitics', which could be a French science, would create institutions in conformity with 'tradition' and the 'national disposition', preparing the way for 'a transfiguration' of the people and its élites.[3] French society was a collective that it was necessary to cure and direct in accordance with the advice of experts in the social sciences, without the slightest reference to humanity or human rights.

Jouvenel stopped short of the conclusion in favour of collaboration that would logically have rounded off his thesis.[4] France, he declared, was in the eye of the cyclone, in a deceptive calm that must be put to good use to 'bung the leaks and consolidate the rigging'.[5] Neither resistance nor collaboration, just a respite to be used to strengthen the country: Jouvenel was a wait-and-see man, keen to conciliate the Germans without breaking with the Anglo-Saxons. At the time of the founding of the Rassemblement National Populaire (RNP), in February 1941, he told Déat: 'You cannot rally people to collaboration; in Germany, they were rallied against France; here, it could only be done in reverse. If it is impossible, we must wait.'[6] His departure to Switzerland in September 1943 expressed his refusal to make a choice and completed his withdrawal from political action.

A number of men fluttered moth-like around the German Institute. One was Giraudoux who, after checking that he was *persona grata*, despite his function of propaganda minister during the phoney war, would make himself known from time to time. Another was Marcel Arland who was already acquainted with Bremer, and who on his own initiative renewed and discreetly maintained contact with him. Bremer later supported the translation of his novel *Terre natale*.[7] Then there was the extremely interesting case of Montherlant, a writer drawn to Nazism by his love of combat and war, his cult of the body and sport, and his amoral heroism and anti-christianism, but distanced from it by his intransigent élitism and individualism and an aristocratic brand of morality that considered unpredictability and repudiation to be the marks of a superior spirit.

In 'Le solstice de juin', written in July 1940, he represented the German victory as a revolution that had toppled a rotting world (in another text, he identified himself with the enemy and his 'exterminator' planes: 'Why am I not them? Why is it not permissible for me to be one with their joy?'[8]). The victory belonged to the pagans, and the swastika flying from the towers of Notre Dame proclaimed to the whole world: 'You have been defeated, Galilean.' Now it was up to France to 'play its part bravely' and 'profit from the many kinds of lessons that the conqueror could teach it'.[9]

Vichy's authority and élitism were to his liking, but not its churchiness. Trouble with the police, over his pederasty, brought to a head his distaste for the free zone where he felt he was stifling,[10] while Grasset was promising a great welcome in Paris and Bremer, his translator before the war, was urging him to return and be fêted.[11] Montherlant himself reckoned that there was 'political action for him to take in Paris, of exactly the kind desired by the Germans' who, he was sure, would win the war, just as he was sure that it was France that would have to pay for the new order. He advised Roger Peyrefitte, his companion and confidant in pederasty, who had been sacked from his diplomatic post in the autumn of 1940, after a scandal in Vichy, likewise to move to the capital.[12]

Peyrefitte was himself already of a mind to 'get what he could out of what was happening in Europe'. He was counting on his friend obtaining the necessary permission for his return to Paris and on him ensuring a place for their brotherhood in the new Europe. 'And what revenge that will be for a certain order of ideas and sentiments! Who knows how it will be, this famous New Order, if people like you take enough trouble? There can be no doubt that the Germanic ideal is closer to the ancient ideal – and hence to ours – than to that of the civilization of N[otre] D[ame] and sentimental girls. All this, by the way – as of course you very well know – if it is not too late, is to remind you that before "the man of Weimar" (or rather of Munich) [Hitler], you represent not only yourself, which is already a great deal, but also an élite (we may as well call it that) that has struggled, that suffers, that groans at the stupidity and incomprehension of what passes for civilization.'[13] The above shows the extent of the delusions that people could harbour on the score of Nazism, even homosexuals for whom it was not exactly a saintly protector.

Once in Paris, Montherlant showed discretion, although he set up 'relations of close friendship'[14] with the German Institute. 'Le solstice de juin' was his clearest statement on collaboration, but when he published this text in a collection of essays of the same title, in the autumn of 1941, he added a postscript that emptied it of substance ('In truth, events have never been important to me. All that I loved about them were the rays that they produced, as these passed through me. So let them be what they will and let the world make of them what they will').[15]

In January 1942, in an interview in *La Gerbe*, he referred to 'the heroic struggle of the new European civilization against the lower Europeans'. Was this implicit approval for the German war in the East? Or a reference to a struggle that set heroes and slaves in opposition in all societies, including Germany, and that no 'European peace' would ever bring to an end? The interpretation was left open. When questioned about the construction of Europe, he gave his approval on the project, then immediately disengaged himself. 'The construction of Europe following a heroic path is an adventure. A dangerous adventure. There is a risk of failure. There is also a risk that this construction might turn out to be an illusion.' The perfection of the individual remained the paramount rule, 'whatever the social and political structure of the world, and whatever its victorious gods'. The journalist had asked him what place his heroism left for the masses, to which his reply was as follows: 'When certain communities eventually learn from experience that theirs is the nature of slaves, the heroes belonging to those communities will, if necessary, detach themselves morally and adhere elsewhere . . . The notion of patriotism is in the process of changing. Those who have taken too narrow a view of it will be unhappy.'[16] Clearly, his concept of the heroic individual carried within it the seeds of dissolution for traditional patriotism. Montherlant was indicating the path down which the fanatics of collaboration would rush, abandoning their own and going over to the conqueror. From his lofty vantage point he then proceeded to make his way down the other incline, towards the writing of *La Reine morte*.

As for Peyrefitte in Vichy under a cloak of secrecy, he was working away at the novel of manners that was to make his reputation, *Les Amitiés particulières*. In May 1943, he recovered his job, thanks to the intervention of Achenbach, who mentioned the matter to Laval. He was assigned to the governmental delegation in occupied territories directed by Brinon, to whom he wrote a letter of thanks singularly lacking in Greek moderation ('I shall employ all my zeal and, I may say, all my heart in, to the best of my modest ability, furthering the so very noble and essential task that you are so gloriously tackling. It will be my honour, in response to the trust that you have been so kind as to place in me, to profit from your lessons and your example').[17]

Paul Morand was another diplomat-writer. He was an elegant and cosmopolitan author who wrote as though always on the wing, but around 1933 he had begun to sink into the bogs of xenophobia. After the defeat, he found himself jobless: having left London for Vichy in June 1940 with no authorization, he had been suspended by Baudouin. Upon his return in 1942, Laval then reintegrated him and appointed him chairman of the commission for cinematographic censorship. Up until then, in Paris mostly, he shone in circles close to the occupiers, retreating into the shadows whenever the spotlight fell on him, and meantime busied himself revising his work. For the second edition, in 1942, of his book *1900*, which had first appeared ten years earlier, he summarily cut the following passage: 'The antisemitism that played a capital role in this period, only to disappear a few years later, today seems incomprehensible to us: a sort of besetting frenzy. France had no cause to resent its Jews, who are among the best and most assimilated [of its citizens].'[18]

In his *Chroniques de l'homme maigre* (1941), he presented an oblique version of his view of things. Though never using the word collaboration, he pointed his reader in the right direction by praising the advantages brought by the defeat: frugality, the rediscovery of essentials, the 'exoticism at home', 'with no Americans and no Polish Jews', the deliverance from politicians and the powers of money, the wider horizon opening on to Europe. Throughout the world what was taking place was 'a magnificent and irresistible coagulation of ethnic masses and the formation of a truly world-wide economy set upon gigantic foundations'.[19] As evidence of his clairvoyance he added a reminder of his earlier views, particularly on immigration. Then he tossed the end of his scarf over his shoulder: he would go his own way, content to 'take time as his adviser'. By 1943 time no longer seemed a reliable adviser and Morand got himself appointed ambassador to Romania. Jünger's comment was 'Autumn is coming, the swallows are leaving.'[20]

To occupiers so keen to parade representatives of their own culture, it was gratifying that the natives were hospitable and prepared to treat the intruders as guests. A number of artists and musicians agreed to work with German groups. In May 1941, for the twenty-fifth anniversary of the death of Max Reger, the singer Irène Joachim thus appeared with the Passani Quartet.[21] That same month, Germaine Lubin, a distinguished Wagner specialist, took the role of Isolde in performances given by the Berlin Staatsoper, under the direction of Karajan: she even did so, as a somewhat astonished Bremer was quick to point out, for the performance reserved for members of the Wehrmacht.[22] A number of musicians and musicologists, at the Institute's request, formed a Mozart society, designed to establish close links with the Salzburg Mozarteum. Its chairman was Adolphe Boschot, from the Institute, and the honorary committee included the director of the Conservatoire, the secretary general of the Opéra and a number of professors.[23] As for Lifar, with German support he organized an exhibition devoted to ballet and dance in the Romantic period. He invited Baldur von Schirach, the head of Hitler Youth and governor of Vienna, to attend its opening.[24]

The exhibition of the works of the sculptor Arno Breker, in the summer of 1942, constituted the climax of all this artistic hospitality. On the French side, the honorary committee, formed essentially by the Groupe Collaboration, was placed under the chairmanship of Bonnard and included a series of artists (Belmondo, Derain, Despiau, Van Dongen, Segonzac, Friesz, Landowski, Vlaminck), the architect Auguste Perret and René Delange, the director of *Comoedia*.[25] Perhaps more interesting, from our present point of view, is the welcome offered by Cocteau, who on 23 May 1942 provided *Comoe-*

dia with a 'Salut à Breker': 'I salute you, Breker. I salute you from the lofty land of poets, a land where countries do not exist except in so far as each individual brings the treasure of his national work to it.'

Since the defeat, Cocteau had concentrated solely on his art. His diary shows to what extent French people could live on separate planets: how many others were going into ecstasies over 'the prodigious beauty of Paris' in 1942?[26] In the course of his professional activities, he discovered that tolerance was a Nazi virtue. In 1941, his play *La Machine à écrire* was banned by the prefect of police. This decision was then overruled by Propaganda-Abteilung, which slyly claimed to 'desire to allow the artistic life of Paris to flourish harmoniously'. 'Each people has its own artistic and cultural ideas, and it is in order to safeguard the country's originality that the occupying authorities are leaving French creative artists their liberty.'[27]

By extending a welcome to Breker, Cocteau, who had been professing to be above current affairs, perversely entered into them – in his own way, to be sure. He was not a man of war and, in 1942, was pinning his hopes on a rapid peace emerging from the exhaustion of both sides. He wrote as follows: 'The honour of France may one day lie in the fact that it refused to fight.'[28] Besides, Nazi Germany was not without its attractions for him, in particular its leader. The picture that he created of him would rate a place in a museum of imaginary representations of Hitler. Cocteau religiously noted all Breker's remarks about the Nazi leader who, he claimed, would reveal his capabilities in peace even more than in war. He was fascinated by the notion of an artist-leader, all powerful politically, yet at the same time a patron and protector of the arts, at once Napoleon and poet ('In Hitler, we have a poet beyond the comprehension of the souls of drudges',[29] he wrote, referring to the French leaders of the pre-war period).

He was also beguiled by the prospect of European unification. On 2 July 1942, he recorded the pronouncements of the new director of the municipal police: 'He speaks of Hitler with eloquence but no pomposity and no narrow-mindedness. He believes, as I do, that it would be tragic to prevent such a soul from pursuing his task to the very end and to strangle it on the way. Already the "European" cards are ready at the Prefecture: *Mr So-and-so, European (District, France)*. No more customs, no more frontiers . . .' Compared with Hitler, Pétain was small and faded, totally lacking any 'sense of grand theatre' and incapable of producing any response other than 'the sentiments of an usherette'.[30] In early 1943 he produced another astonishing representation: 'Hitler is a civilian. The military will get him . . . He was dragged into a war that he detests. His pacifism was doomed in advance.' Then he took hold on himself: 'On no account allow myself to be distracted from the things that count by the dramatic frivolity of the war.'[31]

A number of artists and writers were by no means averse to a trip to Germany in the course of a high season that lasted from mid-1941 to mid-1942. What the organizers had in mind were propaganda operations that would not lead to contact with the German public, but at the most a meeting with other French nationals resident in Germany either voluntarily or under compulsion. Those invited were either artists or the directors of institutions that had given their German colleagues the warmest of welcomes to France. A number of these visits never progressed beyond the planning stage: one such was a trip for architects in 1942, another for representatives of the artistic world, planned for 1941 with a provisional list of guests that included the composers Marcel Delannoy and Marcel Dupré, the violinists Jean Fournier and Ginette Neveu, the theatre directors Charles Dullin, Gaston Baty and Pierre Renoir, the actresses Annie Ducaux, Elvire Popesco and Madeleine Renaud, plus opera singers and directors – thirty people in all.[32]

The most important of these visits involved music, arts and cinema circles. The first was to Vienna, in November/December 1941, for the Mozart celebrations. The group of travellers included the composers Arthur Honegger, Florent Schmitt, Marcel Delannoy and Gustave Samazeuil, the director of the Opéra, Jacques Rouché, several journalists and music critics, including Delange, Rebatet, Robert Bernard, the director of *La Revue musicale,* and Paul-Marie Masson, the professor of the history of music at the Paris faculty of letters.[33] At the beginning of the following year it was the turn of a selection of artists: the sculptors Paul Belmondo, Charles Despiau and Paul Landowski; the painters André Derain, Cornelis Van Dongen, André Dunoyer de Segonzac, Othon Friesz and Maurice de Vlaminck. On their return a number of them expressed their enthusiasm for the consideration enjoyed by artists in the Nazi regime.[34] Next, in March, it was film actors who went off: Albert Préjean, Danielle Darrieux, Viviane Romance, Junie Astor and Suzy Delair. Another trip for theatre people, planned for the summer of 1942, with Henri Decoin, Marcel L'Herbier, Abel Gance, Edwige

Feuillère and Gaby Morlay, fell through.[35] People from the world of entertainment were also sent beyond the Rhine to cheer up the French voluntary workers there: including Maurice Chevalier, Édith Piaf, Charles Trenet and Raymond Souplex.

The two trips for writers opened and closed this season of travels. The organization of the first, in the summer of 1941, occasioned such rivalry between the embassy and Propaganda-Abteilung that Berlin had to beg them to stop quarrelling. In October, Drieu, Ramon Fernandez, André Fraigneau, Brasillach, Jacques Chardonne, Abel Bonnard and Jouhandeau went off to Weimar, to honour with their presence the first congress of the writers of the New Europe, held, as was fitting, within the framework of 'the Week of the German war book' (Arland, Baroncelli, Combelle and Morand appeared on the provisional lists).[36] One year later, the same little group, with one or two changes – Drieu, Fraigneau, Chardonne, Thérive and Georges Blond – returned to Weimar for the second congress of the Association of European Writers, created by Goebbels in a bid to impose his own domination over European culture.

The first trip had been quite enough for Jouhandeau. The entries in his diary convey his unease: 'How could I not have tried to justify, legitimize my presence in this enemy country at such a time?' The excuses he produced were his love for Germany and its culture, and the need for the two countries to get along together. 'All I am trying to prove is that a Frenchman is not necessarily germanophobic, even in the present circumstances. Indeed, I would use my own body to create a fraternal bridge between Germany and ourselves.'[37] This was more than a mere figure of speech, since Jouhandeau was at the time pursuing a young German poet with his attentions. By early 1942, he was distancing himself, while still remaining favourably disposed towards Germany, to some extent by default, out of his fear of Soviet hegemony or American domination.

Another writer who was not present on the second trip to Weimar was Giono. Although his home was in the free zone, he went to Paris at the beginning of 1942 and 'immediately', 'on his own initiative', made contact with Heller, who found him 'extremely well disposed' to collaboration.[38] Although invited to Weimar, he did not go. In September, he told the German consulate in Marseilles that he was unable to leave on account of his mother being ill. The subterfuge one might have suspected was belied by his emphatic regret. Giono declared himself 'desolated' not to be able to take part in this trip, 'the more so given that I have been looking forward to it impatiently and [it] would have enabled me to continue with even more faith in the task of bringing France and Germany closer together that I have been working at ever since 1933'. His protestations continued: 'I am truly very disappointed, but I hope that it will be possible to take part in a future visit and a future meeting of the Association of European Writers, which has done me the much appreciated honour of choosing me to take part.'[39] Along with Cocteau, Giono provides an example of someone beguiled by the figure of Hitler himself, rather than by the regime. 'What is Hitler, the man, if not a poet in action?', he is reputed to have asked Fabre-Luce:[40] Hitler, enchanting the whole world with his strength, his power and his mystery.

In general, reciprocity was singularly lacking in these cultural demonstrations. The artists involved were not slow to notice this, and recriminations mounted, even amongst those best disposed towards Germany. Musicians, in particular, were critical of the ban affecting French music in Germany and the ostracism meted out to French performers. True, Alfred Cortot was invited to the 1942 Berliner Festspiele, but that exception was due to his personal importance as an ardent Pétainist, a member of the National Council and chairman of the Organization Committee for music. The following year, he was invited to make a tour, giving fifteen concerts. The same concern to keep a hold on the faithful resulted in the cellist, Pierre Fournier, another partisan of collaboration, receiving an invitation to give three concerts. The embassy, which was by now finding it difficult to organize musical events, considered these measures insufficient and pressed for more. In November 1943, Goebbels magnanimously authorized the playing of French music in the Reich, on condition that it should not take up more than one quarter of the programme.[41]

Scientific relations were cultivated out of the glare of publicity. Here, for tactical reasons, there was a measure of reciprocity. In the summer of 1940, the occupying power considered ordering all international organizations and associations based in Paris to be transferred to Berlin. But this project was soon deferred, so as not to damage the policy of collaboration, and was replaced by the idea of renewing old contacts, with the aim of accustoming the French scientific community to the dominant role of its German counterpart, a role that would be formalized after the war.[42] In July 1941, invitations to visit the Reich for French scientists were once again authorized.[43] A respectable number were issued by German associations (of dermatologists, botanists, mathematicians, geographers, economists, etc.) desiring the presence of French colleagues at their annual congress or at some colloquium. The embassy filtered these invitations and suggested names. A few scientists received personal invitations, for instance in the field of botany, agronomy and astronomy, but for the most part these led to no follow-up.[44] In these overtures from the German side, it is hard to distinguish between a spontaneous desire to prolong earlier links, and mere obedience to the official directive to establish contacts with French scientists.

In Vichy, cultural collaboration aroused considerable interest, along with hopes of reciprocity. By the summer of 1941, Jean-Édouard Spenlé, a distinguished Germanist and a man of commitment, was pressing the government to create an organism that would be the counterpart, in Berlin, of the German Institute in Paris. This would 'reassure those with certain reservations who are at present hesitating to accept any invitation or appeal of a "unilateral" nature'.[45] The idea resurfaced when Bonnard took over the Ministry of National Education. Now the proposal was to create a 'Comité Culturel Franco–Européen' designed to promote relations between universities, develop school exchanges and standardize diplomas, and even to set up a Franco–German *lycée*, the philosophy being to 'enable French culture to profit from the zone of influence of German culture, and vice versa'.[46] Needless to say, nothing could have been further from the conquerors' plans.

Bonnard's impetus made itself felt in several quarters. Deans of faculties were invited to contribute to a German review that centralized scientific and university documentation.[47] Here and there, various university officers made their own contributions; Jean Joseph Bertrand, for example, another Germanist and the rector of the Academy of Besançon, who launched a scheme for an exchange of books with German universities.[48] The resumption of school exchanges was considered by a mixed committee composed of a representative of the German Institute and five French teachers (René Lasne, Georges Lefranc, André Meyer, Robert Fortier and Pierre Velut). From it emerged the idea of a Franco–German holiday camp, which the minister's office found appealing as 'a beginning of Franco–German collaboration at the university level'.[49] Efforts were also made to send scholars and lectors beyond the Rhine. In 1942, for the first time, the Germans offered scholarships for summer courses in Munich,[50] which found plenty of applicants. At that time, the German Institute was receiving five or six enquiries a week about

German studies, study trips or holiday courses in Germany.[51] In 1943, at the beginning of the academic year, the Germans even appointed French Germanists as university assistant lecturers, to replace reservists who had been called up.[52]

In almost all disciplines, there were individuals, occasionally figures of some importance, who helped to establish contacts or relations, as a few examples will show. Germanists were particularly exposed, wooed by both the government and the occupiers, and some allowed their sudden importance to go to their heads. At the very least, the situation was conducive to gestures: in the spring of 1941, the Institute of Germanic Studies at the Sorbonne, with Epting's support, organized a series of public lectures (Maurice Boucher, Henri Gouhier, Spenlé, etc.) on German culture, which the *Pariser Zeitung* was careful to announce regularly.[53] Yet in the autumn of 1941, Epting painted a gloomy picture of the situation. The attitude of most Germanists was reserved or hostile, although a rather better state of mind was evident among the younger generation of professors who had visited Germany before the war – which was why, he thought, it would be advisable to resume the exchange programmes.[54]

This picture is confirmed by the enquiry requested by Bonnard in 1942 into 'professors whose teaching brings them into contact with foreign countries'. Its real purpose was to make sure, so to speak, that teachers of English were not anglophile and teachers of German were germanophile. However, it turned out that only a tiny minority among the latter expressed any collaborationist sympathies.[55] A few, however, did so in their teaching or their writing: apart from Spenlé and Bertrand, André Meyer, René Lasne – the co-editor, alongside Georg Rabuse, of an *Anthologie de la poésie allemande* (Stock, 1943) – Maurice Betz, Philippe Lavastine, Eugène Bestaux and Robert Pitrou.[56]

Among the historians, the catch was meagre. Michel Lhéritier, in charge of lecture courses in Dijon and a specialist on the Revolution in Bordeaux, carried very little weight. However, since 1926, he had been the secretary general of the Comité International des Sciences Historiques, in which capacity he had defended the Comité's universal vocation and on that account opposed breaking with Nazi Germany.[57] As early as August 1940, he had approached Epting, to obtain authorization for the reappearance of the Comité's bulletin. Epting was sympathetic to his request, having it in mind to transfer the association to Berlin.[58] Lhéritier considered it essential to keep the Comité going even without the English and despite the fact that the Americans wanted to put it to sleep. In the first issue of its bulletin, he justified his opinion in ingratiating vein: 'Like the monuments that Chancellor Hitler was careful to respect here in the war, [the Comité] is not only an organ of scholarship but also an impersonal and disinterested organ of civilization that deserves to be preserved for future humanity.'[59] Lhéritier managed to obtain paper even after the introduction of restrictions, by promising more space for German historians writing on subjects such as peoples, history and race.[60] He also tried to organize a Franco-German colloquium to take place in Weisbaden in the autumn of 1942, but was unsuccessful as all the French historians made themselves unavailable.[61] His efforts were none the less rewarded when after pulling a few strings he got himself appointed by Bonnard to a chair at the Sorbonne.[62]

In the field of mathematics, the Germans achieved a much better trawl. Gaston Julia was a veteran of the 1914–18 war whose serious facial wounds had caused him to wear a black mask ever since. He was a professor at the Sorbonne and at the Polytechnique, a member of the Académie des Sciences, a commander of the Légion d'Honneur, the recipient of numerous prizes, and secretary of the International Union of Mathematicians. In the latter capacity, he was contacted at the end of 1940 by a German colleague charged with taking over the association, who recorded with satisfaction that Julia was well disposed to collaboration.[63] It was an attitude that had no doubt been encouraged by the existence of an authentic scientific community capable of solidarity, even during the war – the only one of its kind, so far as I know. German mathematicians had made representations to the OKW in favour of their French colleagues who were prisoners of war, pressing for their release and securing the right to establish a scientific correspondence.[64]

In France, Julia busied himself trying, apparently without much success, to persuade the other university mathematicians to resume publication in and exchange articles with German journals.[65] In July 1942, he was invited to Göttingen, where he delivered a lecture in which he presented himself as a friend of national socialism.[66] The warmth of his convictions and his excellent contacts no doubt explain how it was that Bonnard thought of him to direct the Comité Culturel Franco-Européen, mentioned above.[67] He was to be one of the few university teachers invited to a German university, along with another leading academic in the exact sciences, Louis Dunoyer, professor of physics at the faculty of sciences in Paris and president of the French Society of Physics, who was a convinced Pétainist.[68]

Medicine seems to have been a discipline particularly tempted by contacts. Asked by the Germans to encourage exchanges of professors, Carcopino, the then Minister of National Education, in February 1942 replied as follows: 'If the experiment is to be made in Paris, it is in the faculty of medicine that it has most chance of success.'[69] This can be explained partly by a state of mind quite widely favourable to Vichy, which had granted a number of long-standing professional demands, and partly by the popularity of certain ideas, in particular to do with hygiene, that might encourage sympathy for some aspects of Nazi politics. Such sympathy was naturally particularly developed in the restricted circles interested in racism which, it should be remembered, at this date still found exponents and attracted research workers with scientific pretensions.[70]

At any rate, a number of leading lights in the medical world manifested no hostility. Underlying their behaviour, one senses, was a combination of Pétainism, professional ambition, institutional defensiveness, and professional links established with German colleagues before the war. The director of the Pasteur Institute was Gaston Ramon, a member of the Institut de France and a man whose every audience with Pétain evoked all the fervour of a pilgrim.[71] In the autumn of 1941, he travelled to Germany to assess 'the recent progress accomplished there in the field of vaccination against foot-and-mouth disease'.[72] In April 1942, the Germans asked him for twenty litres of anti-typhus vaccine, which he supplied without a qualm: 'According to the thinking of the Marshal, this will be added to whatever else will later count in France's favour.'[73]

Emmanuel Leclainché, the president of the Académie des Sciences, former president of the Académie de Médecine, and former chairman of the board of directors of the Pasteur Institute was director of the International Institute for Epizootic Diseases. In 1941, he reopened it 'in agreement with the occupation authorities and under their supervision'.[74] The following year, he was preparing to hold an international veterinary congress, with the Germans indicating which states to invite.[75] Professor Rist, regarded by the occupiers as the best French specialist in the field of research into tuberculosis,[76] went off in November 1941 to attend the Congress of German Organizations for the Struggle against Tuberculosis. And there were some even more committed doctors, for whom the German Institute organized a trip in March 1942; Dr Céline was among the travellers.[77]

Even the tiny circle of psychoanalysts was affected, in the person of René Laforgue, one of its historic figures. He was born in Alsace and fought in the Great War under German colours. In 1918 he became French and in the 1930s was a member of the International League against Antisemitism (LICA). So impressed was he by the successes of Nazi Germany that he even decided to resume his earlier nationality. He tried, unsuccessfully, to set up a society run on the lines of the Nazi version of psychotherapy, as an offshoot of the International Society of Pysychotherapy, which had fallen into German hands.[78]

Let us briefly consider one last case: that of Alexis Carrel. Since 1904 he had been living in the United States, working at the Rockefeller Institute. In 1912 he was awarded a Nobel Prize and went on to become famous with his book *L'Homme, cet inconnu*. It presented a plan to reconstruct society that was founded upon ideas from the extreme right on, for example, the inequality of the sexes and the hierarchy of races. When the author expressed sympathy for La Rocque and Doriot in the 1930s, it came as no surprise to anyone. At the beginning of 1941, Carrel returned to France and suggested that Vichy create 'a sort of think-tank, which would provide the head of government with solutions to all fundamental problems', in particular those relating to 'the regeneration, protection and progress of the individual and the race'. Significantly, he immediately added, 'For reasons of a psychological nature, it is imperative not to pronounce the word "race".'[79]

In November 1941, a law instituted the Fondation Française pour l'Étude des Problèmes Humains (French Foundation for the Study of Human Problems), its task being 'to protect, improve and develop the French population in all its activities'. Prudent as ever, Carrel kept aspects such as eugenics in the background, despite the fact that he advocated the development of a 'biocracy'.[80] Had he not been so reticent, he would have been seen as hitching his wagon to the Nazi regime and would thereby have compromised the future of his research. It is an example that shows how, under the conditions of the occupation, general intellectual agreement could sometimes check closer ties rather than facilitate them.

As early as June 1941, Carrel went to Paris, where he was welcomed with open arms and offered every assistance for setting up his Foundation. He maintained continuous and cordial relations with the embassy, requesting to be supplied with scientific data relating to, among other subjects, the improvement of races.[81] In May 1942, his principal collaborators, Dr André Gros and Dr Jacques Ménétrier, two specialists in occupational medicine, visited Germany on a study trip.[82] Carrel was always discreet in public and was reserved in his meetings with the occupiers.[83] It was not his intention to become involved with politics, which he despised. He felt little sympathy for the Germans. Although, owing to both his antidemocratic opinions and his views on the biological cure for society, there were evident convergences between his views and Nazism, he was repelled by its politics of the masses, so different from his own ideal of a team of scientists guiding the Prince along the path to regeneration. All the same, in September 1943, he did declare that 'only the Germans were capable of imposing order upon Europe, and in particular France' and that they were 'by no means beaten yet'.[84]

Under interrogation after the war, Epting produced a list of thirty-six academics with whom he had been in contact under the occupation. Most were professors of law or letters, while scientists accounted for less than one quarter of the group.[85] Some had declared their partisan commitment (for example, Bardèche, Fay, Fourneau, Labroue and Le Fur). Others (Gidel and Ripert) held an official position in the university that prevented them from opposing the policies of the government. The rest were men such as those mentioned above (Boucher, Carrel, Dunoyer, Julia, Lhéritier, Pitrou, Schmidt, Spenlé, etc.) or others who might equally well have been mentioned (Dauphin-Meunier, Louis Hourticq, Édouard Dolléans, Jean Thomas and Georges Dumézil). One other deserves a special mention: René Maunier, professor in the faculty of law in Paris and a great specialist on imperial questions, who was one of the few French academics, along with Emmanuel Leclainché, to publish articles in a German periodical during the war.[86] All in all, these people made up only a tiny majority of the scholarly world, but they represent a phenomenon that is by no means insignificant. It shows that no circles constituted exceptions, not even those of people from whom a critical sense might have been expected. By no means everybody regarded Nazism as a radical negation of all intellectual values.

PART III

Commitment

QUITE a few men and women in French society opted for collaboration. Unlike their compatriots who breached the code of dignity or ignored it for reasons not primarily politico-ideological, these people rejected the very validity of that code, believing, as Chardonne did, that it was necessary to break the chain of disasters. Instead of practising a surreptitious accommodation, they embraced opinions and adopted modes of behaviour that made them collaborationists and partisans of the politics of collaboration.

Along with the French state, their leaders all shared a common ambition: to reach agreement with the occupier before the current conflict came to an end, in order to obtain the best possible peace conditions. But they had no power and consequently none of the elements of state authority such as a territory, armed forces or a degree of freedom of action. Their only resource was speech and persuasion, their best hope and bet being to gather as much support as possible, as a stepping-stone towards power and towards the implementation of a policy of collaboration that they believed they would make a success of. In the meantime, they made most of a political situation organized and controlled by the occupier, a situation which, by reason of its scope and diversity, had no equivalent in Nazi Europe. The widely diversified nature of French society made for a variety of forms of accommodation. Similarly, the plurality of the political groups in France caused collaborationism to take a diversity of forms, which it tried to exploit so as to extend its appeal and audience.

From 1942 on, that diversity decreased. Most of those in French society tempted by accommodation disentangled themselves at the latest and for good in November 1942. Even the Vichy regime made two moves to extricate itself, the first in November 1943, when it endeavoured to reorientate its internal policies, the second in the summer of 1944, when its principal leaders suspended their functions, although without formally resigning. But in the partisan world, things took a different turn. Although a fraction of this world did follow society's general movement of distancing itself, the rest drew even closer to an occupying power whose ultimate victory seemed less and less certain, and they became even more radical in their fanatical commitment. This shows that collaborationism was more than a matter of accommodation. Though engendered by society, it tore itself away from society in such a way as to set itself apart from it and seek to reconstruct it with the aid of the enemy. Collaborationism had been launched with fanfares in the name of defence of the nation, but ended up insisting that the interests of those occupied coincided directly with those of their occupiers.

23

Anti-France

IN THIS modern age, occupying forces always discover a number of fault lines that they can exploit. The widest and most tempting to use is separatism when, within a state's boundaries, one section of the population demonstrates that it is rebellious or wavering in its allegiance. Towards the end of the First World War, all the belligerents made use of the weapon provided by nationalistic claims in their bids to destroy their own opponents and prepare for an international order that would serve their own interests. While the central powers pressed for the dismantling of the Russian empire, the *entente* powers did likewise in respect of the Austro-Hungarian empire and the Ottoman empire. Even in Western Europe, where the nation-state had long been established, the map was not altogether stabilized. The Germans were pressing the Flemish movement to break away from Belgium so as to pave the way for German domination along the Channel coastline. And after 1918, the French banked on the regional identity of the people of the Rhineland and, in fits and starts, endeavoured to establish an autonomous or independent state there – as would later be held against them.

The Nazi regime, more than any other, was prone to play this card whenever it was in its interests to do so. Its ethno-racist principles provided powerful encouragement for dissatisfied nationalities and its victories opened up the prospect of vindication for their claims. Croatia and Slovakia thus achieved their objectives, unlike the Ukraine and other nationalities inhabiting the 'vital space' of the master-race. In the West, the occupier reopened the Flemish question and for the first time tried out the French keyboard. In Berlin in the summer of 1940 amid the euphoria of victory, plans proliferated for splitting France apart, some of which derived their inspiration from abroad. In 1938, in a work translated into German, the 'Burgundian' writer Johannès Thomasset had suggested dividing up France in a most orderly fashion: southern France would pass under an Italian protectorate, Brittany would either be independent or attached to Ireland, the Basque country would be attached to Catalonia, Flanders to the Netherlands, and a vast 'Germanic' region comprising Burgundy, Champagne, Alsace and Lorraine would be placed under the protection of the Reich. In the summer of 1940 the SS journal hardly surprisingly devoted a complimentary review to this work, which the author was to send in July 1942 to an Alsatian autonomist, dedicated as follows: 'Homage to liberated Alsace from Burgundy, which is waiting'.[1]

The French state itself made a number of gestures. On 11 July 1940, Pétain spoke of provinces and governors, hinting at recognition for regional identities and a decentralization of the administration. It is hard to tell to what extent he was fearful of movements that might play into the hands of the Germans or whether he was simply voicing certain historical aspirations of the traditionalist right. In any case supporters of a moderate regionalism discovered reasons for hope and for supporting the new regime, even though it rapidly became clear that, largely because of the prevailing circumstances, it was in practice instead veering in the direction of a reinforced centralism.[2] For autonomists and above all for separatists, the time for fine words and benevolent reforms was long past. The German victory brought their incarcerated leaders one immediate benefit, for it restored their liberty. This encouraged their expectations of another more decisive benefit, namely the realization of their objective. But that miracle never did come to pass.

The Alsatian autonomists were the first to discover that, as with a medal, there were two sides to the German victory. The fifteen leaders arrested at the beginning of the phoney war, then transferred to southern France, were handed over to the occupation authorities by Vichy. Every tendency of autonomism was represented within this little group, from the Christian right of a man such as Rossé to the Nazifying wing of one such as Bickler, but all aspired to an Alsace that would affirm its personality and enjoy some kind of sovereignty. There were some among the new masters who shared that aspiration, for example Ernst, the leader of the people of Alsace-Lorraine in the Reich, that is to say those who had opted for Germany in 1919. Ernst favoured the creation of a state of

Alsace-Lorraine, which would be part of a belt of vassal states on the western and southern flanks of the Reich, stretching from the Netherlands to Liechtenstein and taking in Luxemburg, Flanders, and German Switzerland. It was a dream of autonomy that had been shared by the Nazis of the Sudetenland and Austria, before becoming Mussert and Quisling.

However, what Hitler wanted was for these lands to be purely and simply incorporated into the Reich. Alsace was handed over to the Gauleiter of Baden, Robert Wagner, who perceived an advantage in proceeding by gradual stages. Having dispelled Ernst's illusions, he entrusted to him the task of using autonomism to rally the population to annexation. To this end, Ernst created the Alsatian auxiliary service (the *Elsässischer Hilfsdienst*: EHD) into which he enrolled the autonomist leaders. First, however, he got them to sign a message addressed to Hitler, in which they 'entreated him to integrate their native land with the Great Reich'. Some signed gladly, Bickler for one, as he had already been won over to Nazism. Others agreed to do so because the power of Germany was such that separatism no longer seemed viable. Others resigned themselves, not without a struggle, for instance Rossé and his Catholic autonomist friends, who wanted the Alsatian people to be consulted first, France's renunciation of Alsace to be recorded in a peace treaty, and also assurance from the Reich that it would respect religious liberties.[3] In the end they too signed: the German victory had made a strong impression, France was bound to lose Alsace and was already resigned to this. It was better to play along.

Nor were they alone in reacting in this way. Two-thirds of the 410000 odd Alsatian evacuees or refugees decided to return, while the remaining third chose to remain in the free zone.[4] The return of these people did not, of course, amount either to a plebiscite or to approval of German domination. After the trials of evacuation and living as refugees in southern France for almost a year, the prospect of returning home had many attractions. All the same, it did mean going to live in a region that everybody knew to be destined for annexation. The hope of some special status played its part, as did the return of Alsatian prisoners, conceded by Hitler so that the atmosphere was not sour from the outset.

The autonomists did, despite everything, still hope to turn the EHD into a force for the defence of Alsatian interests or even the framework for a future autonomous administration. In the meantime, Wagner assigned them to the immediate tasks: screening the returning evacuees and prisoners, providing assistance for the needy, and disseminating propaganda on the themes of French oppression and the new era that was dawning. The meetings held in the summer of 1940 were well attended, and the autonomist leaders conveyed the message efficiently. In the meantime, Wagner set up an administration that he filled with officials brought in from Baden.[5] In the autumn, the EHD was gradually absorbed into the Opferring, a Nazi organization for Alsace that was designed as a stage on the way to membership of the Nazi party. At the beginning of 1941, the EHD was dissolved and Wagner installed the autonomist leaders in his administration, in showy but solidly monitored positions. They were eventually admitted to the Nazi party and took German nationality in 1942.[6]

The autonomists thus became mere auxiliaries to the new masters. In August 1942 they even gave their approval to their young compatriots being incorporated into the German army (out of 130000 incorporated there were to be 36000 dead or lost without trace). Instead of safeguarding the Alsatian identity, they applied a policy of germanization and nazification that made the politics of first the German empire, then the French Republic seem admirably benign. It was a cruel blow, especially for the Catholic autonomists. They had fought to preserve the religious identity of Alsace against republican secularism. Now they were forced to look on helplessly as the Nazis struck repeatedly against Catholicism (such as suppressing the concordat, closing down Catholic schools and expelling Jesuits). Catholics and non-Catholics alike had to swallow a policy that was not content – as they had hoped – to 'de-Frenchify' Alsatian life by germanizing family and first names and banning the French language, but was designed to stamp out the very Alsatian dialect by forbidding its use in the administration.[7]

At the end of the day, they turned out to have served the Reich's interests well by encouraging a particular state of mind before the war and then, after the war, encouraging acquiescence or resignation, mostly through the hope of a measure of autonomy. The enrolment of two-thirds of the Alsatian population in various Nazi organizations is not particularly significant, for it testifies above all to the presence of very real pressure, in many cases compulsory membership, in particular for officials and those employed in certain sectors. The same applies to the Opferring, which boasted 169235 members in June 1942. But all the same, 30000 people had actually joined the Nazi party by 1944 and 20000 or more of them were probably

Alsatians.[8] Furthermore, 2100 Alsatians voluntarily joined the Wehrmacht and the Waffen-SS, even before obligatory military service was introduced.[9] According to German records, 20 per cent of the population were favourable to the Reich in 1941, and 10 per cent were still expecting a German victory in 1944.[10] But for most Alsatians the effect of this whole experience was to tighten their links with France.

The Flemish separatists welcomed the German victory with open arms, particularly those who favoured the idea of a Greater Netherlands. In Belgium, the head of the VNV, Staff de Clercq, who posed as a unifier, demanded that all the Flemings be gathered together into a single state. A little later he was to demand that French Flemish prisoners be liberated like the Belgian Flemings, and that French Flanders become 'the living space' of the Flemish people, following the expulsion of the population of French stock living north of the Somme and their replacement by Flemish colonizers.[11]

Abbé Gantois, ordered by Cardinal Liénart to choose between the priesthood and politics and later relieved of his priestly functions, also welcomed the conqueror. In a note that he had delivered to the occupation authorities even before the signing of the armistice, he represented northern France, down to the Somme, as a racially Germanic territory. He stressed the strategic desirability for Germany of a territory comprising Boulogne, Calais and Dunkirk, and pressed for the constitution of a federal Flemish state that would include, as well as Holland and Belgian Flanders, a 'state of Southern Flanders'.[12] At the end of the year he wrote directly to Hitler to plead once again for the integration of 'Southern Flanders' 'within a Dietschland' that would form 'the marches of Germanity and of the Reich in the West, against the sea and Roman influences'. He now recognized Hitler as 'the Führer of all Germans' and declared himself in favour of attachment: 'We are lower Germans and we wish to return to the Reich', still in the hope that, within it, the Flemings would enjoy some autonomy.[13]

By defeating France, Nazi Germany eliminated one obstacle on the road to separatism but immediately erected another no less obstructive: what the Nazis wanted was to absorb their Flemish cousins. In Lille, the military authorities had in mind a probable annexation of the region they were administrating (the guides distributed to their troops stressed its Germanic character) and they considered it to be in their interest to encourage a sense of regional identity that would separate it from the rest of France. They therefore authorized Gantois to revive his Flemish League of France and his bilingual monthly, *Le Lion des Flandres*. But they forbade him to spread any propaganda in favour of separatism or the idea of a 'Greater Netherlands', being convinced that it would have the effect of pushing the population a little closer to Gaullism and would provoke difficulties with Vichy. The German authorities in Brussels also forbade the VNV to propagate the solution of a 'Greater Netherlands' and the idea of a 'living space' in French Flanders.

Gantois wished to steer clear of the political field, partly so as to avoid breaking with his superiors and partly because political activism did not belong to his world of traditionalist values. He limited himself to complaining of the French 'yoke', dwelling on the shortcomings of the Republic (the death of the provinces, the falling birthrate, the social levelling, dechristianization) and of Latin France generally, using a racist turn of phrase akin to that of the Nazi press. At the same time, he was striving to reawaken the Flemish identity of the 'French Netherlands' and a sense of their belonging to the Germanic community. With the support of the occupying power, he created clubs, libraries, evening classes and even a Flemish Institute in Lille, which offered predictably slanted courses on the history of Flanders. He worked indefatigably organizing exhibitions of art, congresses on the Flemish culture and a youth movement ('La Jeunesse de la Flandre du Sud').

His efforts were rewarded with a measure of success. The 1942 congress on Flemish folklore drew 1200 participants; and the fortnight of Flemish art, that same year, attracted 12000 visitors.[14] The Germans represented all this as confirmation of their belief that regionalism was a better card to play than separatism, even if its political impact was more diffuse and less immediate. That is why they encouraged the creation of an illustrated magazine, *La Vie du Nord*, which 'apolitically' fostered regionalist feeling and set out to forge the identity of a minority exploited by the rest of France, adding a dose of racism and antisemitism.

The disparity between the relative power of attraction of this cultural regionalism and the insignificance of Flemish separatism was flagrant. Gantois's movement never involved more than a few hundred people, many of them 'notables', almost all from conservative Catholic circles. These were joined by a few activists who in 1943 broke away to form an organization in the service of the SS. In contrast to Alsace and to Brittany, there was no real linguistic basis, nor any problems of existence for the different communities, as there were in Belgium. Furthermore, Gantois's movement was of an archaic nature rarely found in organizations attracted by Nazism. The adoption of ethno-racist notions left untouched a bedrock of profoundly reactionary ideas, unconcerned with social discourse or even anticommunism, and petered out amid nostalgia for a patriarchal, rural, Catholic society.

The Breton leaders had long since overstepped the safeguards that held back a man such as Gantois. They had been won over by Nazism before the war and, as refugees in Germany, had there sought support for their cause. During the phoney war, the Abwehr, which had taken them under its wing, entrusted them with the preparation of radio broadcasts for Brittany and allowed them to select recruits from amongst the Breton prisoners. Their efforts were hampered by the limited numbers of soldiers taken prisoner, but when the Germans relaunched their attack, they were resumed.[15] Having picked out all the Breton prisoners, the autonomist leaders were allowed to select likely recruits before returning to France.[16]

Their return to Brittany in Germany's luggage vans heralded a brief period of high hopes and confusion. As the Germans were opposed to their immediately proclaiming a Breton state, on 23 July the separatists created a Breton National Council. They found the funds to produce a weekly paper, *L'Heure bretonne*, which made some impact when it held out the hope of release for Breton prisoners of war. They petitioned the occupation services to support the independence of Brittany – a national socialist Brittany, to stand 'sentinel' for the new order, in the west of the European continent. The climax of this period came when a communiqué from the German press appeared, announcing the appointment of a military governor of Brittany, a decision that was interpreted as recognition of a special future for the region.

In the grey-green ranks of the German Military Command there was much confusion. In some circles, the separatist cause aroused considerable sympathy, as – for instance – in the Abwehr. While it could not claim the priority that German or Germanic peoples deserved, it did, on the other hand escape some of the drawbacks that went with that priority, namely absorption into the Reich. In the MBF, the head of the administrative section, Werner Best, a member of the German Society for Celtic Studies, had for several years taken an interest in the Breton question and was firmly in favour of independence. A Brittany where German troops could be stationed would, along with Norway, form a base from which it would be possible to control the western seaboard of the continent, keeping Britain under surveillance once it had been defeated – with the added possibility of interfering in its internal affairs by exploiting the kinship of the Bretons, the Welsh and the Irish – and protecting the continent against the United States.[17]

Other services, following the example set by Ribbentrop, were more sensitive to the needs of the moment, in particular the importance of dealing tactfully with the French regime. Himmler himself, learning of the creation of the Breton National Council, let it be known that it was not in the interests of Germany to weaken Pétain. Not only did his priority go to the Germanic peoples, but he added a second argument, in direct opposition to Best's – an example of the malleability of ethno-racist reasoning! – namely, the danger that a Breton state might be attracted into the orbit of the Welsh and the Irish, thereby ultimately damaging the interests of Germany.[18]

After the false news of the appointment of a military governor for Brittany, which caused consternation in Vichy, some clarification seemed called for.[19] While the need to deal tactfully with France came first, there was no point in ruling out options for the future. Abetz was keen to reserve the possibility of detaching Brittany; it made sense to hold on to the separatism card. With Best's agreement, given grudgingly (he was to return to the attack in July 1941),[20] it was decided not to support the Breton movement officially, but to protect it secretly, mainly by preventing it from being bullied by the French state.

This was a bitter disappointment for the Breton leaders. It was at the expense of both them and the Flemings that the Reich pursued its tactical collaboration with Vichy. On top of this, other surprises were soon to come. As in northern France, the Germans were keeping several irons in the fire. They noted the weakness of the separatists' appeal: the population was affronted by their anglophobia and philonazism, and the Church publicly condemned them: a group of priests who had published a manifesto favouring separatism were reprimanded. Priests were forbidden to give absolution to the Breton nationalists.[21] As for the French administration, it harassed them in a very determined way and German protection could not always ward off the effects of it.

In the autumn of 1940, the occupiers took a twofold decision. The leadership of the PNB was purged; its historic leaders who were definitely too disruptive – they had just condemned Montoire – were pushed aside; Mordrel was even sent to live in Germany. The new leadership, grouped around the Delaporte brothers, was expected to guarantee a moderate and reliable orientation. At the same time, the Germans decided to fish in the richer waters of regionalism. They began to broadcast a weekly radio programme in Breton, and also supported the creation of a daily newspaper, *La Bretagne*. Its director, Fouéré, the young sub-prefect of Morlaix, accompanied by six other leaders of cultural movements, had approached them, in September 1940, asking for support for the teaching of the Breton language.[22] Fouéré, who was opposed to separatism but kept the bridges to it open, was himself a partisan of broad autonomy. With German support, he was able also to acquire *La Dépêche de Brest*, which gave him total circulation of close to 100000 copies.[23]

From the German point of view, the combination of separatists and autonomists was ideal. As the commander of the Rennes Staffel remarked: 'For a moderate organization to be effective, it is necessary for the extremist organization to continue to exist with a measure of support.'[24] Separatism remained an option for the future and, in the meantime, regionalism and autonomism, by cultivating the Breton identity, paved the way for a possible future separation, without clashing head-on with Vichy. The existence of separatism enhanced Fouéré's position. By attacking the government and above all the French administration but at the same time professing loyalty to Pétain, he appeared the least undesirable of the Bretons and one who should be managed with tact.

Fouéré managed to rally a number of 'notables' and to make himself the spokesman for the demands that were proliferating in Brittany in the wake of the defeat. Some were institutional demands, ranging from the creation of a Breton province to that of a Breton state and taking in fiscal autonomy and the 'bretonization' of the administration; other demands were cultural and gave rise to a plethora of organizations (a centre for Breton studies, an École Supérieure for Breton, a Celtic Institute, and Celtic clubs, etc.) designed to reanimate and propagate Breton culture. To prevent a slide towards the extremists, Vichy made a few concessions, the principal one being the creation, in October 1942, of a Comité Consultatif de Bretagne. This committee, composed of the representatives of many Breton associations, but not the PNB, secured the appointment of Breton civil servants, a Breton language test for certain administrative posts, and the creation of a number of agencies designed to defend Breton interests in the socio-economic domain, including an association for the protection of Breton workers in Germany. Quite clearly, this moderate autonomism, which made the most of the situation to promote its own interests, was extremely useful to the occupying power. Although discreet on the subject of collaboration, it supported German propaganda by chiming in with its own anglophobic, anticommunist and antisemitic tirades. After November 1942, the tendency represented by Fouéré inclined towards a neutralist position – Brittany for itself alone, you might say, paraphrasing Maurras – which at least presented the advantage of blocking the progress of the resistance.

As for the PNB, German policy was to keep it in a subordinate position, even when it became more moderate, going so far as to make a gesture in Vichy's direction by settling for a federal solution. Needless to say, its leaders passionately desired French politics to fail, both the politics of Vichy and the politics of the parties in Paris, of which they were no less distrustful.[25] Their only hope was that the Reich might change its mind and, in the meantime, to seize upon every opportunity to demonstrate their support for the new European order, persistently seeking recognition of a special status for Brittany. Although keen to participate in the struggle against communism, they rejected enrolment in the Legion of French Volunteers against Bolshevism and begged, in vain, to be allowed to form a unit of volunteers within the framework of the Waffen-SS.[26]

Belonging as it did to the category of parties merely tolerated, the PNB was not allowed to hold public meetings and this restricted its powers of attraction, which remained limited without being negligible. It could boast at least 3000 militants and a zone of influence which, thanks to its newspaper, comprised about 10 000 people.[27] In the summer of 1942, its leaders once again requested authorization for their party, once again without success. The SS was of the opinion that a change of policy would upset Laval, who was very suspicious of separatists. Abetz approved, underlining how dangerous it could be to reinforce the Catholic element in Europe. Besides, it seemed to him pointless to use Breton independence to weaken France, given the state in which the latter already found itself.[28]

In November 1942 the separatists experienced another surge of hope when the free zone was occupied. However, the detestable Vichy–Berlin link was still not broken and continued to block a Rennes–Berlin axis. From the spring of 1943 on, most of the PNB leaders swung towards neutralism and sought to dissociate their struggle from Germany's. A minority, led by Célestin Lainé, the head of the party's combat group, opted for total commitment. Following the assassination of Abbé Perrot in 1943, it set up the Perrot unit – the Bezen Perrot – a militia of SD auxiliaries which Lainé declared to be 'the first armed Breton unit since the Chouan army was dispersed'.[29] At the liberation, these extremists departed in the luggage vans that had brought them.

All things considered, the Germans exploited the autonomist and separatist faultlines only to a limited degree. This was not because it might have been in their interests to do so (that is, to exploit separatist faultlines only to a limited degree), but because for them the priority was to keep Vichy sweet, and for this a price had to be paid. They also had to bear in mind the interests of other friendly or allied states. When, in the autumn of 1941, the military indicated the possibility of action in concert with the Basque autonomists, the embassy counselled prudence for fear of damaging relations with Madrid.[30] As for Corsica, the year of Italian occupation, from November 1942 to October 1943, was not long enough to exploit more than a handful of supporters amongst Rocca's former partisans. There remained the nationalists of North Africa, whom Weygand kept an eye on and who, for their part, were distrustful of Italy's colonial ambitions. After November 1942, the Germans tried to use them against the Anglo-Saxons, with no more than very mediocre results, finding at most support from a fraction of the Néo-Destour in Tunisia, while Bourguiba remained aloof.

24

The Paris Fronde

ALTHOUGH the occupiers were measured in their support of the Breton and the Flemish separatists, in the very capital of France they actively encouraged a political opposition to Vichy. In 1941, a whole collection of parties were strutting on the Paris stage, flanked by men of letters, all in favour of collaboration and spurring on the government. At the time of the débâcle, Weygand had had the fearful vision of a Commune. As in 1871, the capital would resist the government that had departed to the provinces. However, this time, far from attracting a group of 'patriotic diehards', Paris, once invaded, became home to men and groups leading the way into collaboration, who had much more in common with the Fronde than the Commune – the Fronde being a revolt of vassals who broke with neither the regime nor its leader.

This body of opposition did not emerge immediately after the defeat. It took shape gradually, drawing its support from a number of quarters and encouraged by the occupying power, which was keen to infiltrate its own policies into French society by any means or channels available. No sooner were they installed than Abetz and Propaganda-Abteilung entered into competition in their efforts to relaunch the press, making the most of the evacuation of most of the major newspapers, with a view to remodelling the media scene: here installing new directorial teams or finding a *modus vivendi* with existing newspaper proprietors, there creating periodicals whose contents and tone were carefully designed to reach a wide variety of circles (*Aujourd'hui, La Vie industrielle, Les Nouveaux Temps, La France au travail, La Gerbe*, etc.).

Where politics were concerned, Abetz had plenty of elbow room. He set out to locate past contacts and chatted up other people who interested him. If they were prisoners of war, he got them released: Bucard, for example, interned in Switzerland, and Benoist-Méchin, Gustave Bonvoisin, Marcel Braibant, Brasillach, Darquier de Pellepoix, Marion and Roger de Saivre.[1] In Paris he found, as well as communists, a whole throng of agitators from the extreme right. Some owed him their freedom – Boissel, for instance, who had been found guilty of Hitlerian activities. Others hastened to approach him. Costantini, who wanted a declaration of war against England and offered to form a legion of airmen, and Deloncle, the head of the Cagoule, who seemed to regard the defeat simply as an opening for a career befitting his conspiratorial talents.

Abetz had scant interest in these small groups of dubious reputation and disorganized activity with their strong-arm tactics against Jewish businesses, clashes between rival gangs, internal rifts, and mutual denunciations to the Germans. The obscure Christian Message, head of the PNSF (the French National Socialist Party), who provoked clashes with the police and whose law and order gangs (black uniforms adorned with skulls) assumed the right to keep order not only in the streets but even in people's homes,[2] ended up in prison, having exceeded the patience of the occupiers. Equally obscure at the time was Robert Hersant, head of the Jeune Front, a subsidiary of Clementi's PFNC. Having distinguished himself by smashing the windows of Jewish shops in the Champs Elysées, he was denounced by one of his own militants whom he had ticked off for his Nazi talk: 'I don't want any Germans or Boches around me. I make use of Germans, but I detest them.'[3] Soon after this, Hersant left Clementi to take over the direction of the Centre Maréchal Pétain in Brévannes, an offshoot of Vichy's Secrétariat de la Jeunesse. Here, he kept his distance from the Paris scene, but did not abandon collaboration. In the summer of 1941 he was busy organizing a charity gala for the liberated prisoners of war, a gala 'placed under the sign of collaboration', as his assistant Balestre – a former hope of Lecache's LICA, who was to enlist in the Waffen-SS in 1943 – was careful to point out, when he wrote inviting the German services to attend.[4]

But Abetz was out to catch bigger fish in his nets. He did not need to put out many signs or to issue many invitations. Men simply came to him either out of curiosity or hoping to promote their interests. Marquet was one, who told the SS, newly arrived in Paris, that the government was inadequate, Pétain too old, Laval too parliamentary, and Vichy full of Jews.[5] Outside the government the cohort of the discontented was swelling daily. Flandin, who had returned to the occupied zone, made contact with the embassy and expressed his doubts about the government, adding incidentally that he had advised Laval to take measures against the Jews and the freemasons. In his view, France and Germany had two common enemies: Russia, which sooner or later would march on the West, and America, the great economic rival of the future. Europe needed to bury its quarrels and make common cause, starting by eliminating England from the continent and the Mediterranean, then by designating particular spheres of influence: the eastern Mediterranean for Italy, the western Mediterranean and North Africa for France, and central and Danubian Europe for Germany. Between these spheres of influence, economic cooperation would be desirable, even going so far as customs and economic union.[6] Soon after this, those close to the former president of the Council, with the aid of Propaganda-Abteilung, launched a newspaper for business circles, *La Vie industrielle.*

The organizers of the plan for a single party, Déat and Bergery, were also looking towards Paris, especially after Pétain had refused to consider the idea. Abetz, learning of their dissatisfaction, signalled to them: here was a fine chance to set up a left-wing opposition! Déat was encouraged by the managers of *L'Œuvre,* who wanted it to reappear in Paris and to entrust the direction of the paper to him. Unlike Bergery, he decided he would return to the capital, with the blessing of Laval, whom he had regarded as his political mentor since his arrival in Vichy and whose actions he would now support in his newspaper, in the hope of entering the government when there was a reshuffle. In the meantime, much to the satisfaction of Abetz, he took on the role of an effective left-wing opponent, taking up the defence of parliamentary representatives, mayors and teachers, virulently attacking the 'little white terror' of the Church, the military and the followers of Maurras, and firmly pleading the cause of collaboration.

Marquet, who was dropped from the government in September, took the same road. If Déat had revived *L'Œuvre,* he would revive *Le Petit Parisien,* whose proprietors were likewise seeking a protector. But hardly were they in business than Marquet's team was pushed aside by Propaganda-Abteilung and replaced by followers of Doriot, led by Claude Jeantet. Doriot, who professed to be 'the Marshal's man', was also thinking that he ought to be in Paris. Even if not authorized to revive his party,[7] he could create a newspaper. Abetz, who entertained many misgivings where he was concerned and under no circumstances wished for a political force to be present in both zones at once, was nevertheless afraid of pushing him into the opposite camp. So he allowed him to launch *Le Cri du peuple* with funding from Pétain's office.[8]

In the autumn of 1940, in a Paris where intrigues were flourishing whatever the season, the idea of a gathering of forces was making headway amongst men who disapproved of Vichy's internal policies while applauding its foreign policy. That gathering would carry weight with the Germans and above all with the government, parked the other side of the demarcation line. Nobody was at this point considering trying to unseat it, not even Déat, whose political future depended on Laval. To all of them, the reassurance that Pétain represented seemed indispensable: without it they would be excluded from the game that pivoted on him and would be seen as creatures of the occupier. On 13 October, Portmann, a senator and Flandin's right-hand man, beat a path to the embassy to explain that a group of men of note – Flandin, Marquet, Déat and Doriot – wished to establish a relationship with the population and find a basis for political action.[9] Because of the ban on all political activity ordered by the military, those involved were thinking of using the umbrella of a social aid organization, Winter Assistance, for example. Abetz promptly gave his agreement:[10] here was his chance to form a reserve team to be kept in waiting in the corridors of power for later use. On 19 October, the circle of rebels met at the headquarters of the PPF. The moderate right and the moderate left predominated, with Doriot and his men in the minority. As well as friends of Flandin, who was himself absent, and former neo-socialists grouped around Déat, it included leaders of former veterans' associations (Goy and Rivollet), trade unionists (Bureau, Guireau and Delmas), socialists (Paul Faure and Spinasse), Chateau and a number of pacifists, Benoit-Méchin and Barthélémy, who was representing Doriot.[11] Laval who was always on the lookout for followers and wanting a finger in every pie, was keeping an eye on the operation and obtained approval for the project from Pétain.[12] On 5 November, General La Laurencie announced the creation of the Entr'aide d'Hiver, under the wing of the Secours National.

But no sooner had Montoire been celebrated than the sacking of Laval upset everything. Flandin who was now in the government, was regarded as a defector, if not a traitor. Doriot, who was more than ever the 'Marshal's man', covertly approved of the dismissal of the wily Auvergnat. Déat was furious. He had believed the time for a ministerial shuffle was at hand and had precipitated the crisis by his articles (for which he was briefly imprisoned) and now the last bridge to Vichy was collapsing. Laval, who allowed Abetz to bring him back to Paris, found himself drawn closer to Déat by misfortune. The two men railed against Pétain and, with the embassy abetting by spreading false rumours, convinced themselves that the episode represented a national catastrophe. They spread the word that the Germans had prepared peace terms that exceeded all hopes: the sole loss of Alsace-Lorraine, no war indemnity apart from the occupation costs, an economic agreement, a guarantee for the African empire; and all this had been lost through the stupidity and irresponsibility of the men of Vichy![13]

Abetz had been struck by the ease with which Laval had been ousted: the man was a lone wolf. He accordingly encouraged Déat to form a political movement to support him. At the same time, in conformity with the directive to foster division, he got ready to grant authorization to other political parties. On 7 January, he explained to the other occupation services that it was necessary to attract men favourable to Germany and to show that collaboration was not unpopular. He mentioned Boissel, Bucard, Clémenti, Darquier de Pellepoix, Deloncle, Costantini and Delaunay, recommending 'the greatest reserve' towards Doriot, on account of his links with Vichy.[14] Neither Laval nor Déat were mentioned: after all, the whole point was to create some rivals to oppose them.

Déat was very disappointed when Abetz told him that the movement that he was preparing would have no monopoly. Reluctantly he accepted the ambassador's explanations: 'As I understood it, the Germans are engaged in some political gardening, to see if anything will grow. And Abetz appears to believe that one day all this might be federated and joined together.'[15] He nevertheless threw himself into advancing his own cause. The circle of those involved remained more or less the same as in the preceding autumn, minus the Flandinists and the Doriotists but plus Deloncle, whom nobody had wanted then and who, true to form, was toying with the idea of a violent coup if the government refused to listen to reason.[16]

What is rarely known is that Laval played a central role in the birth of the future movement. He approved of the idea, reckoning that it would put pressure on Vichy and convince the Germans that collaboration enjoyed popular support. Step by step, he pursued its realization, either personally or through his faithful follower, Cathala.[17] Achenbach attributed to him not only the decision to found the movement but also the intention to become its leader.[18] At this time, it was designed as an organization that would have to support him after his return to government (considered to be imminent), not as an opposition party in the occupied zone, which is what it later became. The wily Auvergnat had a plan up his sleeve: Deloncle would found a 'Militia' designed to protect him, Laval. That is why he badgered Déat to name the movement the 'Popular Legion'.[19] He wanted a praetorian guard to protect him from nasty surprises. This explains the presence of Deloncle, which cast a chill over the former leftists. When he eventually did create the Milice in 1943, Laval, who was still distrustful of the parties and still keen on an armed bodyguard, was simply pursuing the same line.

In early February, the creation of the Rassemblement National Populaire was announced. Its board of directors comprised Cathala, Déat, Deloncle and his lieutenants Fontenoy and Vanor, Goy, the leader of the largest veterans' association, and the trade unionist Perrot. But a few days later some of these men withdrew.[20] For Perrot and his friends, associating with Deloncle definitely posed a problem. Cathala and others close to Laval withdrew for a different reason. Abetz had just told Laval, whose hopes had still been high at the end of January, that he should no longer count on returning to the government. Laval immediately distanced himself: left outside the government, his credit with Pétain and with the people generally could only be damaged by association with a movement limited to the occupied zone which, through its criticisms of Vichy, would be taken for an agent of the occupying power. He nevertheless encouraged Déat to press on, bringing him 'a few hundred thousand francs' collected from his contacts; subsequently he intimated that he himself might speak at some public demonstration and occasionally he sported the party badge.[21] After all, one advantage of the new party was that it made him look like a moderate alternative to it. To Déat, who remained undismayed, Fontenoy confided his suspicion that 'sheltered by the RNP and without committing himself openly, Laval was playing with Vichy, taking now the role of arsonist, now that of firefighter'.[22] All this suited Abetz: Laval's semi-retreat was presenting Vichy with the threat of a counter-government, just as Hitler had demanded.

Early in 1941, Paris was composed of a number of circles all of which depended on the support or favour of the occupier. At the centre was Abetz's finest catch, Laval, whose presence in Paris, even before Déat's in Vichy in 1944, showed that one could come and go between the two capitals and that it was not only in the case of marginal figures that the occupiers figured large in political calculations. Laval put in an appearance at the more important functions in collaborationist Paris, for instance at the opening of the 'La France européenne' exhibition, and the send-off ceremony for the LVF in August, at which he and Déat were both wounded. But he spent most of his time spinning his spider's web, keeping in touch with everybody, listening, making arrangements and manipulating.

Abetz loyally supported him and several times tried to get him back into the government. But he was held back by the directives of his superiors and the logic of his own politics. Once Darlan had been received by Hitler and seemed to fit the bill, Laval became less valuable. During the summer of 1941, the ambassador, who was expecting a rapid victory in Russia, tried to realign the teams in Paris and Vichy in preparation for an imminent shift of operations to the West and France's hoped-for participation in the conflict. In the two-headed government that he favoured, led by Laval (Foreign Affairs and the Interior) and Darlan (the Armed Forces), there would be Déat (National Education), Luchaire (Press and Information), Georges Bonnet (Finance), Marquet (Public Works), Pucheu (Economy), Barnaud and Lehideux in their current posts, Marion (Propaganda), and Doriot (Jewish questions).[23] Laval had to be patient until the following spring. He spent this new period in the wilderness as he had spent the last one before the war – in frustration and convinced that others were missing opportunities that he could have seized. But what could he do on his own? He was as dependent on German support as the party leaders were, and he shared their dilemma. He could only hope for power if Vichy displeased the Germans or if the situation deteriorated: in other words only if he took the risk of putting himself even more under the control of the occupying power.

Laval was surrounded by erstwhile parliamentary representatives, several of whom had taken part in the consultations of the autumn of 1940, who wanted no public positions but sometimes wrote in the Paris press, and above all maintained excellent relations with the embassy, at least up until 1942. Several ministers of the defunct Republic were in this position. Fernand Bouisson, a dissident socialist, former president of the Chamber of Deputies, fleetingly president of the Council in 1935, and one of the managers of *L'Œuvre*, wanted to revive parliamentarianism in Vichy, with the support of the Nazis. At the beginning of December 1940 he, along with Laval and the embassy, was active in planning a new government, to include Paul Faure, Flandin and Déat.[24] Marquet, who had been present at the founding of the RNP but, like those close to Laval, had then distanced himself, created a 'centre de propagande français pour la reconstruction européenne' (a centre of French propaganda for European reconstruction) in Bordeaux, and meanwhile kept in touch with his Paris contacts. The former Minister for Foreign Affairs, Georges Bonnet who was very much at home at the embassy, where he lunched on 11 March 1941 in the company of Laval, Déat and Scapini, and later attended a reception in honour of Göring on 2 December 1941 accompanied in particular by Marquet,[25] was held in high enough esteem by Abetz to be included in his plan for a government in the summer of 1941. Bonnet kept up his relations with Déat and Laval with whom he again met, for example in December 1941 at a breakfast at the Ritz hosted by Achenbach, at which Laval made them all laugh with anecdotes about the Senate's Jews and freemasons.[26]

Another minister of the defunct Republic was Anatole de Monzie, who wrote to Brinon on 5 November 1940, inviting him to lunch, along with Abetz, in terms that betrayed his sensitivity to the infraction of the code: 'I asked M. Achenbach to sound out M. Abetz about a meal in my home. I said "in my home", being anxious to continue our cordial relations, initiated under your auspices, on the same personal footing.'[27] Monzie had plans for intellectual collaboration centred on the *Encyclopédie française*, the publication of which he had been directing for years. He agreed with Déat that the French people 'would be won over to collaboration by a change of line in internal politics'.[28] He did not push himself forward too much in public, but saw to it that he remained welcome at the embassy, publishing his book *Ci-devant* (Flammarion 1941) in consultation with embassy staff.[29] At the turn of 1942, foreseeing a return to power for Laval, he was seen again, alongside Bonnet and Montigny, in meetings of former parliamentary representatives organized by Déat, who was now relieved of Deloncle's presence, to consider the convocation of a National Assembly in the event of Pétain's death.[30] In November 1943, with the outcome of the war now obvious he called upon Pétain to convoke the National Assembly and bring about 'internal pacification through a return to the normal life of a Republic'.[31]

Other members of this circle included a few deputies who were supporters of Flandin or Caillaux, chief among them Montigny and

Roche. Montigny was frequently seen at the embassy, where he was invited along with Brinon on 21 April 1941, and then again on 17 July, with Monzie. Roche was a member of the RNP's commission on propaganda and organization at the beginning of February 1941; he then distanced himself but remained in contact with Déat. In November 1941, he discussed drawing up a governmental list with him.[32] All these former parliamentary representatives, who had been ardently pro-Munich and who found Vichy too reactionary, were anxious to remain in the game, but without taking too many risks. Their behaviour was yet another sign of the atmosphere of those first two years that encouraged many French people to plan for the future bearing the Germans carefully in mind.

The circle of the supporters of collaboration, for its part, took centre stage in the full limelight. Obviously, the most in view were the parties granted authorization by the occupying power: Le Feu and the Groupe Collaboration in January 1941, the RNP and Constantini's Ligue Française in February, Boissel's Front Franc in April, and Bucard's Francism in May. Doriot's PPF, which was initially merely tolerated, did not gain authorization until the autumn. Other groups continued to exist on suffrance, the PNB for example, Pétanist organizations such as the Amis du Maréchal, with a following centred in the Bordeaux and Rouen regions, and Les Jeunes du Maréchal.

The leaders of these groups chose to conduct their political activities under the control of the occupying power, that is to say initially the military authorities, then, from 1942 on, the SS. Their activities were subjected to a series of conditions. They had to request permission for every public event, for the wearing of uniforms, and for processions and parades. Tricolor flags and pennants were tolerated indoors, but singing or playing the *Marseillaise* was prohibited absolutely.[33] The Germans did not want to risk things slipping out of control or to provide them with the means of winning popularity cheaply, by playing on French nationalism. They were also concerned not to give these parties any open support, both so as not to lower them in public opinion and in order not to be under any obligation to them. Members of the occupation services were under orders not to take part, except in the line of duty, in any political meetings or functions organized by the collaborationists.[34]

In return for those constraints and a finicky censorship, the political groups were free to try to whip up support, recruit followers and organize. But to what end? Political competition went round in circles on this artificial stage, given that both elections and any attempt at a coup were ruled out. Only Pétain and the occupying authorities held the keys to the accession of power. All the Paris leaders could do was demonstrate, by rallying as much support as possible, that they were the people to do business with, that their rightful place was in the government, and that it was in the Germans' interest to deal generously with France.

When they launched themselves into these activities, they were well aware of being a minority in the country. On the day of Montoire, Déat scribbled in his diary: 'The Parisians, excited by the English radio, were making fools of themselves at full blast.'[35] In January 1941, Doriot wrote that 'reforming the public mind' would be 'a long and difficult process', and put his finger on the difficulty: 'Dragging an old democratic country into an authoritarian regime is not an easy matter. No more is changing France's external orientation.'[36] François Mauriac who, on 26 February 1941, was dining with Fernandez and Drieu La Rochelle, noted: 'They are afraid, speak of the reprisals that they are risking in the event of defeat, and consider themselves heroes.'[37]

In these mixed circles, professional leaders of tiny groups seeking stable partners rubbed shoulders with opportunists and fanatics, but also with men not moved by base motives. Their most generally shared characteristic was their position as outsiders, men in the minority, in many cases as a result of clashing with some political family and also of mounting frustration in the period immediately before the war, when their aspirations and hopes had been enormously stimulated by the concurrent events of the French crisis and the fascist successes. Their rejection of the *ancien régime* and their instinct to engage in a politico-ideological vendetta was compounded by their cast of mind, which was that of political professionals who would under no circumstances settle for retreat or abstention. Although aware of the attitude of most of their compatriots, these men had not given up hope of making them see reason, if necessary, by force. It was an attitude that progressively became more deeply rooted, as in fact it also did for Pétain, who in August 1941 declared that he would save the French from themselves.

The embassy men were prepared to indulge and cajole their pets, without being too fussy about who they were. They gave considerable support to Delaunay, a moderate former deputy, now leader of the Feu movement, whose ambition was to get the French to understand their role in the new Europe, 'just as the Bretons have understood theirs in France'.[38] Abetz found the fellow a bit confused but, after all, he was, as he put it, fanatically bound in the right direction,[39] meaning that he was fully prepared for France to become a satellite. Le Feu was the first party to be granted authorization and was launched with a prodigious expenditure of propaganda, but it was soon to fizzle out. After only a few months, its leader, quite exceptionally, retired from politics.

Abetz and Achenbach kept Déat's hopes boosted by conjuring up the image of a Hitler who was interested in his movement and by talk of the famous struggle between different tendencies within the Nazi regime, a struggle in which it was important to take part in order to orientate the future. In reality, Hitler took a very distant view of his supporters in Paris, whom he regarded with cynicism and scorn. If ever he spoke of them it was with a mixture of astonishment at an attitude that he could not understand, deep-seated distrust of the French as a whole, and delight at the thought that these men were detested, impotent and dependent upon his protection.[40] He never ascribed the slightest importance to them and certainly never considered raising them to power so long as Pétain, Darlan and Laval played their parts satisfactorily. They were no more than tools, and weak ones at that, for achieving his objectives: namely, to divide the French and to soften up Vichy.

It should be pointed out that the leaders in Paris entered into the Germans' game all the more eagerly given that they did not believe the situation in Vichy to be a closed one. To all of them, Pétain's personal legitimacy seemed essential: every one of them claimed the Marshal's support. The ban on the Légion Française de Combattants in the occupied zone afforded them a space that they could claim to fill as supporters of Pétain, even as they continued to criticize his government. There was no doubt that their activities caused plenty of teeth to gnash in Vichy. The regime, bent on authority, could tolerate only those who fell into line and detested rebels of whatever persuasion. Massively drawn from the ranks of the 'notables' as it was, it looked down upon men without any social standing such as the former communist Doriot and even Professor Déat, let alone the rest of them. In Pétain's eyes, these men were harmful to the unity of the country, contravening the authority of his government and challenging his own claims to know best and to lead. They were bringing back all that political debate that he had been hoping to eliminate in order to heal France.

However, any image of fierce antagonism stems from a false perspective. Relations between the two capitals were in fact a tissue of rivalry and complicity. There was more to Paris than Déat; other party leaders were made welcome in Vichy, occasionally received by Pétain or one of his ministers, and benefited from both facilities and funding. In November 1941, Darlan gave authorization for the Groupe Collaboration to operate in the free zone, although the activities of all the political parties had been banned there since the summer. He also opened up first the free zone, then North Africa, to recruitment for the LVF, then, at the beginning of 1942, began to provide it with funding.[41] Pétain, Darlan and the various ministries, in particular the Ministry for Information, were regularly slipping sealed envelopes to Bucard, Clémenti, Deloncle and Doriot. Following Laval's return to power, there was a gush of funds for the RNP, but without drying up those for the rest, for Laval was prone to make liberal use of financial manipulation.[42]

The fact was that disagreements did not affect principles. Pétain was indicating the right path, the path of the national revolution and collaboration. But these principles were sometimes badly applied or converted into misguided measures. The Paris leaders were rivals, not opponents, extremists of Pétainism, not anti-Pétainists. Even in foreign policy, they took more or less the same line. Although they were more aggressive towards the Anglo-Saxons and from time to time pressed for the need to recover the dissident colonies, giving as good as they got, they never demanded war against England until November 1942, the point at which they began to press for a military alliance with the occupier. Pétain, Darlan and Laval would no doubt have been delighted to wring their necks, or at least some of them. But they were careful to avoid any official condemnation that might rebound against themselves. They limited themselves to a policy of corruption and division, playing their rivals off one against another: in 1941, Bucard and Doriot against Déat; the following year, when Laval was back in power, all the parties against Doriot. In these circumstances, the party leaders did not see themselves as impotent protégés of the occupier, despite the fact that their dependence steadily increased owing to their lack of popular support and the fact that Vichy kept the door that interested them well and truly closed.

Abetz was to devote all his energies to his political gardening, to return to Déat's expression. The Paris scene, a mixture of parties and journalists, arranged itself in the traditional pattern, with a left, a centre and a right. But it was a truncated scene, shrunken and preoriented: you had to stand firm for collaboration in external policies and agree to modulate your attacks against Vichy, dancing to the tune of the embassy and the military censorship. Yet within these limitations, it presented a remarkable diversity, unmatched anywhere else in Nazi Europe. Collaborationism incorporated every pre-war political family, with the notable exceptions of the radicals and the Christian Democrats, and each produced a team, however small, to elaborate a discourse based on its own heritage, which it naturally distorted but did so according to a certain law of distortion, so to speak, which made it possible still to recognize its point of departure and which prepared the route for its evolution. That initial plurality testified to the degree to which the French political world had been shaken in the course of the 1930s and by the shock of the defeat.

In every quarter the arguments for collaboration rested upon the idea that adaptation was both necessary and inevitable. Thereafter, four main themes were hammered home, with the emphasis varying from one current of thought to another, as follows. First, political collaboration was in the national interest: France was bound to collaborate in its own interest, so this collaboration could be identified with traditional nationalism. Second, collaboration was an effective means in the struggle against common enemies, Jews or communists, which isolated nations and could not fight effectively. Third, collaboration was a factor of peace: a desire to bring to an end the cycle of Franco-German wars and to establish concord between neighbours. Fourth, collaboration was the way to construct a new Europe which was essential in order to take on intercontinental competition and safeguard the standing and civilization of Europe.

To start with, it was the argument of national interest, definitely distinct from the interests of the occupier, that tended to predominate. Then what came to the fore was the idea that the interests of both sides in fact coincided and that this meant joining forces against common enemies. At this point, a 'European' argument, overlapping with Nazi propaganda, became more and more general, whereas in the early days this argument had seemed more of an extension of a pre-war theme particularly favoured on the left and in the centre. This Europe was for the time being a negative community, and the principles of its future organization were left somewhat nebulous by propaganda, until such time as victory afforded Hitler total freedom of manoeuvre.[43]

25

Abetz's left wing

IN Abetz's garden the flowerbed on the left was small, but it boasted a fine variety of plants. The men to be found there all rejected a sweeping condemnation of the past and likewise Vichy's verdict on where the responsibility for the defeat lay. The orientation of the new regime largely accounted for their commitment. It revolted them to the point of driving them beneath the occupier's umbrella and, what was more, made them feel that they were remaining loyal to their republicanism, or at least to their earlier commitment to peace and to forging closer ties with Germany. Here, as elsewhere, it was a loyalty and a continuity that were largely spurious: the defeat had precipitated a revision of values.

Criticism of Vichy was harsh and incisive, yet limited. Former men of the left declared their allegiance to Pétain, stressed the need for the national revolution and collaboration, and expressed their longing for an authoritarian regime founded upon one great popular party that would introduce profound changes. Even if they criticized the Labour Charter, they approved of its principles, the prohibition of strikes and lock-outs, the one-union system and the right to work. They became the heralds of a national socialism that rejected Marxism, drawing its inspiration from pre-Marxist or anti-Marxist thinkers.

Characterized by a denunciation of nationalism and attached to the idea of an economic organization of the continent, these circles were ready to swallow the occupiers' bait of European propaganda: an organized, regulated Europe as dreamed of by both Briand and Jaurès and brought into being by Nazi Germany; a functional unification that would accommodate peace and mutual respect between the partners by establishing 'such a network of interdependence that this would seem the very condition of each nation's independence'.[1]

Nazism represented the avant-garde of a historical transformation increasingly perceived on all sides to be essential. 'Through its anticapitalist and popular nature, the revolution that brought forth the new Germany had already spilled over beyond its national framework; it had taken on a universal meaning, and in the first instance a European meaning.'[2] These men credited the conqueror's regime with not only social policies and anticapitalism, but also anticlericalism if not antichristianism, and devotion to the community. Misconceptions about Hitler ran riot in this left-wing minority. Alongside the military genius respected by Vichy, and the artistic genius and great-hearted patron of the arts dear to Cocteau, here they celebrated the man of the people, the socialist, the architect of Europe. On 29 June 1940, Déat incredulously noted in his diary: 'Chateau says that the Führer is staying in Paris in rue Jean-Goujon, in an unpretentious hotel where he is paying for his own room.'

Hardly surprisingly, it was this leftist band that was Abetz's favourite. Nothing could delight him more than the quarrels going on between the two sides of the demarcation line over where responsibility for the defeat lay, with one side blaming the schoolteachers, the other the military. Here were men who would be useful in detaching the people from the influence of Vichy and, it was to be hoped, turning them against it. And their pacifism, their condemnation of nationalism and their lack of enthusiasm for military might anticipated his own plan for a France that would turn itself into a satellite of its own accord. His support of people who persisted in harking back to the Republic and socialism frequently irritated the other German services, which were always ready to accuse the embassy of rampant liberalism without seeing how effective its policies were, in the first two years at least.

Since the autumn of 1940, Déat had stood at a crossroads amid these circles. But his association with Deloncle scattered those who had gathered round him. The former men of the left may have held similar views, shared a common political past and the same socio-professional profile – they were teachers, journalists and trade unionists – but there remained quite a few differences between them, connected with how long ago they had broken away and above all stemming from the ongoing effects of the fragmentation of the French left.

We need not linger over the long-standing wholehearted pacifists, individualists with little taste for organization but plenty for the sound of their own voices, always convinced that they were in the right. They were to be found with *Aujourd'hui* which was launched in September 1940 under the direction of Henri Jeanson, formerly on the *Canard enchaîné*, who had been imprisoned for pacifism during the phoney war and was now condemning reactionary Vichy and arguing for collaboration with Nazi Germany, which had taken the lead in the 'crusade of emanicipation for the peoples of Europe'.[3] Jeanson was soon to be sacked and even imprisoned: there was no place for a *Canard* substitute in the new landscape. However, the other pacifists continued to write, self-righteous to the last, in organs of the collaborationist left, which were distinguished by the signatures of Victor Marguerite (who died in 1942), René Guérin, Georges Pioch, Félicien Challaye, Marcelle Capy and Robert Jospin.

The trade unionists were represented by a group of men repelled by the Vichyism of Belin and the bulk of the former *Syndicats* tendency. These were more critical of the new regime, more explicitly committed to collaborationism, and determined to operate in the occupied zone.[4] *L'Atelier*, which appeared at the beginning of December 1940, provided them with a mouthpiece, even if this 'French working weekly' was massively funded by the embassy and, to a lesser extent, by Eugène Schueller, who occasionally also wrote for it.[5] Around the directors of the paper, Gabriel Lafaye and René Mesnard, a team was formed composed of trade unionists from the old CGT, some of whom were quite well known: Georges Dumoulin, Aimé Rey, Pierre Vigne, Marcel Roy, Gaston Guiraud and Marcel Lapierre.

This group proclaimed its loyalty to 'socialism' and demanded the construction of a 'community-based state, a true association of producers, through their respective organizations the co-owners of property, co-participants in the organization of production, and co-beneficiaries in the distribution of products'.[6] It committed itself early and deeply to collaboration, motivated by a concern not to lose ground, stimulated by a profound antiliberalism that made it easy to adopt corporatist and authoritarian concepts, and spurred on by pacifism and a virulent anticommunism. Its members made much of the fact that Jaurès had been a supporter of Franco-German reconciliation and took the 'socialism' of Nazism extremely seriously. Aimé Rey, a long-standing trade unionist went into raptures over a 'popular, anticapitalist and socialist [Germany] that had derived from its faith a military and revolutionary strength that astonishes the whole world'. For him, 'the realization of socialism in Europe is conditional upon collaboration between German and French popular and anticapitalist movements'.[7] In March 1941, a delegation led by Dumoulin went to Germany on a fact-finding trip organized by the embassy, which was keen to encourage the recruitment of volunteer workers. On their return, the trade unionists sang the praises of the impeccable cloakrooms and washrooms, the roomy and comfortable canteens, and the organization of leisure and recreation.[8]

In April 1941, this group set up the Centre Syndicaliste de Propagande (CSP), joined most notably by Georges Albertini, a socialist and trade-unionist professor and member of the 'Redressement' tendency. Soon afterwards the CSP attached itself to the RNP, bringing some 800 members.[9] Recruitment among workers had proved a failure. In June 1941, Dumoulin, who had just completed a propaganda tour, noted: 'The grassroots are hostile, indifferent or refractory.'[10] His team met with more success higher up the social ladder, particularly among local leaders of the former CGT. The leaders of fifteen or so federations wrote for the paper, which initially, in July 1941, published 21000 copies, 64 per cent of which were remaindered, then between 15000 and 18000 copies.[11] In March 1944, the CSP managed to assemble 685 delegates for a national conference. They came from seventy departments; most were the chairmen of local trade unions, and about half the major departmental unions were represented.[12] This gives an idea of how very limited, albeit not negligible at the level of the local leaders, the influence of this new-look trade unionism was, once it had made peace with the authorities in the name of organization, and with Nazi Germany in the interests of 'socialist' and anticommunist reconstruction.

Several groups split off from the SFIO, particularly those with a Paul-Faurist tendency. Paul Faure limited himself to a discreet role of influence and intercession, holding conciliatory talks in both Paris and Vichy and, above all, urging Pétain to achieve 'sacred union', and halt 'partisan struggles, social conflicts, and religious and philosophical quarrels', 'for the time that it takes, in so far as is possible, to ensure the salvation and independence of our country'.[13] A number of his old supporters wanted to act out in the open, and in Paris. They were headed by Francis Desphelippon, who had helped with the preparations for setting up the RNP, then distanced himself with the blessing of Laval, who was keeping a fatherly eye on him.[14] Shortly afterwards, assisted by René Chateau, a pacifist, radical deputy and member of the League of Human Rights, and Paul Rives, a socialist deputy, he formed a group with a name very much in tune with the times, France-Europe, for which he tried to get embassy recognition. His companions came for the most part from the SFIO: local party leaders (Charles Pivert, the federal secretary for the Seine department), trade unionists (Raymond Froideval, Roland Silly, the secretary of the National Union of CGT engineers), mayors and deputies (Paul Perrier, Jean Garchery, Camille Planche and Louis Sellier) and a few intellectuals, including Claude Jamet. None were men of the top rank, but a few held a measure of power in the middle echelons. Membership never rose above a few hundred.

This group declared itself in favour of an authoritarian and popular republic: a head of state chosen by the nation, advised and controlled by assemblies elected by universal suffrage, a single and hierarchical revolutionary party, the nationalization of key industries, and the management of the economy by tripartite corporations. In foreign policy it demanded 'the construction of a Europe that will at last ensure peace'. Franco-German reconciliation would have to be achieved through, on the one hand, 'France sincerely renouncing all isolationist policies and revenge and, on the other, Germany renouncing the idea of a peace that would constitute revenge for the Treaty of Versailles'.[15]

Charles Spinasse was another who had gravitated from Paul-Faurism, a professor at the Conservatoire Nationale des Arts et Métiers, who had served as Minister for the Economy, then for Finances, under the Popular Front. In the summer of 1940, he took charge of *L'Effort*, a daily paper created in the free zone to take the place of *Le Populaire*. The change of title was as telling as the change of contents was instructive. The newspaper, to which more than twenty former socialist parliamentary representatives contributed, proclaimed the death of the Socialist party and the continuation of socialism. It approved of collaboration, with dignity and in peace.[16] In the summer of 1941, Spinasse requested permission from the embassy to publish, in Paris, a weekly aimed at working-class circles in the capital.[17]

In *Le Rouge et le Bleu*, a 'review of French socialist thought', which began to appear in November 1941, he developed the idea of a community-based order inspired by Proudhon, at the same time emphasizing the need, in the short term, for an authoritarian state based on a popular party.[18] Where collaboration was concerned, he pressed for equal rights, professing himself prepared to abandon one particular view of national sovereignty: France must give up its aspirations for military might and be satisfied with economic health and intellectual influence.[19] This weekly carried articles by several socialist deputies, Georges Lefranc from the 'Redressement' tendency, Anatole de Monzie, and the writers Pierre Hamp and Nino Frank. It published around 35 000 copies.[20]

The last of these groups had split off from the PCF following the German–Soviet pact, when one-third of the French deputies had left the Communist party, unlike the party officials. These remained loyal, with only a few exceptions, one of whom was Marcel Gitton, a member of the Politburo.[21] After the defeat, Gitton and his friends (Capron, Clamamus and Parsal) drew closer to Doriot, as if in the disarray of the rupture the only option was to join up with the most senior dissident. However, there were personality clashes, and in the spring of 1941 Gitton created the POPF (Parti Ouvrier et Paysan Français).[22] Its programme for foreign policy was collaboration with a view to a peace treaty that would guarantee political independence and territorial integrity for France; for internal policy, it included the nationalization of certain industries, the institution of a corporative organization for trade unionism, and the promulgation of a constitution that provided for a leader responsible to the nation, elected consultative assemblies, and a single party.[23] Membership seems never to have risen above one thousand, its following limited to the Paris region, where the POPF directed its action against communist circles, thereby exposing itself to revenge on the part of the PCF, which arranged the assassination of Gitton and a number of his comrades.

The embassy crowd was coursing several hares at once. Chateau, Spinasse and Gitton all insisted on an egalitarian concept of collaboration and held out the hope of a united and pacified Europe. Their views did not extend to the military sphere, where they refused to adopt any line on the score of either methods or aims. On antisemitism and the struggle against freemasonry, they were virtually silent.

Meanwhile, Déat had launched himself into the RNP, along with Deloncle. Already for several years he had been proclaiming the need to bypass the left–right rift. He remained attached to the idea of a single party, even if he had stopped talking about it since his return to Paris. And he was convinced that collaboration was vital for France. He set out two aims for the new movement: 'to accomplish the national revolution promised in July but betrayed by the Vichy government'; and 'to save all that can be saved, making sure that the policy of collaboration triumphs'.[24] Saving meant 'preserving France, saving it from massive amputations. And then saving our part of Africa.'[25] Déat clung to the belief that his movement could play a decisive role by taking over from a government that he considered to be irresponsible. Having listened to Achenbach's somewhat pessimistic assessment of Hitler's attitude at the end of January 1941, he wrote: 'All the more reason to get our Rassemblement [RNP] going, for it will become France's only chance not to appear as the conquered party when peace comes, but rather as an European associate.'[26] His conviction that he was acting for the good of the country should be acknowledged. He made it clear in a letter from the RNP to Pétain in March 1941: 'We wish to tell you, Monsieur le Maréchal, that we shall not allow France to be assassinated, and that we are most definitely resolved upon anything to ensure general salvation.'[27] In July 1941, he even told Abetz that 'saving France has become a private matter'.[28] This was the exact counterpart to resistance seen as a private matter, nothing to do with institutions and possibly even opposed to them.

Déat was a man with an intellectual conceit that isolated him from the surrounding world. This was accompanied by an unexceptional desire for power: that of a deputy who had had more downs than ups but had briefly been a minister in early 1936, an experience that had left him with dazzling memories. But he also had an activist bent and was fascinated by the idea of one great dynamic party that would bring all its members together on a common project. Also, he aspired to a strongly organized society, as could be seen from his concept of collaboration and his image of a Europe in which solidarity would be ensured by the analogous natures of its regimes and the links between their respective economies. France would fit into this Europe, exchanging its territorial integrity for an economic integration that would dispense the conqueror from insisting on pledges. It was an idea that he had no hesitation in ascribing likewise to Hitler: 'We are, all things considered, extremely lucky to be dealing with a conqueror who is a great man . . . Extremely lucky that, having led Germany to victory, he conceives hegemony to be a higher responsibility and now considers his essential mission to be the reconstruction of Europe. For, after all, things might have gone very differently.'[29]

Déat was an austere and singleminded man. Money did not come into his commitment. He was of a rather timid nature, more a follower than a leader. He found it very difficult to keep his own end up faced with Laval, upon whom his political fortunes depended and who for a long time led him by the nose. Deep down, he was naive, as if he did not realize that manipulation was a part of politics and that arguments were judged just as much by their utility as by their intrinsic value. Abetz and Achenbach guided him with great tact, encouraging him to believe that 'economic collaboration will intertwine all European interests' and that 'territories will remain placed under the sovereignty of their respective countries'.[30]

When Déat hitched up with Deloncle, his ideas underwent further modification. Although his ambition was to make the RNP the basis of a single party, he took an authoritarian rather than a totalitarian view: 'When the Party finds a Leader, it will follow him. But it is not certain that a single, undisputed leader will be discovered in France.'[31] In external politics, he showed the same moderation, denying any intention of swinging over into a German alliance: 'How could France accept that supreme betrayal and become Germany's ally after being England's?'[32]

The RNP did not produce the hoped-for results. Déat's differences with Deloncle soon became apparent. It was not only an opposition of experiences, mental frameworks and reflexes, but also a fundamental clash over the very nature of the party. Déat wanted 'as wide a party as possible, able to incorporate goodwill from as many quarters as possible', whereas Deloncle had set his sights on 'a minority party, steadfast and pure, rather than an amorphous, invertebrate mass'.[33] Tensions developed during the summer of 1941, when Deloncle drew closer to Vichy; then came the assassination attempt on Laval and Déat, in which both men detected his hand. An intervention by the embassy made the split definitive, leaving Déat master of the RNP, with an invitation to resume his efforts to win over the masses. After a rapid start, recruitment had run out of steam, with a membership of no more than 20000 or so.[34]

The split precipitated paradoxical developments: on the one hand, an attempt to reconnect with former leftists, which resulted in the integration of groups that had until then preferred to remain aloof, and a resumption of talks with former parliamentary representatives; on the other, a radicalization of ideas which resulted in the RNP falling into line with the Nazi model and plunging into virtually unlimited collaboration. The *Atelier* team had joined the RNP in the spring. Albertini now took on the post of secretary general of the party. The people from France-Europe became associates as a subsidiary of the RNP, the Front Social du Travail (FST), the function of which was to organize supporters into professional categories. To help rake in more people, the embassy provided them with a newspaper, the daily *La France socialiste*. Chateau, who took charge of it, turned the paper into a platform for a renovated socialist and authoritarian republicanism, opening it up to every current in the collaborationist left. It had considerable success, with an average publication of between 110000 and 115000 copies, almost as many as *L'Œuvre*, with its backing of a long-standing readership. The newspaper provoked the ire of the collaborationist right and prompted criticism from both Propaganda-Abteilung and the Abwehr, which were scandalized by its defence of the Republic and above all by its discretion on the subject of antisemitism. The embassy covered for its protégés, pointing out that the objective was, after all, to attract Leftist circles.[35]

The integration of these new groups into the RNP, which the POPF and Spinasse eluded, proved no more solid than its association with the Cagoulards. Déat and those around him threw themselves into frantic radicalization, spurred on by a darkening horizon. Laval's return to power looked further off than ever, the embassy was making do with Darlan, collaboration was marking time, the population was hostile, and the war was dragging on. By the summer of 1941, after the German attack against the USSR, Déat was voicing pessimistic thoughts: 'One has to accept one's lot calmly: not before twenty years has passed, enough time for the next generation to grow, will there be a majority in this country willing to accept the new order, let alone help to bring it about.' His conclusion was: 'So there will be no spiritual renaissance in France except by dint of the determined, fanatical efforts of one great party that will allow nothing to stand in its way.'[36]

Now he began to underline the military dimension to collaboration, speaking of reconquering the dissident colonies and Syria, which had been captured by the British, and supporting the idea of an authentically European army, 'not just one made up of a collection of national contingents'.[37] He also declared his rejection of state collaboration founded upon a quid pro quo basis, advocating instead commitment without bargaining. 'To win everything, you have to give everything and ask for nothing: an attitude quite beyond our horse-dealing diplomats.'[38] Above all, he fell into line with the ideas of Nazism, adopting the principle of one leader and proclaiming the totalitarian vocation of the party.

This radicalization was reinforced by the frustrations occasioned by the change of government in April 1942. Laval kept him out, consoling him with sympathetic words and encouraging him to prepare for the single party, then inventing a series of pretexts for putting off his appointment. Déat, who now took to appearing in uniform, completed his transformation of the RNP. The party was to become the pillar of the regime, ensure the replacement of the élites, organize the totalitarian retraining of the nation, and guarantee the maintenance of order. (Albertini said: 'Who can deny that the departure of the German army at this point would probably give rise to an internal crisis and social disturbances of exceptional gravity?')[39]

An accentuation of antisemitism, which up until now had played a relatively modest part, was accompanied by a general turn to racism. Déat called for 'the rational and selective breeding of little Frenchmen' and sang the praises of sterilization, declaring 'We are half-breeds but aryan ones.'[40] Nazi rituals were introduced into party demonstrations, with one remarkable variant: in October 1942, in commemoration of party members who had died wearing the LVF uniform, a legionnaire announced that they had 'fallen for Europe'.[41] At the time of the landing in North Africa, Déat was at one with the right-wing extremists in calling for an unlimited alliance with the occupier. He was forced to depend more and more upon the latter now that he could not count upon Laval getting him into government. Whereas originally his concern for French might, which was relatively strong in the context of the collaborationist left wing, had contributed to his radicalization, he now found himself in the position of a man rejecting the most obvious aspects of state collaboration. On 24 November 1942 he bitterly reproached Laval for persisting in asking for compensation from Germany, saying: 'Would it not be better, would it not be more in conformity with both the nature of things and a Hitlerian view, to offer proofs and pledges straight away, by plunging in regardless?'[42]

The course of Déat's evolution brought about splits first with Spinasse, then with Chateau and the former France-Europe group. In July 1942, when Déat relaunched the idea of a single party, Spinasse attacked him for 'mimetism': 'What can be said of the idea of a leader as the founder of a religion and the creator of myths, a leader who stands alone before his conscience, before God and before his people, a leader who leads because the law of his own being is confused with that of his race? All that can be said is that it is totally incomprehensible to the French people.' For him, the real problem was 'to sweep away anarchy by organizing society', to found a society in which collective powers limited each other, and not to force it into the strait-jacket of a single party – an idea that revived the Leninist heresy condemned by French socialism in 1920. His own hope was for a union of peoples within a pluralist Europe.[43] His periodical was banned soon after this, and Spinasse withdrew from all public activity.

Chateau, a Jacobin devoted to the ideal of the general will, accepted a single party, perceiving it as a pedagogical instrument: not a barracks, but a 'school where one can free spirits from their bonds, where they can be taught all that one needs to know in order to declare one's opinion, and where they can be delivered from prejudice and ignorance'.[44] Déat's totalitarian ideas widened the gap between them: in the present conditions, Chateau could see, a single party did imply the use of force.[45] Their disagreement resulted in Chateau's exclusion from the RNP at the turn of the year, then his eviction from *La France socialiste* during the following summer, at the same time as the France-Europe team distanced itself.[46]

By the autumn of 1942, Chateau had launched a new movement, the Ligue de la Pensée Française, the aim of which was to unite the French around freedom of conscience and to establish peace between all European peoples. The association refrained from pushing freedom of thought to its ultimate conclusion, no doubt as repayment for being granted German authorization: it remained closed to Jews, and former dignitaries of freemasonry were excluded from positions of authority. The movement, under the direction of Chateau and Jamet, comprised convinced pacifists (such as René Guérin and Robert Jospin), disciples of Alain, led by Alain himself, a fair number of trade unionists, socialists and members of POPF, and a number of celebrities, including Robert Denoël, Lucienne Delforge, Marcelle Capy, Germaine Decaris, André Salmon, Édouard Chaux, and Gabriel Cognacq.[47] Most had made their views on collaboration clear enough in 1941–42. But they now beat a prudent retreat towards positions of universal peace and internal concord, with the support of Laval, who counter-balanced Déat, and with the permission of the occupiers, who preferred pacifism to resistance.

Chateau and the Ligue de la Pensée Française continued their efforts right to the end, petitioning Pétain and Laval in 1944 to work for reconciliation amongst the French and to launch an appeal for peace, proposing the formation of a 'European economic community'.[48]

Déat and his friends, for their part, were slipping into boundless collaboration in the hope of forcing the occupier to trust them. But this should not lead us to forget that earlier Déat had won considerable sympathy because he attacked Vichy in the name of values that may have looked familiar to an audience not in the mood to be discriminating. On 1 March 1942, he spoke in Orleans before a large crowd. According to the police, there were many people drawn there by curiosity amongst whom were 'numerous supporters of the Popular Front and former masonic leaders, who vigorously applauded M. Marcel Déat's critique of the government's internal policies'.[49] At the beginning of 1943, again according to a police report from Seine-et-Marne, Déat, 'through his anticlericalism, his violent attacks on "paternalism" (*sic*) and the satirical cachet that he has managed to preserve in *L'Œuvre*, incontestably enjoys a definite prestige amongst quite a wide readership of minor employees and teachers, in short a fair proportion of the former readers of the paper from the rue Louis-le-Grand'.[50]

While Déat's path had diverged greatly from that of most of the collaborationist left he preserved something of their common past. Having adopted much of the Nazi ideology, he tried, as if to compensate, to root it in the ideological soil of the French left: he traced the forging of closer ties between France and Germany back to Jaurès, totalitarian democracy back to Rousseau, and went back to the French Revolution for a parallel with the 'national socialist revolution'. As a symbol of that almost erased imprint of the left, on the occasion of his fiftieth birthday, in March 1944, his lieutenants presented their leader Déat with Diderot and d'Alembert's *Encyclopédie*.[51]

26

The 'notables'

Alongside former militants of the left was a by-no-means-undistinguished centre, whose members were from the start notable in both their tone and their methods. Unattracted to military action and still less to rowdy politics, they held the floor in the press, gave lectures, and wrote books, bestowing upon collaboration a certain distinction, celebrity and social sheen. In contrast to the left wing, where academics abounded and a variety of groups pursued the complicated political lines of the pre-war days, the moderate wing was made up of figures whose attitude was determined by connections and temperament. This was collaboration for respectable people, defended by respectable people, who became less respectable once they got as carried away in their commitment as more vulgar partisans.

In truth, the 'notables' fell into two distinct groups. Some were liberals who had rallied to the idea of a new order, without renouncing certain elements of liberalism. Others were conservatives or reactionaries – many of Catholic inspiration, a few Maurrasians – who now surmounted the barriers of conformism. All manifested the greatest respect for Pétain. The homage they paid the old soldier was solemn, their criticism of the government measured. It was communism that was regarded as the essential danger: their attacks against the Anglo-Saxons were muted, at least up until 1942; and their condemnation of Jews and freemasons was restrained.

At the roots of this rallying to the new order lay a rejection of the claims of the populace, of 'the populace as king', and a fundamental resistance to a mass society and the historical evolution that had produced it; a protest against materialism on the part of sensitive liberals, those nostalgic for the high days of spirituality, and orthodox reactionaries. What they appreciated in Nazi Germany was the opposite of its plebeian and 'socialist' element, namely its reputed restoration of order and hierarchy and also of faith and spirituality. When it advocated collaboration, this branch stressed the 'national interest': acceptance of necessity in the name of reason. Without being nationalistic, it was sensitive to the importance of prestige and power, but at the same time developed a rhetoric on Europe and its economic unity, or on Europe and the Christian civilization under threat from foreign competition, or even aggression, such as Asiatic bolshevism or Anglo-Saxon imperialism.

What on earth can liberals have found to attract them in a Nazi Europe? Certainly not respect for human rights, the limitation of state power or self-fulfilment for the individual. But these were liberals who had modified their views in the crisis years, subduing freedom by interventionism, rethinking the meaning of democracy, and regressing in the direction of fundamental élitist values. They reacted to the defeat as experts in compromise, adaptation, backers of the least of all evils, men aware of how much a prolonged war would cost them. Besides, economics recognized no frontiers; perhaps the time had come to demolish stifling barriers. Necessity and calculated self-interest provided the bases for a familiar line of argument. Loyal to a measured optimism, or perhaps to an inbuilt scepticism, they refused to see things in the worst light: France had not been free before the war, nor would it be enslaved after it. In the new situation, there were human beacons to whom they could turn: Briand for the European idea, Caillaux for closer links between France and Germany.

A number of prominent newspapers and journalists argued in the name of such continuity, in the first place Jean Luchaire, the director of *Les Nouveaux Temps*, whose Briandism dated from way back. His newspaper was aimed at a readership of the centre influenced by a right-wing anticommunist and pro-Munich radicalism and well enough represented by a man such as Émile Roche, who published a few articles, along with other politicians ranging from the liberal right to pro-conciliation socialists.[1] This paper followed the embassy line, supporting Laval and criticizing Vichy. Collaboration was justified by a battery of arguments drawn from history, common sense and the idea of the least of all evils. Hitler, by himself taking the first step at Montoire, had shown that he was not a conqueror in the usual mould, that what he wanted was *entente* and the welfare of

Europe, and that France had everything to gain in grasping his outstretched hand.

Further to the right, *La Vie industrielle* was run by the Flandinist wing of the Alliance Démocratique which, in the days immediately before the war, had evolved towards the reform of institutions and acceptance of organized capitalism. Austere and didactic, this paper acted as the mouthpiece of the liberal tendency that had rallied to Pétain and authority in the name of competence, efficiency and stability. It was a rallying movement shot through with criticism directed against excessive interventionism and the administrative inflation of the French state. It was aimed at business circles, and defended a 'positive' collaborationism that reasoned in economic terms and proposed a functional type of Europeanism, many aspects of which were to be resuscitated in the 1950s.

Before being brought into the government, Flandin had himself set out the main lines of this collaborationism. The new Europe ought to form a large economic space, allowing the free circulation of goods and capital, and this would be facilitated by the adoption of a single currency and the constitution of a monetary union 'on the basis of a European fixed exchange rate mechanism, guaranteed by unifying the methods of monetary creation and management of central banks'.[2] The newspaper stuck to this line after Flandin's departure and continued to look favourably upon the organization of the continent, safeguarding as much liberalism as possible and maintaining exchanges with the rest of the world. In an article entitled 'The European economic community', the leader-writer of the newspaper wrote on 14 June 1941 as follows: 'The constitution of Europe as an economic unit will not result in the disappearance of nations, but the community of interests will to a large extent create a political community.'

Such ideas extended the pre-war theses of the Alliance Démocratique and technocratic circles such as Nouveaux Cahiers and Redressement Français, which had favoured European unity achieved through a rationalization of production and economic interdependence. They converged with the approach of some German leaders and testified to a European tendency that thought in terms of vast economic spaces. Although close to the collaborationist left in their insistence upon the economy, where they differed was in their concern for rationalization and productivity, as opposed to the attitude of men such as Déat and Spinasse who focused primarily upon social organization and who seemed virtually unconcerned with the ideal of economic growth. No more than on the left did anyone address the question of the balance of forces or the extent to which Germany would monopolize all advantages. The French economy was considered to be best served by a new Europe: it was, after all, not without advantages of its own, competition would stimulate it to modernize, and its voluntary insertion into such a Europe might temper the territorial consequences of the defeat.

The readership was rather limited: between 15000 and 20000 copies were printed. But that readership was composed of businessmen some of whom, at least, must have been affected by the arguments and views put before them. From the end of June 1942 onwards, the paper modified its position, when hopes of economic collaboration collapsed in the face of the unequivocal evidence of the Germans' exploitation of the French economy.[3]

A few intellectuals of liberal provenance belonged to the team that created this moderate and reasonable version of collaborationism, one far removed from the idea of a society controlled and mobilized by a single party, and that favoured an outcome to the war that would leave the door open for reconciliation with the Anglo-Saxons. Drieu had a point when he lumped together the names of Chardonne, Fabre-Luce and Monzie, describing them as 'liberal minds liberally open to the opposite of liberalism'. He added that they were incapable of committing themselves thoroughly to that negation, and that this had the effect of reviving his own hatred of liberals. ('And that is why we – myself and I don't know who else – are all for violence.')[4]

We may as well leave aside Monzie, whose public commitment was as limited as it was prudent. Of the other two, one had a political past. Alfred Fabre-Luce had an agile mind and was an observer with a keen eye for detail but was frequently misled on major issues. He was a frustrated politician, a prince's adviser who never found a prince to listen to him. In the 1920s, along with Luchaire and Jouvenel, he was a stern critic of Poincaré and French nationalism, a supporter of the League of Nations, of closer relations between France and Germany and of European organization. At the turn of the following decade, he saw that liberalism was declining and moved towards authority, which led him to Doriot, whom he abandoned after Munich. After the defeat he declared himself for collaboration, in a measured and oblique fashion, particularly in the second volume of his *Journal de France*, which covered the period from the defeat up to Laval's return in 1942: a book that provides a fine example of the calculated liberalism of the occupying power.

This was quite a well-informed chronicle that contained some sharp comments on French life and was written with a certain freedom of tone. In it, Fabre-Luce castigated both the detractors of collaboration and those who profit from it, and he criticized the Jewish Statute for its 'pointless infringements of humanity, property, and the rights of war veterans',[5] but without – of course – challenging it in principle. In page after page, he listed arguments recommending collaboration as the only reasonable policy – too bad if public opinion was not convinced: '"Public Opinion" has only ever favoured policies of national suicide', he remarked, with a certain aplomb.[6] To win the reader over, he sometimes used the argument of historical necessity, sometimes that of the national interest, and he did not hesitate to spell out an alternative that was in no way flattering to the conqueror with whom he was aiming to get along: 'The choice that is offered us is a simple one. A new Europe is being set up. We are invited to take part in its construction. If we accept, we join its blood aristocracy and benefit from its privileges. If we refuse, the place prepared for us after the war will be that of slaves.'[7]

He approved of Laval, seeing in his return a new chance for collaboration, and described his vision of the future as follows: 'Today, we must take as our point of departure one fact: the German victory . . . European history shows us the fragility of conquests achieved through violence that are not supported by consent. The Roman empire remains the ideal for civilized nations; but it has never been possible to recreate it through the strength of a single people. What we must construct is a collective Rome. In this task, we shall be not subjects but collaborators; we may even – at the end of the process – become co-emperors.'[8] Although Fabre-Luce believed a German victory likely, he looked forward to eventual 'reconciliation between the combatants', with France establishing the liaison with the Anglo-Saxon world. What was important was that Europe should be able to stand up to the other continents: 'Our quarrel with Germany has masked another danger: the decline of the whole of Europe.'[9]

France was not going back on all that it stood for by following a policy of collaboration; on the contrary, it was rediscovering the best part of itself. The *Anthologie de la nouvelle Europe* that he was preparing in the first half of 1941 aimed to establish that French letters had 'their own place of honour and responsibility in the world into which we are entering'.[10] In this curious anthology, Hitler, Mussolini, Maurras, Gobineau and Barrès rubbed shoulders with Valéry, Péguy, Gide and Bergson, to the sole end of presenting a table of values upon which the founders of a 'collective Rome' could agree: a rehabilitation of strength, with sovereignty passing from the people to the leader, and imperialism transposed from a national to the European level. Fabre-Luce, who resisted the importation of Nazism, believed the two countries might develop in opposite directions. 'The war will have brought to democracy national socialism, a certain austerity of mores, a taste for authority, an instinct of biological preservation. It will have brought to dictatorships supranational problems and inspired them with a certain desire for *détente* . . . Seen from Sirius, these frightful convulsions will simply have constituted the birth-pangs of a new world.'[11]

The coming together of the two countries, written in the stars as it was, would be speeded up by their common trials. 'Already, in the twilight of the long war in which ideologies are becoming moderated, 1789 and 1933 seem less like two enemies and more like a single Revolution, with bolshevism lying in ambush.' Fabre-Luce, who wrote this in the summer of 1941, was looking forward to the victory banquet: 'Europe will only be able to organize itself in a lasting fashion by drawing inspiration from the national and social doctrine the elements of which are all present here. I take pleasure in declaring this even as battle still rages and with the future still uncertain.'[12] In 1943, the future no longer looked uncertain, and Fabre-Luce published the third volume of his *Journal de France* without authorization; it would not have passed the censorship. The Germans were irritated by this calculated volte-face by a man whose earlier well-disposed sentiments they had much appreciated.[13] Fabre-Luce was imprisoned for a few weeks, only to find himself once again behind bars after the liberation, at which he put on a great show of indignation at having been persecuted by both sides. It was the very least due to the man whose German publisher, quoting a review by Chardonne, had introduced him to the public as 'the most intelligent man in France'.[14]

If liberalism stands for marking out a private sphere and protecting it, Jacques Chardonne was a practised liberal: a novelist of intimate feelings, a champion of subtlety, quality, and the most delicate forms of civilization, and also the cantor of Barbezieux, a little society in the Charente region, set up as the ideal of a bourgeois and provincial France, hard-working, peaceful, and well-deserving. It is worth underlining that in the 1930s he had remained publicly uncommitted. It was only at the defeat that he was propelled on to the public stage: during the phoney war, he had been very indignant at the Germans and very critical of totalitarianism.[15] He justified acceptance of the defeat by the judgement that history would pass, just as Fabre-Luce and Montherlant did: accept what is, because it is, if necessary taking an age-long view and speculating upon the happy consequences that may unpredictably follow from great disasters. It was a view of the situation condemned by Raymond Aron, who read his words in London.[16] Chardonne went on to remark that, however much national feeling might rebel, it was necessary to overcome a reaction of ill-judged resentment and, rather than rail against the conqueror, try to make the best of the situation. The defeat had revealed a deep sickness, not military but civil, and the remedy was clear: 'To cure ourselves, we must learn from our conquerors.'[17]

Chardonne used the word 'conversion' to describe his change of attitude. He had suddenly become aware of the danger hanging over Barbezieux and of the historical opportunity to dispel it that was offered. In *Voir la figure* ('Seeing the Pattern'), he recalled the beginning of the century, a happy period when he had known 'contented workers' and when people lived peaceful lives, without the despicable distractions of the cinema and the press.[18] The greatest virtue of the defeat was that Barbezieux would recover from 'the addiction to the easy life that touched all classes of society', and would rediscover the salutory austerity of the old days, returning to 'truer views on the great things of life and the value of human beings'.[19] His attitude provides a good illustration of the kind of restorative aspirations which, overcoming more immediate reactions, seized hold of some liberals – those who, like Chardonne, were deeply conscious of a threat hanging over the individual and the bourgeois.

Once converted, he set about converting his uncomprehending compatriots. Like Fabre-Luce, he looked down on them. 'Never have I been more sensible of the honour of knowing how to think that has devolved upon some, and the wretchedness of the great mass.'[20] He, far superior, would teach them 'to see the pattern', to piece together all the elements of the situation so that they made sense: collaboration was a necessary policy and also a desirable one. Exhorting his poor compatriots to 'think against the inclination of their very being and their old and frequently faulty education',[21] and to bow to the inevitable and discover the greatest good in whatever existed, he piled up his arguments. Some related to France's situation: defeat was inherent in the facts, there was no appeal against German superiority; reconquest by England, were it possible, would ruin the country; France needed to be remade from within. Others concerned the conqueror, who was showing moderation and great understanding of his historical task. And into these arguments he slipped a warning that the conqueror was perfectly capable of behaving quite differently: by refusing to recognize 'the benevolent nature of the German occupation', the French were condemning themselves 'to a far more tragic servitude'.[22]

Chardonne did not sing the praises of Nazism. Nazi Germany was simply fulfilling a historical role, accomplishing a revolution dictated by the state of the continent, a revolution to which the French themselves confusedly or secretly aspired, without the ability to bring it about. Like Fabre-Luce, he was counting on the creation of closer ties through a partial and mutual assimilation of the two countries' respective views of the world. 'France now desires more rigour in society; Germany will come to desire more flexibility.'[23] For France had failed to accomplish its mission: 'The individual is salvation . . . The community ideal is never any more than a passing necessity, a cure for a degenerate individualism.'[24] So there was a place for Barbezieux in the Europe of Berchtesgaden: 'The people of Barbezieux were people of an age gone by; without changing very much, they will become the people of the future.'[25] Returning to the present, Chardonne ended with a new condemnation: 'It is essential that the French be forced into silence . . . What is needed is a government that is implacable: tyrants, but tyrants who know their job.'[26] Chardonne, Bonnard and many others among these writer-'notables' all displayed the same scorn for the French and could hardly find words harsh enough to revile their waywardness, their blindness, addictions and madness. None of them were prepared to try to understand the arguments of those compatriots of theirs who argued differently; instead, they all clung to their position as superior beings. The more conscious they were of their fragility, the more inflexible they became.

After 1942, Chardonne turned his back on this theory of historical necessity: even when probable, even when certain, an allied victory did not appeal to him. Now he kept his opinions to himself, still obsessed by the communist danger ('It is with despair that I see German towns being destroyed. It is our own fortress that is crumbling'[27]), but prudently gave up the idea of publishing a book already at proof stage, *Le ciel de Nieflheim*, which would certainly have blackened his name: 'National socialism has created a new world around the human individual', he declared in it; and 'the SS make a proper use of their absolute power, with the population making no complaints, once it has become accustomed to this'.[28]

The well-known figures who adorned the pediment of the Groupe Collaboration attracted more attention to themselves than any book would have done. But they always remembered their manners: political commitment, to be sure, but of the right kind and in the right company. The Groupe took over from the Comité France–Allemagne and aimed, as it had, to enrol the élite of the nation. It held a number of trump cards, starting with its legitimacy. Placed under the patronage of Fernand de Brinon, it consistently proclaimed its loyalty to Pétain and unfailingly supported the national revolution and the politics of Montoire. In Vichy, it enjoyed the support of Darlan, who in November 1941 authorized it to operate in the free zone, and also of Laval, who in January 1943 directed the prefects to protect it. It declared, equally steadfastly, that it was not a party, for it was above parties; and it is true that it did not go in for the criticisms and backbiting that marred the discourse of the other political groups in Paris. The activities that it encouraged were peaceable ones, essentially public lectures and cultural functions. Its propaganda was diffused through press releases, and recruitment was mainly a matter of asking well-known people to join, or of offering membership to the public who attended its functions.

Its preponderantly 'notable' character was reflected in its honorary committee, which included, as well as five members of the Institute de France, Cardinal Baudrillart, Georges Claude, Pierre Benoit, Abel Hermant and Abel Bonnard (the latter three were members of the Académie Françaіs), Drieu la Rochelle, Melchior de Polignac, Claire Croiza (a professor at the Conservatoire de Musique) and René Moulin (a member of the Conseil Supérieure des Colonies). As for the board of directors, it comprised Alphonse de Chateaubriant, the chairman of the Groupe, and two vice-chairmen (Jean Weiland and René Richard du Page) and a secretary general (Ernest Fornairon). Its ranks had been much depleted since the days of the Comité France–Allemagne. Only three members of the new honorary committee had been leaders of the CFA (Drieu, Benoit and Polignac). Alphonse de Chateaubriant, who would have seemed a fiendish choice then, was now enthroned in honour. There were no more parliamentary deputies or politicians, no more ambassadors.

The predominance of cultural life was reflected in the way in which the Groupe was organized: an economic and social section (directed by the architect Paul Marme); a scientific section (the surgeon Charles Claoué with, as other section leaders, Charles Laville, François Maignan and Dr Robert Soupault); a literary section (Bonnard and

José Germain); a legal section (Professor Le Fur); and an artistic section, subdivided into three: dramatic art (the dramatist Jean Sarment, who in 1944 succeeded Vaudoyer as head of the Comédie-Française); music (Max d'Ollone, the director of the Opéra-Comique, with, as honorary chairmen, Alfred Bachelet and Florent Schmitt, both from the Institut de France); and the plastic arts (Georges Grappe, the curator of the Rodin Museum, with, as vice-chairmen, Othon Friesz and Paul Belmondo). There was also a youth group, the Jeunesses de l'Europe Nouvelle, led first by Marc Augier, who came from the left and then went off to join the LVF in the autumn of 1941, then Jacques Schweizer, the former leader of Taitinger's Jeunesses. The JEN maintained the élitism of the parent group, recruiting in the *lycées* and amongst the children of 'notables'.

Although very much a minority in their own circles, taken all together these few clusters of people produced a far from negligible social sheen that no other group could boast. Most of its leaders were middle-aged and their commitment to collaboration, with all its diverse motives, as it were, mirrored in miniature the tensions and temptations experienced by some French people ever since the Great War. Several, like Chardonne, had come round to that commitment since the defeat. All were prone to antidemocratic tendencies or came from antidemocratic backgrounds, were inclined to conservatism if not traditionalism, and had an image of Germany that was blurred by their own phobias and disgust at the state of their country.

Cardinal Baudrillart, the rector of the Catholic Institute of Paris provides an illustration. During the First World War he had led a Catholic committee charged with defending the allied cause abroad and denouncing German crimes. Since then he had remained anti-German and in 1939 had condemned Nazism as the 'renewed barbarity of paganism'.[29] Then he changed his mind, no doubt after mulling things over for several years. His hostility to Germany and his distrust of Nazism were blotted out by his detestation of communism, a difficulty with which he had not had to cope during the earlier world conflict. The fear of Soviet communism and horror at the notion of another Commune in France got him to 'see the pattern' and decide that Germany was the lesser evil or even, after 22 June 1941, an evil out of which great good might come.

Alphonse de Chateaubriant was another Catholic untouched by Maurrasian sympathies. He had been won over to Nazism before the war, interpreting it in the light of his own aspirations for a restored France and his heterodox Christian spiritualism. The world had fallen into 'decadence' because it had lost its link with religion and its symbols, replacing these by the materialism of *homo oeconomicus*, with his money and his machines: communism was the logical consequence of this. The world needed to be respiritualized within community frameworks that would allow human beings once again to experience the warmth of solidarity and shared beliefs. Seen in this perspective, collaboration appeared as the cure for a diseased civilization, not just a diseased France. It promised to usher in a new historical cycle, which could also be justified in terms of the existing situation: European unity under German direction was imposed by a kind of law of continental unification and intercontinental competition.[30]

Abel Bonnard had been influenced by Maurrasism but shared certain elements of the same vision, to that extent identifying with a traditionalist current of thought that regarded Vichy as a machine for going back in time and that was also favoured by a number of other academicians – Henri Bordeaux, Maurice Donnay, La Varende and Pesquidoux. But around the mid-1930s, Bonnard had become enraged with the 'moderates' of the liberal and conservative right, and accused it of being largely responsible for the decadence of France. He drew closer to Doriot and the PPF, being much attracted by this party (in a very un-Maurrasian way). In even more un-Maurrasian fashion, he then conceived a great admiration for Nazi Germany. In 1941, he completed the break: having attacked the 'moderates', he now rounded on the 'reactionaries', that is to say Maurras, because he persisted in his 'patriotism leading to an impasse', instead of 'fully accepting the association of France and Germany in a great Europe'.[31] All in all, he was a curious figure, 'this academician of shock tactics', to borrow Céline's expression: in many ways he was a traditionalist, attached to the image of a rural, virtuous, unchanging France, but at the same time he had fallen under the spell of fascism, mobilization and communion in action, and summed this up well enough in his own image of a desirable society: 'We shall live in a hierarchical organization, animated by a spirit of fraternity.'[32]

Alongside letters, science had an important place. Charles Laville and Ernest Fourneau were well-known figures and convinced collaborationists. Fourneau was a long-standing partisan of closer ties with Germany who in 1941 did not hesitate to help the occupier by examining the full range of scientific journals and selecting those whose continued publication seemed essential.[33] George Claude's career had been less conventional, for he was an inventor gifted in the field of practical application, far removed from theory and pure science. He was a man who had tasted success and was prosperous and well known, but who in 1928 had failed to win election as a deputy. He then turned to Maurrasism, although apparently without great enthusiasm, for soon he was pressing for closer Franco-German ties. After becoming one of the most popular lecturers for the Groupe Collaboration, in 1942 he suffered from a bout of depression and conceived the bizarre idea of committing suicide in public, at the end of a lecture. He had set out his reasons in a statement entitled 'Died for France', in which he dedicated the gesture itself to someone else: 'It is my wish that my sacrifice be accepted by the Führer whom I know to be a man sensitive to such sentiments, that he accept it as the ardent expression of my trust that Germany and Italy will be indulgent towards this people whose misfortune it has been not to be able to rid itself of its wretched leaders, and keep for a France at last regenerated a place that is worthy of it in this new Europe that it will, I hope, help them build and organize.'[34]

With an array of 'notables' such as this, it is not surprising that the message of the Groupe Collaboration was above all historical and cultural. Its lecturers aimed to help their audiences to discern 'the real Germany'[35] and to reveal to them the 'intellectual affinities' between the two countries and the complementarity of the two peoples, teaching them to understand the need for a reconciliation in which Germany would play the role of 'guide', by reason of its particular responsibilities. The Groupe was to make full use of Goebbels' Europeanist propaganda: the construction of a Europe made up of free and independent peoples was worthy of sacrifices that would help Germany protect the continent and liberate it from the evil powers that beset it.

The high profile of the Groupe's leaders, its support from the government, and the nature of its activities all contributed to its impact which was by no means negligible. Chateaubriant's weekly, *La Gerbe*, published 130000 copies, 100000 of which were sold.[36] It was partly thanks to the Groupe's official cachet that its touring lecturers, whether French or German, such as Professor Grimm, spoke to full halls. The front rows would usually be filled by the prefect or his representative, the regional and municipal authorities, delegates from the Vichy services, representatives of the Order of Doctors, the chambers of commerce, and sometimes the Church, not to mention the local collaborationist groups.

In June 1942, Grimm made a lecture tour of the free zone. For all his talks (in Lyons, Avignon, Cannes, Marseilles, Nîmes, Narbonne, Perpignan, Carcassonne, Montpellier and Toulouse), he attracted full houses. In most places there was also a crowd outside the building, which listened to the lecturer through a loudspeaker. The audience numbered over 2000 people every time, substantial applause was forthcoming, and references to Hitler and assurances of his friendly disposition towards France were greeted by ovations. The German professor was fêted at private receptions organized by chambers of commerce (of Marseilles and Toulouse), by the rector of the University of Toulouse, and in Montpellier by an honorary committee comprising the mayor, the chamber of commerce and the university authorities. Grimm's impression was that his public had changed since the pre-war days when he used to give lectures for the Comité France–Allemagne: fewer of the respectable bourgeoisie, and a wider social mix, probably the groups brought in by the collaborationist parties.[37]

According to the embassy, the Groupe's lectures reached an audience of 200000 people.[38] Many no doubt came purely out of curiosity, but curiosity is itself indicative of a certain state of mind. On 1 June 1942, Abetz reported that the Groupe could claim 38000 members, 12000 of them in the free zone; at the end of the year, one of its organizers mentioned a figure of 100000; then in May 1944 the embassy again produced a detailed statement of membership numbers standing at 42283.[39] The figure included a good many 'notables', but also some hotheads – not that the one description necessarily excludes the other. The organizer of the Lyons Groupe was a *docteur ès sciences*, an assistant lecturer at the Faculty of Sciences. In June 1942, he asked Abetz for financial aid for his section: 'I beg you, Excellency, to pardon my request: but it also comes from people of real merit who are fiercely struggling to open the eyes of all French people to the merits of the Führer and the magnanimous sentiments of the German people towards their brothers, the people of France, who have in past times shared with it the "yoke" of British slavery.' The letter signed off as follows: 'With you for the new Europe! Heil Hitler!'[40]

27

The hard right

THE right or rather extreme right wing brings us back to the militants. Unlike Abetz's left, here the reference was military, the rhetoric arrogant and trenchant, and the primordial value was authority, the basis for a total rejection of democracy. These militants were the Marshal's men, or even his aggressive partisans, and exhorted the government to press on strongly, starting by meting out punishment to those responsible for the war, as a measure of justice or revenge and, above all, a pledge of its break with the past. At the end of 1940, the Doriotists were demanding that something 'irremediable' be done by digging a deep dividing trench 'with, at the bottom, a little blood, to make it impassable – the blood of those responsible for all our misfortunes'.[1] Purges, exclusions and repression were at the heart of their programme, with a throbbing, indefatigable call to strike back: against those responsible for the war, those in opposition, those resisting, the communists, the freemasons and the Jews. Antisemitism held a place of prime importance for them and Nazi politics constituted the sole model.

In these circles of nationalists, it was of course believed that collaboration must restore France's might, it being taken for granted that it would be coordinated or associated with that of the conqueror. The army and the empire were the holy Arks, the very basis of national life. The rhetoric of collaboration revolved around the national interest: in the early days at least there was no eulogistic discourse on Europe, little or no concern for the economy, interdependence or the opening of frontiers, and no more than a limited interest in the 'socialist' dimension to Nazism. On the other hand, its ability to generate energy and strength clearly did exert a strong attraction, as did its totalitarian determination to make people fall into line and train them to stay there.

In these circles Déat, even in the later stages of his evolution, would never find favour. No more would Laval, who was violently detested. And here the movement of withdrawal, as the war evolved, was less marked than elsewhere, and there were fewer changes on points of principle between the beginning of the period and its end. There was nevertheless some evolution, if only in the abandonment of the germanophobia that had originally marked French nationalism but had already been on the wane in the period leading up to the war. That abandonment was startlingly attested by the radical revision of a number of works. *L'Histoire du cinéma*, by Maurice Bardèche and Robert Brasillach, had first appeared in 1935, when it contained the following remarks on the German cinema: 'In [the cinema] Germany indulges its deep romanticism and that taste for sadism, fear and shock, and the mixture of sexuality and death that went to the heads of so many of its sons after the war.' In the second edition, published after the defeat, the end of that sentence is altered and prolonged with an addition: '. . . of sexuality and death that went to the heads of so many of its Jews after the war; for, as everywhere else, the Jews had rushed to the cinema'.[2] All the negativity in the earlier judgement passed on Germany was now shifted and concentrated on the Jews. That reference to the common enemy laid the foundations for an *entente* without reservations.

The evolution of the attitude of the extreme right was also and above all reflected in its inflated approval of totalitarianism, in its increasingly radical racism, and in its assimilation of political action to military combat. The use of force against political adversaries was now deemed legitimate or even natural. The representations of civil war, which had surfaced around the middle of the preceding decade, established their hold in a situation where those doing the threatening leaned for support on the strength of an occupier. This evolution was also reflected at the level of nationalism, the rhetoric of which, after the German attack on the USSR, began to incorporate the 'European' theme. After November 1942 the confusion of French and German interests was justified in the name of a 'European revolution' which, through a transposition of the twofold internal struggle against democracy and communism to the continental level, became first and foremost a struggle against common enemies. The conqueror was regarded less and less as a nation and more and more as a regime that provided a model, thanks to which the French nation could be newly founded.

The extreme right wing comprised, first, a small cohort of leaders broken in to militant action in the pre-war period, who had since then taken over at least some of the trappings of fascist movements: their special shirts and raised-arm salutes, and their swearing of oaths and cult of the dead. They had established more or less close relations with neighbouring regimes from which some of them had even received financial support. None had really made any political breakthrough except Doriot, briefly, in 1936–37. After the defeat, most of these men remained the professional organizers of small political groups. The only reason for singling out Clémenti, a journalist who launched himself into political life in 1934, becoming the object of a number of legal charges and convictions, is his decision, in the autumn of 1941, to settle in Lyons, where he published his paper, *Le Pays libre*, with funding from Vichy, and was soon forgotten by everybody. Jean Boissel, a pensioned-off war veteran and an unsuccessful architect in civilian life, became convinced of his destiny thanks to a medium who directed him to effect a reconciliation between France and Germany and Italy, a mission that he endeavoured to accomplish using the bridge afforded by racism and antisemitism. Found guilty of spying for Germany in 1939, he was submitted to a psychiatric investigation that pronounced his delusion to be that he was 'a predestined man who suffered for the sake of his mission and on that account deserved to triumph over the enemies bent on destroying him'.[3] Once extricated from prison by the Germans, he resumed his struggle in the same obsessional fashion. The editor-in-chief of his newspaper, *Le Réveil du peuple*, Auguste Féval, was very much in the same mould, holding occult powers responsible for his material troubles and the mental illness of his wife.[4] As for Pierre Costantini who, as a good Corsican, was a passionate admirer of Napoleon, he had had a chaotic professional career before the war and only after the defeat devoted himself to politics, finally finishing up in an asylum for the mentally disturbed.

Deloncle, Bucard and Doriot were figures of more account. Deloncle, an engineer and company manager, was propelled into politics by the riot of 6 February 1934. He pulled out of Action Française, which he reckoned to be impotent, and opted for the *putsch*, setting up networks of men and obtaining arms with the help of fascist Italy, which he repaid by assassinating its opponents in exile, meanwhile relying on a strategy of tension and provocative assassination attempts to topple the Republic. Understandably, he was glad to seize the opportunity provided by the defeat, unlike some of his companions who took posts in Vichy or else went off to join de Gaulle.

Cunning, secretive and vain, he surrounded himself with henchmen and adventurers, a few respectable figures such as General Lavigne-Delville and the industrialist Eugène Schueller, and one or two intellectuals, the most notable of whom was Georges Soulès. Soulès, like his leader, was from the École Polytechnique, but had been a militant in the SFIO in the 1930s, when he belonged to the 'Redressement' tendency. He was beguiled and fascinated by 'this man without ideas'.[5] Being a former leftist militant, he attempted to organize the MSR, and in doing so discovered just how far apart different worlds could be. Deloncle, who kept a tight hold on the reins, was interested only in military organization and intelligence activities. What he wanted from his men was not so much a communion of ideas, but rather gang solidarity. And in his actions he continued to show a taste for violence which, as is easy to understand, soon separated him from Déat. In June 1941, for example, he suggested to the Germans that he might hunt down Jews and Gaullists for them in exchange for their liberating some French prisoners of war.[6] In October he used plastic bombs to blow up seven Paris synagogues, acting in league with the SD, which supplied him with explosives.[7] After his split from Déat, he renewed his allegiance to Pétain, placing his movement at his disposal and explaining the great importance of his intelligence network, with its twenty-four sections devoted to specialized investigations.[8] At the same time, he launched himself into diplomacy, dispatching emissaries to the SS, fascist Italy and, later on, Franco's Spain.[9] In Paris, the embassy, which was distrustful of him, kept him on the list of parties that were merely tolerated. Yet Deloncle was perfectly explicit in his declarations: 'Today, it is Germany that sets us the example to follow in order to realize the truth of the twentieth century. Thanks to the energy and genius of the Man it has found to be its leader and at the cost of determined labour and courage, it has built the prototype for the European national socialist regime.' France's task was to support 'through its political action, the Nation that has taken on the responsibility of unifying Europe'.[10]

In May 1942, this advocate of *putsch* was himself the victim of one, in which Soulès had a hand.[11] Grudges had been building up on many scores, ranging from methods of leadership to links with Vichy and including Deloncle's dubious entourage. The *coup de grâce* was dealt by Laval's return to power. Laval had regarded the former Cagoulard chief with the deepest suspicion ever since the assassination attempt of the previous year. The plotters now took possession of the party headquarters and denied Deloncle's men admittance, at which Deloncle announced his retirement from political life. He was followed by Schueller, and a fair number of his party's members transferred to the PPF. It was an astonishing end for this man who had been feared on so many sides. He continued with his plots for a while until, at the beginning of 1944, he was murdered by the German police, apparently as the result of a misunderstanding.

Reduced now to a few hundred militants, Soulès's MSR, financed by Laval, developed a discourse on 'race and soil'. It presented itself as 'the party closest, in ethics, doctrine and methods, to the German national socialist party'. In its programme, it declared its wish to 'purify Europe racially, by eliminating the Jews', and to unite it 'politically, economically, and spiritually', with Nazism and Hitler setting 'a grandiose example'. What was new about the second MSR was its desire to 'constitute a new order of chivalry', but one without a leader, designed to bring together all the collaborationist forces.[12] Having shared in Déat's efforts to create a single party, the MSR became more of a secret society, withdrawing from active politics and dreaming of a Franco-German reconciliation.

Bucard was a war veteran who had never got over his war experiences and had for a while worked as a professional agitator who hired himself out to others (such as Valois, Coty and Hervé); then, from 1933 onwards he had worked on his own account. Of all the Paris leaders, it was he who had the best contacts in Vichy: Pétain received him on several occasions and felt that he could count on his allegiance. He also had good relations first with Darlan, then with Laval, at least up until the end of 1942. His party functioned in the free zone and his newspaper, *Le Franciste*, was published in both Marseilles and Paris. Bucard tried to make the most of his contacts in both towns.

He started out as a nationalist in extreme right leagues, then moved over to fascist totalitarianism, retaining something from his Catholic past and prone to emphasize the spiritualism and 'mysticism' of Francism. For the rest, he had a plebeian and popular style of speech ('There's a hell of a lot of dirty washing to do and muck you'd need a knife to scrape away') and was somewhat short on analysis and reason, compensating for this with a rhetoric of indignation and calls for repression.[13] Initially he carried over from his nationalism a vocabulary of grandeur, honour and heroism, making out that this set him apart from the common herd. He professed to reject the 'bleating kind of collaborationism',[14] criticized the spinelessness of others, and called for respect for the territorial integrity of defeated France. In Orleans, in February 1942, his adjutant, Guiraud, declared that there could be no question of collaboration if France were to lose the northern region and Alsace-Lorraine, then rounded off the meeting by singing the *Marseillaise*. It was this double lapse that earned him a warning from the Germans.[15] Francism continued to pipe away at its own particular tune to the last. In 1943, it attacked Laval, criticizing his version of collaboration, full 'of baseness and platitudes' and called for a government that would treat 'frankly and without evasions' with Germany.[16]

As early as the autumn of 1941, Bucard had formalized the dilemma and pronounced his choice: 'Should we wish for the victory of England, hence also of the USSR, on the pretext that they promise to maintain France's territorial integrity? Or should we accept the victory of Germany which, at this moment and with other peoples, is leading a veritable crusade for European salvation against all the communist and judeo-masonic international forces? For us, the situation is very clear. We hope for the victory of those who will deliver Europe from bolshevism and will at the same time liberate it from judeo-capitalistic power, for only then will Europe be able to live! '[17]

In the spring of 1942, following the Orleans incident, Francism had adopted a lower profile, telling its militants that equal rights and duties for conqueror and conquered must be deferred until after the war and that, for the moment, France should agree to recognize only its duties: if it did not help Germany now, there would be no chance of real collaboration in the future. It was therefore necessary to 'trust' the conqueror. This position was justified by an exceptionally fragile argument: namely, Hitler could have destroyed France in 1940, but did not; on the contrary, he had held out a helping hand.[18] After November 1942, Francism adopted the theme of 'Europe', an entity above nations, and even looked beyond a federation of states to a future in which a European nation-state would arise.[19] Bucard was to stick to this right to the end, but was always regarded by the Germans with some suspicion on account of his Pétainism and rumours about his homosexuality, as a result of which he was funded 'according to his going value'.[20] The membership of his party never rose above about 10 000.

Doriot stood head and shoulders above the rest of the small group of Paris leaders.[21] His party attracted the most members, probably a maximum of between 40 000 and 50 000, including those in North Africa. On the right wing, Doriot alone benefited from the collaboration of professional journalists and the support of a ring of intellectuals. He was a vigorous, unscrupulous man, and had retained from his time as a communist a sense of the importance of organization, manoeuvrability, analysis in terms of the power struggle, and open-mindedness with regard to international questions and strategic considerations. During the winter of 1940–41 he went along with the government line. Collaboration was a realistic policy, he explained to one of his adjutants; since a German victory was a probability, it was necessary to minimize its adverse effects by demonstrating goodwill and using the time afforded by the prolongation of the war to struggle back up towards the Germans. 'If we were no more than a handful of men surrounding the Marshal, this would be betrayal', he went on to say, 'but we are several million: that amounts to a legitimate opinion'.[22] This was a view that he was later to forget.

In the spring of 1941, he realized that he was marking time. Although he had reactivated his party in both zones, with newspapers to support him in both (*L'Émancipation nationale* in Marseilles, *Le Cri du peuple* in Paris) and could boast a solid following in North Africa, the political horizon was no clearer. *Le Cri du peuple* had been a flop, with its circulation plummeting from 150 000 to 16 000 in March 1941.[23] The PPF was no more than tolerated in the occupied zone so it could not hold public meetings. The dearth of prospects in Vichy, the stagnation of the party in both zones, and financial needs impelled Doriot to accentuate his collaboration policy.

At the PPF congress in the occupied zone in May 1941, he took a significant step forward, for the first time adding the 'European' argument to that of the national interest. 'I have three reasons for pursuing the policy of collaboration: as a Frenchman, I am saving my country from the worst; as a European, I am helping to unify the continent; as a revolutionary, I am propelling France into a national and social revolution, the only means to restore its unity.'[24] On this occasion he openly adopted a racist programme, always absent in pre-war days, calling for not only a hardening of the Jewish Statute, but also the prohibition of mixed marriages and even, implicitly, the sterilization of Jewish 'metics': in short, all the ideas of the SS.[25]

The German attack on the USSR thrust him completely into collaboration. His chance came with the creation of the Légion des Volontaires Français contre le Bolchévisme (LVF), proposed by various party leaders, supported by Abetz, but held in check by Hitler. In this new war, Doriot detected an opening: a rapid victory, a satisfied Germany, a France that would be better treated, and reward for himself. He joined up and in the autumn departed with the first contingent. He decided to try to turn the LVF into his own tool. His efforts at politicization displeased the Germans, who sent him back to France at the beginning of 1942, in time for them to take the LVF in hand.

Doriot's politics between the spring and the winter of 1942 shows how unusual he was in Paris circles, in particular with regard to the scope of his ambitions and his powers of manoeuvre. He had maintained contact with Laval while the latter was in Paris, although the distrust between the two men continued.[26] After returning to power, Laval gave him a little money but refused him not only a post in the government but also authorization to undertake a lecture tour in the free zone and North Africa. Doriot then launched himself into a major propaganda campaign in the occupied zone, vigorously criticizing Laval, albeit not directly, for the inadequacy of both his internal and his external policies, and posing as the pretender to power. His challenge would have been grotesque had he not been counting on backing from the occupier. Doriot was the only Paris leader who systematically set out to exploit the diversity of tendencies in the occupation apparatus.[27] He had won a degree of sympathy from the leaders of Propaganda-Abteilung by getting his militants to organize propaganda campaigns, and also from the Abwehr by volunteering information on the resistance movement. He had also established good relations with the SS, whose authority had increased with the arrival of Oberg and which was using him to exert pressure on Laval, just as the embassy had used Laval and Déat to put pressure on Darlan. With all of them, Doriot exploited their growing need for French auxiliaries.

However, all this adverse support from the German services was not enough to put him in the saddle, despite the publicity surrounding the congress that he organized in Paris at the beginning of November and that he tried to use to impress them all. It was Laval, who complained to the German authorities,[28] who came out on top. Hitler needed him and eventually made this known – thereby putting a stop to Doriot's campaign. By the end of 1942, the PPF was on its knees owing to the expenses to which it had committed itself, the embassy's suspension of its funding, and the threat of dissolution that was looming.[29] At the beginning of 1943, Doriot returned to the Eastern front, hoping for a renewal of credit as he proved his loyalty. It is quite true that for him anticommunism was a powerful source of motivation. Now that danger was increasing all the time, the idea of pulling back, retreating, let alone doing a U-turn was to him unthinkable, despite the fact that he, more than anyone, might have had the effrontery to do so.

Throughout the right-wing sector, antisemitism ruled, with all the parties supporting the propaganda of the German services and sometimes their actions: the PPF assisted the police in the Vélodrome d'Hiver round-up. Some men and some chapels even made this their exclusive speciality, continuing their line of action of pre-war days. There was scant evidence of concern for the national interest here, or rather this was from the outset defined as coinciding with the cause and victory of Nazi Germany, whose entire struggle was seen from this angle. Germany was certainly attacking the problem at its root, in a way that exceeded all their hopes and that was opening up possibilities for fulfilling even the most extreme aspirations of antisemites in all countries. Those in France certainly did not hang back; on the contrary, they supported the policies of the occupier, clamouring for them to be hardened. For these people there could never be enough discrimination against the Jews, they could never be despoiled, isolated and punished enough until such happy time as they disappeared altogether from Europe.

Their commitment to this task was strengthened by the advantages in the situation. Wide-eyed, they all welcomed such a fine opportunity, in which, simply by indulging their own passions, they would be rewarded by official support, assured employment and liberal remuneration. The chairman of the Association of Anti-Jewish Journalists, Jacques Mesnard, who was also the editor-in-chief of *Le Matin*, wrote to the official in charge of Jewish questions at the embassy, with every reason to assure him of 'the affectionate gratitude of the members of the AJA, of which you are certainly the founder and the most precious friend that we have been lucky enough to meet in our anti-Jewish struggle'.[30]

Antisemitism had its own special centres. The Institut d'Études

des Questions Juives (IEQJ), funded by the Germans, was directed by Paul Sézille, a retired captain in the colonial infantry, an alcoholic, quarrelsome, incompetent man who eventually wore out the patience even of his protectors.[31] According to him, the Friends of the IEQJ could boast 30000 members and sympathizers and 7000 subscribers, and he claimed that they came from all classes of society, beginning his list with doctors, followed by engineers, shopkeepers, lawyers, clerks and, lastly, workers.[32] The Centre d'Action et de Documentation, installed in the former headquarters of the Grand Lodge of France, was run by Henry Coston, who had been close to Nazism since the 1930s. In the summer of 1942, Coston, deeming propaganda 'in favour of closer ties between France and Germany' to be inadequate, advised the Germans to order compulsory screenings of the film, *Le Péril juif*, explaining that it was, in his opinion, the only way to get the population to understand 'the excellent administrative and policing methods that have been followed'.[33]

Antisemitism was served by a number of newspapers. The most important was *Au pilori*, run by Jean Lestandi. At the end of 1941 it was printing 60000 copies and selling close on 50000, a remarkable success for a paper carrying such rabidly antisemitic articles. No doubt for a small minority of French people it chimed with their own antipathies. One of their number may have been the Parisian widow who, at the end of 1943, sent her greetings for the New Year to Brinon. She wrote as follows: 'Excuse me for taking the liberty of writing to you I must send you my best wishes for the New Year of 44 and above all for long life I would beg you to excuse me from taking fizzy drinks the Jews put the powder from invisible diamonds in it's unforgiveable it cuts up all the fibres of the intestines and the doctors as usual think its a natural death. The year will be terrible I think but I keep hoping the Germans will be victorious if they are not what a disaster for France if it loses. But let us hope for better days for me life is sad I have an old-age pension and am unwell and 68 years old if you send me a small donation it would help me out.'[34]

A handful or so of intellectuals, some with quite a name as men of letters, used their talents to foster anti-Jewish hatred, and incorporated it deeply in their collaborationist commitment. In the forefront was the *Je suis partout* team, whose antisemitism was, if anything, even stronger than before the war and whose political attitudes were diverging more and more from those of their old master. Maurras was an ardent supporter of Pétain and spent most of his time railing against the enemies within. But he was suspicious of collaboration (without going so far as to attack it, out of respect for the Marshal) and certainly hostile to collaborationism. 'I am not European,' he snapped at the people in Paris, 'I am French, French from the sole clan of France.'[35] His disciples were already breaking away from the orthodox line, rallying to the idea of a leader and a single party, the two institutions of totalitarian regimes, the former still apparently related to monarchism, the latter clearly not. On the issue of collaboration they severed their last ties with Maurras. Having begun by supporting it in the name of realism and the national interest, they were soon defending it in the name of the common struggle and representing Nazism as a model that would make it possible to regenerate Europe and France itself.[36] They were, however, deterred from militant membership of any party by reason of their élitism and their tenacious antipathy to any mobilization of the masses. If they did go so far as to commit themselves, it was in most cases by enrolling in the Waffen-SS, where they could continue to fantasize about belonging to a heroic aristocracy. In December 1941, their newspaper was printing 78000 copies. Of the 64000 put on sale by Hachette, 55000 were sold, quite apart from those that went out to subscribers.[37] In 1943 the number of copies printed rose to over 150000 but, at this point, this reflected the support of the occupying force more than the sympathies of the French public.

Meanwhile, Céline was continuing along his pre-war course, distancing himself from the parties, but indicating his sympathy for Doriot. Fired with enthusiasm for the war against the USSR, he considered joining the health corps of the LVF. In the spring of 1942, he was eagerly following the German offensive and welcomed Laval's return to power.[38] In the open letters that he wrote to the most committed newspapers (*Au pilori, Je suis partout, L'Appel,* etc.), he declared his political position, following an altogether coherent line of thought.[39] He was as much racist as antisemitic: the elimination of Jews, desirable, indeed essential, was not enough. The French race needed to be purified, to be made to follow a cure of abstinence, to be recleansed, bodily and physically re-educated. In *Les Beaux Draps* (1941), the tone of which reflected the heated bitterness of his colleagues, he lambasted the French who had understood nothing and continued to squint towards England and Gaullism. Vichy was the worst of all and, until such time as a new kind of education could produce results, it was necessary to attract those French fools who thought only of money, by means of a 'Labiche version of communism', for example by allocating to them the property of the Jews: it seemed the only way to awaken the racist awareness that was so sadly lacking.

Along with Céline, Drieu la Rochelle was one of the French intellectuals closest to Nazi racism, the most inclined to think in terms of race, biological differences, superiority and inferiority, corruption, half-breeds, and decadence and, conversely, purging, purification and elimination. Eventually he reached the logical enough conclusion that he recorded in writing on 8 November 1942: 'I belong to a race, not to a nation.'[40] Just as Céline, after the war, was able to use his racism to underpin a surprising and self-interested philo-semitism – in which the Jews became the companions of the white race in opposition to the dangerous yellow and black races – similarly Drieu, watching young members of the SS in their tanks on the Champs Elysées, in June 1944, wrote: 'I love this blond race to which I belong, but it is also to be found amongst the English, the Americans and the Russians.'[41] Hence his latter-day philo-sovietism, which was in no way an ideological switch, but purely a matter of admiration for a triumphant force.

Alongside the idea of race was another concept, that of empire. This was a political form that the era of the nation-state had swept away in Europe but that resurfaced as soon as German hegemony was accepted. But the empire of the future was to safeguard nations and would be an empire of nations – 'a collective Rome', as Fabre-Luce put it – a political organization that would 'reconcile the notion of a nation and the notion of an empire or a federation'.[42] It was the only way to restore Europe's might at a time of intercontinental conflict, and to afford it domination over the 'vital space' to which it had a right, in Africa, the Near East and Russia.[43] Drieu, who had not wanted war with Germany and had never dreamed of expansion for France, now sketched out a future of grandeur and expansion for a Europe unified by Hitler.

28

Party members and military men

THE politicians who produced the discourse of collaboration were not ranting to empty houses. They could surely not have led the way so fervently had they not sensed some ferment of excitement amongst the mass of their compatriots. We have already noted Doriot's words in the autumn of 1940: 'If we were no more than a handful of men surrounding the Marshal, this would be a betrayal; but we are several million; that amounts to a legitimate opinion.' Most of those whose opinion inclined to collaboration never signed up with any political movement. But there was without doubt something fermenting, as some of the extreme forms that that opinion took in their own way show, foremost among them the cult of Hitler. In 1941 and 1942, several dozen French people sent their good wishes to the Nazi leader for his birthday or for the New Year, and some – the ladies in particular – added a poem.[1] Another poet was a retired professor who begged Brinon to pass on to Hitler the sonnet that he had composed to thank him for liberating prisoners from the Dieppe region following the unsuccessful Canadian landing in August 1942 (Ah! What a subtle diplomat the Führer is/And wherever he goes, what a clever victor'[2]). Others wrote begging for the honour of being sent a picture of him, for none were on sale in France. For example, a former member of the Comité France–Allemagne, working for one of the occupation services, wrote: 'If you possibly can, I would like you to send me a portrait of the Führer, to hang in our office. I already have Marshal Rommel and would like the Führer to be there too, as he should be everywhere.'[3]

The collaborationist parties comprised the activist elements from a current of opinion that was far more extensive. Up until 1942 they essentially employed all the classic methods of political action: propaganda, recruitment, political education, and mobilization, with a view to their members taking part in some well-publicized action that would enable them to be seen and would demonstrate their importance. They spent lavishly, with permanent officers and a profusion of propaganda, funded by subscriptions and gifts from supporters and above all subsidies from Vichy and the German services, in particular the embassy, which regulated the flow as seemed opportune. Certain groups, in particular the PPF, enjoyed the support of Propaganda-Abteilung, which financed a good many of their propaganda campaigns, since their ideas coincided.[4]

The various parties also endeavoured to target recruitment on particular professions, groups of intellectuals or young people. Some, in particular the RNP, specialized in organizing social assistance for prisoners of war or retired workers, or in making administrative suggestions to the French or German authorities. They had no hesitation in roping in captive or dependent audiences, such as the families of prisoners, promising to intercede for them (in 1941, this was a speciality of the RNP and the MSR) or the voluntary workers in Germany, among whom they would have liked – but were not allowed – to recruit (the Groupe Collaboration was the only group to be authorized to do so).[5] They also attracted members by obtaining jobs for them in services working for the occupiers, for instance recruitment offices and black market agencies.

They kept in contact with their supporters through the party newspaper, local meetings and above all organized demonstrations. In 1941–42, Déat and Doriot spoke to packed audiences in the provinces, particularly Doriot, who undertook a lecture tour to boost the LVF in April–May 1942. Anticommunism was, in every sense, a productive theme. This was a cause to which businesses were willing to contribute,[6] and was the only one with the power to attract crowds large enough to fill the Vélodrome d'Hiver. Thus on 1 February 1942, 20000 spectators gathered there to hear, in particular, Doriot, who was just back from the eastern front.[7] In the autumn of 1942, just before the landing, the principal parties held their congresses, one after another, each attracting a few thousand militants. It was a matter of rivalry and making a big impression with a show of force. Strenuous efforts were made to muster as many supporters as possible and the events were made as spectacular as possible, on the Nazi model. These miniature Nuremburg rallies provided an opportunity to show off the party's units for the maintenance of order, which were becoming increasingly important, especially in the Francist party and the PPF.

By 1942 party groups, albeit small and fragile, were established all over the place. They were at their most active between the spring and the autumn of 1942, with the PPF considered the most dynamic and the best organized by the French and German authorities. Among the militants, particularly the younger ones, activism developed in increasingly aggressive forms in the face of a society less and less tolerant of them. There were clashes, even with the police. In May 1942, after their congress had ended, 500 uniformed young Doriotists spread through the streets of Paris, clashing with policemen, twenty-four of whom were wounded. Elsewhere, militants would vandalize busts of Marianne, street signs guilty of republican overtones, or anything that referred to the Anglo-Saxons. In Paris, also in May 1942, young members of the PPF entered a dry-cleaners and tore down a notice bearing the English word 'pressing', while young RNP militants insisted on the removal of a photograph of Roosevelt displayed in the window of a photographer's shop.[8] On 14 July 1942, in Marseilles, PPF militants fired on a crowd demonstrating in the front of the party headquarters, killing two women.

Less visibly, another form of activism, every bit as alarming and far more dangerous, was developing: informing, spying and denunciation. Deloncle's MSR and above all the PPF made this their speciality. A unit run by Beaugras for the PPF collected both political and military intelligence, particularly on the resistance, which it passed on to the Abwehr in exchange for funds.[9] The RNP did not operate in this field until Laval's return to power, when it had hopes of becoming a government party. At this point it took it upon itself to organize surveillance of the administration and public life generally, becoming increasingly assiduous following the landing in North Africa, when local officials were requested to 'report all individuals dangerous to the government and the occupying authorities'.[10]

None of this was likely to improve an image that had been unfavourable right from the start. The administration frequently made difficulties or was grudging when the supporters of collaboration asked for help. In January 1942, the proprietor of a castle in Maine-et-Loire wrote to Abetz to complain: 'Ever since the establishment of the regime that has made Germany greater and enabled it to become the nation that guides the whole of Europe, my family and I have admired both your doctrines and your Great Leader. So right from the start we have wholeheartedly supported the political movements dedicated to ''collaboration''.' The count, the countess and their son wished to spread the ideas of collaboration through the neighbouring villages, with the aid of a projector. But although the Staffel of Angers had given them permission to do so, the prefecture and the chamber of commerce had been keeping them waiting for months. 'What can be done, Excellency? Our most ardent desire is to make your country known to our compatriots. Above all, we should like to show them that that country can be our best friend; and finally that, if they learn to know it, they will be bound to love it.'[11]

The militants were surrounded by distrust, if not hostility. The icy circle mentioned by Guéhenno concerning the occupiers also surrounded their friends. As early as the summer of 1941, here and there windows of party offices were smashed and warnings, followed by threats, were addressed to local leaders. From the autumn of 1941 on, acts of violence took place. Deadly injuries were still isolated in 1942, but they were no less disturbing on that account, encouraging an embattled mentality amongst the militants and making ordinary supporters increasingly prudent. Many had been discreet from the start. Now they became doubly careful or withdrew altogether. A report by the RNP leader in Bernay (Eure), written in the summer of 1942, is probably representative of the situation in small provincial towns at this time. It states that the local section could boast no more than fifty supporters out of a population of 7000 inhabitants; and even those fifty had only agreed to join 'on condition that their membership be kept strictly secret'.[12]

Throughout France, membership numbers for the collaborationist groups were highest during the first two years, peaking in 1942. This was clearly at odds with the graph of public opinion. But the general climate, although manifestly unfavourable to collaboration, did not exert pressure of a uniformly constricting nature, and uncertainty as to the outcome of the war weighed heavily upon many people. It was actually because of the prolongation of the war in the East that some people were prompted to commit themselves, for it seemed to indicate that the communist danger was even greater than had been thought. Still, these people committed themselves in the hope of a final victory for Germany. Others joined because of the decline of the national revolution, the deterioration of the climate inside France, and the resurgence of old enemies. It was a reaction that goes a long way towards explaining the phenomenon of the Milice.

The supporters of collaboration constituted a tiny society within civil society generally, and were attached to it by links of many kinds. But as those links were not uniformly tight, two different tendencies soon became detectable: some partisans pulled away and moved back towards the majority; others, on the contrary, detached themselves altogether from the majority and pledged themselves utterly to collaborationism, 'to the very end'.

Partisan commitment was essentially a masculine phenomenon: women constituted only a minority of about 15 per cent. Even so, their very presence was remarkable at a time when they had no political rights. It was also an urban phenomenon, particularly prevalent in the larger cities. The Paris region on its own accounted for a large proportion of the members of each party. In May 1944, the Groupe Collaboration had a total of 42283 members, 21983 of them in Paris (overall, 32882 were in the northern zone and 9401 in the free zone).[13] There is a social explanation for this distribution: urban life is characterized by separations between the places where one resides, works and pursues leisure activities. It is therefore possible for an individual to form several different networks of relations so that more opportunities for political commitment arise for him. It is easier to join parties; one is less visible and less likely to be labelled.

The socio-professional composition of the partisan world over the 1940–44 period displayed a great diversity. The whole of French society was reflected in this microcosm, but in a very distorted fashion.[14] Peasants and workers were no more than weakly represented (27.5 per cent as compared to 62.9 per cent of the active population of 1936); all the same, they accounted for one out of every four supporters. The middle and upper classes made up the major battalions (71.4 per cent as compared to 30.3 per cent in 1936). Business proprietors (industrialists, retailers and artisans) were as numerous as the workers and peasants put together. Their over-representation (27 per cent as compared to 13.8 per cent) was about double, as was that of office workers (managers, employees, officials: 36.3 per cent compared to 16 per cent), but way behind the liberal professions (7.2 per cent as compared to 0.5 per cent). In the last category a number of professions were disproportionately strong: doctors, for example (whereas lawyers hardly figured at all), managers, travelling salesmen and commercial representatives – all professions with above average contact with the general public. However, it is not possible to verify whether their commitment was determined by this specific context or whether it reflected their normal involvement in political action. All in all, the preponderance of rather well-to-do social strata might suggest that collaborationism was a classic social reaction. However, the strong presence of the salaried middle classes and the minority but by no means negligible weight of the working classes (workers, service personnel) indicates a more widespread pull that confers upon these movements quite a marked cross-class character.

The analysis may be pushed a little further, thanks to a national sample composed of individuals purged for having belonged to some collaborationist group – as it were, the foot-soldiery of the partisan troops.[15] If one examines the socio-professional composition of new members year by year, two sub-categories emerge distinctly, one before 1942, the other after that year. It turns out that the overall statistics given above result from an average taken between two contrasting sets of figures, and that they conceal the fact that a considerable and continuous change in the relative weight of the various categories took place as time passed: social categories followed one another, gradually descending the social scale. In 1941, retailers, civil servants, employers, the liberal professions and retired people were, in relative terms, the most strongly represented. The next year they were superseded by managers, teachers, clerks, people with no profession and technicians. In 1943, these were replaced by technicians, artisans and service personnel who, in 1944, were in turn replaced by students, workers and agricultural labourers. In that last year, 1944, the farmers, teachers, employers and liberal professions provided no new members at all.

If we put the figures together on a two-year basis, the full picture of this changing pattern of behaviour for the various social categories is revealed. Of all the employers in the sample, 87.5 per cent joined in 1941 and 1942, as did 83 per cent of the retailers, individuals from the liberal professions and retired people, 81 per cent of the teachers, 80 per cent of the technicians and 70 per cent of the civil servants. Those joining in 1942 and 1943 comprised 73 per cent of all the clerks, 72 per cent of the service personnel, 70 per cent of the artisans, 67 per cent of those without any profession, 66 per cent of the farmers and 58 per cent of the workers. Finally, 75 per cent of the students and 83 per cent of the agricultural labourers joined in 1943–44 (the strong presence of students in 1943 is linked with the establishment of the STO and the creation of the Milice: 40 per cent of the students in the sample went into the Milice). The same phenomenon is detectable where the women are concerned (15 per cent of the sample). On average, these were younger and less well educated than the men. The women of the early days, who did not go out to work and were drawn from the more prosperous circles, were later replaced by younger girls, manual workers or employees. These mostly joined in 1943.

This shifting of social categories was accompanied by a noticeable decrease in age, a drop in levels of education, and an increase in people with relatively chequered careers behind them. The older people were, the earlier they joined (the average age in 1941 was forty-two, whereas in 1944 it was twenty-six), and the earlier they subsequently pulled out. Given that some professions are closely linked with age – running a business or taking part in one of the liberal professions, for instance – their concentration in the first two years is easily explained. As for the other categories, in particular those that seem less affected by the watershed of 1942, the generation factor offers a key. Thus, roughly the same proportions of craftsmen joined in 1942 and 1943, but in the earlier year their average date of birth was 1891, in the next year it was 1913. One quarter of the civil servants in the sample joined in 1943: not only were they younger, they were also lower in the hierarchy, most being PTT auxiliaries or young SNCF agents.

Finally, the factor of social instability is at least as important as socio-professional positions. If we put in one group people with a chequered professional history and those with a police record – let us call them 'unstable people' – we obtain 19 per cent of the sample, that is to say one-fifth of the total. But the 'unstable' category makes up 38 per cent of all agricultural labourers, 36 per cent of the workers, 30 per cent of the technicians, and one-quarter of service personnel and employees. There are no such people among the farmers, the teachers or the employers, practically none in the liberal professions or among the retired people and managers. Thus, even in the first period, the minority from the popular strata and some of the middle strata is characterized by certain features – in particular instability – that distinguish it from the majority, which is composed of prosperous, stable, and securely rooted people. After 1942, the falling away of the latter is accompanied by their replacement by a younger generation and greater instability among the popular strata (the proportion of 'unstable people' among the workers joining in 1944 shoots up to 68 per cent). If there is a conclusion to be drawn from this sample, it is that the relatively cross-class nature of collaboration masks a more complex reality: on the one hand, we find people representative of their social category, mature, educated people who joined early and withdrew early, behaving in politics as they were accustomed to behave in their ordinary lives; on the other, many social misfits who had broken their ties with their original backgrounds or had been detached by the vicissitudes of their lives. Broadly speaking, the former group provided the collaborationist groups with members, the latter with militants and also most of the recruits for military units wearing German uniforms.

In this sample, on average one person in four had a political past: more amongst the retailers, teachers, civil servants and people from the liberal professions. Amongst people with no profession and agricultural labourers, virtually none had a political past; amongst employers, the number was definitely below average. After 1942, fewer had any political past: one-third of members in 1941, 7 per cent in 1944. As time passes, the role played in people's commitment by political memories of the pre-war period steadily diminishes. Increasingly, what mainly prompts them to commit themselves to collaboration is the disorientation that the occupation itself produced amongst dispersed fractions of the popular strata.

Of the collaborationist members with a political past, just over two-thirds came from the extreme right (out of 108 cases, 43 were veterans who had supported La Roque, 38 were PPF, 10 were AF, etc.), 22 per cent were from the left (out of thirty-five cases, fifteen were SFIO, four were USR, six were PCF, etc.), only 8 per cent came from the moderate right. Pillars of the *ancien régime*, particularly radicals, were conspicuous by their absence. These people were distributed across the board of the various collaborationist movements in accordance with a certain pattern. The RNP attracted three people from the extreme right for every eighteen from the left; the PPF attracted fifty-eight from the right for every eight from the left, Groupe Collaboration attracted six from the right for every four from the left. In short, the presence of former men of the left was by no means negligible; but continuity with the extreme right was more pronounced. Yet even the number from the right was only a tiny fraction of the members of that political family in the 1930s.

The greatest proportion of party members with a political past belonged to the PPF (41 per cent); the next greatest belonged to Francism, and in both cases the party dated from before the war. But only 23 per cent of the people registered with the PPF under the occupation had belonged to that party in the past, and many of those had suspended their membership for a period of several years. Similarly, although 32 per cent of the Francists had a political past, only 10 per cent had belonged to Bucard's party before the war. So to a large extent these two parties found new memberships under the occupation, as they did new local leaders. Of the thirty or so names of departmental leaders mentioned in the PPF press in 1937–38, only about ten reappeared after 1940. In 1942 the party weekly cited the names of seventeen departmental leaders who had joined since the defeat.[16]

Whether new or old, the collaborationist parties were strongly characterized by instability, and as time passed that instability increased. Of those who had joined in 1941, one-third had left by the end of the following year; almost half those who joined in 1942 had disappeared one year later; but one out of every two members dating from 1941 and 1942 stayed on to the very end. The local party leaders appear to have been even more unstable, perhaps because they were more exposed. Out of thirty-eight PPF departmental organizers operating in the occupied zone at the beginning of 1942, only seven were still at their posts at the end of 1943. Some had been transferred or promoted, but most seem to have retired around November 1942. In the case of the RNP, out of thirty-six departmental organizers recorded in 1942, only five were still at their posts in the summer of 1943.[17] From this we can gauge the fragility of these organizations and the hardline obstinacy of their leaders, not only in comparison with grass-roots members but also with local leaders, who were more sensitive to the atmosphere and what was happening around them.

Our sample suggests that the collaborationist groups only filled out their ranks by attracting people who had previously avoided political commitment of any kind, although that does not necessarily mean that they had no political inclinations. To judge from the declarations made by people caught in the purges, the motives for their mobilization varied considerably. For many, self-interest was certainly a major motive: it appears in the defence of one in five people, or even one in four in the cases of those enrolled in 1942: a party card made for easier relations with the occupiers. Motives such as a desire for protection or influence, or even constraint exercised by a member of the family or a superior affected one in ten of all those involved and a good third of those who joined in 1943 and 1944. But conviction was the motive invoked by 75 per cent of these people (80 per cent in 1941, but only 41 per cent in 1944). Three factors emerge from statements made at the time of the purges: support for Pétain, frequently invoked; anticommunism, omnipresent; and reference to social justice, usually mentioned in connection with the difficulties of life under the occupation. This last point, stressed in particular by people from the more popular strata does not, however, turn these parties into protest movements. Despite the criticisms aimed at the government, these were movements that supported the official policy – that of Pétain and the French state.

For total membership numbers, we are reduced to approximations. Up until the end of 1942, the parties as a whole mustered possibly a total of 150000 members.[18] Assuming the membership for 1943–44 to have been half that for 1941–42, as in our sample, the total for the period of the occupation, adding in the Milice, might have come to 250000, that is to say the equivalent of the SFIO at the time of the Popular Front. Of course, this kernel of party members was surrounded by quite a wide circle of sympathizers: people who did not actually join for various reasons – insufficient commitment or a distrust of 'politics' in general, absence of enticement, prudence, etc. – although they may well have held strong enough opinions. One such was a woman in the Eure department who declared, as if in confirmation of Queneau's *Un rude hiver*: 'We're better governed with the Germans than with the French, and they have more discipline than there is here. The French were stuffing their faces while the Germans were turning out weapons. It's enough to make you sick, being French is.'[19]

The readership of the weekly political press gives a vague idea of the number of these sympathizers, certainly a better idea than the circulation of the daily newspapers, which were often read simply for administrative information and the sales figures had fallen to half their pre-war level.[20] The purchase of a political weekly, after all, indicates a positive choice, with no practical justification. In 1942, the total number of copies of these weeklies, all (except *Je suis partout*) created since the defeat, came to about 500000. Taking into account a considerable number of unsold copies, 300000 must have been sold each week in the occupied zone.[21] Assuming twice or three times as many readers and adding in the readers of periodicals such as *Grin-*

goire and *Candide* in the free zone, of which several hundred thousand copies were printed, it would appear that at least one or two million French people leaned toward collaborationism.

Alongside partisans and sympathizers of this political movement, there were Frenchmen who donned the uniform of the occupier. The Légion des Volontaires contre le Bolchévisme was controlled by the Paris parties. However, they did not provide many recruits for it; these mostly came of their own accord. Anticommunism certainly was an opinion, a feeling that was widely shared and deeply felt. For some French people, the German-Soviet conflict, instead of alienating them from collaboration, as it did most of their compatriots, actually consolidated or precipitated their commitment. Here is what a couple of aristocratic residents of Versailles, 'vibrant with enthusiasm', wrote to Abetz to congratulate him on this event that gave the Montoire gesture 'all its noble and profound meaning': 'It is with fervent enthusiasm that my wife and I venture to tell your Excellency of the deep admiration that we feel for the heroism of the German armies, led by the genius of their Führer into the most noble of wars. Our French hearts are with those knights battling for Europe, whose magnificent bravery will deliver us once and for all from the Jewish, Anglo-American and Bolshevik vermin.'[22]

Others actually joined up, donned German uniform and swore an oath of allegiance to Hitler as leader of the struggle against communism. Some did so encouraged by the assent of Pétain, loudly publicized by propaganda and publicly confirmed by the Marshal himself in November 1941 ('You are responsible for part of our military honour'). These volunteers included men of conviction ('I am proud to fight in German uniform alongside our German comrades under the Reich') as well as plenty of hotheads. One lieutenant, a practising Catholic and PPF militant who was confident of victory, wrote as follows in October 1941: 'Next it will be the turn of England and France, for it is above all in our own dear land that we long to use bombs, grenades, machine guns and daggers.' He signed off with 'Long live France! Long live Hitler!'[23]

In the autumn of 1941, the Germans reckoned 30 to 40 per cent of these volunteers to be idealists, the rest probably adventurers or jobless.[24] The first of those categories no doubt included the more mature men, many of them veterans from 1914, whose relatively strong presence so struck observers in the early days. In March 1942, the Germans complained that not one of a large contingent of volunteers from Marseilles could be retained for service, as the very youngest was already forty-five years old.[25] That serves as a reminder of the fact that there was a generational dimension to anticommunism, and that the first to join the volunteers were probably men who had already been anticommunist for some time. Alongside these were many unemployed, social outcasts, men with failed marriages, adventurers and old soldiers, whose presence made the LVF a relatively ill-disciplined body. In the summer of 1943, one member of a delegation visiting the Légion that included Brinon and Brasillach described the undisciplined, violent atmosphere: 'Blows are sometimes exchanged, men have fought with officers, officers have been killed.'[26]

Right to the end, the Légion retained its motley composition, but with a falling off among the 'idealists'. Among the latter were men of the old France, such as Comte Mayol de Lupé, a prelate though not a priest, who joined up at the age of sixty-seven and for whom 'crusade' remained the sacred watchword. In November 1943 he declared himself delighted that the level of recruitment was 'noticeably rising', thanks to the arrival of 'society' people: 'We may have lost Bernard de Polignac, but we have amongst us lieutenants or legionnaires [by the name of] de Villefranche, de Monfort, de Lapeyrouse, de Veilmont, de Parzie, etc., all of whom do their names great credit.'[27]

In the first half of 1944, postal censorship testified to the presence of people motivated by a taste for adventure ('You know how adventurous I am: I like action, travel and danger and here I am really living'), by material needs ('Pay is falling, that's the main thing, and meanwhile this shit of a war is still not over'), and by romantic disappointment ('I joined up with the LVF because I felt everything with you was going wrong'). Only a minority, those convinced of the communist danger, mentioned their political motives and also spoke of their cameraderie with the Germans, taking responsibility for their decision: 'I left with the LVF because the Germans were and still are the only ones capable of overthrowing bolshevism. The only thing that deterred me was the green uniform, but it is now dearer to me than our own because it is unsullied by any defilement of my honour.'[28]

As Frenchmen in German uniform, torn between allegiances, the legionnaires were in a very trying position. As one of them lamented, they were estranged from their families, received icily when they went home on leave and had been abandoned by the government and the administration. In short, they felt rejected by the French community.[29] Some came to terms with their double allegiances and worked out their priorities, as did one lieutenant who, in March 1943, declared that the LVF had sworn allegiance to Hitler, not to Pétain and, if forced to choose between the two, he would obey the leader he had chosen freely, namely Hitler.[30] Others moved away from their country but still found no place for themselves. On 7 September 1943 Charles Braibant wrote as follows: 'The other day one of our doctor friends noticed a Boche who spoke very bad German. He made enquiries. He discovered that he was a chap from the "French" Legion against bolshevism. Tired of being insulted by upright Frenchmen, these wretches pocket the tricolor cockades that are part of their German uniform and chatter away in German as well as they can, so as to pass themselves off as pure Boches.'[31] In all, 5800 Frenchmen joined the LVF, 3000 of them during the first year of recruitment: a meagre number, achieved at huge financial expense. But there had been 13 400 volunteers, many of whom had been rejected for reasons of health or on account of their criminal records.[32]

From 1943 on, there was another fighting body seeking French recruits: the Waffen-SS. In December 1942, Himmler, alarmed at the German losses, suggested to Hitler the formation of a French unit, to be known as Gobineau or Charlemagne.[33] After somewhat protracted negotiations, which he tried yet again to use as a lever to secure some kind of political promise, Laval authorized the enrolment of volunteers (the Law of 23 July 1943), having been assured that the unit would not be used on French territory or engaged against Free France and that its members would be disarmed when demobilized.[34]

By this date, the new unit, in competition with the LVF anyway, was never likely to produce miracles, even if it did arouse curiosity in some quarters. In 1944 a promotional exhibition of photography was put on in Paris for ten days. To the delight of its German organizers, it attracted about 2000 visitors each day, even more at the weekends.[35] The results were certainly not too bad: by the summer of 1944, 3000 men had been recruited out of an unknown number of volunteers, probably twice as many.[36] The volunteers swore allegiance to Hitler, as the 'Germanic and reforming leader of Europe', not simply the commander of the antibolshevik struggle. Nearly all came from popular circles, many of them joining up after altogether chaotic careers. Some had been recruited from the STO, possibly under pressure, or from amongst petty delinquents offered a choice between prison and mobilization. Only a minority appear to have been motivated politically. There were virtually no officers or local leaders of any calibre, apart from a few drafted in from the Milice (the LVF had been faced with exactly the same problem).

Other Frenchmen donned the uniforms of auxiliary Wehrmacht units. About 2000 joined the Kriegsmarine, in which they serviced ships or acted as armed guards in submarine bases.[37] The NSKK-Motorgruppe Luftwaffe was a motorized unit belonging to the Nazi party and engaged in military tasks such as transport assistance for the Luftwaffe. The French volunteers, who were to serve as drivers or manual staff, wore the uniform of the German airforce, with a tricolor tab. They promised 'to fight with Germany and its allies against all enemies of the New Order in Europe, wherever necessary and until definitive victory'.[38] In June 1943, the number of enrolled men was 1982;[39] it probably reached a total of 3000. There was a large shortfall: by 31 March 1943, 1374 men had been enrolled out of 3755 volunteers.[40] Others joined the Todt Organization as foremen or armed guards, wearing the organization's khaki uniform with a tricolor tab. By the spring of 1943, the number of French armed guards already stood at over 3000.[41]

By the summer of 1944, 9000 Frenchmen had been enrolled in combat units and a few months later these were joined by 1800 men from the Milice now in the Charlemagne division and several hundred collaborationists who had taken refuge in Germany: a total of about 12000 men. At least 10000 other Frenchmen wore the uniform of auxiliary units in the German army. In the background were probably twice as many who had volunteered but been rejected, making a total of at least 40000 Frenchmen prepared to wear the German uniform. Apart from the militants and those who genuinely believed in what they were doing, a high proportion, if not the majority, of these men seem to have made their choice in conditions and for reasons similar to the workers who volunteered to go to Germany, many of them sharing similarly disadvantaged social origins, a low level of education and previously unstable careers. Other factors behind their choice must have been their impressionability to propaganda, admiration for the Germans' strength, and antipathies and prejudices of a political nature. Although not all these men may have perceived the full political significance of their choice with equal clarity, it was certainly evident to them all.

29

Militias

THE landing in North Africa caused the collaborationists to stampede. Once Vichy had lost its trump cards, it was as if they themselves had. To regain their footing, all they could do was raise the stakes. All now clamoured for military alliance and unlimited collaboration, and all heaped violent criticism on Laval. Even Déat could hardly restrain himself. The theme of Europe was on all their lips, accompanied by declarations of solidarity with Nazi Germany. 'We consider ourselves ideal brothers of the leaders of the Reich', declared one PPF leader. Costantini spoke of turning his party into 'the French section of the European union of national socialist forces'. 'The duty of France coincides with the duty of Europe. It orders us to make straight for our goal: union through national socialism'.[1]

The situation created a vacuum around collaboration, and a crushing hostility descended upon the collaborationists, particularly those who continued to voice their opinions and demonstrate their commitment. Many chose to beat a retreat or resign. Except in major cities, after the beginning of 1943 the faithful slunk along in the shadows and met in secret. The parties fell back to cluster round their local leaders and a handful of hardliners, who faced their compatriots as they would a hostile people. Symptomatic in this respect was the reaction of one 'notable', a member of the Groupe Collaboration, a professor at the Conservatoire National des Arts et Métiers and chairman of the Société d'Encouragement pour l'Industrie Nationale (the Society for the Encouragement of National Industry). In a letter to Brinon, he observed that in 1941 French people who favoured collaboration could operate out in the open. In 1942, the situation was quite the reverse. Now, 'loyal Frenchmen have entered the night'. What could be done with the rest, the great majority that refused to understand? 'They must be made to obey by force.'[2]

In the parties, classic political methods gave way to paramilitary organization and policing activities. Unable to prove that collaboration enjoyed popular support, the extremists set about demonstrating what they could do in other ways. This was the time of militias, men in uniform, and clandestine activities. But now the Paris parties were no longer on their own. From the heart of Vichy, a new actor emerged upon the collaborationist stage – the Milice.

Collaborationism had never come exclusively from Paris. In the free zone, it certainly represented one current of opinion that was articulated in the press and was manifested in the activities of parties such as the PPF and Francism, which were present in both zones. But certain Vichy-based groups had also adopted a line that was indistinguishable from that of the Paris parties. The major one was the SOL, the 'Service d'Ordre Légionnaire', which had emerged in 1941 from the Pétainist Légion Française des Combattants, with the blessing of Darlan and the support of Pucheu, who hoped to turn it into an extra police force. The SOL attracted activists from amongst the legionnaires, those who flaunted their loathing of parliamentary representatives, communists and Jews. Its leader, Joseph Darnand, was a war veteran and an old militant from the extreme right, who had gravitated from Maurras to Deloncle's Cagoule. Of the 15000 or so men whom he recruited, most came from the right-wing leagues, or at least from a right-wing background. With its parades, its public swearing of oaths and above all activities that were prone to overstep the bounds of legality, small wonder the SOL soon came to be generally seen as an imitation of the SA or the SS.[3]

Darnand's career was to benefit from Laval's return. The two men, the one a former Cagoulard, the other a former parliamentary representative, were mistrustful of each other, but self-interest on both sides overcame this. Laval was looking for an instrument that he had lacked in 1940. He wanted to get back at Doriot, and he believed he could manipulate Darnand. Darnand, for his part, wished to shake off the Légion's control and was seeking an area of power that extended beyond the free zone: in June 1942, he was already asking the Germans for permission to move the SOL into the occupied zone, arguing that this would be as much to their advantage as to his.[4]

Not long afterwards, he publicly took up a position spearheading collaboration. Laval had sent him to Poland to visit the LVF, which he was hoping to bring under the control of the French state. Darnand returned much impressed by the prostration of the conquered Poles and above all by his encounter with their conquerors. 'I have seen this people at war, clustered around its leaders in unwavering solidarity. I sensed the sincerity of this people's desire to avoid a return to the useless wars that for centuries have set it in opposition to France for which, even in its defeat, it retains esteem and respect. I was painfully aware of its astonishment in the face of the hesitancy and reservations of our people, who appear not fully to appreciate the generosity of Germany's gesture.' Accordingly, what was needed was positive collaboration, a first pledge of which was the LVF, even if the French failed to understand the action of its men, even if they could not recognize 'what the acceptance of a foreign uniform and foreign commanders inspired in the way of lucid sacrifices and the rejection of traditions and preferences – all that has shaped our souls – to leave room solely for what is essential: the will to sacrifice oneself for one's country, whatever the conditions of that sacrifice.' Now that the government wished to create a tricolor Legion, it was the duty of the SOL to be present in the 'avant-garde of the European struggle'.[5] This openly collaborationist position brought Darnand into line with the Paris party leaders. He was alongside them again in November, after the landing, supporting co-belligerence against the Anglo-Saxons for the sake of reconquering the AFN.

The creation of the Milice, at the turn of the following year, was a product of Laval's plan to amalgamate all the collaborationist parties into a single formation – a plan that failed, despite his 'extraordinary interest' in it.[6] In default, he at least created the Milice that was to have accompanied the single party. The regime, now without an army, needed a praetorian guard. Darnand, for his part, kept his own political objectives in view, from the start stressing the double mission of the Milice Française: to maintain order and to reform the country politically. He intended it to be his stepping-stone to power.[7]

The movement was organized on the model of the Nazi party. Alongside the general Milice, which received all those who joined, women as well as men, and the Avant-Garde, for girls and boys between the ages of fourteen and eighteen, was a voluntary Franc-Garde for militants of an age to fight, and a permanent Franc-Garde run as a military unit living in barracks, designed to serve as an armed force. An extra statute envisaged the permanent Franc-Garde developing an external section: 'a political and military formation composed of persons wishing to demonstrate their political beliefs by fighting bolshevism beyond the territory of France, alongside analogous formations constituted by other European countries'.[8] Darnand had his eye on absorption of the LVF.

In the course of the SOL's transformation into the Milice, membership had fallen considerably. Some of the *miliciens* had evolved along the same lines as Darnand himself. Others were young people in search of employment, attracted by the exercise of authority or intent upon eluding the STO by enlisting in the permanent Franc-Garde. The Milice differed from the Paris parties in that a high proportion of those enlisting in it were farmers (although definitely fewer than in the SOL) and while students, soldiers and police were strongly represented, relatively few teachers were. Its leaders included many 'notables' and even members of the nobility, mostly from conservative, Catholic circles, many of them traditionalist or Maurrasian. Anticommunism was fundamental: it absorbed all the phobias and allergies of these circles and, since the summer of 1941, had prompted many people to revise their ideas about Germany.[9] More generally, the Milice was made up of men strong on order, who set the greatest store by the legitimacy of Pétain and the French state and could not tolerate the rise of resistance on their territory, finding this far more unbearable than the presence of the Germans and even believing it to justify closer cooperation with the latter. Whereas the collaborationists in the occupied zone committed themselves in order to defend one particular political option at a time when the population was still withdrawn, although already defiant to collaboration, the Milice was, right from the start, a rear-guard organization created by a regime that had forfeited all credibility in the eyes of public opinion: it was, in fact, a force for civil war.

Recruitment did not match up to expectations, as was recognized by Darnand, who was aware of the disproportion between the heavy administrative apparatus and the small and insufficiently active force of militants. But he did not give up his goal. 'Our most determined enemies would like us to remain a militarized, hierarchical movement, solely devoted to extra policing missions', but it was equally important to create 'the political movement alone capable of influencing the country deeply and training the leaders who must take over and who are so badly needed in France'.[10]

However, on the political front disappointments continued. Darnand wanted to carry the Milice into the northern zone; Laval resisted this, fearing to find himself faced by a new, more powerful Doriot. As usual, however, he did not actually say 'no', but asked Darnand to study the matter with the Germans. Darnand's idea was to gather all the parties around his 25000 *miliciens*, creating a total of 40000 to 50000 men. In this way, the Milice would become single party. Negotiations were held in Paris in July 1943, under the aegis of the embassy. Most of the Paris leaders were unwilling to do more than set up a coordination committee,[11] and the embassy, which favoured an amalgamation, could not insist upon it because of its directive to encourage divisions. Laval was only too pleased not to have to do anything, and did nothing, even though the Germans proved agreeable to the Milice moving into the northern zone.[12]

From the early summer on, a wave of resignations developed, caused by difficulties of all kinds, above all the turn taken by the war.[13] Darnand, who around May–June does not seem to have ruled out rallying Free France,[14] presented Laval with his resignation. He complained of the hesitancy of the administration, the lack of means, in particular for setting up the Francs-Gardes quartered in barracks, and Laval's own procrastinations. Again he declared that only collaboration 'can make it possible for France once more to take up a place and rank worthy of its past amongst the finally reconciled countries of Europe'. He remained 'convinced that viable *entente* between the European nations will always be conditional upon the unity of Europe's political ideal and the harmony of internal regimes'. In other words, he was exhorting Laval to place internal politics on the same level as external politics.[15]

Although he subsequently retracted his resignation, matters did not improve. The frame of mind of his lieutenants was equally dissatisfied. As the resistance movement grew, assassinations were beginning to take their toll of *miliciens*. Meanwhile the Milice was inadequately armed, a fact for which Laval blamed the distrust of the German services. The departmental leaders of the Milice, who met him in August, did not believe him and decided to turn to the local occupation authorities, pointing out that it was essential for them to be armed if they were to maintain order and cope with Gaullist or communist uprisings that might accompany the Anglo-Saxon invasion.[16]

In this climate of unrest and mistrust of Laval, Darnand was seeking allies. In the preceding autumn he had made contact with Déat. Both were dependent upon Laval and had plenty of reasons to complain of him, and each could help the other: Déat by facilitating the implantation of the Milice in the northern zone, Darnand by facilitating the creation of a single party throughout the land. What had to be done was hitch the single party and the Milice together. Working with Bucard, the Groupe Collaboration and Soulès's MSR, Déat revived the idea of amalgamation that had been abandoned the previous autumn, and this time included in the agenda the merging of their respective militias, as a step towards joining up with Darnand.

As a result, the paramilitary question also came to the fore in the northern zone. The parties' own respective militias were small forces, always competing for attention. In the spring of 1943, the Germans for the first time authorized them to parade in the streets. They were now allowed to prove their resolution and keenness to fight and throw out signals in the direction of opponents and the general population. Between April and August, all the principal militias held parades, none mustering more than 2500 men, the RNP even fewer.[17] The PPF had been the last to provide itself with a militia, having previously made do with its force for maintaining order, and it was the last to march. According to an observer from the resistance, the Vélodrome d'Hiver was only half-full, the procession along the Champs-Élysées mustered no more than 2200 participants, women and girls included. Amid what passed for the party's shock troops, he spotted a hunchback and several cripples. Most of the faithful were thin, stooping, and looked undernourished (they came from the lower classes and were hard hit by the restrictions). Many of those curious enough to be onlookers barely concealed their hostility, and the few passive sympathizers in the crowd reacted not at all to the insults and jibes from other bystanders. This observer concluded that the Germans had given up all political action and were now concerned solely to encourage the formation of combat units that they might use as auxiliaries in their struggle against the resistance.[18]

The Déat–Darnand alliance produced a declaration – the Plan of 4

September – addressed to the principal Nazi leaders. The two men, supported by Luchaire, requested Germany's help in fusing together the militias, creating a single party, and thoroughly reshuffling the government. They also asked for a pact to be concluded guaranteeing France its territorial integrity, and requested administrative and political sovereignty and aid for the reconquest of its empire, in return for their military assistance.[19]

In the meantime, Darnand had also been seeking support elsewhere: from the SS, which itself needed help in setting up a French Waffen-SS unit. Oberg had met with resistance on the part of Doriot, who began by refusing, saying that he could not countenance any germanization, then promised to help recruitment in the name of the European battle.[20] Darnand responded more positively and promised to provide between 200 and 300 Francs-Gardes. As an extra pledge, he himself volunteered for the Waffen-SS and swore an oath of allegiance to Hitler, 'the Germanic and reforming Führer of Europe', promising obedience unto death. It is worth stressing the importance of this gesture. Darnand was the first French politician to swear loyalty to Hitler unconditionally, not solely within the framework of the struggle against bolshevism, as Doriot and the LVF legionnaires had. He entered fully into the SS system, based upon a man-to-man allegiance and overstepping the boundary of nationality, while the SS professed to believe him to be descended from a 'Germanic' people. He furthermore committed himself to active service at such time as his superiors should require it, thereby tying his own hands in the event of disagreement arising.

Darnand pushed ahead in this way in order to obtain aid and allies, to force Laval to make a move, and to manoeuvre himself closer to power, for this had clearly become his goal. In the immediate instance, he wanted weapons for his Franc-Garde. The increasing number of assassinations alarmed him and above all, as he explained to the Germans, he wanted a reasonable force at his disposition in case of internal difficulties, one that would enable him to avoid having to call for their intervention: the French state must be in a position to maintain order on its own, as Pétain and Laval themselves wished.[21]

At the end of September, the occupation authorities decided to allow the collaborationists the means to protect themselves. Weapon permits would be issued, with precautions. Family protection would be organized and plans would be made with a view to a possible evacuation in the event of an 'invasion'. The SS granted the Milice the right to open training camps in twenty-one departments, for a total of 600 *miliciens*, who would receive policing and military instruction under the direction of SD officers. The weaponry could be procured from arms caches seized from the resistance. As for the leaders of the Milice, they would be issued with arms to defend themselves.[22]

The Germans were less generous to the Paris parties, a fact that indicated the importance the Milice had acquired in their eyes, to the detriment of, for example, Doriot, to whom the SS had been sympathetic just the previous year. The Paris parties would be given a few arms, but the men handling them would be placed at the disposition of the German police. It was thus that, in November 1943, the decision was taken to create a Selbstschutz (a self-protection unit), a paramilitary force composed of members of the collaborationist parties, who would be given two weeks' training in a camp at Taverny.[23]

By the end of 1943, the militant force of collaboration was shrinking. The figure of 40000 to 50000 seems acceptable if it refers to those still active after the summer lull. By now the situation was bringing them all closer together and stereotyping them as never before. Darnand had caught up with the Paris leaders and was now speaking as a 'European', stressing the need for a Europe united in the face of the perils threatening it: American imperialism and, above all, communism. 'The communist Internationale and its allies must be opposed by the union of European nationalists. For nobody can any longer claim that this war is an ordinary conflict with merely a few provinces at stake. What this world revolution has set in opposition are the very same forces that were opposed in the Germany of 1920 and the Spain of 1936.'[24] During the summer, Brasillach, for his part, had dropped his *Je suis partout* friends, as he disapproved of this shift. Although 'germanophile and French', he was 'more French than national socialist'. He rejected what he called the 'denationalization' towards which they were moving as they adopted the single slogan, 'Fascism, all for fascism', in which he detected 'an inside-out Maurrasism' and a denial of France's best interests.[25]

The faithful – 'We are not quitters' was the theme of a meeting held in the Salle Wagram on 15 January 1944 – emitted an aggressiveness that was to make all the excesses of the following year possible. Since the summer of 1943, clashes with not only the public but also the forces of law and order had been increasing. In

Paris, on the second anniversary of the LVF, 27 August 1943, legionnaires attacked the police, wounding forty-seven of them.[26] Groups of young militants, usually PPF or Francists, sometimes uniformed LVF on leave, would embark on vengeful rampages, ripping away street signs, smashing town-hall busts, demanding money with menaces from shopkeepers, and sometimes beating up people who refused to salute them or accept their tracts. When rounded on by ordinary people, they would brandish their weapons and call for German protection. In Elboeuf, in the autumn, young PPF supporters, armed with revolvers, stopped passers-by, searched them and marched some off to the Kommandatur.[27] In the southern zone, the Milice assumed policing powers, encroaching upon the functions of the administration and giving rise to mounting friction.

Here is just one of many examples to illustrate the state of mind of the hardline brigade. It is a letter from a PPF member to a friend in the LVF, dated 15 December 1943: 'Here, joy of joys, we have at last discovered combat. Death awaits us on every side, but we at last feel we are not shirkers. Every day the party pays with its blood for its attachment to Europe and our leader.' The letter ends as follows: 'Forward to victory for Europe and for Christianity over the brute [of communism]. Long live Doriot! Long live France! Long live Hitler! '[28]

The leaders made no attempt to curb this exaltation – quite the contrary. Guiraud, Bucard's adjutant, demanded that 'antiterrorism fight terrorism with the means and methods of terrorism' and called for the creation by any means of 'a climate of fascist terror' that would neutralize resistance.[29] Darnand exhorted his followers to fight with their backs to the wall: 'Today we must either conquer or die. Better to die free than to live as slaves of Israel, in a world from which all the high values of our western ideal will be banished.'[30] Since the spring, thirty-three *miliciens* had been killed and 165 wounded,[31] and on 16 October the Milice weekly, *Combats*, carried the following inset on the front page: 'Militiamen, you may be attacked in cowardly fashion tomorrow. Provide your commanding officer with the names of hostages immediately.' In Perpignan, in the Milice headquarters, a poster read as follows: 'Be strong. Greet blows with blows. You may be attacked in cowardly fashion. Give your commanders the names of hostages immediately. Strike hard and keep quiet.'[32]

In November, Darnand authorized reprisal operations, with

Oberg's approval. In Annecy, six people reckoned to be close to the resistance were killed, to avenge an equal number of *miliciens* assassinated in the region. Two of the victims were chosen because they were Jewish, a third because of his freemasonry.[33] The PPF was acting in similar fashion in Lyons, where its leader, Francis André, had seven people killed between the autumn of 1943 and the spring of 1944. A note would be left on the victim's body: 'Terror against terror. This man has paid with his life for the death of a nationalist.' In Nice, the officer in charge of the PPF's service for maintaining order, with the agreement of the Germans, removed six men held in the municipal prison and had them executed as reprisals for the assassination of one party member.[34]

The counter-terrorism was murderous violence that was unleashed amidst ideological frenzy far more than as an antiguerilla strategy. If the perpetrators of assassinations could not themselves be reached, 'ideological opponents' were struck down, first and foremost Jews, in accordance with perfect Nazi logic. It was not enough to isolate them, brand them, seize their possessions, send them to concentration camps: they were now to be used as hostages, one hundred to be shot for every Frenchman assassinated.[35]

This state of mind was a crucial factor in the horrors that followed. Civil war may be too excessive a description, to the extent that there was no struggle involving a large proportion of the population: the members of the resistance and the collaborationists were two small minorities, the former of which enjoyed massive sympathy while the latter were generally loathed. Nevertheless, the climate resembled that of a civil war in that, on both sides, the enemy was diabolicized. The attacks on collaborationists were aimed as much at symbols as at men guilty of harmful acts against their compatriots. While some were killed as a result of precise accusations – denunciations leading to dire consequences, operating as auxiliaries of the German police, etc. – others paid the price purely for their political commitment, sometimes a political commitment already in the past, as in the case of one PPF leader in Grenoble, a university professor who had resigned from the party in 1942, yet was killed the following year.

The extremists represented themselves as victims who merely responded to the aggression directed against them. But they were forgetting their desire to make the majority of their compatriots fall into line, their exaltation of violence, the forceps that they wielded for the delivery of the new France, the value they set on virility and war, and their calls for vengeance and reprisals. They were all the more unpardonable because they were supported by an occupying force using its power in an increasingly brutal fashion.

30

The rout

At the end of 1943, the government co-opted Darnand as secretary general for the Maintenance of Order and Philippe Henriot, a *milicien* and proud of it, as Secretary of State for Propaganda and Information. The Milice extended its authority to the forces of order, the prison system and propaganda and continued to strive to infiltrate the rest of the administration. France was a virtual militia-state. All it lacked were a popular base, means in the form of men and skills, and the support of the regime's highest authorities. It none the less held a number of strategic advantages, first and foremost the maintenance of order. Its operations, coordinated with those of the occupying power, certainly dealt the resistance some heavy blows.

Two months after Darnand and Henriot, another extremist, and the only Paris leader to be singled out in this way, acceded to power. Déat was at last rewarded for his loyalty to Laval, but rewarded somewhat meanly, with a post that brought with it more responsibilities than real power. Darnand's position seemed all the stronger in that he enjoyed the steady support of the SS, some of whose leaders were even considering enforcing the unification of the collaborationist parties, a step that would certainly be to his advantage. Gottlob Berger was one who favoured this. He was in charge of the armed troops of the SS and was seeking every possible means to strengthen the struggle against the resistance. As he explained to Himmler, no German mother wept when a foreigner died for Germany. Oberg, on the other hand, was against the idea and successfully intervened, reminding Himmler of Hitler's directive: although it was necessary to treat collaboration as a showcase, the final goal should never be obscured, namely the destruction of France: to achieve this, it was important to retain the possibility of playing off the French political parties one against another.[1]

Darnand was at least able to carry the Milice into the northern zone, for Laval now withdrew his opposition to this. The SS insisted that the Paris leaders press their partisans to enrol in it and promise to respond to any order for mobilization in the event of 'troubles'. Darnand was now in a strong position in the small world of extremists, far outstripping Doriot in both men and means, now that he had the authority of the state behind him, as well as a sizeable budget that he was constantly clamouring to have increased. According to German records, at the turn of the year the Milice comprised between 26000 and 30000 men, half of them Francs-Gardes, as well as fifteen or so units of Francs-Gardes stationed in barracks (probably about a thousand men). So the resignations of the summer and autumn must have been compensated for,[2] no doubt by an intake of men in the mould of Lacombe Lucien: dubious characters with criminal records, admirers of violence, brawlers in search of good pay and warlike adventures, a few 'daddy's boys' swept up in the movement, and hotheads who preferred the Franc-Garde to the STO.

As for the other parties, their only option was increasingly to become auxiliaries of the occupiers. They wanted weapons, and were given some on condition that the men who carried them be placed at the service of the German police. The 'self-protection force' planned in the preceding autumn was set up although, according to Oberg, the Paris leaders failed to produce the requisite numbers of men and no more than 400 individuals were trained at Taverny.[3] However, the SS appears to have had no trouble using other means to find the auxiliaries for whom it had more and more work. They recruited from amongst collaborationists, former voluntary workers in Germany, people in trouble with the law, or by filling the breach with teams of black marketeers. Armed and carrying German cards, the auxiliaries could not be touched by the French police. They created havoc by their work of surveillance on public opinion and infiltration into the resistance. It is not possible to make out how many swelled the pool of agents employed by the occupiers throughout this period, but after the liberation an investigating judge reckoned that they may have totalled 9000 to 10000.[4]

At the beginning of 1944, the parties were asked to set up another supplementary force, this time to assist Sauckel. The 'slave-trader of Europe' wanted to block the drain of STO dodgers and correct the curve of departures for Germany. The SS had neither the time nor the means for this task; and counting on the French police was these days out of the question. The new force was known sometimes as the 'Committee for Social Peace', sometimes as the 'Action Group for Social Justice' and its primary task was to track down STO dodgers. Its secondary mission was to protect French employees of the German administration, the families of volunteer workers in Germany and also those of LVF volunteers. It was first set up in Marseilles, where Sauckel obtained the help of Sabiani, the local head of the PPF, who appears to have forced the hand of the other party officials.[5] At any rate, on 10 March 1944, 431 of the 460 members of the forces were stationed in Marseilles. Later, a small stream of recruits presented themselves at the Mortier barracks in Paris. By August, when the retreat eastwards began, 1800 men had been enrolled.[6]

It was hard for Laval to put up with Darnand's rising power, but it did have the advantage of checking the activities of the Paris extremists. So far as ideas went, policy distinctions between them were clear, but in practice they were confused. The extremists in both Vichy and Paris wanted a resolute policy of association with the occupier. The highest authorities of the French state were still hoping for a compromise peace and were by now emphasizing as best they could that they were acting under German pressure. Pétain clung, as if to a life-saving spar, to the remnants of his popularity, which revived slightly when he toured the northern zone in the spring of 1944, and was fêted there by modest crowds. Surprised by this, the German propaganda services' explanation for his emotional welcome was that he was seen as a symbol of the French motherland and a fixed point to which to cling in the climate of anxiety produced by the bombing raids and the risk of upheavals when the liberation came.[7] With the unknown round the corner, in the eyes of the timid, Pétain now recovered his function as a refuge, which had been his major role a few years earlier. Not everybody would greet the liberation with unalloyed delight. In October 1944, Galtier-Boissière wrote: 'If a Gallup poll had existed in France, I think it would have revealed 95 per cent *maréchalists* immediately after the armistice, 50 per cent up until the invasion of the southern zone, and still 30 per cent at the time of the Allied landings.'[8]

In practice, differences of policy lost their importance since the concern of all sides was to maintain order, even at the price of a repression that fostered a climate of civil war. On this point there was no difference at all between Darnand's position and Pétain's, or Maurras's. In February 1944, the latter wrote: 'As we repeat several times a week, the best response to the threats of terrorists is to subject them to a legitimate counter-terror.'[9] Pétain and Laval were exhorting their agents to redouble their severity and were manifesting support for Darnand. Pétain received him several times, and sometimes alluded to the mutinies of 1917.[10]

Darnand needed no encouragement. Like Henriot, he hammered home the theme that order must be maintained, a 'French order' that was in the national interest, and emphasized that he was not in the business of working for the occupier. Since its leader had joined the government, the Milice's newspaper was less strident in its exaltation of the European struggle. Its line now was that the Milice was carrying out a French operation, but it was one parallel to the action of the Germans, on French soil, against French people. Court martials, introduced at the beginning of the year, were summarily executing anyone caught red-handed in terrorism, whether their action had been directed against Germans or against French agents: that is an indication of the hardening of attitudes and the coincidence of policies.

Vichy's forces for maintaining order worked in close coordination with the SS, which guided them and used them to further its own interests. In reality, the Milice was not so much a force for maintaining order as a policing force of low calibre. As soon as matters became serious – where a combative maquis existed, as at Glières, or where large-scale resistance action was involved – it handed over to the Germans. In many operations its men served as scouts or infiltration agents, preparing the way for the occupier's intervention. Their role or vocation, if one can call it that, was to carry out tasks that the occupiers would find difficult left to themselves, given that they were not exactly on their home ground: detection, surveillance, capturing suspects, even interrogation, in which torture was beginning to be used systematically. The Milice set itself above the law and was soon operating outside it. As well as brutality and summary execution, it went in for robbery and looting, particularly at the expense of Jews, the main target of its frenzied hatred, as is attested by the murder of, among others, Victor Basch, the former chairman of the League of Human Rights, and his wife, both in their eighties, and – later – the murders of Jean Zay and Georges Mandel.

Meanwhile, more or less everywhere, collaborationists were themselves the targets of attacks that were steadily increasing in number. In June, Abetz produced figures of 300 *miliciens* killed, 270 PPF supporters, 130 Francists, 100 members of Groupe Collaboration, and 50 members of RNP.[11] Other individuals also fell victim to this wave of assassinations: Vichy officials, organizers of the Légion des Combattants, people accused of denunciations or other activities that assisted the occupier. By 6 June 1944, over 2000 French people had been assassinated.[12] The struggle against collaborationists became inexpiable, running alongside the fight against the occupier, but with more hatred, as between enemy brothers.

When the allied troops landed in Normandy on 6 June, Pétain and Laval appealed to officials to remain at their posts and to French people to obey their government, declaring 'We are not in the war.'[13] The position they adopted was in conformity with the logic of 'France for itself alone'. This satisfied the occupier, as it was designed to deter the population from assisting the Allies. The French state mobilized its last remaining forces to maintain 'French' order behind the German lines. Laval appointed Darnand Secretary of State for the Interior and provided him with 'tribunals for the maintenance of order' that operated alongside the court martials and, like them, passed judgements that were executed on the spot. The Paris leaders kept their word and exhorted their militants to 'offer and provide the party's full collaboration with forces loyal to the French state and the security organizations of the European armies, with the aim of maintaining internal order' (to quote the PPF).[14] Yet again, they were scandalized by the position adopted by Vichy and clamoured to be admitted into the government and for all-out repression and unconditional commitment to the German side.

On 14 June, they asked Abetz to arrange for the return of the LVF and the Waffen-SS to France, so that they could be thrown into the struggle against the 'invaders'. Abetz, who favoured the idea, set out the details of these possible French reinforcements for the German war: 3000 Waffen-SS, 1050 NSKK, 400 Kriegsmarine guards, 300 members of the Walloon Legion, and several thousand men in armed service for the Todt organization or as auxiliaries to the German police. These 8000 to 10000 Frenchmen were supposed to be joined by the 10000 *miliciens* already mobilized, plus between 5000 and 10000 men to be provided by the Paris parties.[15] Adding to these figures the 2000 LVF then serving in the East, 25000 to

30000 Frenchmen would then be on active service on the occupier's side, either maintaining 'French order' or in 'German uniform'.

But Oberg and the military authorities were unwilling to bring back the LVF and the Waffen-SS.[16] The French would fight better against the Soviets than against the Allies. Nor was Darnand in favour, no doubt fearing that his Milice would be swallowed up in this amalgamation of collaborationist forces. Meanwhile, he was employing it relentlessly in the mission assigned to it by the Vichy leaders, tracking down members of the resistance and boosting the action of the German forces. The brutalities and exactions were unimaginable: the sense of having their backs to the wall fostered a venomous desire to make others pay dearly for the predictable defeat. Hence all the torture, the orgy of brutalities inflicted upon bodies at their last gasp, in which police efficiency was the most tenuous of justifications for a frenzied desire to humiliate and degrade.

In Vichy, at the beginning of August, when the allied breakthrough was irreversible, Pétain set about distancing himself from all this. He wrote to Darnand, expressing his disapproval of the excesses committed by the Milice in the defence of 'French order'.[17] While the Marshal was trying to make contact with de Gaulle, at the same time reaffirming his own legitimacy, Laval was manoeuvring with Herriot to get the National Assembly reconvened, with himself presiding over a transitional government that would welcome the victors, checkmate de Gaulle, and plead for national reconciliation in the name of the anticommunist struggle. The Germans soon put a stop to his efforts, which in any case were doomed to failure.

By mid-August, the outcome was no longer in doubt. A retreat was organized and, while Pétain and Laval were carried off in its train, the extremists hurriedly flocked to join the German convoys. Some had a trying journey from the south, struggling through ambushes set by the resistance and in some cases dragging into the débâcle family members who had no say in the matter. For those who decided to remain or who were unable to flee, the time of trials was just beginning. About 4000 French people were summarily executed between 6 June and the end of the liberation.[18]

Pétain and Laval chose to regard themselves as prisoners, not without the former seeking to differentiate himself from the latter. Pétain had decided that there was no longer a government, but that a French state remained and that he was its embodiment. He asked for Laval's resignation, which Laval refused, objecting that the Marshal, having renounced all activity, would be performing an act of government by accepting his resignation.[19] The extremists, for their part, were certainly not resigned to the situation. Between 23 August and 1 September, they had a series of meetings with Ribbentrop, and were then received by Hitler. Doriot, Déat, Darnand, Marion and Brinon were all present; Bucard was not, no doubt discredited as a result of a recent shoot-out between his bodyguard and the French police. At this point, when they still held a part of French territory, the Germans were keen to reassemble the collaborationist forces, if possible with Pétain's blessing, and to use them to create a maquis in France and foment a 'national' opposition to de Gaulle and his communist allies.

This time their preference definitely went to Doriot, and they tried to persuade the other leaders to back him up. Doriot insisted upon the leadership of the government and asked for a guarantee of integrity for both France, minus Alsace-Lorraine, and the empire. He was the only one to show any signs of a political attitude, however derisory in the existing situation. But the others were not prepared to fall in behind him and in the end Ribbentrop decided that, with Pétain's blessing, Brinon should head an unofficial government, charged with the mission of working upon the Marshal to get him to appoint Doriot.

As the allied advance continued, the French collaborationists pulled back to German territory and installed themselves in Sigmaringen, to which the Axis countries then sent delegations. Abetz headed the German embassy and the Italy of the Salo Republic was represented, as was Japan. In this cardboard world, rivalry and squabbling once more took over. The sixth of September saw the creation of the 'Délégation Gouvernementale Française pour la Défense des Intérêts Français en Allemagne'. Déat, Darnand and Bridoux were members, as were Luchaire and Brinon, while Marion, Bonnard and Bichelonne followed Pétain and Laval into retreat and the preparation of their defence. The extremists, who clung to a belief in a miraculous reversal of the military situation, busied themselves reconstructing the semblance of a state, complete with ministries, planning charts, laws and a *Journal officiel*. But most of their efforts were devoted to doing down the claims of Doriot, who had marked his distance from them by settling first in Neustadt, then in Mainau on Lake Constance. They all tried to make themselves useful to the Germans by broadcasting propaganda to France and setting up schools to train intelligence and sabotage agents: of the 200 or so agents trained apparently no more than a handful were ever parachuted into France.[20]

How many were there of these new *émigrés*? Probably between 10000 and 15000, including 4000 *miliciens*, several thousand Doriotists, and a few hundred RNP supporters and Francists, some of whom were accompanied by wives and children.[21] The Germans were not about to leave them without employment. Only a few hundred people remained with the Delegation and the party leaders. While the wives and some of the men were sent off to work, those able to fight were enrolled in the Charlemagne division of the Waffen-SS, which included all the French already in German uniform (in the LVF, the Waffen-SS, or various other German services), as well as some 1500 *miliciens* – in all about 7000 men. Darnand had volunteered his *miliciens*, in the hope that he would be leading the new unit. But once his men were enrolled, the Germans slammed the door in his face. Cut to the quick, he asked, equally unsuccessfully, to join the troops of the Belgian leader Degrelle, whose ambition was to head all the French-language speakers and imbue them with a sense of their true Germanic nature.[22] Possibly one-fifth of the men of the Charlemagne division survived the war; the rest died to prolong the agony of Nazism.

By the end of 1944, the situation had swung in Doriot's favour, and on 6 January 1945 he announced the creation of a Comité de libération, headed by himself. Brinon rallied to this, to the initial fury of Déat and Darnand, who then gradually resigned themselves. It was on the eve of a meeting with his two latest rivals that Doriot met his death, gunned down by unidentified, but probably Anglo-Saxon planes. The débâcle had arrived. It was soon followed by capture and trials. Laval, Bucard and Darnand were shot; only Déat escaped, hidden in some cloister in Italy.

The gap between the men of the state and the men of the parties endured right to the end. With the state no more and French soil beneath their feet no more, Pétain and Laval were, in their own way, logical enough and went on strike. The extremists were too, in their fashion, as they tried to cling on even to what was no more than the appearance of state power. It had been the object of their ambitions from the start and in their pursuit of it they had slipped further and further towards the occupier. They ended up in a position they would have found hard to imagine back in 1940, when they had launched themselves into their policies in the name of the protection of their country and defence of its interests.

The French Revolution had found supporters more or less everywhere in Europe, as it had spread. Those who gave a warm welcome to its armies called themselves 'patriots': for them, the salvation of their motherland lay in foreign aid that would make it possible to shake free from the *ancien régime*. As Toqueville wrote, the French Revolution had wiped out the old frontiers and either brought men together or divided them 'despite laws, traditions, characteristics and language, sometimes turning compatriots into enemies and foreigners into brothers; or rather, over and above all individual nationalities, it had created a common intellectual motherland whose citizens men of all nations could become'.[23] Déat used to like to compare the two expansions, drawing the no doubt consoling conclusion that Nazism too was revolutionary. Yet the difference was obvious: Nazism swept over Europe in the name of a particularist and racist vision of the world, not a universalist mission, and with only force to justify the domination of the superior race and the crushing of those conquered.

Yet it too found supporters more or less everywhere in Europe, and men willing to die for it. In this respect a comparison is justified and worth considering. Again citing Toqueville, it could be said that, in different forms and with a different spirit, this did constitute the repetition of a phenomenon already experienced in Europe at the time of the religious wars and then again with the French Revolution: 'All foreign wars took on something of the character of civil wars; and in all civil wars foreigners appeared.'[24] However, unlike those earlier periods, the 1940s in Europe represented the zenith of the era of nationalism. Everywhere Nazi Germany's collaborators justified themselves in the name of a national imperative: for some, accession to independence, for others the safeguarding of an identity and a chance to develop it.

They did remain attached to defending the interests of their own countries. The trouble was that they could no longer see how to dissociate these from the interests of Nazi Germany. In the course of their struggles as minorities, they had loosened their ties with their national societies and placed themselves in the position of outsiders. As they become more radical, they remained faithful to the high value they placed on strength and combat and to their rejection of liberal and democratic principles. But they allowed themselves to be dragged into the occupier's camp in their struggle against common enemies and they ended up placing that struggle above the defence of their natural nation. It certainly was an age of totalitarianism.

The penetration of the totalitarian spirit did the rest. Men such as Déat and Doriot may have derived from their previous cultural luggage or partisan experiences the idea of a nation needing to be reformed from scratch. But what about nationalists such as Bucard and Darnand? Traditionally, the right had always attacked the artificiality of revolutionary thought, the notion of a *tabula rasa* and a new society. Pétainism held to that line of thinking in its belief that the nation was itself capable of producing the energy and means for its own renewal, if the state would only provide the appropriate framework. The collaborationist nationalists, for their part however, no longer believed in anything but permanent training and mobilization. Their evolution shows that the notion of human adaptability had found a welcome on the right and could be put to serve its values, which was precisely what the fascist movements had discovered. For this minority, the physical nation was of small account compared with the ideal nation that needed to be created. The occupier was at once a national partner and a political model: by creating the new France, they would at the same time be saving the French nation. But for that the occupier needed to be a real partner and the alliance of nationalists needed to be something other than wishful thinking that concealed the reality of men who had simply become turncoats serving a new colonial power.

In the summer of 1944, Drieu La Rochelle, who would not be leaving for Germany and who committed suicide soon after, had taken a pitying and accusing look at himself: 'I am crushed by the banality of everything: the commonplace has overwhelmed me. My concierge was right: "The Germans are always stupid", she said, "Hitler is copying Napoleon. England or America always win the last battle." I have fought against whatever is commonplace for four years, in vain and against the wisdom of nations.'[25] His concierge had been right, but at least Drieu was honest: 'To the last, I still like Hitler, despite all his mistakes, all his ignorance, all his lies. On the whole he presented me with my political ideal: physical pride, a quest for charisma, prestige, warrior heroism – and an equally romantic compulsion to exhaust himself, destroy himself in a spontaneous, unmeasured, excessive, fatal thrust.'[26] These are the words of a man who never lived up to his own image of himself and was forever lamenting his own softness, weakness and decadence. But what he said touched upon one of the most profound traits of Nazism. Drieu was not altogether mistaken about the darkly destructive, suicidal character of the movement that had fascinated him.

Conclusion

After the liberation, Europe was the scene of a vast purge that affected millions of people. There was no precedent for the phenomenon in the occupations that had punctuated history since the French Revolution. The fact is that this occupation had been different. Nazi Germany had imposed a heavy yoke and had reduced the occupied peoples to wretchedness. The weight of its jackboot had become increasingly crushing. It had exterminated millions of people, leaving behind it Auschwitz as a symbol of modern barbarity. Furthermore, it had set out to annihilate all modern ideologies, liberalism, democracy, socialism, communism and, eventually Christianity. It had infringed the rights of nations by attempting to impose the domination of a master-race that would exercise the power of life or death over them. It is not surprising that those who, in one way or another, associated themselves with this force that was not simply a national occupier but also a regime implementing a policy of ideological hegemony should have brought down retribution upon themselves.

France was the first liberated country to demand a reckoning. After an extra-judicial purge that claimed 8000 to 9000 victims, the judicial purge began by investigating 300000 cases and ended by passing sentence upon 124613 individuals. Slightly under 50000 of these received prison sentences; of the 6763 condemned to death, 767 were executed, plus an equal number who had been sentenced to death by military tribunals. Slightly over 50000 others were stripped of their civic rights. There was also a professional purge, especially in the administration, in which at least 25000 people were penalized. In all, about 150000 French people were probably affected in one way or another.[1]

This purge, which contributed to the fixing of the image of the recent past, sought to settle the account for the experience of the occupation by identifying and singling out a group of people deemed accountable, upon which the collective feelings of the French were then concentrated and vented, thereby purging the ambivalences, ambiguities and uncertainties that had characterized the experience of many individual French people. Thanks to the cold war, the myth of an entire people committed to resistance logically enough soon led to an amnesty designed to bring peace through the reintegration of a handful of traitors. But from the 1970s onwards, this image of the past became increasingly cracked: now the purge seemed flawed and a growth of suspicions, encouraged by the perception of a long-standing oblivion or a long-standing lie, produced an impression of crimes unpunished, accountability insufficiently identified, and a French people that had been besmirched as a whole by the murky waters of the period. Attention now focused upon the persecution of the Jews and the new sensitivity to human rights that had taken over from nationalism and the major ideologies bestowed upon those years a black image that spread to envelop virtually everyone who had lived through it.[2]

It is impossible for historians to ratify either of these two images. They have to remember that accommodation is a regular phenomenon in almost any occupation, where certain points or interfaces of contact are inevitably created and some adjustment to the new situation has to be made. Like a dictatorship, an occupation does not function purely by dint of constraint; it usually finds some more or less stable and lasting basis in shared interests, and by constructing networks of accommodation that link occupiers and occupied together and make it possible for the machine to continue to operate. The French, with their colonial past, are well placed to understand that there can be no domination without a minimal degree of acceptance, however fragile, and that divisions and diverging interests in the subjugated societies are bound to play into the hands of imperial dominion. Besides, it would not be fair systematically to ascribe either a positive or a negative connotation to the phenomenon of accommodation. After the Nazi catastrophe, the Germans – or at any rate those lucky enough to find themselves in the zones occupied by the western Allies – reckoned that it was in their interest to enter into association with their conquerors and together establish the basis for a new state.

Accommodation takes forms and incorporates degrees that need to be distinguished so that they are not all muddled together. The first form is a structural one imposed by the need to have public services that continue to function and an economy that does not collapse. This is all the more inevitable when the society involved is diversified, the division of labour is highly developed, and interests and sectors are deeply interconnected. Once an occupier seeks to exploit the economy for his own needs, choices for the least of evils cannot be avoided, choices in which survival for the national community must be weighed against assistance given to the enemy, assistance thanks to which that enemy might win its war and perpetuate its domination. These are painful, agonizing choices, with the scales always tipping to the same side, towards the stronger party, but it would be hard to avoid them, given that an entire society cannot take to the maquis as an individual can. But such an adaptation should at least involve calculating one's concessions as precisely as possible, abstaining from anticipating the occupier's demands and, even more, from adopting policies that commit the country's future. That is what most of the French did; how could they have avoided doing so?

But with some people accommodation went further. It took on a deliberate character, went beyond a minimal adaptation, and involved initiatives that betrayed a desire for closer ties or some agreement. Such behaviour amounted to providing, directly or indirectly, material or moral assistance for the occupier's policies. These people did not simply make the best of the occupation; they tried to adapt to the occupier in two distinct ways. The first may be described as opportunist accommodation, for want of a better term. It occurred within certain limits, with one eye always kept on how the situation was developing, and was chiefly motivated by a desire to defend or promote interests of either a personal or a corporative nature, in a situation of uncertain outcome. But it meant going more than halfway to meet the enemy and his policies: as when people entered into social relations with him, chose to produce or work for him, to frequent his propaganda centres or learn his language, to adjust to the framework imposed by him, even though other choices were possible and abstention involved no great sacrifices. The term opportunism does not mean that this pursuit of one's own interests was necessarily purely cynical or regardless of values. Although most of the accommodation in this category may not have been primarily prompted by politico-ideological motives, these were often present in some limited or diffuse form, establishing a connivance that rendered such gestures of cooperation all the easier to make.

The second form of deliberate accommodation was, in the widest sense, political. In these cases, people were seeking to come to an agreement by taking a long-term view and were making a decision that was fundamentally political, even if their motives were mixed, even if their desire for such an agreement was prompted by resignation more than enthusiasm, and even if they did set some limits upon it. Political accommodation could range all the way from declared support for a policy of *entente*, through sympathy for the occupier's propaganda, to enrolling in his forces and wearing his uniform. In all these cases, it was necessarily combined with a measure of ideological connivance, however limited and weak.

These three forms of accommodation are to be found under occupations generally. They allow for an analysis both broad and differentiated, unlike the concept of collaboration, with its essentially politico-ideological point of view, punitive inspiration and denunciatory and polemic effect. At the liberation, the offence of collaboration was defined and condemned in the complex context of the current political balance of forces, principles of law and judicial practices, and in accordance with a logic and with criteria that it is impossible for a historian to accept integrally or to take over. For that logic, based on criteria that focused primarily on aid knowingly given to the enemy, left out of account structural accommodation, despite the fact that this had been far and away the most important from the occupier's point of view. For at least three years the Germans managed both to maintain their domination and to keep the yoke in place, despite cutting to the minimum the number of their troops assigned to maintaining order, and thereby making it possible to reinforce other fronts and also to exploit the economic resources of France in a most effective way. Including prisoners of war and those forced into the STO, over four million French people were working directly for the Germans in 1944 (2600000 in France and 1314000 in Germany), that is to say 37 per cent of the male population between the ages of sixteen and sixty.[3] And that is not counting all the labour further up the pipeline of the French economy that was contributing indirectly to the German war effort. Objectively, this massive assistance, obtained by dint of constraint and intimidation and facilitated by the obvious desire of the French not to starve to death, far outweighs the courageous action of members of the resistance, even if this did make a remarkable contribution at the level of information, symbolism and both the political and the armed struggles, particularly in the last months.

Collaboration clearly did include political accommodation as defined above; and at the same time it incorporated a measure of opportunistic accommodation. But from an intellectual point of view there are no imperative reasons for drawing the exact demarcation line within this second category of collaboration at any particular level. The level of what was considered actionable would vary, particularly in relation to the political forces present; no doubt the communists would have set it considerably lower than others. It is not the historian's task to say whether there should have been more punishment or less; a historian's perspective is quite simply different from that of those who carried out the purges. Consider the case of the people who set about learning German, particularly in the German Institute: was this collaboration or not? According to the rules laid down in the purge and from the point of view of liberal law, in which each case must be judged on its own merits, with a particular emphasis laid on intention, such behaviour could be regarded as providing no immediate aid to the enemy, quite apart from the matter of establishing whether such aid was intended by those involved. However, from a historian's perspective, there could be nothing more significant than that movement towards the occupier's language, nothing more interesting than the everyday, ambiguous, furtive forms of French society's adjustment to the presence of the occupier.

At the end of this enquiry it would at any rate appear that deliberate, voluntary accommodation extended well beyond the circle of those punished in the purges. It is understandable that its widespread nature – paradoxically enough felt more strongly with the passing of time, possibly because the extent of Pétain's popularity became more and more shocking – should, over the past twenty years, have given rise to suspicions. Yet it is worth repeating that the great majority of French people had no faith in collaboration and wanted none of it, and that they did behave worthily, even if their uncertainty and passivity in the first two years allowed a certain latitude to those who were venturing further towards accommodation. Many French people assuredly lived through a kind of prolonged phoney war from 1939 to 1944, in the hope that their country would be spared as much as possible: their memory of earlier trials and their sense of the national weakness are explanation enough. But, however inactive, their wait for liberation was certainly impatient. To be a hero is honourable; not to be one is not necessarily dishonourable.

The fact remains that, at the level of opinion, for a time at least and in a spirit of resignation or scepticism, many millions of French people did go along with the government's policy of collaboration. At the level of behaviour, several hundred thousand of those occupied went to work for the occupiers or sought to obtain orders from them. Others, tens if not hundreds of thousands, tried to learn their language, attended the cultural events they organized and flocked to their propaganda exhibitions or even made social, sentimental or sexual overtures to them. Finally, at the partisan level, several hundreds of thousands held definitely positive opinions on collaboration and some expressed these through political or military commitment. These people came from every walk of life, with the working class strongly represented in certain roles. Proportionately, even if they remained in the minority, the more affluent classes were even more affected, by reason both of their political and social reflexes reinforced by grudges left over from the pre-war period and also of the situation itself, which propelled many of them into the front line in an administrative or entrepreneurial capacity. Since there was more at stake for them, rejection of accommodation was more costly just as its rewards were greater.

To understand the widespread nature of the phenomenon, we must take into account the conditions that determined it in this – as in any other – occupation, conditions that operated with particular force in the first two years. The first conditioning factor, which decides everything else, is the policy that the occupier adopts, for it is the occupier who marks out the playing field and kicks off. By making a martyr of Poland, with the aim of destroying it not only as a state but also its national identity, the Nazis paralysed any attempts at cooperation on the part of its inhabitants in advance. In France, by contrast, they adopted a policy far less brutal than in Eastern Europe and more flexible than in the other, so-called 'Germanic' countries of Western Europe.

The second conditioning factor stems from the alternatives that exist, alternatives that are circumscribed by people's assessment of the conqueror's power and the likely duration of his domination, and also by their view of their possible liberators. With regard to the first point, the prospect of lasting domination largely explains the resignation to the imperial yoke that was encountered in the

European empires: a resignation, or even acceptance, encouraged by the advantages brought by the conqueror, which in part compensated for his domination. In the case of France between 1940 and 1944, the fact that the war was continuing all around it was bound to foster hope, and this acted as a check on widespread resignation. As to the second point: if France had had the Soviet Union as a neighbour and a potential liberator, as the peoples of Eastern Europe did, it would probably have been far more prone to political accommodation. The prospect of liberation by the Soviets was viewed quite differently from the possible arrival of the Anglo-Saxons.

The third conditioning factor is the degree of cohesion that exists within the occupied society. A society's receptiveness to the policies of the occupier and its disposition towards accommodation are likely to be greater if it is in a state of crisis or is divided against itself. French society, like the other European societies occupied by Nazi Germany, was fraught with tensions and these weakened its patriotic rejection of occupation, even though the fundamental value of that rejection was for the most part recognized, as is shown by the swift and widespread realization that the fact of occupation called for a particular pattern of behaviour – the observance of a code of conduct for exceptional times.

Some of those tensions were of a social nature and went beyond mere feelings of resentment between different categories or layers of society. We have already noted the serious effects that can be produced by the phenomenon of social fragmentation and weakened civic and national reactions in consequence of difficult social conditions, inadequate education, or a subordinate position, all of which erode people's ability to reject collaboration with the occupier and encourage them to grasp at any opportunity to profit from the situation. The same attitude can be fostered by conflict between one's national loyalty and the protection of one's personal interests. Other tensions were political: aspirations for renewal, authoritarianism, anticommunism, and antisemitism made people shortsightedly detect positive aspects to Nazism. The nationalism that had been at the source of most of these attitudes was weakened by the recognition of a partial solidarity with the occupier in the struggle against common enemies. This was a tendency that, in the case of collaborationists, went so far as to encourage the idea of rebuilding the nation with the aid of the conqueror. Finally, there were other tensions that had to do with pacifism, a sense of the country's weakness and a desire to preserve French blood, which made people regard an enforced unification of the continent as necessary or even desirable. All these elements were already present before the defeat. They assumed even greater weight when Vichy highlighted and sanctioned them.

As it pursued its policy of collaboration, the French state not only made grave concessions in order to achieve an illusory regeneration, recuperate France's sovereignty and restore its standing in the midst of a war that had no end in sight and was assuming world-wide proportions; in its desire to perpetuate its regime, it also drew closer and closer to the occupier. Even if its slogan was 'France for itself alone', the end result of its policies was to turn it into a stepping-stone for the criminal activities of Nazism. The occupier might possibly have managed to deport as many Jews by giving direct orders to the French police, as it did in the countries whose governments were established in London. But the fact remains that Vichy lent a hand by turning in foreign Jews, denaturalizing some French Jews and arresting Jews with French nationality.

It should not be imagined, however, that, without Vichy, there would have been no collaboration. French society possessed mechanisms of its own for accommodation. But the French state did confer a legitimacy upon them, exerting an influence that, without being unequivocal, was heavily negative. When one compares the situation with that of the other occupied countries in Western Europe it emerges, despite the diversity of their pasts and their national contexts, that in respect of marked forms of political accommodation – membership of collaborationist groups or commitment that involved wearing the German uniform – France comes at the bottom of the scale. The existence of the French state and above all the popularity of Pétain probably had a deflecting effect: in many cases the support given to Pétain may have prevented more radical commitment. On the other hand, in its behaviour French society does seem to have been more prone to opportunist accommodation, for in this area the existence of Vichy had the opposite effect, lending encouragement to interests in need of defence or promotion. Although the other occupied societies of Western Europe produced more supporters and recruits for collaborationism, they at the same time provide examples of civil resistance the like of which are not to be found in France: the Amsterdam strike in support of the Jews, and in Holland and Norway the movements of refusal to cooperate on the part of academics and the medical profession, etc.[4] These constituted demonstrations of opposition to the local Nazis' attempts to make those under occupation fall into line; whereas in France the French state fostered an appearance of legality that disarmed open rejection of this type.

The years of occupation indubitably left a painful splinter lodged in the memories of French people; for a cherished image of France was damaged by all the compromising deals struck with one of the worst regimes of modern Europe. The experience of the Second World War overturned the glorious image of the Great War, which had not only ended in victory, but had also produced a sacred unity in times of tribulation. The defeat of 1940 toppled the institutions of France and paved the way for a regime for which, right up until the moment when it collapsed in infamy, the redefinition of a political pact took priority over the salvation of the nation. Meanwhile, over the question of who it was that embodied political legitimacy and the national interest, opinion had been deeply divided. In circumstances such as those of an occupation, individual men and women sometimes discover who they really are. But it is difficult for a whole society to do so. France entered upon its trial pursuing a course that it was hard to correct in the short term, despite the great figure of one rebel general and all the sacrifices made by a minority of French people.

Table 1 Social composition of the principal collaborationist groups

	Fran.	*GC*	*PPF*	*RNP*	*SOL*	*Milice*	*LVF*	*Waffen-SS*	*Total*
Industrialists	7	57	111	52	48	56	–	–	331
	1.7	***3***	***3.6***	***2.2***	***3.5***	***2.2***	–	–	***2.9***
Shopkeepers	37	189	376	334	124	199	6	–	1265
	9.3	***10***	***12.4***	***14.3***	***9.1***	***7.8***	***4***	–	***11.4***
Artisans	33	110	231	163	72	206	16	6	837
	8.3	***5.8***	***7.6***	***7***	***5.3***	***8.1***	***10.8***	***4.8***	***7.5***
Farmers	16	95	221	107	428	465	12	11	1355
	4	***5***	***7.3***	***4.6***	***31.7***	***18.3***	***8.1***	***8.8***	***12.2***
Agricultural workers	5	7	34	22	13	42	22	13	158
	1.2	***0.3***	***1.1***	***0.9***	***0.9***	***1.6***	***14.8***	***10.4***	***1.4***
Liberal professions	28	136	235	100	88	137	6	1	731
	7	***7.2***	***7.7***	***4.3***	***6.5***	***5.4***	***4***	***0.8***	***6.6***
Cadres	12	94	126	123	82	123	2	2	564
	3	***4.9***	***4.1***	***5.2***	***6***	***4.8***	***1.3***	***1.6***	***5.1***
Commercial travellers	5	21	40	35	3	9	–	–	113
	1.2	***1.4***	***1.3***	***1.5***	***0.2***	***0.3***	–	–	***1***
Teachers	16	28	44	80	12	17	–	–	197
	4	***1.1***	***1.4***	***3.4***	***0.8***	***0.6***	–	–	***1.7***
Civil servants	23	44	190	90	96	155	4	–	602
	5.7	***2.3***	***6.2***	***3.8***	***7.1***	***6.1***	***2.7***	–	***5.4***
Workers	49	45	246	249	102	210	36	43	980
	12.3	***2.3***	***8.1***	***10.7***	***7.5***	***8.2***	***24.3***	***34.4***	***8.8***

Table 1 Continued

	Fran.	*GC*	*PPF*	*RNP*	*SOL*	*Milice*	*LVF*	*Waffen-SS*	*Total*
Employees	80	267	505	430	139	347	15	27	1810
	20.1	***14.1***	***16.7***	***18.5***	***10.3***	***13.7***	***10.1***	***21.6***	***16.3***
Service personnel	9	12	55	50	3	31	1	2	163
	2.2	***0.6***	***1.8***	***2.1***	***0.2***	***1.2***	***0.6***	***1.6***	***1.4***
Students	34	21	85	49	12	130	4	7	342
	8.5	***1.1***	***2.8***	***2.1***	***0.8***	***5.1***	***2.7***	***5.6***	***3***
Retired people	5	82	115	95	54	57	2	–	410
	1.2	***4.3***	***3.8***	***4***	***4***	***2.2***	***1.3***	–	***3.7***
No profession	28	164	321	273	37	222	6	4	1055
	7	***8.6***	***10.6***	***11.7***	***2.7***	***8.7***	***4***	***3.2***	***9.5***
Army	5	8	23	25	8	58	5	1	133
	1.2	***0.4***	***0.7***	***1***	***0.5***	***2.2***	***3.3***	***0.8***	***1.2***
Police	1	2	12	11	20	19	1	2	68
	0.2	***0.1***	***0.3***	***0.4***	***1.4***	***0.7***	***0.6***	***1.6***	***0.6***
Clergy	–	6	9	9	5	1	–	–	30
	–	***0.3***	***0.2***	***0.3***	***0.3***	***0.03***	–	–	***0.2***
Others	4	102	38	25	2	47	10	6	234
	1	***5.4***	***1.2***	***1***	***0.1***	***1.8***	***6.7***	***4.8***	***2.1***
Total	397	1490	3017	2322	1348	2531	148	125	11 047
	100	***100***	***100***	***100***	***100***	***100***	***100***	***100***	***100***

The figures in bold italics indicate the percentages.

Source: Table based on thirty-eight departmental enquiries carried out by the correspondents of the Comité d'Histoire de la Deuxième Guerre Mondiale, IHTP, Enquiry into collaboration.

Table 2

	Active population 1936[1] %	*Combination of the collab. groups in Table 1*[2] %	*Civic Courts sample*[2] %
Industrialists and shopkeepers	13.8	27	19
Farmers	23.5	15	5.5
Farm workers	8.1	1.7	2.3
Liberal professions	0.5	8.1	7.8
Cadres and employees (including civil servants)	16	36.3	35.5
Workers	31.3	10.8	23.6
Domestic servants	3.3	1.8	4.3
Army, police	2.8	2.2	1.4
Clergy	0.6	0.3	0.1

1 Claude Thélot and Olivier Marchand, *Deux Siècles de travail en France: population active et structure sociale, durée et productivité du travail*, INSEE, 1991, pp. 186–7.
2 Percentages recalculated after eliminating the following categories: retired people, students, no profession, others. The category of domestic servants is very inaccurate, given that the enquiry into collaboration used the much larger category of service personnel.
3 The proportion of farmers is 5.9 per cent in the four principal groups (PPF, RNP, Groupe Collaboration, Francism). It is their greater preserve in the SOL and the Milice that pushes up the average.

Notes

ABBREVIATIONS IN THE NOTES

AA	Auswärtiges Amt (Foreign Ministry)
AA-PA	Auswärtiges Amt-Politisches Archiv, Bonn
ACS	Archivio Centrale dello Stato, Rome
AD	Archives départementales
ADAP	*Aketen zur Deutschen Auswärtigen Politik*
AN	Archives Nationales, Paris
ASMAE	Archivio Storico-diplomatico, Ministerio degli Affari esteri, Rome
BAK	Bundesarchiv, Coblenz
BA-MA	Bundesarchiv-Militärarchiv, Fribourg-en-Brisgau
CDJC	Centre de Documentation Juive Contemporaine, Paris
DFCAA	Délégation Française auprès de la Commission Allemande d'Armistice
dr.	dossier, file
FRUS	*Foreign Relations of the United States*
IfZ	Institut für Zeitgeschichte, Munich.
IHTP	Institut d'Histoire du Temps Présent, Paris
MAE	Archives du Ministère des Affaires Etrangères
RHDGM	*Revue d'Histoire de la Deuxième Guerre Mondiale*
RHMC	*Revue d'Histoire Moderne et Contemporaine*

Notes

PREFACE

(The place of publication is Paris, unless otherwise indicated.)

1. *See*, in particular, Stanley Hoffmann, *Essais sur la France. Déclin ou renouveau*, Paris, Seuil, 1974; Robert O. Paxton, *Vichy France, Old Guard and New Order 1940–1944*, New York, Columbia University Press, 1972.
2. *See* H. R. Kedward, *Occupied France. Collaboration and Resistance 1940–1944*, Oxford and New York, Blackwell, 1985, and *In Search of the Maquis. Rural Resistance in Southern France 1942–1944*, Oxford, Clarendon Press, 1993; John F. Sweets, *Choices in Vichy France. The French under Nazi Occupation*, Oxford University Press, 1986.
3. See the experience of the Channel Islands, Madeleine Bunting, *The Model Occupation. The Channel Islands under German Rule*, London, HarperCollins, 1994.

INTRODUCTION

1. I am thinking, in particular, of the works of Jean-Pierre Azéma, Stanley Hoffman, Eberhard Jäckel, H. R. Kedward, Pascal Ory, Robert Paxton, John Sweets and, of course, the team at the Institut d'Histoire du Temps Présent. Among the many works devoted to other countries occupied by Nazi Germany, I should like to single out those by Gerhard Hirschfeld (*Fremdherrschaft und Kollaboration. Die Niederlande unter deutscher Besatzung 1940–1945*, Stuttgart, Deutsche Verlags-Anstalt, 1984, English translation, 1988) and Mark Mazower (*Inside Hitler's Greece: the Experience of Occupation 1941–1944*, New Haven, Yale University Press, 1993). For a working aid, see Donna Evleth, *France under the German Occupation. An Annotated Bibliography*, New York, Greenwood Press, 1991.
2. On the evolution of the word 'collaboration', see Hans Lemberg, 'Kollaboration in Europa mit dem Dritten Reich um das Jahr 1941', in K. Bosl (ed.), *Das Jahr 1941 in der europaïschen Politik*, Munich, Oldenbourg Verlag, 1972, pp. 143–62.

1 THE FUTURE OF A DEFEAT

1. Robert Aron, *Histoire de Vichy*, Fayard, 1954, p. 16.
2. Marc Ferro, *Pétain*, Fayard, 1987, p. 80.
3. The expression appears in a letter from Pétain to Reynaud, dated 26 May 1940 (cited by Jean-Louis Crémieux-Brilhac, *Les Français de l'an 40*, vol. I, *La guerre oui ou non?*, Gallimard, 1990, p. 572).
4. Text in Emmanuel Berl, *La Fin de la IIIe République*, Gallimard, 1968, pp. 81–2.
5. Henri Michel, *Vichy année 40*, Laffont, 1966, p. 39.
6. Ferro, *Pétain*, *op. cit.*, p. 97.
7. See Jean Lacouture, *De Gaulle*, vol. I, *Le Rebelle*, Seuil, 1984.
8. *FRUS*, 1940, vol. 2, pp. 462–9.

2 AN UNDECIDED PRESENT

1. Antoine de Saint-Exupéry, *Écrits de guerre*, Gallimard, 1982, p. 431.
2. Edmond Duméril, *Journal d'un honnête homme pendant l'occupation, juin 1940–août 1944*, introduced by J. Bourgeon, Thonon-les-Bains, L'Albaron, 1990, pp. 26–7.

3. Guy de Pourtalès, *Journal*, vol. II, *1919–1941*, Gallimard, 1991, p. 387 (24 June 1940).
4. *Ibid.*, p. 397 (18 July 1940).
5. Paul Claudel, *Journal*, vol. II, *1933–1955*, Gallimard, 1969, p. 317 (25 June 1940); Gérald Antoine, *Paul Claudel*, Laffont, 1988, p. 320.
6. Crémieux-Brilhac, *Les Français de l'an 40*, *op. cit.*, vol. I, p. 602.
7. See Jean Vanwelkenhuyssen and Wichert Ten Have on Belgium and Holland, in Jean-Pierre Azéma and François Bédarida (eds), *Vichy et les Français*, Fayard, 1992, p. 689ff.
8. Duméril, *Journal d'un honnête homme*, *op. cit.*, pp. 27–8.
9. 'Ce reste de fierté', *Le Figaro*, 29 June 1940, reprinted in Jean Touzot, *Mauriac sous l'occupation*, La Manufacture, 1990, pp. 199–200.
10. Cited by Daniel Cordier, *Jean Moulin. L'inconnu du Panthéon*, vol. II, J.-C. Lattès, 1989, p. 365.
11. Paul Léautaud, *Journal littéraire*, vol. III, Mercure de France, 1986, p. 82 (21 June 1940).
12. Jacques Copeau, *Journal 1940–1948*, vol. II, *1916–1948*, Seghers, 1991, p. 493 (21 June 1940).
13. Léautaud, *Journal littéraire*, *op. cit.*, p. 164 (5 September 1940).
14. Théodore Fontane, *Aus den Tagen der Okkupation*, in *Sämtliche Werke*, vol. XVI, Munich, Nymphenburger Verlagshandlung, 1962, pp. 252–3.
15. *'Lagebericht für die Zeit bis 31.7.40'*, BA-MA, *RW 24* 15.
16. Léon Werth. *33 Jours*, Viviane Hamy, 1992, p. 118.
17. Simone de Beauvoir, *La Force de l'âge*, Gallimard, 1960, pp. 467–8.
18. *'Tätigkeitsberichte'*, 21 and 28 August, AN, *AJ 40* 1232.
19. Cited by Paul Christophe, 'Le cardinal Baudrillart et ses choix pendant la Seconde Guerre mondiale', *Revue d'histoire de l'Église de France*, no. 200, January–June 1992, p. 60.
20. Yves Farge, *Rebelles, Soldats et Citoyens. Carnet d'un commissaire de la République*, Grasset, 1966, p. 199. Maurice Martin du Gard heard people saying 'Germany will teach them some order', *Chronique de Vichy*, Flammarion, 1948, p. 32.
21. Pourtalès, *Journal*, *op. cit.*, p. 409 (2 August 1940); pp. 421–2 (30 August 1940).
22. Werth, *33 Jours*, *op. cit.*, p. 86.
23. See the entries for the end of May and early June 1940 in his *Journal 1939–1945*, Gallimard, 1992.
24. Cited by Ginette Guitard-Auviste, *Chardonne*, Orban, 1984, p. 204.
25. Henri Guillemin, *Parcours*, Seuil, 1989, p. 400.
26. 'Le dernier coup', *Le Figaro*, 15 July 1940, in Touzot, *Mauriac sous l'Occupation*, *op. cit.*, p. 205.
27. Mauriac to Édouard Bourdet, 25 July 1940, *Lettres d'un vie*, Grasset, 1981, p. 244.
28. 'Les Cahiers de la petite dame, 1937–1945', *Cahiers André Gide*, no. 6, Gallimard, 1975, p. 180 (22 July 1940).
29. André Gide, *Journal*, *1939–1942*, Gallimard, 1946, p. 57 (9 July 1940); p. 83 (5 September 1940).
30. Copeau, *Journal 1901–1948*, vol. II, *op. cit.*, p. 493 (21 June 1940).
31. *Ibid.*, p. 501 (6 July 1940).
32. Bibliothèque nationale (BN), Journal d'Alain, vol. III, p. 122.
33. Jean Paulhan, *Choix de lettres*, vol. II, *1937–1945. Traité des jours sombres*, Gallimard, 1992, p. 181 (letter to Henri Pourrat, 13 August 1940).
34. See the first months of his *Journal des années noires*, Gallimard, 'Folio', 1973.
35. Reports from *Rü In Paris*, 2 and 5 August 1940, BA-MA, *RW 19*, *Wi I A* 3 99.

36. 'Kriegstagebuch', 13 August 1940, BA-MA, *RW 24* 2.
37. Pose to Voigt, 2 August 1940, AN, *AJ 40* 823. Negotiations undertaken 'with a view to limiting the damages from an absence of earnings that the consequences of the war seem likely to produce', as the minutes of the council meeting of the BNCI delicately put it on 23 September 1940 (AN, *F 12* 9564).
38. Letter from Pose, 12 August 1940, AN, *AJ 40* 823.
39. 'Kriegstagebuch', 5 September 1940, BA-MA, *RW 24* 2.
40. Éts. Querel, 18 September 1940, AA-PA, *Botschaft Paris* 2404.
41. AN, *AJ 40* 862, dr. 7.
42. AN, *F 12* 9623, dr. Félix Potin.
43. *Chronique de Vichy, op. cit.*, p. 30.
44. 'Lagerberichte des Wi-u.Rü.-Stabes Frankreich', report for the month of October 1940, BA-MA, *RW 24* 15.
45. Léautaud, *Journal littéraire, op. cit.*, p. 124.
46. Pascal Fouché, *L'Édition française sous l'Occupation (1940–1944)*, vol. I, Bibliothèque de littérature française contemporaine de l'université Paris-VII, 1987, p. 46f; also appendix VI, letters of 30 and 31 July, pp. 348 and 350.
47. *Ibid.*, pp. 20–1.
48. Lifar to Abetz, 21 August 1940; Schleier to Lifar, 30 August 1940 AA-PA, *Botschaft Paris* 1379; *Botschaft Paris* 1101A.
49. Stéphane Courtois, 'Un été 1940. Les négociations entre le PCF et l'occupant allemand à la lumière des archives de l'Internationale communiste', *Communisme*, no. 32-33-34, 4th term 1992, 1st and 2nd terms 1993, p. 88.
50. *Mémoires d'un français rebelle*, Laffont, 1948, p. 197; letter from Loustaunau-Lacau to the German embassy, AA-PA, *Botschaft Paris* 1298.
51. Adam Philibert to Streicher, 3 August 1940, AA-PA, *Botschaft Paris* 1318.
52. Édouard Daladier, *Journal de captivité (1940–1945)*, Calmann-Lévy, 1991, p. 170.
53. Guéhenno, *Journal des années noires, op. cit.*, p. 222.
54. Pourtalès, *Journal*. vol. II. *op. cit.*, p. 441.

3 A PRESENT PAST

1. Jean-Louis Crémieux, *Les Français de l'an 40, op. cit.*
2. Maurras, *Devant l'Allemagne éternelle*, Éditions À l'étoile', 1937, p. 215.
3. See, for example, the disarray among radical circles: Serge Berstein, *Histoire du Parti radical*, vol. I, *La Recherche de l'âge d'or*, Presses de la FNSP, 1980; and by the same author, *Édouard Herriot ou la République en personne*, Presses de la FNSP, 1985.
4. Serge Berstein, *Histoire du Parti radical*, vol II, *Crise du radicalisme (1926–1939)*, 1982; William Irvine, *French Conservatism in Crisis*, Baton Rouge, Louisiana State University Press, 1979; Paul Christophe, *Les Catholiques et le Front populaire*, Éditions Ouvrières, 1986.
5. Daniel Lindenberg, *Les Années souterraines 1937–1947*, La Découverte, 1990.
6. Jean-Jaques Becker and Serge Berstein, *Histoire de l'anticommunisme en France*, vol. I, *1917–1940*, Orban, 1987.
7. William H. Schneider, *Quality and Quantity. The Quest for Biological Regeneration in Twentieth-Century France*, New York, Cambridge University Press, 1990.
8. See his articles given to *Le Figaro* in 1935–36 and reprinted in *Pleins Pouvoirs*, 1939.
9. Bloch to Lucien Febvre, 3 May 1940, AN, *318 Mi* 1.
10. The expression 'pacifist depression' was used by the Greek ambassador Politis (Jean-Baptiste Duroselle, *La Décadence 1932–1939*, Imprimerie Nationale, 1979, p.

179). For the return of war at the beginning of the decade, see Ladislas Mysyrowicz, *Autopsie d'un défaite. Origines de l'effondrement militaire français de 1940*, Lausanne, L'Âge d'Homme, 1973.

11. Rémy Pithon, 'Opinions publiques et représentations culturelles face aux problèmes de la puissance. Le témoignage du cinéma français (1938–*1939*)', *Relations internationales*, no. 33, spring 1983, p. 101.
12. See Ralph Schor, *L'Opinion français et les étrangers 1919–1939*, Publications de la Sorbonne, 1985; by the same author, *L'Antisémitisme en France pendant les années trente*, Brussels, Complexe, 1992; and by Pierre Birnbaum, *Un mythe politique: la République juive*, Fayard, 1988.
13. Schor, *L'Antisémitisme en France, op. cit.*, p. 2.
14. Paul Lévy, *La Langue allemande en France. Pénétration et diffusion des origines à nos jours*, vol. II, *De 1830 à nos jours*, IAC, 1952, P. 225.
15. See Fernand L'Huillier, *Dialogues franco-allemands 1925–1933*, Publications de la Faculté des Lettres de l'Université de Strasbourg, 1971; Jean-Claude Delbreil, *Les Catholiques français et les tentatives de rapprochement franco-allemand (1920–1933)*, Metz, SMEI, 1972; Hermann Hagspiel, *Verständigung zwischen Deutschland und Frankreich? Die deutsch-französische Außenpolitik der zwanziger Jahre im innenpolitischen Kräftefeld beider Länder*, Bonn, Ludwig Röhrscheid Verlag, 1987.
16. Claudel, *Journal, op. cit.*, p. 53 (18–19 March 1934); p. 92 (21 May 1935).
17. *Correspondance générale*, vol. VI, *1933–1936*, Gallimard, 1990, letter to Colonel Meyer, p. 490 (16 March 1936).
18. Teichler, *Internationale Sportpolitik im Dritten Reich*, Schorndorf, Verlag K. Hofmann, 1991, p. 153.
19. *Les Carnets de la drôle de guerre. Novembre 1939–mars 1940*, Gallimard, 1983, p. 274 (20 Feburary 1940).
20. *L'Allemagne nouvelle*, Flammarion, 1936, pp. 262–3. French thought was 'profoundly disconcerted by the national-socialist phenomenon' (Ladislas Mysyrowicz, 'L'Image de l'Allemagne nationale-socialiste à travers les publications françaises des années 1933–1939', in *Les Relations franco-allemandes 1933–1939*, Éditions du CNRS, 1976, p. 134).
21. Alain Fleury, *La Croix et l'Allemagne*, Cerf, 1984, p. 409.
22. George Pistorius, *L'Image de l'Allemagne dans le roman français entre les deux guerres (1918–1939)*, Nouvelles Éditions Debresse, 1964, p. 206.
23. François Garçon, *De Blum à Pétain. Cinéma et société française (1936–1944)*, Cerf, 1984, pp. 165–6.
24. *Statistisches Jahrbuch für das Deutsche Reich, 1928–1938*. It is interesting to note that in 1935 almost three times as many British people and four times as many Dutch were visiting Germany (the French accounted for no more than about 5 per cent of the foreigners entering Germany).
25. Gordon Dutter, 'Doing Business with the Nazis: French Economic Relations with Germany under the Popular Front', *Journal of Modern History*, June 1991, pp. 296–326.
26. 'Échanges practiqués entre la France et l'Allemagne avant la guerre', n.d., AN, *70 AJ* 29. The data on school exchanges come from Dieter Tiemann, *Deutsch-französische Jugendbeziehungen der Zwischenkriegszeit*, Bonn, Röhrscheid, 1989, pp. 170, 310.
27. On young Christians, see Allain René Michel, *La Jeunesse étudiante chrêtienne face au nazisme et à Vichy (1938–1944)*, Lille, Presses Universitaires de Lille, 1988, p. 46. On scouts, see the *Völkischer Beobachter*, 29 December 1938, p. 11.
28. Epting, 'Bericht der Zweigstelle Paris des DAA über ihre Tätigkeit vom 1 April 1936

bis 30. September 1937', AA-PA, *Botschaft Paris* 1053/4. There were still 2000 in 1937–38 (Gigeon report, 29 March 1939, AN, *70 AJ* 4).

29. Epting, 'Bericht der Zweigstelle Paris des DAA über ihre Tätigkeit vom 1 Oktober 1937 bis September 1938', AA-PA, *Botschaft Paris* 1053/4.
30. See Marius-François Guyard, *La Grande-Bretagne dans le roman français 1914–1940*, Marcel Didier, 1954. On the cinema, see Garçon, *De Blum à Pétain, op. cit.*, p. 137f; and newspaper cartoons, Christian Delporte, *Les Crayons de la propagande. Dessinateurs et dessin politique sous l'Occupation*, CNRS Éditions, 1993, pp. 87–8.
31. Ignatius Frederick Clarke, *Voices Prophesying War 1763–1984*, London, Oxford University Press, 1966, p. 166f.
32. For example, Henry de Farge and Jean Mauclère, *Feuilles français dans la tourmente. Les héros de la presse clandestine dans le Nord envahi*, Berger-Levrault, 1932 and Louise Thuliez, *Condamnée à mort*, with a preface by Weygand, Flammarion, 1933.
33. Annette Becker, 'Mémoire et commémoration: les "atrocités" allemandes de la Première Guerre mondiale dans le Nord de la France', *Revue du Nord*, no. 295, April–June 1992, pp. 339–54.
34. See, for the period before 1914, Marieluise Christadler, 'Politik, Mythos und Mentalität. Französische und deutsche Jugendliteratur vor dem I. Weltkreig', in *Deutschland-Frankreich. Alte Klischees-Neue Bilder*, Duisburg, Verlag der Sozialwissenschaftlichen Kooperative, 1981, pp. 73–5, and Michael Jeismann, *Das Vaterland der Feinde. Studien zum nationalen Feindbegriff und Selbstverständnis in Deutschland und Frankreich 1792–1918*, Stuttgart, Klett-Cotta, 1992.
35. Maxence Van der Meersch, *Invasion 14*, vol. II, Lausanne, Grand-Chêne, 1948, p. 327 (1st edition, Albin Michel, 1935).
36. Garçon, *De Blum à Pétain, op. cit.*, pp. 161–2.
37. Queneau, *Journal 1939–1940*, Gallimard, 1986, 27 August 1939, p. 35.
38. Queneau, *Un rude hiver*, Gallimard, 1939, pp. 132–3.

4 THE MASTERS OF THE MOMENT

1. Éditions Coopération, 1939, pp. 27 and 23.
2. Eugen Weber, *La Fin des terroirs. La modernisation de la France rurale 1870–1914*, Fayard, 1983, p. 108f. On what follows, see in particular Christian and Solange Gras, *La Révolte des régions d'Europe occidentale de 1916 à nos jours*, PUF, 1982; and Christian Gras and Georges Livet (eds), *Régions et Régionalisme en France du XVIIIe siècle à nos jours*, PUF, 1977.
3. See Gérard Cholvy, 'Régionalisme et clergé catholique au XIXe siècle', in *Régions et Régionalisme en France du XVIIIe siècle à nos jours, op. cit.*, pp. 187–201.
4. See, for example, the work by Kleo Pleyer, *Die Landschaft im neuen Frankreich*, Stuttgart, 1935; and H. Brühl, 'Das französisches Nationalitätenproblem', *Die Westmark*, February 1939, pp. 249–56.
5. See in particular Franz Petri, *Germanisches Volkserbe in Wallonien und Nordfrankreich*, Bonn, Röhrscheid, 1937, 2 vols.
6. See F. Pomponi, 'Le régionalisme en Corse dans l'entre-deux-guerres (1919–1939), in *Régions et régionalisme en France du XVIIIe siècle à nos jours, op. cit.*, pp. 393–415.
7. Paul Lévy, *La Langue allemande en France*, vol. II, *op. cit.*, pp. 235–38, 250.
8. E. Defoort, 'Jean-Marie Gantois dans le mouvement flamand en France (1919–1939)', in *Régions et Régionalisme en France du XVIIIe siècle à nos jours, op. cit.*, pp. 327–36.
9. Willem Meyers, 'Les collaborateurs flamands de France et les contacts avec les milieux flamingants belges', *Revue du Nord*, no. 237, 1978, p. 338.

10. Lévy, *La Langue allemande en France*, *op. cit.*, pp. 240–1. On Alsatian autonomism, see Philip Bankwitz, 'Les Chefs autonomistes alsaciens 1919–1947', *Saisons d'Alsace*, no. 71, 2nd term, 1980.
11. See Bernard Reimeringer, 'Un communisme régionaliste? Le communisme alsacien', in *Régions et Régionalisme en France du XVIIIe siècle à nos jours*, *op. cit.*, pp. 361–92; also, Samuel Goodfellow, 'From Communism to Nazism: the Transformation of Alsatian Communists', *Journal of Contemporary History*, 27, April 1992, pp. 231–58.
12. On Bickler, see Francis Arzalier, *Les Perdants. La dérive fasciste des mouvements autonomistes et indépendantistes au XXe siècle*, La Découverte, 1990.
13. Alain Déniel, *Le Mouvement breton (1919–1945)*, Maspero, 1976, pp. 380–4.
14. Cited by Michel Denis, 'Mouvement breton et fascisme. Signification de l'échec du second EMSAV', in *Régions et Régionalisme en France du XVIIIe siècle à nos jours*, *op. cit.*, p. 500.
15. Déat, *Journal de guerre*, 28 June 1940 (AN, *F 7* 15342).
16. See Pierre Milza, *Fascisme français. Passé et présent*, Flammarion, 1987.
17. Maurice Merleau-Ponty, 'La guerre a lieu', *Les Temps modernes*, no. 1, October 1945, pp. 49–50. On Abetz, see Rita Thalmann, 'Du Cercle de Sohlberg au Comité France–Allemagne: un exemple d'évolution ambiguë de la coopération franco-allemande', in *Les Relations culturelles franco-allemandes dans les années trente*, colloquium DAAD and IHTP, Paris, *6–8* December 1990, pp. 103–21 (published under the title: *Entre Locarno et Vichy: les relations culturelles franco-allemandes dans les années 1930*, ed. Hans Manfred Bock *et al.*, Éditions du CNRS, 1993, 2 vols).
18. See AA-PA, *Botschaft Paris* 1049/1.
19. *Cahiers franco-allemands*, May 1937.
20. At the General Assembly of March 1937, the treasurer of the CFA announced 419 recent new members (*Cahiers de l'UF*, 20 March 1937, p. 4). One of Déat's adjutants, Levillain, who had joined in 1938, held card no. 955 ('Exposé', AN *Z 6* 415, Maurice Levillain). On the attitude of the Ancien combattants see Antoine Prost, 'Les anciens combattants français et l'Allemagne *1933–1938*, *La France et l'Allemagne* 1932–1936, CNRS, 1980, pp. 131–48.
21. *Cahiers franco-allemands*, October 1936, p. 353; nos. 3–4, 1937, p. 126; February 1938, p. 87; AA-PA, *Botschaft Paris* 1049/2.
22. *Cahiers franco-allemands*, September 1937, p. 307.
23. AA-PA, *Botschaft Paris* 1060/4. Sacha Guitry seems to have been prevented at the last moment from attending the congress.
24. Köster, 22 May 1935, AA-PA, *Abt. Pol. II*, vol. XXIII.
25. Michel Grunewald, 'L'idéologie du "rapprochement franco-allemand" dans les *Deutsch-französische Monatshefte/Cahiers franco-allemands (1934–1939)*' in *Les relations culturelles franco-allemandes dans les années 1930*, *op. cit.*, pp. 12–33. See also Barbara Unteutsch, *Vom Sohlbergkreis zur Gruppe 'Collaboration'. Ein Beitrag zur Geschichte der deutsch-französischen Beziehungen anhand der Cahiers franco-allemands, 1931–1944*, Münster, Kleinheinrich, 1990.
26. Pichot, 'Pour être lu à Berlin', *L'Œuvre*, 16 November 1938.
27. Welczek to Goebbels, 25 January 1939, AA-PA, *Botschaft Paris* 1057d.
28. Hans-Joachim Teichler, *Internationale Sportpolitik im Dritten Reich*, *op. cit.*, p. 188.
29. Welczek, 8 August 1939, AA-PA, *Botschaft Paris* 1056b.
30. Feihl, 19 November 1936, AA-PA, *Botschaft Paris* 554d.
31. Céline, *L'École des cadavres*, Denoël, 1938, pp. 95, 98. See Philippe Alméras, *Les Idées de Céline*, Bibliothèque de Littérature Française Contemporaine de l'Université de Paris-VII, 1987.

32. *Devant l'Allemagne éternelle. Gaulois, Germains, Latins. Chronique d'une résistance*, Éditions À l'étoile', 1937, p. vii.
33. See Pierre-Marie Dioudonnat, *Je suis partout, 1930–1944. Les maurrassiens devant la tentation fasciste*, La Table Ronde, 1973.
34. See Philippe Machefer, 'Les Croix de Feu devant l'Allemagne', *La France et l'Allemagne 1932–1936, op. cit.*, pp. 109–29.
35. Jouvenel, 'Das französische Weltreich', *Cahiers franco-allemands*, nos. 3–4, 1938, pp. 103–5; Fabre-Luce, 'La race blanche joue sa vie', *Candide*, 23 June 1939.
36. Doriot, 'La Chine, champ de bataille pour la suprémacie mondiale', *Revue de Paris*, 15 August 1937, pp. 814–20.
37. Flandin, 'Weltsorgen der Gegenwart', *Europäische Revue*, November 1933, pp. 588–95.
38. Burrin, *La Dérive fasciste. Doriot, Déat, Bergery, 1933–1944*, Seuil, 1986, pp. 72–5. See Norman Ingram, *The Politics of Dissent. Pacifism in France 1919–1939*, Oxford University Press, 1991; and Patrick de Villepin, 'Plutôt la servitude que la guerre! Le pacifisme intégral dans les années trente', *Relations Internationales*, no. 53, spring 1988, pp. 53–67.
39. René Belin, 'Les avertissements de la raison au-dessus des mouvements du cœur', *Syndicats*, 30 October 1936.
40. See, for example, Soulès, 'Le socialisme doit-il réviser sa critique du fascisme?', *Redressement*, April 1939, pp. 10–12.
41. *Le Journal*, 30 April 1936, in Philippe Pétain, *Actes et Écrits*, Flammarion, 1974, pp. 421–2.
42. *Paroles aux Français, Messages et Écrits, 1934–1941*, Lyons, Lardanchet, 1941, p. 14f (speech to the congress of the Union Nationale des Anciens Combattants).
43. 'Conversazione R. Ambasciatore-Maresciallo Petain', ASMAE, *Affari politici Francia* 20.
44. See François Monnet, *Refaire la République. André Tardieu, une dérive réactionnaire (1876–1945)*, Fayard, 1993.
45. Landini to the Ministero della cultura populare (Italian propaganda ministry), reports of 9 March, 18 March and 6 April, NA (National Archives, Washington), T 586/475.
46. Report of 6 April 1938, *ibid.*.
47. Duroselle, *La Décadence, op. cit.*, p. 125. In October 1940, Charles Rist, who had accompanied Laval on an official visit to the United States in 1931, told Barnaud: 'Laval has always been wrong in his foreign politics, and knows nothing of the feelings of others, whether they be German, Italian, American or English' (Charles Rist, *Une saison gatée*, Fayard, 1983, p. 9, 19 October 1940).
48. *Ibid.*, p. 398.
49. *Ibid.*, p. 371.
50. Welczek to AA, 12 April 1937, AA-PA, *Pol. II 109*, vol. III. This committee published *Cahiers du Rassemblement national pour la reconstruction de la France*.

5 FRANCE FOR ITSELF ALONE

1. See Stanley Hoffmann, *Sur la France*, Seuil, 1976, and *Essais sur la France*, Seuil, 1974; Jean-Pierre Azéma, *From Munich to the Liberation 1938–1944*, translated by Janet Lloyd, Cambridge, Cambridge University Press and the Editions de la Maison des Sciences de l'Homme; Azéma and Bédarida (eds), *Vichy et les Français, op. cit.*.
2. See Pierre Laborie, *L'Opinion française sous Vichy*, Seuil, 1990.

3. See Robert Paxton, *Vichy France 1940–1944*, New York, Alfred Knopf, 1972 and *Parades and Politics at Vichy. The French Officer Corps under Marshal Pétain*, New Jersey, Princeton University Press, 1966.
4. See Michèle Cointet, *Le Conseil national de Vichy*, Aux Amateurs de Livres, 1989; Jean-Paul Cointet, *La Légion française des combattants*, Henri Veyrier, 1991.
5. Pétain to Baudrillart, 28 November 1940, AN, *2 AG* 493, dr. CC 74 17.
6. *Discours aux Français*, Albin Michel, 1989, p. 172.
7. Henri Du Moulin de La Barthète, *Le Temps des illusions. Souvenirs (juillet 1940–avril 1942)*, Geneva, Éd. du Cheval Ailé, 1946, p. 93.
8. *Ibid.*, p. 392.
9. See Baudouin, *Neuf mois au gouvernement (avril–décembre 1940)*, La Table ronde, 1948, p. 366.
10. Maurice Moch, *L'Étoile et la Francisque. Les institutions juives sous Vichy*, ed. A. Michel, Cerf, 1990, p. 69 (conversation of 15 March 1941).
11. Du Moulin, *Le Temps des illusions, op. cit.*, p. 427.
12. Leahy to Roosevelt, 18 March 1941, *FRUS*, vol. II, *Europe*, p. 129; Valeri to Maglione, 25 September 1941, *Actes et Documents du Saint-Siège*, Rome, Libr. Editrice Vaticane, vol. V, no. 99.
13. Pierre Limagne, *Éphémérides de quatre années tragiques 1940–1944*, vol. I, Bonne Presse, 1945–47, p. 566 (2 May 1942); Claudel, *Journal, op. cit.*, p. 413 (3 September 1942).
14. Du Moulin, *Le Temps des illusions, op. cit.*, pp. 196–7.
15. Baudouin, *Neuf mois au gouvernement, op. cit.*, p. 256.
16. Benoist-Méchin, *De la défaite au désastre*, Albin Michel, 1984, vol. I, p. 79.
17. Philippe Masson, *La Marine française et la Guerre 1939–1945*, Tallandier, 1991, p. 24f., p. 292.
18. Hervé Coutau-Bégarie and Claude Huan, *Darlan*, Fayard, 1989, p. 338.
19. Nerin E. Gun, *Les Secrets des archives américaines. Pétain–Laval-De Gaulle*, Albin Michel, 1979, p. 96.
20. Du Moulin, *Le Temps des illusions, op. cit.*, p. 147.
21. *Ibid.*, pp. 359–60.
22. *Ibid.*, p. 146.
23. Claudel, *Journal, op. cit.*, p. 358 (8–10 May 1941).
24. See Jean-Baptiste Duroselle, *L'Abîme 1940–1944*, Imprimerie nationale, 1982.
25. Coutau-Bégarie and Huan, *Darlan, op. cit.*, pp. 288–9.
26. *Ibid.*, pp. 315–16.
27. Baudouin, *Neuf mois au gouvernement, op. cit.*, p. 265f.
28. Conversation between Bouthillier and Hemmen, 27 August 1940, DFCAA, vol. I, pp. 182–5.
29. Abetz to AA, 14 July 1940, AA-PA, *Büro des St. S., Frankreich* 2.
30. Grimm, 'Besprechung mit Minsterpräsident Laval im Hause von Marcel Ribardière am 28 August 1940', BAK, *Nachlaß Grimm*. The idea of deriving compensation from the British colonies was also circulating in the French delegation at Wiesbaden (Paxton, *Vichy France, op. cit.*, p. 66).
31. Maurras, *La seule France*, Lyons, Lardanchet, 1941.
32. See Robert Frank, 'Vichy et le monde, le monde et Vichy: perceptions géopolitiques et idéologiques', in Azéma and Bédarida (eds), *Vichy et les Français, op. cit.*, p. 105f.
33. Huntziger to Weygand, 30 August 1940, AN, *AJ 41* 148, dr. Archives historiques.
34. Von Neubronn to DWStK (the German armistice commission), 20 February 1941, AN, *AJ 40* 1233.
35. *Carnets du pasteur Boegner*, Fayard, 1992, p. 186 (27 June 1942).

36. Jouvenel, *Un voyageur dans le siècle*, Laffont, 1979, p. 435–6.
37. Carcopino himself, talking to Achenbach in June 1941, paid homage to 'Strength through joy' ('Notes prises au cours de l'entretien du 5 juin 1941 à l'ambassade d'Allemagne', AN, *F 60* 429, dr. Organisation générale de l'enseignement).
38. AN, *F 60* 1433, dr. Études-traités de paix.

6 THE MACHINERY OF OCCUPATION

1. See Hans Umbreit, *Der Militärbefehlshaber in Frankreich 1940–1944*, Boppard-sur-le-Rhin, Harald Boldt Verlag, 1968, and Eberhard Jäckel, *La France dans l'Europe de Hitler*, Fayard, 1968.
2. For references to the six million to be expelled, see W. Wagner, *Belgien in der deutschen Politik während des Zweiten Weltkrieges*, Boppard-sur-le-Rhin, Harald Boldt Verlag, 1974, p. 176. On plans concerning Burgundy, see Conrad F. Latour, *Südtirol und die Achse Berlin–Rom 1938–1945*, Stuttgart, Deutsche Verlags-Anstalt, 1962, pp. 74–5.
3. *Monologe im Führerhauptquartier 1941–1944*, ed. W. Jochmann, Munich, Heyne Verlag, 1980, p. 245.
4. W. A. Boelcke, *Kriegspropaganda 1939–1941. Geheime Ministerkonferenzen im Reichspropagandaministerium*, Stuttgart, Deutsche Verlags-Anstalt, 1966, p. 420 (9 July 1940).
5. There were 531 in Paris, 325 in the regions and 596 in the Feldkommandanturen (Best, 'Die deutschen Aufsichtsverwaltungen', BA-MA, *RW 24* 319). See also Lucien Steinberg, *Les allemands en France*, Albin Michel, 1980; and Rita Thalmann, *La Mise au pas. Idéologie et stratégie sécuritaire dans la France occupée*, Fayard, 1991.
6. *Die faschistische Okkupationspolitik in Frankreich (1940–1944)*, a selection of documents edited by L. Nestler and F. Schultz, Berlin, Deutscher Verlag der Wissenschaften, 1990, pp. 31–2.
7. Ernst Jünger, *Premier Journal parisien*, Christian Bourgois, 1980, p. 107 (23 February 1942).
8. *Ibid.*, p. 108.
9. See Heinrich Bücheler, *Carl-Heinrich von Stülpnagel*, Berlin, Ullstein, 1989.
10. Helmut Krausnick, *Hitlers Einsatzgruppen*, Frankfurt-on-Main, Fischer, 1985, pp. 191–2.
11. *Die faschistische Okkupationspolitik in Frankreich, op. cit.*, p. 31, note 44.
12. *Tätigkeitsbericht der Propaganda-Abteilung Frankreich für die Zeit vom 8.1.–25.1 1941*, p. 14, AN, *AJ 40* 1001.
13. *Die faschistische Okkupationspolitik in Frankreich, op. cit.*, p. 31.
14. Umbreit, *Der Militärbefehlshaber in Frankreich, op. cit.*, p. 106.
15. 'Übersicht über den Einsatz deutscher Firmen im Bereich des MBF', 28 June 1944, BA-MA, *RW 35* 854.
16. *Die faschistische Okkupationspolitik in Frankreich, op. cit.*, p. 31.
17. See Klaus Kirchner, *Flugblattpropaganda im 2. Weltkrieg*, vol. II, *Flugblätter aus Deutschland 1939/1940*, Erlangen, Verlag D+C, 1982.
18. See the Wiesbaden recriminations in AN, *AJ 40* 1368, dr. *Allg. Bd.2.*
19. AA-PA, *Botschaft Paris* 1930.
20. Benoist-Méchin, *À l'épreuve du temps*, vol. II, Julliard, 1989, p. 220.
21. André Weil-Curiel, *Le Temps de la honte*, vol. II, Éd. du Myrte, 1946.
22. See the documents in AA-PA, *Botschaft Paris* 1050/1, and Tiemann, *Deutsch-französische Jugendbeziehungen der Zwischenkriegszeit, op. cit.*, pp. 117–18.

23. See his file, SS-Personal-Akte Abetz, Berlin Document Centre. The SS backed his return to France at the end of 1943.
24. *Ibid.*
25. Feihl hearing, 1 September 1946, AN, *3 W* 358, dr. Feihl.
26. Abetz to Speidel, 22 June 1940, CDJC, LXXI-1.
27. *'Politische Arbeit in Frankreich'*, 30 July 1940, CDJC, LXXI-28.
28. Best, *'Grundsätzliche Richtlinien für die politische Behandlung des besetzen Gebietes'*, 19 August 1940, CDJC, LXXI-1.
29. According to Albert Wenceslas, member of the Information Section of the Embassy, AN, *F 7* 15 307.
30. *Monologe, op. cit.*, p. 254 (2 February 1942); p. 53 (2 August 1941).
31. *Pétain et les Allemands. Mémorandum d'Abetz sur les rapports franco-allemands*, Gaucher, 1948, pp. 87–9, report of 23 June 1941. One week earlier, Abetz had explained to an Italian diplomat: 'Tomorrow, France will be what it was at the time of the Roman empire: a province, a very important province of course, which will enjoy its liberty and autonomy, but still a province and not the most important one' (note by Anfuso, 15 June 1941, ACS, *MCP 168*, dr. 168⁄124.
32. *Die Tagebücher von Joseph Goebbels*, vol. IV, edited by E. Fröhlich, Munich, K. G. Saur, 1987, p. 370 (20 October 1940); p. 411 (26 November 1940).
33. Abetz, *Das offene Problem. Ein Rückblick auf zwei Jahrzehnte deutscher Frankreich-politik*, Cologne, Greven Verlag, 1957, p. 217.
34. *Monologe, op. cit.*, p. 305 (27 February 1942).
35. Here are two examples of this solidarity: on 11 July 1942, Brinon asked Laval, on Abetz's behalf, for some information that Berlin required on an aspect of Vichy's politics, explaining: 'The ambassador did not conceal from me that, if he is to pursue his personal efforts, he also needed to be completely informed on the position adopted by us' (Brinon, 'Message for President Laval', 11 July [1942], AN, *F 60* 1479). When Achenbach left Paris in 1943, Laval, who had been unable to attend his farewell dinner, sent him a message of 'friendship': 'I have known him in difficult times and it will be a joy to meet him on the day when we can together contemplate the happy result of our common efforts' (telephone message from Laval to Brinon, no. 611, 17 May 1943, *ibid.*).
36. Knochen hearing, 6 January 1947, AN, *3 W* 358, dr. Knochen.

7 MONTOIRE

1. Jäckel, *La France dans l'Europe de Hitler, op. cit.*, p. 162. See also the thesis by Karl-Volker Neugebauer, *Die Errichtung der deutschen Militärkontrolle im unbesetzten Frankreich und in Französisch-Nordestafrika. Eine Studie zum Problem der Sicherung der Südwestflanke von Hitlers Kontinentalimperium*, Cologne, Diss, 1977.
2. Yves Bouthillier, *Le Drame de Vichy*, Plon, 1950, p. 56; Baudouin, *Neuf mois au gouvernement, op. cit.*, p. 372 (19 October 1940).
3. *Discours aux Français, op. cit.*, pp. 88–9.
4. Schmidt, 22 October 1940, *ADAP*, D 11/1, no. 212.
5. Schmidt, 24 October 1940, *ADAP*, D 11/1, no. 227.
6. Déat, *Journal de guerre*, 25 October 1940.
7. *Discours aux français, op. cit.*, pp. 94–6.
8. Schleier to AA, 15 November 1940, *ADAP*, D 11/12, no. 338.
9. Armistice meeting of 20 November 1940, AN, *AJ 41* 33, 'PV réunions d'armistice 1940–1941'.

10. As well as Du Moulin, see Pastor Boegner who recorded the testimony of several people in Vichy on 21 and 22 December, and then that of Peyrouton on 4 February (*Carnets du pasteur Boegner, op. cit.*, pp. 63–4, p. 77).
11. Tasca notebooks, 18 December 1940 (I should like to thank Denis Peschanski for allowing me to consult these notebooks).
12. Abetz to AA, 26 October 1940, *ADAP*, D 11/1, no. 234.
13. See Benoist-Méchin's 'Journal de La Ferté-Hauterive', reproduced in *À l'épreuve du temps*, vol. II, *op. cit.*, p. 66.
14. Boegner, *Carnets du pasteur Boegner, op. cit.*, p. 77 (4 February 1941).
15. Bouthillier, *Le Drame de Vichy, op. cit.*, p. 77 (4 February 1941).
16. Ferro, *Pétain, op. cit.*, p. 202.
17. That is what Darlan said to Hitler on 25 December (Schmidt, *ADAP*, D 11/12, no. 564).
18. Baudouin, *Neuf mois au gouvernement, op. cit.*, p. 422.
19. Gun, *Les secrets des archives américaines, op. cit.*, p. 211f.
20. On the Laval–Bouthillier disagreement over Bor's actions, see the study by Michel Margairaz, *L'État, les Finances et l'Économie. Histoire d'un conversion 1932–1952*, Imprimerie nationale, 1991, pp. 632–3.
21. He said so to Göring, for example, see Abetz to AA, 9 November 1940, *ADAP*, D 11/1, no. 306.
22. Armistice meeting of 7 December 1940, AN, *AJ 41* 33, 'PV réunions d'armistice 1940–1941'.
23. 'Réunion d'armistice franco-allemande du 10 décembre 1940 à l'ambassade allemande à Paris', AN, *AJ 41* 138, dr. 13.
24. See R. T. Thomas, *Britain and Vichy. The Dilemma of Anglo-French Relations 1940–1942*, New York, St. Martin's Press, 1979; and Robert Frank, 'Vichy et les Britanniques 1940–1941: double jeu ou double language?', *Vichy et les Français, op. cit.*, pp. 144–63.
25. Llewellyn Woodward, *British Foreign Policy in the Second World War*, vol. I, London, Her Majesty's Stationery Office, 1970, pp. 429–30.
26. Hervé Coutau-Bégarie and Claude Huan, *Lettres et Notes de l'amiral Darlan*, Économica, 1992, p. 203.
27. Leahy to Roosevelt, 13 May 1941, *FRUS*, 1941, vol. II, *Europe*, p. 170.
28. Telegram from Tuck on 20 July 1942, cited by Gun, *Les Secrets des archives américaines, op. cit.*, p. 262.
29. Note from Darlan for Pétain, 8 November 1940, *Lettres et Notes de l'amiral Darlan, op. cit.*, doc. 142, p. 248.
30. 'Note relative aux négociations pour la suppression de la ligne de démarcation', 7 December 1940, AN, *AJ 41* 39, dr. Cab. 62 'dossier préparé par le ministère des Finances pour M. Flandin 15 décembre'.
31. 'Note pour le Ministre. Réflexions sur la politique de "collaboration" ', 6 November 1940, not signed, probably by Barnaud, AN, *F 37* 1, dr. b.
32. Several of these arguments were raised by Darlan himself in a note for Pétain on 8 November 1940 (see above, n. 29).
33. Note by Darlan on 17 November 1940, *Lettres et Notes de l'amiral Darlan, op. cit.*, doc. 144, p. 252.
34. Leahy to Roosevelt, 13 May 1941, *FRUS*, 1941, vol. II, *Europe*, p. 167.
35. Note by Darlan on 22 July 1941, cited by Hervé Coutau-Bégarie and Claude Huan, *Darlan, op. cit.*, p. 449.

8 THE DARLAN ERA

1. Abetz to AA, 18 December 1940, *ADAP*, D 11/2, no. 531.
2. Schmidt, wrongly dated 24 December 1940, *ADAP*, D 11/2, no. 564.
3. Hencke, 16 December 1940, *ADAP*, D 11/2, no. 521; Schuchardt, 'Unterredung mit Botschafter Abetz am 29.1.41', AN, *AJ 40* 1202, dr. *V.O. zur Deutsch Bot. Paris.*
4. Benoist-Méchin, *À l'épreuve du temps*, vol. II, *op. cit.*, p. 71, 11 January 1941.
5. Schuchardt, 'Unterredung mit Botschafter Abetz am 29.1.41', AN, *AJ 40* 1202, dr. *V.O. zur Deutsch Bot. Paris.*
6. Brinon to Pétain, 30 January 1941, in Alain Darlan, *L'amiral Darlan parle*, Amiot-Dumont, 1952, p. 271–4.
7. Abetz to AA, 31 January 1941, *ADAP*, D 11/2, no. 736.
8. Déat, *Journal de guerre*, 30 January 1941; 'Niederschrift über die Besprechung bei der Deutschen Botschaft', 6 February 1941, AN, *AJ 40* 539.
9. Notes by Huntziger, cited in Coutau-Bégarie and Huan, *Darlan*, *op. cit.*, p. 369.
10. 'Niederschrift über die Besprechung bei der Deutschen Botschaft', 6 February 1941, *AJ 40* 539.
11. Note dated 8 February 1941, AN, *AJ 40* 1202, dr. *V.O. zur Deutsch Bot. Paris.*
12. *Pétain et les Allemands*, *op. cit.*, pp. 79–84.
13. See Richard F. Kuisel, 'The Legend of the Vichy Synarchy', *French Historical Studies*, spring 1970, pp. 365–98.
14. Note of 30 January 1941, in Coutau-Bégarie and Huan, *Lettres et Notes de l'amiral Darlan*, *op. cit.*, doc. 165, p. 288.
15. Another note of 30 January 1941, *ibid.*, doc. 166, p. 290.
16. Barthélémy, *Ministre de la Justice*, Pygmalion, 1989, p. 345 (reporting on remarks made by Darlan in June 1941).
17. Hearing on 18 November 1945, AN, *3 W* 358.
18. Stohrer, Madrid, 17 February 1941, *ADAP*, 12/1, no. 62.
19. Letter from Pétain to a northern industrialist, 5 July 1941, reprinted by Étienne Dejonghe, 'Le Nord isolé: occupation et opinion (mai 1940–mars 1942)', *RHMC*, January–March 1979, pp. 92–3.
20. G. Wagner (ed.), *Lagevorträge des Oberbefehlshabers der Kriegmarine von Hitler, 1939–1945*, Munich, J. F. Lehmann, 1972, 18 March 1941, p. 203.
21. See AN, *AJ 40* 1201, dr. 18A *'Syrien'*.
22. Memo by Abetz, p. 101 (6 May 1941); see Benoist-Méchin, *De la défaite au désastre*, vol. I, *op. cit.*, p. 68f.
23. Pétain to Hitler, 5 May 1941, *ADAP*, D 12/2, no. 491; Benoist-Méchin, *ibid.*, p. 89.
24. Schmidt, 11 May 1941, *ADAP*, D 12/2, no. 491; Benoist-Méchin, *ibid.*, p. 89.
25. Coutau-Bégarie and Huan, *Darlan*, *op. cit.*, p. 406.
26. Pétain, *Discours aux Français*, *op. cit.*, p. 132.
27. Text of the additional protocol in Benoist-Méchin, *De la défaite au désastre*, vol. II, *op. cit.*, pp. 435–6.
28. *Ibid.*, p. 141f.
29. Recapitulatory file 'Négociations avec l'Allemagne 7 mai 1941–31 juillet 1942', AN, *AJ 41* 138.
30. Vogl, 11 June 1941, AN, *AJ 40* 1203, dr. 27 *Pariser Besprechungen*. See also dr. 25 Biserta.
31. Louis Noguères, *Le Véritable Procès du maréchal Pétain*, Fayard, 1955, p. 308.
32. *DWStK Abordnung Paris*, 8 July 1941, AN *AJ 40* 1203, dr. 25 Biserta. The recapitulatory file 'Négociations avec l'Allemagne 7 mai 1941–31 juillet 1942' (AN, *AJ 41* 138) explains that, on 14 July, 'the French government, tired of discussing French

concessions without obtaining any political advantages in return, had two notes handed to M. Abetz by M. Benoist-Méchin'.

33. Coutau-Bégarie and Huan, *Darlan*, *op. cit.*, p. 434.
34. *Ibid.*, p. 435.
35. Text in Benoist-Méchin, *De la défaite au désastre*, vol. I, *op. cit.*, p. 440f.
36. Coutau-Bégarie and Huan, *Darlan*, *op. cit.*, pp. 441–2.
37. 17 November 1941, *ADAP*, 13/2, no. 478; see also Abetz's memo of 4 December 1941 cited in note 16 of no. 529.
38. 'Note sur des études préliminaires à des négociations de paix', not signed, n.d. [late 1941), AN, *F 37* 1, 'Doc. générale'.
39. Schmidt, 21 December 1941, *ADAP*, E/1, no. 45.
40. AN, *AJ 41*, dr. Juin–Göring negotiations.
41. Schleier, 22 December 1941, *ADAP*, E/1, no. 47.
42. A commentary by a high-ranking French civil servant: 'Transit through Tunisia, which we have been denying to Germany since 28 May (Paris protocols) is thus granted to Italy' (recapitulatory file 'Négociations avec Allemagne 7 mai 1941–31 juillet 1942', AN, *AJ 41* 138).
43. Ribbentrop, '*Bemerkungen zur französischen Antwort*', 31 December 1941, *ADAP*, E/1, no. 76.
44. Woermann, 21 January 1942, *ADAP*, E/1 no. 153.
45. Abetz, 5 January 1942, *ADAP*, E/1, no. 94.
46. Benoist-Méchin, *À l'épreuve du temps*, vol. II, *op. cit.*, pp. 304–5.
47. Benoist-Méchin, *De la défaite au désastre*, vol. I, *op. cit.*, pp. 358–63.
48. *Ibid.*, p. 251.
49. Abetz, *Pétain et les Allemands*, *op. cit.*, p. 139.
50. Leahy to Roosevelt, 11 December 1941, *FRUS*, 1941, vol. II, *Europe*, p. 199.
51. 'Pol. und wirt. Probleme des unbesezten Gebietes', 14 August 1941, not signed, AA-PA, *Botschaft Paris* 1329.
52. Déat, *Journal de guerre*, March 1942.

9 ENDLESS NEGOTIATIONS

1. See Isabelle Boussard, 'Les négociations franco-allemandes sur les prélèvements agricoles: l'exemple du champagne', *RHGDM*, no. 95, July 1974, pp. 3–24.
2. See AN, *AJ 41* 336, 'Problèmes concernant les fonctionnaires'.
3. 'Abschlußbericht der Verwaltung Allgemein und Gruppe Allgemeine und innere Verwaltung', p. 17, AN, *AJ 40* 536, dr. 2.
4. Boemelburg, 'Präfektenversammlung Vichy 19.2.42', AN, *AJ 40* 539. On the movements of prefects under Vichy, see Sonia Mazey and Vincent Wright, 'Les préfets', in Jean-Pierre Azéma and François Bédarida, *Vichy et les Français*, *op. cit.*, p. 275f.
5. Note by Abt. Verwaltung, Gruppe VI (in), 21 April 1942, AN, *AJ 40* 539.
6. 'Tätigkeitsbericht der Gruppe Allgemeine und Innere Verweltung', p. 20, AN, *AJ 40* 536, dr. 4.
7. 'Lagebericht über Verwaltung und Wirtschaft Oktober–Dezember 1942', AN, *AJ 40* 444.
8. Hervé Villeré, *L'Affaire de la Section spéciale*, Fayard, 1973, document no. 7 in the appendix.
9. See Michaël R. Marrus and Robert O. Paxton, *Vichy et les Juifs*, Calmann-Lévy, 1981.
10. Serge Klarsfeld, *Vichy-Auschwitz*, vol. I, Fayard, 1983, pp. 49–50.
11. Marrus and Paxton, *Vichy et les Juifs*, *op. cit.*, p. 91, p. 111.

12. *Carnets du pasteur Boegner, op. cit.*, p. 86.
13. See Michel Margairaz, *L'État, les Finances et l'Économie, op. cit.*
14. 'Note sur la conduite de la négociation générale avec l'Allemagne', 6 November 40, AN, *AJ 41* 39, dr. DSA Négociation générale.
15. 'État résumé des négociations économiques à Wiesbaden au 15 novembre 1940', appendix XI to report no. 34, *DFCAA*, vol. III, pp. 104–6.
16. As Doyen explained to Huntziger on 8 March 1941, 'The German government is very careful to present all its demands in separate chapters, and in this way it makes sure that the discussion remains strictly fragmented. It knows that it thereby puts the French government in a difficult position, since it is forced to formulate in an unsystematic order the demands that it wishes to be considered during the talks' (note from Doyen to Huntziger, 8 March 1941, appendix IV to report 47, *DFCAA*, vol. IV, p. 195). On the economic exploitation of occupied France, see Alan Milward, *The New Order and the French Economy*, Oxford University Press, 1970.
17. Margairaz, *L'État, les Finances et l'Économie, op. cit.*, p. 616f.
18. Note by Bouthillier, 7 November 1940, AN, *AJ 41* 168, 'Négoc. générales'.
19. 'Note sur les rapports économiques franco-allemands depuis l'armistice', August 1941, *AN, AJ 41* 168, 'Négoc. générales'.
20. Henry Rousso, 'Vichy face à la mainmise allemande sur les enterprises françaises', in Claude Carlier and Stefan Martens (eds), *La France et l'Allemagne en guerre. Septembre 1939–novembre 1942*, Institut historique allemand, 1990. pp. 469–87; Margairaz, *L'État, les Finances et l'Économie, op. cit.*, ch. XIX, p. 631f.
21. See Michel Gratier de Saint-Louis, 'Les dessous d'une négociation: la main-d'œuvre française en Allemagne (8 septembre 1941–février 1943)', *Bulletin du Centre d'histoire économique de la Région lyonnaise*, no. 4. 1987.
22. Meeting of 14 January 1942 at the Majestic, AN, *F 37* 4.
23. Note from Berthelot to Hemmen, 8 May 1941, AN, *AJ 41* 101; 'Ier rapport du Comité d'étude des autoroutes françaises', *Revue économique franco-allemande*, December 1942, p. 15.
24. Benoist-Méchin, *De la défaite au désastre*, vol. II, *op. cit.*, p. 71.
25. Margairaz, *L'État, les Finances et l'Économie, op. cit.*, pp. 599–600.
26. AN, *F 37* 27, dr. Aid given by Germany to the French economy.
27. Milward, *The New Order, op. cit.*, p. 273.
28. Margairaz, *L'État, les Finances et l'Économie, op. cit.*, pp. 599–600.
29. See Margairaz, *ibid.*, p. 601f., and the notes in AN, *F 37* 20, 'Études sur la collaboration économique franco-allemande'.
30. 'Wirt. Berichte des MBF', report for December 1941–January 1942, BA-MA, *RW 35* 304.
31. Huntziger to Weygand, 19 August 1940, DFCAA, vol. I, pp. 155–6.
32. Armistice meeting of 29 January 1941, DFCAA, vol. IV, p. 71.
33. See Peter F. Klemm, 'La production aéronautique française de 1940 à 1942', *RHDGM*, no. 107, 1977, pp. 53–74; Patrick Facon and Françoise de Ruffray, 'Aperçus sur la collaboration aéronautique franco-allemande (1940–1943)', *RHDGM*, No. 108, 1977, pp. 85–102.
34. Claude Huan, 'La construction navale française 1940–1942' in *La France et l'Allemagne en guerre, op. cit.*, pp. 197–210.
35. Klemm, 'La production aéronautique', *op. cit.*, p. 67; Huan, 'La construction navale', *op. cit.*, p. 210.
36. Klemm, 'La production aéronautique', *op. cit.*, pp. 72–3.
37. Note by Huntziger, 10 July 1941, DFCAA, vol. IV, p. 631.

38. Arnaud Teyssier, 'L'armée de l'Air d'armistice face à l'Allemagne (juillet 1940–novembre 1942)', in *La France et l'Allemagne en guerre, op. cit.*, p. 187; Coutau-Bégarie and Huan, *Darlan, op. cit.*, p. 308f.
39. 'Mise au point à la date du 15 septembre des questions principales traitées par la Sous-commission des forces terrestres'; and note by Allier (armaments sub-commission), 24 September 1941, AN, *AJ 41* 38, dr. Historiques.
40. Bridoux, 'Note pour les Délégations françaises près des Commissions d'armistice de Wiesbaden et de Turin', 12 June 1942, AN, *AJ 41* 627, dr. Armée d'armistice.
41. Yves Durand, *La Captivité. Histoire des prisonniers de guerre français 1939–1945*, FNCPG-CATM, 1980, p. 34.
42. See for example Leroy-Beaulieu's note, 'Note pour le délégué général aux relations économiques franco-allemandes', 8 July 1941, AN, *AJ 41* 167, 'Poudres et explosifs'.
43. Coutau-Bégarie and Huan, *Darlan, op. cit.*, p. 557.

10 THE RETURN OF LAVAL

1. Pétain, *Discours aux Français, op. cit.*, p. 245.
2. Leahy, 27 April 1942, *FRUS*, 1942, pp. 181–2.
3. Kupferman, *Laval*, Balland, 1987, pp. 333–4.
4. Klarsfeld, *Vichy–Auschwitz*, vol. I, *op. cit.*, p. 221.
5. Benoist-Méchin, *De la défaite au désastre*, vol. II, *op. cit.*, p. 50.
6. Abetz, 1 June 1942, in *Pétain et les Allemands, op. cit.*, p. 179.
7. Krug, 20 August 1942, *ADAP* E/3, no. 205.
8. Benoist-Méchin, *De la défaite au désastre*, vol. II, *op. cit.*, pp. 63–4.
9. Statement by Barnaud, 'Réunion franco-allemande du 27 septembre 1942 à l'Hôtel Majestic', AN, *AJ 41* 83. See Michel Gratier de Saint-Louis, 'Les dessous d'une négociation', *op. cit.*, pp. 48–51.
10. *La Vie industrielle*, 22 October 1942.
11. See Jean-Pierre Husson, 'L'itinéraire d'un haut fonctionnaire: René Bousquet', in *Vichy et les Français, op. cit.*, pp. 287–302.
12. Panlucci, 16 October 1941, ASMAE, *Affari politici Francia*, B. 49.
13. Daladier, *Journal de captivité, op. cit.*, pp. 168–70 (16 September 1942).
14. Bousquet to Oberg, 18 June 1942, in Klarsfeld, *Vichy–Auschwitz*, vol. I, *op. cit.*, p. 209.
15. Note by Hagen, 4 July 1942, on the conversation of 2 July between Oberg and Bousquet, in *ibid.*, pp. 228–9.
16. Schleier to AA, 9 September 1942, AA-PA, *Botschaft Paris* 1125a.
17. Zeitschel to Schleier, 28 February 1942, in Klarsfeld, *Vichy–Auschwitz*, vol. I, *op. cit.*, p. 196.
18. *Ibid.*, p. 231.
19. *Ibid.*, p. 233.
20. Klarsfeld, *Vichy–Auschwitz*, vol. I, *op. cit.*, p. 192.
21. Hearing of 4 January 1947, AN, *3 W* 358.
22. Klarsfeld, *Vichy–Auschwitz*, vol. I, *op. cit.*, p. 184.
23. *Carnets du pasteur Boegner, op. cit.*, p. 205 (11 September 1942).
24. Klarsfeld, *Vichy–Auschwitz*, vol. I, *op. cit.*, p. 308, p. 312.
25. *Ibid.*, p. 408.

Notes

11 PUPPET VICHY

1. 'Gespräch mit Marschall Pétain Vichy am 20. Oktober', note from Rohan passed on by von Grote on 20 November, *ADAP*, E/4, no. 202.
2. Strack to the embassy in Paris, 6 November 1942, *ibid.*, no. 141.
3. Duroselle, *L'Abîme*, *op. cit.*, p. 383; the text is slightly different in Couteau-Bégarie and Huan, *Darlan*, *op. cit.*, p. 595.
4. Schmidt, 14 November 1942, *ADAP*, E/4, no. 176.
5. Benoist-Méchin, *De la défaite au désastre*, vol. II, *op. cit.*, p. 238.
6. Schleier, 11 November 1942, *ADAP*, E/4, no. 161.
7. *Discours aux Français*, *op. cit.*, p. 288 (19 November 1942); see also the 23 November appeal to the French of French West Africa, p. 289.
8. Barthélémy, *Ministre de Justice*, *op. cit.*, p. 388f.
9. AN 2 AG 26, dr. Special French North Africa file (reprinted in Albert Kammerer, *Du débarquement africain au meurtre de Darlan*, Flammarion, 1949, pp. 675–6).
10. Abetz, 15 November 1942, *ADAP*, E/4, no. 182.
11. Abetz, 16 November 1942, *ADAP*, E/4, no. 184.
12. *Discours aux Français*, *op. cit.*, p. 288 (19 November 1942).
13. Schleier, 22 November 1942, *ADAP*, E/4, nos 217 and 220.
14. Ribbentrop to Laval, and Hitler to Pétain, 26 November 1942, *ADAP*, E/4 nos 226 and 227.
15. Jäckel, *La France dans l'Europe de Hitler*, *op. cit.*, p. 372.
16. Memorandum dated 23 December 1942 on a meeting of the German services concerned with France, IFZ, *Mfm* MA 167 (OKW 131).
17. Schmidt, 19 December 1942, *ADAP*, E/4, no. 310.
18. Abetz to Ribbentrop and Ribbentrop to Abetz, 19 November 1942, AA-PA, *Büro des Staatssekretärs, Frankreich*, vol. X.
19. Von Rundstedt, 11 December 1942, AN, *AJ 40* 1382, dr. 8 *Politische Angelegenheiten 1943/4*.
20. Schleier, 15 December 1942, *ibid.*
21. Schmidt, 19 and 24 December, *ADAP*, E/4, nos 310 and 314.
22. Barthélémy, *Ministre de la Justice*, *op. cit.*, p. 351.
23. Abetz, 23 December 1942, AN, *AJ 40* 1382, dr. 8 *Politische Angelegenheiten 1943/4*.
24. Schleier, 31 December 1942, *ADAP*, E/4, no. 334.
25. *Discours aux Français*, *op. cit.*, p. 297.
26. Laval to Rundstedt, 12 January 1943, AN, *AJ 41* 615, dr. New Army.
27. Jäckel, *La France dans l'Europe de Hitler*, *op. cit.*, p. 376, n. 49.
28. See AN, *AJ 41* 615, dr. New Army.
29. Laval's letter to Hitler is reproduced in a telegram from Schleier dated 11 March 1943, *ADAP*, E/5, no. 193.
30. Hitler to Pétain, 28 April 1943, *ADAP*, E/5, no. 353; on the Hitler–Laval meeting, Schmidt, 3 May 1943, *ADAP*, E/6, no. 7.
31. See Marc Ferro, *Pétain*, *op. cit.*
32. Klarsfeld, *Vichy–Auschwitz*, vol. II, *op. cit.*, p. 145f; Susan Zuccotti, *The Holocaust, the French and the Jews*, New York, Basic Books, 1993, p. 190f.

12 PUBLIC OPINION

1. Georges Bernanos, *Le Chemin de la Croix-des-Ames*, Gallimard, 1948, p. viii.
2. Claude Mauriac, *Bergère ô tour Eiffel. Le Temps immobile 8*, Grasset, 1985, p. 462 (22 September 1983).
3. 'Zusammenfassung der seit 1940 bis heute von der Informationsabteilung der Deutschen Botschaft Paris geleisteten Arbeit', AA-PA, *Botschaft Paris* 1125b/2 (the reports in question do not appear to have survived).
4. Denis Peschanski, 'Le régime de Vichy a existé', in Denis Peschanski (eds), *Vichy 1940–1944. Archives de guerre d'Angelo Tasca*, Fondazione Giangiacomo Feltrinelli, CNRS, and Feltrinelli, 1986, p. 41f. See also Antoine Lefébure, *Les Conversations secrètes des Français sous l'occupation*, Plon, 1993.
5. 'Kulturpolitische Arbeit in Frankreich', n.d. [late 1942], AA-PA, *Botschaft Paris* 1125b/2.
6. See Pierre-Marie Dioudonnat, *L'Argent nazi à la conquête de la presse française 1940–1944*, Jean Picollec, 1981.
7. François Garçon, 'Nazi Film Propaganda in Occupied France', in David Welch (ed.), *Nazi Propaganda. The Power and the Limitations*, London, Croom Helm, 1983, p. 173.
8. Denis Peschanski, 'Contrôler ou encadrer? Information et propagande sous Vichy', *Vingtième Siècle*, no. 28, October–December 1990, pp. 65–75.
9. Étienne Dejonghe, 'Être occupant dans le Nord', *Revue du Nord*, no. 259, 1983, pp. 723–4. See, by the same author, 'Le Nord isolé: occupation et opinion (mai 1940–mars 1942)', *RHMC*, XXVI, January–March 1979, pp. 48–97.
10. 'Lagebericht für die Zeit bis 31.8.40', BA-MA, *RW 24* 15.
11. 'Synthèse hebdomadaire des interceptions des contrôles téléphoniques, télégraphiques et postaux, 20 décembre 1940–5 janvier 1941', AN, *AJ 41* 25, 'Contrôles techniques'.
12. 'Synthèse décadaire du contrôle téléphonique', 1–13 May 1941; 1–30 July 1941, AN, *F 7* 14930.
13. 'Synthèse décadaire', 1–15 March 1941, *ibid.*
14. 'Synthèse des interceptions', 7 September–7 October 1941, AN, *AJ 41* 25, 'Contrôles techniques'.
15. Regional inspection of Clermond-Ferrand, telephone commission, 1–10 November 1940, AN, *F 7* 14927.
16. 'Synthèse décadaire', 1–13 May 1941, AN, *F* 7 14930, 'Commission Centrale de contrôle téléphonique'.
17. 'Synthèse hebdomadaire des interceptions', 6 June 1941, AN, *AJ 41* 25, 'Contrôles techniques'.
18. 'Synthèse décadaire', 1–31 August 1941, AN, *F 7* 14930, 'Commission centrale de contrôle téléphonique'.
19. See the 'Tätigkeitsbericht' of the Kontrollinspektion (K.I.), AN, *AJ 40* 1232.
20. K.I., 'Tätigkeitsbericht', 1 August 1941, AN, *AJ 40* 1234.
21. Reports of 15 and 25 August 1941, AN, *AJ 40* 1234; report of 16 October 1941, *AJ 40* 1235.
22. 'Synthèse des interceptions', 7 November–7 December 1941, AN, *AJ 41* 25, 'Contrôles techniques'.
23. K.I., 'Tätigkeitsbericht', 7 April 1942, AN, *AJ 40* 1235.
24. 'Synthèse hebdomadaire des interceptions', 30 June 1942, AN, *F 7* 14926, 'Direction des contrôles techniques'.

25. 'Synthèse des interceptions', 10 September–10 October 1942, AN, *AJ 41* 25, 'Contrôles techniques'.
26. 'Statistique des contrôles techniques', AN, *F 7* 14926, 'Direction des contrôles techniques'; *2* AG 461, 'Synthèse des contrôles'.
27. 'Synthèse hebdomadaire des interceptions', 18 November 1941, AN, *F 7* 14926, 'Direction des contrôles techniques'.
28. AN, *Fla* 3 689, dr. Reports from prefects of the free zone.
29. 'Synthèse des interceptions', 7 September–7 October 1941, AN, *AJ 41* 25, 'Contrôles techniques'.
30. 'Synthèse hebdomadaire des contrôles', 17 November 1942; 24 November 1942, AN, *2 AG* 461, 'Synthèse des contrôles'. The work by Sarah Fishman (*We Will Wait. Wives of French Prisoners of War, 1940–1945*, New Haven and London, Yale University Press, 1991) leaves out this aspect of the subject.
31. 'État d'esprit des prisonniers', appendix II to the synthesis of 6 June 1941, *AJ 41* 25, 'Contrôles techniques'. See also Yves Durand, *La Captivité, op. cit.*, p. 341f.
32. 'Synthèse des interceptions', 7 October–7 November 1941, AN, *AJ 41* 25, 'Contrôles techniques'.
33. K.I., 'Tätigkeitsbericht', 20 January 1942, AN, *AJ 40* 1235.
34. 'It is the lack of positive results that seems to elicit criticisms of collaboration from the public, far more than the principle of it' ('Synthèse hebdomadaire des interceptions des contrôles téléphoniques, télégraphiques et postaux', 25 November–4 December 1940, AN, *AJ 41* 25, 'Contrôles techniques'). 'It seems that if the occupier used a little psychology, much of public opinion would rally round' (1 September 1942, *ibid.*).
35. See Pierre Laborie, *L'Opinion française sous Vichy, op. cit.*
36. See for example Guéhenno, *Journal des années noires, op. cit.*, p. 233 (25 January 1942) and p. 260 (27 May 1942).
37. Hans Pfahlmann, 'Fremdarbeiter und Kriegsgefangene in der deutschen Wirtschaft 1939–1945', Dissertation, Wurzburg, 1964, pp. 77–8. In July 56 800 workers had left for Germany from all the occupied countries in Western Europe; in September this figure fell to 8300 (*ibid.*, p. 144).
38. Charles Bettelheim, *Bilan de l'économie française 1919–1946*, PUF, 1947, p. 234.
39. See the colloquium *Les Ouvriers en France pendant la Seconde Guerre mondiale*, ed. D. Peschanski and J.-L. Robert, Actes du colloque Paris-CNRS, 22–24 October 1992; also no. 158 of *Le Mouvement social* (January–March 1992), devoted to workers in France during the Second World War.
40. See the Manifesto of November 1940, Daniel Cordier, *Jean Moulin*, vol. I, *op. cit.*, pp. 25–8.
41. AN, *F 60* 408, dr. Death sentences.
42. Hans Umbreit, 'Auf dem Weg zur Kontinentalherrschaft', in *Das deutsche Reich und der Zweite Weltkrieg*, Stuttgart, Deutsche Verlags-Anstalt, 5/1, 1988, p. 199.
43. Bobkowski, *En guerre et en paix*, Montricher (Switzerland), Éditions Noir sur Blanc, 1991, p. 178 (16 December 1940).
44. Guéhenno, *Journal des années noires, op. cit.*, p. 242 (26 February 1942); p. 320 (22 February 1943); p. 406 (30 April 1944).
45. Paulhan to Jouhandeau (March 1941), in Paulhan, *Choix des lettres*, vol. II, *1937–1945*, *op. cit.*, p. 213.
46. Doyen, 'Note sur l'état d'esprit en zone occupée', 28 April 1941, AN, *F 60* 502, 'Situation politique intérieure'.
47. Bloch to Febvre, 8 May 1942, AN, *318 Mi* 1.

48. Guéhenno, *Journal des années noires, op. cit.*, p. 141 (21 May 1941).
49. François Mauriac to Fernandez, 12 February 1941, *Lettres d'une vie, op. cit.*, p. 238.
50. Report by the prefect of Finistère for September 1941, AD Rennes, *43 W* 1.
51. Claude Mauriac, *Bergère ô tour Eiffel. Le Temps immobile 8, op. cit.*, p. 209 (18 December 1942). Pierre Mauriac, senior professor of the faculty of medicine of Bordeaux, was a committed collaborationist.
52. Tasca, Notebook B–B, 27 July 1941.
53. Guéhenno, *Journal des années noires, op. cit.*, p. 182 (26 August 1941); Paulhan to Jouhandeau, 5 September 1941, *Choix de lettres*, vol. II, *1937–1945*, *op. cit.*, p. 232.
54. Jules Jeanneney, *Journal politique (Septembre 1939–Juillet 1942)*, Colin, 1972, p. 192 (10 September 1941).

13 THE FRENCH AND THE GERMANS

1. Werth, *33 jours*, *op. cit.*, pp. 134–5.
2. *Ibid.*, p. 139.
3. *Ibid.*, both quotations on p. 127.
4. Reproduced in *Chronique privée de l'an 1940*, Stock, 1941, p. 143.
5. Chardonne, *Voir la figure*, Stock, 1941, p. 11.
6. On the reconstruction of the image of the enemy, see Margaret Atack, *Literature and the French Renaissance. Cultural Politics and Narrative Forms, 1940–1950*, Manchester, Manchester University Press, 1989, p. 64f.
7. Text in appendix IV, Henri Noguères, *Histoire de la Résistance en France*, vol. I, Laffont, 1967, pp. 468–71.
8. 'La guerre a eu lieu', *Les Temps modernes*, no. 1, October 1945, p. 52.
9. Léautaud, *Journal littéraire, op. cit.*, p. 107 (25 June 1940). A similar echo is to be found in Maurice Martin du Gard, *Chronique de Vichy, op. cit.*, p. 73. Some authorities greeted the occupiers with a bouquet, the prefect of the Gironde, for one (René Terrisse, *Bordeaux 1940–1944*, Perrin, 1993, p. 18).
10. Marie Bonaparte, *Mythes de guerre*, London, Imago, 1946, p. 103.
11. *Ibid.*, p. 106.
12. *Ibid.*, pp. 76–7.
13. 'A certain admiration for the might of the German army is detectable' ('Synthèse hebdomadaire des interceptions des contrôles postaux, télégraphiques et téléphoniques', no. 136, 25 April, AN, *F 7* 14926, 'Direction des contrôles techniques').
14. Léautaud, *Journal littéraire, op. cit.*, p. 293 (9 October 1942).
15. Bobkowski, *En guerre et en paix, op. cit.*, p. 293 (9 October 1942).
16. Guéhenno, *Journal des années noires, op. cit.*, p. 293 (9 October 1942).
17. Charles Braibant, *La Guerre à Paris* (8 November 1942–27 August 1944), Corréa, 1945, pp. 370–1 (1 December 1943).
18. Maupassant, *Boule de Suif et autres histoires de guerre*, GF-Flammarion, 1991, pp. 66–7.
19. See Étienne Dejonghe, 'Être occupant dans le Nord', *Revue du Nord*, no. 259, 1983, pp. 708–45; and Jacques Natali, 'L'Occupant allemand à Lyon de 1942 à 1944, d'après les sources allemandes', *Cahiers d'histoire*, XXII, no. 4, 1977, pp. 441–64.
20. See, for example, the directive from the *Kommandostab Ic* of 17 February 1942, AN, *AJ 40* 451, dr. AG 106.
21. Guéhenno, *Journal des années noires, op. cit.*, p. 321 (22 February 1943).
22. Léautaud, *Journal littéraire, op. cit.*, p. 178 (24 September 1941).
23. *Ibid.*, p. 720 (17 October 1942).

24. Felix Hartlaub, *Das Gesamtwerk. Dichtungen, Tagebücher,* Frankfurt-on-Main, Fischer, 1955, p. 459.
25. Jünger, *Premier journal parisien, Journal II. 1941–1943*, Christian Bourgois, 1980, pp. 178–9 (18 August 1942).
26. Jünger, *Second Journal parisien, Journal III. 1943–1945*, Christian Bourgois, 1980, p. 170 (29 September 1943).
27. Guéhenno, *Journal des années noires, op. cit.*, p. 45 (19 September 1940).
28. *Ibid.*, p. 324 (22 February 1943).
29. Braibant, *La Guerre à Paris*, op. cit., p. 271 (3 September 1943).
30. Sartre, 'Paris sous l'occupation', *Situations*, vol. III, Gallimard, 1949, p. 20. Guéhenno had the same feeling, *op. cit.*, p. 321 (22 February 1943).
31. Léautaud, *Journal littéraire, op. cit.*, p. 999 (16 January 1944).
32. Sartre, 'Paris sous l'occupation', *op. cit.*, pp. 20–1.
33. Letter dated 19 December 1870, *Correspondance*, Librairie de France, vol. II, 1928, p. 492.
34. Léautaud, *Journal littéraire, op. cit.*, p. 999 (16 January 1944).
35. Claude Mauriac, *Bergère ô tour Eiffel. Le Temps immobile 8, op. cit.*, pp. 464–5 (28 December 1940). After the war, François Mauriac was to look back at this experience, referring, on the defensive, to Vercors, whose advice had become the norm and forced him to justify himself: 'With regard to everything to do with that, we are still living in the midst of hypocrisy and it will take a long time for everyone to recount their own experiences freely' (Jean Touzot, *Mauriac sous l'Occupation*, La Manufacture, 1990, p. 361).
36. Jünger, *Premier Journal parisien, II, op. cit.*, p. 14 (7 March 1941); p. 115 (5 March 1942); pp. 38–9 (13 June 1941).
37. Ministère de la Défense, État-major de l'armée de terre, Service historique, *Rapports d'activité du XXVe corps d'armée allemand en occupation en Bretagne (13 décembre 1940–20 novembre 1944)*, Château de Vincennes, 1978, p. 95.
38. *Boule de Suif et autres histoires de guerre, op. cit.*, pp. 45–6.
39. Louis Chevalier, *Les Relais de la mer*, Fayard, 1983, p. 382.
40. Georges Vigne, 'Voyage d'enquête en Normandie et en Bretagne (15 November–1 December 1940)', AN, *2 AG* 454.
41. Claude Mauriac, *Bergère ô tour Eiffel. Le Temps immobile 8, op. cit.*, pp. 45–6 (2 March 1942).
42. Rist, *Une saison gâtée, op. cit.*, pp. 97–8 (17 October 1940).
43. *Ibid.*, p. 240 (22 March 1942); pp. 262–3 (24 July 1942); p. 227 (24 September 1942).
44. Jünger, *Premier Journal parisien. II, op. cit.*, p. 49 (8 October 1941).
45. Claude Mauriac, *Bergère ô tour Eiffel. Le Temps immobile 8, op. cit.*, pp. 262–3 (19 February 1943). On Gould, see Gilles Cornut-Gentille and Philippe Michel-Thiriet, *Florence Gould, une Américaine à Paris*, Mercure de France, 1989.
46. Jünger, *Premier Journal parisien, II, op. cit.*, p. 159 (22 July 1942).
47. Corinne Luchaire, *Ma drôle de vie*, Sun, 1949, p. 138.
48. Hearing of 10 June 1947, AN, *3 W* 358, dr. Epting.
49. AN, *3 W* 359, 'Origines diverses'.
50. Hearing of 6 January 1947, AN, *3* W 358.
51. Fabre-Luce, *Journal de la France*, vol. II, p. 133.
52. *Ibid.*, pp. 147–8.
53. Copeau, *Journal*, vol. II. *op. cit.*, p. 504.
54. Franz Seidler, *Prostitution, Homosexualität, Selbstverstümmelung, Probleme der*

deutschen Sanitätsführung 1939–1945, Neckargemünd, Vowinkel Verlag, 1977, pp. 145 and 171.

55. *Ibid.*, p. 156f.
56. See, for example, 'Le lit 29', IN *Boule de Suif et autres histoires de guerre, op. cit.*
57. Ernst Fraenkel, *Military Occupation and the Rule of Law. Occupation Government in the Rhineland, 1918–1923*, Oxford University Press, 1944, p. 143.
58. Ulrich Herbert, *Fremdarbeiter. Politik und Praxis des 'Ausländer-Einsatzes' in der Kriegswirtschaft des Dritten Reiches*, Berlin, Verlag Dietz, 1985, p. 126.
59. Michèle Bood, *Les Années doubles. Journal d'une lycéenne sous l'occupation*, Laffont, 1974.
60. Jünger, *Premier Journal parisien. II, op. cit.*, p. 22 (1 May 1941).
61. See Edmonde Charles-Roux, *L'Irrégulière ou mon itinéraire Chanel*, Grasset, 1974.
62. Pierre Gounand, *Carrefour de guerre, Dijon 1940–1944*, Besançon, Éditions Franc'Albert, 1990, p. 294; Paul Jankowski, *Communism and Collaboration. Simon Sabiani and Politics in Marseille, 1919–1944*, New Haven and London, Yale University Press, 1989, p. 132.
63. François Rouquet, 'Une administration française face à la Seconde Guerre mondiale: les PTT', History doctorate, Toulouse-Le-Mirail, vol. III, p. 118f. (and, by the same author, *L'Épuration dans l'administration française*, CNRS, 1993).
64. Marguerite Duras, *Hiroshima mon amour*, Gallimard, 'Folio', 1991, Appendices, p. 125f.
65. Henri Michel, *Paris allemand*, Albin Michel, 1981, pp. 287–8.
66. AD Gard, *3 U* 7 314, file on M.-L. R.
67. Marcel Baudot, 'L'épuration: bilan chiffré', *Bulletin de l'Institut d'histoire du temps présent*, no. 25, September 1986, p. 50.
68. Dr. Albath to Oberg, 4 September 1942, AA-PA, *Botschaft Paris* 1206.
69. 'Monatsbericht der Staffel für Dezember und Besprechung zwischen Herrn Oberstleutnant Schmidtke und Staffelführer Leutnant Knöbel am 15. 1. 43', AD Bourges, Prop. Staffel/2.
70. See André Halimi, *La Délation sous l'Occupation*, Alain Moreau, 1983, which is devoted to the denunciation of Jews.
71. AD Rennes, *43 W* 1, report of the prefect of Côtes-du-Nord for September 1941.
72. Annie Lacroix-Rix, 'Les relations sociales dans les entreprises', in Peschanski and Robert (n.d.), *Les Ouvriers en France pendant la Seconde Guerre mondiale, op. cit.*, pp. 225–6.
73. Baudot file on the repression, IHTP; Julien Papp, *La Collaboration dans l'Eure 1940–1944*, Éditions Tirésias Michel Reynaud, 1993, p. 181.
74. See the social composition in Marcel Ruby, *La Résistance à Lyon*, Lyons, L'Hermès, 1979, 2 vols.; and Jean Goueffon, 'La cour de justice d'Orléans', *RHDGM*, no. 130, April 1983, p. 59.

14 THE CHURCH AND THE ASSOCIATIONS

1. Abetz to Speidel, 22 June 1940, AA-PA, *Botschaft Paris* 1313.
2. Text of 26 June 1940, in Denis Peschanski, 'La demande de parution légale de *L'Humanité* (17 juin 1940–27 août 1940)', *Le Mouvement sociale*, no. 113, October-December 1980, pp. 88–9.
3. 'Aufzeichnung über die französische kommunistische Partei', 7 July 1940, *AJ 40* 888, dr. 12.
4. Note by Best on 19 August 1940, CDJC, XXIV, 1a.

5. Stéphane Courtois, 'Un été 1940. Les négociations entre le PCF et l'occupant allemand à la lumière des archives de l'Internationale communiste', *Communisme*, nos. 32-33-34, 4th term 1992, 1st and 2nd term 1993, pp. 85–128.
6. Letter of 26 July 1940, AN, *AJ 40* 890, dr. 12.
7. Letter of 7 August 1940, AN, *AJ 40* 890, dr. 2.
8. These organizations were the Union Fédérale des Associations Françaises d'Anciens Combattants, the Union Nationale des Combattants, the Union Nationale des Mutilés, Réformés et Anciens Combattants, and the Comité d'Entente des Grands Invalides (see file UF Randoux, AA-PA, *Botschaft Paris* 1302).
9. Pétain, 'Note pour monsieur le Secrétaire général aux Anciens Combattants', 8 December 1940, AN, *Z 6* 417.
10. Statements by Schleier, note from the Direction des services de documentation.
11. 'Besprechung in der Deutschen Botschaft am 7. Januar 1941', AN, *AJ 40* 551, dr. 3.
12. Circular from Rivollet on 24 March 1941, AN, *Z 6* 417.
13. Abetz, 'Vorschlag zu einer Neuordnung des Gewerkschaftswesen und zu sozialistischen Maßnahmen im besetzen Frankreich', 26 September 1940, AA-PA, *Handakten Etzdorf* 20.
14. See the Abetz–Best correspondence in November 1940, AA-PA, *Botschaft Paris* 1315.
15. List in IHTP 75646, *Mfm* 61.
16. Abetz to AA, 14 January 1941, AA-PA, *Botschaft Paris* 1315.
17. See 'Gewerkschaften' file in AN, *AJ 40* 551, dr. MBF II V pol 21.
18. Schleier, 'Französische Gewerkschaftswesen', 23 April 1941, AA-PA, *Botschaft Paris* 1315; in 1943, a trade unionist reckoned the number of workers belonging to trade unions to be between 100000 and 120000 ('Notes pour une doctrine du FST', *Informations ouvrières et syndicales*, 18 March 1943).
19. *L'Atelier*, 9 May 1942, p. 3.
20. Delmas to Grosse, 25 February 1941, AN, *AJ 40* 551, dr. MBF II V pol 21. See the same file for the rest of the Delmas affair.
21. Note by Dahnke, 'Berufsverbände der Hochschullehrer', referring to a communication from Grosse, *ibid.*
22. Claude Langlois, 'Le régime de Vichy et le clergé d'après les *Semaines Religieuses* des diocèses de la zone libre', *Revue française de science politique*, XXII, no. 4, August 1972, p. 762.
23. Wilfred D. Halls, *Les Jeunes et la Politique de Vichy*, Syros, 1988, p. 108 and p. 440, n. 9.
24. 'Rapport sur la situation présente de la jeunesse et sur les conditions de son organisation et de son éducation', n.d. [late 1941], AN, *Fla* 3687.
25. Jean-Paul Cointet, 'L'Église catholique et le gouvernement de Vichy. Église et Légion', in *Églises et Chrétiens dans la IIe Guerre mondiale*, vol. II, *La France*, n.d. Xavier de Montclos *et al.*, Presses universitaires de Lyon, 1982, pp. 438–9.
26. After the summer of 1941, Pétain's speeches ceased to be reprinted in the *Semaines Religieuses* (Langlois, 'Le régime de Vichy et le clergé', *op. cit.*, p. 755). On the Church during this period, see Jacques Duquesne, *Les Catholiques français sous l'occupation*, Grassnet, 1986; Renée Bédarida, 'La hiérarchie catholique', and Étienne Fouilloux, 'Le clergé', in Jean-Pierre Azéma and François Bédarida (eds), *Vichy et les Français*, *op. cit.*, pp. 444–62; pp. 463–77.
27. Hubert Claude, 'La hiérarchie catholique, le gouvernement de Vichy et l'occupant, dans la zone réservée', *Églises et Chrétiens pendant la Seconde Guerre mondiale dans le Nord–Pas-de-Calais*, 5–6 November 1977, in *Revue du Nord*, vol. LX. no. 237, April–June 1978, pp. 271–2; Pierre Barral, 'Le clergé lorrain sous l'occupation', *Églises et*

Chrétiens dans la IIe Guerre mondiale, vol. II, *La France*, *op. cit.*, p. 94; Baudrillart, *Le Testament politique d'un Prince de l'Église*, Guillemot and Lamothe, 1942.

28. Hubert Claude, 'La hiérarchie catholique', *op. cit.*, pp. 272–3.
29. *La Croix*, 9 November 1940, cited by Alain Fleury, *La Croix et l'Allemagne*, Cerf, 1984, p. 391.
30. 'Bericht über die Aktion gegen die Erzbischöfe und Bischöfe im Bereich der Assenstelle Dijon', 17 December 1940, AN, *AJ 40* 927.
31. On Tricot, see AA-PA, *Botschaft Paris* 1372; and on Renaud, see von Bose, 'Aufzeichnung', 19 March 1942, *Botschaft Paris* 1299; and 'Aufzeichnung', 24 July 1943, *Botschaft Paris* 2481.
32. Abetz to AA, 12 October 1942, AA-PA, *Botschaft Paris* 2481. See also Hans Umbreit, 'Les services d'occupation allemands et les Églises chrétiennes en France', *Églises et Chrétiens pendant la Seconde Guerre mondiale dans le Nord–Pas-de-Calais*, 5–6 November 1977, in *Revue du Nord*, vol. LX, no. 237, April–June 1978, pp. 299–309.
33. Jean Vinatier, *Le Cardinal Suhard*, Le Centurion, 1983, p. 121.
34. 'Le cardinal Suhard et le Conseil national', 6 February 1941, unsigned, but by Suhard or someone close to him, AN *2 AG* 493, dr. CC 74 17.
35. Abetz to AA, 13 December 1940 and 28 January 1941, AA-PA, *Botschaft Paris* 1372.
36. Klassen, 'Aufzeichnung', 2 December 1943, AA-PA, *Botschaft Paris* 2481.
37. Knochen to Abetz, 31 July 1941, and Schleier at AA, 6 August 1941, AA-PA, *Botschaft Paris* 1372.
38. AN, *F* 37 1, dr. b: the government wished to give the ceremony 'as much brilliance as is compatible with the present difficulties'. See Benoist-Méchin, *De la défaite au désastre*, vol. II, *op. cit.*, p. 171f.
39. Note by von Thienen, 14 November 1941, AA-PA, *Botschaft Paris* 1372; list of guests invited to the embassy, *Botschaft Paris* 1101a.
40. Beaussart to Abetz, 5 January 1942, AA-PA, *Botschaft Paris* 1372.
41. 29 December 1941, AN, *F 60* 1492, dr. Chevrier.
42. Abetz to AA, 28 January 1941, AA-PA, *Botschaft Paris* 1372.
43. 'Note pour le Ministre', unsigned, 10 December 1941, AN, *Fla* 3687.
44. Suhard to Abetz, 3 May 1941, AA-PA, *Botschaft Paris* 2452.
45. Nonce Valeri to Cardinal Maglione, 29 July 1942, in Klarsfeld, *Vichy–Auschwitz*, vol. I, *op. cit.*, p. 297.
46. Laval–Knochen meeting 3 August 1942, in *ibid.*, p. 312, and Hagen-Bousquet conversation, 8 October 1942, p. 475.
47. Krug to Abetz, 30 October 1942, AA-PA, *Inland I D*, R 98802.
48. Claudel, *Journal*, vol. II, *op. cit.*, pp. 400–1.
49. 30 June 1942, AN, *2 AG* 492, dr. CC 72 AC.
50. Suhard to Pétain, 24 June 1943, AN, *2 AG* 493.
51. Klarsfeld, *Vichy–Auschwitz*, *op. cit.*, p. 106.
52. Suhard to Pétain, 22 February 1943, AN, *2 AG* 492, dr. CC 72 AC; Suhard to Abetz, 18 February 1944, AA-PA, *Botschaft Paris* 2481.
53. Mgr. Chappoulie to Bérard, 15 May 1943, AN, *2 AG* 492, dr. CC 72; Schleier to Krug, 24 June 1943, AA-PA, *Botschaft Paris* 2481.
54. Gossmann, 'Aufzeichnung für Herrn Gesandten Schleier', 4 August 1943; Schleier to Suhard, 28 June 1943, AA-PA, *Botschaft Paris* 2841.
55. 'Aufzeichnung für Herrn Gesandten Schleier', 4 August 1943, AA-PA, *Botschaft Paris* 2841.
56. See Markus Eikel, 'Die religiöse Betreuung der französischen Zivilarbeiter in

Deutschland 1943–1945', *Revue d'Allemagne*, XXIII, October–December 1991, pp. 467–85.

57. Klassen, 'Aufzeichnung', 22 March 1944, AA-PA, *Botschaft Paris* 2481.
58. Vinatier, *Le Cardinal Suhard*, *op. cit.*, p. 192.
59. Abetz to AA, 14 July 1944, AA-PA, *Inland I-D*, R 98802.
60. Weekly report on the situation in the occupied territories, 8 October 1942, AN, *F 60* 1536.
61. Alain Dantoing, *La 'collaboration' du cardinal. L'Église de Belgique dans la guerre 40*, Brussels, De Boeck, 1991.
62. Klassen, 'Aufzeichnung', 2 December 1943, AA-PA, *Botschaft Paris* 2481.
63. Renée Bédarida, 'Dans la tourmente 1940–1944: des droits de la personne aux droits de l'homme', in Pierre Colin (ed.), *Les Catholiques français et l'Héritage de 1789*, Beauchesne, 1989, p. 205.

15 BUSINESS LEADERS

1. See Richard Vinen, *The Politics of French Business 1936–1945*, Cambridge University Press, 1991 (a stimulating and controversial book).
2. On the CO, see Henry Rousso, 'L'Organisation industrielle de Vichy', *RHDGM*, no. 116, 1979, pp. 27–44; Adrian Jones, 'Illusions of Sovereignty: Business and the Organization of Committees of Vichy France', *Social History*, II, no. 1, 1986, pp. 1–32; Richard F. Kuisel, *Le Capitalisme et l'État en France. Modernisation et dirigisme au XXe siécle*, Gallimard, 1981, p. 237f.; Margairaz, *L'État, les Finances et l'Économie*, *op. cit.*, p. 511f.
3. Rousso, 'L'aryanisation économique: Vichy, l'occupant et la spoilation des Juifs', *Yod*, nos. 15–16, 1982, pp. 66–9.
4. See the reports of the various directives of the Ministry of Industrial Production (MPI) for 1943–4 in AN, *F 12* 10030.
5. G. Liet-Veaux, 'L'organisation professionelle 1939–1946', *Revue d'économie politique*, no. 6, November–December 1947, p. 1282.
6. The directors of the two major sections of the MPI (chemical products and mechanical construction) between them supervised thirty-five committees ('Étude sur les CO', produced by the CETS, 10 September 1941, AN, *F 37* 20, dr. Organisation professionelle). For an example of relations between the commissioners and the CO, see AN, *F 12* 10070, dr. CO electric energy.
7. 'Wirtschaftsberichte des MBF', April–May 1941, BA-MA, *RW 35* 303.
8. On the incidents, see the report of the Rüstungsinspektion Paris, 23 May 1941, BA-MA, *RW 24* 56; and on the negotiations on the role of the CO, AN, *AJ 40* 776, dr. 1.
9. Jones, 'Illusions of Sovereignty', *op. cit.*, p. 5.
10. AN, *AJ 40* 781, dr. 3.
11. André Dubois, 'La Collecte du cuir brut dans les temps présents et l'Organisation d'un marché dans une économie nouvelle', April 1941, AN, *AJ 40* 777, 'Cuir'.
12. 'Wirtschaftsberichte des MBF', report for December 1940–January 1941, BA-MA, *RW 35* 303, and report for February 1941, *RW 24* 15.
13. Bichelonne's plan for the meeting of January 1941, 7 January 1941, in Jörg Raubaum, 'Die Entwicklung der Kollaboration zwischen den deutschen und französischen Monopolen in einigen wichtigen Industriezweigen und der Raub von französischen Unternehmen und Beteiligungen durch deutsche Konzerne in der ersten Periode der faschistischen Okkupation (Juni 1940–Juni 1941)', Dissertation, Berlin (East), 1968. Appendices, p. 9.

14. See AN, *F 37* 20, 'Chambres de commerce'.
15. Letter of 29 January 1942, AN, *AJ 40* 784, dr. 2.
16. *La Vie industrielle*, 27 February 1941.
17. Note of 4 December 1941, AA-PA, *Botschaft Paris* 1382. The trips continued up until the eve of the liberation (see BAK, *R 13* XIII 238).
18. Report of the Wi, Rü. u. Rü.-Stab Frankreich for November 1940, BA-MA, *RW 24* 15.
19. 'Bericht über Verhandlungen in Paris vom 30. Oktober bis 3. November 1942', BAK, *R 13 VI* 55.
20. *La Vie industrielle*, 8 February 1941; see also 'Pucheu: Wir haben gleiche Interessen', *Pariser Zeitung*, 13 April 1941, p. 4.
21. *La Vie industrielle*, 19 March 1941.
22. Raubaum, 'Die Entwicklung der Kollaboration', *op. cit.*, pp. 70–8.
23. See the Frankreich-Bericht of the Reichsgruppe Industrie, in Dietrich Eichholtz, *Geschichte der deutschen Kriegswirtschaft 1939–1945*, Berlin, Akademie-Verlag, 1969, pp. 352–64.
24. Raubaum, 'Die Entwicklung der Kollaboration', *op. cit.*, p. 181f.
25. AN, *F 37* 28, 'Accords franco-allemands'.
26. See Hermann Wandschneider, 'Pläne der deutschen Elektrokonzerne zur "Neuordnung der europäischen Wirtschaft" im Zweiten Weltkrieg', *Jahrbuch für Wirtschaftsgeschichte*, 1970/4, pp. 219–43.
27. Address by Guérard at the banquet of the Société de Géographie on 17 June 1941, AN, *F 37* 11, 'Assurances'.
28. AN, *AJ 40* 838, dr. 2.
29. G. Cheneaux de Leyritz, 11 September 1940, *AJ 40* 835, dr. 1. Jean Fourastié described Cheneaux de Leyritz as 'a high-ranking civil servant of exceptional value' ('Les assurances', *Revue d'économie politique*, no. 5, September–October 1947, p. 1184).
30. AN, *AJ 40* 835, dr. 2.
31. Report by Hemmen for the July-December 1941 period, BAK, *R 91* 721; see also AA-PA, *Ha Pol IIa Frankreich*, R 107 478.
32. Cheneaux de Leyritz, 'Note pour M. le Kriegsverwaltungsrat Docteur Capitan', 12 September 1941, AN, *AJ 40* 835, dr. 2.
33. 'Conférence plénière au Reichswirtschaftsministerium le 16 décembre à 10 h.', *F 37* 11, 'Assurances'; see also a note from the RWiM (German economics ministry), 'Vermerk', 18 December 1941, *AJ 40* 836, dr. 17.
34. Dr Sondermann, 'Vermerk', 7 November 1942, *AJ 40* 836, dr. 17. The negotiations made hardly any more progress. By February 1942, the German companies had taken over about 20 per cent of the policies formerly held by British companies (note of 16 February 1942, *F 37* 11, dr. Insurances).
35. According to *La Vie industrielle*, 5 August 1941, p. 4, 'Quelques précisions sur l'accord internationale de Berlin'.
36. *La Vie industrielle*, 26–28 September 1942, p. 3.
37. See, for example, the remarks of a German delegation of industrialists, AN, *F 37* 32, 'Fabrication de pigments plombiques'.
38. Norguet to Barnaud, 'Avantages que l'industrie française peut retirer de sa situation actuelle vis-à-vis de l'industrie allemande', AN, *F 37* 27, 'Aide apportée por l'Allemagne à l'économie française'.
39. Benoist-Méchin, *De la défaite au désastre*, vol. II, *op. cit.*, p. 124.

40. Weekly report by the DGTO, (Délégation générale du gouvernement français dans les territoires occupés), 2 July 1942, AN, *F 60* 1536.
41. Meetings of 8 and 9 July 1942 of the CO of optical equipment and precision instruments, BA-MA, *RW 19 WiIA3* 156.
42. *Ibid.*
43. 'Protokoll', BAK, *R 13 XIII* 236.
44. Letter of 2 November 1943 to the secretary general of the CO of leather industries, BAK, *R 13 XIII* 238.
45. AN, *F 12* 9 595, dr. Ugine.
46. See AN, *AJ 40* 824, dr. 1.
47. Letter to Dr Keobe, 30 May 1944, AN, *AJ 40* 838, 'Personnel des sociétés d'assurances'.
48. Dr Michel, 'Vermerk', 17 March 1943, AN, *AJ 40* 779, dr. 1.
49. File in AN, *72 AJ* 1928.

16 CAPTAINS OF INDUSTRY

1. 'Lagebericht des Wi-u. Rü.-Stabes Frankreich', December 1941, BA-MA, *RW 24* 17. For a synthesis on the situation of businesses, see Michel Margairaz and Henry Rousso, 'Vichy, la guerre et les entreprises', *Histoire, Économie et Société*, no. 3, 1992, pp. 337–67.
2. Note of 5 September 1941, AN, *AJ 41* 73, 'Commissaires allemands'.
3. 'Lagebericht des Wi-u. Rü.-Stabes Frankreich', November 1940, BA-MA, *RW 24* 15.
4. Reports of February and March 1941, *ibid.*
5. 'Lagebericht der Rü In A' for February 1941, BA-MA, *RW 24* 48.
6. 'Schlußbericht über die Deutsche Technische Ausstellung im Petit Palais zu Paris', 11 November 1941, AN, *AJ 40* 775, dr. 5.
7. 'Lagebericht der Rü In A', BA-MA, *RW 24* 49.
8. Richard Vinen, 'The French Coal Industry During the Occupation', *The Historical Journal*, March 1990, pp. 105–30.
9. Peter Lessmann, 'Industriebeziehungen zwischen Deutschland und Frankreich während der deutschen Besatzung 1940–1944, Das Beispiel Peugeot–Volkswagenwerk', *Francia*, 17/3, 1990, p. 141.
10. Philippe Mioche, 'Les sidérurgistes', in Azéma and Bédarida (eds), *Vichy et les Français*, *op. cit.*, pp. 604–5.
11. Final report of the bank group, AN, *AJ 40* 820.
12. François Marcot, 'Les ouvriers de Peugeot, le patronat et l'État', in Peschanski and Robert, (n.d.), *Les Ouvriers en France pendant la Seconde Guerre mondiale*, *op. cit.*, pp. 252–3.
13. Dr Giebel to RWiM, 28 May 1941, and note by Schlotterer, 28 May 1941, AN, *AJ 41* 813, dr, *Kapitalinvesttiionen*.
14. 'Kriegsgeschichte des Wi-Rü, 1. Oktober 1940–31. Dezember 1941', BA-MA, *RW 24* 19.
15. *Die faschistische Okkupationspolitik in Frankreich (1940–1944)*, *op. cit.*, doc. 221, extract from a report of the Feldwirtschaftsamt im OKW for the January–April 1944 period, pp. 310–11.
16. *Pariser Zeitung*, 9 April 1941.
17. Fernand Picard, *L'Épopée de Renault*, Albin Michel, 1976, p. 185 (12 January 1943).
18. See, for example, the Basset affair in BA-MA, *Wi I A 3* 108, dr. James Basset; 'Licences' in *AJ 40* 812 is not very full; on public works, see Dominique Barjot,

'L'Industrie française des travaux publics', *Histoire, Économie et Société*, no. 3, 1992, p. 425.

19. Referat Handel, 'Deutsch-französische Zusammenarbeit', n.d., *AJ 40* 782, dr. 2.
20. The director of the chemical industries, 'note pour Monsieur le Ministre', 11 November 1941, AN, *F* 37 32, dr. Buna.
21. M. Margairaz, *L'État, les Finances et l'Économie, op. cit.*, pp. 662–4.
22. Pucheu to Duchemin, 23 April 1941, *ibid.*, pp. 650–1.
23. Peter Hayes, 'La stratégie industrielle de l'IG Farben en France occupée', *Histoire, Économie et Société*, no. 3, 1992, pp. 493–514, and also his *Industry and Ideology. IG Farben in the Nazi Era*, New York, Cambridge University Press, 1987.
24. Pierre Cayez, 'Négocier et survivre: la stratégie de Rhône-Poulenc pendant la Seconde Guerre mondiale', *Histoire, Économie et Société*, no. 3, 1992, pp. 483–4; by the same author, *Rhône-Poulenc 1895–1975*, Colin/Masson, 1988, pp. 147–50.
25. Summary of the report to the shareholders' meeting, *La Vie industrielle*, 12 November 1942, p. 6.
26. See AN, *F 37* 32, dr. Aluminium, and Margairaz, *L'État, les Finances et l'Économie, op. cit.*, pp. 624–8.
27. Jean Dupin to the Minister of Industrial Production, 11 June 1941, AN, *F 37* 32, 'Construction usine d'alumine'.
28. Note from Terray, 4 September 1941, *ibid.*
29. Leroy-Beaulieu to Barnaud, 'Entretien avec M. Hemmen', 23 April 1941, AN, *F 37* 1, dr. b.
30. Milward, *The New Order and the French Economy, op. cit.*, p. 105.
31. See the file on the Ugine purge, AN, *F 12* 9595.
32. From the lists of the Round Tables of 13 May, 1 July and 28 October 1942 (AA-PA, *Botschaft Paris* 1101b) and the police enquiry at the liberation (AN, *F 12* 9559, 'Papiers relatifs aux affaires de banques'.
33. Picard, *L'Épopée de Renault, op. cit.*, p. 143 (27 February 1942).
34. Achenbach to AA, 7 January 1943, *ADAP*, E/5, no. 20.
35. Claude Lévy, *'Les Nouveaux Temps' et l'Idéologie de la collaboration*, Presses de la FNSP, 1974, pp. 40–1.
36. See the Société cotonnière du Nord et de l'Est affair in AN, *AJ 40* 816, dr. 92b.
37. Hearing of 6 January 1947, AN, *3 W* 358. The purge proceeding against Boussac ended with the case being withdrawn. See Marie-France Pochna, *Bonjour, Monsieur Boussac*, Laffont, 1980.
38. AA-PA, *Botschaft Paris* 1122 and 1309; a card index of about 1000 cards is to be found in the purge file on Chaux, AN, *Z 6* 249 and 250. Chaux had inherited a fortune (banking, hotels) but was ruined in the early 1930s; he then played an active role in planning circles.
39. AN, *Z 6* N.L. 11108.
40. Picard, *L'Épopée de Renault, op. cit.*, p. 214 (23 September 1943).

17 MONEY MANIPULATORS

1. See Henri Laufenburger, *Les Banques françaises depuis 1914*, Sirey, 1940; Jean Bouvier, *Un siècle de banque française*, Hachette, 1973; Hubert Bonin, *L'Argent en France depuis 1880. Banquiers, financiers, épargnants dans la vie économique et politique*, Masson, 1989.
2. See Claire Andrieu, *La Banque sous l'Occupation. Paradoxes de l'histoire d'un profession*, Presses de la FNSP, 1990.

3. Dieter Wolf, *Doriot*, Fayard, 1969, p. 212.
4. 'Bericht über die Tätigkeit des Bankenaufsichtsamtes in Paris (Juli 1940 bis August 1941)', AN, *AJ 40* 822, dr. 4.
5. Final report by Dr Koebe, AN, *AJ 40* 820, dr. 2.
6. Note from the embassy dated 1 March 1941, AA-PA, *Ha Pol IIa Frankreich, Paket* 7 *Finanzwesen* 20, vol. II.
7. Scheffler to the vice-chairman of the Reichsbank, 11 August 1941, AN, *AJ 40* 833, dr. 5.
8. 'Übersicht über den Einsatz deutscher Firmen im Bereich des MBF', 28 June 1944, BA-MA, *RW 35* 854.
9. Andrieu, *La Banque sous l'Occupation, op. cit.*, p. 155.
10. *Ibid.*, p. 188f.
11. *Ibid.*, p. 221f.
12. *Ibid.*, pp. 195–6.
13. On the Aerobank, see AN, *AJ 40* 824, dr. 3.
14. For an assessment of the activities of this company, see the note of 17 June 1943 in AA-PA, *Botschaft Paris* 2405.
15. See, for example, the comments of Scheffler in his letter to the Reichsbank dated 11 August 1941, *AJ 40* 833, dr. 5.
16. 'Lagebericht des Wi-u. Rü.-Stabes Frankreich', March 1941, BA-MA, *RW 24* 15.
17. Note from Gerstner, 10 September 1941, AA-PA, *Ha Pol IIa Frankreich.* R 107 413.
18. Gerstner to RWiM, 17 March 1942 and 6 October 1942, AA-PA, *Ha Pol IIa Frankreich,* R 107017.
19. Note from the RSHA on 16 April 1943, AA-PA, *Ha Pol IIa Frankreich, Paket 7 Finanzwesen* 20, vol. II; Knochen hearing of 6 January 1947, AN, *3 W* 358.
20. See Annie Lacroix-Ruiz, 'Les grandes banques françaises de la collaboration à l'épuration, 1940–1950. I. La collaboration bancaire', *RHDGM*, no. 141, January 1986, p. 32f.
21. See the reports to general assemblies in *La Vie industrielle* for July and August 1942.
22. Rist, *Une saison gâtée, op. cit.*, p. 267 (23 August 1942).
23. Report on accounting expertise, AN, *Z 6* N.L. 74.
24. In January 1942, Bouthillier, informing the CO for banks of his refusal to give a guarantee for war risks to the banks which gave credits to aeronautical companies for their German orders, nevertheless underlined the fact that the government was very keen that these orders should be met, and he concluded: 'I consequently feel it is very important that the banks give as much help as they possibly can to the financing of such operations' (AN, *F 37* 35, Bouthillier and Ardant, 22 January 1942). On the role of the state in mixed companies and aryanization affairs, see the remarks of Henry Rousso, 'Vichy face à la mainmise allemande sur les entreprises françaises', in Carlier and Martens (n.d.), *La France et l'Allemagne en guerre, op. cit.*, pp. 486–7, n. 40.
25. Boyer to Stiehr, 13 October 1942, AN, *32 AQ* 46.
26. Administration council of 23 December 1941, AN, *F 12* 9565.
27. Final report of the Bank Group of the MBF, AN, *AJ 40* 820.
28. In these four banks, the Office des Changes arranged without delay for the exports to Germany made by their business clients, allowing them a quite exceptional month in which to produce their justificatory documents. This was a facility well calculated to attract new clients, of which the banks took full advantage; it also afforded an opportunity to levy a commission (Lacroix-Riz, 'Les grandes banques françaises de la collaboration à l'épuration', *op. cit.*, p. 28).

29. 'Compte rendu de la visite de M. Masson [of the Crédit Lyonnais] le 15 juillet 1941'; 21 July 1941, AN, *F 37* 27.
30. In connection with Paribas: Ardant wanted the banks' stake to take a collective form, mediated by the Comité des Banques. He gave up this idea at the request of Barnaud, who judged it preferable that the CO should not officially patronize a company supposed to function like all private companies. Each bank thus had to decide on its own stake (see the notes of 17 and 22 April 1941, 'Rapports Terray', AN, *F 37* 2). On Radio Monte-Carlo, see AN, *F 37* 27.
31. Note of 12 April 1943, *AJ 40* 823, dr. 1.
32. See Philippe Marguerat (with the collaboration of L. Jilek), *Banque et Investissement industriel. Paribas, le pétrole roumain et la politique française 1919–1939*, Geneva, Droz, 1987.
33. See *F 12* 9565, dr. Paribas.
34. Rist, *Une saison gâtée, op. cit.*, pp. 272–3. Rist then resigned from the Banque des Pays de l'Europe Centrale.
35. *Ibid.*, p. 164 (24 May 1941); p. 250 (21 May 1942).
36. *Ibid.*, p. 267 (23 August 1942).
37. Statement of 18 October 1945, AN, *F 12* 9559.
38. Note by Gerstner, 15 October 1941, AA-PA, *Ha Pol IIa Frankreich, Paket Finanzwesen* 20, vol. II.
39. Chéradame to MBF, 22 March 1943, AN, *AJ 40* 823, dr. 2. Pose was the author of a work that appeared in 1942 (*La Monnaie et ses institutions*, PUF, 2 vols.), in which he spoke of 'France in the German school' (vol. II, pp. 818–20). In 1953 he was elected to the Académie des Sciences Morales et Politiques.
40. See the documents in AN, *F 12* 9566.
41. Chéradame to the MBF, 22 March 1943, AN, *AJ 40* 823, dr. 2.
42. Various statements in AN, *F 12* 9564.
43. Coutau-Bégarie and Huan, *Darlan, op. cit.*, p. 696f.; p. 716f.
44. The commissioner was retired after a few months because of the continuing commitment of the bank in German businesses and in exchange for the retirement of several of the company's executives who were deemed to be unreliable (AN, *AJ 40* 823, dr. 2).
45. Ziegesar to the MBF, 5 May 1941, AN, *AJ 40* 827b.
46. His annual pay came to 500000 francs in 1941 and 700000 in 1944 (AN, *Z 6* N.L. 74).
47. On the circle around Le Roy Ladurie, see Drieu La Rochelle, *Fragment de mémoires 1940–1941*, Gallimard, 1982, pp. 55–6, 77; on the dinner of 20 January 1941, see AA-PA, *Botschaft Paris* 1101a.
48. Reports by Ziegesar of 20 November 1940 and 20 January 1941; report by Falkenhausen, 24 November 1941, AN, *AJ 40* 827b, dr. 1.
49. See the correspondence of Ziegasar and Karl Hettlage, AN, *32 AQ* 35 (archives of the Commerzbank's representatives in Paris).
50. 'Gründung einer französischen Gesellschaft zur Entwicklung der wirtschaftlichen Beziehungen zwischen Frankreich und Deutschland', AN, *AJ 40* 75, dr. 5.
51. See the Dr Hettlage file in AN, *32 AQ* 53.
52. Letter from the Worms Bank to the Paris representatives of the Commerzbank, 23 June 1942, AN, *32 AQ* 46.
53. There are many examples in AN, *32 AQ* 6, 38, 42, etc.
54. Letter from Stiehr, Paris to the Berlin headquarters, 25 September 1941, *32 AQ* 46. For an example where this happened, see the file on Moteurs Salmson, *32 AQ* 42.
55. See the SPEB file in AN, *32 AQ* 42. A comparison between the archives of the

Commerzbank and the statements of Le Roy Ladurie at the time of his trial is illuminating.

56. Report by Falkenhausen, 12 October 1942, AN, *AJ 40* 827b, dr. 1.
57. Drieu La Rochelle, *Fragment de mémoires, op. cit.*, p. 80.
58. 'Lagebericht über Verwaltung und Wirtschaft Juli/September 1943', *AJ 40* 444.
59. See *La Lutte en France contre le travail forcé pendant l'Occupation. Monographie relative aux banques*, FDT, 1949, p. 62.
60. File in AN, *AJ 40* 833, dr. 1.
61. Bloch-Lainé, 'Le financement de la résistance', *RHDGM*, no. 1, November 1950, p. 13.
62. Hearing of 18 October 1944, AN, *Z 6* N.L. 74. Le Roy Ladurie was also to produce a statement by Joliot-Curie, for whom, since the end of 1942, and no doubt not without political afterthoughts, he had been providing financial assistance that enabled him to pursue studies on radioactivity that were designed in part to make up for France slipping behind other countries as a result of the occupation (Joliot-Curie, 'Note for M. Denivelle', n.d., AN, *F 12* 9566).
63. AN, *F 12* 9569, the Public Ministry's indictment of Ardant.

18 ROGUES AND MENIALS

1. AN, *F 12* 9619, dr. Gilet and Descas.
2. Descas to Boemers, 12 May 1942, *ibid.*
3. Descas to Boemers, 18 October 1943, *ibid.*
4. For all that follows, see Jacques Delarue, 'Les dessous du marché noir', in *Trafics et Crimes sous l'Occupation*, Fayard, 1968.
5. *Ibid.*, p. 61f.
6. BAK, *R* 121 893.
7. Purge files in AN, *F 12* 9629 and the report by OSS, 'The Göring Collection', 15 September 1945, in *F 12* 9596.
8. Purge files in AN, *F 12* 9596.
9. AN, *32 AQ* 38, Éts. Sanéfo.
10. BAK, *R 9 I* 575 to 578.
11. BAK, *R 9 I* 578/1, letter of 9 May 1942.
12. AN, *AJ 40* 816, dr. 77, letter of 18 June 1941.
13. AN, *AJ 40* 815, dr. 83. In this particular case, the economic officials of the MBF decided to do without the authorization of the French government, reckoning that to apply, making known the change of ownership, would ruin the company's chances of prospering.
14. AN, *32 AQ* 36, 'Stés parisiennes de Travaux biochimiques', 7 October 1941.
15. 'Lagebericht ü. Verwaltung u. Wirtschaft Okt. Dez. 1943', AN, *AJ 40* 444.
16. Correspondence in *AJ 40* 814, dr. 1.
17. 'Übersicht der vom Generalkommissariat für Judenfrage erfassten jüdische Unternehmen von Aufnahme der Tätigkeit an', 10 May 1944, AN, *AJ 40* 615, dr. 4. Marrus and Paxton (*Vichy et les Juifs, op. cit.*, p. 146) put the total at 7400, whereas Henry Rousso speaks of 10500 temporary administrators appointed in May 1941 ('L'aryanisation économique: Vichy, l'occupant et la spoliation des Juifs', *Yod*, nos. 15–16, 1982, p. 60).
18. Paul Pesquet to MBF, 17 July 1941, AN, *AJ 40* 783, dr. 6.
19. Letters of 12 May 1941 and 8 June 1941, AN, *AJ 40* 621, dr. 2.
20. Intendant beim MBF, 'Tätigkeitsbericht für die Zeit vom 1.7.1942 bis 31.12.1942', BA-MA, *RW 35* 98.

21. 'Lagebericht des Wi-u. Rü.-Stabes Frankreich', report for December 1941, BA-MA, *RW 24* 17; *Die faschistische Okkupationspolitik in Frankreich (1940–1944), op. cit.*, doc. 221, extract from a report of the Feldwirtschaftsamt im OKW for the period of January–April 1944, p. 310–11.
22. Jacqueline Sainclivier, 'Le poids de la guerre sur l'emploi et la vie des ouvriers en Bretagne (1938–1944)', *Les Ouvriers en France pendant la Seconde Guerre mondiale, op. cit.*, p. 87. See also Rémy Desquesnes, 'L'Organisation Todt en France (1940–1944)', *Histoire, Économie et Société*, no. 3, 1992, pp. 535–50.
23. Figures taken from 'Lageberichte' of the Abteilung Ia, AN, *AJ 40* 443.
24. *Pariser Zeitung*, 5 July 1942, p. 7.
25. Abetz to AA, 6 July 1944, AN, *AJ 40* 846, dr. MBF C4 LVII IC4.
26. 'Wochenkurzbericht für die Woche vom 23.7–29.7.44', AN, *AJ 40* 866, dr. 12.
27. Alan S. Milward, *The New Order and the French Economy, op. cit.*, p. 124, table 13. The data on figures fluctuate from one source to another, for this period in particular.
28. See the reports of Dr Petzsch of 27 February and 29 May 1941, AN, *AJ 40* 860, dr. 2.
29. Ulrich Herbert, *Fremdarbeiter*, Berlin, Verlag J. H. W. Dietz, 1985, p. 99. It is worth noting that only a very small minority of voluntary workers were indicted at the liberation.
30. Report by Dr Petzsch, 15 October 1941, AN, *AJ 40* 860, dr. 2.
31. See the dr. 1, AN, *AJ 40* 896.
32. Pfahlmann, *Fremdarbeiter und Kriegsgefangene, op. cit.*, pp. 32–3.
33. Herbert, *Fremdarbeiter, op. cit.*, p. 272.
34. Pfahlmann, *Fremdarbeiter und Kriegsgefangene, op. cit.*, p. 134.
35. See the monthly reports of medical visits in AN, *AJ 40* 860, dr. 2.
36. Jean-Marie Guillon, 'Y a-t-il un comportement ouvrier spécifique? Les ouvriers varois', in *Les Ouvriers en France pendant la Seconde Guerre mondiale, op. cit.*, pp. 472–3.
37. See Henri Raczymov, *Maurice Sachs*, Gallimard, 1988.
38. Brinon to the DFCAA, 24 August 1943, AN, *AJ 41* 461.
39. AD Gard, CC 307/308.
40. BA-MA, *RW 35* 1157.
41. E. Aubert-Weiss, 'Tätigkeit der Abt. Auswertung', 22 September 1942, AA-PA, *Botschaft Paris* 1125b/2.
42. Letter of 19 October 1940, AN, *AJ 40* 860, dr. 5.
43. Dr Kohl, 'Anwerbung von Arbeitskräften in Frankreich', 26 August 1941, AN, *AJ 40* 846.
44. N.d. [autumn 1940], AN, *AJ 40* 864, dr. 1.
45. MBF to the embassy, 27 December 1941, AN, *AJ 40* 864, dr. 3.
46. Julien Papp confirms the efficacy of this propaganda of proximity for the Eure, *La Collaboration dans l'Eure, op. cit.*, p. 168.
47. See AN, *AJ 40* 856, dr. 3 to 5.
48. 'Gastarbeiter. Bericht über das vierte Quartal 1941', BAK, *R 41* 264.
49. 'Conditions d'existence d'un ouvrier français ayant travaillé en Allemagne', 10 July 1942, AN, *AJ 41* 346, 'Informations diverses'.
50. Yves Durand, *La Captivité, op. cit.*, p. 331f.
51. *Dommages subis par la France*, vol. IX, DPI Monograph: Exploitation de la main-d'œuvre française par l'Allemagne, pp. 108–10.
52. AN, *AJ 40* 859, dr. 1 and 2.
53. AN, *F 12* 9610, dr. Panoma and Paros.

Notes

19 *SPRECHEN SIE DEUTSCH?*

1. Goethe, *Aus meinem Leben. Dichtung und Wahreit*, Leipzig, Inselverlag, 1922, p. 116.
2. See Martin Süss, *Rheinhessen unter französischer Besatzung. Vom Waffenstillstand im November 1918 bis zum Ende der Separatistenunruhen im Februar 1924*, Stuttgart, Franz Steiner Verlag, 1988, p. 41f, p. 136; and Gerhard Brunn, 'Französische Kulturpolitik in den Rheinlanden nach 1918 und die Weisbadener Kunstausstellung des Jahres 1921', in Peter Hüttenberger and Hansgeorg Molitor (eds.), *Franzosen und Deutsche am Rhein 1789–1918–1945*, Essen, Klartext, 1989, pp. 219–42.
3. Abetz to AA, 15 October 1940, AA-PA, *Botschaft Paris* 1319. Newspapers delighted in showing the queues of visitors (*Paris-Soir*, 15 October 1940, and *L'Œuvre*, 16 October 1940).
4. There were 49428 visitors in Bordeaux in February–March 1941, 42805 in Lille in August–September, 21697 in Rouen in December 1941–January 1942 (on this exhibition see the files in AA-PA, *Botschaft Paris* 1339–40 and 2497).
5. 'Bericht über die Freimaurerausstellung in Paris', AA-PA, *Botschaft Paris* 1339.
6. See Dominique Rossignol, *Vichy et les Franc-Maçons*, J.-C. Lattès, 1981.
7. AA-PA, *Botschaft Paris* 1340.
8. 'Zusammenfassung der seit 1940 bis heute von der Informationsabteilung der Deutschen Botschaft Paris geleisteten Arbeit', AA-PA, *Botschaft Paris* 1125b/2.
9. *Ibid.*
10. André Kaspi, 'Le juif et la France, une exposition à Paris en 1941', *Le Monde juif*, no. 79, July–September 1975, pp. 8–20, and by the same author, *Les Juifs pendant l'occupation*, Seuil, 1992, pp. 104–10.
11. See the file in AA-PA, *Botschaft Paris* 1191.
12. AA-PA, *Botschaft Paris* 1192.
13. See the reports of the Propaganda-Abteilung for June and July 1942, BAK, *R 55* 1337.
14. A note from Gidel to Bonnard on 16 July 1942 (AN, *F 17* 13360) contains a list of the teachers who organized visits to the exhibition. The Lycée Condorcet heads the list (forty-five teachers), followed by Janson (sixteen), Voltaire (thirteen), Pasteur (eleven), Charlemagne (ten), Henri IV (two), Louis-le-Grand and Montaigne (one), etc.
15. Taubert to Goebbels, 31 March 1943, BAK, *R 55* 964.
16. Note from the German Consulate of Toulouse, 13 June 1944, AA-PA, *Botschaft Paris* 1111b.
17. Luther to Krüger, 8 September 1942, AA-PA, *Handakten Luther* 13.
18. There were 2559038 visitors to the embassy's exhibitions ('Zusammenfassung der seit 1940 bis heute von der Informationsabteilung der Deutschen Botschaft Paris geleisteten Arbeit', AA-PA, *Botschaft Paris* 1339).
19. Letter of 25 October 1940, AA-PA, *Botschaft Paris* 1339.
20. Feger, 'Rilkes schöpferische Freundschaft', *Pariser Zeitung*, 7 March 1942, p. 5. On the German Institute, see Eckard Michels, *Das Deutsche Institut in Paris 1940–1944*, Stuttgart, Franz Steiner Verlag, 1993.
21. Serge Added, *Le Théâtre dans les années Vichy, 1940–1944*, Ramsay, 1992, pp. 104–7.
22. 'La musique allemande à Paris', *Pariser Zeitung*, 13 September 1941.
23. Gertrud vom Steeg, 'Zwei Jahre deutscher Musik und deutschen Theaters in Frankreich. Ein Tätigkeitsbericht des Deutschen Instituts', *Deutschland-Frankreich*, no. 3, 1943, pp. 134–7.
24. 'Arbeitsbericht Mai 1942–Juli 1943', AA-PA, *Botschaft Paris* 1124.

25. Fabre-Luce, *Journal de la France*, vol. II, Imprimerie J.E.P., 1942, p. 154.
26. 'Akademische Abteilung', n.d. [summer 1942], AA-PA, *Botschaft Paris* 1112a.
27. See his articles, 'Die Formung des französischen Geistes durch den Legisten', *Deutschland-Frankreich*, no. 2, 1942; and 'Souveraineté d'État et liberté des mers', in *Quelques aspects du droit allemand*, Sorlot, Cahiers de l'Institut allemand, no. 6, 1943.
28. Schleier to AA, 16.9.41, AA-PA, *Botschaft Paris* 1376.
29. Epting, 1 May 1942, AA-PA, *Pol. II Richtlinien 15, Deutsches Institut (Berichtsdoppel)*.
30. Rist, *Une saison gâtée, op. cit.*, p. 247 (27 April 1942).
31. 'Akademische Abteilung', n.d. [summer 1942], AA-PA, *Botschaft Paris* 1112a.
32. See his annual reports in AA-PA, *Botschaft Paris* 1053/4.
33. Letter from the office of the rector of Paris to the Ministry of National Education, 8 June 1941, *AJ 16* Provisional/6, 'Rapports du rectorat'.
34. Abt. Ia, 'Lageberichte' report from March 1941, AN, *AJ 40* 443; Schleier, 22 November 1941, AA-PA, *Botschaft Paris* 1374.
35. Paul Lévy, *La Langue allemande en France, op. cit.*, p. 212.
36. Lévy, 'Les incidences des guerres sur l'enseignement des langues vivantes', *Revue universitaire*, no. 3, May–June 1947, p. 135.
37. In the absence of statistics on the language choices of the new pupils in particular, this is a rough calculation based on a comparison of the increased numbers of pupils following German courses between 1940 and 1941 and the estimated number of pupils entering secondary education. Epting confirms this proportion of two-thirds in one of his reports ('Entwicklung der Germanistik in Frankreich', 11 December 1941, AA-PA, *Botschaft Paris* 13374). The basic figures are taken from Paul Lévy (*La Langue allemande en France, op. cit.*, pp. 215–16) and from the statistical tables for the years 1939–45 kindly made available to me by the Centre de Documentation de la Direction de l'Évaluation et de la Prospective – Ministère de l'Éducation Nationale. The statistics by sex are missing for the years following 1941. I have been unable to find any statistics for private education.
38. Fabre-Luce, *Journal de France*, vol. II, *op. cit.*, p. 121.
39. Pierre Girard, 'La SNCF sous l'occupation', in Institut Hoover, *La Vie de la France sous l'occupation (1940–1944)*, vol. I, 1957, p. 327.
40. Bobkowski, *En guerre et en paix, op. cit.*, p. 178.
41. Figures provided by Richard Cobb (*Vivre avec l'ennemi. La France sous deux occupations: 1914–1918 et 1940–1944*, Éditions du Sorbier, 1985, p. 146), source not indicated.
42. AN, *AJ 40* 563, dr. V Kult 409.
43. *L'Œuvre*, 19 December 1940.
44. See the 'Miméphone' file, in particular the note 'Résultats de la première année du Miméphone', in AN, *AJ 16* provisoire 1939–1944, box 39.
45. BAK, *R 51* 61, see also Besançon, *R 51* 64.
46. 'Arbeitsbericht Mai 1942–Juli 1943', AA-PA, *Botschaft Paris* 1124.
47. 'Liste der Lehrkräfte', 15 January 1943; 'Einzelbericht über eine Inspektionsreise zur Zweigstelle Wassy am 19.5 1943', BAK, *R 51* 110.
48. Epting to Abetz, 17 and 18 October 1941, AA-PA, *Botschaft Paris* 1368.
49. 'Vergleichszahlen der Kursteilnehmer von 1942/43 und 1943/1944', BAK, *R 51* 476.
50. 'Arbeitsbericht Mai 1942–Juli 1943', AA-PA, *Botschaft Paris* 1124.
51. 'Bericht der Sprachabteilung des Deutschen Instituts . . . vom 1.11 1943 bis 30. 6 1944', BAK, *R 51* 171.

52. 'Bericht über die Arbeit des Lektorats Paris für die Monate Mai–Juni 1944', BAK, *R 51* 171.
53. Calculation obtained by assuming 50 per cent of the students re-enrolled at the end of the school year.
54. In Bordeaux, of the 1783 people enrolled at the end of 1942, 30 per cent were less than twenty years of age, 23 per cent between twenty and thirty, 24 per cent between thirty and forty, 20 per cent between forty and sixty, 3 per cent over 60 (Bak, *R 51* 110).
55. Reassessment of various comparable data – a comparison between all categories involved being incomplete for the first two years – at various dates in 1941 and 1942 for Paris (BAK, *R 51* 169–70), Angers (*R 51* 93), Dijon (*R 51* 131), Nantes (*R 51* 159).
56. The figures of the Paris Institute for February 1943 (4284 cases known) make it possible to pinpoint certain categories, the distribution of the various groups remaining the same. Shopkeepers, 6 per cent (254 individuals); artisans and workers, in separate groups, the former 3 per cent (137), the latter 2.6 per cent (114). In the liberal professions (9 per cent), 5 per cent (216) held some university diploma (doctors, pharmacists, etc). Finally, public officials, isolated here, make up a total of 13 per cent: 7.3 per cent lower officials (317), 1.6 per cent higher ranking officials (71), 22 per cent primary teachers (97) and 1.5 per cent secondary teachers (66). Source: BAK, *R 51* 170.
57. See the report of the special Besançon police commissioner on the clientèle of the local German Institute, 19 August 1941, AN, *F 60* 408, 'Propagande anti-nationale en zone occupée'.
58. BAK, *R 51* 131 and *R 51* 170.
59. 'Arbeitsbericht Mai 1942–Juli 1943', AA-PA, *Botschaft Paris* 1124.
60. *Ibid.*
61. Note by Funke, 8 April 1941, BAK, *R 51* 64.

20 INTELLECTUALS AND SELF-PRESERVATION

1. Circular from Faral, 5 August 1940, Archives of the Collège de France, H-II-e-36.
2. Text relating to the pencilled note 'handed to the General Delegation on 25 January 1941', *ibid.*, H-II-e-65.
3. 7 November 1940, *ibid.*, H-II-e-62.
4. Report of the Abteilung Verwaltung for the month of October 1940, AN, *AJ 40* 566, dr. École Libre des Sciences Politiques.
5. Benoist-Méchin, *À l'épreuve du temps*, vol. II, *op. cit.*, p. 28.
6. Pierre Birnbaum, *La France aux Français*, Seuil, 993, p. 176; Joseph-Barthélémy, *Ministre de la Justice*, *op. cit.*, pp. 303–4, n. 6.
7. Epting, 'Liste der deutschen und französischen Persönlichkeiten, die in den Monaten Januar und Februar an Frühstücksveranstaltungen des Deutschen Instituts teilgenommen haben', AA-PA, *Botschaft Paris* 1368. On Siegfried, see Birnbaum, *La France aux Français*, *op. cit.*, pp. 145–86.
8. Leriche informed Ménétrel of his colleagues' fear of changes to the statutes of the Collège de France (lettre of 22 May 1941, AN, 2 *AG 77*). For Vichy's bad image of the Collège, see AN, 2 AG 459, 'Éducation nationale'. Béraud considered the institution to be a den of Jews (*Sans haine et sans crainte*, Les Éditions de France, 1942, p. 233).
9. Faral to the secretary of State for National Education, 23 August 1941, Archives of the Collège de France, H-II-e 62.
10. Hand-written note, n.d. [1944], *ibid.*, H-II-e dr. Réparations and sanctions.

11. See the entry by Nicole Racine in Jean Maîtron (ed.), *Dictionnaire biographique du mouvement ouvrier français*, vol. XXXII, Éditions ouvrières, 1988.
12. Spencer R. Weart, *Scientists in Power*, Massachusetts, Harvard University Press, 1979, p. 155; Bertrand Goldschmidt, *Les Rivalités atomiques 1939–1966*, Fayard, 1967, pp. 55–6.
13. Letter cited by Maurice Goldsmith, *Frédéric Joliot-Curie. A Biography*, London, Lawrence and Wishart, 1976, p. 97. See also Rosalynd Pflaum, *Marie Curie et sa fille Irène. Deux femmes, trois Nobel*, Belfond, 1992.
14. See the 'Historique' left by Faral, Archives of the Collège de France, H-II-e-66, dr. Occupation of the Joliot laboratory.
15. David Irving, *The German Atomic Bomb. The History of Nuclear Research in Germany*, New York, Da Capo Press, 1983, p. 71.
16. Wolfang Gentner, *Entretiens avec Frédéric Joliot-Curie à Paris occupée 1940–1942*, Heidelberg, Max-Planck Institut für Kernphysik, 1980, p. 2 (I am grateful to Nicole Racine for letting me have a copy of this text).
17. All the citations that follow are taken from the file 'Laboratoire Joliot-Curie' (AN, *AJ 41* 71), in particular the overall report by Faral, n.d. [18 August 1940].
18. General Koeltz annotation on the file, *ibid.*. The information clause does not appear to have been used.
19. 'Note pour le secrétaire d'État à l'Instruction publique', 3 October 1940, AN, *F 17* 13 385, dr. Collège de France.
20. Gentner, *Entretiens avec Frédéric Joliot-Curie, op. cit.*, p. 7.
21. Pierre Biquard, *Frédéric Joliot-Curie et l'Énergie atomique*, Seghers, 1961, p. 74.
22. Kommandostab Ic, 'Aktennotiz', 20 November 1940, AN *AJ 40* 566, dr. 21. The suspicions hanging over Joliot came to the surface in March 1941, when the embassy, alerted by the SD, which had picked up a rumour that Joliot was to be appointed the administrator of the Collège de France, immediately told the Ministry of National Education of his opposition (notes of 24 and 29 March 1941, dr. 19, AN *AJ 40* 566).
23. Kommandostab Ic (I), 'Aktennotiz', 23 November 1940, AN *AJ 40* 566, dr. 21. Langevin had been arrested by the SD, at Epting's request, without the MBF, which held all policing powers, being informed. This quarrel about responsibilities facilitated the success of the pressure exerted by Joliot and the intervention of the Heereswaffenamt.
24. Letters of 10 and 11 February 1941, Archives of the Collège de France, H-II-e-66.
25. Letter from Faral to the Minister of National Education, 23 August 1941, H-II-e-62.
26. Gentner, *Entretiens avec Frédéric Joliot-Curie, op. cit.*, p. 5.
27. The experience gained in Paris helped the Germans in the construction of their own cyclotrons, and caused them to modify their plans (see *Archiv Max Planck Gesellschaft, Nachlaß Walther Bothe* 78, Bothe to Bauinspektor Treiber, 10 March 1941) and also helped them in their experiments on artificial radioactivity (*ibid.*, 101). I am grateful to Mark Walker for having provided me with information relating to Joliot's laboratory drawn from the German and American archives, and also for his invaluable advice.
28. On the subject of nuclear research in general, Joliot wrote in 1943; 'This research, if carried to its conclusion, could have momentous consequences; it has been suspended in France since June 1940' ('note remise à M. Trefouel, directeur de l'Institut Pasteur le 22 novembre 1943'), AN Fontainebleau, *Archives du CNRS*, 800 284–55, 'Papiers Joliot-Curie'.
29. Bobkowski, *En guerre et en paix, op. cit.*, pp. 303–4 (4 March 1942). In *L'Avenir de la science* (Plon, 'Présences', 1941), alongside a contribution by Louis de Broglie, which refers to the subject in an erudite way, there is an imaginative piece of

science fiction by Pierre Devaux, in particular the following scenario, which was to enjoy great success after 1945: 'Despite the Draconian surveillance over the disintegrators, placed under the authority of counter-espionage, a disintegrable mass as large as a fist is stolen by an extremist, and is launched by means of a rocket on to a foreign capital which goes up in flames and collapses like a house of cards. The riposte arrives and Paris is reduced to rubble; the survivors resort to making stone axes' ('Prophètes et inventeurs', p. 212).

30. See Mark Walker, *German National Socialism and the Quest for Nuclear Power*, Cambridge, Cambridge University Press, 1989.
31. See Bloch's letter to Febvre on 22 June 1938, AN, *318 Mi* 1. On Bloch, see Carol Fink, *Marc Bloch: A Life in History*, New York, Cambridge University Press, 1989.
32. Febvre to Bloch, n.d. [autumn 1940], AN, *318 Mi* 1.
33. 'Memento de questions à traiter oralement', n.d. [autumn–winter 1940], *ibid.*; letter, n.d. [autumn 1940], AN, *318 Mi* 2.
34. Febvre to Bloch, 13 April 1941, *ibid.*
35. Bloch to Febvre, 16 April 1941, AN, *318 Mi* 1.
36. Febvre to Bloch, 19 April 1941, AN, *318 Mi* 2 (there are two versions of this letter). The last passage has been cited by Massimo Mastrogregori, 'Le manuscrit interrompu. *Métier d'historien* by Marc Bloch', *Annales ESC*, January–February 1989, p. 149.
37. Bloch to Febvre, 16 April 1941, AN, *318 Mi* 1.
38. Bloch to Febvre, 16 May 1941, *ibid.*
39. Bloch to Febvre, 7 May 1941, *ibid.*
40. Bloch to Febvre, 16 May 1941, *ibid.*
41. Febvre to Soustelle, 16 July 1945, AN, *F 41* 1028, dr. *Annales ESC*.
42. Febvre to the director of the press, 14 September 1945, *ibid.*
43. 'Note pour M. Roy', 8 February 1943, AN, *F 17* 13381, Presse pédagogique et scientifique'.
44. On the administrative form requesting authorization to reappear, filled in by Charles Morazé (10 August 1945, *F 41* 1028, dr. *Annales ESC*), in reply to the question asking whether the periodical had been 'scuttled', the reply runs as follows: 'Yes, in its regular form.' 'At what date?': 'In June 1940. It continued to appear in the form of *Mélanges*.' This covered up the request to the German authorities for authorization in 1941, and the publication of the periodical under the title of *Annales* for one year. Febvre himself, in his letter to the director of the press (above, n. 42), did allude to the change of title in 1942, but represented this as an act of quasi-resistance to Vichy's 'proscriptions'.

21 *INTER ARMA SILENT MUSAE*

1. Cocteau, *Journal 1942–1945*, Gallimard, 1989, p. 557 (23 September 1944).
2. Evelyn Ehrlich, *Cinema of Paradox. French Film-making under the German Occupation*, New York, Columbia University Press, 1985, pp. 148–50.
3. Léautaud, *Journal littéraire*, *op. cit.*, p. 464 (11 December 1941).
4. *Adjutantur der Wehrmacht beim Führer*, 31 March 1942, a circular distributed by the Propaganda-Abteilung, AD Bourges, *Außenstelle Bourges der Prop. Staffel NW*, dr. 2.
5. Jean-Pierre Bertin-Maghit, *Le Cinéma sous l'occupation*, Olivier Orban, 1989, pp. 98–9.
6. Bremer, 'Lage des französischen Schriftums', 17 June 1941, AA-PA, *Botschaft Paris* 1377.
7. See, for example, Léautaud, *Journal littéraire*, vol. I, *op. cit.*, p. 19f.
8. Added, *Le Théâtre dans les années Vichy*, *op. cit.*, p. 129.

9. Ehrlich, *Cinema of Paradox*, *op. cit.*, p. 43f.
10. Pascal Fouché, *L'Édition française sous l'Occupation*, vol. I, *op. cit.*, p. 19f.
11. *Ibid.*, p. 52.
12. Heller, 'Arbeits und Lagebericht', 20 March 1942; 'Fur das Tätigkeitsbericht', 27 December 1941; 'Tätigkeitsbericht vom 17.5.–bis 23.5.41'; 'Tätigkeitsbericht vom 15–bis 22.1.41', AN, *AJ 40* 1005, dr. 7.
13. Note by Epting, 31 January 1941, AA-PA, *Botschaft Paris* 1377.
14. 'Kulturpolitische Arbeit in Frankreich', n.d. [late 1942], AA-PA, *Botschaft Paris* 1125b.
15. Claire Girou de Buzareingues, 'La traduction en France', in *Le Livre français*, n.d. Julien Cain, Robert Escarpit and Henri-Jean Martin, Imprimerie nationale, 1972, p. 269; Herbert Lottman, *La Rive gauche*, Seuil, 1981, p. 209.
16. Mercure de France published six translations between 1940 and 1944 out of a total of ten for the 1919–44 period; Denoël four out of eight; PUF seven out of seventeen; Masson two out of eight; Hachette eight out of fourteen (figures obtained from perusing Liselotte Bihl and Karl Epting, *Bibliographie französischer Übersetzungen aus dem Deutschen 1487–1944*, Tübingen, Max Niemayer Verlag, 1987).
17. AN, *AJ 40* 1007, dr. 1.
18. Note by Epting, 8 February 1941, AA-PA, *Botschaft Paris* 1377.
19. Note by Bremer, 15 February 1941, AA-PA, *Botschaft Paris* 1377.
20. Heller, 'Tätigkeitsbericht vom 13.–19.2.41', AN, *AJ 40* 1004, dr. 7.
21. Gérard Loiseaux, *La littérature de la défaite et de la collaboration*, Publications de la Sorbonne, 1984, pp. 91–2; Fouché, *L'Édition française sous l'Occupation*, vol. I, *op. cit.*, pp. 268, 389–406.
22. Fouché, *L'Édition française sous l'Occupation*, vol. II, *op. cit.*, p. 231.
23. Heller, 'Tätigkeitsbericht vom 20. bis 27. September 1941' and 'Tätigkeitsbericht vom 28.9 bis 4.10.41', AN, *AJ 40* 1005, dr. 7.
24. Girodias to Hartmann, 22 October 1941, AA-PA, *Botschaft Paris* 1378. Hartmann, who recommended him to Abetz, described him as 'absolut deutschfreundlich', 23 October 1941, *ibid.*
25. 'Les cahiers de la petite dame, 1937–1945', *Cahiers André Gide*, no. 6, Gallimard, 1975, p. 198 (5 October 1940).
26. *Henry de Montherlant–Roger Peyrefitte, Correspondance*, Laffont, 1983, p. 122 (October 1940).
27. Fouché, *L'Édition française sous l'Occupation*, *op. cit.*, p. 68f.
28. *Pariser Zeitung*, 19 August 1942, p. 5. On 18 September 1941, the same newspaper carried an article by A. Salar, 'Le programme de la NRF', p. 7, which ran as follows: 'I went to ask M. Queneau, the helpful literary director of the NRF, if he would be so kind as to give me some idea of his plans, and I learnt that a most interesting effort is to be made to introduce the French public to some of the most striking works of German literature.'
29. AN, *AJ 40* 1007, dr. 1.
30. Fouché, *L'Édition française sous l'Occupation*, *op. cit.*, p. 126f.
31. Drieu, *Journal 1939–1945*, *op. cit.*, p. 289f.; Paulhan, *Choix de lettres*, vol. II, *1937–1945*, *op. cit.*, p. 266f. After the liberation, at the time of the purge, Paulhan spoke of the 'complete' separation and 'absolute break' between the publishing house and the periodical, 'which the German authorities had taken over in 1940' (Pierre Assouline, *Gaston Gallimard*, Balland, 1984, p. 382).
32. Letter of 7 July 1942, unsigned (but certainly from Gaston Gallimard), *Botschaft Paris* 1203. The second Otto list, which appeared soon after, eliminated all books by Jewish authors, except scientific works.

33. 'Neues deutsch-französisches Kulturzentrum in der Hauptstadt', *Pariser Zeitung*, 22 April 1941, p. 4.
34. Wiemer to Abetz, 'Aufzeichnung', 12 August 1942, AA-PA, *Botschaft Paris* 1139a.
35. Note from the Sipo/SD, 19 March 1943, AA-PA, *Botschaft Paris* 1141b.
36. See Assouline, *Gallimard*, *op. cit.*
37. Guéhenno, *Journal des années noires*, *op. cit.*, pp. 73–4 (30 November 1940).
38. 'Les cahiers de la petite dame, 1937–1945', *op. cit.*, letter from Professor A. Marcou, p. 217 (4 January 1941).
39. Léautaud, *Journal littéraire*, *op. cit.*, p. 172 (18 September 1940).
40. Paulhan, *Choix de lettres*, vol. II, *1937–1945*, *op. cit.*, letter to Mauriac, p. 333 (28 August 1943).
41. Louis Guilloux, *Carnets 1921–1944*, Gallimard, 1978, pp. 270–1.
42. On the reception of Sartre's dramas, see Ingrid Galster, *Le Théâtre de Jean-Paul Sartre devant ses premiers critiques*, vol. I, Jean-Michel Place, 1986. See also Annie Cohen-Solal, *Sartre*, Gallimard, 1985.
43. Déat, *Journal de guerre*, 26 August 1940.
44. Roger Vailland, *Écrits intimes*, Gallimard, 1968, pp. 72–3 (6 June 1942).
45. Letter to Drieu, 11 December 1940, in François Mauriac, *Lettres d'une vie*, *op. cit.*, pp. 244–5.
46. Henri Guillemin, *Parcours*, Seuil, 1989, p. 401.
47. Letters from Mauriac to his wife, 24 February and 1 March 1941, cited by Touzot, *Mauriac sous l'Occupation*, *op. cit.*, pp. 31–2.
48. Bremer, 'Lage des französischen Schriftums', 17 June 1941, AA-PA, *Botschaft Paris* 1377.
49. Letter to his wife, 7 June 1941, cited by Touzot, *Mauriac sous l'Occupation*, *op. cit.*, p. 34.
50. Letter to Drieu, 18 July 1941, *Lettres d'une vie*, *op. cit.*, p. 255.
51. Touzot, *Mauriac sous l'Occupation*, *op. cit.*, p. 56.
52. Bremer, 'Lage des französischen Schriftums', 17 June 1941, AA-PA, *Botschaft Paris* 1377. Duhamel after the war: 'I went to the German Institute having been expressly summoned there to receive warnings tinged with threats' (Georges Duhamel, *Le Livre de l'amertume*, Mercure de France, 1983, p. 377).
53. Léautaud, *Journal littéraire*, *op. cit.*, p. 363 (26 June 1941).
54. See Jean-Marc Morjean, 'Camus ou le prix des mots (June 1940–August 1944)', in *La littérature française sous l'Occupation*, Presses universitaires de Reims, 1989, pp. 27–41; and Jean-Pierre Rioux, 'Camus et la Seconde Guerre mondiale', in Jeanyves Guérin (ed.), *Camus et la Politique*, L'Harmattan, 1986, pp. 97–106.
55. Saint-Exupéry, *Écrits de guerre*, *op. cit.*, p. 255.
56. Pierre Chevrier, *Antoine de Saint-Exupéry*, Gallimard, 1949, p. 177.
57. See 'Saint-Exupéry traduit en allemand', *Pariser Zeitung*, 5 February 1941.
58. *Pariser Zeitung*, 1 August 1941, 'Tagebuch aus dem Kulturleben', p. 8; 14 October 1941, p. 5.
59. On these publishing up and downs see Fouché, *L'Édition française sous l'occupation*, *op. cit.*, vol. I, pp. 174–5; vol. II, pp. 110–11.
60. Michel Apel-Muller, 'L'édition de 1942 des *Voyageurs de l'impériale*: une entreprise "diabolique"', *Recherches croisées*, 1988, p. 196f.
61. Cited in *ibid.*, p. 188.
62. Apel-Muller inclines in this direction, *ibid.*, p. 204.
63. See the extracts from the correspondence in *ibid.*, pp. 180–1.
64. Aragon to Paulhan, 8 April 1943, cited in *ibid.*, p. 203.

22 THE SIGNING-UP OF THE MUSES

1. AA-PA, *Botschaft Paris* 1101a.
2. Jouvenel was twice present (on 29 October 1941 and 2 June 1942) at these breakfasts that the ambassador enjoyed hosting (AA-PA, *ibid.*). He himself mentions in his memoirs other meetings (*Un voyageur dans le siècle, op. cit.*, p. 402f., p. 426f.). He was on the list of guests for the commercial section of the embassy for the 'Heldengedenkfeier' at the Grand Palais on 15 March 1942 (AA-PA, *Botschaft Paris* 110Ab).
3. Jouvenel, *Après la défaite*, Plon, 1941, p. 229f.
4. 'La France en Europe. À propos d'un livre de Bertrand de Jouvenel', *Pariser Zeitung*, 13 February 1941.
5. *Après la défaite, op. cit.*, p. 238.
6. Déat, *Journal de guerre*, 10 February 1941.
7. Note by Bremer, 18 June 1941, AA-PA, *Botschaft Paris* 1377.
8. 'Midi', in *Le Solstice de juin*, Grasset, 1941, p. 89.
9. *Ibid.*, pp. 292, 310, 311–12.
10. Pierre Sipriot, *Montherlant sans masque*, vol. II, Laffont, 1990, p. 177f.
11. In one of his reports Bremer cites a letter from Montherlant in which the latter complains of the stifling atmosphere in the free zone, Bremer, 'Lage des französischen Schriftums', 17 June 1941, AA-PA, *Botschaft Paris* 1377.
12. *Henry de Montherlant–Roger Peyrefittre, Correspondance, op. cit.*, p. 282 (27 April 1941).
13. Peyrefitte to Montherlant, *ibid.*, pp. 284–5 (2 May 1941).
14. Epting to the Vichy consulate, 18 April 1942, AA-PA, *Botschaft Paris* 1111a. Montherlant attended a 'Rive Gauche' reception at the embassy on 3 November 1942 (AA-PA, *Botschaft Paris* 1101b).
15. *Le Solstice de juin, op. cit.*, pp. 316–17.
16. Reprinted in Sipriot, *Montherlant sans masque, op. cit.*, pp. 192–94.
17. Peyrefitte to Brinon, 17 May 1943, AN, *F60* 1496.
18. Ginette Guitard-Auviste, *Paul Morand*, Hachette, 1981, pp. 172–3.
19. *Chroniques de l'homme maigre*, Grasset, 1941, pp. 64, 66, 98–9, p. 182.
20. Jünger, *Second Journal parisien, op. cit.*, 29 August 1943, p. 144.
21. Gertrud vom Steeg, 'Zwei Jahre deutscher Musik und deutschen Theaters in Frankreich. Ein Tätigkeitsbericht des Deutschen Instituts', *Deutschland-Frankreich*, no. 3, 1943, pp. 134–7.
22. Bremer to Schleier, 13 November 1941, AA-PA, *Botschaft Paris* 1379.
23. Note by Bremer, 19 August 1941, AA-PA, *Botschaft Paris* 1380.
24. Schleier to Epting, 15 January 1942, AA-PA, *Botschaft Paris* 1379.
25. See AA-PA, *Botschaft Paris* 1111b; see also Laurence Bertrand Dorléac, *Histoire de l'art, Paris 1940–1944*, Publications de la Sorbonne, 1986.
26. Cocteau, *Journal 1942–1945, op. cit.*, p. 34 (13 March 1942).
27. Propaganda-Abteilung to Brinon, 6 May 1941, AN, *F60* 1488.
28. Cocteau, *Journal, op. cit.*, 5 May 1942, p. 111.
29. *Ibid.*, p. 188 (24 July 1942).
30. *Ibid.*, p. 173 (2 July 1942).
31. *Ibid.*, p. 234 (9 January 1943); p. 335 (18 August 1943).
32. Note for Schleier, 7 August 1941, AA-PA, *Botschaft Paris* 1379.
33. AA-PA, *Botschaft Paris* 1142.
34. Bertrand Dorléac, *Histoire de l'art, Paris 1940–1944, op. cit.*, p. 94f.
35. Rita Thalmann, *La Mise au pas, op. cit.*, pp. 209–12.

36. Heller, 'Tätigkeitsbericht vom 6. bis 13. September 1941', *AJ 40* FF 1005, dr. 7; AA-PA, *Botschaft Paris* 1378.
37. Jouhandeau, *Journal sous l'Occupation*, Gallimard, 1980, pp. 83–4 (5 October 1941).
38. Heller, 'Kurzbericht', 7 March 1942, AN, *AJ 40* 1005, dr. 7.
39. Giono to the German consul in Marseilles, 27 September 1942, AA-PA, *Botschaft Paris* 1111a.
40. Fabre-Luce, *Journal de la France*, vol. II, *op. cit.*, p. 195.
41. Knothe to AA, 23 August 1943, and the reply from Berlin on 15 November 1943, AA-PA, *Botschaft Paris* 1142; for criticism of the absence of reciprocity in the theatre, see Added, *Le Théâtre dans les années Vichy, op. cit.*, p. 120.
42. Gr.4 to Best, 20 August 1941, AN, *AJ 40* 567, dr. *Angeleg. der intern. wissenschaft. Organis. in Frankreich.*
43. Note by Best, 8 July 1941, *AJ 40* 567, dr. *Wissensch. Beziehungen D. zu Fr.*
44. See *AJ 40* 567, dr. *Wissensch. Beziehungen D. zu Fr.*; also AA-PA *Botschaft Paris* 1382.
45. Spenlé to Brinon, 5 July 1941, AN, *F 60* 1496. See Spenlé's *Nietzsche et le Problème européen*, Armand Colin, 1943.
46. AN, *F 17* 13359, dr. Franco-European Committee.
47. Circular by Mouraille, 25 December 1942, AN, *F 17* 13343, 'Correspondance avec les dir. 1942'.
48. Bertrand to the office of the Ministry of National Education, 23 October 1942, AN, *F 17* 13359.
49. Velut to Bonnard, 11 July 1942, and note from the minister's office on the subject of Velut's report, n.d., AN, *F 17* 13359, dr. Valut. The camp planned for the late summer of 1942 does not seem to have taken place.
50. AA-PA, *Botschaft Paris* 1210.
51. 'Akademische Abt.', n.d. [1942], AA-PA, *Botschaft Paris* 1112a.
52. AN, *AJ 40* 556, dr. *Franz. Germanisten an d. Universit.*
53. Lectures collected in the volume entitled *Esquisses allemandes*, Cahiers de l'Institut d'Études germaniques no. 1, Aubier, 1942. See the review in the *Pariser Zeitung*, 5 July 1942, p. 5 (Alfred Buesche, 'Erneuerte Universitas').
54. Epting, 'Entwicklung von der Germanistik in Frankreich', 11 December 1941, AA-PA, *Botschaft Paris* 1374.
55. AN, *F 17* 13360, 'Relations culturelles avec l'étranger'.
56. Most contributed to the periodical *Deutschland-Frankreich*. See also Lionel Richard, *Le Nazisme et la Culture*, Maspero, 1978, p. 297f.
57. See the correspondence in AA-PA, *Botschaft Paris* 1055a.
58. Epting to AA. 7 August 1940, and the reply of 19 August 1940, AA-PA, *Botschaft Paris* 1138.
59. 'Avant-propos', *Bulletin of the International Committee of Historical Sciences*, no. 46, June 1941, pp. 6–8; see also 'L'activité du Comité internationale des sciences historiques en 1940–41', archives of the CISH Doriguy Lausanne, dr. 1941–1944.
60. Correspondence in AA-PA, *Botschaft Paris* 1138.
61. Karl-Dietrich Erdmann, *Die Oekumene der Historiker. Geschichte der Internationalen Historikerkongresse und des Comité International des Sciences historiques*, Göttingen, Vandenhoeck und Ruprecht, 1987, p. 257.
62. AN, *F 17* 13343, dr. Lhéritier.
63. Report by H. Geppert, 20 December 1940, AA-PA, *Botschaft Paris* 1382. On Nazi plans to take over the mathematics, see Reinhard Siegmund-Schultze, 'Faschistische Pläne zur "Neuordnung" der europäischen Wissenschaft. Das Beispiel Mathematik',

NTM-Schriftenreihe für die Geschichte der Naturwissenschaft, Technik und Medezin, 1986/2, pp. 1–17.

64. AN, *AJ 40* 567, dr. *Wissensch. Beziehungen D. zu Fr.*
65. Note of 5 December 1941, *ibid.*
66. Note of 10 October 1942, AA-PA, *Botschaft Paris* 1115a.
67. AN, *F 17* 13359, dr. Franco-European Committee. Julia does not appear to have been purged at the liberation.
68. AA-PA, *Botschaft Paris* 1138; see his efforts to improve the lot of his two prisoner-of-war sons by getting them transferred into German industry, letter from Dunoyer to Bonnard, 15 July 1942, accompanied by the letter from the Dunoyer sons to their father, 23 June 1942 in AN, *F 17* 13360, 'Professeurs d'allemand et d'histoire prisonniers'.
69. Note of 11 February 1942 on a conversation between Carcopino and Dr Rilke at the Majestic on 10 February 1942, AN, *AJ 16 provisoire 6*.
70. See the presence at the head of the Institut d'anthroposociologie, created by the Commissariat aux questions juives, of 'notables' such as Claude Vacher de Lapouge (a doctor of medicine and law), Saint-Germes (a professor of political economy in the faculty in Caen), Professor Achard (secretary general of the Académie de Médicine), Professor Gruveilhier (of the Institut Pasteur), Professor Guillermond (a member of the Académie des Sciences), Professor Martial (Faculty of Medicine), the Reverend Bergougnioux, a professor of the Catholic University of Toulouse ('Antijüdische Propaganda', unsigned, n.d., AA-PA, *Botschaft Paris* 1190).
71. 'As on all my trips, I return comforted and confident for the future after seeing the Marshal. He is the pillar who, all by himself, holds up the entire edifice and that pillar seems to me more unshakeable and solid than ever. May God . . . preserve him for a long time for us and France, once again, will be saved by him' (Ramon to Ménétrel, 2 April 1942, AN, *2 AG* 77).
72. Ramon to Ménétrel, 16 November 1941, *ibid.*
73. Ramon to Ménétrel, 2 April 1942, *ibid.*
74. Leclainché to Brinon, 10 July 1941, AN, *F 60* 1494.
75. Note by the DGTO of 8 July 1942, AN, *F 60* 1494.
76. See AA-PA, *Botschaft Paris* 1376.
77. François Gibault, *Céline 1932–1944*, Mercure de France, 1985, p. 245.
78. See Elisabeth Roudinesco, *Histoire de la psychanalyse en France*, vol. II, Seuil, 1986, p. 170f.; and by the same author, 'Documents concernant l'histoire de la psychanalyse en France durant l'Occupation', *Confrontation*, autumn 1986, pp. 243–78; Alain de Mijolla, 'La psychanalyse et les psychanalystes en France entre 1939 et 1945', *Revue internationale d'histoire de la psychanalyse*, no. 1, 1988, pp. 167–222; by the same author, 'Document inédits. Les psychanalystes en France durant l'occupation allemande, Paris, November 1943', *ibid.*, no. 2, 1989, pp. 463–73.
79. AN, *2 AG* 75, letter of 16 June 1941, reprinted in Alain Drouard, 'Alexis Carrel et la Fondation française pour l'étude des problèmes humains', thèse d'État, Paris-IV, 1989, Appendix II/21, pp. 113–15 (thesis published under the title *Une inconnue des sciences sociales: la fondation Alexis Carrel, 1941–1945*, Éd. de la Maison des Sciences de l'Homme, 1992).
80. Alexis Carrel, *Jour après jour 1893–1944*, Plon, 1956, p. 235 (for 4 December 1942).
81. Note by Unger for Schleier, 12 August 1941, AA-PA, *Botschaft Paris* 1376.
82. Carrel to Schleier, 13 May and 22 July 1942, *ibid.*
83. Alice Apting-Kullman, *Pariser Begegnungen*, Hänner-über-Säckingen, Privatdruck, 1972, p. 73.

84. Letter of 14 September 1943 in Drouard, *Alexis Carrel et la Fondation française, op. cit.*, p. 524. Carrel died soon after the liberation.
85. The names cited by Epting, some given with a forename, are the following: Angelloz, Marcel Aubert, Maurice Bardèche, Georges Blondel, Boucher, Carrel, Cazamian, Clement, Dauphin-Meunier, Desmarets, Dolléans, Dumézil, Dunoyer, Esmein, Fauconnet, Bernard Fay, Fourneau, Gilbert Gidel, Gouhier, Paul Hazard, Houticq, Julia, Henri Labroue, Le Fur, Lhéritier, René Maunier, Mestre, Mignon, Robert Pitrou, Réau, Ripert, Roussy, Albert-Marie Schmidt, Jacques Seydoux, Spenlé, Jean Thomas (hearing of 10 June 1947, AN, *3 W* 358, dr. Epting). Epting may have confused a few of these names, for instance those of Jacques and Roger Seydoux, or made some mistakes, for instance over Paul Hazard, who worked at some point for the resistance (although very little was clearly either black or white at this time). The presence on this list of the name of Dumézil, who was then quite unknown, makes it impossible to close the file on his philonazism (see Didier Eribon, *Faut-il brûler Dumézil?*, Flammarion, 1992).
86. René Maunier was present, on 21 October 1941, at the breakfast hosted by Abetz in honour of Carl Schmitt, as were Gidel, Le Fur, Pierre Gide, Ripert and Germain Martin (AA-PA, *Botschaft Paris* 1101a). He made a number of contributions to the *Weltwirtschaftliches Archiv* (July 1942 and January 1943), as did Joseph Saint-Germès, the professor of economics in Caen (*ibid.*, July–September 1944). Emmanuel Leclainché published in German medical periodicals in 1942 and 1943 (see the *Bibliographie der deutschen Zeitschriftenliteratur*).

23 ANTI-FRANCE

1. On German plans in the summer of 1940, see Lothar Kettenacker, *Nationalsozialistische Volkstumspolitik im Elsass*, Stuttgart, Deutsche Verlags-Anstalt, 1973, pp. 49–51. The work by Thomasset (*Pages bourguignonnes*, Brussels, Éditions de la Phalange, 1938) is discussed in *Das Schwarze Korps*, 22 August 1940 (see Robert Specklin, 'La frontière franco-allemande dans les projets d'Adolf Hitler', *Recherches géographiques à Strasbourg*, no. 24, 2nd term 1986, p. 21, n. 36).
2. See Pierre Barral, 'Idéal et pratique du régionalism dans le régime de Vichy', *Revue française de science politique*, XXIV, October 1974, p. 911–39.
3. Philp Bankwitz, *Les Chefs autonomistes alsaciens 1919–1947*, *Saisons d'Alsace*, no. 71, 2nd term 1980, p. 76.
4. Kettenacker, *Nationalsozialistische Volkstumspolitik*, *op. cit.*, p. 163f.
5. *Ibid.*, p. 115f.
6. Bankwitz, *Les Chefs autonomistes alsaciens*, *op. cit.*, pp. 83–4.
7. See Kettenacker, *Nationalsozialistische Volkstumspolitik*, *op. cit.*, p. 163f.
8. *Ibid.*, pp. 212–13.
9. *Ibid.*, p. 218.
10. Bankwitz, *Les Chefs autonomistes alsaciens*, *op. cit.*, pp. 78, 95. There were no summary executions in Alsace during the war or after it, so there was no violent reprobation on the part of the population against autonomism which, nevertheless, was identified with collaboration after the liberation: with regard to civic chambers, Alsace (6953) came just behind Paris (8245) for the number of condemnations.
11. See Willem Meyers, 'Les collaborateurs flamands de France et les contacts avec les milieux flamingants belges', *Revue du Nord*, no. 237, 1978, pp. 337–49.
12. Note by Gantois on 11 June 1940, AN, *AJ 40* 12, dr. 5.
13. Document reprinted in Étienne Dejonghe, 'Un mouvement séparatiste dans le Nord

et le Pas-de-Calais sous l'occupation (1940–1944), le "Vlaamsch Verbond van Frankrijk", *RHMC*, January–March 1970, p. 74.

14. *Ibid.*, p. 61.
15. Note by the *Abwehr* II/1W, 27 May 1940, AN, *559 Mi*.
16. Alain Déniel, *Le Mouvement breton (1919–1945)*, Maspero, 1976, p. 224.
17. Best, 'Die Bretagne als Eckpfeiler der deutschen Wacht am Atlantik', n.d. [July 1940], AN. *AJ 40* 547, dr. *MBF* III Vin 40; see the translation in Henri Fréville, *Archives secrètes de la Bretagne 1940–1944*, Rennes, Éditions Ouest-France, 1985, pp. 29–31.
18. Himmler to Heydrich, 4 July 1940, AN, *F 7* 15144, dr. 1.
19. See AN, *AJ 40* 547, dr. MBF III Vin 40; the essential documents have been translated and introduced by Henri Fréville, *Archives secrètes, op. cit.*, See also Hans Umbreit, 'Zur Behandlung der Bretonenbewegung durch die deutsche Besatzungmacht im Sommer 1940', *Militärgeschichtliche Mitteilungen*, 1968/1, pp. 145–65.
20. Best to Schilling, 17 July 1941, AN, *F 7* 15 144, dr. 1.
21. Déniel, *Le Mouvement breton, op. cit.*, p. 232.
22. Fréville, *Archives secrètes, op. cit.*, p. 65. On the broadcasts in Breton from Radio-Rennes, see the report by Weisgerber in Gerd Simon, 'Zündschnur zum Sprengstoff. Leo Weisgerbers keltologische Forschungen und seine Tätigkeit als Zensuroffizier in Rennes während des 2. Weltkreigs', *Linguistische Berichte*, no. 79, June 1982, pp. 47–50.
23. The journal appears on the list of periodicals owned or influenced by the embassy (note by Feihl, 2 April 1942, AA-PA, *Botschaft Paris* 1134).
24. H. von Delwig Tiesenhausen to Roeder, 13 December 1940, AN, *AJ 40* 547, translated in Fréville, *Archives secrètes, op. cit.*, pp. 52–3.
25. See, for example, the report of the prefect of Ille-et-Vilaine of 16 August 1941, AN, *FICIII* 1156.
26. See correspondence in AN, *F 7* 15144, dr. 1.
27. Christian and Solange Gras, *La Révolte des régions d'Europe occidentale de 1916 à nos jours*, PUF, 1982, p. 164; Déniel, *Le Mouvement breton, op. cit.*, pp. 268–9.
28. Note by the VI B, 13 August 1942, 'Sprachregelung in der Frage der Umorganisation der PNB in MvtNB zwecks evtl. Erlangung der offiziellen Zulassung'; VI, 'Aktennotiz', 20 August 1942, AN, *F 7* 15144, dr. 1.
29. Arzalier, *Les Perdants, op. cit.*, p. 115.
30. Achenbach to MBF, 14 October 1941, AN, *AJ 40* 547, dr. *MBF* III Vin 42.

24 THE PARIS FRONDE

1. AA-PA, *Kult. Pol. II*, R 67018. A number of prisoners were freed as a result of interventions by other German services – Pierre Brisson, the editor-in-chief of the *Figaro* thanks to the German Ministry of Foreign Affairs, two members of the Polignac family at the request of Ribbentrop, Fernand de Rohan-Chabot thanks to the intervention of a high-ranking SS officer – or by French leaders – Georges Izard at the request of Laval, General Bridoux at the request of Brinon (AA-PA, *Kult. Pol. II*, R 67018). Some of these men, Izard in particular, later entered the resistance.
2. AN, *AJ 40* 551, dr. V pol 256/01.
3. Report passed on by the Propaganda-Staffel of Paris, 12 September 1940, AN, *AJ 40* 888, dr. 12.
4. Balestre to the head of the SD, 5 August 1941; Hersant to Brinon, 30 September 1941, AN, *F 60* 1480/2. Hersant appears on the list of guests to be invited to a tea

party at the embassy on 31 January 1942, along with Marc Augier, Blond, Bonnard, Benoist-Méchin, Brasillach, Fraigneau, Luchaire, Drieu (AA-PA, *Botschaf Paris* 1101b).

5. Heydrich to Ribbentrop, 27 July 1940, *ADAP,* D/10, No. 247.
6. Grimm, report of 16 July 1940, BAK, *Nachlaß Grimm, Frankreich-Berichte.*
7. Janvier to MBF, 12 September 1940, and the reply of 19 September 1940, AN, *AJ 40* 888, dr. 12.
8. 100000 to 150000 francs per month according to Fossati (hearing of 27 June 1946, AN, *Z 6* 99).
9. Note by Schleier, 16 October 1940, AA-PA, *Botschaft Paris* 1328.
10. Abetz to MBF, 'Aufz. über die wichtigsten politischen Besprechungen in der Zeit vom 1. bis 20. Oktober 1940', AN, *AJ 40* 1367, dr. 43; Déat, *Journal de guerre,* 15 October 1940.
11. *Ibid.*, 19 October 1940.
12. *Ibid.*, 31 October and 1 November 1940.
13. *Ibid.*, 26 December 1940.
14. 'Besprechung in der Deutschen Botschaft am 7. Januar 1941', AN, *AJ 40* 551, dr. 3.
15. *Journal de guerre,* 3 January 1941.
16. *Ibid.*, 6 January 1941.
17. *Ibid.*, 31 December 1940; 19 January 1941.
18. Major Schuchardt, 'Aufzeichnung über politische Morgenbesprechung in der Botschaft am 22.1.41', AN, *AJ 40* 1202, dr. V.O. zur Deutsch Bot. Paris.
19. Déat, *Journal de guerre,* 16 January 1941.
20. 'La première semaine du RNP', unsigned, n.d., AA-PA, *Botschaft Paris* 1312.
21. Déat, *Journal de guerre,* 13 February 1941; 4 March 1941; 12 April 1941.
22. *Ibid.*, 4 March 1941.
23. *Ibid.*, 21 August 1941.
24. *Ibid.*, 9 December 1940.
25. AA-PA, *Botschaft Paris* 1101a.
26. On Bonnet and Déat, *Journal de guerre,* 30 October 1941; 12 March 1942. On the meal at the Ritz, 'Aktenvermerkung über Besprechung am 4.12.41', AN, *AJ 40* 544, dr. *MBF* II F 22.
27. Monzie to Brinon, 5 November 1940, AN, *F 60* 1495.
28. Déat, *Journal de guerre,* 29 November 1940.
29. 'Tätigkeit Dr. Klassen', n.d. [1942], AA-PA, *Botschaft Paris* 1125b/2.
30. Déat, *Journal de guerre,* 18 December 1941, 29 January 1942, 6 March 1942.
31. Letter reprinted in Martin du Gard, *Chronique de Vichy, op. cit.*, pp. 390–2.
32. 'La première semaine du RNP', unsigned, n.d., AA-PA, *Botschaft Paris* 1312; Déat, *Journal de guerre,* 18 November 1941. Roche attended a Round Table lunch in 1942 (Roche hearing on 13 December 1945, AN, *F 12* 9559, 'Papiers relatifs aux banques').
33. See the circulars of the MBF of 23 June 1941 and 15 March 1942, and also that of the Befehlshaber der Sipo und des SD of 7 July 1942, AN, *AJ 40* 551 and *F 7* 15 145.
34. Circular of 17 February 1942 and note by the MBF on 5 March 1943, AN, *AJ 40* 451, dr. AG 106.
35. Déat, *Journal de guerre,* 24 October 1940.
36. Doriot, 'Ordre nouveau', *Le Cri du peuple,* 3 January 1941; 'la collaboration franco-allemande', *ibid.*, 4 January 1941.
37. Cited by Jean Lacouture, *Mauriac,* Seuil, 1980, p. 364.
38. Delaunay to Abetz, 9 October 1940, AA-PA, *Botschaft Paris* 1301.
39. 'Besprechung in der Deutschen Botschaft am 7. Januar 1941', AN, *AJ 40* 551, dr. 3.

40. Note by Etzdorf, 20 February 1942, 'Führer über die "Cooperation" mit Frankreich', AA-PA, *Handakte Etzdorf* 3.
41. Darlan to Pucheu, 9 December 1941, AN, *Fia* 3652, dr. LVF; Déat, *Journal de guerre*, 26 January 1942.
42. See the purge files on Lebrun (AN, *Z 6* 580), Buchard (*Z 6* 181), Ménétrel (*Z 6* N.L. 10605), Albertini (*Z 6* 8), Fossati (*Z 6* 99). See also Pierre Assouline, *Une éminence grise, Jean Jardin*, Balland, 1986, pp. 94, 96–7; Soulès-Abellio, *Ma dernière mémoire*, vol. III, *Sol invictus 1939–1947*, Ramsay, 1980, p. 313.
43. See Paul Kluke, 'Nationalsozialistische Europaideologie', *Vierteljahrshefte für Zeitgeschichte*, no. 3, July 1955, pp. 240–7, and Peter Longerich, *Propagandisten im Kreig. Die Pressabteilung des Auswärtigen Amtes unter Ribbentrop*, Munich, Oldenbourg, 1987, p. 77F.

25 ABETZ'S LEFT WING

1. Charles Albert, *L'Angleterre contre l'Europe*, preface by M. Déat, Denoël, 1941, p. 113.
2. *Ibid.*, pp. 90–1.
3. *'Aujourd'hui*: sa raison d'être', *Aujourd'hui*, 10 September 1940, p. 3.
4. 'Bericht über einen Besuch des Herrn Vigne', 3 October 1940, AA-PA *Botschaft Paris* 1315.
5. Report by Feihl on the press controlled by the embassy, 2 April 1942, AA-PA, *Botschaft Paris* 1134. For the funding by Schueller, see the report by the temporary administrator of the paper, 15 October 1944, AN, *Z 6* 561 (G. Lafaye).
6. Speech by Roger Paul at the national trade union conference, *L'Atelier*, 22 November 1941.
7. Rey, 'Pourquoi nous sommes collaborationnistes', *ibid.*, 21 February 1942.
8. Dumoulin, 'On n'a pas voulu de moi à Vichy', *L'Atelier*, 4 April 1941.
9. Lafaye hearing, 14 February 1945, AN, *Z 6* 561, dr. G. Lafaye.
10. Dumoulin, 'Convient-il d'organiser un congrès syndical national?', *L'Atelier*, 28 June 1941.
11. Pierre Alber *et al.*, *Documents pour l'histoire de la presse aux XIXe et XXe siècles*, CNRS, 1977, p. 78.
12. Abetz to AA, 29 February 1944, AA-PA, *Botschaft Paris* 1315. See also *L'Atelier*, 4 March 1944.
13. See his letter to Pétain's office, 6 December 1941, AN, 2 *AG* 449. See Marc Sadoun, *Les Socialistes sous l'Occupation. Résistance et collaboration*, Presses de la FNSP, 1982.
14. Desphilippon to Achenbach, 2 September 1941, AA-PA, *Botschaft Paris* 1304.
15. Desphilippon to Achenbach, 16 September 1941, AA-PA, *Botschaft Paris* 1311.
16. Spinasse, 'Au service de la France', *L'Effort*, 5 September 1940; 'Il n'y a pas de collaboration sans espoir', *ibid.*, 10 October 1940.
17. Spinasse to Feihl, 30 July 1941, AA-PA, *Botschaft Paris* 1242.
18. Spinasse, 'Ce que nous voulons', *Le Rouge et le bleu*, 15 November 1941; 'La République des sages', *ibid.*, 20 June 1942.
19. Spinasse, 'Réponse à des amis', *ibid.*, 17 January 1942.
20. *Documents pour l'histoire de la presse, op. cit.*
21. Claude Pennetier and Denis Peschanski, 'Partir, se taire, rester: les choix des élus de la Seine', Azéma, Prost, Rioux (n.d.), *Le Parti communiste français des années sombres 1938–1941*, Seuil, 1986, pp. 222–3.

22. Note by von Nostitz on a conversation with Gitton and Capron, 10 May 1941, AA-PA, *Botschaft Paris* 1304.
23. See AN, *AJ 40* 1008, dr. 5.
24. Statement by Déat at the conference of local leaders of the Région Parisienne, dispatch from the AFIP, 15 February 1941, AN, 72 AJ 1832, dr. RNP.
25. *L'Œuvre*, 9 January 1941.
26. Déat, *Journal de guerre*, 28 January 1941.
27. Letter cited by Martin du Gard, *Chronique de Vichy, op. cit.*, pp. 170–1.
28. Déat, *Journal de guerre*, 9 July 1941.
29. 'Aspects d'un grand destin', *L'Œuvre*, 20 April 1941.
30. Déat, *Journal de guerre*, 15 October 1940, 5 and 17 December 1941.
31. Déat, 'Structure et fonction du Parti', *L'Œuvre*, 23 December 1940.
32. Déat, 'Les Allemands n'ont rien demandé', *ibid.*, 25 January 1941.
33. Fontenoy, 'Nous savons ce que nous voulons', *Révolution*, 12 October 1941. See also the report by Bard of 1 July 1941, AN, *2 AG* 520, dr. CC 104 H; see also AN, *F 60* 234.
34. On the RNP, see Reinhold Brender, *Kollaboration in Frankreich im Zweiten Weltkrieg. Marcel Déat und das Rassemblement National Populaire*, Munich, Oldenbourg, 1992.
35. Notes by the Propaganda-Abteilung of 23 and 30 June 1942, reply from the embassy of 11 September 1942, AA-PA, *Botschaft Paris* 1238.
36. Déat, 'Incompréhensions majeures', *L'Œuvre*, 21–22 July 1941.
37. 'Valeurs anciennes, valeurs nouvelles', *ibid.*, 13 January 1942.
38. 'Nous n'avons rien à marchander', *ibid.*, 2 January 1942.
39. Report to the national council, *Le National populaire*, 8 August 1942. See also Déat's articles in *L'Œuvre*, 13 and 20 July 1942.
40. Déat, 'Le sol et le sang', *ibid.*, 25 September 1942; speech by Déat to the congress of the Jeunesses Nationales Populaires, *Le National populaire*, 10 October 1942.
41. 'Jugendpressedienst', 6 October 1942, in AA-PA, *Botschaft Paris* 1374.
42. Déat, *Journal de guerre*, 24 November 1942.
43. Spinasse, 'Contre tout mimétisme', *Le Rouge et le Bleu*, 4 July 1942; 'La fuite en avant', *ibid.*, 1 August 1942.
44. Chateau, 'Partis et parti', *La France socialiste*, 8 April 1942.
45. Chateau, 'Le parti unique et le climat présent', *ibid.*, 26–27 September 1942.
46. Schleier, 6 September 1943, AA-PA, *Botschaft Paris* 2463.
47. *La France socialiste*, 23–24 January 1943, p. 2; 16 February 1943. Delmas and Lefranc appear on the first list of the Comité central de la Ligue (AA-PA, *Botschaft Paris* 1308). On the statutes, see AN, *Z 5* 270 (Chateau).
48. Chateau to Pétain, 25 April 1944, AA-PA, *Botschaft Paris* 1308; letters from the Ligue to Pétain and Laval of 10 January and 16 February 1944, MAE, *Alger-CFLN* 1442.
49. Prefect's report for March 1942, AN, *FI CIII* 1163.
50. Renseignements généraux, Melun, 18 March 1943, AN, *F 7* 14904.
51. *Le National populaire*, 11 March 1944.

26 THE 'NOTABLES'

1. Claude Lévy, *Les Nouveaux Temps et l'Idéologie de la collaboration*, Armand Glin, 1974, pp. 88–9.
2. Flandin, 'Échangisme européen', *La Vie industrielle*, 11 December 1940; see also, by the same author, 'Collaboration', 21 November 1940.

3. See Olivier Wieviorka, 'Une droite moderniste et libérale sous l'occupation: l'exemple de *La Vie industrielle*', *Histoire, Économie et Société*, no. 3, 1985, pp. 397–431.
4. Drieu La Rochelle, 'Libéraux', *NRF*, November 1942, p. 607.
5. Fabre-Luce, *Journal de la France*, vol. II, *op. cit.*, p. 300.
6. *Ibid.*, p. 119.
7. *Ibid.*, p. 285.
8. *Ibid.*, p. 307.
9. *Ibid.*
10. *Anthologie de la nouvelle Europe*, Plon, 1942, p. vi.
11. *Journal de la France*, vol. II, *op. cit.*, pp. 308–9.
12. *Anthologie de la nouvelle Europe*, *op. cit.*, p. xlv (same page for the last quotation).
13. See the notes on the affair in AA-PA, *Botschaft Paris* 1139b. The Propaganda-Abteilung had decided that the second volume of the *Journal de France*, which had, besides, been prepared in close consultation with the embassy ('Tätigkeit Dr. Klassen', AA-PA, *Botschaft Paris* 1125b/2), was particularly appropriate for the French prisoners of war; it presented an interesting perception of developments in France since the defeat, from the point of view of German propaganda (Heller, 'Kurzbericht', 10 July 1942, *AJ 40* 1005, dr. 7.
14. Chardonne, when attending a concert at the German Institute for the first time, had scrutinized the faces around him, then been reassured when he noticed that Fabre-Luce was present: 'One is reassured when one sees the most intelligent man in France alongside' (*Voir la figure*, Grasset, 1941, p. 42).
15. See his *Chronique privée*, Stock, 1940.
16. Raymond Aron, 'Au service de l'ennemi' (I and II), in *L'homme contre les tyrans*, New York, La Maison Française, 1944, p. 186F.
17. *Chronique privée de l'an 1940*, Stock, 1941, p. 118.
18. *Voir la figure*, *op. cit.*, pp. 48, 52.
19. *Ibid.*, pp. 198, 206.
20. *Ibid,*, p. 43.
21. *Ibid.*, p. 78.
22. *Ibid.*, p. 80.
23. *Ibid.*, p. 63.
24. *Ibid.*, p. 62.
25. *Ibid.*, p. 72.
26. *Ibid.*, p. 89.
27. Guitard-Auviste, *Chardonne*, *op. cit.*, p. 224.
28. *Ibid.*, p. 227.
29. Paul Christophe, 'Le cardinal Baudrillart et ses choix pendant la Seconde Guerre mondiale', *op. cit.*, p. 58.
30. See L.-A. Maugendre, *Alphonse de Chateaubriant*, André Bonne, 1977.
31. Bonnard, 'Les réactionnaires', *Je suis partout*, 26 May 1941.
32. Bonnard, *Pensées dans l'action*, Grasset, 1941, p. 93. See J. Mièvre, 'L'évolution politique d'Abel Bonnard', *RHDGM*, no. 108, October 1977, pp. 1–26.
33. Heller, 'Tätigkeitbericht vom 19.12. bis 25.12.40', AN, *AJ 40* 1005, dr. 7; note by the ABt. Verw. of the MBF, 5 February 1941, *AJ 40* 560, dr. 4.
34. *Procès Georges Claude*, Bleuet, BDIC, pp. 90–1.
35. 'Les statuts de notre groupement', 'Collaboration 1940–1944', mémoire de maîtrise, Paris, I, 1977–8; and Barbara Unteutsch, *Vom Sohlbergkreis zur Gruppe 'Collaboration'*, *op. cit.*
36. *Documents pour l'histoire de la presse*, *op. cit.* p. 78.

37. 'Bericht über ein Vertragsreise in das unbesetzte Gebiet Frankreichs vom 4.–22. Juni 1942', BAK, *Nachlaß Grimm.*
38. Schleier, 6 September 1943, AA-PA, *Botschaft Paris* 2463.
39. Abetz,, 'Notiz für III', 19 June 1942, AA-PA, *Botschaft Paris* 1122; Schleier, 19 January 1943, *Botschaft Paris* 1121/3; von Bose, 16 June 1944, *Botschaft Paris* 1304.
40. G. Duch to Abetz, 19 June 1942, AA-PA, *Botschaft Paris* 1134.

27 THE HARD RIGHT

1. Henri Lèbre, 'Le fossé', *Le Cri du peuple,* 12 December 1940.
2. Alice Taeger Kaplan, 'Fascist Film Aesthetics: Brasillach and Bardèche's "Histoire du cinéma"', *Modern Language Notes,* vol. 95/4, May 1980, p. 867.
3. See AN, *Z 6* 233 (Boissel).
4. Féval Report, n.d., AN, *AJ 40* 1014, dr. 5 bis.
5. Raymond Abellio (pseud. for Georges Soulés), *Ma dernière mémoire,* vol. III, *Sol invictus, op. cit.*, p. 192. See also Philippe Bourdrel, *La Cagoule,* Albin Michel, 1970; and Bertram Gordon, 'The Condottieri of Collaboration: Mouvement social révolutionnaire', *Journal of Contemporary History,* April 1975, pp. 261–75.
6. Schleier to Knochen, 23 June 1941, AA-PA, *Botschaft Paris* 1311.
7. See the file on the affair, IHTP, *MFM all.* 110, H 2646.
8. Deloncle, 'L'Organisation du MSR en zone occupée', n.d. [autumn 1941], AN, *FIA* 3684.
9. See ASMAE, *Affari politici Francia* 49 and *Archivo del Gabinetto,* reel 11, UC 62.
10. Speech by Deloncle on 23 November 1941, AA-PA, *Botschaft Paris* 1313.
11. Abellio, *Sol invictus, op. cit.*, p. 282f.
12. 'Note sur le Mouvement social révolutionnaire', 23 May 1942, unsigned, CDJC, XIXa-15.
13. Bucard, 'Hardi! La France!', *Le franciste* (Paris), June 1941; 'Où sont les guillotines?', *ibid.*, 30 June 1941. See Alain Deniel, *Bucard et le Francisme,* Jean Picollec, 1979.
14. Speech by Bucard to the congress in the occupied zone, *ibid.*, 11 October 1941.
15. He was to give a written assurance that such an infraction would not be repeated (letter of 14 April 1942, AN, *AJ 40* 1008, dr. Francism).
16. See the dr. Francism, AN, *F 41* 347.
17. Speech by Bucard to the congress in the occupied zone, *Le Franciste* (Paris), 11 October 1941.
18. 'Quelques idées premières du francisme', *ibid.*, 11 April 1942, p. 4.
19. F. Antona, 'Faire de l'Europe une réalité vivante', *ibid.*, 6 February 1943.
20. Röhrig, 28 October 1943, 'Note sur la conversation avec le SD-Hauptsturmführer Dr. Kuntze a.s. de Bucard', AA-PA, *Nachlaß Schleier,* III/14.
21. See Dieter Wolf, *Doriot,* Fayard, 1969, and Jean-Paul Brunet, *Doriot,* Balland, 1986.
22. Beugras Notebooks, 1939–1941/1. I am most grateful to Marie Chaix for allowing me to consult this source.
23. 'Pariser Journalisten 1941', n.d., and 'Aufbau der Pariser Presse', n.d. [both spring 1941], AN, *AJ 40* 1008, dr. 3.
24. Speech reprinted in Doriot, *Réalités,* Éditions de France, 1942, p. 106.
25. *Ibid.*, p. 114.
26. See the Abwehr's report, 'Bericht über die Beziehungen Laval-Doriot', 21 October 1942, IHTP, *MFM all.* 85, III C A *Heeresarchiv* Potsdam.

27. See the analysis that he produced, with a measure of realism but also a number of illusions, Beugras Notebooks, 1941–1944/1.
28. Note by Lischka, 12 August 1942, AN, *F 7* 14937, dr. PPF.
29. The PPF had accumulated debts of six million francs by the end of November 1942, forcing Doriot to dismiss a series of permanent staff (Knochen to Schellenberg, 25 November 1942, AN, *F 7* 15145, dr. 3). Within the party, there was talk of possible dissolution and organizers of the apparatus were mentioning the possibility of becoming illegal (see reports from the Nord department, AN, *F 7* 14610).
30. Ménard to Zeitschel, 27 September 1942, AA-PA, *Botschaft Paris* 1225a.
31. *Ibid.*
32. Sézille, 'Création de l'IEQJ', n.d. [spring 1942], AA-PA, *Botschaft Paris* 1190.
33. Coston to Buscher, 3 August 1942, with two appended notes, 'Note sur la propagande en faveur du rapprochement franco-allemand' and 'Note sur la propagande anti-judéo-maçonnique', AA-PA, *Botschaft Paris* 1170.
34. AN, *F 60* 1498.
35. Maurras, *La Seule France*, *op. cit.*, p. 36.
36. Dioudonnat, *Je suis partout*, *op. cit.*, pp. 356, 437.
37. AN, *AJ 40* 1013, dr. S.P.10.
38. François Gibault, *Céline 1932–1944*, *op. cit.*, pp. 229, 249.
39. Philippe Alméras, *Les Idées de Céline*, *op. cit.*, p. 149f.
40. *Journal 1939–1945*, *op. cit.*, p. 302.
41. *Ibid.*, p. 385.
42. 'Le sens de tragique', *Idées*, November 1941, in *Chronique politique 1934–1942*, Gallimard, 1943, p. 329.
43. 'Nécessité continentale', *La Gerbe*, 9 July 1942, in *ibid.*, pp. 363–4.

28 PARTY MEMBERS AND MILITARY MEN

1. See AA-PA, *Botschaft Paris* 1344.
2. Ernest Lacroix to Brinon, 23 September 1942, AN, *F 60* 1494.
3. A. Caruel to the German Ministry of Propaganda, 2 September 1942, AA-PA, *Botschaft Paris* 1187.
4. See in AN, *AJ 40* 1011.
5. See, for example, the letter from Beugras, 'Rapport sur les travailleurs français en Allemagne', 20 October 1941, and his second report of 15 December 1941, AN, *AJ 40* 864; and the AA-PA file, *Botschaft Paris* 2445.
6. See the case of the big department stores of Paris, AN, *F 12* 9621.
7. See the report by Schmidtke, 2 February 1942, BAK, *R 55* 1337.
8. Police Prefecture, 'Incidents quotidiens signalés', announcements of 22, 25 and 26 May 1942, AN, *AJ 40* 884.
9. See the Beugras trial and his Notebooks 1941–1944/1.
10. Letter from the RNP organizer for Beauvais to Levillain, 23 November 1942, AN, *F 7* 14904, dr. Oise.
11. Lucien d'Avvigné to Abetz, 16 January 1942, AA-PA, *Botschaft Paris* 1186.
12. Letter from the organizer of the Bernay section to the departmental organizer, 15 August 1942, AN, *F 7* 14710, dr. Eure.
13. Von Bose, 16 June 1944, AA-PA, *Botschaft Paris* 1304; at the liberation, the police found a card index containing 18226 cards at the headquarters of the Groupe Collaboration, note by the Sureté nationale, 16 October 1945, AN, *3 W* 145.
14. See Tables 1 and 2, pp. 468 and 470.

15. The sample is made up of 648 individuals tried by the civic courts for having belonged to a collaboration movement. Thus these were people against whom there were no more serious charges than bearing arms for the Germans, denunciation, etc. The files, in groups of fifty, were examined in the following archive centres: Aix-en-Provence, Amiens, Angers, Besançon, Bordeaux, Caen, Chambéry, Lille, Limoges, Lyons, Montpellier, Nancy, Nîmes, Rennes, Rouen, Toulouse. Of these 648 people, 158 were members of the PPF, 99 of the RNP, 96 of the Groupe Collaboration, 74 of the Francist movement, 73 of the Milice, 31 of the LVF, 28 of the SOL, 19 of the MSR, 17 of the JEN, etc. The enrolment figures are as follows: 12 in 1940, 152 in 1941, 220 in 1942, 137 in 1943, 52 in 1944. The socio-professional composition is not significantly different from Table 1, except for the workers, who make up 21.1 per cent instead of 8.1 per cent; there are probably several reasons for this, the main one being that the IHTP correspondents only counted workers from industry in this category, whereas I also counted workers from artisan workshops, rather than including them in the category of artisans.

    For a pioneering analysis, see François Marcot and Jean-Pierre Massonie, 'Les collaborateurs dans le Doubs (factor analysis)', *RHDGM*, no. 115, July 1979, pp. 29–54.
16. *L'Émancipation nationale*, 28 November 1942, p. 3; see also Canobbio, the organizer: 'The number of new militants who are coming to us is . . . considerable', Canobbio, 'Où en sommes nous?', *L'Émancipation nationale*, 8 August 1942.
17. Lists of the organizers of the collaboration parties, AD Bourges, Archives of the Propaganda Staffel/6; and the press of the PPF and the RNP, in particular, for the latter, the *Bulletin des cadres*, September 1943.
18. The calculation is as follows: 40000 to 50000 for the PPF; 50000 for the Groupe Collaboration; 15000 to 20000 for the RNP; 10000 for Francism; a few thousand for other groups, plus the separatists. To this we should add about 20000 members of the Amicale des Travailleurs Français en Allemagne, and at least as many members of the Amis de la LVF, bearing in mind that some memberships were multiple.
19. Papp, *La Collaboration dans l'Eure, op. cit.*, pp. 154–5; Papp stresses the importance of this extra-partisan collaboration.
20. Claude Lévy and Henri Michel, 'La presse autorisée de 1940 à 1944', in Claude Bellanger *et al.*, *Histoire de la presse française*, vol. IV, PUF, pp. 36–7.
21. AN, *AJ 40* 1013, dr. S.P.10 and S.P.11.
22. From Saint-Quentin to Abetz, 27 June 1941, AA-PA, *Botschaft Paris* 1313.
23. Letters of 10 and 12 October 1941, AN *FIA* 3684, dr. LVF.
24. MBF to OKW, 23 September 1941, AN, *AJ 40* 1204, dr. *Akte* Nr. 40; see also Rémy Ourdan, 'Rapport concernant l'esprit, l'organisation et l'activité de la LVF', 12 December 1941, Service historique de l'armée de terre (SHAT), *2 P* 14, dr. 4.
25. Account of the 13 March 1942 meeting of the central committee of the LVF, AN, *F 7* 14956.
26. 'Rapport d'un member de la mission de Brinon à son retour d'un voyage en Pologne et en Russie', 16 July 1943, AN, *FIA* 3748, dr. LVF.
27. Mayol de Lupé to Brinon, 5 November 1943, AN, *F 60* 1495.
28. Statistical reports on the LVF, May–July 1944, AN, *F 7* 14933, dr. Milice and LVF.
29. Head of the Simoni battalion, 'Rapport sur la situation de la LVF dans l'Est', May 1943, SHAT, *2 P* 14, dr. 4.
30. Note by the prefect, 11 March 1943, AN, *F 7* 14904, dr. Vienne.
31. Charles Braibant, *La Guerre à Paris, op. cit.*, pp. 225–6.
32. Maurice Delarue, *Trafics et Crimes sous l'Occupation, op. cit.*, pp. 225–6.

33. Note by Himmler for Hitler, 12 December 1942, IfZ *Mfm*, MA 326 (T 175).
34. Brinon to Laval, n.d. [July 1943], AN, *F 60* 1479, dr. Laval 1942–4.
35. Reinbold, 'Bericht über die Propagandaausstellung für die Gründung einer französischen Waffen-SS Division', AA-PA, *Botschaft Paris* 1111b.
36. The figure of 3000 is provided by Abetz, 14 June 1944, AA-PA, *Inland IIg* 304. During the month of December 1943, there were 154 volunteers, only half of whom turned up to be inspected and sixty-four of whom were accepted (Germanische Leitstelle, 'Monatsbericht für Dezember 1943', *Inland II g* 294).
37. Albert Merglen, 'Soldats français sous uniformes allemands 1941–1945: LVF and Waffen-SS français', *RHDGM*, no. 108, October 1977, p. 80.
38. Copy of the contract in AA-PA, *Botschaft Paris* 1175.
39. Schleier to AA, *AJ 40* 848, dr. 1.
40. See AN, *AJ 40* 848, dr. 1.
41. Abetz, 'Notiz für Herrn LR Wagner', 10 April 1943, AA-PA, *Inland II g* 304. According to Merglen (*op. cit.*, p. 80), there were about 5000 foremen on these work sites.

29 MILITIAS

1. Note by the prefect of the Vosges, 2 December 1942, AN, *F 7* 14904, dr. Vosges; note from the Amiens police station, 10 March 1943, *ibid.*, dr. Somme; report by Costantini, 16 April 1943, AN, *AJ 40* 1007, dr. 1.
2. H. M. Magne to Brinon, 18 January 1943, AN, *F 60* 1495.
3. See J. Delperrie de Bayac, *Histoire de la Milice*, Fayard, 1969; Jean-Paul Cointet, *La Légion française des combattants, op. cit.*; Jean-Pierre Azéma, 'La Milice', *Vingtième Siècle*, no. 28, October–December 1990, pp. 83–105.
4. Krug, 11 June 1942, AA-PA, *Botschaft Paris* 1303.
5. Tract of 4 pp. entitled *Investiture des SOL de Lyon 12 juillet 1942. Discours du Chef Darnand.*
6. Abetz, 'Vorschläge Lavals nach seinem Empfang im Führerhauptquartier', put out on 23 December 1942 by the AMt Ausland of the Abwehr, *IfZ OKW* 999, Mfm Ma 190/5.
7. Tract entitled *Mission politique de la Milice française. Discours pronouncé par J. Darnand à Vichy le 30 janvier 1943.*
8. 'Annexe aux statuts de la Milice française', 3 July 1943, AN, *F 60* 514, 'Milice'.
9. See the remarks by Jean Boudet-Gheusi, 'Avec un camarade retour du front de l'Est', *Combats*, 10 July 1943.
10. Letter from Darnand to the heads of departments, 7 June 1943, AN *FIA* 3747, 'Milice'.
11. Guilbaud, 'Note sur l'Organisation des forces collaborationnistes en France', 21 June 1943, and 'Annexe à la note du 21 Juin', 19 July 1943; the latter was passed on to Laval, the embassy and the SS, AA-PA, *Botschaft Paris* 2463/2.
12. Schleier suggests that by June 1943 the embassy was favouring this extension (CDJC, CLXXXIV–30a, 13 June 1943).
13. See AN, *AJ 40* 1210, dr. *Frz. Miliz*, and *AJ 40* 1261, dr. *Heer*/19; according to the Milice, on 30 June 1943 there were 30412 *miliciens*, 12945 of whom were franc-gardes; the Germans were not convinced ('Sonderbericht Nr.9 betr. die frz. Miliz', 1 December 1943, *AJ 40* 1210, dr. as above).
14. Azéma, 'La Milice', *op. cit.*, p. 93.
15. Darnand to Laval, 14 July 1943, IHTP, Mfm all. 155, *OKW* 1056.

16. Report by Colonel Tessier, General Armistice Commission to Control Commission of Bourges, 22 August 1943, OKW 1362, IfZ *Mfm* MA 34.
17. According to its chief (a captain from the fire brigade of Paris), in May 1943 the Milice of the RNP had 1463 members ('Note de renseignement', 25 May 1943, AN, *F 7* 15301, 'Milice, divers 1943–1944).
18. An unsigned note, 'Paris au 3 Août 1943', AN, *FIA* 3956.
19. AN, *3 W* 145.
20. Note by Achenbach, 19 March 1943; see also Abetz's note of 10 April 1943, AA-PA, *Inland II g* 304.
21. Bran, Frankreich-Komitee, 'Bericht über die Sitzung am 4.11.', AA-PA, *Inland II g* 304.
22. 'Besprechungsnotiz betr. Besprechung beim Militärbefehlshaber wegen französ. Milizbewaffnung am 23.11.43', IHTP, Mfm all. 152, *OKW* 1492; see also AN, *AJ 40* 1210, dr. Frz. Miliz.
23. HSSP to Knochen, 12 February 1944, IHTP Mfm 152, *OKW* 1492.
24. *Combats*, 4 December 1943.
25. Dioudonnat, *Je suis partout*, *op. cit.*, pp. 366–7.
26. Reports in AN, *FIA* 3959.
27. See AN, *F 7* 14904, dr. Rouen.
28. AN, *FIA* 3747, 'Milice'.
29. Guirand at the Wagram meeting, *Le Franciste* (Paris), 20 November 1943.
30. Darnand, 'Alerte miliciens', *Combats*, 6 November 1943.
31. Darnand/Herriot meeting in Nice, *Combats*, 4 December 1943.
32. Police note, Perpignan, 24 December 1943, AD Hérault, *III W* 18.
33. Delperrie de Bayac, *Histoire de la Milice*, *op. cit.*, p. 216.
34. Police reports of 8 October 1945 and 4 June 1946, AN *Z 6* 580.
35. Statements by Sicard, 'Il faut résoudre la question juive', *Le Cri du peuple*, 24 January 1944.

30 THE ROUT

1. Berger to Oberg on 8 February 1944, Oberg to Himmler, 10 February 1944, IfZ, *T 175* 125 (MA 327).
2. KI Bourges, 'Ergänzungs-und Abschlußbericht zu Sonderbericht Nr. 9 betr. die französische Miliz', 4 April 1944, AN, *AJ 40* 1210, dr. Frz. Miliz.
3. CDJC, Oberg-Knochen trial, CCCLXIV–2, pp. 86–8, CCCLXIV–6, p. 27.
4. H. Michel, *Paris allemand*, *op. cit.*, p. 131. See Yves Lecoutrier, 'Au service de la Gestapo en Normandie', *RHDGM*, no. 156, October 1989, pp. 37–44. The figure of 30 000 auxiliaries, often cited, lacks evidence to support it.
5. Victor Barthélémy, *Du communisme au fascisme. L'histoire d'un engagement politique*, Albin Michel, 1978, p. 374f.
6. 'Arbeitseinsatz in Frankreich, Stand: 20.8.44', AN, *AJ 40* 847, dr. MBF C64.
7. 'Stimmungsbericht', reports of 30 April 1944 and 1 June 1944, *Aussenstelle Bourges der Prop. Staffel NW*, AD Bourges, dr. 3.
8. Galtier-Boissière, *Mon Journal depuis la libération*, La Jeune Parque, 1945, pp. 38–9 (18 October 1944).
9. Delperrie de Bayac, *Histoire de la Milice*, *op. cit.*, p. 265.
10. *Ibid.*, p. 233; see also Ferro, *Pétain*, *op. cit.*, p. 533f.
11. Abetz, 14 June 1944, AA-PA, *Inland II g* 304.
12. Marcel Baudot, 'L'épuration: bilan chiffré', *op. cit.*, p. 52.

13. Speech by Laval on 4 June 1944, cited by Delperrie de Bayac, *Histoire de la Milice*, vol. II, *op. cit.*, p. 69.
14. Barthélemy, *Du communisme au fascisme*, *op. cit.*, p. 400.
15. Abetz to AA, 14 June 1944, AA-PA, *Inland II g* 304. According to the Milice, by the end of July, 10 400 volunteer francs-gardes had been mobilized, 6600 in the southern zone and 3800 in Paris ('Effectif de la Milice française à la date du 25 juillet 1944' AN, *F 60* 514, 'Milice'). To these we should add 2000 permanent francs-gardes, 415 francs-gardes in the northern zone and 1540 in the southern zone (Henri Longuechaud, *'Conformément à l'ordre de nos chefs . . . '. Le drame des Forces de l'Ordre sous l'Occupation 1940–1944*, Plon, 1985, appendix p. 225).
16. Wagner, 19 June 1944, AA-PA, *Inland II g* 304.
17. Delperrie de Bayac, *Histoire de la Milice*, vol. II, *op. cit.*, pp. 221–6.
18. Baudot, 'L'épuration: bilan chiffré', *op. cit.*, p. 52. On the purge, see Peter Novick, *L'Épuration française 1944–1949*, Balland, 1985; Herbert Lottman, *L'Épuration* 1943–1953, Fayard, 1986.
19. See Henry Rousso, *Pétain et la Fin de la collaboration, Sigmaringen 1944–1945*, Brussels, Complexe, 1984.
20. Beaugras hearings, 22 January 1946 (AN, *Z 6* 514) and 4 July 1946 (*Z 6* 511).
21. Abetz gave the figure of 10 000 in his memoirs (*Das Offene Problem*, *op. cit.*, p. 300). The same figure is given in a German document of December 1944 (Arnulf Moser, *Das französische Befreiungskomitee auf der Insel Mainau und das Ende der deutsch-französischen Collaboration 1944/45*, Sigmaringen, Thorbecke Verlag, 1980, p. 8). On the number of *miliciens*, see Abetz, 10 September 1944, AA-PA, *Inland II g* 369, and on the number of the others, see AN, *Z 6* 413.
22. Degrelle to Himmler, 10 December 1944, *IfZ Mfm T 175* 130, MA 332.
23. Tocqueville, *L'Ancien Régime et la Révolution*, vol. I, Gallimard, 1952, p. 87.
24. *Ibid.*
25. Drieu La Rochelle, *Journal 1939–1945*, *op. cit.*, p. 403 (12 July 1944).
26. *Ibid.*, p. 416 (7 August 1944).

CONCLUSION

1. Henry Rousso, 'L'épuration en France: une histoire inachevée', *Vingtième Siècle*, no. 33, January–March 1992. See also Klaus-Dietmar Henke and Hans Woller (eds), *Politische Säuberung in Europa. Die Abrechnung mit Faschismus und Kollaboration nach dem Zweiten Weltkrieg*, Munich, Deutscher Taschenbuch Verlag, 1991.
2. See Henry Rousso, *Le Syndrome de Vichy*, Seuil, 1987.
3. Extract from a report by the liaison officer of the Befehlshaber des Ersatzheeres über den Gesamteinsatz der franz. Arbeiter, for the period of January to April 1944, in *Die faschistische Okkupationspolitik in Frankreich (1940–1944)*, Berlin, Deutscher Verlag der Wissenschaften, 1990, doc. 221, pp. 310–11.
4. See Jacques Semelin, *Sans armes face à Hitler. La résistance civile en Europe, 1939–1943*, Payot, 1989.

Index

Index

Burrin, Philippe.

France under the Germans.

DATE			